Adomnan's Life of Columba

Adomnan's Life of Columba

Edited with Translation and Notes
by the late
Alan Orr Anderson
and by
Marjorie Ogilvie Anderson

Thomas Nelson and Sons Ltd
London Edinburgh Paris Melbourne Johannesburg
Toronto and New York

THOMAS NELSON AND SONS LTD
Parkside Works Edinburgh 9
36 Park Street London W1
312 Flinders Street Melbourne C1
302-304 Barclays Bank Building
Commissioner and Kruis Streets
Johannesburg

THOMAS NELSON AND SONS (CANADA) LTD
91-93 Wellington Street West   Toronto 1

THOMAS NELSON AND SONS
19 East 46th Street New York 17

SOCIÉTÉ FRANÇAISE D'EDITIONS NELSON
97 rue Monge Paris 5

Printed in Great Britain
by T. and A. CONSTABLE LTD., Hopetoun Street
Printers to the University of Edinburgh

Contents

Facsimiles

between pp. 176-7

Schaffhausen, Generalia 1, page 55, lines 7-26
Schaffhausen, Generalia 1, page 14, lines 2-20
Schaffhausen, Generalia 1, page 93, lines 11-30
Schaffhausen, Generalia 1, page 108.

Preface

ADOMNAN's Life of Columba is a historical document for life and culture among the Scots of Britain and Ireland in Adomnan's own time, and for the beliefs and practices of the Irish church. It is also important evidence for the Irish language in the seventh century.

The Schaffhausen manuscript of the Life was sumptuously written by or for a scholar who was a close contemporary of Adomnan, and apart from slight spelling variations, and a few errors, it must be accepted as a true representative of the original fair copy of the author's work.

This edition presents a literatim copy of the Schaffhausen manuscript, and a collation with the three other, much later, surviving texts of the unabridged Life.

We thank Dr E. Schellenberg, the Stadtbibliothekar of Schaffhausen in Switzerland, for his permission to publish the text, and to give some specimen facsimiles of its writing. A fine photographic facsimile, made at Zürich, is now in the National Library of Ireland. We wish to express our great indebtedness to Dr R. J. Hayes, through whose courtesy we were in the first place enabled to have access to that facsimile. Later, Dr Schellenberg kindly permitted Mr H. Koch, of Schaffhausen, to make for us independent photographic copies of the manuscript, and we owe it to Mr Koch's skill that these are clear and legible. They are slightly reduced in size, and there is some loss of margins, but faded writing in red ink is made readable.

We are under obligation to the keepers of manuscripts in various libraries for permitting us to have photographic copies made from manuscripts within their care. We have thus obtained from the British Museum complete facsimiles of the manuscript versions B1, B2, B3, and L ; from the Bodleian Library, facsimiles of §28 of the Cáin Adamnain, and of the earlier part of the Annals of Tigernach ; from Trinity College, Dublin, facsimiles of the earlier part of the Annals of Ulster, made by the photographer of the National Library of Ireland (a special courtesy, since the manuscript is frail and faint). We owe acknowledgements also to the Library of Saint-Omer, Pas-de-Calais, for facsimiles of a text of the abridged Life that we call pseudo-Cummene ; and to the Bibliothèque Nationale of Paris, for the text of P.

We have used the facsimile editions of the Book of Armagh (edited by Edward Gwynn), and of the Annals of Inisfallen (edited by R. I. Best and Eóin MacNeill).

The important edition of Adomnan's Life of Columba, made by William Reeves one hundred years ago, was justly praised for his great industry and learning. His ' copious notes and dissertations ' were based upon much study of printed literature and Irish manuscript material. His treatment of the subject was encyclopaedic, and it is still useful ; but many of his sources were of later date than a modern historian would choose to accept as evidence.

In Reeves's time the published editions of Irish writings were very unsatisfactory. The scientific study of the early Irish language had then only begun : the *Grammatica Celtica* of J. C. Zeuss had not appeared until 1853.

During the last half-century, the comparative study of Irish palaeography has developed. See Lindsay 1915, pp. vii-xii. In this development, W. M. Lindsay played an important part ; compare Lowe 1935, p. vii, and the encomium ibid. at the end of p. xvii.

We make no attempt to cover the same ground as Reeves. In questions of history we have endeavoured as far as is possible to confine our references to the least unhistorical sources. Many nearly-contemporary Latin notes of events were written in Easter tables, in various Irish monasteries, and were copied by early annal-collectors. At least one of these collections was preserved independently in the two chronicles that are known to us as the Annals of Ulster, and the Annals of Tigernach. Thus we have in those late chronicles, where they agree, fairly good evidence for early events.

Adomnan makes some apology for the language in which his names of persons, tribes, and places, are written. Actually he delighted to put his Irish into writing ; and his spellings were a contribution to Irish scholarship. He used archaic Old-Irish forms, often with Latin terminations ; and it is necessary to retain, as far as possible, the spellings that he knew.

In *Early Sources of Scottish History*, which covered many centuries, early Middle-Irish forms of names were adopted as standard, except when modern English names could be used as substitutes. That method had advantages for the English reader ; but it is entirely inappropriate in an edition of Adomnan. Our principle has been to retain in translation his Irish names, whether latinized or not, giving them in their nominative case. This involves the retention of some Old-Irish forms that are not found in Adomnan. Thus we retain one word, Dal-Réti, which would have been Adomnan's form if he had used that tribal name (later Dal-ríata) ; since the genitive *Rēti* occurs, both in Adomnan and in some of the earliest notes in the Annals of Ulster. Our study includes later writers also, and we have found it impossible to be entirely consistent in the spelling of names.

A.O.A.

M.O.A.

I wish to add a personal postscript. This book has been a collaboration, in the fullest sense of the word. Hardly any part of it could have been completed without my wife's help. The Schaffhausen manuscript in facsimiles was for my sight more legible than print, and I was able to transcribe all but the most faded passages. In the later stages of our work all reading and searching have had to be done by my wife. The collation of the other texts was made by her ; and she also contributed to the discussion of the pseudo-Cummene problem the textual analysis that is decisive. The linguistic and palaeographical sections of the Introduction were rough-drafted by me, but they too owe much to the industry of my wife, who both checked my references and sought out additional instances.

Our work together has been largely restricted to books in our own possession ; and we hope that we have not for that reason failed to consult recent publications that ought to have been noticed in our Introduction.

A.O.A.
December, 1957.

A. O. Anderson died in December 1958, when our typescript had been completed and was in the publisher's hands.   Since then I have re-written one paragraph (p. 13) and added a note on the excavations in Iona (p. 108), and have added or corrected a few references.

The four facsimiles are reproduced from photographs made for the purpose by the firm of Foto-Koch, Schaffhausen, in August 1958.

M.O.A.
July, 1960.

Letters, Numbers and Signs

A, B1, B2, B3	texts of the unabridged Life. See pp. 3-5.
C, D, F, L, S	texts of the shortened version. See pp. 11-12.
P	a different abridged version. See pp. 17-18.
A.S.	Anglo-Saxon.
M.I.	Middle Irish.
N.B.	North British.
O.I.	Old Irish.
S.B.	South British.
S.G.	Scottish Gaelic.
m.h.	' a minuscule hand.' (For definition see p. 172).
s.l.	sic lege : ' to be read in this way.'

$\beta, \gamma, \delta, \mu$ Greek letters, β, γ, δ, μ, and others, are occasionally used as symbols of spirant forms of b, g, d, m, and other letters (as in Thurneysen 1946, §29). After an O.I. word containing one of those letters, the equivalent Greek letter, placed in brackets, indicates that the equivalent O.I. letter had its spirant, or ' lenited ', sound.

bb, gg, dd The doubled letters, bb, gg, or dd, within brackets after an O.I. word in which a letter p, c, or t, occurs, indicate that that letter was voiced, sounding like non-spirant b, g, or d.

f, s f and s, in O.I. words, represent lenited f and lenited s.

$æ$ $æ$ in O.I. words : see pp. 1, 130.

n The prosthetic n of Irish eclipsis is here written in O.I. names before vowels only.

When we refer to manuscript volumes that have been numbered in folios or in pages, we give first the number of the folio, or of the page ; secondly, a letter numbering the column in the folio, or in the page ; and thirdly, the number of the line within the column. Thus the numbers and letters in the margin of our Latin text of Adomnan indicate the pages and columns of manuscript A. The book-and-chapter numbers given with the translation are those of Reeves.

| A vertical stroke is used in our Latin text to mark the end of a column of the manuscript. Elsewhere, it is used in the conventional manner, to mark the end of a line of manuscript.

An acute accent, placed above a vowel, indicates that the vowel is long. This is used in Irish names, (1) in transcripts, only when an accent was used to mark length in the manuscript ; (2) elsewhere, above a vowel that is both long and under the word-stress. See pp. 162-4. An acute accent is placed after a vowel or syllable, (1) in transcripts, to show that the vowel or syllable was marked for stress in the manuscript ; or (2) elsewhere, when we wish to indicate on what syllable the word was stressed.

‥ A mark of diaeresis is used by us over the first of two consecutive vowels, to show that a double accent appears in a manuscript above the two vowels.

– The macron is sometimes used by us in transcripts or quotations, to indicate length when a vowel is not marked long in the manuscript. The absence of a macron does not show that the vowel was short. The macron is also used to show length of vowel in theoretical ancient forms of words ; and to distinguish eta and omega from epsilon and omikron, when we quote Greek words in Latin letters.

~ The tilde is sometimes used, in transcription, after a letter over which a bar-sign of abbreviation stands in the manuscript.

‥ Two full stops represent the major stops that are placed, in A, at the end of headings, and chapters or sections.

… Three points show that words have been omitted in a quotation or translation.

[ ] Square brackets are used to introduce letters or words that have been omitted in a quoted source ; and to supply identifying names in the English version.

][Reversed square brackets show that letters at the beginning, or at the end, of quoted words are missing in a source (see p. 2).

- A hyphen separating two elements of Irish names and words shows that the syllable following the hyphen bears the word-stress.

* An asterisk is placed before word-forms that are inferred, but that do not actually occur.

> The arrow-sign after a word or letter means ' giving rise to the later form.'

= The equal-sign, before a year-number, indicates not the true date, but the year intended by the compiler of a chronicle.

× The multiplication-sign (conveniently read ' by ') means ' not earlier than ' a date that precedes it, and ' not later than ' a date that follows it.

Terminology

The terms Britannic, Gallic, and Goidelic, are here used for those Celtic languages in the stage at which they still retained their inflexional terminations. After the loss of those terminations, the names British, Gaulish, and Irish, are used.

North-British (N.B.) indicates the P-Celtic language or languages that were spoken in Britain north of the Forth. South-British (S.B.) includes the P-Celtic languages of Britain south of the estuaries of Clyde and Forth. North-Cumbrian is occasionally used for that branch of the British language that was spoken in the south of Scotland, between the upper Forth and the Solway Firth.

The vague term ' Picts ' is used as a translation of the Latin *Picti*, when no more precise term is justified by the evidence. ' Scots ' (Adomnan's *Scoti*) are the people who spoke the Irish language (*scotica lingua*) in Ireland and in northern Britain to the west of the water-shed.

Abbreviated Book-References

Achery and Mabillon, *Acta Sanctorum ordinis S. Benedicti* (Paris 1668). Contains notes by Mabillon.

Adomnan's *De Locis.* See Geyer 1898.

A.I. *Annals of Inisfallen,* edited in facsimile by R. I. Best and Eóin MacNeill (R.I.A. Dublin 1933).

Amra Coluimchille. Edited in *Liber Hymnorum* 1898.

Anecdota from Irish Manuscripts. Edited by O. J. Bergin, R. I. Best, K. Meyer, J. G. O'Keeffe (Halle and Dublin, 1907 onwards).

Arbroath. *Liber S. Thome de Aberbrothoc* (Bannatyne Club, 1848-56).

A.S.C. *The Anglo-Saxon Chronicle,* edited by Benjamin Thorpe (Rolls Series 23, London 1861).

Atkinson 1887. Robert Atkinson : *The Passions and the Homilies from the Leabhar Breac* (R. I. A. Todd Lectures, II, part 2, Dublin).

A.U. *Annals of Ulster.* The volume numbers, I and IV, refer to the edition by W. M. Hennessy and B. MacCarthy (Stationery Office Dublin, 1887 and 1901). Most of our references are to the manuscript, Trinity College Dublin H. I. 8.

B.B. *The Book of Ballymote,* an Irish collection copied about A.D. 1400, published, in photolithographic facsimile, by the R.I.A. (Dublin 1887).

Bede, *Historia Ecclesiastica.* See Plummer 1896.

Bede, *Life of Saint Cuthbert.* See Colgrave, 1940.

Bede, *Opera de Temporibus.* See Jones 1943.

Berchan's Prophecy. 'The Prophecy of Berchan,' edited by A. O. Anderson, in *Z.C.P.* XVIII (1929), pp. 1-56.

Bergin 1932. Osborn Bergin : ' Varia II ', §10, in *Ériu,* XI, pp. 140 ff.

Best 1908. See Life of Adomnan.

Book of Armagh, manuscript T.C.D. 52. Our references are to the facsimile edition of folios 2-24, edited by Edward Gwynn : *Book of Armagh, the Patrician Documents* (Dublin 1937). Folios 20-4 were written by a scribe Ferdomnach, who wrote most of the later part of the book in A.D. 807, and died in 846. Folios 2-19 were written about the same time, perhaps by another hand. Cf. Kenney 1929, p. 338.

Brüning 1917. Gertrud Brüning : ' Adamnans Vita Columbae und ihre Ableitungen ', in *Z.C.P.* XI, pp. 213-304.

Cáin Adamnain. *Cáin Adamnáin, an Old-Irish treatise on the Law of Adamnan*, edited and translated by Kuno Meyer (Oxford 1905). For the text of §28 we have consulted the Oxford version, Rawlinson B 512, folios 49c-50a, in facsimile.

Cáin Domnaig ('Law of Sunday'). Text edited by J. G. O'Keeffe in *Anecdota from Irish Manuscripts*, III, pp. 21-7 (1910).

Canones Adomnani, text in Haddan and Stubbs 1873, pp. 111-14.

Childe 1935. V. Gordon Childe : *The Prehistory of Scotland* (London).

Colgrave 1940. *Two Lives of Saint Cuthbert*, edited and translated by Bertram Colgrave (Cambridge).

Collingwood 1927. W. G. Collingwood : *Northumbrian Crosses of the Pre-Norman Age* (London).

Columbanus. *Sancti Columbani Opera*, edited by G. S. M. Walker (Dublin 1957).

Cormac 1862. *Cormac's Glossary*, edited from L.B. by Whitley Stokes in *Three Irish Glossaries* (London).

Cormac 1912. *Sanas Cormaic*, edited by Kuno Meyer from the Yellow Book of Lecan in *Anecdota from Irish Manuscripts*, IV.

Crawford 1933. O. G. S. Crawford : 'Iona', in *Antiquity*, VII, pp. 453-467.

C.S. *Chronicon Scotorum*, edited by W. M. Hennessy (Rolls Series 46, London 1866).

Cummene : *Liber de virtutibus sancti Columbae*. See 108a, and pp. 103-05.

Cummene, Life of Columba attributed to. See under Pseudo-Cummene.

De Locis. See Geyer.

Dieckhoff 1932. Henry Cyril Dieckhoff : *A pronouncing Dictionary of Scottish Gaelic, based on the Glengarry Dialect* [Inverness-shire] (Edinburgh).

Dio Cassius. *Dio's Roman History*. Edited in the Loeb Classics by E. W. Cary.

Duald's Annals. Dubhaltach mac Firbisigh : *Annals of Ireland, Three Fragments copied from Ancient Sources*. Edited by J. O'Donovan (Dublin 1860).

Duan Albanach. The latest edition ('The Poem *A eolcha Alban uile*') by Kenneth Jackson is published in *Celtica*, III, pp. 149-67 (Dublin 1955). This poem includes a metrical Middle-Irish version of the Scottish regnal list.

E.C.   *Scottish Annals from English Chroniclers*, by A. O. Anderson (London 1908).

E.S.   *Early Sources of Scottish History*, by A. O. Anderson (Edinburgh 1922).

Evagrius : translation into Latin of Athanasius's *Life of Antony* (quoted from the edition in P.L. LXXIII, in Brüning 1917).

Feachem 1955.   R. W. Feachem : ' Fortifications ', in *The Problem of the Picts* (1955), pp. 66-86.

Féilsgríbhinn 1940.   *Essays and Studies presented to Professor Eóin MacNeill* (Dublin).

Fland Mainistrech (' of Monasterboice ') :   *Synchronisms*. This work incorporates a version of the list of kings of the Scots in Britain. See E.S. I, pp. lvi, cxlii-cl. Cf. the edition by Thurneysen in *Z.C.P.* XIX, which we have not seen.

Fowler 1894.   *Adamnani Vita S. Columbae*, edited by J. T. Fowler (Oxford). The second edition, prepared in 1915, before the appearance of Brüning 1917, was published in 1920.

Fowler 1895.   J. T. Fowler : *Prophecies, Miracles, and Visions of St Columba* (London). An English translation of the above.

Geyer 1898.   *Itinera Hierosolymitana saeculi IIII-VIII*, edited by Paul Geyer (Vienna ; Corpus Scriptorum Ecclesiasticorum Latinorum, XXXVIIII). Adomnan's *De Locis Sanctis* is on pp. 219-97 ; with a useful index of words, pp. 455-80.

Gougaud 1932.   Dom Louis Gougaud : *Christianity in Celtic Lands* ; translated from the author's manuscript by Maud Joynt (London).

Haddan and Stubbs 1873.   Arthur W. Haddan and William Stubbs : *Councils and Ecclesiastical Documents relating to Great Britain and Ireland*, II, part i (Oxford).

Haldane 1952. A. R. B. Haldane: *The Drove Roads of Scotland* (Edinburgh).

H.E.   *Historia Ecclesiastica*.   See Plummer 1896.

Hogan 1910.   Edmund R. Hogan : *Onomasticon Goedelicum* (Dublin).

Irish Life of Columba.   *Betha Coluim-chille*, edited and translated by Paul Grosjean, S.J. in *S.G.S.*, II (1928), pp. 111-71. The text was taken from Advocates' Library Gaelic manuscript 40. Other texts of the Irish Life were edited by Whitley Stokes in *Three Middle-Irish Homilies* (1877) and in *Lismore Lives* (1890).

I.T.   Ernst Windisch and others : *Irische Texte* (Leipzig, 1880 onwards).

Jackson 1953.   Kenneth Jackson : *Language and History in Early Britain* (Edinburgh).

Jackson 1954.   ' Two Early Scottish Names ', in *S.H.R.* XXXIII, pp. 14-18.

Jackson 1955. 'The Pictish Language', in *The Problem of the Picts* (1955), pp. 129-66.

Jones 1913. J. Morris Jones : *A Welsh Grammar* (Oxford).

Jones 1943. Charles W. Jones : *Bedae Opera de temporibus* (Cambridge, Mass.).

Joynt 1908. See Life of Adomnan.

Kenney 1924. James F. Kenney : 'The Earliest Life of St Columcille', in *Catholic Historical Review*, new series, v (1926), pp. 636-44. A paper read in December 1924.

Kenney 1929. *The sources for the Early History of Ireland*, 1 (Ecclesiastical) (New York).

Knowles 1951. *The Monastic Constitutions of Lanfranc*, edited and translated by David Knowles.

L.B. Leabhar Breac, manuscripts in the R.I.A. library.

Levison 1946. Wilhelm Levison : *England and the Continent in the eighth century* (Oxford, photographic replica 1949).

Liber Hymnorum 1898. J. H. Bernard and R. Atkinson : *The Irish Liber Hymnorum* (Henry Bradshaw Society, London).

Life of Adomnan. *Betha Adamnáin*, edited by R. I. Best in *Anecdota from Irish Manuscripts*, II (1908), pp. 10-20 ; translated by Maud Joynt in *Celtic Review*, v, pp. 97-107 (1908, Edinburgh). This Irish Life was originally composed possibly as early as the eighth century, some generations after the death of Cellach Cualann, king of the Lagin (†715).

Life of Antony. See Evagrius.

Lindsay 1894. Wallace Martin Lindsay : *The Latin Language* (Oxford).

Lindsay 1910. *Early Irish Minuscule Script* (Oxford).

Lindsay 1915. *Notae Latinae* (Cambridge).

Lindsay 1922. 'The Letters in Early Latin Minuscule', in *Palaeographia Latina*, part i, pp. 7-61.

Lindsay 1923. 'Collectanea Varia', ibid. part ii, pp. 5-55.

L.L. *The Book of Leinster*, Trinity College, Dublin, manuscript H.2.18, edited by R. Atkinson (Dublin 1880), in hand-copied facsimile.

Lowe 1935. E. A. Lowe : *Codices Latini Antiquiores*, part ii, Great Britain and Ireland (Oxford).

Lowe 1956. *Codices Latini Antiquiores*, part vii, Switzerland.

MacBain 1922. Alexander MacBain : *Place Names, Highlands and Islands of Scotland*, edited by W. J. Watson (Stirling).

MacCarthy 1901. B. MacCarthy : *Annals of Ulster*, iv : Introduction and Index.

MacNeill 1907. Eóin MacNeill : ' Mocu, Maccu ', in *Ériu*, iii, pp. 42-9.

MacNeill 1909. ' The Irish Ogham Inscriptions ', in *P.R.I.A.* xxvii, C, no. 15 (pp. 329-70).

MacNeill 1911. ' Early Irish Population-Groups ', in *P.R.I.A.* xxix, C, no. 4 (pp. 59-114).

MacNeill 1930. ' The Vita Tripartita of St Patrick ', in *Ériu*, xi, pp. 1-41.

Martyrology of Donegal, collected by Michael O'Clery in 1630 ; edited by J. H. Todd and W. Reeves (Dublin 1864).

Meyer 1892. *Aislinge Meic Conglinne*, edited by Kuno Meyer (London).

Meyer 1908. ' Brian Borumha ', in *Ériu*, iv, pp. 68-73.

Meyer, Contributions. ' Contributions to Irish Lexicography ' (1906-1907). Supplement to *Archiv für celtische Lexicographie* (Halle).

Meyer, Wortkunde. ' Zur keltischen Wortkunde.' Published in *Sitzungs-berichte der Königlich-Preussischen Akademie der Wissenschaften* (Berlin), 1912-19.

Miracula Nynie episcopi, edited by Karl Strecker in Monumenta Germaniae Historica ; Poetae Latini Ævi Carolini, iv (1923), pp. 943-62.

Muirchu mocu Machtheni : Latin Life of Patrick, in the Book of Armagh, 2a-8d. (Another copy is in Brussels, Bibliothèque Royale, no. 64.)

New Oxford History of Music, ii : *Early Medieval Music up to 1300*, edited by Dom Anselm Hughes (Oxford 1954).

O'Davoren 1904. ' O'Davoren's Glossary ', edited by Whitley Stokes in *Archiv für celtische Lexicographie*, ii.

Oengus 1905. *The Martyrology of Oengus the Culdee*, edited by Whitley Stokes (Henry Bradshaw Society).

O'Máille 1910. Tomás O'Máille : *The Language of the Annals of Ulster* (Manchester).

O'Rahilly 1946. Thomas F. O'Rahilly : *Early Irish History and Mythology* (Dublin).

O'Rahilly 1950. Contributions to *Celtica*, I (Dublin) ; including, on pp. 387-402, notes on O'Rahilly 1946.

Palaeographia Latina, I-VI, edited by W. M. Lindsay, as a St Andrews University publication (London 1922-9).

Patrick : *Confessio*, and *Epistola*. Edited by Newport J. D. White : *Libri Sancti Patricii* (S.P.C.K., London 1918).

Pedersen 1909. Holger Pedersen : *Vergleichende Grammatik der keltischen Sprachen*, I (Göttingen).

Pedersen 1913. The same, volume II.

Piggott 1949. Stuart Piggott : *British Prehistory* (Oxford).

Piggott 1953. ' Excavations in the broch and hill-fort of Torwoodlee, Selkirkshire, 1950 ', in *P.S.A.S.* LXXXV, pp. 92-117.

Piggott 1955. ' The Archaeological Background ', in *The Problem of the Picts* (1955), pp. 54-65.

P.L. *Patrologia Latina*, edited by Migne.

Plummer 1896. *Venerabilis Baedae Opera Historica*, edited by Charles Plummer (Oxford).

Plummer 1910. *Vitae Sanctorum Hiberniae* (Oxford). Latin Lives.

Plummer 1922. *Lives of Irish Saints* (Oxford). Irish Lives, with English translation.

Pokorny. Julius Pokorny : *Indogermanisches etymologisches Wörterbuch* (Bern, 1949 onwards).

P.R.I.A. *Proceedings of the Royal Irish Academy*.

Problem of the Picts. Edited by F. T. Wainwright (Edinburgh 1955).

P.S.A.S. *Proceedings of the Society of Antiquaries of Scotland*.

Pseudo-Cummene. *Vita Columbae des sogenannten Cummeneus*, edited in Brüning 1917, pp. 291-304.

Ptolemy 1883. *Claudii Ptolemaei Geographia*, edited by C. Müller, I, part i (Paris). The Greek text is edited from many manuscripts, with a Latin translation. The section on Ireland is believed to have been derived from material that was considerably older than the British material. The North-British material was derived, in part at least, from a Roman source, written after Agricola's conquest. The spellings of Ptolemy's names are not strictly phonetic, and it is usually better to represent them in Latin letters. Omikron is not distinguished from omega, nor epsilon from eta ; *ou*, representing the sounds of long *u* and also *w*, is confused with short *u*, short *o*, and *b* (β). Many confusions resulting from itacism occur in the manuscripts. The spellings are discussed in Jackson 1953, pp. 31-5, referring to the analysis in Max Förster's *Der Flussname Themse* (Munich 1942).

Ravenna Geographer 1949. *The British Section of the Ravenna Cosmography* (Oxford) ; edition by I. A. Richmond and O. G. S. Crawford, with philological notes by Ifor Williams.

R.C. Revue Celtique (Paris, to 1934).

Reeves 1857. *The Life of St Columba . . . written by Adamnan*, edited by William Reeves (Irish Archaeological and Celtic Society, Dublin ; issued also by the Bannatyne Club).

Regnal Lists. We use this term to designate the lists of kings, with reign-lengths, contained in the so-called Chronicles of the Kings of the Picts, and of the Kings of Dalriata. See E.S. I, pp. cxix-cxxxvi.

Rhys 1904. J. Rhys : *Celtic Britain* (London). Third edition.

R.I.A. Contributions. *Contributions to a Dictionary of the Irish Language* (Royal Irish Academy).

R.I.A. Dictionary. *Dictionary of the Irish Language.*

Rule of Colum-cille, edited by Kuno Meyer in *Z.C.P.* III, pp. 28-30 ; from Bodleian manuscript Rawlinson B 512.

Ryan 1931. John Ryan, S.J. : *Irish Monasticism* (Dublin).

Ryan 1936. 'The *Cáin Adomnáin*', in *Studies in Early Irish Law*, pp. 269-76 (R.I.A. Dublin).

Ryan 1940. 'The Abbatial Succession at Clonmacnoise', in *Féilsgríbhinn* 1940, pp. 490-507.

Saltair na Rann, edited by Whitley Stokes from Rawlinson B 502 (Oxford 1883).

Sanas Cormaic. See Cormac.

S.D. See Symeon of Durham.

Senchus. *Miniugud Senchusa fer nAlban*, in the *Book of Ballymote*, facsimile edition p. 148 ; and edited in Skene 1867, pp. 308-14. The translation in E.S. I, pp. cl-cliii, needs revision.

S.G.S. Scottish Gaelic Studies (Oxford).

S.H.R. Scottish Historical Review (Edinburgh).

Skene 1867. W. F. Skene : *Chronicles of the Picts, Chronicles of the Scots, and other early memorials of Scottish History* (Edinburgh).

Skene 1874. *Historians of Scotland*, VI ; *Life of Saint Columba . . . written by Adamnan . . .* edited by William Reeves (Edinburgh). This contains a reprint of Reeves's text and textual notes. Reeves's other editorial matter was abbreviated and rearranged by Skene, who added some material of his own.

Skene 1876. 'Notes on the History and probable situation of the earlier establishments at Iona', in *P.S.A.S.* XI, pp. 330-49.

Skene 1886. *Celtic Scotland,* second edition, 1 (Edinburgh).

Skene 1887. The same, volume II.

Sommer 1914. Ferdinand Sommer : *Handbuch der lateinischen Laut- und Formenlehre* (Heidelberg).

Souter 1949. Alexander Souter : *A Glossary of later Latin, to 600* A.D. (Oxford).

Stenton 1947. Sir Frank M. Stenton : *Anglo-Saxon England,* second edition (Oxford).

Stevenson 1949. Robert B. K. Stevenson : 'The nuclear fort of Dalmahoy ', in *P.S.A.S.* LXXXIII, pp. 186-98.

Stevenson 1955. ' Pictish Art ', in *The Problem of the Picts* (1955), pp. 97-128.

Stokes 1887. *The Tripartite Life of Patrick* . . . edited by Whitley Stokes (Rolls Series 89).

Stowe Missal 1906. *The Stowe Missal,* edited in facsimile, by Sir George F. Warner, from manuscript D. II. 3 in R.I.A. Library, Dublin (Henry Bradshaw Society, London). This Missal of Tallaght dates from the beginning of the ninth century ; it represents a liturgy of the seventh century.

Stowe Missal 1913. Transcription of the same, with notes, by Sir G. F. Warner.

Sturtevant 1920. E. H. Sturtevant : *The Pronunciation of Greek and Latin* (Chicago).

Sulpicius Severus. *Sulpicii Severi Libri qui supersunt,* edited by Carolus Halm (Vienna 1866 ; Corpus Scriptorum Ecclesiasticorum Latinorum, 1).

Symeon of Durham. *Symeonis monachi Opera Omnia,* edited by Thomas Arnold (Rolls Series 75 ; 1882, 1885).

T. *Tigernach's Annals.*

Tacitus. *Cornelii Taciti Vita Agricolae,* edited by Henry Furneaux (Oxford 1898).

Tallaght Discourse. E. J. Gwynn and W. J. Purton : ' The monastery of Tallaght ', in *P.R.I.A.* XXIX, C, no. 5 (1911). This important tract was first brought into notice by W. J. Purton.

Thesaurus 1901. Whitley Stokes and John Strachan : *Thesaurus Palaeo-hibernicus,* 1 (Cambridge).

Thesaurus 1903. The same, volume II.

Thompson 1912. Edward Maunde Thompson : *An Introduction to Greek and Latin Palaeography* (Oxford).

Thurneysen 1946.   Rudolf Thurneysen : *A Grammar of Old Irish* ; revised and enlarged edition, translated by D. A. Binchy and Osborn Bergin (Dublin).

Tigernach's Annals.   Bodleian manuscript Rawlinson B 488, folios 7 ff. Edited by Whitley Stokes, in *R.C.* XVII-XVIII (Paris 1896-7).   Our references to this chronicle are taken from facsimiles of the manuscript. In the annal that mentions Tigernach's death, in 1088, it is said that he *hucusque scribsit* (T. 1961 3).   The writing is much later, and there is no change of hand here.   The chronicle continues to 1178.   It was unfortunate that in E.S. preference was given to T. over A.U.   Notwithstanding the later date of A.U., their common source is very often more correctly copied in A.U. than in T.

Walsh 1921.   Paul Walsh : ' Uí maccu Uais ', in *Ériu*, IX, pp. 55-60.

Watson 1912.   William J. Watson : ' The Circular Forts of north Perthshire ', in *P.S.A.S.* XLVII, pp. 30-60.

Watson 1914.   ' Circular Forts in Lorn and north Perthshire ', in *P.S.A.S.* XLIX, pp. 17-32.

Watson 1926.   *The History of the Celtic Place-names of Scotland* (Edinburgh).

Windisch 1880.   Ernst Windisch : *Irische Texte mit Wörterbuch* (I.T. 1).

Z.C.P.   *Zeitschrift für celtische Philologie* (Halle).

Genealogical Tables

THE ROYAL FAMILY OF THE DAL-RÉTI
(The kings are numbered.   See pp. 36-59)

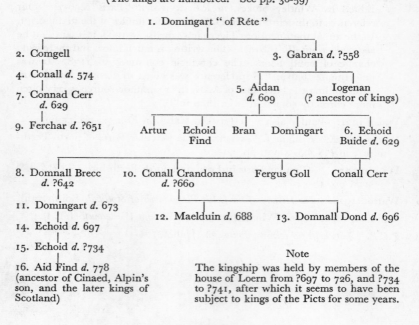

1. Domingart " of Réte "

2. Comgell

4. Conall d. 574

7. Connad Cerr
d. 629

9. Ferchar d. ?651

3. Gabran d. ?558

5. Aidan
d. 609

Iogenan
(? ancestor of kings)

Artur   Echoid   Bran   Domingart
Find

6. Echoid
Buide d. 629

8. Domnall Brecc
d. ?642

10. Conall Crandomna
d. ?660

Fergus Goll   Conall Cerr

11. Domingart d. 673

12. Maelduin d. 688   13. Domnall Dond d. 696

14. Echoid d. 697

15. Echoid d. ?734

16. Aid Find d. 778
(ancestor of Cinaed, Alpin's
son, and the later kings of
Scotland)

Note
The kingship was held by members of the
house of Loern from ?697 to 726, and ?734
to ?741, after which it seems to have been
subject to kings of the Picts for some years.

THE NORTHERN UI-NÉILL

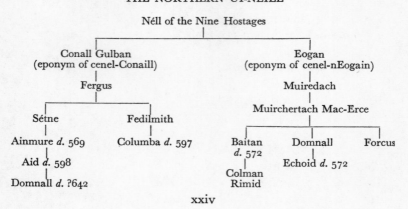

Néll of the Nine Hostages

Conall Gulban
(eponym of cenel-Conaill)

Fergus

Eogan
(eponym of cenel-nEogain)

Muiredach

Muirchertach Mac-Erce

Sétne

Fedilmith

Ainmure d. 569

Columba d. 597

Baitan
d. 572

Domnall

Forcus

Aid d. 598

Colman
Rimid

Echoid d. 572

Domnall d. ?642

xxiv

Introduction

OUR text is that of the Schaffhausen manuscript (A). Some chapter-headings and other passages in A that were originally written in red ink have faded badly ; but thanks to the skill of the photographers, in only three places has the writing remained illegible to us, and in none of these is there any doubt as to the reading. See notes on 5b and 43b.

We have followed exactly the spelling and accents of the original hand, extending the abbreviations. Vocalic *u* (whether written in a *u* or a *v* shape) is printed as *u* ; and consonantal *u* (of either shape), as *v*. So also vocalic *i* (of various shapes) is printed as *i*, and consonantal *i*, as *j*. The *ae* symbol (of various forms) is printed as *ae* when it stands in a Latin word, or a latinized form of an Irish name ; and as *æ* when it stands in an unlatinized Irish name or word. The punctuation of the text hand, the use of enlarged letters, the separation of words and of paragraphs, have been everywhere studied, but we have given in our text and translation the punctuation (including question-marks), and the capital letters, that seemed necessary for a modern reader.

We have described in the footnotes all alterations and additions made in A by later hands, including added accents, but excluding added punctuation marks except where they have some special interest. We have noted all variations between A and B1, B2, or B3, in the spelling and accentuation of Irish, British, and Saxon names and words, including latinized forms ; excepting the name of Iona, which is always *iova* etc. in A, B1, and B2, and always *iona* etc. in B3. In purely Latin words, accents in the B manuscripts have been noted, as a rule, only in words that are noted for some other reason. Variations in the spelling of Latin words have been noted, with certain exceptions. The Latin spelling of each of the B manuscripts is to a great extent the normal spelling of its own time, and as such can throw no light on the origins or relationships of the B text. In order to avoid cumbering the notes with variants of this kind, we have not noted the following variants except when a word has to be noted for some other reason : *ae* in A / *e* in the B manuscripts : similarly *oe* / *e* ; *y* / *i* ; *bt* / *pt* ; *c* / *ch* ; *ch* / *c* ; *f* / *ph* ; *g* / *gu* ; *h* added or omitted ; *h* / *ch* (in *michi* B3) ; *mn, mpn,* used interchangeably ; *mqu* / *nqu* ; *mt* / *mpt* ; *ncx* / *nx* ; *np* / *mp* ; *qu, cu* / *quu* ; *qu* / *cu* ; *sp* / *sb* ; final *t* / final *d* (e.g. *haut, inquit*) ; *ti* before a vowel / *ci* ; *u* / *uv* or *vu* ; unassimilated consonants in A, assimilated in the B manuscripts (e.g. *subfulto* / *suffulto*) ; fluctuation between single and double consonants.

We have, however, noted all variations between *i* and *e*, and between *u* and *o*, because in some cases they affect the sense (e.g. in the prefixes *di* and *de* ; *-cid-* and *-ced-* in compounds of *cedere*; *mutare* and *motare*).

In giving a variant spelling of a Latin word, we have sometimes quoted only the relevant part of the word, substituting hyphens for the unquoted parts. In such cases, we have ignored in the unquoted parts of a word any accents, and any of the spelling variations that are included in the above list. This not altogether satisfactory method has avoided much repetition of virtually identical readings from the different B manuscripts.

Square brackets are used in notes of readings, to indicate that part of a word is missing or illegible in the manuscript cited. The closing-bracket (]), placed before a reading, means that something is missing before it ; the opening-bracket ([), placed after a reading, means that something is missing after it. This applies almost solely to readings of B2, in which, owing to damage by fire, many letters are missing, or are illegible in the photostatic copy from which we have worked.

For our method of printing accents, see p. 163.

THE MANUSCRIPTS

Adomnan's Life of Columba is known to exist in four manuscripts, representing two slightly different versions : A ; and B1, B2, B3.

A, the Dorbbene manuscript, is Generalia 1 in the Stadtbibliothek of Schaffhausen, Switzerland. This manuscript was written by an Irish hand, apparently early in the eighth century, and probably in Iona ; and was taken to the Continent perhaps before A.D. 800, certainly not later than the ninth century. See pp. 12, 103, 175. A library signature at the bottom of page 1, apparently *liber augie majoris*, is nearly all decipherable, and shows that in the thirteenth century the manuscript belonged to the monastery of Reichenau, an island in Lake Constance. That may not have been its first continental home, for ninth-century catalogues of Reichenau manuscripts make no mention of it (Brüning 1917, p. 218). In 1621, it was still in Reichenau. By 1795 it was in the Stadtbibliothek of Schaffhausen, where it now is. For the details of its history, see Reeves 1857, pp. ix, xv, xxii ff. ; Lowe 1956, p. 45. Miss Brüning referred to the *Verzeichnis der Inkunabeln und Handschriften der Schaffhauser Stadtbibliothek*, by H. Boos (1903).

A copy of A was made in 1621 by Stephen White, a Jesuit scholar. His transcript provided the text of the Life of Columba in Colgan's *Trias Thaumaturga* 1647, and also that edited by Baertius for the Bollandists' *Acta Sanctorum*, 1698. These editions are occasionally cited by Reeves 1857. Reeves used A as the basis of his own text. His edition provided, for the first time in print, a fairly accurate text of the work. As an edition of the Schaffhausen manuscript, it is unsatisfactory, judged by modern standards. It contains errors of transcription, some of which result from misunderstanding of the writing ; for instance, he transcribed $d \sim m$ as *dominum* instead of *deum*. He normalized the Latin spelling of A, and made some silent changes of grammatical forms. We have drawn attention to his errors in a few cases.

Reeves's text, and much of his illustrative material, were reprinted in Skene 1874. The text was again reprinted, with ' slight variations ', in Fowler 1894 (second edition, 1920).

B1 is in the British Museum manuscript, Additional 35110, folios 96 verso to 143 recto. The manuscript was probably written at Durham. B1 is preceded, in the same Anglo-Norman hand, by a list of bishops of Durham, ending within the episcopate of Hugh of Pudsey (1154-1195). B1 is followed (after the list of Columba's monks and relations, see Appendix) by extracts from Bede concerning Columba (Brüning 1917, p. 219). To judge from the handwriting, B1 was written not many years before or after 1195. One point, however, suggests an earlier date. In the Life of Oswald attributed to Reginald of Durham, and composed in 1165 (Symeon of Durham, 1, pp. 367, 382), there is a passage derived from Adomnan (8a–9b). One of its readings, *expergefactus*, suggests that the manuscript of Adomnan that was used was B1, since the reading is peculiar to B1, and resulted there from an alteration by the text hand ; see note under 8b. That would mean that B1 was written × 1165, unless the passage was a later interpolation in the Life of Oswald. B1 was rather carelessly transcribed, but was carefully corrected by the text hand in accordance with a reviser's notes, many of which are visible in the margins. The rest of the volume Add. 35110 contains a Life of Augustine of Hippo, Bede's Life of Cuthbert, and other matter relating to Cuthbert, Bede's Lives of king Oswald and bishop Aidan, and Ailred's Life of Edward the Confessor. B1 has not hitherto been used by editors of the Life of Columba.

B2 is in the British Museum Cottonian manuscript, Tiberius D III, folios 192 recto to 217 recto. It is written in a hand of about the end of the twelfth century, or very early in the thirteenth. The whole volume was badly damaged by the fire of 1731, and parts of every page of B2 are missing or illegible. Before the fire (cf. Reeves 1857, p. xxviii), and before the folios were numbered, six folios of B2 were lost from one of the quires, leaving only the two central folios, now numbered 195 and 196. For the gaps thus created, see 13b, 37a. The volume is a collection of Lives of Saints, arranged under the saints' days, mostly in May and June. At the end of the Life of Columba, after the list of monks and relatives, is a poem evidently copied by the writer of B2 from his exemplar, and throwing some light on the history of his text; see below. B2 was collated by Reeves after most of the work of his edition had been done. The results of his collation are printed in Reeves 1857, pp. 456–8.

B3 is in the British Museum manuscript Royal 8 D IX, folios 1 recto to 70 recto. B3 is written in a very legible book-hand of the fifteenth or perhaps early sixteenth century. The beginning of the volume is lost, including about the first eight folios of the Life, presumably a quire. After the Life, and the list of monks and relatives, the remainder of folio 70 recto is left blank. The rest of the volume is occupied by a Rule of Augustine and commentaries upon it. B3 was used by John Pinkerton in his *Vitae Antiquae*, 1789. The manuscript was collated by Reeves, and the results were given in his footnotes, where he calls it B.

For further details of the editions, see Reeves 1857, pp. ix–x ; Brüning 1917, pp. 225–6 ; Kenney 1929, p. 430.

A is not the source of the text preserved in the B manuscripts. Many small errors and omissions in A are not shared by them. See e.g. 5a, 37a (*jugulentus*), 60b, 65b, 105a, 115b, 129b. The B manuscripts show no trace of the insertion made by the writer of A in 108a. In the spelling of Irish names, the B manuscripts preserve some forms that are more archaic than those of A. It is clear that the common ancestor of A and the B version must have belonged to a date earlier than the writing of A. This gives the B manuscripts considerable textual value, in spite of their late date.

There is reason to think that Adomnan wrote the greater part of the Life between the years 688 and 692 ; see p. 96. References here and there in the text to earlier, or later, parts of the Life give an impression that the whole work was written consecutively as it now stands. Some of these references, however, could have been supplied in the process of revision, and they are not always evidence of the order in which the work was composed.

At the end of the preliminary first chapter of Book I (I 1, 10b), Adomnan says that what he has to tell ' will be related more fully below, in three books, with the help of God ' ; as though the bulk of the work was still to be written. The contents of the chapter, however, strongly suggest that it was composed after the work, or the greater part of it, was already in writing. In that chapter, Adomnan provides the reader with a foretaste of what is to come, giving prominence to some of the more dramatic miracles from the second book. The language of the summary is largely made up of phrases that recur in the chapters themselves, and that seem better suited to the full narrative style of those chapters than to a proleptic survey. The phrases in I 1 would seem to have been quoted by Adomnan from memory, and not always accurately (see note on *optatum* under 6b ; cf. p. 20). Two stories that are told at length in I 1 are almost certainly afterthoughts. Their natural place would seem to have been at the end of the second book, among miracles that happened after Columba's lifetime.

The opening of I 1 refers back to the ' second preface ', which serves several of the purposes of an Introduction, and which may actually have been the original beginning of the work. The first ' preface ', the author's apology for his book, was perhaps added later ; otherwise it is difficult to see why there should have been two prefaces.

The latest section to be included in Adomnan's draft was perhaps the incomplete contents-list of the first book. Its items are largely derived from the chapter-headings, which had apparently been composed as integral parts of the work. The list omits the chapter on Aid the Black (I 36), and the composite chapter I 37, so that there is a possibility of those having been added after the list was drawn up. The composite chapter, indeed, on a miraculous fragrance, and on the power of Columba's voice, seems to intrude rather oddly into a sequence of chapters on the punishment of wicked men. If the story of Aid the Black was indeed one of Adomnan's last additions to his draft, it would be tempting to suppose that the story was added during his visit to Iona in, or shortly before, 697, and that it was written in indignation at the murder in 695 of the high-king Fínsnechtae, who, according to later accounts, had been Adomnan's friend.

The contents-list omits also the last seven chapters of the first book, but this may mean only that Adomnan left the list unfinished. Apparently he never made contents-lists for the second and third books.

That the common source of A and the B text was itself a fair copy of Adomnan's work is suggested by a closely parallel use, in A and the B manuscripts, of large and decorative initial letters, especially when these do not seem to be urgently required by the sense. (See e.g. 53b, and *Alia* in 100b.) The common source was not quite free of error. Mistakes common to the two versions, and so presumably present in the source, are detectable at 6a, 23b, 56a (*Crastina* beginning a new sentence), 101b, 109b (perhaps an author's omission), 125b ; cf. an unwanted punctuation point in both versions after *frequentationes*, 7b. At 67b and 107a we have suggested that sentences have been misplaced, pointing to marginal additions having been made, by Adomnan or on his instructions, either in the common source itself or, perhaps more probably, in the draft from which it was derived.

There are some phrases in A that do not appear in the B text : an exclamation on Columba's having restored a boy to life (7a) ; the explanation that a boar encountered by Columba was being chased by hunting-dogs (74a) ; and at the end of a chapter concerning the vindication of Columba at a synod that would have excommunicated him, the statement, ' This utterance was made in Teiltiu ' (106b). It is difficult to see why these phrases, if they had been in the common source, should have been omitted in the B text. The last in particular looks like an addition to the original text, since the natural place to say where the incident happened would have been at the beginning of the chapter, not the end. Each of these phrases adds something substantial to the sense, and is the kind of thing that an author, looking over his work, would add where he felt it was needed. If A was, as it could have been, copied directly from the common source, these phrases would have been added to the source after the progenitor of the B manuscripts had been transcribed from it.

The only other additions of substance in A's text were made by the writer of A himself : the insertion at 108a ; and the Dorbbene colophon on 136a.

The B text contains one substantial passage that is not in A, the story of Vigenus, which we print as a continuation of II 20 (68a). There is reason, apart from its absence in A, to think that this was not a part of the original text.

Of minor changes made in the B text, some are undoubtedly early. The chapter 44 in Book II concerns a drought in Iona in Adomnan's time, and the B text adds to A's heading (98b) : ' The miracle that we are now . . . about to describe was performed in our time, and we beheld it with our own eyes '. It is hardly credible that if this had been in A's original the writer of A would have left it out. The addition evidently purports to be in Adomnan's words, and there seems no reason to doubt that it was in fact added by him, presumably for the benefit of readers outside Iona, to whom the Iona drought was not a living memory. Adomnan may have taken to Ireland, and revised there, the copy of his work that became the ancestor of the B manuscripts. There are other possible author's alterations in the B text at 44b and 96b.

It seems that for some reason the chapter-headings from II 19 to II 28 were extensively altered and expanded in the B text, taking most of their extra substance from the chapters themselves. It is in this same part that the B text adds the story of Vigenus. That addition and the work on the headings may have been done at one time and by one person. As to whether that person was Adomnan, it can only be said that the style is not inconsistent with his authorship. The heading at II 28 in the B text seems to have been composed outside

Iona, for A's *hujus insulae* appears in the B text as *insule Iove* ; and since copyists of the B text elsewhere left unaltered Adomnan's references to Iona as ' this island ', the change at II 28 was presumably made at the same time as the rest of this group of changes.

In the heading of II 13 (62b) the B text adds *in vortice Brecain* ' in Coire-Brecain '. This piece of information is not to be found in the chapter itself. It is not in the corresponding heading in the contents-list of B2 B3, and may have been a comparatively late addition, by some one who knew Irish. It may be noted that Adomnan might have been expected to write a latinized form *Brecani*, as in 17a. Some words also, in praise of Columba, added in the B text to the heading of the last chapter, III 23, are not in the heading as it is given in the contents-list, and were perhaps a later addition.

At the end of the B text were added a list of the monks who went with Columba to Britain, and a list of some of his relatives. The language is early ; see p. 545. Of Columba's companions, only Baithene, Ernan, and Diormit (the first three in the list) are mentioned by Adomnan in the Life.

Contents-lists were added at the beginnings of the second and third books, in the B text (B2 B3 ; there are no contents-lists in B1). This was done after the story of Vigenus had been inserted, and after the alterations had been made in the headings of II 19–28 and 44. The maker of the lists copied, for the most part, the chapter-headings of the B text. It is impossible to be sure whether the lists were made by Adomnan. Some discrepancies between them and the text could have been the doing of copyists. If Adomnan had made the lists, we might have expected him at the same time to have finished the contents-list of the first book, but that is as incomplete in the B text as in A. In the heading of II 11 (61b), for *in Pictorum regione* the contents-list reads *ultra Brittannicum dorsum*, and this might suggest that the list had been made later than the middle of the ninth century, at a time when there was no longer a kingdom of the Picts. We have treated the contents-lists of

c

the second and third books as not being by Adomnan ; see note on 52b.

Stories taken from Adomnan are to be found in the Irish Life of Columba, composed in the eleventh or twelfth century. Some are in Latin Lives of other Irish saints (Brüning 1917, pp. 290–1) : but those Lives may be late, and comparison would be needed to see whether they took the stories from a complete text of Adomnan's work (most probably a B text), or from a shortened continental version (see below).

In the first quarter of the twelfth century a transcript of the B text was made in Scotland. We know of it from the Latin poem that is preserved in B2 (printed in Reeves 1857, p. xxix : reprinted in Haddan and Stubbs 1873, p. 276). The poem had evidently been attached to a copy of the Life of Columba made by a scribe called William at the command of a Scottish king Alexander. The handwriting of B2 can hardly be as late as the reign of Alexander II, so that the king who ordered the transcript must have been Alexander I. The work was apparently done in a religious house that the poet calls *insula pontificum*. There is no reason whatever to suppose that Iona was meant. Further study is needed to establish the identity of this *insula*, but it may be said that the most likely place seems to be the house of Celi-dé on the island of St Serf in Loch Leven.

Our three B manuscripts may all be descendants of William's copy. Certainly they are very closely related to one another, and seem to be derived from an original whose scribe was ignorant of Irish. He wrote *Clocherum filium* (57b), as if *clocher*, literally ' stony place ', had been a man's name ; and *vita anteriorum* for *provincia anteriorum* (109b), not realizing that this was a place-name, ' province of the Airthir ', or ' Easterners '. He used diaeresis accents on double vowels that were in fact merely Irish long vowels.

The spelling of Latin in the B text, very different from that of A, may be largely due to twelfth-century scribes. A few of what were probably Adomnan's own spellings have survived in the B manuscripts : *visionem*, an error for *iusionem* (38b), must go back to *iusionem* with single *s* ; the B text several times had Adomnan's *cognitio, cognitionalis*, for *-nat-* ; *incedens, incedet*, probably Adomnan's spelling, *-ced-* for *-cid-* (85a) ; *alio* as a dative (103a) ; *dimersis, dimersi*, probably Adomnan's *di-* for *de-* (114a) ; *honorificantia* instead of *-centia* (116b) ; *ad notandum* (118a) ; *draignichae* (121a).

Small grammatical variations between A and the B manuscripts are probably in most cases the result of attempts at improvement by copyists of the B text. The same is probably true of differences in vocabulary, especially where the B text has substituted a more familiar word for an uncommon one : e.g. *culpas* for *peccantias* (32a) ; *leprosi* for *lepri* (61b) ; *natante* for *nante* (75a) ; *lapis* for *lithus* (80b) ; *leticia* for *laetatio* and *laetamen* (123ab, 125b).

As for the relationship between the B manuscripts, it can be said that none of them is the source of another. B2 and B3 seem to be more closely related to one another than either is to B1 (see for example their readings of *Ernene*, 132a ; *noscibilis,* 135b). This makes B1 important for establishing the common B text.

Later users of the B text do not much concern us. The Life of Oswald (A.D. 1165) has already been mentioned. Fordun, in the fourteenth century, made use of a version of the B text, including the list of Columba's monks ; but his text was not that of B2, as Reeves thought, since it contained the words *quia . . . deligeret* (107a), which B2 omits (see Fordun's *Chronica*, edited by Skene (1871), p. 113).

Derived Versions

Most of the medieval Lives of Columba are found in continental manuscripts. Miss Brüning classified about twenty texts that take their material partly, in most cases wholly, from Adomnan (Brüning 1917, pp. 220–3, 269, 277). Only two of them (each existing in several manuscripts) need concern us here.

A shortened version of Adomnan's work was made about

the middle of the ninth century or earlier. The earliest known copy of it (S) was written in the monastery of St Gall, in Switzerland, between 841 and 872 (ibid. p. 220). With the exception of some omissions and changes designed to adapt the Life for reading aloud in a continental monastery (ibid. pp. 216 ff.), the shortened version is a straightforward copy of Adomnan, and has generally been treated as a separate text of his work, on a level with A and the B text. But there can be no reasonable doubt that A was in fact its source, and its textual interest is therefore very small. The passage inserted in 108a by the scribe of A was copied in its entirety in the shortened version. The story of Vigenus, added in the B text, is absent from it. There are about a dozen errors in which the shortened version follows A. A few examples of omission common to both are : *describo* 58a ; a phrase in 65b ; *libro* 121a ; *ab* 131b. Sometimes a variety of readings among manuscripts of the shortened version marks an unsatisfactory reading of A, which different copyists have independently tried to improve, e.g. at 31a, *qu(a)e displicent* B1 B2 B3, rightly ; *quae displicet* A ; *quod displicet* S D C ; *quod displicent* F ; *quae displicent* L.

Reeves, in his notes, gave readings from four texts (S F D C) of the shortened version, with various degrees of thoroughness. We ourselves have used, from a photographic facsimile, an eleventh-century copy of the version, in the British Museum manuscript, Additional 19726, folios 59 recto to 97 recto, which Miss Brüning listed as an unclassified text. We have compared it throughout with our other texts and with Reeves's readings of S F D C, and have occasionally referred to it as L. It seems to be closely related to F, a tenth-century manuscript. A few of C's readings have been checked in the reprinted edition (1725) of Canisius's *Antiquae Lectiones* (i, pp. 678-708). It appears from Reeves's few readings of the St Gall manuscript that, although earlier than the others, it was not itself their source. See errors cited from S in Reeves 1857, pp. 30 (two), 62, 143, 144 ; in all these cases, L agrees with A.

The other medieval Life of Columba that we have to

discuss is the one that we call pseudo-Cummene. It was edited by Miss Brüning from three manuscripts of the thirteenth and fifteenth centuries, and from early printed texts. (Brüning 1917, pp. 291–304 : cf. pp. 260 ff.) We have used also photographs of one of her manuscripts, St Omer no. 716.

The passage that the scribe of A inserted in 108a begins : ' Cummene the White, in the book that he wrote concerning the miraculous powers of Saint Columba, said this ... '. Naturally scholars have hoped to identify among the Lives of Columba that lost work of Cummene the White, abbot of Iona from 657 to 669. The text of pseudo-Cummene printed in 1668 in Achery and Mabillon, 1, pp. 361 ff., has the heading *Vita S. Columbae Abbatis Hyensis in Anglia, auctore Cummeneo Albo perantiquo. Ex MS. cod. Compendiensis Monasterii.* It was supposed by Reeves, and later by Kenney, (Kenney 1929, p. 428), that the attribution to Cummene was taken from the manuscript. But Mabillon's note which follows the heading makes it clear that the attribution was an inference. After a quotation from the passage of 108a, citing Canisius's edition (1604) of the shortened version (he does not seem to have known Colgan's edition (1647) of the entire text) he adds : *Haec verba reperiuntur in subjecta Vita num. 5* [pseudo-Cummene, chapter 5] *quae proinde ipsius Auctoris Cummenei fetus est.* He inferred, illogically, that since chapter 5 omits the reference to Cummene it is therefore the work of Cummene himself. The Compiègne manuscript is lost ; no attribution to Cummene is made in any of the known surviving manuscripts of the work. But the supposed authority of Mabillon has carried great weight. Fowler, in his edition of Adomnan, went so far as to print in italics those words that are in pseudo-Cummene to show the use that Adomnan had made of this supposed source.

Miss Brüning formed the definite opinion that pseudo-Cummene was not Cummene's lost work, and was not a source used by Adomnan, but was itself extracted from the work of Adomnan. Dr J. F. Kenney was not completely convinced by Miss Brüning's arguments, and reopened the case for Cummene's authorship (Kenney 1924 ; cf. Kenney 1929, pp. 428–9).

The question is much more than a formal one, affecting as it does a great deal of Adomnan's work, historically as well as textually. We need not here recapitulate the more general arguments of Miss Brüning and Dr Kenney. But it does seem to us that even a general survey makes it almost impossible to regard pseudo-Cummene as an original work and a source of Adomnan. The stories that it contains are bare bones, lacking not merely much of Adomnan's literary art, but almost all the detail and local circumstance that give life to his stories, and all but a very few proper names. (Cf. E.S. 1, p. 55.) If Adomnan had really made use of pseudo-Cummene, he would have had practically to rewrite many of the chapters, drawing heavily on other written sources, oral tradition, or his own invention. Yet, as can readily be seen from the italics in Miss Brüning's edition, he would at the same time have meticulously preserved almost every word of pseudo-Cummene's text ; and it is difficult to see why he should have done this. The only story that Adomnan actually tells us he found in writing (131b) is not in pseudo-Cummene.

The matter can only be settled, however, by a detailed comparison. Chapters 25–27 of pseudo-Cummene, consisting of very brief summaries of stories from Adomnan's first and second books, are admittedly derived from Adomnan. Kenney, in order to sustain his argument, was obliged to regard these three chapters as a later medieval addition. The following points are selected from chapters 1–24.

At the end of III 4 (107a), Adomnan says ' In those days ' (i.e. after Columba's visit to his old master Finnio) ' the saint sailed over to Britain with twelve disciples '. There is reason to think that the sentence was attached to the wrong chapter in the common source of A and the B text, and that Adomnan meant it to stand at the end of the previous chapter, which tells of a much later episode in Columba's life. The author of pseudo-Cummene copied the sentence in its wrong position, after the visit to Finnio. (In Miss Brüning's text it is printed as the first sentence of the following chapter, but there is no division into chapters in the St Omer manuscript, and the division seems to be due to Mabillon.)

The next chapter of pseudo-Cummene begins *Quo perveniens*, i.e. 'when he reached Britain', and goes on to relate the changing of water into wine in the church of bishop Finnio (here called Finnian). But that miracle belonged to Columba's youth ; and Finnio's church was of course, as Adomnan says, *in Scotia* 'in Ireland' (53a). The writer of pseudo-Cummene seems to have thought that *Scotia* was 'Scotland', a meaning that it did not take on until centuries after Adomnan's time. Kenney considered that the water-changing chapter was a later addition to pseudo-Cummene, on the ground that its position as chapter 4 is awkward, and because it comes from Adomnan's second book, whereas nearly all the rest of chapters 1–24 corresponds to stories in his third book. But in fact the story comes in naturally enough, in the scheme of pseudo-Cummene which, unlike Adomnan's scheme, attempts to be chronological. Both it, and the story of the visit, which in pseudo-Cummene preceded it, belong to Columba's youth, and both concern bishop Finnio. There seems to be no reason to doubt that chapter 4 was an original part of pseudo-Cummene, and if so it is evidence that pseudo-Cummene was a late composition by someone ignorant of Irish tradition and the circumstances of Columba's life.

Miss Brüning tabulated quotations from Sulpicius Severus and the Life of Antony, as they appear in Adomnan and in pseudo-Cummene. These are further abbreviated by pseudo-Cummene than by Adomnan : and Kenney explained this by supposing that Adomnan was familiar with the originals, and quoted them from memory more fully than his source had done. In one case, however, where it is an idea that is borrowed rather than words, pseudo-Cummene has failed to understand it. It is the idea, in the Life of Antony, of the soul as a deposit entrusted to man by God. Adomnan (125b) makes Columba, shortly before his death, speak of an angel's coming to claim ' a *depositum*, dear to God ', meaning his own soul. In pseudo-

Cummene chapter 18 the angel has been sent *pro cujusdam missus depositione deo cari*, which should mean 'for the death' (if not 'the burial') 'of a man dear to God' (cf. *depositio* in Souter 1949, p. 96). It would be straining Kenney's argument too far, to suppose that pseudo-Cummene's is here the earlier version, and Adomnan's the later.

In 120a Adomnan describes a supernatural light that filled, 'not without an effect of great terror', the room where the boy Virgno was hiding. In pseudo-Cummene chapter 15, the room itself is 'filled with great terror'; an impossible statement resulting from careless abbreviation. By a similar unfortunate abbreviation, in the account of Columba's fight with demons (110b), pseudo-Cummene chapter 9 reads : 'Nor were the many [demons] able to overcome the one [Columba], until angels of God came to help'. The meaning of the sentence is destroyed by the omission (before 'until') of Adomnan's words 'nor was the one able to repel them from his island'.

In Adomnan's III 23, after the death of Columba there is a long digression, in which Adomnan describes visions that were seen in Ireland on that night. He then reverts to the moment of the saint's death in Iona, taking up his story again with the word *Interea*, 'Meanwhile' (133a). In pseudo-Cummene chapter 23, the visions are omitted, and the story of Columba's death and obsequies is continuous, but the now pointless *Interea* is retained.

The story of Virgno had been told to Adomnan himself (*mihi Adomnano*, 120b) by Virgno's nephew. Pseudo-Cummene repeats the story in Adomnan's words, but more briefly. He does not refer to Adomnan or Adomnan's informant.

Columba's prophetic warning to king Aidan, which was inserted by the scribe of A in 108a, and which is absent from the B version, appears in pseudo-Cummene chapter 5, empty of its historical and political content. The references to Columba's kinsmen in Ireland (the cenel-Conaill) are cut out, leaving the reader of pseudo-Cummene with the impression that Aidan's descendants were warned merely against infrin-

ging the rights of Columba's successors in Iona. The story of
how the prophecy was fulfilled, *temporibus nostris*, in the battle
of Roth and its consequences, is reduced to *Quod ita factum est* ;
mandatum namque viri dei transgredientes regnum perdiderunt.

Apart from the passage in 108a, there is evidence that the
source of pseudo-Cummene was A, and not a B text. In the
B text, Adomnan makes the angel say to Columba's mother :
Viro enim cui matrimoniali copula es juncta . . . filium editura es. The
writer of A omitted the grammatically-necessary noun *copula* ;
and various texts derived from A show various attempts at
restoring a grammatical construction (see note under 105a).
Pseudo-Cummene omits *cui* and *es*, as well as *copula*, and makes
matrimoniali qualify *viro*, thus : *viro enim matrimoniali juncta . . .
filium editura es.* The unusual phrase *vir matrimonialis* is a clumsy
expression for ' married husband ', but is intelligible as an
attempted emendation of A's text.

Other passages might be mentioned, none of them conclusive in itself, but all pointing to the same conclusion, that
pseudo-Cummene was not an original or early work, and that
it was derived ultimately from manuscript A of Adomnan's
Life of Columba.

The text of pseudo-Cummene seems to have originated in
Flanders or northern France, and may have been prepared as
part of a great collection of saints' Lives that was made not
earlier than the middle of the twelfth century (see Brüning
1917, pp. 270–2).

Miss Brüning mentioned, but did not classify, a Life of
Columba in a thirteenth-century manuscript, Paris, Bibliothèque Nationale, Latin 5323, folios 133 recto to 140 recto.
We have collated it with our text from a photostatic copy, and
have cited it occasionally as P. It is evidently a close cognate
of a twelfth-century fragment in Le Mans 217. Both begin
with the same introductory paragraph (in P, *De beato Columbo
. . . infigatur* ; cf. Brüning 1917, pp. 222–3). This is followed
in P by extracts from Bede. From 133d onwards, the text is
copied from Adomnan. Folios have been lost before and after
folio 135.

P, when entire, may have contained the greater part of Adomnan's text, omitting the chapters I 27, 34, 35, II 43, and III 20, unless those were included, out of order, in the missing folios. There are no contents-lists. The chapter-headings are sometimes abbreviated, and some proper names and some of Adomnan's comments are omitted. The text is treated much more freely than in the shortened version ; whole sentences are reconstructed, and some difficult clauses left out.

There is no doubt that P's text of Adomnan was derived from A. It contains the inserted passage of 108a (including the attribution to Cummene) ; and several of its readings seem to result from the omission of a word by the writer of A (see e.g. notes on 97a and 105a).

In both P and the shortened version, the first book begins at *Sanctus igitur* (4a). In P there is a large and highly ornate initial *S*, and the heading in the line above (*Incipit liber I in vita sancti ac beatissimi Columbi presbiteri*) may be compared with the heading in D (Reeves 1857, p. 8). This, and a few readings common to P and the shortened version (*recessum* for *secessum*, 108b ; *provincialibus*, 109a ; *rationabilem* for *rationalem*, 127b), suggest the possibility that both versions were derived from a single copy of A. It is an interesting question, outside the scope of the present edition, whether all the versions derived from A could in fact be descended from a single ninth-century copy.

Adomnan's Sources, Historical Value, and Teaching

The biographer of a saint had a task that imposed certain obligations. His special function was to prove the sanctity of the person whose life he wrote. Sanctity meant the merit that God rewarded with miracles, and therefore it was necessary for Adomnan to devote his book to miraculous occurrences (3b). It was not necessary to follow chronological order, and he makes little attempt at writing a consecutive narrative. His purpose was to show Columba as a saint. Our regret is that he could not tell us more of Columba as a man.

About the supernatural powers of Columba, as described by

Adomnan, there will be different opinions. But before forming any opinion, it is necessary to consider whether Adomnan's statements are evidence for the facts involved. The historian is entitled to require at least as good evidence for less credible phenomena as he would need for matters of everyday experience.

Adomnan wrote nearly a hundred years after the death of Columba, and could have had no direct knowledge of Columba's life. In his second preface he says that he has obtained some information from writing, and some from speech, preferring the authorities that he thought the most trustworthy (3b–4a). But he gives no indication by which we should judge whether his written sources were the work of men who had direct knowledge of Columba's time and place ; and so the necessary historical basis is lacking.

He appears to have used, without naming it, a book written by Cummene, who succeeded to the abbacy of Iona sixty years after Columba's death (see under 108a and pp. 91, 104). Cummene also would not have been a direct witness for Columba's life.

Bede seems to imply that some account of Columba had been written by Columba's disciples. Bede says : *De cujus vita et verbis nonnulla a discipulis ejus feruntur scripta haberi* (H.E. III 4). Since there were no disciples of Columba living in Bede's time, this ambiguous sentence should mean : ' Some writings describing Columba's life and words, written by his disciples, are said to be preserved '. If these existed, they would have been earlier than Cummene, and they would have been sources available to Adomnan.

Adomnan relates only one story that he says he took from a written source, of a vision seen on the night of Columba's death, and that he had heard also from monks of Hinba (131b–132a).

In a few stories, two of which are of events within Columba's lifetime, Adomnan mentions the stages by which the stories reached him. They include the blessing of Ernene Crasen's son by Columba at Clonmacnoise (15b) ; Virgno's experience of flashes of heavenly light in a chapel of Columba's church in Iona (120b–121a) ; the story of Finten's desire to leave Ireland and live as a pilgrim with Columba in Britain (13b) ; and the vision of Columba seen by king Oswald (9b). In every one of these cases the information reached Adomnan through a single intermediary, whom he names.

There is one instance in which Adomnan, when he was young, heard from an old man, Ernene mocu-Fir-roide, of a light in the north-eastern sky that he had seen from Donegal on the night of Columba's death (132a). Adomnan describes the last moments of Columba's life (130a) as, he says, he had learned of them from some who were present ; but his words were partly derived from Evagrius's Life of Antony (see Brüning 1917, p. 246). In some other instances Adomnan mentions the person from whom he derived the story, but does not name the source of that person's knowledge (e.g. 26ab, 50ab).

Stories that are associated with the name of Diormit, Columba's attendant, may have been handed down in Iona, orally, or possibly in writing. Others of Columba's monks are named in other stories. But the naming of a monk as a source for some matter concerning Columba was not always a guarantee of veracity. Adomnan says (44a–45b, I 43) that Lugbe mocu-Blai begged for elucidation of the manner in which Columba received prophetic manifestation of things that were not present to him. Columba gave Lugbe an answer, after exacting from him a promise of secrecy. But in Adomnan's introduction (10b, I 1), composed somewhat later, he says that the request was made by more than one of the brothers, and the answer was given apparently without any pledge of secrecy. In both replies, the explanation attributed to Columba was in fact drawn from the Dialogues of pope Gregory I (†604). (See Brüning 1917, p. 250.) It is to be noted that the reply in 10b adheres more closely to Gregory's words than does the text of 44b–45a.

Adomnan certainly did not neglect traditions, and he says that he was careful to take them from *experti*. But in a hundred years traditions spread widely ; and the same tradition might occur in different forms, at different places. Thus the stories of Nesan (67b) and Colman (68a) look like one story told in two ways.

In the legend that songs praising Columba protected the singers from injury and fire (9b–10a), Adomnan claims to have had a hundred witnesses or more, in districts of Ireland and of Britain. He implies that the magical effect had occurred in many places, in all of which he had inquired into it, but the impression given is that there might have been one such episode, the fame of which was wide-spread.

It happens that some of Adomnan's stories are associated with certain places or objects, which were regarded as confirming the tradition. It is also possible that such stories might have arisen out of an attempt to explain a place-name, or a conspicuous or unusual object. Adomnan's story of the death of Ernan, Columba's uncle (46ab), seems to rest upon a conjectural explanation of two crosses that stood beside the way leading from the monastery of Iona to the harbour, and of which at least one was still standing in Adomnan's time. It is conceivable that a cross might have been put up, as Adomnan says, to mark the spot where Ernan died, but our conjecture is that the other cross would not have been put up to show the place from which Columba saw him die, and that the cause of its erection had been forgotten.

In the tale of Libran, Adomnan says that Libran returned to Columba in Iona the ivory-hilted sword that Columba had given to him. But the description of the ivory-hilted sword appears to have been derived from an account of Irish swords, written by Solinus in the beginning of the third century ; and in that case, Columba's sword was a literary product of Adomnan's imagination. He does not actually say that such a sword existed in Iona in his time.

Adomnan based some of his stories upon oral literature. This explains his touching upon some tales that he does not tell completely ; as for instance that of the butler's bottle, 23b ; the tales of Luguid the Lame, 40a, and of Neman Gruthrech's

son, 40b ; the dispute between two rustics, in the house of
Foirtgern, 66a ; the visit to Columba of four abbots, 118a ;
perhaps also the salmon-fishers on the river Sale, 67a.

Popular literature was without doubt the source of Adomnan's stories of Góre, Aidan's son, 47ab ; and of the death of
Aid Dub, 37ab. The story of the magic stake (83b–85b) has
all the appearance of a popular tale. Gallan Fachtne's son,
35b–36a, and Lugne surnamed Tudicla, 93b, are spoken of as
if they were already known to the reader. Adomnan's stories
of the abbot Cainnech of Aghaboe show the same unworldly
absent-mindedness that distinguishes him in the late Latin
Life of Cainnech : they suggest that Cainnech's character had
already in Adomnan's time become a literary convention.

The voyages of Cormac, grandson of Léthan, are described
(17a, 94b–97b), but not in full (96b). Cormac is one of the
four founders of monasteries who came from Ireland to visit
Columba, and who found him in Hinba, 118a. The others
were Comgell of Bangor, Cainnech of Aghaboe, and Brenden
mocu-Alti of Clonfert. The chapter tells that Brenden saw a
ball of fire over Columba's head while Columba celebrated
Mass in the dark church, and that he reported it afterwards to
Comgell and Cainnech. Cormac has no further place in that
chapter of Adomnan, so that it looks as if the incident in Hinba
was originally part of a longer story.

In another chapter (94b–95b) Adomnan says that Columba,
in his visit to the province of the Picts, requested king Brude to
command his subject, the king of Orkney, that if Cormac and
other Columban monks came in their voyaging to Orkney, no
harm should be done to them there. In Adomnan's account,
Columba had gone to king Brude with unnamed companions ;
Columba had opened the locked fortress-gates with the sign
of the cross, and the king had received him with reverence
(82b). In the Latin Life of Comgell (in Plummer 1910, II,
p. 18), the three abbots, Comgell, Columba, and Cainnech,
went together to the ' pagan king called Brude '. Comgell
broke the locked gates with the sign of the cross ; Columba
broke the door of the king's house in the same way. The king

threatened them with a sword, and Cainnech caused the king's
hand to wither, until he believed in God. This may simply be
a late development of the story told by Adomnan. But possibly
there was a popular tale of Saints that was known to Adomnan,
and to the author of the Life of Comgell, and in which the
abbots set out from Hinba to visit king Brude, while Cormac
set out on the voyage that took him to Orkney. If there was
such a tale, and Adomnan had heard a version of it in Hinba,
he did not accept it entirely. He excluded Comgell and
Cainnech from the expedition to king Brude, did not say that
Brude was a pagan, and represented the opposition of Broichan
to Columba's departure as a sign of enmity, not of amity.

Adomnan's writing contains many quotations, echoes, and
words, from the Bible (Vulgate, or other version), some from
early Christian writers of Latin (especially Juvencus), and some
from Vergil. The biblical quotations have been collected by
Haddan and Stubbs, *Councils*, I, pp. 170–86 (cf. Fowler 1894,
p. 174) ; and quotations from other writers, in Brüning 1917,
pp. 240–55. We have not attempted to extend Miss Brüning's
admirable work.

Certain passages of the substance of Adomnan's Life of
Columba have been derived from books that were in his time
specially well known. We have mentioned his borrowing
from pope Gregory I's Dialogues. Other additions of substance were made from Evagrius's translation of the Life of
Antony by Athanasius ; Sulpicius Severus's Life of Martin,
Epistles and Dialogues ; Constantius's Life of Germanus ; and
the Actus Silvestri.

Adomnan had too little genuine tradition from which to
write a Life of Columba without falling back upon other
sources. He supplies from his own experience, and training
in the doctrine and practice of the Irish church, deficiencies
in his knowledge of Columba. His value is less for the history
of Columba than for his own ideas, and for the circumstances
of his own time.

The long tale of Libran of the Reed-patch (87a–92b) may
be partly fiction ; but it is full of allusions to social customs and

law. Points of law appear also in the story of the magic stake (84b). The history of Aid Dub (36a–37b) exhibits conduct that Adomnan most strongly condemned, in ecclesiastical and civil life. The pleasant story of the storm-driven crane (48a–49a) surely shows the gentle humanity of Adomnan himself.

The laws that are mentioned were presumably Irish laws prevailing in Adomnan's time ; and the penances imposed by Columba were probably such as would have appeared just to Adomnan.

He enlivens his stories with conversations that were un-questionably derived from imagination. He did not in fact expect his readers to suppose that the speeches he gave were the actual words of the speakers. For instance, he quotes the last words of Columba (129a), on the authority of Diormit, without qualification ; but in the next column (129b) he says that Columba's words have been given in an abbreviated form.

It seems to us that next to the object of extolling his pre-decessor, Adomnan is in this work inspired by a desire to instruct his readers in what they should believe, and what they ought to do. He was an abbot, and did not forget his obliga-tion to his community. In every contestable matter that he touches upon his words pronounce his own opinion, expressed by him as a teacher. Apparently-casual remarks were intended to influence his monks, and we must take them seriously.

Columba's ' last words ' might have been held in memory by Diormit, to whom they were spoken (129ab). On the other hand, the attribution of last words to a saint had become a literary convention, which was sometimes used to express the personal views of the narrator. As an instance of this, compare the last words attributed to Cuthbert, on the authority of Herefrith, a priest of Lindisfarne, given in Bede's prose Life of Cuthbert (see Colgrave 1940, pp. 282–4, and 356). So the last words attributed to Columba, expressing the importance of concord as pronounced in the mandate of Jesus, would have fittingly expressed Adomnan's own feelings, in the controversy of his time ; implying that dissension over the date of Easter (cf. 15b) was a sin greater than error in its date.

One instance of a narrative that conveys instruction is the story of the bishop Cronan (45b–46a). In this story Adomnan impresses upon his readers that bishops must be treated with great deference. After studying monastic life in Northumbria Adomnan saw that the subordinate position of a bishop in an Irish monastery was hardly compatible with episcopal dignity ; and he seems to have installed a bishop's chair in Iona (see p. 102).

It is related as an illustration of Columba's prophetic power (113a–114a) that he entered in the commemoration list of Iona the name of a bishop of the Lagin, less than a day after the bishop had died. In this story Adomnan communicated to his monks, and has conveyed to us, some knowledge of the manner in which a name was added to the list.

Adomnan says incidentally also that for this mass-day the brothers were bidden to refrain from their outdoor labour, to prepare the Eucharist, and to provide an additional meal as on a Sunday. (His words suggest, although they do not explicitly say, that the instructions to refrain from outdoor labour, and to prepare the Eucharist, also applied to Sundays.) They went accordingly to the church wearing albs, as on a ' solemn day ' ; and sang the office ' with modulation '.

The narrative of the death of Brito (or ' a Briton '), the first monk who died in Iona, 108a–109a, contradicts a false rumour, and also reminds the abbot that, as a priest, he must not be polluted by presence at a death.

The conditions that in Adomnan's opinion should be accepted by a candidate for monkhood in Iona are mentioned in the tale of Libran (87b), and appear to have been modelled upon the Rule of Benedict.

In Adomnan, *sabbatum* ' sabbath ' means Saturday, the seventh day of the week. He puts into Columba's mouth a reminder that Sabbath was not Sunday (126b–127a). Sunday, the first day of the week, is ' Lord's-day '. Adomnan's attitude to Sunday is important, because he wrote at a time when there was controversy over the question whether the ritual of the

D

biblical Sabbath was to be transferred to the Christians' Lord's-day.

The Jews were not the first people who reckoned days in seven-day periods. But Jewish law decreed that every seventh day should be a day of abstinence from work, a sabbath ; and this inhibition became one of the fundamental principles of their ethics, and the fourth commandment of their decalogue. The Jewish Sabbath extended from Friday evening to Saturday evening.

The early Christians commemorated the crucifixion and resurrection in their celebrations of Fridays and Sundays. In the east, they continued for some time to observe the Jewish Sabbath. Elsewhere, although respect was shown for the Sabbath, the Jewish laws regulating it were abandoned, with other laws of Jewish ritual. But since the Jewish Sabbath was included in the decalogue, there was a recurring tendency to assume that the fourth commandment had not been rescinded, and must therefore have been meant to apply to Sunday. Early Christian scholars argued that the commandment in the decalogue could not be transferred to Sunday without derogating from the original purpose of the Christian festival, and violating the injunctions of the apostle Paul. But the transference had been accepted by many people in Gaul, Britain, and Ireland, long before Charlemagne issued the decree of 789, that labour on Sunday was a breach of the fourth commandment.

The doctrine that Sunday should be kept as a sabbath seems to have been promoted by Caesarius of Arles, early in the sixth century. The councils of Orleans and Mâcon, in 538 and 585, rejected that principle, but prohibited field-work and commerce on Sundays. (Some of the evidence for the period is collected in Cabrol and Leclercq, *Dictionnaire d'Archéologie Chrétienne et de Liturgie*, IV (1921), columns 938–43, 950–6.)

In England, the question of Sunday may have been among the ' other ecclesiastical matters ' discussed at the synod of Whitby in 664, in addition to those that Bede mentions explicitly : namely the method of computing the date of Easter, and the form of the tonsure, in both of which Adomnan accepted the Roman practice, in or before his second visit to Northumbria, in 688.

The transference of the laws of Sabbath to Sunday was accepted in Wessex when king Ine imposed penalties for working on Sunday (× A.D. 694), and soon afterwards by Wihtred, the king of Kent. Bede, writing 698 × 721, in his Life of Cuthbert, added to the account given in the Anonymous Life a statement that Cuthbert instructed king Ecgfrith's widow (on 20 May 685) to put off from Saturday until dawn on Monday her journey from Carlisle to the royal city, since to drive on a Sunday was not permitted (Colgrave 1940, p. 244). This was presumably derived by Bede from a monk of Lindisfarne. The alleged prohibition was an inference from the prohibition against employing ' ox, or ass, or any draught animal ', on the Jewish Sabbath (Vulgate, Deut. v. 14).

In some Lives of early Irish saints, passages, often in the form of comminatory anecdotes, were intended to persuade their readers that those saints had observed Sunday as a Sabbath. The earliest that we know of is a story in the Latin Life of Patrick, composed by Muirchu, at the direction of Aid, bishop of the monastery of Sleibte (Sletty, county Leix). Aid died in 700 (A.U. 699 = 700). Muirchu says (I 25 ; Book of Armagh, 6c) that Patrick, resting on the Lord's-day, heard pagan labourers noisily building earthworks not far from the strait called the Ox's Neck, near a salt-marsh above the sea ; and he forbade them to work on the Lord's-day. But they mocked him, and in the night an inundation of the sea destroyed their work. In another passage of the Latin Life (II 3 ; Book of Armagh 7d, × 846 ; × ?807), it is said that ' It was (Patrick's) custom not to travel between vespers of Lord's-night (Saturday evening) and dawn of the second day of the week (Monday) '. These are among the earliest Irish attempts to persuade Christians to observe Sunday as Sabbath. Obviously after two hundred years such statements about Patrick were assumptions without historical value. Tirechan, somewhat earlier than Muirchu, said that Patrick went from

Ferte Fer Feicc to Teiltiu on an Easter Sunday. (Book of
Armagh 10b). Cf. Muirchu (Book of Armagh 4d.)

Aid, the bishop of Sletty, is called an anchorite. What the
attitude of early Irish anchorites was to the sabbatical observance of Sunday is not clear. But the Celi-dé, who appear to
have owed much to the teaching of eighth-century anchorites,
were ardent supporters of the sabbatical observance.

The sabbatical movement culminated in the production of
a ' Letter of Jesus ', or ' Letter of Lord's-day ', alleged to have
been found on the altar of Peter in Rome ; and said in the
annals to have been brought to Ireland by a pilgrim (A.U.
886 = 887). Upon this basis, laws were promulgated, imposing
heavy penalties for those that violated on Sunday certain
regulations derived from Jewish prohibitions for Sabbath.
See O'Keeffe's editions of the Cáin Domnaig, and of the
' Letter of Jesus ' in Ériu, II, pp. 189–214 ; and comminatory
narratives edited by Kuno Meyer in Z.C.P. III, p. 228. The
account given in Kenney 1929, pp. 476-7 should be consulted.

The confusion between the days was carried so far that in
a homily in the Leabhar Breac, ' Lord's-day ' was substituted
for ' Sabbath ' in the decalogue of Exodus xx (Atkinson 1887,
pp. 247, 480).

There is in fact no historical evidence that Ninian, or
Patrick, or Columba, or any of their contemporaries in Ireland,
kept Sunday as a Sabbath.

In Jewish law, washing on Sabbath was prohibited. But
Columbanus, who was more than twenty years younger than
Columba, and had been trained at Bangor in Dal-nAridi,
instructed his penitent monks to wash their hair on Sunday,
in his rule (Columbanus, p. 154 ; cf. ibid. p. 180).

Travelling on Sabbath was prohibited by Jewish law. But
Adomnan says that Columba arrived at Trioit (Trevet, county
Meath) on a Sunday (41a). More significant is the fact that
Adomnan describes how Columba caused wayfarers to be
ferried across the strait, and to be received in Iona, on a Sunday
(33b). This is in strong contrast to the story told in the much
later Latin Life of Cronan of Roscrea, of how Cronan's rela-

tives, who were bringing food to his monastery for the festival of Easter, were stopped by the vesper bell of Saturday, at the side of a river, and did not proceed further until Monday morning (Plummer 1910, II, p. 25).

The collecting and preparation of food on Sabbath were prohibited, and penalties for fishing on Sunday were prescribed in the Cáin Domnaig. But Adomnan says without comment that witnesses of supernatural phenomena seen on the night of Columba's death, a Sunday, included men who were fishing at that time (132ab). One of them became a holy monk and a *miles Christi*.

The implications of what Adomnan says are strengthened by what he does not say. Any comminatory narratives that he gives are condemnations of conduct, not of the neglect of any ritual obligation. But after the sabbatical observance of Sunday had been accepted, Irish writers (no doubt with the thirty-first chapter of Exodus in mind) made a practice of introducing comminatory anecdotes that threatened calamity to any violators of the sabbatical rules on Sunday.

It seems to follow that the sabbatical Sunday had not yet been accepted by Adomnan or in Iona at the time when Adomnan wrote. The Irish Life of Adomnan perhaps shows that the successors of Adomnan, in Ireland, continued to resist the sabbatization of Sunday, down to the end of the eighth century, or later. It has one curious tale of the lavish supply of food to Adomnan and his fellow-travellers ' on one Sunday' , and although this may be classed as a comminatory narrative, it is directed not against the provision of food on a Sunday, but against the cooking of a dog (Best 1908, p. 16). The story involves a discord between Adomnan and the mocu-Uais of northern Brega. Adomnan similarly regarded the eating of mare's flesh as an act of great depravity (26b).

Many of the Canones Adomnani are concerned with the question of what foods were permissible. Those canons were based on Hebraic sources.

In Adomnan's narrative, evil consequences follow from murder, plundering, niggardliness, exaggerated penitence, and disobedience to an abbot. The sin of bearing false witness is not touched upon at all. The poaching of seals by Erc of Coll is very gently treated.

HISTORICAL BACKGROUND

Adomnan does not use Patrick's Latin term for Ireland, *Hiberio* ; nor the Latin *Hibernia* of Caesar, Pliny, and Tacitus. *Hibernia* was copied from Cummene by the writer of A (108a), in the inserted passage. Adomnan calls Ireland either *Scotia*, or *Evernia* (spelt also *Ebernia* and *Hevernia*), like Ptolemy's *Iouernia*. In Adomnan's usage, these two terms are geographically synonymous, and we have translated them both by ' Ireland '.

The people of Ireland are called by Adomnan *Scoti*, and their language is *scotica lingua*. The Irish in Scotland are *Scoti Brittanniae*, and their language also is *scotica lingua*, but the territory that they occupied is not included in the term *Scotia*. Adomnan derived the name *Scoti* from Latin writers, who gave it to the invaders, from Ireland, of the Roman province in Britain. About the middle of the fifth century, Patrick seemed to imply that there were Scoti in Britain as well as in Ireland ; and in his repeated phrase, *filii Scottorum et filiae regulorum*, showed that the Scoti could have been of noble rank. He did not otherwise distinguish the Scoti in Ireland from among the *Hiberionaces* and the *Hibernas gentes*, some of whom might not have spoken a Goidelic language. Adomnan's implication is that the Scoti were the Gaelic-speaking population of Evernia.

Adomnan's term *Brittannia*, for the whole island of Britain, was taken from Latin writers. His *Brittones* (a hypocoristic derivative of *Brittanni*) meant the non-Saxon inhabitants of what had been the Roman province. Adomnan's *Saxonia* was (or included) the territory of the Angles of Northumbria. The term had been used in a similar sense by bishop Wilfrith ; and was later so used by Bede's abbot, Hwætberht (Plummer 1896, I, p. 383 ; II, p. 368).

Picti are first named by Latin writers in the end of the third century. Adomnan applies the name to the people of Brude's kingdom in the latter part of the sixth century.

The Greek name Orcades was derived by Adomnan from Latin writers (only in the accusative, genitive, and ablative, *Orcadas* (Greek), *Orcadum* (Latin), *Orcadibus* (Latin), 95a). See Watson 1926, pp. 28–9. The Greek word was adjectival in form. From it, or from its source, came an Irish noun **Orc*, which appears in the plural as a name for the people (genitive *Orc*, A.U. 579 = 580, 580 = 581) ; and as a name for the islands (dative *Orcaib*, A.U. 708 = 709). The dative plural has in S.G. become a name of Orkney (*Arcaibh*).

Tacitus, before A.D. 100, used the Latin noun *Caledonia* as the denomination of Britain to the north of the Forth ; and he called the inhabitants of Caledonia *Britanni*. Agricola with his army pressed forward against the tribes of these Britanni, from the valley of the Forth probably to the Moray Firth, until he forced them to make a final stand and suffer total defeat in the battle of Mons Graupius, perhaps near Forres. After this battle, and a naval expedition to Orkney (*insulas quas Orcadas vocant*), the Romans claimed that they had reduced all Britain to their dominion.

The tower-builders of Orkney appear to have held the principal headland of Caithness, called *Tarouedoum* or *Orkas* by Ptolemy, and the remains of their towers (' brochs ' in modern terminology only) show that at some time they occupied Caithness and eastern Sutherland. Builders of similar towers appear to have settled in Berwickshire, and to have spread from there, not later than the end of the first century, and not in opposition to the Romans. The broch would have been no defence against the Roman army. At least one of these southern brochs was destroyed, perhaps in a Roman punitive expedition, early in the second century. The history of the southern brochs needs further elucidation. (See Piggott 1953, p. 114.)

It may be inferred from Ptolemy's Geography that early in the second century the people called Kaledonioi were an inland people, surrounded by other tribes, but reaching the sea at two

points : one, at their southern limit, an inlet of the sea between
the mouth of the river Clyde and the promontory of Kintyre ;
the other, at their northern limit, where the river Farrar enters
the Beauly Firth.   On the west, a boundary of the Kaledonioi
was the primeval forest (*Kaledonios drymos*, perhaps ' oak-wood ').
The country thus indicated (including parts of Inverness-shire,
of Perthshire, and perhaps of Stirlingshire) is geographically
improbable as the territory of a single tribe.

Early in the third century, Dio Cassius, describing events
of A.D. 197 to 211, shows that the Kaledonioi were then a
leading tribe in a group of tribes ; and that the Maiatai,
between the Kaledonioi and the Roman Wall that ran from
Forth to Clyde, were the leading tribe of another group.   Both
of these groups were in negotiation with the Romans, who tried
to play the one group against the other.

The term Kaledonioi may originally have been geographical ; but it is thought to have survived in a small area, where
three place-names may have retained, in a form derived from
Irish speech, the name of a local ruling tribe (in the genitive
plural, S.G. *-cailleann*) : Dunkeld, Rohallion, and Schiehallion.
These may be compared with the hill-name Dumyat, which
seems to retain the name of the Maiatai (Adomnan's *Miathi*,
18a).

The name *Picti* appears first in A.D. 297, and, in a somewhat
uncertain text, in A.D. 310 (see among others Watson 1926,
p. 59, and O'Rahilly 1946, p. 533).   Its origin is unknown.   It
was not the proper name of any people, but was given (perhaps
at first in soldiers' slang) apparently to all the peoples of north
Britain beyond the Forth.   Irish raiders of Roman Britain
(*Hiberni*) are mentioned first along with the first mention of the
Picti ; they are afterwards called *Scoti*, still in association with
the Picti.

In the end of the fourth century, Ammianus, writing of
events of the year 367, says that the Picti were divided into
two nations, the Dicalydones and the Verturiones.   He spells
Verturiones with the Latin accusative plural termination *-ēs*, but
spells *Dicalydonas* either with the Greek termination *-as* (as in

Phaeacas in the immediately-preceding sentence), or with the Gallic termination *-ās*. (The Goidelic equivalent ending was *-ās ; see Thurneysen 1946, p. 201.)

The prefix *dī-* in a Celtic language should mean ' without ' ; but ' *calydū*-less ' does not seem to make good sense. ' Two- ' would have been *dwē-* in Celtic (as in Ptolemy's *okeanos douekalledonios* ; apparently ' ocean of two *kalledū's* '). If in this name Ammianus has used the Greek prefix *di-* ' two ', he implies that there were two groups of Caledonians and that the Verturiones were neither of these groups. The Picti of Ammianus would then have included three population groups. But the explanation remains doubtful.

The people that Ammianus calls Verturiones are mentioned here for the first time. It would appear that they had superseded the Maiatai in the leadership of the southern tribes, before the end of the fourth century ; and quite possibly in the beginning of the third century, as a result of the wars between the emperor Severus and the Kaledonioi and Maiatai. Adomnan shows a tradition that the Maiatai continued to occupy a district that was perhaps to the east and south of Stirling.

There is later evidence for the existence of Verturiones. Without doubt that was a North-British or Gallo-Britannic form of their name ; and its Goidelic form is represented by the Old Irish and Middle Irish *Fortrin(n) in the plural, for the people or their territory, and later *Fortriu in the singular, for their territory or their eponym. The nominatives do not occur, and the genitive, *Fortren(n)*, is common to the plural and the singular.

The suggestion that *Verturiones* was of the same origin as Britannic *vertera* > Welsh *gwerthyr* ' fortress ' (Rhys 1904, pp. 322–3), implying that *Verturiones* meant ' fortress people ', has not been established. *Verter* survived into the tenth century as an element in a place-name *Wertermōras* which was taken by Symeon of Durham from an Anglo-Saxon note or panegyric, describing the limits of Æthelstan's invasion of Scotland in A.D. 934 (S.D. II, pp. 93, 124 : *usque Dunfoeder* (Dunnottar) *et*

Wertermorum, where *morum* is the dative of the A.S. *mōras*, meaning ' mountains ', ' moors ', or ' marshes ').

North-British *verter*, or Gallo-Britannic *vertera*, would no doubt have been translated by speakers of Old Irish into *forter* > *fortar*. *Forter* survives in several Scottish place-names (cf. Watson 1926, p. 69) ; but it is not as yet clear whether all of these were translated from North-British names. There may have been a Goidelic noun **vertero-* or **vertera*, with the same origin and meaning as Britannic *vertera*. Both North-British *verter* and Irish *forter* > *fortar* could have been formed from the preposition *uer* and the adverbial suffix *-ter-*, exactly as Old Irish *fother* was formed from the preposition *uo*, ' under ', and suffix *-ter-*. In that case *verter* and *forter* would have meant ' upland '. (Cf. note by Ifor Williams in Ravenna Geographer 1949, p. 48.)

Verter does not appear to mean ' fortress ', and *Verturiones* is not exactly the form that ' people of Verter ' would be expected to take.

There is as yet no conclusive evidence to show whether the Verturiones were another tribe of the group previously led by the Maiatai, or were an alien tribe, perhaps brought into Fortriu by the Romans, as a plantation, to ensure the loyalty of those southern tribes. If the ring-forts, or round castles, of Perthshire should be proved by archaeological investigation to have been built in the third or fourth century, it would be impossible to avoid the conclusion that they were the defence-works of the Verturiones. The ring-fort people appear to have entered Perthshire from the region of Loch Awe, by a mountain pass to Glen Lyon ; and to have extended their defences later into the valleys and heights of Atholl. There were other possible lines of approach, from a high point above the north of Loch Lomond to the valleys of the rivers Forth, Teith, and Earn (cf. Haldane 1952, p. 99) ; and ring-fort builders appear to have entered in this way the district of Menteith. (See Watson 1912, 1914, and 1926, p. 69.)

Round castles of this type resemble the ring-forts of Ireland, and may have developed from the Irish type, with slight variations. (Cf. Childe 1935, p. 198.) It appears probable that the brochs were another and specialized development of the same tradition of building.

The region of Fortriu bordered upon the kingdoms of Scots, Cumbrian Britons, and Northumbrian Angles. It was the most important of the group of Pictish provinces. It was perhaps the ' province of the Picts ' that for a generation in the seventh century was subordinate to the kings of Northumbria. Brude Bile's son, and some later kings of the eastern kingdom of North Britain, were called ' king of Fortriu ' in the Irish annals. The names of the kings of Fortriu show that their families were of mixed North-British, Cumbrian, and Irish, origin.

The ' chief bishop of Fortriu ' (or of ' the Fortrinn '), Tuathal, Artgus' son, at his death in 865, was the abbot of Dunkeld (A.U. 864 = 865). Dunkeld was probably included in Fortriu at that time. The kingdom of Fortriu varied in extent, but it can be said that the western boundary of Fortriu in conjunction with Atholl was nearly the same as the modern western boundary of Perthshire.

The peoples whom Adomnan knew as ' Scots of Britain ' were comparatively late settlers from Ireland. They appear to have brought Q-Celtic speech (Goidelic) into Argyllshire. The term *Scoti Brittanniae* is synonymous with the Irish term *fir Alban* ' men of Britain ' ; and the Irish name *Alba* gradually changes its meaning, from ' Britain ' to ' Scotland '. The *fir Alban* were regarded as an extraneous province of Ireland. In Fland's Synchronisms, compiled in the eleventh century, their kings are still named beside the Irish kings.

The principal ruling family of the Scots of Britain belonged to the Dal-Réti (' division of Réte '), who occupied also the northern part of county Antrim. Cf. Adomnan's *Korku-Rēti* (47a), meaning ' tribe of Réte ' ; and the *maccu-Rētai* of A.U. 25b21–22, 677 = 678. The masculine genitive -*Rēti* (dd) becomes later -*Ríata*. Therefore the *t* was non-palatal. The name has no immediate connexion with the feminine noun *reidte*, in which the group *dt* (δt) was palatal, and from which was derived the Irish and Scottish Gaelic *réite* ' agreement '.

Down to the tenth century, the name Dal-Réti (> Dalríata) is found for the people, not the land, of Argyllshire ; under 988 = 989, it means the territory, in A.U. 32d19, but in the corresponding entry in T. 15b48 it still means the people.

The Dal-Réti were said in Irish tradition to have been Erainn, and to have gone from the counties of Kerry and Cork, in Munster, at a time when there was famine there, and to have landed partly in Britain, and partly in north-eastern Ireland. It is hard to tell whether any tradition existed that the Dal-Réti in Argyllshire had gone there from Antrim. The position of the Irish Dal-Réti, in a small territory entirely enclosed between the sea and the Cruithnian kingdom of Dal-nAridi and Eilne, suggests rather that they had gone there from Britain. Their leader in the migration from Munster is said to have been Conaire's son, Coirpre or Echoid. (For the confusion in the legend and pedigree, see O'Rahilly 1946, pp. 202–3.) ' Coirpre's knoll ' (*Cnocc Coirpri*) was the place of a battle in A.D. 736, near Ederline, at the upper end of Loch Awe.

The Dal-Réti of Ireland and of Scotland in historical times were usually under one king, until late in the eighth century. The kingdom included also Rathlin, and other islands. The Irish district was sometimes distinguished as the Dal-Réti of Muirbolg, because their chief harbour was Murlough in county Antrim. (See p. 57. For its extent, see MacNeill 1930, pp. 27–8.) The military service due to the high-king of Ireland from Dal-Réti was a question negotiated at the council of Druimm-Céte (see p. 40).

Domingart, father of the kings Comgell (17b) and Gabran (49b), is not mentioned by Adomnan, but may be regarded as the first historical king of the Dal-Réti, although the dates of his reign cannot be ascertained. He is called ' Domingart Mac-nisse of Réte ' at the time when he withdrew into religion (*Domhangart Mac-nisse Reti secessit*) in A.U. 506 = 507 ; and ' Domingart of Kintyre ' at his death in religion (*Quies Domon-*

gairt Ci[n]d-tire) in A.I. 10b1, under [?501]. With the Irish genitive *Réti* cf. the Latin genitive *Retis*, in *Mors Comgaill maic Domongairt Retis*, A.I. 10b31–32.

In the regnal lists and royal pedigrees, Domingart is called the son of Fergus Erc's son. In the latter half of the ninth century, ' Fergus Mór, Erc's son ', is represented as having been a young man in the time of Patrick's mission to northern Ireland (Tripartite Life, in Stokes 1887, 1, p. 162). An early reference to Fergus is among memoranda that were written in the Book of Armagh (folio 18d27), probably in the early part of the ninth century. There and elsewhere Fergus, like Domingart, receives the epithet *Mac-nise*. The annal-collection of Tigernach notes the occupation of ' part of Britain ' by Fergus Mór, Erc's son, with the nation of the Dal-Réti (misspelt *Dalraida*, T. 7a47–48), under the year of his death [A.D. 501] (E.S. 1, p. 1). This was certainly not a contemporary note. It is not in the Annals of Ulster, is not necessarily earlier than the tenth century, and should not be regarded as historical.

Loern was reputed to have been another son of Erc. The tribe of Loern in northern Argyllshire had some right to military service from two tribes of Airgialla (see p. 57), an inland group of minor kingdoms to the west of the Cruithni of Dal-nAridi. In an assessment of the military strength of the tribe of Loern, it is stated that they could draw from the Airgialla a hundred men, out of their total strength of seven hundred. (E.S. 1, p. clii, from B.B. p. 148.) Thus it appears that while the Dal-Réti of Britain were akin to the Dal-Réti of Ireland, the tribe of Loern were akin to tribes among the Airgialla ; and doubt is thrown upon the assumption in the pedigrees that the founders of the colonies in northern and southern Argyllshire were two brothers, Loern and Fergus.

A third colony is said to have been founded by a third brother, Oingus, whose territory is not clearly defined. He is associated with a settlement made in the island of Islay, where three of his great-grandsons are said to have inherited territory formerly possessed by their mother's father, a Cruithnian. The island is less than thirty miles from the coast of Eilne, which was held by the Irish Cruithni.

There was doubtless some population-group that the Senchus designates the tribe of Oingus Erc's son, and it seems probable that the region of Angus in eastern Scotland was named after that group. It would reasonably be suggested that the Isla river, which is a boundary of Angus, was named after the divinity whose name had been given to the island of Islay (cf. Watson 1926, p. 87). It is rather less safe to assume that the king, Oingus Forcus' son, who by conquest in the eighth century reduced the Dal-Réti to the dominion of the eastern kingdom, had some pretension to leadership of the tribe of Oingus, besides being a claimant through his mother to the kingship of Fortriu.

Irish colonists in Britain whose names were remembered belonged to the ruling families in the colony. But there may have been many Irish settlers of other families, and of other tribes. Presumably also there must have been many dependents who were not of Irish origin.

The descendants of Domingart of Réte seem to have held the supremacy among the confederate tribes of Scots in Britain in the sixth and seventh centuries.

Domingart's son, Comgell, is said to have reigned for thirty-five years. His name was given to the region of Cowal, between Loch Fyne and Loch Long. By adding that region to the dominion of the Dal-Réti, Comgell, or his descendants, made Loch Fyne safe for travellers between Ireland and the eastern shore of Argyll.

Comgell was succeeded by his brother, Gabran, at the end of whose life the Scots in Britain (i.e. the Dal-Réti) had been forced to yield ground before Brude Maelchon's son. The Irish annals used as a source a collection of the tenth or ninth century, which is here copied in Latin in A.U. 20b11–12, 557 = 558, *fuga ante filium Maelchon* ; and translated into Irish in A.U. 20b20, 559 = 560, *immirge* (' withdrawal ' or ' evacuation ') *re mac Maelchon*. It is translated and expanded in T. 8a34–35 : *Teichedh* (' flight ') *do Albanchaib riam Bruidhi mac*

Maelchon righ Cruithnech. T.'s version was made in the end of the eleventh century, or later. For its use of *Cruithnig*, see p. 63. The death of Gabran immediately precedes the Latin entry, and immediately follows the Irish entries.

If the Scots who fled were Gabran's people, it must follow that Gabran and Brude had a common frontier, and in consequence that Brude's dominions included Fortriu. Adomnan seems to place a royal fortress of Brude near the Beauly Firth, and he gives no clear indication that Brude's dominion extended south of the river Ness. But Bede calls Brude a *rex potentissimus*, and also implies that Brude reigned over southern as well as northern Picts.

Gabran was succeeded by his nephew, Conall, Comgell's son. Adomnan implies (17b) that when Columba set out to take up his pilgrimage in Britain he visited Conall for a time. Conall's place of abode may very probably have been in the district that is now called Argyll, which includes Dun Add, the traditional and symbolical capital of the Dal-Réti in Britain. Dun Add was besieged in 683 (*obsesio duin Att*, A.U. 25c27), and was taken by Oingus Forcus' son when he laid waste the lands of the Dal-Réti in 736 (A.U. 735 = 736, and T.). It was probably a stronghold in Columba's time, and may then have been a royal residence. (Cf. J. Hewat Craw, in *P.S.A.S.* LXIV, pp. 111-27 ; and Stuart Piggott, in *P.S.A.S.* LXXXVII, p. 193.)

The *caput regionis* to which Columba went with Lugbe mocu-Min (31a) was perhaps Dun Add. They met a ship arriving there from Gaul. The ship-harbour for Dun Add was Loch Crinan, from which the river Add gave access by boat to the eastern slope of the castle hill.

King Conall reigned for about fifteen years. The year of his death, A.D. 574, is inferred from the annals. Conall had sons who survived him, but Aidan Gabran's son was chosen as his successor. Adomnan, perhaps following Cummene, says (107b) that Columba would have preferred Iogenan, Gabran's son ; and the inference may be made that some later claimants may have been descendants of Iogenan (see p. 49).

A conference between Aid Ainmure's son, king of the northern Ui-Néill and high-king of Ireland, and king Aidan Gabran's son, was held at Druimm-céte in county Londonderry, in the summer of 575 (49b, 58b ; A.U. 574=575). Columba was present at this conference. Adomnan says nothing of its purpose or result. He implies that the subject in dispute concerned relations between the two kingships, and that it ended amicably.

Much later than the time of Adomnan, it was believed that the Irish territory of the Dal-Réti had been a principal subject of dispute. (Cf. E.S. 1, pp. 81–5.) The most intelligible account of the terms of settlement is given in the second preface (? of the eleventh century) to the Amra Choluimchille : ' Colman Comgellan's son of Dal-Réti gave the judgement, that the levying and hosting of (the Dal-Réti go) with the men of Ireland, since hosting always (goes) with lands ; their tax and tribute (go) with the men of Britain '. There is no doubt that the ' lands ' intended were the lands of the Dal-Réti in Ireland. No claim of the king of northern Ui-Néill to military service from lands in Britain is implied, and possibly none was ever made. It is equally clear that such an agreement would have left Irish Dal-Réti as part of king Aidan's dominions. The Irish Dal-Réti, like the Cruithnian Dal-nAridi, were merged in the kingdom of the Ulaid in the period of the Scandinavian settlements in Ireland.

In the year after the council of Druimm-céte, a battle was fought in Kintyre (*bellum Delocho*, A.U. 20d28–29 ; *cath Delgon*, T. 8c7–8), and Dunchad, the son of king Conall, and ' many others of the allies of the sons of Gabran ', were killed, fighting on one side. The battle is unexplained, unless it could have been one of the legendary battles that Baitan Cairell's son, king of the Ulaid, fought against king Aidan in Britain (cf. Berchan's Prophecy, stanzas 23–26 ; E.S. 1, pp. 87–88).

Without accepting as historical the legend of Baitan's wide dominion in Ireland and Scotland, we may use the legend to point out the real danger that the Dal-Réti, if they had not preferred a modified direct allegiance to the king of northern

Ui-Néill, might have been subordinated by force to kings of the Cruithni and the Ulaid.

Aidan became king at a time when the Dal-Réti had gained some stability in Argyllshire, and were pushing eastward into the territory of the Fortrinn. According to the Tripartite Life of Patrick (Stokes 1887, 1, p. 162), the territory conquered by Aidan, and called Fortriu, was in the secure possession of descendants of Fergus Mór. That was written after the time of Cinaed Alpin's son. Evidently the author of the Tripartite Life accepted the pedigrees that make Alpin and Aidan descendants of Fergus Mór ; and believed that Cinaed had hereditary right to the kingdom of Fortriu. The facts are stated as the fulfilment of a prophecy by Patrick.

In an earlier Life, which was the basis of the Tripartite Life, Fergus Mór Mac-nise was mentioned, and his name is repeated among the memoranda in the Book of Armagh 18d27 (perhaps × 807, and certainly × 846). If that mention implies that there was already in the earlier Life a prophecy of Patrick about the descendants of Fergus, it would show that earlier than the time of Cinaed Alpin's son that prophecy was thought to have been fulfilled.

Berchan's Prophecy, stanza 116, seems to imply that Aidan invaded territory of the eastern kingdom to avenge an attack that had been made upon him (E.S. 1, p. 76).

Aidan's battle against the Miathi was fought only a short time after Columba's visit to Aidan and his sons, when Echoid Buide was a young child (18a, 19a). This is the only evidence given by Adomnan of the date of the battle.

Adomnan writes as if the battle of the Miathi had been one of the most strenuous of Aidan's victories, dearly bought, with the loss of 303 men, including two of his sons, Artur and Echoid Find. Another of Aidan's sons, Domingart, was killed in a disastrous battle in England (19a). The natural assumption is that that disaster was one of Aidan's greatest defeats, and so very probably it was the battle of Degsastan, which is dated by Bede in A.D. 603 (H.E. I 34).

The common source of A.U. and T. about this time entered

E

events some two or three years earlier than their true date.
A.U. and T. enter the ' killing (*jugulatio*) of Aidan's sons, Bran
and Domingart ', one year after the death of Columba ; and
what must have been the battle of Degsastan, ' the battle of
the Saxons in which Aidan was defeated ', four years later
(A.U. 599 = 600). Probably Adomnan's account is to be
preferred.

Tigernach 8d48–49 adds to the *jugulatio* the names of
Echoid Find and Artur, and makes all four brothers victims
of the battle of Circhenn. But that is a late and corrupt
conflation, and it must not be used, as has been done by Skene
and others (Skene 1886, p. 161 ; O'Rahilly 1946, p. 504), to
identify the battle of Circhenn with the battle of the Miathi.
The battle of Circhenn is not mentioned in A.U. Circhenn
was apparently the region of Mearns or Angus, remote from
the Maiatai, who were near the Roman Wall ; and the time
of the battle of Circhenn (?598) appears too late for the battle
of the Miathi. The battle of Circhenn was a defeat, that of
the Miathi was a victory.

These Miathi are regarded as descendants of the ancient
Maiatai (see p. 32). Their name is thought to have survived
in the names of two hills : Myot Hill, to the south of Stirling ;
and Dumyat, north-east of Stirling, to the north of the Forth.
The high losses incurred in the battle of the Miathi suggest
that the assault was made against a well-defended stronghold.
There is on Dumyat the site of an ancient fortress, which could
perhaps have been the scene of the battle. (See Feachem 1955,
pp. 77–8.) Dumyat was formerly a boundary between the
counties of Stirling and Clackmannan, and it may have been
on an ancient frontier.

Both the hills are within the British territory of Manau,
which included Clackmannanshire and extended to the south
of the Roman Wall, as far as Slamannan. The Maiatai had
occupied part at least of Manau. How far their land may
have reached to the eastward is a matter for further investigation.

It is not surprising that the ' battle of the Miathi ' should have been entered as the ' battle of Manau ' in the Irish annals (genitive *Manonn*, in A.U. 21a24, of O.I. *Manu* > *Mana* ; *Manonn* also in A.U. 710 = 711 ; elsewhere in the annals genitive *Manann* and *Manand*). The battle of Manau, and the death of Brude Maelchon's son in the year after that battle, must have been entered in consecutive years in a source of the annals, since they appear together twice in A.U. (503 = 504 and 504 = 505 ; 582 = 583 and 583 = 584) ; twice in T. (7b4–5, 8c32–35) ; and once in A.I. (10d). (Cf. E.S. 1, p. 89.) The battle appears also in A.U.21a under 581 = 582, and that may have the best reading of the text : *Bellum Manonn in quo victor erat Aedhan mac Gabrain* ; cf. T. 8c30–31. (In A.U. 21b2, 582 = 583, *fri* is an error for *la*.) But very probably A.U.'s entries of 582 = 583 and 583 = 584 represent most nearly the dating of the source. The source was probably an Iona chronicle.

It has been suggested that this battle was fought not in Manau, but in the island of Man. The Irish forms of the two place-names are indistinguishable. Where the Latin forms (*Eumania* and *Eufania*) occur, in the annals for years 577 and 578, they show that the island of Man was intended. These items of the common source of T. and A.U. are best represented by A.U., which reads under 576 = 577 : ' The first peril (*periculum*) of the Ulaid in Man ' ; and under 577 = 578 : ' Withdrawal (*reversio*) of the Ulaid from Man '.

An Irish antiquarian tract (E.S. 1, pp. 87–8) says that Man (*Manann*, *Manand* ; *Manu*, in Laud 610, *Z.C.P.*, VIII, p. 327) was cleaned out (*glanta*) by Baitan Cairell's son ; and that the Góidil left Man in the second year after Baitan's death (†580 = 581, A.U.). That would have been in 582 or 583.

O'Rahilly 1946, p. 504, argued that the first peril of the Ulaid in Man must have been followed by a second peril, not mentioned by the Irish annals ; and, interpreting *periculum* as ' expedition ', that the second expedition must have been ended by Aidan's victory in the *bellum Manonn*, in 582 or 583. The word *periculum* may mean ' invasion ' ; but whatever it means, there seems to be no reason why a second *periculum* should not have ended in the retreat of 578.

If the author of the tract really meant that Aidan caused the Ulaid to withdraw from Man, his statement is inappropriately worded, since he would not have meant to say that Aidan and his followers were not Góidil. The author seems to have imagined that the Ulaid were fighting against Saxons, as is stated in the Book of Lecan version ; though it is thought unlikely that Saxons had at that time occupied Man. The date given in the tract was almost certainly taken from the annals, which place the *bellum Manonn* two years or one year after the death of Baitan, but which show no connexion between the two events. It is clear that the tract, which is the basis of O'Rahilly's argument, is unhistorical and inconsistent, and is not evidence either for the date of the retreat from Man, or for the place of the *bellum Manonn*. The annals are evidence of traditions according to which Aidan's victory in the *bellum Manonn* would have been gained four or five years after the withdrawal of the Ulaid from Man.

The Annals of Ulster enter under 579 = 580 ' an expedition to the Orkneys ' (or ' against Orkneymen '), ' by Aidan Gabran's son ', and they repeat *fecht Orc* under 580 = 581. Both of these annals are written in Irish, which shows that they are not drawn from the earliest sources. The repetition of the item suggests that the annal had been entered in two of the later sources of A.U. On the other hand, this expedition is absent from all the other Irish annal-collections, and this fact throws doubt on the validity of the item.

The alleged expedition to Orkney may have been derived from some literary legend that claimed for Aidan that he had dominion over the whole of Scotland, and in that case the expedition would be unhistorical. Adomnan says that Brude (Maelchon's son) was the overlord of the king of Orkney, and that good relations continued between Columba and Brude until the end of Brude's life (95a, 83a). An attack by Aidan upon Brude's vassal would have been an act hostile to Brude, unless it had been undertaken in alliance with Brude. In the year 580 ' Cennalath, king of the Picts, died ', according to the common source of A.U. and T. He is said, in the regnal list, to have shared Brude's kingdom for one year (E.S. I, pp. cxxiii, 86). Nothing is known of these affairs. It is not impossible that Cennalath was king of Orkney and the north-east mainland, and was for a time the successful rival of Brude, and that his death resulted from Aidan's campaign against the Orkneymen.

Thus Aidan's campaigns against the Orkneymen and the Miathi may have been directed against peoples hostile to Brude's kingdom, on Brude's northern and southern borders. Adomnan shows no instance of warfare by Aidan against king Brude.

If by the battle of the Miathi in ?583 Aidan gained control over the territory of Manau, the part of Manau to the south of the Forth would be his point of contact with the Northumbrian dominion, and the place of the battle of Degsastan (in 603) might be looked for there, or from there towards the south-east.

According to Bede (H.E. I 34), king Æthelfrith had so depopulated the lands of the Britons that Aidan was prompted to lead a great and powerful army against him. Many Northumbrians fell, but Aidan's losses were so overwhelming that ' from that time, no king of the Scots in Britain dared to come to battle against the nation of the Angles down to the present day ' (A.D. 731).

When the battle of Degsastan was fought, Aidan was an old man. Berchan's Prophecy, stanza 118, seems to be speaking of Aidan when it says : ' At the time when he dies, he will not be king ; on Thursday, in Kintyre '. That would imply that he had renounced the kingdom, and had entered a monastery in Kintyre in his last years.

Since a weekday is an insufficient date for any genuine tradition, we should imagine that *dia dardaoin* 'day between two fasts' means here Maundy Thursday, the Thursday before Easter. In the Martyrology of Tallaght (L.L. 359a) the commemoration day of Aidan's death is 17 April. That day was Thursday in the years 598, 609, 615. If these data could be trusted, Aidan would have died on 17 April 609. It is of interest to observe that in B. MacCarthy's tables of the calendar according to the 84-year cycle system, 17 April 609 would have been Maundy Thursday (MacCarthy 1901, Tables N, O).

Aidan's death is entered in A.U. under 605 = 606, which allowing for the prolepsis of this part of the annals would stand for A.D. 609 ; and is placed in A.I. 11b3 ten years after 599. (Cf. E.S. 1, p. 125, notes 3–5.)

Aidan was succeeded by his son Echoid Buide. Adomnan implies (18b–19a) that Echoid received his father's whole dominion, and we may assume that it passed to him when Aidan retired into monastic life. Echoid seems to have had some dominion in Fortriu, since at his death he was called *rex Pictorum* in Cuanu's book (A.U. 628 = 629), though he is not named among kings of the Picts in the regnal lists. Cuanu's Book may have meant that Echoid had claimed the kingdom of Fortriu through his mother, who might have been a daughter of Brude Maelchon's son, or of some other king of Fortriu. It is said that a daughter of Aidan was Maithgein of Monid, and she may have been a full sister of Echoid (see Oengus 1905, pp. 116, 117).

The claim of Connad Cerr, son of Conall, Comgell's son, to the kingship of Dal-Réti had been passed over. But after the death of Echoid, Connad became king, and he is called ' king of Dal-Réti ' when he died, in the battle of Fid-eóin later in the same year (A.U. as above, and T.).

The next king of Dal-Réti was Domnall Brecc, Echoid Buide's son. Other sons of Echoid are named as ancestors of families in the east : Fergus Goll, in Gowrie (*Gabranaig*), and Conall Cerr, in (northern) Fife (*fir* [*F*]*ibe*). (See E.S. 1, p. cliv.)

About eight years before Domnall's death he was defeated in a battle fought ' in Calathros ' (E.S. 1, pp. 158, 159 note 6). The district of Calathros included Ederline (*Etar linddu*, A.U. 29c30, 735 = 736), and so was probably near the border between Argyll and Lorn. If Calathros ' harbour point ' was a name of Craignish promontory, it might have been extended to include a district inland from Loch Craignish.

Four years later, Domnall Brecc took part in a disastrous campaign, in which he is said to have brought considerable forces from Scotland to the aid of Congall Caich, the king of the Cruithni of Dal-nAridi, and of the Ulaid. Congall Caich was defeated and killed in the battle of Roth, or Moira, in county Down, by Domnall, son of Aid, son of Ainmure, at that time the high-king of Ireland. There is a legend that Congall was a sister's-son of Domnall Brecc. Domnall Aid's son was Columba's kinsman, and head of the cenel-Conaill, and in boyhood he had received Columba's blessing (19ab).

The legendary accounts of the battle assert that Domnall Brecc was captured, or that he narrowly escaped, and that three of his brothers were killed. The only nearly-contemporary account of these things is that given by Cummene (657 × 669), and quoted in an insertion in the Dorbbene manuscript (108a). As abbot of Iona, Cummene had monasteries under him in Britain and Ireland, and had an active interest in affairs of state. His connexion with Columba's monastery of Derry would have given him the knowledge of what happened on the coasts of cenel-nEogain and cenel-Conaill. According to Cummene, Domnall Brecc's share in the war was his ravaging of the province of Domnall Aid's son. That was the territory of cenel-Conaill, at a considerable distance from Moira, which was near the western boundary of the Cruithni of Dal-nAridi. The Irish annals do not say that Domnall Brecc fought in the battle of Moira.

On the same day on which the battle of Moira was fought, Conall Coil, Mailcobo's son, an ally and nephew of Domnall Aid's son, defeated the cenel-nEogain in the battle of Sal-tire (genitive *Sailtire* A.U. 23c2 and T. 10a30). The name Sal-tire was known to the Scandinavians, who believed that it meant Kintyre (cf. Heimskringla, Magnus Barelegs' Saga, c. 10). If we accept that meaning, and assume that Domnall Brecc's force was naval, the course of events can be explained in the following way. Domnall Brecc's fleet, led or sent to attack the cenel-Conaill coast, was joined by ships of the cenel-nEogain, and with them withdrawn to Kintyre. The fleet of cenel-

Conaill then followed them, and arrived there about the same time as Domnall Aid's son reached Moira with his land army.

These victories of Domnall Aid's son confirmed him in the high-kingship of Ireland. By supporting the high-king's enemies, Domnall Brecc had ended the amicable relations that had existed since the council of Druimm-céte between the cenel-Conaill and the descendants of Aidan.

According to Cummene, Domnall Brecc had violated an injunction expressed by Columba at the time when Columba ordained Aidan as king, that neither Aidan, nor any of his descendants, should injure Columba, or his relatives in Ireland. Cummene wrote that through violating this injunction Domnall Brecc had caused Aidan's descendants to lose the ' sceptre of this kingdom ' from their hands. The place where Cummene wrote was very probably the territory of the Dal-Réti of Ireland; and the time, probably 661 × 669 (see p. 91). The ' sceptre ' that was lost was dominion over the Irish Dal-Réti.

Cummene's statement is our only evidence of the loss of the kingdom, and that part of his statement must be accepted. He wrote at a time when the position of Aidan's descendants was widely known, and if his version of the facts had not been true, Columba's prophecy, of which those facts were supposed to be the fulfilment, would have been rendered ridiculous.

After Domnall Brecc had lost dominion over the Irish Dal-Réti, a belief that he had incurred Columba's curse would have injured his position as the king of his tribe ; but he continued to be the leader of an army.

Two episodes are mentioned together in the Irish annals, in the year after the battle of Moira : a flight of the people of Domnall Brecc at Glenn Mairison (T. 10a32–33 ; *bellum glinne Mureson*, A.U. 23c7–8, 637 = 638) ; and a ' siege of Etin ' (A.U.), or ' of Etain ' (T.). The *s* of *Mureson* or *Mairison* looks as if it may stand for English *st*. These annals seem to imply that Domnall Brecc's supporters were besieged in Etin. In this context, the place besieged would have been a fortress (in Carriden ?) not so far east as Edinburgh.

That these episodes occurred to the south of the Forth is suggested by the circumstances of Domnall's death, four years after the battle of Moira. Domnall Brecc was killed, after reigning for fifteen years, or in the fifteenth year of his reign, in the battle of Srath Caruin, by Eugein (*Ohan*), the king of the Britons (of Dumbarton) ; in December of the year in the January of which Domnall Aid's son had died ; i.e. in 643 or 642. Eugein was a son of Beli Neithon's son. (See E.S. 1, pp. clviii, 167–8.) The river Carron is here the Carron of Stirlingshire. Between it and the Avon which bounds West Lothian there was a 'plain of Manau' (A.U. 27b18–19, 710 = 711 ; T. 12b30 ; A.S.C.DE, year 710). Domnall Brecc was apparently attempting to hold southern Manau (which his grandfather may have subjugated) not against the Northumbrians, but against the Britons. We have Bede's assurance that no king of the Scots had led an army against the nation of the Angles after 603.

After Domnall Brecc, the next king of Dal-Réti seems to have been Ferchar, Connad Cerr's son, of the family of Comgell. In the source of the regnal lists he was entered before Domnall Brecc, perhaps through a scribal error. It is uncertain how much of the territory of the Dal-Réti was under the rule of Ferchar during Domnall's lifetime. Ferchar died in ?651 (E.S. 1, p. 170).

A 'Dúnchad Duban's son' appears as king in Fland's Synchronisms at about this time. He may have been the grandfather of Fiannamail 'Dúnchad's grandson', who was king of Dal-Réti in about 700 (see below). There is a possibility that Dúnchad Duban's son was a descendant of Iogenan, Gabran's son. A Dúnchad Eoganan's son died in ?621, and the name recurs in a later generation at the death of Dúnchad Euganan's son, about 680. (See E.S. 1, pp. 118, 145, 190.) *Duban* 'little black one' was a nickname of a type that served to distinguish between men who had the same baptismal name. Old-Irish nicknames were quite often substituted for real names, and Dúnchad Duban's son may have been identical with the second Dúnchad Euganan's son.

When Cummene wrote, the descendants of Aidan had not yet recovered the kingship. Aidan's grandson, Conall Crandomna, a brother of Domnall Brecc, died in 659 or 660, and he is entered as king in the regnal lists. According to the version of the list in the Duan Albanach he shared the kingdom with Dúnchad (called *Dunghal*). Conall could have held dominion over the Dal-Réti of Britain, while Dúnchad was king over the Dal-Réti of Ireland.

Domnall Aid's son, high-king of Ireland, died in 643 or 642. He was succeeded by his nephews, who died in 654 and 658. After they died, the high-kingship of Ireland was held by two sons of Aid Slane. These, and their successors, belonged to the southern Ui-Néill, and from 658 onwards the offence done by Domnall Brecc against the cenel-Conaill would hardly have prevented a descendant of Aidan from obtaining the kingship of Dal-Réti.

The earliest indication in the annals that a descendant of Aidan had regained the kingship of Dal-Réti is in 673, when Domingart, Domnall Brecc's son, at his death is called ' king of Dal-Réti ' (A.U. 672 = 673. The text is grammatically ambiguous, but must be understood in this way). He seems, therefore, to have recovered the kingdom over the Dal-Réti of Ireland after the time at which Cummene wrote.

When Cummene wrote, the descendants of Aidan had not only lost the kingship ; they had come under the domination of *extranei*. Neither the house of Comgell, nor the descendants of Aidan's brother, could properly have been called *extranei* in relation to Aidan's descendants. It seems probable that by *extranei* Cummene meant the Northumbrians.

After the overthrow and death of Æthelfrith, the king of Northumbria, in 616, his sons took refuge among the ' Scots or Picts ' (H.E. III 1). This brought future rulers of the Northumbrians into peaceful contact with the Scots and Picts.

One of Æthelfrith's sons was Anfrith (or Eanfrith), whose son Talorcan became later a ' king of the Picts ' (653–657). A second son of Æthelfrith was Oswald, who reigned over Northumbria from 633 to 641 (Stenton 1947, pp. 81–2), or from 634 to 642 (Levison 1946, p. 272). Adomnan says that king Oswald with twelve men had been baptized during his exile among the Scots. (Cf. H.E. III 3.) King Oswald attributed his victory, through which he obtained Northumbria, to the intercession of Saint Columba (8a–9a).

Oswald is said by Adomnan to have been 'ordained by God as emperor of the whole of Britain'. Bede also says that Oswald received under his dominion all the peoples and provinces of Britain, speaking the four languages, British, Pictish, Irish, and Anglo-Saxon (H.E. III 6). The extent of Oswald's dominion had obtained for him the title of Bretwealda. (For a lucid account of the title *Bret(en)-(án)wealda* 'ruler of all Britain', see Stenton 1947, pp. 34–6.)

Adomnan and Bede approach this matter from different points of view, and taken together they seem to prove that the 'outsiders' who, according to Cummene, dominated the descendants of Aidan were the Angles of Northumbria. Cummene definitely places the subjugation to outsiders after the battle of Moira ; we may suppose that the loss sustained by Domnall Brecc in that warfare, with the resulting forfeiture of the kingship of the Irish Dal-Réti, had induced him to accept the Bretwealda Oswald (who was probably his friend) as overlord.

Cummene's book *De virtutibus sancti Columbae* was written during the reign of Oswiu, Oswald's brother, who had succeeded to the kingdom of Bernicia at the time of his brother's death. Bernicia extended on the eastern side of Britain from the Tees to the Forth, and westward to the Solway. Oswiu did not become Bretwealda until he had defeated Penda, the king of Mercia, in 654 or 655. Bede says of Oswiu that 'for the most part he subdued also the nations of the Picts and Scots, and made them tributary' (H.E. II 5 ; cf. III 24). Unless Bede is inconsistent, he implies that the submission of some Picts and Scots to Oswiu was made under force or threat, and differed in this from their submission to Oswald. Probably also tribute had not been exacted by Oswald from Domnall Brecc.

At the height of Oswiu's power, the king of the Picts was Talorcan (†657), a son of Anfrith, and nephew of Oswiu. After Talorcan, two kings of the Picts are called ' son of Domnall ', and it seems possible that they were sons of Domnall Brecc, by a Pictish mother. These were Gartnait, who died in 663 ; and his brother, Drust, who was expelled from his kingdom in 672, and died in 678. (Cf. E.S. 1, pp. cxxiv–cxxv, 178, 181, 184.) Cummene's lament over the descendants of Aidan was written 657 × 669 (or 661 × 669), while one of these sons of Domnall was ' king of the Picts '.

The position of Domnall Brecc's successors in relation to Northumbria is very obscure. His son, Domingart, as king of the Scots in Britain, would seem to have owed tribute to Oswiu, his overlord in Britain ; when he was king of the Dal-Réti in Britain and in Ireland, he would have owed military service from the Dal-Réti of Ireland to the high-king of Ireland.

Oswiu's death in 670 seemed to offer the northern peoples an opportunity of throwing off the Northumbrian overlord-ship. Æddi's Life of Wilfrith gives a florid and vague account of what followed. In the early years (670 × ?672) of the reign of Ecgfrith Oswiu's son, the Picts collected a great horde of peoples on their frontier, refusing to be subject to the Saxons. Ecgfrith, with Beornhæth ' a bold under-king ', went against them with a mounted force, and defeated the Picts with great slaughter (cf. E.C. p. 37). Two fordable rivers were filled with the Pictish dead, and can hardly have been other than the Avon and Carron, where those rivers are separated, near their mouths, by three or four miles. Between them was the plain of Manau, in which the battle of 711 was fought.

As in 643, so still in 670 × ?672, the plain of Manau was not within Bernician territory. The Scots in Britain had lost any hold that they had had upon Manau, which continued to be disputed land lying between the Angles and the Britons of Strathclyde. The Picts endeavoured to hold it in 711, when one of them, a boy, *Finnguine filius Deileroith*, was killed by the

'Saxons'. His brother, *Garnat filius Deileroith,* died in 716 (A.U. 27b18–20, 27d10).

The warfare described by Ædddi very probably led, directly or indirectly, to the expulsion of Drust Domnall's son from his kingdom in 672, and perhaps to the setting up of Brude Bile's son as king of Fortriu. Brude was called 'king of Fortriu' in the common source of A.U. (692 = 693) and T. (11d22–23). (T. 11c23–26 reads *la Bruidhi mac Bili regis Fortrenn,* in which *regis* is a scribal error for *regem.*) According to the verses attributed to Riaguil (see below), Brude fought (in 685) 'for the heritage of his grandfather'. The natural inference would be that Brude's grandfather, but not his father, had been king of Fortriu. A verse quoted in the Irish Life of Adomnan (Anecdota, II, p. 17) says that Brude was the son of a king of Ail-Cluaithe (Dumbarton). In a genealogy appended to the Historia Brittonum, it is said that Brude the king of the Picts was a cousin (*fratruelis*) of Ecgfrith.

These sources are not the best of historical evidence, but they do not necessarily conflict with one another. Ecgfrith and Talorcan, Anfrith's son, were *fratrueles,* in the strictest sense of that word. If the mother of Brude Bile's son had been the wife of Beli Elfin's son, king of Dumbarton, and a daughter of Talorcan, all the relationships could agree. The death of Beli Elfin's son in 722 is entered in Annales Cambriae (under [722]), and in the Irish annals ('Bile Eilphin's son', A.U. 721 = 722) ; and he would have survived his son Brude by twenty-nine years. He had perhaps the epithet *Búan* 'long-lived' in Irish tradition, misrepresented in Duald's Annals, p. 40 (E.S. I, p. 220). Talorcan was probably born 617 ×, so that if Brude was Talorcan's grandson he would have been not more than forty years old when he died, and very young when Drust was expelled.

In 684 Ecgfrith sent an army into eastern Ireland. He took prisoners, invaded churches, and earned the curses of the monks of Brega (H.E. IV 24 ; A.U. 684 = 685, 686 = 687 ; cf. the verses of Riaguil, as below). In the spring of 685, he collected a strong force, defying remonstrances, set out to waste

a ' province of the Picts ', and was led, by the usual with-
drawing tactics, not, as Bede says, *in angustias inaccessorum
montium* (H.E. IV 24), but into the swamps of Angus. The
Northumbrian army was almost annihilated by the forces of
Brude Bile's son at a place called Nechtan's Mere, apparently
the Mire of Dunnichen, on 20 May 685, a Saturday. Ecgfrith
was killed or mortally wounded in the battle. His death was
commemorated on 27 May, according to an addition in
Oengus 1905, p. 136. The statement of Symeon of Durham
that Ecgfrith was buried in Iona (*in Hii*, 1, p. 32) appears to
have been taken by Symeon from some source, written or oral,
that had misunderstood the lines of Riaguil : *Cia do rada aitirge* .
is hí indhí iar n-assa (Duald's Annals, p. 110), ' Although he
have repented, it is penitence too late '. (The true meaning
was first shown by W. J. Watson, literally ' she is the she too
late '.)

After the death of Ecgfrith, his brother Aldfrith, Oswiu's
son, was erected to the kingdom of Northumbria. According
to Bede, he was of illegitimate birth (*nothus* ; Colgrave 1940,
p. 238). He was apparently trained for the priesthood.
Bishop Aldhelm wrote of him as of one who had been his
adopted son, implying that Aldfrith had been his pupil, perhaps
at Malmesbury (Stenton 1947, p. 89 ; Plummer 1896, II,
p. 312). Aldfrith had studied among Irish monks. There was
a tradition in Ireland that he was a writer of Irish, and was
called in Irish Fland Fína ' blood of wine ' (perhaps meaning
' of noble parentage ' ; cf. *fínfuil* in R.I.A. Dictionary).
Adomnan calls him his friend (103b). In the notice of his
death, in Duald's Annals, p. 110, Aldfrith is said to have been
' a renowned scholar, Adomnan's pupil '.

An alleged prophecy of Cuthbert (in the Anonymous Life
of Cuthbert ; Colgrave 1940, p. 104, cf. 329) implies that
Aldfrith was in Iona in May 684. This may be evidence that
Aldfrith was in Iona at some time before he became king,
but there is no evidence to show where he was at the time
of Ecgfrith's raid upon eastern Ireland.

At the time of the battle of Dunnichen, the king of Dal-Réti

was Maelduin, Conall Crand-omna's son, who had succeeded
Domingart, Domnall Brecc's son, in 673, and who died in 688.
The agreement with the Picts (see p. 59) must have been made
either by Maelduin or by his successor, his brother Domnall
Dond, who died in 696.

Adomnan probably finished his Life of Columba in the
reign of Domnall Dond. Since the kingdom of Dal-Réti was
again held by a descendant of Aidan, it must have seemed to
Adomnan that what had been written by Cummene about the
sceptrum was no longer appropriate, and so he did not include it
in his work. If Cummene's reference to *extranei* was understood to mean Northumbrians, that also would have become
inappropriate, since their defeat in 685.

Domnall Dond was apparently succeeded by his kinsman
Echoid (or Echu), son of Domingart, son of Domnall Brecc.
Echoid's name is entered among the guarantors of Adomnan's
Law in 697 with the simple title ' king ' : *Euchu ūa Domnaill rī*
(Cáin Adamnain, §28). None of the guarantors is called ' king
of Dal-Réti '. Echoid was killed in the same year (A.U.
696 = 697).

(Beside the Irish name *Echoid* (> *Eochaid*), gen. *Echdach*
(see p. 146), there is another guttural stem *Echu* (> *Eochu*), gen.
Echach, which is used as though it were a hypocoristic form of
the longer name. These two stems may be of different origin,
but in use they became synonymous, and so, to avoid misunderstanding, we render them both as ' Echoid ' in our
translations, and generally when we mention the name ; but
of course we retain the spelling actually used, when we quote
directly from a text.)

Ferchar Fota, the head of the descendants of Loern, also
died in 697. In 698, his son Ainfcellach ' was thrown out from
the kingdom, and taken, bound, to Ireland ' (A.U.). The
words *de regno* imply that Ainfcellach was king, and the event
suggests that he had claimed to be king of Dal-Réti, as well
as of the descendants of Loern. Both he and Ferchar Fota are
included among the kings in Fland and the regnal lists.
Historical sources do not tell us what claim Ferchar or his

son could have had to the kingship of Dal-Réti. Neither of
them is included among the guarantors of Adomnan's Law.

If it was in fact the kingdom of Dal-Réti that Ainfcellach
had held, that seems to have been taken from him by a claimant
of another line, Fiannamail Ossene's son, who at his death in
700 is called ' king of Dal-Réti ', though he is not included in
the lists of kings. He is named among the guarantors of
Adomnan's Law, without any title (*Fiannamuild ua Dunchatai*) ;
and cannot have obtained the kingdom of Dal-Réti until after
the death of Echoid Domingart's son. He was a grandson of
Dúnchad, who may have been the ' Dúnchad Duban's son '
of the regnal lists ; and it is possible that he was a descendant
of Aidan's brother Iogenan (see above).

The Life of Adomnan is not a historical source, but it does
show (chapter 5) a tradition that there was another claimant
of the kingdom, Cathusach, son of Echoid, son of Domingart ;
but that he was not able to hold it, and his descendants did
not receive it. (The name Cathusach occurred in two previous
generations of the royal family : E.S. 1, pp. 169, 198.)

After the death of Fiannamail it appears that Ferchar
Fota's son Selbach obtained the kingdom of Dal-Réti. His
name is entered in Fland and the regnal lists (see M. O.
Anderson, in *S.H.R.* xxviii, pp. 109 f.). In 723, he is called
' king of Dal-Réti ' in Tigernach's Annals. He entered a
monastery in that year, and his son Dúngal took his place as
king ; but in 726 ' Dúngal was thrown from the kingdom '.
In 726, according to Tigernach's Annals, ' Echoid son of
Echoid began to reign '. Accession notes are usually later
additions in a chronicle, but there seems to have been in this
instance some reason why the accession was memorable.
(Compare the note in A.U. 732 = 733, and T., of the assumption by Muiredach son of Ainfcellach of the kingdom of
cenel-Loairn.)

The accession of Echoid brought the kingship of Dal-Réti
back, after twenty-nine years, to the descendants of Aidan :
Echoid was the son of Echoid, son of Domingart, son of
Domnall Brecc.

Here we must return to the insertion in 108a. It is ostens-ibly a quotation from the *Liber de virtutibus sancti Columbae*, composed by the abbot Cummene, A.D. 657 × 669, when the descendants of Aidan had lost the kingdom ; warning, and inciting them, to accept the authority of Columba's successor, and to resist the domination of Northumbria. Adomnan had taken material from the same chapter of Cummene, but omitted this passage, which in his time had lost its original significance.

The insertion was elaborately made, by or for Dorbene, and was almost certainly prompted by some circumstance existing at the time when A was written. It could just possibly have been done under instructions from Adomnan (× 704), but there seems to be a strong balance of probability in favour of a later date (704 × 713). Cf. pp. 104-05. In either case an obvious reason for inserting an incitement to resist aggression was the fact that the tribe of Loern had usurped the leadership that pertained to the line of Domingart, Gabran, and Aidan.

In 727, ' Selbach, and the *familia* of Echoid, Domnall's grandson, met at Irros-foichnae, and there some men fell, of the two peoples of Airgialla ' (A.U. 28c22–25, 726 = 727). This seems to imply that Selbach, returning from an Irish monastery, was accompanied by an Irish escort from the Airgialla. (Cf. p. 37.) Nothing more is known of this conflict. Selbach died in 730.

Echoid is included in Fland and the regnal lists (see *S.H.R.* as above). ' Echoid son of Echoid ' is named also in the list of kings of Dal-nAridi (*Eochaid macc Echach*, L.L. 41e). The latter title was perhaps obtained as a result of the battle of 731, described in the Irish annals, from an Old-Irish source : *Bellum inter Cruithne et Dalriati in Murbuilgg, ubi Cruithni devicti* ' A battle between the Cruithni, and the Dal-Réti of the Muirbolg, and in it the Cruithni were conquered ' (A.U. 29a8–9, 730 = 731). This quotation was omitted in E.S. 1, p. 228. In A.U., *Cruithni* means Irish Cruithnians, and here, as usual, stands for ' people of Dal-nAridi '. The ' Dal-Réti of Muir-

F

bolgg' are the people of Irish Dal-Réti, of which Muirbolc
was the harbour. (See p. 36.)

The high-king of Ireland, Flaithbertach, king of the cenel-
Conaill (Columba's branch of the northern Ui-Néill), was
defeated in battle by the rival branch, the cenel-nEogain, in
732 (A.U. 731 = 732). In 734 (or 733) he obtained help from
the Scots in Britain : ' Flaithbertach led the fleet of Dal-Réti
to Ireland ; and a great slaughter was made of them in the
island of Hoine . . . and many were drowned in the river that
is called the Bann. Echoid Echoid's son, king of Dal-Réti,
and Conall Conchobar's son, died ' (T. ; cf. E.S. 1, pp. 229–30).
Flaithbertach was defeated also in a battle in Mag Itho (in
Donegal). Among the killed were *nepotes Echdach*, and it is not
known whether they were grandsons of king Echoid's father, or
were members of one of the several kindreds called Ui-Echach.

It may be inferred from Tigernach's Annals that Echoid's
death resulted from the battle on the Bann. After that the
history of the kingship of the Dal-Réti is very obscure. In
?733, Ainfcellach's son, Muiredach, had ' assumed the kingship' of cenel-Loairn (A.U. 732 = 733). It is implied that he
became the leader of the Dal-Réti in Britain : in 736, the
districts of the Dal-Réti were wasted by Oingus Forcus' son,
king of the Picts, who took as hostages Muiredach's cousins,
the sons of Selbach ; and Muiredach, leading the Dal-Réti at
Ederline, was routed by the Fortrinn under Talorcan, the
brother of Oingus (A.U. 735 = 736). Dúngal, Selbach's son,
had incensed Oingus, by dragging Oingus' son Brude from
sanctuary in Tory Island off the coast of Donegal (A.U.
732 = 733) ; and in the next year Dúngal had been forced to
take refuge in Ireland, ' fleeing from the power of Oingus '.
In 741, Oingus ' smote the Dal-Réti ' ; and until his death in
761 he seems to have dominated the Scots of Britain. Oingus
was succeeded by his brother, Brude Forcus' son, as ' king of
the Fortrinn ' (A.U. 762 = 763) ; and Brude was succeeded
by Cinaed, Feradach's son, ' king of the Picts ' (A.U. 774 = 775).
Cinaed fought a battle in Fortriu with Aid Find in 768. Aid
Find was a son of Echoid, and was king of the Dal-Réti at the

time of his death (A.U. 777 = 778). There is no reasonable doubt that Aid Find's father was the Echoid Echoid's son who died in 734 or 733 (see above). Some pedigrees omit one of the two Echoids, but without any historical justification. Aid Find is an ancestor of Cinaed Alpin's son, and to Aid Find were attributed ' the rights and laws of the kingdom ' that were introduced under Cinaed's brother, Domnall (E.S. 1, pp. clvii, 291).

It has sometimes been asserted that Aid Find was descended not from Aidan, but from the house of Loern, through Muiredach, Ainfcellach's son. This rests upon no historical ground whatever, but upon an addition to the Chronicle of Melrose, made by a thirteenth-century annotator who, using a corrupt list of kings, falsely assumed that each successive king was the son of his predecessor. (See Chronicle of Melrose, facsimile edition (1936), pp. 2, xxiv, xxvii ; cf. M. O. Anderson, *S.H.R.* xxviii, pp. 109, 110, 116.)

The battle of Dunnichen had far-reaching consequences. According to Bede (H.E. IV 24) ' from that time the hope and valour of the kingdom of the Angles began to ebb, recede, and sink. For not only did the Picts recover the land of their occupation that was held by the Angles, but the Scots in Britain and also some part of the Britons recovered their liberty '.

The triumph of Brude would have made it possible for him as king of the Picts to reach the agreement with the Scots that is implied by Adomnan (102b–103a), under which their territories were separated by the central watershed (*dorsi montes Brittannici*). Part of it is still the boundary between Perthshire and Argyllshire. Any Scottish settlements that there may have been in Perthshire or Stirlingshire, in Fife, in Gowrie, or elsewhere to the east of the Spine, would by that agreement have been placed under the government of the Picts ; and any Pictish inhabitants of northern Scotland to the west of the Spine would have been under the Scots.[1] This arrangement

---

[1] We prefer the term ' Spine ', as a literal translation of *dorsum* or *druimm*, because it has a geographical meaning, which is not apparent in the undefined term ' Drumalban '.

did not need to be more exactly defined, or mapped out, because the position of the watershed was shown by the direction in which the rivers flowed. The agreement did not affect the territories of the Britons.

Brude Bile's son died in 693, and was succeeded as king of the Picts by Tarain Ainftech's son, of whom nothing is known except that he was expelled from his kingdom in 697, and went to Ireland in 699. His name is spelt also *Tarachin*, in A.U. 26b23 and T. 11a47, probably from a North-British pronunciation *Taraïn*. Tarain was an uncommon name. The fact that Adomnan, in or before 692, wrote about a Pictish noble, Tarain, who was a friend of Columba, suggests that Tarain Ainftech's son, who must then already have been successor-elect to the Pictish kingdom, was thought to have been a descendant of the earlier Tarain.

Tarain's successor was Brude Der-ile's son. Der-ile or Der-ili (an Irish name, meaning 'daughter of the Isla' or 'daughter of Islay') was evidently his mother's name, and it must have been through her that he inherited the kingdom. The form of her name is uncertain : *-ile* would be the O.I. genitive of a feminine IA-stem ; *-ili*, the O.I. genitive of a masculine IO-stem. *Íle* 'Islay' was generally an IA-stem (see p. 152). *Íle* an IO-stem might have stood for either the island, or the river, for which there is no other O.I. evidence.

Among the guarantors of Adomnan's Law the last-named is Brude Der-ile's son, 'king of the Cruthen-people', *Bruide mac Derilei rī Cruithintuathi* (Rawlinson MS. B 512, 50a25). The list was contemporary, but the forms of its names are affected by Middle-Irish spelling, and misspellings. The writer of this text used final *-e*, *-ei*, and *-i*, interchangeably. It is not possible to say whether *Derilei* stands for *Derile* or *Derili*.

Brude Der-ile's son died in 706, and was succeeded in the kingdom by his brother, Nechtan Der-ile's son (or Der-ili's son). Nechtan sent messengers, probably priests, to abbot Ceolfrith of Wearmouth and Jarrow, asking for a pronouncement upon subjects that were under dispute, namely the time of celebration of Easter, and the form of the clerical tonsure.

This contact with Nechtan's messengers gave Ceolfrith an opportunity of obtaining information about the eastern kingdom. He replied in a long letter, in which he may have had the assistance of Bede (H.E. V 21). It is noteworthy that in this letter Ceolfrith does not address Nechtan by the perhaps offensive title of *rex Pictorum*. But Bede refers to him by that title, which Bede himself popularized. In the letter Nechtan's name is given as *Naitanus*, and Bede refers to him as *Naiton* and *Naitonus* ; these are North-British forms of the name that is in Old Irish *Nechtan*.

After receiving Ceolfrith's letter, king Nechtan ordered the old Easter tables, of the 84-year calendar, to be destroyed throughout his territories. Here Bede implies that Nechtan was king of ' all the provinces of the Picts '.

Presumably because Columban monks (*familia Iae*) in the eastern kingdom did not accept the reform in the date of Easter, or the Roman tonsure, king Nechtan expelled them in 717. At the time of their expulsion, the mother house in Iona had already accepted the Easter reform.

In 724, king Nechtan withdrew to a monastery. During the next five years his kingdom was contended for by Drust, who was possibly a grandson of king Drust, Domnall's son, and who died in 729 ; by Elpin, who was possibly a descendant of the kings of Dumbarton, through Brude Bile's son, and who was finally defeated in 728 ; and by Oingus Forcus' son, who, after defeating the other claimants severally, became ' king of the Picts ', apparently in 729.

It is implied in A.U. 735 = 736 that Oingus (like Brude Bile's son) was king of Fortriu. He is given that title in Duald's Annals ; and his brother, Brude, who succeeded him, is called ' king of Fortriu ' at his death (A.U. 762 = 763, and T.).

The extent of the area that was at any one time included in the term Fortriu is always somewhat uncertain. The areas governed by Brude Bile's son, and the sons of Der-ile, and the sons of Forcus, may have varied in extent, but all these kings seem to have had a hereditary claim to the same kingship of Fortriu.

The ' kings of the Picts ' had one distinguishing feature :
they were elected to their kingship in accordance with a
peculiar custom. What Bede says (H.E. I 1) about their law
of succession was presumably obtained in part from the
messengers of Nechtan Der-ile's son, whose own succession had
followed this law. Bede says that when there was any doubt
about the election of a king of the Picts, they must choose a
king from the female royal *prosapia* rather than the male. In
effect, that means that a claimant's right to the kingdom came
through his mother rather than through his father.

The evidence is too slight to show how, in various circumstances, the succession law was carried out. Except for two
possible instances in the ninth century, we know of no ' king
of the Picts ' who was the son of an earlier king of the Picts.
There is no known instance of the kingdom's being ruled by a
queen. It would seem that a king's right to be elected passed
neither to his son nor to his daughter, but could pass to his
daughter's son. Several times a king's immediate successor
was his brother (presumably his mother's son, as in the case
of the sons of Der-ile) ; and it may be that when this did not
happen the immediate successor was usually a daughter's-son
of an earlier king, as apparently in the case of Brude Bile's son.
It is possible to account for most of the successions, in the
historical period, on these lines.

If this system of succession really was followed, it is neither
matrilinear nor patrilinear, and it could have resulted from a
coalition for mutual defence between a matrilinear and a
patrilinear people, by treaty, and perhaps in no other way.
In the legend of the Picts that Bede obtained from an Irish
source, or perhaps from the messengers of Nechtan Der-ile's
son, some compromise was indicated.

It is noteworthy that we find the system connected with the
district of Fortriu, the district that had retained the name of
the Verturiones, who had dominated it at the end of the
Roman occupation of Britain. The fact that Brude Der-ile's
son was called king of Cruthentuath (see above) suggests that
Cruthentuath was another name for the district of Fortriu.

This is the earliest written evidence that there were Cruithni in North Britain. In his Life of Columba, Adomnan does not mention Cruithni in North Britain. When he speaks of Cruithni , he always means the Dal-nAridi, and kindred states, in northern Ireland.[1] He calls Aid Dub ' a Cruithnian by family, of royal lineage ' (36a) ; the relatives of Comgell of Bangor, ' the peoples of Cruthen ' (50a) ; and Echoid Laib, a ' king of Cruithni ' (18a). Adomnan's use of the name suggests that if there were Cruithni in Scotland, he did not think it necessary to distinguish them from the Cruithni of Ireland ; and that Cruithni was not at first a name used (like the Latin Picti) as a denomination of all the inhabitants of North Britain.

If Bede's story of the arrival of the Picti in Britain from Ireland (H.E. I 1) was derived from the messengers of king Nechtan, it would be a legend of the Cruithni of Fortriu. Later Irish versions of the story connect it with the origin of the Irish Cruithni also.

In the Annals of Tigernach two kings, Brude Maelchon's son and Gartnait Domnall's son, are called in Irish ' king of the Cruithnig ' ; and one, Talorcan Anfrith's son, is called ' king of the Cruithni ', the earlier form of their name. These are translations into Irish of the Latin *rex Pictorum*, which was clearly the title given to kings of the Picts in the common source of A.U. and T., though Gartnait is named without title in A.U. None of these three kings receives a Latin title in T.

No Cruithni in Britain are mentioned in A.U., and apparently none were mentioned in the common source of A.U. and T. The use by Tigernach and others, in the latter part of the eleventh century, of the terms Cruithnig and Cruithni, can have little value as historical evidence, since the Picts had been absorbed two hundred years before in the kingdom of a Scottish dynasty.

The old idea, that Cruithni in Ireland and Scotland were

---

[1] The misleading term ' Irish Picts ' was admitted in E.S., and immediately regretted. Further study has shown no early instance of the name *Picti* or ' Picts ' given to the Irish Cruithni. A. O. A.

survivals of a non-Celtic-speaking, perhaps non-Indo-European population, has been superseded by theories that they were descendants of settlements of Iron-Age A or B, and were among the earliest Celtic-speaking populations in the British Isles. The careful analysis in Jackson 1954, pp. 16–18, involves rather complex reasoning, but gives a quite tenable theory.

There is another possible interpretation of the evidence. We may presume that in the first and second centuries A.D. many refugees from the Romans left Britain by the shortest sea-routes, to the north-east of Ireland. We must assume that the P-Celtic-speaking inhabitants of northern Ireland, since they did not live in Britain, did not call themselves ' Priteni ' or ' Pritani ', but that they called the refugees *Priteni because those had come to them from Britain. When Q-Celtic-speaking settlers in Ireland came into contact with the *Priteni, they would have fitted that name into their language as *Quriteni ; and from a kindred IO-stem *Pritenii, they formed their *Quritenii which developed into O.I. Cruithni.

It seems possible, and indeed probable, that some of these *Pritenii or Cruithni from Ireland settled in Perthshire, and that they were already in Fortriu when Aidan and his descendants took that land ' by force ' (ar éicin, Stokes 1887, 1, p. 162). A tradition to that effect might be inferred from a good deal of legendary material. But whether they were the Verturiones, who gave their name to Fortriu, cannot be decided with confidence. Both the descriptive name Cruithni and the descriptive or tribal name *Fortrinn, were known to Irish speakers, and are known to us only through them.

The Cruithni of Ireland are not known to have spoken P-Celtic in historical times. The *Pritenii must have been P-Celtic speakers when they occupied Fortriu, and for some time afterwards. The Dal-Réti, if when they occupied the north-eastern tip of Ireland they were not already Q-Celtic speakers, must have acquired Q-Celtic speech before they obtained their dominion in western Scotland.

Adomnan's representation of North-British names contains many spellings that result from P-Celtic speech, and that must be attributed to North-British phonology ; but also many other spellings that are distinctively Q-Celtic, and must result from Irish phonology. These could be explained as mis-representations by an Irish writer. But the one name that Bede definitely quotes as Pictish, *Peanfahel* (H.E. I 12), shows the same admixture of North-British and Old-Irish sounds, and his independent testimony confirms the impression that North British was then a mixed language. The change that took place from P-Celtic to Q-Celtic in Scotland had already begun to spread from the west.

One item in Cormac's Glossary assumes some knowledge of Cruithnian speech. What Cormac implies is not that a Cruithnian language survived, but that a dialectal word survived in a Cruithnian district, with a specialized meaning. The Glossary says (Cormac 1862, p. 12) : *Cartit, id est delg, id est bēlra Cruithnech, id est delg for a curt[h]ar a choss*—'*Cartit*, a thorn, Cruithnian language ; a thorn on which it puts its foot'. Very similarly in another manuscript (Cormac 1912, p. 25, no. 301) : '*Catit*, or *Cartait*, a thorn, Cruithnian language ; a thorn before which its foot is put'. *Delg* 'thorn' regularly means 'a pin'. The definitions do not leave any doubt about the meaning of the word : it is a guarded fibula, or safety-pin. 'Charity pin' would be an admirable description of this kind of brooch, and the question arises whether *cart(a)it* is not here a derivative of the Latin word *caritas* 'charity'. If *rt*, and long *a*, remained unchanged in North British (Jackson 1955, pp. 161, 164), a Vulgar-Latin *cartāt-em* would have become *cartāt* (or *cartād*) in North British ; and Cormac's spelling would have been an Irish transformation of this word. Cormac gives separately the Irish word *cartoit* 'love', taken from the South-British derivative of *caritas*. (Cf. Thurneysen 1946, § 925.)

If *cart(a)it* was thus derived from Latin independently of Irish, and was preserved in Fortriu, that would be of impor-tance to the history of Fortriu.

The bishop Cormac, king of Cashel, to whom this glossary was ascribed, died in the battle of Mag-nAilbe, A.D. 908.

Some of the items are old, and may be attributed to the ninth century.

The epithet of Echoid Laib (β), a king of Cruithni (18a), appears also in A.U. 22b16–17, 610=611, at the death of Echoid's son, *Mors Eugain maic Ecach Laibh* (with *l* altered later to *b*). In Middle Irish, *laib* appears to have the basic meaning 'askew'. An epithet *laebderc* meant 'squinting' (Plummer 1910, II, p. 356).

COLUMBA

Apart from what can be inferred from Adomnan's account, very little is known of Columba. The Middle-Irish ' Life of Columba ', a homily, supplies nothing that can be regarded as historical. Any scraps of genuine tradition that it may contain cannot be distinguished from what is legendary.

Bede says that Columba came to Britain from Ireland in A.D. 565, and that he was buried in Iona when he was seventy-seven years old, about thirty-two years after he had come to Britain (H.E. III 4).

In this, Bede's informant differs from Adomnan, who says that Columba was in pilgrimage for thirty-four years (30+4, 123b–124b) ; and that Columba was in his forty-second year when his pilgrimage began (4a), implying that he was seventy-five years old when he died.

Adomnan may have been the source of entries in the Annals of Ulster, which say that Columba sailed to Iona in the forty-second year of his age (A.U. 562=563) ; and that he died in his seventy-sixth year (A.U. 594=595 ; for errors in A.U.'s year-numbers before and after 600, see E.S. 1, p. 118 note 2). There are cognate entries in other Irish annals, with some errors in the numbers (*xlu°* for *xlii°*, T. ; *lxx.uii* for *lxx.ui*, T., C.S., and *aetate lxxui*, A.I.).

The annals all say that Columba died ' v. id. jun.', i.e. on 9 June (a Sunday night, T., C.S., A.I. ; of Pentecost, T., C.S.). 9 June is Columba's day in the calendars. The ' night of Sunday ' could have been taken from Adomnan (127a, 128b). The statement that it was the night of Pentecost is an error. It is probably implied also in A.I. 10c27, where it is said that 'his first night in Britain was Pentecost'. There seems to have been an erroneous traditional assumption that Columba's pilgrimage lasted from Pentecost to Pentecost.

9 June was a Sunday in 597, and that may be accepted as the year in which Columba died. According to Adomnan's figures, Columba's pilgrimage in Britain would have begun in 563, and the year of his birth would have been 521 or 522. Adomnan gives no year-numbers, but inclines to use battles as dating points (4a, 17b).

Columba was a son of Fedilmith, son of Fergus (4a). According to tradition, Fergus was a son of Conall Gulban, a son of Néll of the Nine Hostages. Conall was the ancestor of the cenel-Conaill, the branch of the northern Ui-Néill to which Columba belonged. In, and for long after, the time of Columba the branches of the Ui-Néill were dominant in northern and central Ireland. The cenel-Conaill occupied a large part of Donegal. To the east of them were the cenel-nEogain, the other principal division of the northern Ui-Néill. The territory of the southern Ui-Néill extended from north of the Boyne to the Liffey, and westward to the Shannon. (Cf. O'Rahilly 1946, p. 166.) Between the northern and southern Ui-Néill was the group of tribes known as the Airgialla.

Columba's mother, whom Adomnan calls Ethne, daughter of Mac-Naue, receives a pedigree in late writings (cf. E.S. 1, p. 23). They derive her from the Ui-Bairrche, in the province of the Lagin (cf. O'Rahilly 1946, pp. 32, 37).

Columba was destined by his parents for the priesthood. His original name was said to have been Cremthann or Crimthann ' a fox ' (commentaries, in Oengus 1905, p. 144 ; cf. 147 note ; and in Liber Hymnorum, Thesaurus 1903, p. 306). The name Columba was a Latin one, adopted for monastic use. In Irish, Columb or Colum was the name of a few men before Columba, and continued to be the name of many others after him ; and so he was distinguished in retrospect by the designation *Colum(m)-cille*, ' church-pigeon '. In the Félire Oengusso, under 9 June, he is called *Colomb cille caindlech* ('lustrous', W. Stokes, Oengus 1905, p. 139;) the adjective is chosen for alliteration.

When Columba was a young boy, he was given in fosterage to a priest called Cruithnechan (105ab : III 2). His training for religion began in boyhood (4ab). In early manhood, when he had attained deacon's orders, he studied sacred scripture under the teaching of bishop Findbarr (7a, 53a : II 1), who is also called bishop Vinniavus (53b). It is in this period that Adomnan places Columba's first miracle. Again, it is said that as a young man he went to his aged master, bishop Finnio (106b : III 4). The implication is that Finnio and Findbarr were the same man. Adomnan's Vinniavus and Finnio were Latin renderings of a hypocoristic name formed, under British influence, from the Irish name Findbarr (cf. Thurneysen 1946, p. 175).

There is some difficulty in identifying this bishop. We should expect that the name of Columba's most eminent teacher would have been entered in Columba's commemoration list. Bishops were entered in the Iona list in a separate section, beginning with the name of Martin (113b), as in the Stowe Missal. We should further expect that it would have been known in Iona tradition whether Columba's teacher was a bishop or not ; and Adomnan's statement that he was a bishop would be of fairly good historical value. But there is an apparent discrepancy. The bishop Finnia who was abbot of Mag-bile (Moville, in county Down), died about 579 or 580 (A.U. 578 = 579, A.I. 10d25). He might have taught Columba, though he would hardly have been a bishop at that time, and perhaps was scarcely old enough to have been Columba's principal master. Adomnan says that, when Columba went to Finnio, Columba was a youth, and Finnio was an old man (*suum videlicet magistrum, juvenis senem adiit*, 106b). Latin usage permitted the word *senex* to describe a man of middle age ; and a man of forty-five, or even forty, could be called *senex* in contrast with people of younger age. It is uncertain whether Adomnan would have followed this Latin usage. (Cf. p. 492.)

Finnia of Cluain-iraird (Clonard, county Meath, near the Boyne), the first abbot of his house, might have been an old man when Columba was young. His death is entered at ?550 (A.I. 10c5–6), or 549 (A.U. 548 = 549). He is not called bishop at his death. But the second and fourth abbots of the house were bishops (A.U. 588 = 589, 653 = 654 ; cf. Oengus 1905, p. 177). The third abbot was not called bishop (A.U. 614 = 615).

Among the various forms of the name given to these two men by early writers other than Adomnan, we have found Findbarr(us) applied only to Finnia of Moville, and Vinniavus applied only to Finnia of Clonard. As a result of the mis-spelling Vinnianus, and partly through attraction to the hypo-coristic Finden(us), the spelling Finnian(us) has tended to absorb the earlier forms.

In a calendar of the Old-Irish period in Karlsruhe Codex Augiensis no. 167, Finnia of Clonard is entered under his day, 12 December : *Vinniavi Cluano Irairdd* (Thesaurus 1903, p. 283).

The Stowe Missal represents the liturgy of the community of Tallaght in the early ninth century ; and it may have had a direct connexion with the liturgy of Iona. Its commemora-tion list has only one Vinniavus (*Vinniavi*, genitive ; not *Vinniani*, as in Thesaurus 1903, p. 284), and he is entered the first among the priests (*sacerdotum*) ; and only one Findbarr (*Finbarri*, genitive), who is placed among the bishops, and whom we must presume to be Finnia of Moville.

If Adomnan meant to assert that Columba's teacher was Finnia of Clonard, he would appear to have neglected the evidence of the tradition that went with the commemoration tables ; his words would be the earliest instance of the belief that Finnia of Clonard was a bishop (cf. Ryan 1931, pp. 120–1). If he meant that Columba's teacher was Finnia of Moville, his words *juvenis senem* are misleading.

Finnia of Clonard was later famed as having been the teacher of many of the most notable Irish monks. (Cf. an article by Kathleen Hughes in *Irish Historical Studies*, IX (1954), pp. 13 ff.)

While Columba was still a young deacon, studying divine wisdom in a district of the Lagin, he had a master called Gemman (73ab : II 25). This might have been not very far from Clonard.

Apart from the few chapters mentioned above, in which Adomnan touches upon phases of Columba's childhood, training, and youth, we cannot be sure that any of Adomnan's stories was meant to refer to Columba's life before the battle of Cul-drebene (A.D. ?561).

Three stories are connected with the district of Cell-mór Deathrib, Loch Cé,and the river Bó (Kilmore, Lough Key, and the river Boyle, all in the north of the county Roscommon), 43a, 52a, 67b.

A Latin Life of Munnu (the Finten Tailchan's son of Adomnan's I 2) says that Columba was the master of a school in Cell-mór of Diathrib (Plummer 1910, II, p. 228 ; MS S1) ; and the implied date would be nineteen years before Columba's death, that is about 578. It might possibly be inferred from this that Columba had some earlier association with the house at Kilmore, or that it was later an affiliated Columban house ; but we cannot assume that he was there at the time indicated, or that he himself founded it, any more than we can assume that he founded the many churches that the Irish Life has attributed to him. Adomnan seems to represent him as merely visiting the district, and he gives no clue to the date or number of the visits.

The fishing expedition that Columba is represented as having shared with friends who were keen fishermen, upon the river Sale (67a), is perhaps more appropriate to Columba's life before he became abbot of Iona, and even before he was abbot of Derry, and while he was still a young man in Ireland. In that case the river would probably have been the Blackwater, in county Meath. That river was called Sele in the Book of Armagh, where it is stated that Patrick had cursed the river so that there should be no salmon in it. Adomnan would have known the legend of Patrick's curse, and might have thought that Columba's success in obtaining a salmon demonstrated his sanctity. Adomnan says that the river abounded in fish ; but he implies that only the fish caught for Columba was a salmon. We may compare the story told in the Tripartite Life, and perhaps in the earlier version of that Life, relating that the north side of a river was cursed by Patrick, but became fruitful in fish when Muirgus, the king of cenel-Coirpri (†698), gave as an offering to Columba the unproductive part. The tradition involved is that there was an outlying district of the cenel-Coirpri, to the north of the Erne, near its mouth, within the borders of the cenel-Conaill. In that outlying territory was the land of Drumhome (*dorsum tómme*, 132a), in which there was a Columban settlement. (See p. 106.)

Columba founded a monastery at Daire-Calcig (Derry, in Londonderry county). According to the Annals of Ulster it was founded in 546 (A.U. 545 = 546) ; but that date is based upon a legend that connected the foundation with the death of Mo-Bí, whose death was entered under the previous year. The date is little to be trusted. Adomnan does not mention the monastery at Derry, though he mentions the place three times (11b, 26a, 90a).

Bede also does not mention the monastery of Derry. He says that before Columba came to Britain ' he had made the noble monastery in Ireland that from an abundance of oak-trees is named in the language of the Irish *Dearmach*, that is " Plain of oaks " '. This was the Dairmag (Durrow, in county Offaly) the foundation of which appears to be dated by Adomnan later than the occupation of Iona. (See p. 88.)

The battle of Cul-drebene (4a, 17b) was a turning-point in the history of northern and southern Ui-Néill. It was fought probably in 561 (A.U. 560 = 561) ; according to tradition, in a place between Drumcliff and Sligo (Hogan 1910, p. 319), in northern Connaught. In the battle, Diormit Cerball's son, king of the southern Ui-Néill, ' ordained, by God's will, as the ruler of all Ireland ' (36b), was defeated by the northern Ui-Néill and Aid, king of the Connachta.

Extremely little is known about the cause and purpose of

the battle (E.S. 1, pp. 24 ff.). In later times Columba was held
to have been to blame for it. It was said by some (T, C.S.)
that Columba had given his protection to Curnan, a son of
the king of the Connachta, that Diormit Cerball's son had
killed Curnan, and that Columba had attacked Diormit for that
reason. It was a matter of common belief that Columba
avenged any violation of protection that he had given (cf. 71a,
73ab, 108a).

It might be a reasonable presumption that Curnan had
been the hostage of his father with the high-king Diormit, and
that Columba had befriended him, as he is said to have later
befriended Scandlan Colman's son, who was the hostage of his
father with Aid Ainmure's son, the king of cenel-Conaill
(19b–20a). It would then follow that some rebellious action
of Curnan's father had caused Diormit to put Curnan to death
and to invade the territory of the Connachta. Columba
induced his relatives of the northern Ui-Néill to go to the
assistance of the Connachta, and their combined forces opposed
Diormit at Cul-drebene.

The implication was not that Columba had fought at
Cul-drebene, but that he instigated the battle, and obtained
the victory by prayer (A.U. 20b24–25; T. 8a40). (See
pp. 84-5.)

The idea that Columba held himself to be in some respect
guilty ' on account of the battle of Cul-drebene, which he had
won against Diormit Cerball's son, and of the other battles
that had been fought because of him ', is expressed in a late
preface to the *Altus Prositor*, a Latin hymn that was attributed
to Columba (Liber Hymnorum 1898, 1, p. 62). It is there
stated that the hymn was composed to beg for forgiveness.
(Cf. E.S. 1, p. 97.)

A further stage of this rumour insinuated that Columba's
pilgrimage, or mission to Britain, was undertaken as a penance
for this fault (' in Britain, fear of hell ', in Amra Coluimchille,
Liber Hymnorum, 1, p. 179; E.S. 1, p. 38).

This idea is developed in the Latin Life of Laisran, the
abbot of Daminis (Devenish, county Fermanagh), which says

that Columba went to his confessor, Laisran, and asked his advice how he could best obtain remission of sins and the favour of God after the deaths of many men in the battle of Cul-drebene ; and that Laisran ordered him to release from torment as many souls as those whose perdition he had caused, and further bade him to remain in perpetual exile from Ireland (Plummer 1910, II, p. 139).

If this legend was in existence in Adomnan's time, he deliberately rejected and contradicted it. He describes how Columba attended the council of Druimm-céte in Ireland, about A.D. 575, and how he spent some months founding the monastery of Durrow, apparently in 585 or later (see below) ; and he mentions visits, or a visit, to Ireland, of *aliquot dies* (40a and 97b), and for *aliquantis diebus* (83a). In the words attributed to Columba, *ut me de meo absolveret inculatu* 123b, although *inculatus* ' residence ' might possibly have been an Adomnanian synonym for *perigrinatio*, the meaning of *absolveret* is 'to release ' him, not from ' pilgrimage ', but from his earthly life. As the word is used here, it does not mean that he had taken a vow of lifelong exile, but it might later have been misunderstood in that sense, and have given rise to the legend that his life in Britain was a lifelong penance.

Whether or not the battle of Cul-drebene influenced Columba in his decision to leave Ireland, he had other motives also. He had been trained for the priesthood, and was of royal descent. It was very natural that he should have undertaken the leadership of the Irish church in Britain. His life in Britain was a ' pilgrimage for Christ ' (4a). Adomnan implies that it was not penitential pilgrimage among an alien people. It was monastic life in a place remote from centres of human population, and in the company of some friends and kinsmen chosen for their ideals of a spiritual life.

At a synod in Teiltiu (Teltown, county Meath) a sentence of excommunication was sought, and for a time obtained, against Columba (105b–106b). Adomnan does not explain the charge that had been made, but says merely that it was on the ground of offences that were ' trivial and very pardonable ',

G

and that the excommunication was irregular. The synod was
held within the territory of Diormit Cerball's son, undoubtedly
under his influence, and presumably in August of 562, the year
after the battle of Cul-drebene.

Although Adomnan thought that his verdict needed the
support of a vision seen by Brenden, his verdict did not depend
upon that vision. We must accept the fact that his statement
expressed his own opinion, which he thought was also the final
judgement of the church in Ireland, that Columba was not to
be condemned for blood-guilt, or any crime. So far as Adomnan's evidence goes, the recurrent and increasing rumours to
the contrary were slanders.

Some rumours adverse to Columba appear to have reached
Bede, who regarded them with caution, preferring to ascribe
to him the merit of his successors (H.E. III 4).

Columba sailed to Britain two years after the battle of
Cul-drebene (4a, 17b), that is, probably in 563. According
to what Adomnan, not quite consistently, says about the end
of Columba's life (123b–124b), it would appear that Columba
was thought to have arrived in Britain either in April, or in
Easter week, and to have died shortly after completing thirty-
four years in pilgrimage.

In an addition to his original text (see 107a and note),
Adomnan says that Columba sailed to Britain with twelve
disciples. A list of their names is given in the B manuscripts
(see the Appendix). It contains only three that are mentioned
in Adomnan's Life of Columba.

Adomnan implies (17b) that when Columba left Ireland
he went first to the king of Dal-Réti, Conall, Comgell's son.

While he was with king Conall, the battle of Ond-móne
(mm) was fought in Ireland. This appears to be the ' battle
of Móin Daire-lóthair ' of the Irish annals (A.U. 562 = 563 ;
T. ; C.S.), in which the northern Ui-Néill, together with some
Cruithnian supporters, defeated the kings of Dal-nAridi and
other Cruithnian districts. The king of Dal-nAridi, Aid
Brecc, was killed in the battle (L.L. 41e). Echoid Laib, the
king of another Cruithnian district, survived (18a). The

victors were Ainmure Sétne's son, king of the cenel-Conaill and first-cousin of Columba ; and Domnall and Forcus, two sons of Muirchertach macc-Erce, who were joint kings of cenel-nEogain (18a). These had also been among the victors at Cul-drebene.

As a result of the battle of Móin Daire-lóthair, the Ui-Néill annexed Cruithnian lands to the west of the river Bann, including the districts of Lea (28a) and of Ardd-Eolorgg (Book of Armagh, 15b29). They thus approached, though they did not yet join, the land of the Dal-Réti. Between Ui-Néill and Dal-Réti lay a strip of Cruithnian land, called Eilne (51a), bounded by the rivers Bann and Bush. (Cf. Book of Armagh, 15b–c ; Hogan 1910, pp. 394, 482.)

A couple of years later, Diormit Cerball's son was killed (A.U. 564 = 565). His killing by Aid Dub, son of Suibne, was a subject of oral literature. Adomnan calls Aid Dub a Cruithnian of royal blood (36ab), implying that his father was a king of Dal-nAridi, as he is said to have been in the medieval legend of the death of Diormit ('Aided Diarmata', in S. H. O'Grady's *Silva Gadelica* (1892), i, pp. 72 ff.). The regnal lists make Aid Dub the successor of Aid Brecc as king of Dal-nAridi, and successor of Daig Cairell's son as king of Ulaid (L.L., 41e, 41c. Daig's death is entered in A.U. 586 = 587, and that of Aid Dub in 587 = 588). Columba's curse was supposed to have caused the double death of Aid Dub (37ab and footnote).

After the death of Diormit, the sovereignty of Ireland was assumed jointly by Domnall and Forcus, Macc-Erce's sons, who had been victorious in the battles of Cul-drebene and Móin Daire-lóthair. These were the first kings of the northern Ui-Néill to acquire the high-kingship, which, during the remainder of Columba's lifetime, seems to have alternated between the cenel-nEogain and cenel-Conaill. After Domnall and Forcus, Ainmure Sétne's son appears to have obtained the high-kingship. He was killed in 569, and soon afterwards was avenged by his son Aid. Apparently Baitan, Macc-Erce's son, and Echoid, son of Domnall Macc-Erce's son, received the kingship after Ainmure, and were decapitated. When news of their deaths (A.U. 571 = 572) reached Columba, he was in or near Ardnamurchan (20b).

To them succeeded Aid, Ainmure's son, under whom the council of Druimm-céte was held (see below). He was killed by the Airgialla (A.U. 597 = 598), and the southern Ui-Néill then regained a share in the sovereignty. According to a late entry in A.U., after Aid's death the sovereignty was divided between Aid Slane, king Diormit's son, and Colman Rimid, son of Baitan Macc-Erce's son. Adomnan (21b) implies that Aid Slane reigned alone until, against Columba's warning, he killed his nephew, Suibne son of Colman Mór (A.U. 599 = 600); after which he enjoyed a part only of his father's kingship of all Ireland, and died after four years and three months. His death, at the hands of Suibne's son, Conall, is entered in A.U. 603 = 604.

It is possible that Adomnan's mention of Columba's visit to king Conall, Comgell's son, suggested the much later entry in the annals, which say, at the death of king Conall, that he had given ' as an offering the island of Ia Choluimb-chille ' (A.U. 573 = 574 ; T., C.S.). This item was entered in the annals long after Iona had passed from the Pictish to the Irish dominion.

Adomnan does not say that Iona was given to Columba by Conall. But he implies that all the land to the west of the Spine, or watershed, was the territory of the Scots of Britain ; not only in his own time, for which his evidence about this must be accepted, but in the time of Columba, for which he is not evidence. He must have supposed that already in Columba's time Iona was far removed from the dominion of Picts, and was under the dominion of the over-king of Dal-Réti.

A generation later than Adomnan, Bede gave a different account (H.E. III 3-4) : ' . . . That island (Hii) belongs by right to Britain, from which it is separated by only a narrow strait, but long ago was resigned by gift of the Picts who inhabit those parts of Britain to monks of the Irish, through whose teaching they had received the faith of Christ.

' In the year of the Lord's incarnation 565, at the time when Justin the Younger received after Justinian the government of the Roman empire, there came to Britain from Ireland a priest and abbot of notable monastic profession and life, named Columba, to preach the word of God to the provinces of the northern Picts, that is to those that are separated by steep and rugged mountain ranges from their southern regions. For those southern Picts, who have their seats among the same mountains, had a long time before, as they say (*ut perhibent*), abandoned the error of idolatry, and received the faith of truth, when the word was preached to them by the most reverend bishop and most holy man, Ninia, of the race of the Britons ; who had been correctly trained in the faith and mysteries of the truth, at Rome. And the see of his bishopric, distinguished by the name of the bishop Saint Martin, and by a church where he rests in the body along with many holy men, has but now come into the possession of the Angles. That place pertains to the province of the Bernicians, and is called commonly Ad Candidam Casam, because he made there a church of stone, in a manner uncustomary to the Britons.

' Columba came to Britain while Bridius Meilochon's son, a most powerful king, reigned over the Picts, in the ninth year of his reign ; and by word and example he brought that nation to the faith of Christ. Therefore he received from them that island, to hold it for the making of a monastery. . . . His successors occupy it to the present day. And there he was buried, when he was seventy-seven years old, after about thirty-two years from the time when he came to Britain, to preach.'

What Bede says of the regions taught by Columba and by Ninian was doubtless derived in part from the messengers who were sent by king Nechtan Der-ile's son to Bede's abbot, Ceolfrith, about the year 710. Nechtan's appeal was for confirmation of the decisions of Rome, in opposition to the practice of the Irish church. The reply, written in Latin, was interpreted to Nechtan by his most learned men, who, by implication, may have been trained in a Ninianic tradition.

The communications between king Nechtan and Ceolfrith seem to prove that the Ninianic church had extended to Fortriu before the time of Bede, and that Bede thought that Ninian's mission to the Picts had been directed originally to Fortriu. That may have been true, although a Pictish area nearer to Ninian's see appears to have been thought of as the place of his mission, in the Miracula Nynie episcopi, in which *naturae* is an error for ?*Niduderas* : cf. the *Niuduera regio* ' district of the Nith-dwellers ' named in the Anonymous Life of Cuthbert ; and *terram Pictorum qui Niduari vocantur* in Bede's version (Colgrave 1940, pp. 82, 192 ; cf. W. Levison, in *Antiquity* 1940, pp. 288 f. See A. O. Anderson, in *S.H.R.* xxvii, pp. 42–5, emending ' Peohtwine ' on p. 43, line 26, to ' Peohthelm '). Adomnan and other Irish sources show no knowledge of Ninian's mission.

Bede gives no date of Ninian, except that his church was named after Martin, who is believed to have died in 397. The earliest evidence of a mission to the Picti is given by Patrick, who in his letter to the soldiers of Coroticus twice wrote of some ' apostate Picts ', about the middle of the fifth century.

Bede places the conversion of the northern Picts in what he believed to have been the year of Columba's first arrival in Britain, and before the occupation of Iona ; whereas Adomnan seems to place Columba's visit to the province of the Picts (east of the Spine) after the occupation of Iona (95b), and at a time when Columba could be spoken of as an ' old man ' (*senex* ; see under 114b, and p. 81).

Bede's statements that the island was given by ' the Picts that inhabit those parts of Britain ' (III 3), and that Columba received the island ' from them ' (not ' from him ') (III 4), could be imagined to mean that Iona was actually given not by king Brude, but by the inhabitants of the shores near Iona, to whom Columba would already have taught the Christian faith. This interpretation might partly reconcile the conflicting accounts, but we think that it is not what Bede intended to say. By dating the coming of Columba in a year of Brude's reign, he implied that Columba came to a place within the territory of Brude. The same contact between Columba and Brude seems to underlie both Bede's and Adomnan's accounts.

Very little can be inferred from Adomnan of the people who controlled the islands and coasts about Iona in Columba's time. He mentions a *Geona cohors*, whose leader, a man of high principle, went to Columba in Skye. That leader did not speak Irish (34b–35a). Adomnan implies that the southern coasts of Ardnamurchan, and the island of Hinba, were open to attack by great-grandsons of Gabran, who were apparently in command of the sea (69b, 72a). Adomnan mentions without enthusiasm the tribe of Loern, among whom he was stayed by contrary winds in the island of Saine (101b).

A district of early settlement by the tribe of Loern retains the name of Lorn. It is probable that when their power was at its highest they controlled land further to the north-west. When Columba visited Coire-salchain (46b ; cf. p. 87) he may have been the guest of an ancestor of Ferchar Fota, who was king of the tribe of Loern at the time when Adomnan wrote. Coire-salchain seems to have been within the district of Morvern (possibly originally the territory of an ancient mormaer, cf. A. O. Anderson, in *S.H.R.* XXIX, p. 85), and Morvern was traditionally associated with the name of Baitan, who is supposed to have been the Baitan, great-grandson of Loern Erc's son, in the pedigree in B.B. (E.S. I, p. clvi). (Cf. Watson 1926, p. 122.) Cronan Baitan's son (72b) may have been a son of that Baitan, who had a brother called Cronan (E.S. I, p. cliii).

Adomnan says that Columba lived for thirty-four years as an ' island soldier ' (*insulanus miles*). This does not necessarily mean that Iona was the only island in which he lived during that period. Another island monastery founded by Columba was in the island of Hinba, which has not yet been identified (p. 154). There is no clear indication to show which of these islands was occupied first, and we are not told how he divided his time between them. Adomnan speaks of him in three chapters as residing in Hinba ; and while he resided in Iona, he continued to rule Hinba through a *praepositus* or prior.

The later idea that Columba and his monks sailed to Iona directly from Ireland appears in the Irish Life, but it rests upon no source that has value as historical evidence. Columba's pilgrimage was a planned enterprise, not a random exploration like those attributed to Cormac grandson of Léthan, and in later sources to Brenden mocu-Alti. Considerable time would have been needed, not only for the building, but for the obtaining of materials, and the provision of boats, stock, and essential supplies, in a place so remote as Iona.

About one-third of Adomnan's stories of Columba are placed by him in Iona. Very few of them are datable. Adomnan believed that Columba was in Iona at the time of the death of Brenden, the abbot who had founded the monastery of Birra (Birr, in county Offaly). Brenden may have died as late as 573 (A.I., Duald's Annals), or as early as 565 (A.U. 564 = 565 ; T. ; C.S.). (See E.S. 1, p. 37 ; O'Rahilly 1946, p. 245.)

Columba was in Hinba, according to Adomnan, when he was required to ordain Aidan as king, in 574, but the ceremony of ordination was performed in Iona (107ab.) Thus Adomnan implies that ordination by Columba, and therefore by Columba's successors, was a necessary part of the installation of a king of Dal-Réti. It consisted in the laying-on of hands by the priest-abbot. There is no indication that a bishop was present, and there was no anointing.

Adomnan tells circumstantially how Columba, while he remained at Druimm-céte for the conference between the kings Aid Ainmure's son and Aidan Gabran's son, blessed Aid's son, Domnall. Domnall was then a boy, and he lived to old age (19ab). He died in ?643, in the fourteenth, or thirteenth, year of his reign as high-king (E.S. 1, pp. 166–7). Adomnan says also that Columba befriended at Druimm-céte Scandlan, the son of king Colman of Osraige. Scandlan had been fettered as a hostage by king Aid (19b–20a).

After attending the council of Druimm-céte, Columba walked with Comgell of Bangor, on the hill-route from Limavady to Coleraine. They rested near the fortress of Dun-

Cethirn, on the Sconce Hill, beyond which the road descends into the valley of the Bann ; and Columba is reported (49b–50a) to have prophesied about the battle to be fought at Dun-Cethirn (in 629) between the Cruithnians and the northern Ui-Néill. Columba was received with honour at Coleraine, on the Bann.

After the ordination of Aidan, Gabran's son, and his conference and agreement with the high-king of Ireland, the time was appropriate for some understanding between Aidan and king Brude. Columba's visit to that king would have been most fitting in this time. The part that Columba had played in the negotiations at Druimm-céte would have marked him out as a most suitable emissary ; and he was then old enough to have merited the description *senex* given to him by Adomnan (114b).

Aidan's father, king Gabran, had apparently, seventeen years before, encroached upon king Brude's territories in the region perhaps of Fortriu ; and now Adomnan shows us king Brude occupying a fortress in Inverness-shire. A settlement might have been desired by both parties, and Columba's visit to Brude was a demonstration that the Irish in Britain desired peace with the eastern kingdom.

That Adomnan thought that Columba had made only one journey to the ' province of the Picts ' is shown by the beginning of chapter 32 of book II (78a) : *Illo in tempore quo* ' In the time when the holy Columba remained for some days in the province of the Picts '. The chapters that follow (II 33, 34) deal with the same visit (*Eodem in tempore*), and with the end of the visit (*Post supra memorata peracta*).

In the next chapter (II 35), Columba's arrival at the fortress of king Brude is described, rather ambiguously, thus : *Alio in tempore, hoc est in prima sancti fatigatione iteneris ad regem Brudeum.* Eminent scholars whom we have consulted have preferred the translation in E.S. i, p. 49, ' On the saint's first laborious journey to king Brude ', which implies that Columba visited Brude more than once, to the translation of Fowler 1895, p. 86. We cannot, however, infer that the preceding chapters in Adomnan belonged to a later visit by Columba to the province of the Picts, since the *Illo in tempore* passage quoted above definitely implies that Columba made only one such visit. Moreover, if Columba had previously visited the province of the Picts, and had (as Bede asserts) converted the ' northern Picts ' to Christianity before he occupied Iona, it seems incredible that Adomnan could have spoken of any later visit as he does in book II chapters 32–34 (78a–82a), and could have represented the Picts to have been then still pagan.

We must therefore interpret the *fatigatio* passage somewhat differently. The phrase *fatigatio iteneris* does not necessarily mean ' the labour of a long journey ' ; it may equally well mean ' the labour of a steep path '. If as is likely Brude's fortress was thought to have been a hill-fort, the approach to it would have been thought of as steep and arduous, especially for an old man. Adomnan's meaning must have been ' The first time that the saint climbed the exhausting way to king Brude ', presumably from a lodging or encampment near the river Ness. The narrative seems to require that Columba would have gone to the fortress two or more times during his one visit to the province. Every ascent would have been equally laborious.

Occasional indications are given by Adomnan of the route that Columba must have followed in his journey to the province of the Picts. In book I chapter 34 he relates that Columba, with Diormit and others, set out by water to go across the Spine of Britain. They appear to have portaged their boat up the Lochy river (now in Inverness-shire) ; and they passed one night at a place where a stream ran into Loch Lochy, perhaps on its north-western shore. They would after that have crossed the Spine above Loch Oich, and continued by boat down Loch Ness. The journey down Loch Ness may possibly have been broken on its north-western shore, near Urquhart, which, according to Adomnan, Columba reached on foot (114b). He then proceeded to the river Ness. On his return from the province, he embarked with his sailors, presumably in the ship in which he had come, and sailed up Loch Ness.

During his visit to the province Columba seems to have lodged (according to Adomnan's story) on the side of the river Ness nearer to the fortress of king Brude (80a). Adomnan's account does not make it clear whether Brude's fortress was to the north, or to the south, of the river Ness. He thought that it had heavy double gates of wood in a rampart, within which the king's house and presumably other houses stood (82b). He had undoubtedly seen hill-forts of the wood-bound rampart type, and he probably thought that Brude's fortress was similarly constructed.

Adomnan's acquaintance with the route from Lochaber to the river Ness suggests that he may have gone that way himself ; and he may have inquired into local traditions of a visit by Columba. For many matters the interval, of more than a century, would have been too great for the survival of genuine tradition ; but if king Brude really did occupy a fortress near the Ness, that fact might have been remembered for a hundred years. On the other hand, the name of a powerful king could have been attached in false tradition to a prehistoric fortress.

A most prominent wood-bound fort is on the top of Craig Phatrick, near the Beauly Firth, and four miles from where the river Ness leaves the lake ; and it seems to us probable that Adomnan regarded that as the fortress of king Brude. The question whether Adomnan could have thought that a hill-fort was inhabited in the latter part of the sixth century may be answered by his apparent implication that Dun-Cethirn was inhabited in 575 (49b). That hill-fort seems to have been occupied as late as 681, when wooden buildings within it were burned (A.U. 680 = 681).

In any case, Adomnan places king Brude's fortress not far to the south of the Beauly Firth, which was the northern boundary of the Kaledonioi, and is in the boundary zone between the hill-fort people of wood-bound ramparts, and the people of circular defensive towers. The fact that Adomnan brings together in this zone the king of Picti and the king of the Orcades is interesting and significant. The ancient boundary between nations was still thought of as a boundary between populations.

The Brude-and-Broichan chapters are literary in character, but they are of value for the names that they contain.

Bru(i)de is an Irish form derived from a presumably North-British name **Brodjos*. This was a very early borrowing, made before the time of Columba. (See p. 158.) Bede calls Brude ' Bridius son of Meilochon ' (*Bridio filio Meilochon*, H.E. III 4). Where Brude first appears in the Annals of Ulster he is not named, but is called ' Maelchon's son' (or ' Maelchu's son '), under 557 = 558. This note suggests that the father was better known than the son. The Mailcun, king of Guenedota, whose death in 547 is entered in Annales Cambriae, was the Maglocunus whom Gildas calls an ' island dragon ', and whose territory included Anglesey. It is not possible to say that Brude's father was, or that he was not, this Maglocunus.

Adomnan's statement that Brude's foster-father was a wizard, called Broichan, raises difficult questions. Adomnan's Latin form of the name is Broichanus, except in one instance, where it is Froichanus (*de Froichano*, in MS A, 80a[1]). Adomnan's Broichanus is a latinization either of an Irish name, or of a North-British name that had been transmuted into Irish. The initial *B* either represents the Irish spirant (β) that developed from initial *w-* and that had become *f-* in Adomnan's time, or is a Latin substitute for the sound *w-* which had probably remained in North British.

Adomnan describes conversations between Columba and Broichan, without any mention of an interpreter. He tacitly implies that Broichan understood the Irish language.

The Irish form of the name, Froichan, appears as the name of the man who formed for the high-king Diormit Cerball's son a ' druids' fence ' in the battle of Cul-drebene. He is called Fraechan, son of Temnan, in an addition copied into the margin of A.U. 20b, at 560 = 561 ; and Fraechan, son of

---

[1] The reading *de Froichano* was communicated by me in a letter to Professor Jackson of 29 March 1953, but my reading was inadvertently quoted by him as *Uroichan* in Jackson 1955, p. 143. A. O. A.

Teniusan, in the text of T., 8a46. The earliest accounts, in the common source of A.U. and T., said that Diormit was defeated in that battle through the prayers of Columba ; and according to an Irish poem quoted by T. and C.S. Columba's prayer dispelled a mist that concealed Diormit's army.

These entries seem to show that there was a literary tradition in which Froichan was a renowned wizard, who would have been contemporary with Columba. It is incredible that there could have been two wizards called Froichan who interposed magic spells against Columba, one in the interest of the high-king of Ireland, the other as foster-father of the chief king of the eastern kingdom in North Britain. If the Brude-and-Broichan chapters have any historical value, Broichan and Froichan must have been one person.

It seems immediately very improbable that Brude's foster-father could have been the wizard who supported king Diormit at Cul-drebene. The improbability would be only slightly less if Brude's father had been king of Anglesey and Man. On the other hand, druidism had flourished in Anglesey, and the cult might have been continued by settlers from Anglesey among the Cruithni in eastern Ireland.

While Bede speaks of Columba's preaching to ' the provinces of the northern Picts ', Adomnan speaks of his visiting a ' province of the Picts ', implying neither that it was the whole kingdom, nor that it was less than the whole kingdom. He makes no division between northern and southern Picts. But he makes it clear that the district visited by Columba was pagan.

Bede calls Brude a ' very powerful king ', and Adomnan says that Brude held the hostages of the king of Orkney. We have seen that Brude claimed dominion probably over Fortriu (p. 39). If the peoples of Angus and Fortriu were among the Picts who had, according to Bede, become Christians, and if (as is probable) Brude reigned over part of that area, it might be assumed that Brude also was a Christian. And in fact neither Bede nor Adomnan says that Brude became a Christian through the teaching of Columba. In this question, Adomnan's implication is not positive, and his account must not be taken as proof of anything, except that if there was an earlier legend that Brude was a pagan and was brought to Christianity by Columba, Adomnan's reticence would amount to a denial.

Adomnan says that Columba's miracles greatly impressed the king and his subjects, but he gives no account of any general conversion of Picts. Emchath and his family were converted at Urquhart, and baptized (114b). An unnamed man heard the preaching of Columba through an interpreter and was baptized, with his household (78a). This man's son died, and was restored to life by Columba ; and the God of the Christians was glorified among the people (79a). In the river Ness, within the province of the Picts, Columba repelled a water beast, and the pagan barbarians magnified the God of the Christians (74a–75b).

Adomnan did believe that many persons had been brought to Christianity by Columba. This appears in the vision attributed to Ethne before Columba's birth, and in the prophetic utterance of Brenden of Birr at the synod of Teiltiu : ' a son predestined by God as a leader of innumerable souls to the heavenly country ' 105a ; ' him whom I see predestined by God as a leader of the peoples to life ' 106b.

Adomnan's account of Columba's entire occupation with the exercises and employments of monastic life (4b) is given partly in the words in which Sulpicius had described the daily life of Martin of Tours. This passage of Adomnan is perhaps to be taken as doctrinal rather than biographical, but it does show that Adomnan regarded monasticism as the main purpose of Columba's life in Britain, not journeys or missionary enterprise. Adomnan mentions some journeys made by Columba, but gives no hint that any of them was in the nature of a ' preaching circuit ', such as the Irish Life describes (*S.G.S.* II, p. 146). The contrast between Adomnan's Life of Columba and the Irish Life is so marked that we must consider whether already in Adomnan's time a legend of Columba's missionary journeys had arisen, and Adomnan intended to contradict it.

A generation later than Adomnan, Bede says simply that

' Columba was the first teacher of the Christian faith to the Picts beyond the mountains, to the north ', that Columba ' came to Britain to preach ', and that he ' came to preach the word of God to the northern Picts '. Bede's idea of a missionary campaign is shown in his account of the campaign of bishop Aidan, when Aidan was sent for to reintroduce Christianity in Northumbria. He may have imagined that Columba led a campaign to the northern Picts, in a somewhat similar manner, but he does not say so.

What Adomnan does imply is that the fame of Columba led would-be believers to come to him from pagan lands, as in the instances of the man from Crog-reth, and the leader of the *Geona cohors*.

Considered as a settlement showing to pagan peoples the merits of religious life, Iona appears remote and inconspicuous. But monks went from the monastery at Iona to found other monasteries, both among the ' northern Scots ' and among the provinces of the Picts (H.E. III 3 ; see pp. 105-08). The combined influence of this system of monasteries would have been great in Columba's time, and later.

Adomnan mentions the presence of Columba at certain places, to the west of the Spine. Coire-salchain (46b) is perhaps the Coire of Loch a' Choire, below Sgurr Salchain, in the district of Kingairloch. This was beside Loch Linnhe, and accessible to the traveller from the Cruach of Rannoch. A different identification, also in Morvern, quoted by Watson 1926, p. 94, appears to be less probable. In a district of Lochaber, Columba was hospitably received by a layman, Nesan (67b) ; and he was there also when he gave a magic stake to a beggar (83b). Columba visited his friend Colman, a layman (68b), in Ardnamurchan. A spring in Ardnamurchan was named after Columba (61ab), and he is twice mentioned as travelling through the rocky district of Ardnamurchan (20b, 61a).

A visit of some days to Skye is mentioned (*aliquantis diebus*, 74a ; *per aliquot dies*, 34b). The place where Artbranan, the leader of the *Geona cohors*, was baptized and buried, was marked

by a cairn of stones on the shore (35a). Columba was entertained in the island of Rathlin (93b), perhaps on his route from
or to Ireland. One occasion is mentioned on which Columba
visited the home of king Aidan, not long before the battle of
the Miathi (18b–19a).

The only violent opposition to Columba that Adomnan
mentions came from a branch of the descendants of Gabran,
carrying on military or piratical activity in the seas about
Hinba and Ardnamurchan. The *persecutor* who nearly burned
Columba's boat beside Loch Lochy may have been one of this
military group.

We can infer from Adomnan that Columba made a visit
to Ireland, of several months (*per aliquot menses*), when he
founded the monastery of Dairmag (Durrow, in county Offaly).
At that time (14a), Alither was the abbot of Clóin of Saint
Céran (Clonmacnoise, county Offaly). Alither became abbot
of Clonmacnoise 585 ×, and died 599 (see A.U. 584 = 585 and
598 = 599). (Cf. Ryan 1940, pp. 493–4.) If Adomnan is
right, Durrow was founded not earlier than 585.

Bede said that Columba had founded Durrow before he
came to Britain. Bede's informant might have been influenced
by a claim of Durrow to be senior to, and independent of, the
monastery of Iona. But it is not impossible that the land of
Durrow had been given to Columba for a monastery before
563, and that he did not establish a full complement of monks
there until 585 or later. Adomnan's account of the building
by Columba's monks of a ' large ' or a ' larger building '
(*alicujus majoris domus*, 31a) at Durrow, while Columba was in
Iona, could be reconciled with his having had a smaller number
of monks in Durrow before.

The site of the monastery of Durrow was said to have been
given to Columba by Aid Brendan's son (T. 8d27–28 ; addition to A.U. 588 = 589). Aid is called king of Tethbe (Teffia)
in T., and at the entry of his death in the text of A.U. (as
above). It is uncertain whether he became king in succession
to his uncle, Craumthann, Briun's son, who died in 553 (A.U.
552 = 553, and T.), or after the death of his father, Brendan,

Briun's son, who died in 576 (A.U. 575 = 576, and T.). (Cf. Plummer 1896, II, p. 133.) Aid was already the leader of the forces of Tethbe in 562, when they defeated Diormit Cerball's son, at Cul-Uinsen (A.U. 561 = 562, and T.).

We might have expected that Columba would have visited his houses of Derry and Durrow at intervals, but Adomnan mentions no other instance of his visiting either house, unless possibly in a story of his presence at Durrow in the apple season (54a).

Columba died in Iona, apparently in the night of 8–9 June, A.D. 597 (see p. 66). Adomnan devotes the longest chapter of his book to a detailed account of Columba's last days and death. Probably oral tradition was in part the source of this chapter. Since there was a *Liber de virtutibus Columbae* written by abbot Cummene, it may be assumed that that book would have described also Columba's death, and that Adomnan would have used it.

The place of Columba's burial was known to Adomnan (129a, 135ab), and he implies that Columba's stone pillow, standing beside it, was its only memorial. A stone found before 1873 (*P.S.A.S.* x, pp. 614–15), near the northern rampart, is now exhibited as Columba's pillow-stone. The carving on its surface can hardly have been as early as Adomnan's time. Columba's bones had not been enshrined at the time when Adomnan wrote. (Walafridus Strabus believed that they had been enshrined before 825 ; E.S. i, p. 164.)

A few Latin Hymns are or have been attributed to the authorship of Columba. Among these the *Altus Prositor* and part of the *Noli pater indulgere* are the least unlikely to have been composed by him. (Cf. Kenney 1929, § 91.) Very many Irish verses written centuries later were by a literary convention ascribed to Columba. (See ibid, p. 441.) Adomnan's mention of magical *carmina* (9b) sung by laymen shows that Irish verses in praise of Columba already existed in Adomnan's time. A surviving poem, the Amra Coluim-chille, was probably completed after the time of Adomnan's death. (See the account

H

given of it, ibid. § 212. The text is in Liber Hymnorum, 1898, I, pp. 162–183 ; cf. II, pp. 53-80.)

No manuscript survives of which we can say that it was written by Columba's hand. The psalter known as the Cathach of Saint Columba is in Irish majuscule writing for which a date in the latter part of the sixth century is ' palaeographically possible ' (Lowe 1935, p. 41, cf 52). A copy of the Vulgate Gospels, known as the Book of Durrow (Trinity College Dublin 57, A.IV. 5), could possibly have been a later transcript from a manuscript written by Columba. (See Lindsay 1923, pp. 22–3 ; Lowe 1935, p. 43 ; Mario Esposito, in *Irish Historical Studies*, IX (1954), p. 3, note 3.)

ABBOTS OF IONA

Columba's successor as abbot of Iona was his cousin and foster-son (11b, 119a), Baithene, son of Brenden (App.), son of Fergus, son of Conall Gulban. In Columba's lifetime, Baithene appears to have had authority over penitents in Hinba, and he was at another time prior of Mag-lunge in Tiree. His commemoration day was 9 June (102a). He lived until about three years after the death of Columba (E.S. I, p. 119).

The later abbots of Iona were normally chosen from the kindred of Columba. Their relationships were tabulated in Reeves 1857, between pp. 342 and 343.

The third abbot of Iona, Laisran, Feradach's son, had been in charge of the building of Durrow. He died probably in 607 or 608 (A.U. 22a21 ; E.S. I, p. 125).

The fourth abbot, Virgno (119b–121a), died about 623 or 624 (E.S. I, p. 147).

Segene (†652) was the fifth abbot. To him and the anchorite Beccan, a letter on the Easter question was written by Cummian, Beccan's brother, after the synod of Mag-Lene (in Offaly), held in ?630. Cummian writes with authority, and was very probably also an anchorite. His letter is illuminative of Irish scholarship in his time. (See MacCarthy 1901, pp. cxxxv-cxli, and Jones 1943, pp. 89–93, 97–9.) Segene continued to reject the Roman Easter-reform. With other north-Irish heads of monasteries he wrote a letter to pope Severinus ; and they received in answer a letter written in 640 by the pope-elect, John IV, which is quoted by Bede (H.E. II 19). Bede says that, while Segene was abbot, bishop Aidan was sent from Iona to establish the Christian church in Northumbria (H.E. III 3–5 ; A.D. 635). About A.D. 637 (A.U. 634 = 635 ; T.), Segene founded the church of Rechru (Rathlin), which was within Columba's sphere of influence (93b). Segene's name appears in A also as Segine ; and in the B manuscripts is always Segine.

The sixth abbot, Suibne, is not said to have been of Columba's kindred. He died in 657.

Cummene became the seventh abbot, apparently in 657, and died in 669. Eight years before his death, ' The abbot Cummene came to Ireland ', according to T. 10c43–44. This was not a note made in Iona. The absence of an abbot from his monastery, noted like this in the annals, implies that he was absent for a considerable time. Perhaps Cummene did not return to his monastery. His *Liber de virtutibus sancti Columbae* was probably written while he was in Ireland, very possibly in the new monastery of Rathlin, in the territory of the Irish Dal-Réti. (See p. 48.) In 108a, where a quotation from his book was inserted, he is given the epithet *albus* ' the white ', added above the line (by the same hand) after *Cummeneus*. He receives that Latin epithet rather erratically in the Irish annals ; thus its genitive is *ailbi* in A.U. 668 = 669 ; and worse, *ailbe* in T. The Martyrology of Oengus gives him the Irish epithet *find*, also meaning ' white ' (Oengus 1905, p. 62) ; and this confirms the implication of 108a, that *Cummeneus albus* was Cummene the abbot of Iona.

Failbe became the eighth abbot of Iona. He died in 679 ; his death-day was commemorated on 22 March. He also after four years in the abbacy went to Ireland. The common source of A.U. 672 = 673 and T. read : ' Voyage of Failbe, abbot of Iona, to Ireland ' ; and of A.U. 675 = 676 and T. :

' Failbe returns from Ireland '. These notes were evidently
made in Iona. Failbe was Adomnan's predecessor (9b, 15b).

ADOMNAN

Adomnan was the ninth abbot. He was born about A.D.
628. His father is said to have been Ronan, Tinne's son ; and
his mother, Ronnat, of the cenel-nEnna, of the district of
Raphoe, county Donegal. (Cf. E.S. 1, p. 210 ; Oengus 1905,
p. 210.) He was descended, through his father, by six generations from Columba's grandfather, Fergus, son of Conall
Gulban.

Adomnan was an Irishman (cf. *per totam nostram Scotiam*
135b), and he regarded the high-king of Ireland as his temporal
lord (*deo auctore ordinatum* 36b).

Adomnan latinized his own name from the archaic Old-
Irish *A'domnan* (δ, μ) : *mihi Adomnano*, four times in MS A.
Occurrences of the spelling -*dom*- in the B manuscripts prove
that their source, as well as the source of A, read -*dom*-. Also
-*dom*- occurs in one manuscript of Adomnan's *De Locis*
(Geyer 1898, p. 221). Manuscript versions of Bede's *De
Locis* show some surviving spellings with -*dom*-, which suggest
that the copy of Adomnan's *De Locis* that Adomnan gave
to king Aldfrith contained the spelling -*dom*- (ibid. pp. xlvi,
323).

The spelling *Adomnan* prevailed in the earliest writings, and
continued down to the tenth century, and is occasionally found
much later. But already within the Old-Irish period the *o*,
between non-palatal consonants, in a syllable following the
stressed syllable, would have changed to *a*, and *Adamnan* would
have become a normal spelling. Medieval writers generally
substitute *a* for the *o* in this name.

It is agreed that the interpretation ' little Adam ', given to
the name in Cormac's Glossary, is incorrect. The word
appears to have been a monastic name, meaning ' man of
great dread '. It is a compound, stressed on the first syllable,
formed with the intensive particle *ad* prefixed to an abstract

formation (*omnae) from *omun* 'fear', and the derivative suffix -án.

There may perhaps have been some confusion between two words : *adomnae* (δ, μ) 'great fear' ; and ?*adamnae* (δ, mm) 'great hunger', which Pedersen 1909, p. 169, wished to connect with P-Celtic cognates, but for which there is little evidence in Irish. *Adamna* in Colman's Hymn (Thesaurus, 1903, p. 300) rhymes with *adamra* (δ, μ) ; both of these words should have lenited *m*, but imperfect rhyme occurs in the same Hymn. *Adamna* is there explained by a gloss, *id est gorta* 'famine'. Meyer, Wortkunde, § 131 (1917), rejected the gloss as an error. *Adomnae mór* 'great panic' occurs in A.U. 825 = 826 ; cf. *úamon mór* 'great terror' in A.U. 63b2 : A.D. 1096.

That the *d* and *m* in the name *Adomnan* were traditionally lenited is shown by later Irish spellings, and by Scottish place-names in which it occurs as *Eodhnan* and similar forms (Watson 1926, p. 270).

Adomnan shows no personal knowledge of any abbot of Iona earlier than Failbe, and so his early training seems not to have been received in Iona. It is possible that he ruled over the monastery while Failbe was in Ireland. Adomnan was present in Iona, and perhaps in authority there, seventeen years (or fourteen years) before he wrote his Life of Columba (98b–99b).

When he was abbot, or deputy of the abbot, Adomnan entertained for some time in Iona a bishop from Gaul, Arculf, who had travelled in the eastern Mediterranean. Adomnan listened to his accounts of places in Palestine and other eastern countries, and made notes of them on wax tablets. Later he wrote them out on parchment, producing his book *De Locis Sanctis* (Geyer 1898, p. 221). He asks his readers to pray for Arculf, and also for himself, since Arculf had related his experiences very willingly, and he had written them out under great difficulties : ' Although I was occupied throughout the whole day with the laborious cares and responsibilities of the church, almost too heavy to be borne, accumulating on every side ' (ibid. pp. 296–7). Bede, in his own book upon the holy places, acknowledges his debt to Adomnan and Arculf (ibid. p. 323 ; cf. Plummer 1896, pp. 316–19).

In 686, Adomnan went to Northumbria (103b) as an ambassador of Ireland to Aldfrith (*legatus suae gentis . . . missus*), according to Ceolfrith (Plummer 1896, p. 344), and conducted sixty Irish captives, taken by Ecgfrith in 684 from Mag-Breg, back to Ireland (A.U. 25d20–21). Two years later (103b), he visited Northumbria again, went to see Ceolfrith's monastery of Wearmouth and Jarrow, and after studying for some time the customs and practice of the Anglian monks he accepted their guidance in the matters of Easter and the tonsure (Plummer 1896, pp. 315, 344). He returned to Iona, and failing to convince his monks of the need for reform he went to Ireland, where he had considerable success in persuading those Irish monks who were not under the dominion of Iona. Most of the southern Irish monks were not subject to Iona, and had accepted the reformed calculation of Easter many years before. Adomnan refers to the discord arising among the churches of Ireland because they celebrated Easter at different times (15b).

The common source of A.U. and T. said : ' In the four-teenth year after the death of Failbe, Adomnan proceeded to Ireland '. This was evidently an Iona note. The year in-tended was probably 692. As long as the monks of Iona persisted in keeping Columba's Easter, Adomnan would, if he were there, have been obliged to celebrate Easter with them, on the same day. We do not know that Adomnan was in Iona at Easter later than 691 or 692. When he left Iona, he was in all probability accompanied by monks who did accept the reforms that he had adopted.

The monastery of Raphoe (Rath-both) was associated with his name. If indeed it was his foundation, he might very well have founded it in or after 692.

Adomnan's name is met in several Perthshire place-names. (See Watson 1926, pp. 270–1.) Dedications, or names given to churches in honour of a saint, are most uncertain sources of historical information. It seems probable that Adomnan had travelled in Fortriu, but of that there is no other evidence. There was a church of Adomnan (Teunan Kirk, ibid.) at Forglen in Banffshire, where land had been granted ' to God, St Columba, and the Brecc Bennach ' (Arbroath, Registrum Vetus, no. 5). That relic may be as old as the end of Adomnan's life (Francis C. Eeles : ' The Monymusk Reliquary or Brecbennoch of St Columba ', in *P.S.A.S.* LXVIII (1934), pp. 433–8 ; Stevenson 1955, p. 108).

The annals do not mention Adomnan's returning to Iona after he left it in 692. But he had been outside of Ireland, and probably had visited Iona, when, in the centenary year of Columba's death, he ' proceeded to Ireland and gave the Law of the Innocents to the peoples ' (A.U. 26b24–25 ; 696 = 697).

Adomnan's Law was enacted for the protection of women, men in holy orders or in religious communities, and children, against acts of violence, in war and peace. (See Ryan 1936.) The council at which the Law was accepted met at Birr in County Offaly, in 697. The Law was presumably drawn up conjointly by Irish lawmen and by Adomnan. The penalties for infringements of the Law are recounted in Cáin Adamnain, §§ 34–53. The fines exacted were in part payable to ' Adomnan and his community (*munter*)'. Adomnan was still abbot of Iona, and head of the Columban group of monasteries.

The names of the guarantors of the Law are enumerated in § 28, which begins like this : ' These are the terms of enactment of the Law of Adomnan of Iona. At Birra its enactment was imposed upon the men of Ireland and of [northern] Britain, as a perpetual law till Doom, by command of their nobles, clerical and lay (their lords, and their chief heirs, and their bishops, and their scholars, and their confessors) '. The guarantors named are almost equally divided between forty ecclesiastic or monastic persons and fifty-one laymen. We do not know how many of the guarantors were actually present at the council, or on what day the council was held. Among them are four whose place of residence was in Scotland. They are king Brude Der-ile's son, who succeeded in 697 ; king

Echoid Domingart's son, who died in 697 ; Ceti (or Coeddi), bishop of Iona (†712) ; and Curetan, bishop (?of Rosemarkie ; Watson 1926, p. 315). It is very remarkable that a law introduced in an Irish council should have been assumed to be valid also not only among the Scots of Britain but in the kingdom of Brude Der-ile's son (Fortriu), and in the northeast of Scotland.

Bede's account suggests that after Adomnan had gone to Ireland (in ?692), he did not again reside in Iona until the year of his death. In that year he celebrated in Ireland the canonical Easter (which, according to MacCarthy 1901, would have been three weeks earlier than the Irish Easter in 704). Afterwards he returned to Iona, and exhorted his monks very strenuously to accept the catholic time of Easter. He failed ; and died there before the Easter of the following year, which would have produced further discord. (H.E. V 15.) He died in 704, in his 77th year (A.U. 26d26–27, and T.). His deathday was commemorated on 23 September (according to the Tallaght martyrologies, and T.).

The Life of Columba was composed by Adomnan in Iona (6b, 31b, 75b, 76a, 98b, 119b, 135b), while he was abbot (9ab, 15b, 119b), after his second visit to Northumbria (103b). Bede apparently did not know that Adomnan had written a Life of Columba. Adomnan must have written the Life 688 × 704, and almost certainly 688 × 692.

Adomnan's scholarship may have included textual notes on Vergil's Bucolics and Georgics (see Kenney 1929, pp. 286–7).

The body of Brude Bile's son was, according to a tradition, carried to Adomnan for burial in Iona. The tradition is unhistorical, but it has preserved verses that are ascribed to Adomnan himself. In the Life of Adomnan (p. 17) they may be read like this : ' Mor do ingantaib do[g]ni · in ri genair o Muiri · Bet[h]a scuaban i mMuili · ecc do Bruide mac Bili · Is annamh · iar mbeith i rrighe tuait[h]e · Ceppan caue crinndara · im mac righ Ala-Cluaithe '. ' The King that is born of Mary performs many wonders : [giving] life to a *scuapan* in Mull, death to Brude Bile's son. It is strange, it is strange, that after his being in the kingship of the people a block of hollow withered oak should be about the son of the king of Ail-Cluaithe '.

These stanzas are considerably older than the Life in which they stand, and it is not impossible that they might have been composed by Adomnan. They may have been the source of the legend that, out of regard for future abbots of Iona, Adomnan refrained from bringing Brude back to life.

Scuaban, in Best 1908 and Joynt 1908, is regarded as a proper name, although that does not occur elsewhere. The antithesis is between Brude, an able and powerful king, and something which was either a weakling or an inanimate object. **Scōpan > scuapan* means ' little broom ' or ' little sheaf '. Some episode that was well known must underlie these verses, but we know nothing of it. A ' little sheaf' could have been the last sheaf taken from the harvest-field, the ' maiden '. That meaning would involve a perhaps too-complex poetic image, and would require that Brude's death occurred in harvest-time.

Caue is the genitive singular feminine of **cau*, a derivative of the Latin *căvus* ' hollow '. The word could have been derived through British or North British. The survival of intervocalic *w* may be compared with Adomnan's *bou*, **Iou*, and *naue*.

The reading *crín'-dara*, for *crinn'-dara*, is not convincingly right, but *crín* is a possible reading, and neither *cruinn* nor *crann* will do.

The Life of Adomnan is an early-Middle-Irish homily, for his commemoration day, upon the text *Accinge sicut vir*, Job xxxviii. 3. It is a collection of legends, in many of which the names of real persons are mentioned. It is of interest for the importance attached to Adomnan in traditions of a later date ; and it lays stress upon Adomnan's power of controlling, through prophecy, the course of events.

Ceolfrith, Adomnan's contemporary, praised his moderation, humility, and devotion ; and Bede says of Adomnan that he was a good man, and wise, and most nobly equipped with knowledge of the Scriptures, and describes him as a man that took great pains to promote concord and peace (H.E. V 21, 15).

LATER ABBOTS OF IONA

The successor of Adomnan as abbot of Iona was apparently Conamail Failbe's son. It is not known whether he had been a leader of the recalcitrant monks. In the seventeenth-century Martyrology of Donegal, p. 244, Conamail Failbe's son is said to have been ' of the race of Colla Uais ' (or Colla Uas), ' sovereign of Ireland '. This may mean that he was of the mocu-Uais in Airgialla, and so raises an interesting speculation whether Conamail's appointment was promoted by the tribe of Loern, in opposition to the Dal-Réti. But there were other families of mocu-Uais, not within the district of Airgialla (see Walsh 1921 ; and cf. O'Rahilly 1946, p. 223). From the Life of Adomnan, there appears to have been a tradition of some discord between Adomnan and the mocu-Uais of northern Brega. (See above, p. 29.)

In 707, within Conamail's lifetime, Dúnchad son of Cenn-faelad received the office of abbot (*principatum Iae tenuit*). Conamail died (*abbas Iae*) in 710.

Bede says that the old Easter was still celebrated in the monastery of Iona in 715, and that the Roman Easter was accepted *sub abbate Duunchado*, and celebrated there, in 716. The community had been persuaded to make the change by a Northumbrian bishop, Ecgberht, who had spent many years in Ireland (H.E. III 4, V 22). He had been a guarantor of Adomnan's Law in 697. Bede implies that the change of tonsure occurred at the same time as the change of Easter, both in Iona, and in the monasteries that were subject to Iona. He wrote about fifteen years after the event, and his evidence has historical value.

The Irish annals agree with Bede in part. They say that the Roman Easter was accepted ' in the monastery of Iona ' (*in Eoo civitate*, A.U. 715 = 716 ; *in Eo civitate*, T.). But the

monks of some Columban house or houses within the territories of Nechtan Der-ile's son seem to have held out against
the reforms, and in the following year Nechtan expelled them
from his kingdom (*Expulsio familiae Iae trans dorsum Brittaniae a
Nectano rege*, A.U. 716 = 717 ; and to the same effect in T.
12c43, 45). Tigernach says, one year later, that ' the crown
of tonsure was put upon the *familia* of Iona ' (*super familiam Iae
datur*, T. 12d5–6).

   If both of these statements about the *familia Iae* were taken
from one source (although the note on the tonsure is not in
A.U.), *familia* must here have meant the Columban monks to
the east of the watershed, and the note of the tonsure in 718
would presumably have been meant to show that the expulsion
ended then. The alternative to this explanation would be that
Tigernach has used two sources, with differing dates of the
changes.

   The abbot Dúnchad died in 717. On Saturday 29 August
716, Faelchu, Dorbene's son, had received ' the chair of
Columba ', in the 74th year of his age (A.U. 715 = 716 ;
' 87th ' in T. is a textual error). Faelchu died in 724, but in
722 Fedilmith had received the abbacy (*principatum Iae tenuit*,
A.U. ; so read T.). Apparently Fedilmith was abbot-substitute,
since, when Faelchu died, Cillene Fota succeeded him in the
abbacy (*in principatum Iae*, A.U. ; so read T.).

   Cillene Fota died in 726. His successor, Cillene Droichtech,
was an anchorite, and is called *anc(h)orita Iae* in the annals. In
his time, ' Adomnan's relics were carried to Ireland, and his
Law was renewed ' (A.U. 726 = 727, and T.). The relics
remained in Ireland for three years.

   During this abbacy, the scholar (*sapiens*) Cu-chuimne, a
collector of Irish canons, was a monk in Iona, and died in 747
(A.U. 30d17–18, and marginal additions). A Latin Hymn
was attributed to him (Liber Hymnorum, I, pp. 32–4,
cf. II, pp. xvi, 17, 123–5). (See Kenney 1929, pp. 248–9,
269–70.)

   Cillene Droichtech died in 752. He was said to have been
of the southern Ui-Néill (see Reeves 1857, p. 382). The next

abbot, Sleibene, lived until 767, but his successor, Suibne, was already called abbot of Iona in 766.

None of these occasional overlappings in the abbacy is to be taken as evidence of a schism in Iona. Aged abbots of Iona must often have been compelled to relinquish their onerous charge, passing it into the hands of a younger man.

In the time of Suibne's successor, Bresal, 772–†801, the first Norwegian raiders appeared in the western sea. Iona was devastated by them in 795 (A.I. 13f16–17 ; E.S. 1, p. 256). In 802, Iona was burned. In 806, many of the monks were killed. The community had already planned their escape to Ireland, and in 807 their new monastery of Columba began to be built, at Cenandas (Kells, in county Meath); it was finished in 814. The abbot, Cellach, who had superintended the building, then resigned the principate. He died in the following year.

In the time of Cellach's successor, an attempt to carry on monastic life in Iona was made by Bláthmac, Fland's son, who in 825 was killed by ' Danes ', together with many of his companions (see E.S. 1, pp. 263–5). A monastery, under an abbot, was apparently established in Iona about the middle of the tenth century ; but Kells continued to be the chief monastery of the successor of Columba.

Under the title *Chronicon Hyense* (' Chronicle of Iona ') Reeves compiled a collection of historical notes, arranged under the abbacies of Columba and his successors, down to A.D. 1219 (Reeves 1857, pp. 369–410). Reeves wrote these notes in Latin ; sometimes quoting, sometimes adapting or translating, the sources that he used. He states explicitly that his chief source was the Annals of Ulster. He supplemented those from other Irish chronicles, and from Adomnan's Life of Columba. Unfortunately, in the Historians of Scotland edition, (Skene 1874) extracts from Reeves's *Chronicon Hyense* were printed separately (pp. 334–42) from Reeves's editorial comment (pp. cxlvi–cxlvii). Thus it was possible for a careless reader to assume that the compilation was an actual chronicle written in Iona, notwithstanding that it continues for four hundred years after the monastery had left Iona.

No chronicle of Iona has been preserved. But the Irish annal-collections contain some items that must have been derived from the Iona monastery, and many that probably were derived from that source. It may be supposed that the monks of Iona had had an Easter calendar of the 84-year cycle, with a margin in which notes of events could be entered opposite the years in which they happened, or were thought to have happened. The practice of making contemporary notes in Iona began in the abbacy of Failbe, if not earlier. It continued under successive abbots, down to the time when Norwegians made Iona uninhabitable, and the monks migrated to Ireland. After A.D. 814, any chronicle notes that they produced were written at Kells in county Meath.

BISHOPS IN IONA

In early Irish monasteries, at Armagh and some other places, the abbot was usually a bishop. But many monasteries were ruled by priests who were not bishops. These included houses of the important groups that originated in the foundations of Columba, Comgell of Bangor, and Ciaran of Clonmacnoise. As Bede remarks of Iona, and the province of the Scots in Britain (H.E. III 4) : ' That island, however, always has as its ruler an abbot who is a presbyter, so that to his authority the whole province, and even the bishops themselves, contrary to the usual order, must be subject, following the precedent of that first teacher, who was not a bishop, but a presbyter and monk '.

Bishops that were monks were subordinate, in Irish monasteries, to their abbot. Late in the seventh century there are a few instances in which a bishop-monk is spoken of as bishop of his monastery. For example, Dicuill Colman's son was ' bishop of Cluain-eidnech ' in County Leix (†672, A.I.). The common source of A.U. 686 = 687, and of T., had this entry : ' Death of Ossene, bishop of the monastery of Finnten ',

without naming Ossene's father. This bishop may have been
the Oissene, Ernan's son, an aged priest, who had been a monk
of Finten (Munnu), and who gave to Adomnan information
about Finten and Columba (13b). Finten's monastery was
Tech-Munnu, now Taghmon in county Wexford.

Perhaps not much later, canons for the Irish churches
prescribed that there should be one bishop in every civil
district (*tuath*), and that he should be attached to the great
church of the district. Adomnan, in his visits of 686 and 688
to the monastery of Wearmouth and Jarrow, had seen the
honour accorded to bishops in Northumbria. He inculcates
a high respect for bishops in his instructional tale of the bishop
Cronan (45b–46a).

The bishop Ceti who was a guarantor of Adomnan's Law
in 697 is named ' Coeddi, bishop of Iona ' at his death, in
A.U. 711 = 712, and in T. 12b last line (*Ceode*). His death-day
was given as 24 October, in the Martyrology of Donegal. In
713 ' Dorbene obtained the chair of Iona, and after five months
in the primacy (*in primatu*) he died, on Saturday, 28 October
(*v. kal . Novimbris die sabbati*) ' (A.U. 712 = 713, and T.
12c13–15).

It has been supposed that by the ' chair of Iona ' the
abbacy was meant. But while the office of abbot is frequently
called *principatus*, the word *primatus* means ' office of primate ',
and is not elsewhere in A.U. used for ' abbacy ' (see MacCarthy
1901, p. 302). An abbot of Iona had apparently established
there a bishop's high-seat (*kathedra Iae*) comparable with the
abbot's high-seat (*kathedra Columbae*, A.D. 716 ; see above,
p. 99), and symbolizing the bishop's functional authority over
the church of the Scots in Britain. During the episcopate of
Dorbene, the abbot of Iona was Dúnchad. No successor to
the bishop's chair is named. Bede says that the Northumbrian
Ecgberht, a bishop, lived in the monastery from 716 until
his death in 729 (H.E. III 27). But although Ecgberht was
a bishop, and in Iona, he was a very old man, and it
seems unlikely that he held the primacy over the Scots in
Britain.

The Insertion and Colophon in Manuscript A

In the colophon of manuscript A, 136a, the words *pro me Dorbbeneo* have not unnaturally been assumed to mean that the writer of A was called Dorbbene, and that he was the Dorbene who died in 713. The name was a very uncommon one. A Dorbene was the father of Faelchu, who became abbot of Iona in 716, at the age of 73. That Dorbene might perhaps not have been too old to become bishop of Iona in 713, but he would have been much too old to write A, which is the work of a calligrapher of not more than middle age.

There are different possible interpretations of the colophon. (1) The bishop Dorbene might have been a different person from Dorbene the father of Faelchu. In that case the bishop could have been the writer of A. (2) The bishop Dorbene might have been the father of Faelchu, and have employed a calligrapher to write A and its colophon, for the benefit of the monks of Iona, and to obtain their prayers. The colophon does not actually say that Dorbbene was the writer of the manuscript. (3) The writer of A and the colophon might have been a Dorbene otherwise unknown. (4) A, and its colophon, might have been copied by an unnamed scribe from a manuscript that had been written by a known or unknown Dorbene.

In cases (3) and (4) there would be no external evidence for the date of the manuscript.

The first of these interpretations seems to us to be the most probable, that the manuscript was written by the Dorbene who became bishop of Iona, and that he was not the father of Faelchu.

The insertion in 108a was made by the same writer, in a much smaller hand, with a fine, and harder, pen. This minuscule writing is discussed, with a full-size facsimile of part of the page, in Lindsay 1910. There is no doubt that the insertion was made by the writer of A ; slight variations result from compression, and his use of a different kind of pen. Whether the pen used for the text was a reed or a quill may be doubtful, but that used for the insertion was almost certainly a quill. The writer was evidently quite well accustomed to writing in the smaller as well as in the larger hand. Many words were abbreviated, and two abbreviations that he uses, *dc~s* ' dicens ' and *q~m* ' quoniam ', frequent in early Irish minuscule writing, do not occur elsewhere in A.

The insertion was planned in advance. A space was left blank for it between the top and the bottom of column 108a, and the insertion was later entered in the blank space. The extent of the insertion, and the smaller size of the writing, had been allowed for, and the space left was only a little too small. The delay in entering the insertion is sufficiently explained by the need of finding, for the smaller writing, suitable pens and ink.

If the addition had been suggested by Adomnan, we should have expected it to be entered in the larger writing of the rest of A. It seems probable that Dorbene was responsible for the insertion, and decided to show by the smaller writing the extent of his addition to Adomnan's text. This would almost necessarily have been at a time when Adomnan was no longer alive (704 × 713).

A somewhat different explanation might be that the space left blank was intended for a shorter entry in the larger hand, and that a changed plan, involving more writing, forced the writer to use smaller letters. That would not so necessarily imply that Adomnan was not responsible for the addition.

The writer names as the source of his addition Cummene's *Liber de virtutibus sancti Columbae*, and after the words *sic dixit quod*, to the end of the insertion, what he writes is a quotation, if not an exact quotation, from Cummene.

There is nothing in the insertion to show that any part of it was Adomnan's work. It was not Adomnan's practice to name his written sources, or to give verbatim extracts from them. He evidently derived his preceding chapter (III 5) in part from Cummene's book, but in his own words, and without naming Cummene.

Certain words and spellings in the insertion are never used

by Adomnan in his Life of Columba. *Ainmuireg* was spelt *Ainmurech* by Adomnan (confirmed by B1 B3). *Hibernia* does not occur in Adomnan, who uses the forms *Evernia, Hevernia,* and *Ebernia. Quoniam,* used as in the Vulgate for *quod,* is not found either in Adomnan's Life of Columba or in his *De Locis* (Geyer's Index Verborum). *Suus* and *eorum* are slightly confused, in a manner that is not characteristic of Adomnan.

The passage quoted had originally been composed probably 661 × 669, after Aidan's descendants had lost their Irish kingdom, and were subordinated to king Oswiu of Northumbria (pp. 47-51). It contained a lament over their decline, and it was omitted by Adomnan because when he wrote they had recovered their kingdom, and their liberty (p. 55). It was inserted by or for Dorbene, because the descendants of Aidan were again in decline, this time through the encroachment of the tribe of Loern (p. 57).

THE MONASTERY OF IONA

Writing about the mission of bishop Aidan, who was sent from Iona in 635, Bede said nearly a hundred years later (H.E. III 3) : ' That island's monastery held for a long time pre-eminence over almost all the monasteries of the northern Irish (*Scottorum*) and over the monasteries of all the Picts, and was their superior in ruling their communities ' (*populis*). Bede said also that from the monasteries of Iona and Durrow ' very many monasteries were planted by Columba's disciples both in Britain and in Ireland, so that the same island monastery, in which he rests in the body, held the principate over them all ' (H.E. III 4).

Similarly Adomnan speaks of Iona as Columba's *matrix eclesia* (16b), and of Columba as a ' pillar of many churches ' (131a) ; and he says that Columba's ' monasteries, founded within the boundaries of both the peoples ', i.e. of Picts, and of Scots in Britain, ' down to the present time are greatly held in honour by them both ' (103a).

The northern *Scotti* were the Irish of northern Ireland, and

I

of western Scotland. In Ireland, the monastery of Derry is
not mentioned by Adomnan or Bede. It was earlier than the
monastery founded in Iona, and possibly Durrow was also.
Columba's association with Cell-mór Deathrib was probably
earlier than his pilgrimage (see p. 70). It is implied (3a)
that a foundation by Columba was close beside a monastery
founded by Mochta of Louth.

A cemetery used for burial of Columban monks, at Druimm-
Tómme, in the south of county Donegal (132a), was probably
beside a religious house, which was later associated with the
monastery of Derry (A.U. 920=921). Cormac ua-Liathain
was a monk of Columba, and is called the founder of a
monastery ; but where that monastery was, Adomnan does
not say.

We accept from Bede the fact that many monasteries among
the Scots of Britain had been founded by monks from Iona,
but few of them are known to us by name. Adomnan mentions
three monastic establishments existing in Columba's lifetime,
under Iona : one in Hinba ; one at Mag-lunge in Tiree ;
and one called Cella Diuni, near Loch Awe. Each of these
was ruled by a praepositus. A fourth may have been the
monastery in Elena insula, also under a praepositus. A
monastery called Cailli au inde was founded by a man who,
when young, had accompanied Columba on the journey
across the Spine.

Later mentions of Columba in legend, or in dedicatory
place-names, are not sufficient evidence of any direct association with him. It has been suggested that various ancient
churches in Scotland named Annat may be evidence of
foundations by Columba, but the name shows only that an
earlier had been superseded by a later foundation.

The Irish name *Airchartdan* (see p. 157) suggests that a
Columban monastery may have existed at Urquhart in
Adomnan's time, and may have been the principal source of
his account of Columba's visit to the Picts.

Monasteries that were not subject to Iona, among the
Scots in Britain, included Artchain, in Tiree, founded by

Findchan (36a). Other monasteries in Tiree, continuing into Columba's time (111a), were said in Lives of Saints to have been founded by Brenden mocu-Alti and Comgell of Bangor (Plummer 1910, I, p. 143 ; II, p. 11). Brenden is said to have founded also a church in the Garvelloch Islands (Watson 1926, p. 81).

Adomnan relates a pleasant story of Molua, a monk of Iona. Molua is a hypocoristic cult-form of the name Lugid. Its diminutive was Moluoc(c). If Molua was intended to be the Moluoc who founded the monastery of Lismore, between Morvern and Appin (O.I. *apdaine* ' abbacy ', here ' abbot's country' ; see e.g. MacBain 1922, p. 285), the implication would be that Lismore was a daughter house of Iona. Lugid, or Moluoc(c), of Lismore died three years before the death of Columba (A.U. 591 = 592, and T.). But there is no known connexion between Iona and Lismore, and it is improbable that Molua and Moluoc were the same person. Molua, according to Adomnan, belonged to one of the numerous families called Ui-Briúin. This origin seems to exclude an identification of Adomnan's Molua with Molua of Clonfert-mulloe (cf. Plummer 1910, I, p. lxxxiii, and II, p. 206). It is a coincidence that both these Moluas were specially friendly to animals.

A later monastery not of Columban origin was at Applecross in Ross-shire (*Apor-crosan*, A.U.). Mailrubai came to Britain in A.D. 671, and founded the church of Applecross in 673 ; and he died there in 722, aged 80 or 81 years (A.U. 670, 672, 721 = 671, 673, 722 ; and T.). He has been called ' abbot of Bangor ', but incorrectly ; the Bangor list of abbots does not include his name (E.S. I, p. 219 ; Thesaurus 1903, p. 282 ; Kenney 1929, p. 266).

This foundation is evidence that the Scots in Britain had extended their territory beyond the northern boundary of Inverness-shire before the end of the seventh century ; since Bede implies that all the monasteries in the territory of the Picts were founded from Iona.

The *familia Iae* that was expelled in 717 may have been

either one monastery, or all the monasteries, of Columban monks within the territory of the eastern kingdom. Bede's words, written about A.D. 731, show knowledge that monasteries had existed in the territory of the Picts, but he says nothing of the expulsion. His words do not necessarily imply that the expelled monks had been recalled, or even that any monasteries remained in the eastern kingdom.

The past tenses used by Bede in writing of the authority of Iona indicate that the power of Iona had declined. The Columban churches had undoubtedly lost something of their traditional influence by their prolonged resistance to reforms that in the end they had been obliged to accept. Through contact with Northumbria, the Pictish king had preferred the leadership of the Roman church, whose influence had, he was assured, first reached his predecessors through the mission of Ninian. It is possible that Iona had not in Bede's time recovered its dominion over the monasteries in the eastern kingdom.

The area within which Columba's monastery [1] was established in Iona can be inferred, but the sites of its church and other buildings are unknown, with one possible exception.

---

[1] This account of Columba's monastery buildings, based mainly on Adomnan's text and a little ground observation, was written in 1956. In that and the following three years excavations have been carried out in Iona under the direction of Mr Charles Thomas, lecturer in Early British History in the University of Edinburgh, who kindly supplied me with information while this book was in proof. The results, when they have been completed and published, will require that some of our suggestions should be modified or abandoned. But in the meantime it has seemed best not to attempt a partial rewriting, and our account is printed unaltered. A few points must be mentioned. The greater part of the vallum has been satisfactorily traced. Some evidence has been found that would place the site of Columba's buildings roughly in the position of the present Abbey, and if this proves to be conclusive it will rule out our suggestion of a site on the upper, or western, level. The 'hut-foundation' beside the south-western entrance has been examined and pronounced to be not a hut at all, and the entrance itself to be doubtful. Remains of a hut have been found on the partly-artificial hillock called Tor Abb opposite the west end of the Abbey church, and it has been suggested that this was Columba's cell. If our theory is right, that Columba used two huts, one with a floor of earth or stone, and one with a raised wooden floor, the Tor Abb hut might be identifiable with the former. M. O. A.

There is little hope of discovering where the original buildings were, unless an aerial survey can show some traces of them. We have no reason to suppose that they have been obliterated by later buildings.

Irish monasteries were customarily surrounded by a boundary wall, such as the *vallum* that Adomnan mentions round Clonmacnoise (14a), and the little rampart mentioned between a monastery of Columba and a monastery of Maucte (3a). He speaks also of a *vallum* between the monastery of Iona and the cow-pasture (*bocetum*). There is in Iona an earthen rampart, which may be as old as the time of Columba. (See Crawford 1933, p. 460.) It extends for a quarter of a mile, beginning at the high rocky ground that has been called Cnoc nan Carnan, immediately above the medieval abbey-church, and running from there in a north-north-easterly direction to within forty yards of the southern boundary of the Clachanach farm-land (on the six-inch Ordinance Survey map). It there curves towards the east, and continues eastward visibly as far as the high road. In 1933, it was seen continuing for about 600 feet farther towards the sea (Crawford 1933, p. 461). In 1951, we could not detect it beyond the road, but we were told that the field had occasionally been ploughed in recent years.

In the southern end of the existing rampart there is an entrance, and beside the entrance there is a circular foundation, presumably of a small house. From that point two diverging ramparts curve round Cnoc nan Carnan to the south-east, extending to the broken face of the hill. Probably one of them originally continued towards the sea. The western and northern ramparts appear to have been originally two sides of a more-or-less rectangular enclosure.

Among the buildings that survived in Adomnan's time there appears to have been a hut, traditionally known as Columba's writing-house. Adomnan calls this hut Columba's *tegoriolum*, or *tegorium*. This had been built upon a wooden floor (29a), and had presumably been constructed of wood. In his writing-house, Columba is represented to have at times received a guest, or taught a student. While he wrote, two attendant monks sometimes stood beside its door. In it, a shout could be heard from the shore of Mull (29a) ; and from it, rocks of the coast of Mull were visible (123b). The door therefore faced east or south-east. The writing-house was near the gateway by which monks passed to and from the cow-pasture. They had a custom of asking for Columba's blessing, on their way. Thus Molua stopped at the writing-house before he went outside the *vallum* (76b, cf. 65b).

Dr O. G. S. Crawford has made the bold suggestion that the house beside the south-western entrance could have been Columba's *tegoriolum* (Crawford 1933, p. 463). It is the one surviving hut-foundation that is associated with the rampart. It may have been of similar age, and it was probably there in the time of Adomnan. There is no gap in the circle for an entrance. The foundation could perhaps have supported a circular platform of boards upon which a wooden house could have been built (*in tegoriolo tabulis subfulto*). If it had originally been built for a keeper of the gate, its outlook would presumably have been towards the north-west or west. The *tegoriolum* faced in the opposite direction ; but the position of the doorway might have been altered, to fit it for an abbot's writing-house. The rocks of Mull would have been visible to the south-east, although a direct view from the gate-house to the east would have been cut off by Cnoc nan Carnan. The structure and purpose of the gate-house cannot be determined without the most expert investigation.

Adomnan describes dwellings near the river Nile, in some-what similar words : *in domibus transversis tabulis suffultis* (Geyer 1898, p. 283). Those houses were built on piles, to allow for the occasional flooding of the Nile. It is implied that joists (*tabulae*) were attached to the piles, and floor-boards were laid across the joists, and that the construction was rectangular. If the description of the *tegoriolum* was an abbreviated repetition of the words used in describing the Nile houses, Adomnan would imply that the *tegoriolum* also was rectangular, and stood on piles, either to produce a level floor on uneven ground, or to avoid the dampness of the soil. Either alternative was possible in the monastic enclosure. We cannot assume that this was what Adomnan had in mind, but if it were his meaning, the *tegoriolum* and the gate-house site would not be the same.

Columba's connexion with the *tegoriolum* appears to have been derived from a local tradition, which Adomnan associates with the name of Diormit, Columba's attendant. It was in the *tegoriolum* that, according to Adomnan, Columba wrote for the last time, on the last day of his life. No witness is named, but it must be assumed, from Adomnan's account, that Diormit was present. Diormit lived for many years (77b) after Columba's death (see p. 20). There was no long gap between Diormit's death and the succession of abbot Segene, in whose abbacy Failbe, Adomnan's predecessor, was in the monastery. There could have been verbal tradition from Diormit through Failbe. There may also have been written tradition. Diormit or some contemporary might have been among the disciples of Columba that were said, according to Bede, to have written about Columba's life and words. (See p. 19.)

The word *tegoriolum* is perhaps no part of the local tradition. Adomnan uses the word *tegorium* or *tegoriolum*, with the synonym *domuncula*, in his *De Locis* (Geyer 1898, pp. 227–9), for the round rock-chamber in the church of the Sepulchre.

Within the area enclosed by the rampart, two levels are to be distinguished. The upper level borders on the western rampart. The lower level, much wider, extends from the declivity that separates it from the upper level, to the shore. The medieval buildings are on the lower level ; but that could not have been inhabited or cultivated without preliminary draining. The upper level was better drained, and had longer evening sunlight.

It seems to us possible that the flat northern part of the upper level might have been chosen for the earliest settlement. Consistently with this interpretation, the *tegoriolum*, ' constructed on higher ground ' (123a), would have been in the southern part, on Cnoc nan Carnan ; Adomnan's *vallum* (76b) would be the western rampart ; the route between the monastery and the western plain would have been through the entrance at the gate-house ; and the *monticellus* from which Columba looked down upon his monastery and blessed it (128a) would presumably have been the Sgùrr an Fhithich, overlooking the centre of the western rampart.

The *monasterium*, in the wider meaning of that word, appears to have included everything that was within the *vallum*. Within the rampart the buildings, being made of wood, have disappeared. The church of Iona is called by Adomnan synonymously *eclesia*, *oratorium*, and once *sacra domus* (120a). Presumably there was a window on the eastern side, above the altar. We should guess that the door was on the western side, and that the monastic huts were placed somewhat to the west and within sight of the church door (cf. 129b–130a).

There was no vent in the church roof (125b–126a). The roof is spoken of by Adomnan as the *parasticia*.

A feature of the church was the exedra, which was an annexe, apparently built on the outside of the church wall, and entered from the inside of the church. From the words *interior janua* Reeves 1857, p. 358, followed by others, inferred that the exedra had an outer door also, so that the church could be entered through the exedra ; although such an entrance is not involved in Adomnan's story. In our translation of 120a the ' inner door ' is understood to mean the door between the church and the exedra, and the implied outer door is the door of the church. Alternatively, Adomnan's words could be interpreted to mean that the inner door led not into the exedra, but into a *conclave*, or compartment with a lock, within the exedra.

The church seems to have been unlighted for the midnight office except by lamps that the monks carried from their sleeping-quarters (130a). Adomnan does not describe the small houses in which the monks slept. Probably those, and the abbot's sleeping-house, were built of wattle and daub. The monks slept upon litter (*stramen*), while Columba was traditionally believed to have slept upon bare rock (129a).

Columba's sleeping-house (*hospitium* or *hospitiolum*; *domus*, 121b) must not be confused, as was done by Skene, with his *tegoriolum*, which had a wooden floor. His sleeping-house had a divided door, each part with hinges and a key-hole (121b). His house in Hinba had a similar door (119a). The upper part of the divided door would have served as a window.

In addition to their separate sleeping-houses, the monks had a house or houses that they shared in common. In their daily life, they needed a kitchen, a refectory, a common room for conference, and a room where in cold or wet weather they could have the warmth of a fire. A building used for some of these purposes was called in later Irish *tech coitchenn*, a ' common house '. The house, *domus*, in which Columba gave instructions to monks on a stormy day (16a) was presumably not his sleeping-place, but a common house.

Adomnan sometimes uses the term *monasterium*, in a restricted sense, for the common house. He relates that while Columba was sitting in the *monasterium*, beside the hearth, Lugbe mocu-Min sat near by, reading, until he was needed to perform some service in the *monasterium* (28b). A ewer of water stood in the same room. The common room is there thought of as not separate from the kitchen quarters.

Columba's common house, *domus* or *monasterium*, was essential to the domestic management of the monastery, and could hardly have been rebuilt while still in use. Adomnan imported timber for a large common house, *magna domus*, in Iona (100a), and that may have been a different building. Some years later, he imported oak timber, to renovate ' our *monasterium* ' (100b), and it is not clear whether that was the old common house, or the new.

It seems to be implied by Adomnan's words *alicujus majoris domus* (31a) that there was more than one ' larger house ' at Durrow. One of them is called synonymously *monasterium* and *magna domus* (115ab). It was round, and high. The repeated assumption that the ' round *monasterium* ' of Durrow was an early instance of an Irish round stone tower is anachronistic, and appears to have no basis.

The hospice (*hospitium*) in Iona, where guests were received, was built of wattle (54b). It may perhaps have been outside the monastic enclosure. The crane received as a guest on the western plain was housed and cared for, for three days and nights. That was the length of time during which entertainment was afforded to a pilgrim guest (48a–49a). Visitors who were guests of Columba for a much longer period (e.g. *per aliquot menses*, 109a) were very probably given sleeping-houses similar to those of the monks.

In Columba's monastery, there was a small open space among the buildings, in which the monks could walk. It is called by Adomnan the *plateola* (108b), and it may have been paved. It was probably on ground that the monks had to cross to reach the church from their sleeping-houses. We may compare with this the *platea monasterii* on which offerings were laid out, at Coleraine (51a).

The rampart (*vallum*) was the monastic boundary, not a defence against attack ; it would have been useless against marauders from the sea. Within this enclosure (*ar lar croi Ia*) an irregular monastic settlement was dispersed by the Irish clergy in A.D. 1204 (A.U.).

Agricultural buildings mentioned by Adomnan stood outside the monastery. The nearest barn (126a), in which grain was stored, was near the western rampart, and presumably close to a path that ran between the monastery and the cornfields in the western plain of the island. The building of dry-stone enclosures (*opus maceriale*) that was going on in the western plain in the last summer of Columba's life (75b) was presumably intended for the separation of cattle and crops. One house on the western plain is mentioned (48b).

Adomnan seems to have thought it customary for the brothers to carry the harvest back to the monastery on foot (38a) ; a distance of less than a mile, most likely through the smooth valley known as Gleann an Teampuill. The wagon that once carried Columba to the plain must have gone round about, to the south of Cnoc Mòr, near the line of the modern road.

Adomnan mentions a building (*canaba*, 46b) that may in his time have still stood beside the road from Columba's monastery to the harbour. From a story told in a Latin Life of Ciaran of Clonmacnoise, Reeves (1857, pp. 88, 440) argued that a *canaba* or *zabulum* was a kiln. What is actually implied by the story is that a *canaba* ('shed') or *zabulum* ('barn') could be used as a drying-house for grain, by lighting a fire under a wicker wheel, upon which the ears of grain were laid. The story is not lucidly told. But it states that the *canaba* caught fire, and that the *zabulum* was dragged from the ground and thrown into a river. If (as is practically certain) the writer used these words synonymously, he must have thought that the building was made of wood. (Cf. Plummer 1910, I, p. 204.)

Adomnan gives no indication of the use to which the *canaba* in Iona was put. Skene apparently wished to identify with it the remains of a stone kiln that Pennant saw near the water-mill, in A.D. 1772 (Skene 1887, pp. 96–8). But it is unlikely that there was a water-mill of any kind in Iona as early as the sixth century. The mill-stone that in Adomnan's time served as the base of a cross (127a) was presumably a worn-out stone of a handmill, and the cross a wooden one (cf. Collingwood 1927, p. 5). The mill-pond, now dry, but known as the Lochan Mòr, the substantial dam, and the water-mill and other buildings whose remains were noted by Pennant, are works of a time much later than Adomnan's.

Skene assumed that the *canaba* stood midway between the harbour and Columba's *tegoriolum*, but that does not seem to follow from the story told by Adomnan. That assumption, together with his belief that the position of the *canaba* was fixed by the remains of the 'stone kiln', led Skene to place Columba's monastery considerably to the north of the northern rampart. Apparently he had failed to notice that rampart, or its conspicuous north-western corner. The wall that he saw running northward, which he took to be continuous with the western rampart, is in fact a continuation of a much slighter counterscarp that lies outside the western rampart and that is probably of later date (cf. Crawford 1933, p. 461).

The harbour that was used by monks of Iona is not distinctly specified. The best ports for the landing and launching of skin-covered boats were probably the bays that are called in the maps Port nam Mairtir, and St Ronan's Bay. Some creeks to the east of the monastic area, and below Clachanach, would have given access to the sea in very calm weather. One of these was probably the place where a milk-skin was steeped (86a).

Adomnan implies that Columba had among the members of his community men whom he could send on journeys into Britain or Ireland. A ship (*navis*) belonging to Columba is mentioned, 86a, and that or another is implied in other places, e.g. 56a and 90b. Short notice was given to prepare the ship and collect a crew. Sailors were obtainable in or near Iona.

The most usual Irish ship was the curach (*curucus*, 100ab). It was made of hides sewn together (*pellicium tectum navis*, 96a) over a wooden frame-work.

Adomnan uses Latin nautical terms in speaking of a curach's prow, stern, sides, and keel (96a), and these do not imply anything with regard to the construction of curachs. Light boats of this kind were built on one occasion by Julius Caesar, in imitation of a British design (*De Bello Civili*, I 54).

Small curachs were relatively portable. They could be used on land, inverted, as temporary shelters (cf. 35ab, 42a, 47b). Curachs were light, buoyant, and sea-worthy. The larger of them at least were fitted with a mast, which must have been removable. Irish sailors used oars with blades (100b ; *remorum palmulae*, 96ab) when there was no wind behind them. When the wind was favourable, they used a sail. The course of a ship under sail could be to some extent controlled by using oars (cf. 25a).

The material of sails (*vela*) and ropes (*rudentes* ; *funes*) is not mentioned. The sail was apparently of a rectangular lug-sail type, and hung from a yard (*antemnae*) which could be attached to the mast symmetrically (*crucis instar*, 101a) or, by implication, unsymmetrically. The raising of these sails is mentioned by Adomnan twice, in stories (one of them within his own experience) of a change from adverse to following wind. On these occasions, two actions are mentioned : raising the sail, and tightening the ropes (*protensis rudentibus* 101a ; *tensis rudentibus* 91a). The hoisting of the sail meant raising the yard (101a), to which the upper edge of the sail was attached. It is not clear whether the ropes mentioned were the sheets from the lower corners of the lug-sail, or stays from the top of the mast.

In Adomnan's time, a ' long ship ' (*longa navis*) built of pine and oak timbers was made for Iona (100a). That was a sea-going vessel of caulked planks, comparable with the war-ships of Scandinavia. The timbers for this ship had been brought from a distance by land and sea, to Iona. They had been partly prepared (*dolatae*) in advance, and it is possible that the *dolatae materiae* included critical parts (such as the prow) already shaped by carpenters.

Navis and *navicula* are used as synonyms (24a, 34b). *Navicula* is synonymous with *cimba*, *cimbula*, and *navigium* (6b, 82a), and with *caupallus* (74b, 75b). The terms *caupallus*, and *alnus* (74b, primarily ' alder '), may be intended to mean a wooden boat. A variant of *navicula* is *navicella*, 134a. *Ratis* appears as a synonym of *navis* in 91a (cf. 37b). *Scafa*, in 100a, appears to be a small hide-boat, or coracle. *Oneraria navis*, in 54b, was presumably a hide-boat of wide beam. A merchant-ship from Gaul is called *barca*, 31a.

According to Bede (H.E. III 4), the whole island of Iona had been given to Columba. Adomnan mentions, outside the monastic enclosure (*monasterium*), the cow-pasture (*bocetum*, 127b) in which the monks had the right to graze their cattle ; and the arable land in the western plain. Presumably the grant of Iona to Columba had in fact included the whole island, with the small islands that lie beside it, from high-water mark upwards (cf. *cispitem*, 27b).

According to Adomnan (54b) Columba had the right to take a shipload of wattles, as building-material for his hospice, from a layman's field, near the shore (probably not in Iona) ; but made a compensatory gift to the layman of a supply of barley seed. Adomnan says that some Atlantic seals, which frequented a small island not far from sand-hills on the shore of Mull, were owned by the abbot of Iona (42a).

Monasticism reached Ireland through the inhabitants of what had been the Roman province in Britain. Along with Christianity, the Irish learned the use of the Latin language, and of the Latin alphabet. Latin became the necessary basis of their ritual.

Candidates for the priesthood were generally trained in reading from an early age. Patrick deplored his lack of this training. Columba, while still a child, was given in fosterage to a priest ; and he was later taught by noted teachers. He himself was renowned as a teacher of spiritual sons, and in this character he was succeeded by his foster-son Baithene (128b).

Adomnan seems to assume that boys (*juvenes*) were admitted as *alumni* in Iona. One young pupil to whom Columba taught philosophy (*sapientia*, 121b) failed in obedience, and did not persevere in religious life. Adomnan mentions no instance of the admission of a child.

A man who wished to enter monastic life was required to accept in advance the privations and hardships of the monastery. The form of acceptance that Adomnan relates in the case of Libran (87b) is an echo of the form prescribed in the Benedictine Rule, and may be regarded as the form that Adomnan wished to prescribe for his monks.

In Iona, a period of probation was generally imposed, before an applicant could be allowed to take the monastic vow of obedience to the abbot, and be accepted as a monk of the community (33b). If he had transgressed, he could not be accepted until he had expiated his sin by penance. Even then, his taking of the monastic vows might be delayed by his civil obligations (II 39).

Adomnan does not mention any penitents in Iona. They were apparently sent to Columba's monasteries in Hinba and Tiree.

Monastic life was regulated by times and seasons.

Tempus ' period of time ' or ' point of time ' is used for
' year ', ' season of the year ', ' month ', and once for ' calendar
date ' (36a).

The year mentioned in 30b (*antequam praesens finiatur annus*)
is a calendar year. It extended for some months after the time
of speaking. The year mentioned in 112a extended from one
day to the same day of the same month in the following year.
But in 123b the year appears to be from one movable feast to
the same in another year.

Adomnan mentions the seasons of spring, summer, autumn,
and winter. In 54b and 55a, Adomnan uses the words ' after
the middle of summer ' synonymously with ' when fifteen days
of June had passed '. He thus implies that the 92 days of the
summer quarter consisted of two equal parts, 1 May to 15 June,
and 16 June to 31 July. This rests upon a conventional
division of the calendar, not upon any astronomical theory.
But Adomnan may here be accepted as evidence of Irish
custom. What he says agrees with his other references to the
seasons (cf. 98b, 99b ; 75b, 124b). The Irish festivals of
Beltane and *samain* were held at the beginning of the summer
and winter quarters, on 1 May and 1 November.

The autumn quarter was the time of ripe apples (54a)
and pigs fattened with nuts (71ab). The threshing of grain
is apparently mentioned to indicate the time of the year (30a).

The Roman months named by Adomnan are *Martius,
Aprelis, Maius, Junius, Agustus* (54b–55b, 99b, 124b). He does
not use the Roman method of distinguishing the days within
the month. The only month-day that he names, 15 June, is
distinguished by its number in the Latin month. In 34ab,
Adomnan's ' month ' appears to mean four weeks.

Periods of a week (*septem dies, septimana,* or *ebdomas*) are
mentioned by Adomnan. Some of these began with Sundays
(34a, 126a). One began on a Saturday, and ended on Friday ;

the next day after is called the eighth day (22b ; cf. 43b).
Other weeks began on unspecified days (29b–30a, 33a), and
ended on the seventh day following (89a, 90a, 91b). As was
usual, the day counted from, as well as the day counted to,
was included in the reckoning. A period of fourteen days and
nights is mentioned, 95b–97a.

The first day of the week, Sunday, is called by Adomnan
' Lord's Day ' : *dominicus*, 113a ; *dominica dies*, or *dies dominica*,
33b, 41a, 45b, 118a, 125b.

Days of the week (*feriae*) were numbered from Sunday.
Tuesday was the third day of the week (29a). Wednesday,
the fourth day of the week, was a fast (29b). It was later called
' day of the first fast ' (M.I. *dia-cétain* ; S.G. *Di-ciadain*).
Friday, the sixth day of the week (22b) is not mentioned as a
fast by Adomnan. It was *dia óine didine* ' day of the last fast ',
in the Milan glosses of Diarmait (Thesaurus 1901, p. 383) ;
now S.G. *Di-haoine*. So Thursday was *dia-dardain* ' day between
two fasts ' (Saltair na Rann, line 8150 ; S.G. *Diardaoin*). The
fast on Friday appears to have been observed already by
Columbanus, and in Northumbria by bishop Aidan. Saturday
was ' Sabbath ' (*sabbatum*) or ' the day of Sabbath ' (22b,
126ab).

According to the author of the Tallaght Discourse, § 69 :
' In the rule of Columcille, Saturday's allowance of food and
Sunday's allowance are of equal amount, because of the rever-
ence that was paid to Sabbath in the Old Testament. It
differs from Sunday in work only. And in other rules there is
similarity of allowances on Sabbath and on Sunday '. The
Tallaght Discourse represents an early phase of the movement
towards sabbatization of Sunday. The surviving ' Rule of
Columcille ' does not contain the item quoted, but no authentic
Rule of Columba has survived.

Although the astronomical day, which begins at midnight,
was not entirely unknown in Ireland, the monastic calendar of
Ireland, as of other Christian countries, began the day in the
evening (*vespere*, Gen. i. 1–5). Nightfall on the eve of Columba's
festal day was spoken of as ' the beginning of this day.' (101b).

The words *hac in nocte*, spoken in the morning, meant 'last night' (122a).

The day from sunrise to sunset was divided, in theory, into twelve equal hours. In the twelve-hour day, the length of the hours changed with the length of daylight; and that varied in the different seasons and in different latitudes. Only at the equinoxes could those hours have had the same length as astronomical hours of the twenty-four-hour day. Astronomical hours could not have been shown correctly on a primitive sun-dial. But any sun-dial could have shown the time of midday, and when the position of the sun at sunrise had been noted the hours of the twelve-hour day could be roughly estimated. In the latitude of Iona, they varied, according to the time of year, from 30 to 90 minutes of our time.

The first, third, sixth, and ninth hours of the twelve-hour day gave their names to four of the 'canonical hours' at which the monks daily entered the church to perform their religious office. The last office of the day was vespers (*vespertina hora*, 38a; *vespertinales dei laudes*, 40a). We do not know how closely the monks adhered to the theoretical times of their canonical hours.

The earliest daylight was indicated by *mane* (64b), *mane primo* (68b), *diluculo mane* (102a). The tenth hour of the day is mentioned in 96a (*decima hora diei*). The other numbered hours that Adomnan mentions are canonical hours.

The canonical hours that were celebrated at Bangor, in Down, are shown in the Antiphonary of Bangor, written perhaps a little before the time when Adomnan composed his Life of Columba. At Bangor, the first canonical hour of the night was *initium noctis*. But Adomnan shows no sign that that office was celebrated in Iona.

On the night of his death, in Iona, Columba retired to his sleeping-place immediately after vespers (129a). He was roused by the bell that called the monks to the midnight office (*media nocte*, 129b. The Irish name for this canonical hour was *medon-aidche*, or *midnocht*, meaning the 'middle of night'). Columba ran to the church, and died. On that occasion at

K

least, the monks seem to have continued their nocturnal office into the next canonical hour, the morning hymns (*ymni matutinales*, 133a) ; after which they carried back Columba's body from the church.

Adomnan uses the name of a canonical hour as an expression that could include not only the office, but whatever happened immediately after it, while the monks were collected together. Thus at prime (*prima diei hora*, 57a) Columba instructed Lugaid Lathir to make a journey to Ireland ; and at tierce (*hora diei tertia*, 64b) he foretold suitable weather for Colman Beogna's son to return to Ireland. On one 9 June, Adomnan arrived in Iona after the office of tierce (102a).

Sext was originally midday (it was called alternatively *medon lái* in Irish). Midday was the one possible fixed point in the day at all seasons of the year. *Post meridiem* in 65a probably means ' after sext '. In Adomnan's time, Mass was celebrated at sext on Columba's day, 9 June (*hora sexta*, 102a).

The hour of none, in Iona, is mentioned in 48b (*post nonam diei horam*) and 86b (*hora transacta nona*). But in these instances the name of the canonical hour may have included also a meal that followed it. After none, dinner began at Aghaboe with the breaking of holy bread (63a). On the weekly fast-days, as in Lent, the Irish monks in Northumbria took no food before the hour of none (Bede, H.E. III 5). It is implied that on other days they had an earlier meal. According to a Tallaght account, Columba was not specially addicted to fasting. (See Tallaght Discourse, § 68.)

The singing of vespers could be regarded as part of the celebration of the following day, when that was a Sunday or a major feast ; and so we find *vespertinalem dominicae noctis misam* (128b), ' vespers of the Lord's night ', on the evening of Saturday. Here *misa* has its earlier meaning, 'church service', and does not signify ' the Mass '.

Adomnan sometimes uses the word *hora* for an indefinite period of time, as in *hora in hác* (43b). *Eadem hora* is used for the space of time within which events in different places could be regarded as simultaneous (e.g. 93b, 96b). Adomnan says that Colcu Cellach's son noted in a wax tablet the day and hour (*tempus et hora*) of one of Columba's visions, and that the vision was confirmed when Colcu learned of a death that had occurred in his home-country at the same time (*eodem horae momento*, 36a). In this story, Adomnan implies that the community in Iona, and a community probably in Ireland, made reckonings of time that could agree in placing an event within the same hour of the twelve-hour day. But an average, or equinoctial, hour is implied in some phrases that express the idea of one hour's duration : *per unius horae momentum* (66b), *post quasi unius horae interventum* (95b), *post aliquantum quasi horae intervallum unius* (119b).

In 66b and 36a, above, and in 31a and 34a, *momentum horae* means the space of one hour ; but in 101a and 122b, *momentum* and *momentiolum* mean a very short space of time, and in 122a *eodem momento* means ' at that instant '. Bede possibly follows an Irish source where he divides an hour into forty *momenta*. (See Jones 1943, p. 183.)

The season of Lent is mentioned in 88ab ; Easter in 88ab and 124b ; and the Easter controversy, in 15b. The ' completion of the days of Easter ' (60a) seems to be Low Sunday (Pascha Clausum ; cf. *in clausula pasca* in the Stowe Missal 1906, f. 26a) ; but it has been explained also as Whitsuntide (Ryan 1931, p. 346).

The *natalicium domini* (60a) should mean the day of Christmas. The ' feast-day of the birth (*natale*) of the saints Columba and Baithene ' (102a) means their death-day, 9 June. The ' natal day ', that is the death-day, of Brenden of Birr (112b) was celebrated on 29 November (Oengus 1905, p. 237).

Adomnan shows that the Eucharist was celebrated on Sundays (41b, 45b, 118a, 125b). Annual feasts on which it was celebrated were called ' solemn days ' (*sollemnes dies*), and on those days the Iona monks went to the church in white robes (113b). Adomnan mentions the celebration of the Eucharist in Iona at Easter (88ab) ; and in the office of sext, on the feast of Columba and Baithene. The stories in 112b to 113b may imply that the feasts of Brenden of Birr, and of

Colman mocu-Loigse, were Mass-days in Iona, in Adomnan's time.

Adomnan's account of the visit to Iona of Cronan, a bishop in the province of Mumu, is taken as evidence of a custom in Iona, that the breaking of bread in the Eucharist was done by two priests, or by one bishop (45b). (Cf. Gougaud 1932, pp. 327–8.) But on other occasions Columba appears to have celebrated the Mass alone.

In the Stowe Missal, the Gospel reading followed the half-uncovering of the elements. But in Adomnan's account of the Mass performed by Columba at Hinba (118a), the Gospel was read before Columba with his guests entered the church to celebrate the Mass. The custom of reading the Gospel outside a church, and celebrating Mass inside, might have arisen in churches that had no window ; or else in churches that were too small to hold the congregation. This archaic practice was omitted from the story as it was copied in the Pseudo-Cummene.

The story of Columba's visit to the *caput regionis* in the end of one year implies perhaps that the wine that was necessary for celebration of the Mass at Iona was brought to Argyll in Gaulish ships (I 28 ; 30a–31a), and that that was the custom in Adomnan's own time. Adomnan attributes to supernatural power Columba's knowledge of the exact time when the ship would arrive.

ADOMNAN'S SPELLINGS OF LATIN AND IRISH

The Latin alphabet was introduced into Ireland for the writing of Latin, with the phonetic values that it had among the Britons of what had been the Roman province of Britain. (Cf. Jackson 1953, pp. 67 ff., and 124–5.) Some ambiguities resulted when the Latin alphabet was used for writing Irish words.

Initially and medially, the Latin letter *h* had lost its sound-value in speech, long before Adomnan's time. But efforts were made to restore it, as a division between syllables ; and in some instances the sound of *ch* was substituted for it in medial, and even in initial, positions. (See Sommer 1914, § 113.)

Adomnan, or the writer of A, is fairly consistent in writing, or omitting, initial *h* in Latin words, but quite arbitrary in his choice of the words in which he writes it. He fluctuates in *habunde* 118b, *abundanter* 61a, and *abundos* 54a. Adomnan writes the words of Greek origin, *ebdomas, ydria, ymnus*, without initial *h*.

Since the letter *h* had lost its sound-value, Adomnan could not use it to represent the Irish sound of *h*, and that sound remained unwritten until long afterwards. When he wrote *h* at the beginning of Irish words, it represented no sound, but was a silent embellishment (as in *hi* 57a, 62b, 106b, and *Hinba*). (See Thurneysen 1946, § 25.)

In two instances, in A, *ch* has been written for the Latin *h*, between vowels in *vechiculo* 125a, and between *n* and a vowel in *anchellantem* 80a. But all the manuscripts omit *h* in *exalavit* 130b.

The aspirates *ph, ch, th*, occurred in Latin words that were borrowed from Greek. Adomnan appears to have written *f* for *ph* (*profeta, ofthalmia, sofia, anfibalus, scafa, sulfureus, zefirus, foca*). The B manuscripts tended to substitute *ph* for the *f*, but they retained *f* in some of the less familiar words. It is not certain how Adomnan represented *ch* in Greek words. Manuscript A usually has *c* in *pasca* and *monacus*, with their derivatives; in most other words, *ch*. The B manuscripts nearly always have *ch*. All the manuscripts have *c* in the unfamiliar word *parasticia*. Adomnan represented the Greek theta by *th*: it is so written in five words, in A, and is variously written *t* and *th* in the B manuscripts. (Cf. Adomnan's statement in *De Locis*, p. 276, in which he says that Mount Tabor should be spelt in Greek with theta, and in Latin Thabōr *cum adspiratione* 'with *h*'.)

In O.I., at the beginning of words, the Latin letters *p c t* represent the unvoiced stops (or tenues), but medially and finally they may also represent the voiced stops (or mediae, *b g d*). Adomnan wrote *c* for Anglo-Saxon *cg* in the name

Ecfridi 103b, ' of Ecgfrith '. The lenited (or spirant) forms of Irish *c* and *t* were written by Adomnan as *ch* and *th*, with either neutral or palatal quality. In at least one case (*Maucteus* 3a), Adomnan seems to have written *ct* for *cht*. (Cf. Thurneysen 1946, pp. 21, 135.) In the B manuscripts (most often in B1) *c* is frequently written for *ch*, and *t* is occasionally written for *th*. Adomnan did not indicate the lenition of other Irish consonants, except *f*, for which see below.

In O.I. the letters *b g d* at the beginnings of words stand for the voiced stops. Medially and finally, they may represent the spirant (or lenited) sounds (which we indicate by the symbols *β γ δ*). This happens also initially in certain cases of grammatical synthesis. The sounds of *th* and spirant *d* did not lose their dental character in Gaelic speech until more than three centuries after Adomnan's time.

In M.I. the lenited sounds of *b g d* were distinguished by writing above the letters the Greek rough-breathing sign, which was the first half of the capital letter eta (H). (See Sturtevant 1920, pp. 121, 156–7 ; Thurneysen 1946, § 28.) That sign does not appear in A or in the B manuscripts.

Final *g* appears to stand for neutral *ch*, in *Fēch(u)reg* 22b (probably Adomnan's spelling) and 121a (where the B manuscripts read *Fēchrech*) ; and in *lathreg* (certainly Adomnan's spelling). In the insertion of 108a, *Ainmuireg* is written, but Adomnan wrote *Ainmurech* 49b. In two monosyllables, the value of final neutral *g* is uncertain. The epithet *crag* 11a–12a is written *crach* in the B manuscripts, and it is not certain that Adomnan wrote *crag*. *Crog*, in the compound name *Crogreth* 47a, appears in the B manuscripts as *croch*, which was the Irish *crōch*. But if Adomnan wrote *crog*, that could have been a North-British form of the same word. (See p. 159.) A guttural spirant between unstressed vowels appears as *ch* in *draigniche*, and in *Gruthriche*.

Adomnan's *s*, including intervocalic *s*, was the unvoiced *s* of Irish speech, and was not pronounced like *z* either in Irish or in Latin words (cf. the spelling *prespiter* 120b). In his Latin, single and double *s* are often interchanged. *Misus* is written for *missus*, and *Colosus* perhaps stands for *Colossus* (see p. 155). Irish lenited *s* sounded as *h*, and was sometimes marked with a deleting dot above, by later writers. If lenited *s* occurs in Adomnan's Irish names (mocu-Sogin, mocu-Sailni) he did not mark it for lenition. The presence of an unwritten lenited *s* is sometimes apparent in its effect upon the preceding consonant. A media followed by lenited *s* became unvoiced. The name *Finten* 11a–13b represents *find'sen*.

In Irish words, single continuants, in medial or final position, may represent either the lenited or the unlenited sounds. The occasional doubled letters, in A and the B texts (the stops *cc tt bb*, and the continuants *ll mm nn rr ss*), were intended to show that those sounds were unlenited. Doubling is more frequent in A than in the B texts. The unlenited group *rd* could be written in A as *rtd*. Similarly in § 28 of the Cáin Adamnain, *pb* alternates with *bb* and *p*, in the word *abb* ' abbot ', for unlenited *b*.

Domnail (?lenited *l*) varies with *Domnaill*. If *Muirchol* and *Finchoil* contain *coll* ' hazel ', their final consonant was unlenited *l*, like the *l* of *Comgil*, 50b. In *Cailli*, vocalic *l* + *d* have become unlenited *ll*.

In the Irish word *cambas* the group *mb* is retained. In names that were derived from British (or North-British) speech, *m* appears for *mb* : *Colum* and *Colman*, and the latinized *Colmanus*. *Columb*, in A (11b), is the Irish spelling of the name. Adomnan's Latin spellings *Columbus* and *Columbanus* are based upon the Irish pronunciations. *Columba* is not an Irish name, but the Latin word for ' dove '. In the name of a North Briton, Emchat(h), the *b* could have disappeared after *m*, in Irish as well as in North-British phonology. (See p. 160.)

Double *n* for *nd* occurs in names that were derived from British speech : *Finnio*, *Vinniavus*. The *d* of *nd* is omitted before a following consonant, in *finchoil* and *Fendæ* ; and the second *n* of *nn* is omitted before a consonant in *cencalad*. In A, *fint* is once written (19a) for *find*.

In Latin words, Adomnan's choice between single and double consonants seems often to have been quite arbitrary.

Indo-European consonantal *u* (*w*), when it followed *a*, could combine with it, in Irish, to give a vocalic diphthong *áu* ; and when it followed *o*, to give a diphthong *óu*. Both those sounds later became *ó*, but in Adomnan's spelling (A and the B texts) the diphthongs are retained : *nāue* 4a, later *noe*, genitive singular of *náu* ' ship , later *nó* ; *bōu* 63a, later *bó*, genitive singular of *bó* ' cow '. (See Thurneysen 1946, pp. 44, 45, 125.) Similarly, Adomnan's Latin *Iova*, for the island of Iona, is probably formed from an archaic Old-Irish nominative **I'ou*, but we have rendered it *Io* in the translation. (Cf. p. 154.)

At the beginning of a word, consonantal *u* (*w*) normally developed, in Irish, to *β*, and later to *f* ; and disappeared in grammatical positions in which an initial consonant was lenited. In A, this vanished sound is sometimes omitted (as in *Bo end*), and sometimes represented by *f* with a dot (punctum delens) placed above it, to show that it was not pronounced. In the B manuscripts it is sometimes omitted, and sometimes represented by *f* without any mark of deletion (as in *Bofend*). Probably Adomnan, sometimes at least, used the *f* with deletion dot, and in the B text the dot was left uncopied by a scribe who did not understand its meaning. In *Lathreg-inden* (26a), both A and the B manuscripts omit the *f*, and we may suppose that Adomnan himself had done the same.

In certain names, where we should expect an initial *f*, Adomnan used *v*. It is unlikely that his spelling represents the intermediate stage in the development of *w*- to O.I. *f*-. More probably it represents the equivalent British pronunciation of initial *w*. In Adomnan's time, this was in process of becoming *gw* in South British, but the change was still incomplete (Jackson 1953, § 49) ; in North British, it was probably still pronounced *w* (Jackson 1955, p. 163). It seems that Adomnan's *v*- in proper names indicates a British derivation. Virolec was certainly a North Briton. Vinniavus represents a British hypocoristic name for Findbarr of Clonard, or possibly Findbarr of Moville, both of whom are said to have been trained in Britain. Virgno, the abbot of Iona, was later designated Fergna Brit ' the Briton '.

In Latin words, consonantal *u* was presumably pronounced as a bilabial *v*, and in A there is occasional confusion between it and the sound of lenited *b* (β) : *cavallus* 127a, *repedavit* 49a ; *corbus* 85b, *Fabonius* 100b, 101a, *recuperabit* 77b. Consonantal *u*, which we transcribe as *v*, is not distinguished in the manuscripts from vocalic *u*. In A, when consonantal and vocalic *u* come together (as in *vulneribus* 43b), and the vowel is not changed to *o* (as in *rivoli* 35a), the consonant is frequently dropped : *Ulturnus, aunculum, aesteus, longeus, pluia, fluius*.

Doubled vowels, in Irish words, occur in A and the B texts, and are presumably derived from Adomnan's writing. They stand for long single vowels (cf. p. 547, note 25).

When Irish long vowels changed their sounds, their spelling was changed accordingly. At the time when Adomnan wrote, long *e* (from *ei) before a neutral consonant had not yet finally changed to *ia* ; and long *o* (from *ou) had not changed to *úa*. The long *o* is retained both in A and in the B texts. In the B texts, the long *e* is always retained, but in A, which was written later than the source of the B texts, the *ē* is in a few instances changed to *ea* (*Feachnaus* 32a ; ?*Deathrib* 52a, *Ardceannachte* 56a, *Ceate* 58a, *Leathain* 118a), and in one instance to *ie* (*clied* 55b). The word *niath* is disyllabic, and not an instance of the breaking of long *e*. *Lea* 28a, in A and the B manuscripts, is probably a latinized form of *Lé (accusative *Lée* in Book of Armagh, 15b29).

This feature in A does not prove that much time had elapsed between the time when Adomnan wrote and the time when A was written. The change of sound (*é* to *ia*) was introduced gradually ; but within the space of time during which both phases of the sound were familiar, we may suppose that Adomnan adhered to the old spelling, and that the writer of A was more inclined to accept the new pronunciation. In respect of these vowel-changes, *é* to *ia* and *ó* to *úa*, the text of A would appear to have been a little later than the writing of

Muirchu, and a little earlier than the writing of Tirechan, copied into the Book of Armagh.

Adomnan as a rule does not confuse the Old-Irish diphthongs *āi* and *ōi*, but he, or the writer of A, gives *Aíthche* as the Irish genitive of *Oidech* 64a. He never writes these diphthongs as *ae* and *oe*. *Loen* 121b was presumably a disyllable, like *Loern* 101b.

In Latin, the diphthongs *ae* and *oe* were frequently confused. Manuscript A has an instance of this confusion in *proemia* 129b. Latin *ae* and *oe* had changed, some centuries before Adomnan's time, to the sounds of short open *e* and long close *e* respectively (Sturtevant 1920, pp. 48, 60 ; Jackson 1953, pp. 335, 336) ; and both these sounds were frequently written *e*. For Adomnan's use of the Latin diphthongs the B manuscripts fail us, because generally their writers, like all scribes in and after the end of the twelfth century, changed *ae* and *oe* to *e*.

Manuscript A frequently retains the spelling *ae* (more often written in an *ae* symbol), and almost always retains it in the inflexional ending *-ae*, in *caelum*, and in *prae-*. Among instances of *e* for *ae* are : *secunde* 1b, *Columbe* 5a, *prenuntiavit* 16a, *macheram* 88b, *quesso* 109a, *letante* 125b ; and repeatedly in *estimare* and *mestus, sepe* and *sepius*. Similarly, A has *e* for disyllabic *ae* : *eneo* 49b and *eneam* 99a ; but *aere* 99a, 104b, 109a. It often retains the Latin diphthong *oe* (e.g. *coepit, proeliari, oboediens*). But in some words the *oe* is changed to *e* : *penitens*, with its group of related words ; *cenubium* and *cenubialis*.

As a result of this interchange of spellings, an original Latin *e* is occasionally written as *ae* (e.g. *laboriosæ* 17a, *cæleritate* 115b, *interprætatur* 126b; also *Æthneam* 4a, a latinization of the Irish name Ethne, and *Æthici* 24b, *Æthicam* 64b) ; and as *oe*, in *coepissent* 67a.

In Irish words also, the sound of *e* is occasionally written as *ae* or *æ* : *Cúle-drebinæ* 4a, *Abæ* 32b, *Fendæ* 132a, *Lochdae* 5b (possibly also *Nisæ* 81b, 114b, but that is more probably a Latin genitive, in view of the Latin accusative *Nesam*). The B manuscripts retain *ae* in *Abae*, and they have also *draignichae* (see under 121a) ; B2 and B3 have *Nesae* (see under 81b).

In these words, and in the Book of Armagh, and in certain glosses, *ae*, like *e*, can stand after palatal as well as after neutral consonants (cf. Thesaurus 1903, p. xv) : the *a* in *ae* is not an instance of the *a*-glide that in later Old Irish would have been written after a neutral consonant. (See pp. 138-9.)

Often, in Irish words, but not regularly, an *i*-glide appears in Adomnan between a vowel and a palatal consonant. In the penultimate syllable of the genitive singular of an A-stem, an *i*-glide sometimes appears (*Cainle, Clóithe, Róide*), and is sometimes omitted (*Cúle, lunge*). For *Ainmorius* 18a, the B version has *Anmorius* ; but in Irish spelling the genitive *Ainmurech* 49b was common to both versions.

Final unstressed *i* and *e* in Irish words were not confused by Adomnan, as by writers of Middle Irish ; and the final unstressed *o* of genitives in the I-stem and U-stem declensions is not confused with *-a* in Adomnan's writing, as it is in later Old Irish. In *ached* 63a, and *clocher* 57b, Adomnan has preserved an archaic unstressed *e* that in later Old Irish became *a*. Other instances are *Loerni* 101b, and probably the names of Finten, Brenden, and Comgell.

Adomnan's spellings are useful evidence for the sounds of Irish words. But in Latin words, certain vowels are frequently confused, and some of the confusions are probably derived from Adomnan's text. For instance, in *incedens, incedent* (85a), *ced* is confirmed by the B manuscripts, and is attributable to Adomnan, but is a mis-spelling of *cid*. In 114a, both A and B manuscripts have *dimersis* and *dimersi*, where the prefix *di* is an error for *de*. But Adomnan's *navim* (69b26) and *navem* (69b20) are alternative accusatives of the I-stem *navis* ; and *navis* (100a) is a genitive singular, not, as Reeves assumed, a nominative plural. Confusions of *e* with *i* occur very frequently in A. A few other instances are : *Apreli, deligenter, loquemini, sempliciter, habetus, degitulis ; susciperit, discendens, venina, domisticus, praedistinatam.* Confusion occurs also between *o* and *u*. A few instances are : *commone, motuam, pecodibus, incolomes ; lurica, cenubium, suspes.*

In the genitives of Latin common nouns with nominatives

in -*ius*, double *i* is usually retained by Adomnan. But his genitives of Diormitius, Dermitius, and Echodius, are *Diormiti*, *Dermiti*, and *Echudi*. The vocative of *filius* is regularly *filii* in A, and *fili* in the B manuscripts. In 96b, *angustís* appears to be the ablative of *angusta*, not of *angustiae* as in the B version. In 85b and 131b, *reliquiis diebus* is presumably an error in A. It is not supported by the B manuscripts.

OLD-IRISH STEMS, SYNCOPE, AND COMPOUNDS

Adomnan's language was archaic Old Irish. The Q-Celtic language spoken by the Dal-Réti in his time would have been archaic Old Irish also. Adomnan's spellings of North-British names create a presumption that the influence of Irish upon Pictish speech was already apparent. He does not show evidence of P-Celtic survivals within, or the influence of North-British speech upon, the Irish language of the western kingdom. A few North-British words were in fact adopted in the Old-Irish period and remain in Scottish Gaelic. The dominion of Aidan in Fortriu appears to have been called by a North-British name, *Monid* (δ), perhaps retrospectively ; the same name is given in bardic literature to the kingdom of Scotland. *Monid* was adopted in Irish speech from North-British **moni'jos* after that had become *monid'* as it did also in South British. The kingdom of Monid may have received that name because it was reached over moorland, or by mountain tracks, from Argyll.

The exact form of Irish words in Adomnan's time is important for the history of the Gaelic language. When he conceals that form by latinizing Irish names, it is necessary to reconstruct the Old-Irish from the Latin form ; and the reconstruction is possible in so far as Adomnan's methods are consistent, and are known to us. Fortunately Adomnan gives the Irish form of some names that he has also turned into Latin, and some others can be inferred from writings of an early date.

Through a complete study of Adomnan's names, we have

been led to a conclusion that should be mentioned before we go further. His practice was to produce a Latin noun by adding a Latin case-ending (such as *-us*, *-a*) to an Irish noun, and rarely a Latin adjective by adding a Latin case-ending to an Irish adjective. He did not produce Latin adjectives by adding Latin case-endings to Irish nouns. When he wished to produce a Latin adjective from an Irish noun, he did so by adding to the Irish noun the Latin adjectival endings *-icus*, *-ica* ; or *-ensis*. (See pp. 151, 152.)

We must now proceed to study Adomnan's methods of latinizing the various Old-Irish stems, and we shall take them generally in the order of Thurneysen's declensions.

Old-Irish O-stems (Thurneysen's declension I) were masculine and neuter. When Adomnan turned a masculine noun of this declension into Latin, his practice was to add the Latin nominative ending *-us* to the Irish nominative singular, and to inflect the word as a noun of the Latin second declension. For instance, the Irish *Cormac(c)* was rendered in Latin as nom. *Cormac(c)us*, acc. *Cormacum*, gen. *Cormaci*, abl. *Cormac(c)o*. Masculines of this declension are very numerous. An archaic Irish neuter *clocher*, in the accusative case, is similarly latinized as *Clocherum*.

The Irish dative case is represented in Latin by the dative and ablative. In Adomnan these Irish datives of O-stems appear : masculine, *-bulc*, from *bolc* (131b) ; neuter, *clochur*, from *clocher* (57a).

The neuter substantive *ardd* ' height ' receives the Irish plural inflexion of a neuter O-stem : nominative *artda*, genitive *art*, and dative *artdaib* (20b, 70a, 61a). (This word appears, like the Latin *arduum*, to have been originally a WO-stem. Cf. the Irish adjective *ardd*, Thurneysen 1946, p. 124.)

An Old-Irish noun of this declension (I) ended in a neutral (i.e. non-palatal) consonant, in the nominative singular ; and in a palatal consonant, in the genitive singular and nominative plural. The palatal consonant affected the preceding vowel. In Irish names of more than one syllable, Adomnan's Latin forms generally neglect this change of vowel : thus for the

genitives of the Old-Irish name *Cellach* he gives Irish *Cellaig*
(in A), but Latin *Cellachi*, assuming a Latin nominative
Cellachus.

But he does give effect in almost every instance to one
vowel-change of this class. In this matter we accept the
readings of A as truly representing Adomnan's spelling. When
the vowel of the last syllable was unstressed short *e* in the
nominative, it appeared in the Irish genitive singular and
nominative plural as short *i*. Adomnan as a rule represents
names of this group by two Latin stems : he adds the Latin
terminations, *-us* to the Irish nominative singular, and *-i* to
the Irish genitive singular and nominative plural. Every
Irish word that Adomnan treats in this way must have had a
short vowel in the final syllable. For the Irish *Brenden*, gen.
Brendin, he gives Latin *Brendenus*, gen. *Brendini* (thrice), which
he must have pronounced *Bren'denus*, *Bren'dini*. Similarly he
writes *Cainnechus*, *Cainnichi* ; *Comgellus*, *Comgilli*, with the Irish
genitive *Comgil(l)* ; and once *Comgelli* following the Latin
nominative stem. From the Latin nominative stems he forms
the vocatives, *Cainneche*, *Comgelle*.

The genitives *Brendini*, *Cainnichi*, and *Comgilli*, appear also
in the Litany of the Stowe Missal. In the Litany, the names
ought to be in the vocative ; the genitive forms were presumably taken from a Commemoration list.

The same group includes Adomnan's Latin genitives
singular *Cruthini* (see p. 316), *Cethirni*, and *Foirtgirni*. The
nominative of this last name was a compound of *for* + *tigern*,
literally ' overlord '. The Latin ablative plural, *tigernis*, is
formed from the Irish nominative singular, 43b. For the
origin of the name Loern 'fox', Adomnan's Latin genitive
Loerni (101b), see Watson 1926, p. 121, and Jackson 1953,
p. 384 etc.

Adomnan's Latin accusative, *Alitherum*, should stand for
Irish *alither*, ' stranger ' or ' pilgrim ', with perhaps the same
suffix as in the nominative plural masculine *ind Airthir* ' the
Easterners ' (109b), made from the neuter *airther* ' the east '.

In latinizing Irish plural names that had no equivalent

singular number, Adomnan added the Latin plural termination -*i* to the Irish nominative plural. The Latin genitive
plural *Laginorum* (59b) presupposes a nominative *Lagini*,
formed from an Irish nominative plural *Lagin*. At a somewhat
later date the Irish nominative and genitive plural *Laigin* and
Laigen are found ; but a singular *Laigen* is not found.

From Adomnan's Irish genitives singular *Cathir*, *Libir*, *luthir*,
rathin, we infer the nominatives *Cather*, *Liber*, *luther*, *rathen*.

Similar alternations between short *e* and short *i* occur in
some stressed syllables (Thurneysen 1946, §§ 73–9), and affect
the inflexion of many monosyllables in Old Irish. Of these,
very few are met in Adomnan. The Irish word *fer*, genitive
fir, occurs in the family-name *mocu Fir-rōide*, 132a. *Erc*, 42a,
is not of this class ; it had the genitive *Eirc* in the Book of
Armagh, 20b18. One O/A-stem adjective, *brecc*, appears in a
Latin masculine ablative case *brecco*, assuming a Latin nominative *breccus*, in the insertion in 108a. For the adjective *find/
fend*, and the noun *Nes*, see below under A-stems ; and for
?*Nin*, under I-stems.

The strong Irish stress-accent, falling upon the first syllable
of Irish simple nouns and true compound nouns, caused the
vowels of later syllables to lose their length and quality. But
the vowels of certain final syllables, having been lengthened
in compensation for the loss of a consonant between them and
the final consonant, remained half-long, and retained the
quality of a long vowel : these were very commonly marked
with an acute accent, by Irish writers. (Cf. nom. *Librán* 91b ;
gen. *Salchâin* 46b.) Such terminal syllables that occur in
Adomnan are the derivative or diminutive suffixes -*an*, -*en*,
and -*un*, standing probably for -*agn*-, -*ign*-, and -*ogn*- (see
Thurneysen 1946, §§ 271, 272 ; Meyer 1908, p. 68). Cf.
Jackson 1953, p. 461.

Many names with the suffix -*an* appear in Adomnan. Latin
Aidanus is a derivative of *Aid* ; *Gabranus*, of *gabor* ' goat ' ;
Iogenanus and genitive *Eugenani*, of *Iogen* ; *Laisranus*, of *Laisre*.
The Irish genitive *Leathain* is given in A as well as the Latin
Lethani.

Latinizations of Irish names, in Latin verse, show the Irish suffix *-an* either (1) with a long *a*, as in Columbanus's rendering of his own name (in Columbanus, p. 186), and in Alcuin's *Columbānus* (Carmina CX, xv, line 2 ; Monumenta Germaniae Historica, Poetae Latini Aevi Carolini, i, part 1 (1880), p. 342) ; or (2) with a short *a*, after a stressed syllable, as in Alcuin's *Adomnanus* (ibid.). It is uncertain whether Adomnan's Latin *Adomnano* was stressed on the third or on the second syllable. A stress on the second syllable might account for the later occasional spellings with *-mpn-*, and for the non-Irish stress on the second syllable of ' Adamnan ' in modern English speech.

Adomnan calls by the Irish name *Finten*, and in Latin *Fintenus* (11a–13b), a man who appears in Oengus, and in A.U. 634 = 635, as *Fintan*, genitive *Fintain*. Adomnan's Latin genitives *Aileni* and *Daimeni* imply Irish nominatives *Ailén* and *Daimén*. Similarly his Latin genitive *Craseni* assumes an Irish O-stem nominative *Crasén*, notwithstanding that Oengus 1905, p. 177, and A.U. 634 = 635, give the Irish genitive of the same man's name as *Cres(s)eni*, the Irish nominative of which would be *Cres(s)ene*, an IO-stem.

Briuni 65b, 76a, and *Diuni* 32b, are Latin genitives of *Briún* and *Diún*, with the derivative suffix *-ún*.

More than a hundred years later, Irish names ending in *-án* and *-én* were generally uninflected in writing (see O'Máille 1910, pp. 23–4 ; Thurneysen 1946, pp. 178, 677). But of this there is no sign in Adomnan's spellings. Cf. *Leathain* and *Salcháin*, above ; and *Brecain*, in the B manuscripts, under 62b, an early addition by an Irish writer, perhaps later than Adomnan.

Four Irish names that end in unlenited *l*, though they appear to be O-stems, receive from Adomnan a genitive of the Latin third declension, ending in *-is*. These are : *Cerbulis* 36b (the vowel *u* may have been taken from an Irish genitive *Cerbuill* instead of the usual *Cerbaill*) ; *Conallis* 69b, 72a ; *Domnallis* 69b (beside the Irish genitive *Domnaill* 72a) ; *Nellis* 50a (cf. the Irish genitive *Neil* in the Appendix, and the Irish nominative *Neel* in Book of Armagh, 10b36). Nēll, later Níall, was a common ancestor of Adomnan and Columba. Cerball, a grandson of Níall, was a king of the southern Ui-Néill, and king of Ireland. Conall was a son of Domnall ; Domnall was a son of Gabran, 69b. These four men belonged to royal families of the Scots, in Ireland and in Britain.

It must be supposed that these four names, spelt in a manner that differs from Adomnan's usual method, may have been taken from an earlier Latin historical writing. Adomnan renders the names of other men called Conall and Domnall in Latin according to his usual custom : nominatives *Conallus*, *Domnallus* ; ablatives *Conallo, Domnallo*.

Irish IO-stems (Thurneysen's declension II) are masculine and neuter. They formed nominatives singular ending in -*e*, and genitives in -*i*. Instances of this declension are : nominative masculine *coire* ' cauldron ' 46b ; nominative neuter *daire* ' oakwood ' 90a (dative *dairu*, Appendix) ; genitive neuter or masculine *Eilni* 51a. When Adomnan turned a masculine noun of this declension into Latin, he added the Latin nominative ending -*us* to the Irish nominative singular, and inflected the word as a noun of the Latin second declension. The corresponding treatment of neuter IO-stems would have been to add -*um* to their Irish nominative, but that construction does not occur in Adomnan.

Masculine names of this declension are numerous in Adomnan. The full Latin inflexion is shown in the name of Baithéne : nom. *Baitheneus*, voc. *Baithenee* 13a, acc. *Baitheneum*, gen. *Baithenei*, dat. and abl. *Baitheneo*. From Adomnan's Latin genitive in -*ei* we must always infer an Irish nominative in -*e*, with genitive in -*i*. E.g. the Latin genitive *Turtrei* indicates the Irish genitive *Turtri*, which appears as *Tuirtri* in the Book of Armagh.

The Latin genitive plural *Maugdornorum* (43b, 44a) suggests an Irish singular nominative *Maugdorn*, an O-stem. But the B version (B1 B3) had in both instances *Maugdorneorum*, which would have been Adomnan's Latin derivative from a singular *Maugdorne*, an IO-stem. The name occurs early, in both these declensions, and it is possible that Adomnan was responsible

L

for both readings. According to Adomnan's method, the Latin form of an Irish plural that had no corresponding singular was made by adding -*i* to the Irish plural nominative. Thus his genitive *Cruithniorum* 18a assumes a Latin nominative *Cruithnii*, formed by adding -*i* to the Irish nominative plural *Cruithni*, an IO-stem. (See p. 64.)

Variations result from the tonality of consonants preceding the stem-suffix. The IO-stem suffix in some cases caused palatalization of a single consonant preceding it, and that is often shown by the insertion of an *i* in the preceding syllable. When the suffix was preceded by more than one consonant, there was no conflict of tones if those consonants formed a palatal group. E.g. *Suibneum* (accusative) for Irish *Suibne*.

Adomnan's *Failbeus* represents the Irish name *Fáilbe* (λ β) ' wolf-killer ' (*fáil* ' wolf' with non-palatal *l*) ; the Ogamm-inscribed name *Valuvi*, in the genitive case, is almost certainly the same name. (See MacNeill 1909, p. 345 ; Meyer, Wort-kunde §§ 18, 23 (1912).)

The Irish names *Lugne* and *Lugbe* (in Adomnan's Latin, *Lugneus* and *Lugbeus*) were derived from *Lug*, with *u*-tonal *g*, the equivalent of Gallic *Lugus*, a U-stem (Jackson 1953, p. 441). Adomnan's spellings do not show whether the *g* of *Lugne* and *Lugbe* had or had not retained its *u*-tone quality. The same is true of the genitive *Lugni* in the Book of Armagh (17b1). In later language the words develop as though the *g* had been neutral : the Middle-Irish forms are *Lugna* and *Lugba*. *Lugne* and *Lugbe* were very probably derived from Britannic, but were fully adopted in Goidelic. They seem to occur in Ogamm inscriptions, as *Luguni* (gen.), and *Luguvve* (?nom.). (Cf. MacNeill 1909, pp. 357, 361.)

Maucteus 3a should be understood to represent an Irish nominative **Mauchte*, with *u*-tonal spirant *g* changing to *ch* before *t*. Since *cht* could not be palatal, the name became *Mochta* in later Irish.

When the first consonant of a consonant-group that was followed by the Irish IO-stem suffix was neutral, the group became neutral ; and a vowel-glide (an *a*-glide) developed between the consonants and the case-endings. The final -*e* of the nominative became -*ae*, and -*i* of the genitive became -*ai*, and in Middle Irish both these endings became -*a*. The glide is not shown in Adomnan's spellings. Instances of this are the Irish genitives *Fachtni*, *Sētni*, and *Rēti* (with *t* for *d'd*).

A few compound IO-stems have as their second element -(*g*)*no* > -*na*. Some at least of these Irish -*no-jo* stems were probably taken by Irish from British speech. The hypothetical Britannic ending was *-*gnāwjos*, and is compared with the Latin name *Gnaeus* (Jones 1913, p. 108 ; see Jackson 1953, pp. 382–3). The word *gnō* has been variously interpreted (cf. O'Rahilly 1950, pp. 322 ff ; Pokorny, p. 378).

Names of this pattern that occur in Adomnan are *Beogno* or *Beogna*, *Virgno* or *Fergno*, and probably *Fechna*, all with Latin case-endings added ; and in some oblique cases of *Virgno* or *Fergno* a *v* is inserted before the case-ending. The letters *V*- and -*o* suggest a British derivation. To all these names, in archaic Old Irish, -*e* would have been added for the nominative and -*i* for the genitive. It is to be noted that Adomnan does not include the *e* of their nominatives in his latinizations ; and that his Latin genitives (with the exception of *Virgnovi*), and the Irish genitives, are therefore identical.

Fechno in 5b and 31b may be either a Latin ablative, or an Irish dative, case. The nominative appears as *Fechno* in the Appendix ; but is in Latin *Fechnaus* in B2 B3, and *Feachnaus* in A, 32a. The Ogamm genitive *Veqoanai* (cf. MacNeill 1909, p. 357) points to an Irish nominative *Fēchnae*. In these endings, -*ae* and -*ai*, the *a* is part of the stem, and must not be confused with the *a*-glide mentioned above.

There were no masculine A-stems in Irish, except for a few doubtful instances of genitives in -*ias* in Ogamm inscriptions. But some Irish metaphorical or descriptive names of men were feminine nouns. These retained their gender for a time. (See Thurneysen 1946, p. 183.) The feminine epithet *Lam-dess* (μ, δ) 'right hand' appears as a man's name, 72b, and is translated by *manus dextera* 71b, 72a.

Latin feminine A-stems that are used by Adomnan as

masculine names of men are *Columba* ' dove ', and probably
Tudicla ' little hammer '. The Irish name of Columba was
Colum 118a. *Colum(b)* 11ab is latinized as *Columbus* 12a, 51b,
111a, but never where Columba is meant.

Old-Irish A-stems (declension III) were feminine. Their
nominative case ended in a neutral (*a*-tonal) consonant. The
genitive was formed by adding a case-suffix -*e*, for -*ias*, which
caused palatalization of a single consonant preceding it ; but
when it followed a neutral consonant-group (either original or
resulting from syncope), the final consonant remained neutral,
and the suffix -*e* was changed to -(*a*)*e* > -*ae* > -*a* (cf. Thurneysen
1946, pp. 98, 99 ff.).

Irish A-stem nouns that occur in Adomnan are : *lam* (for
lám) ' hand ' in loose composition (above) ; *cuul* (for *cúl*)
' corner ', with genitive *cúle*. The feminine name *Erc* occurs
in Adomnan in the Irish genitive only, *Erce* (see p. 75).
The same genitive appears in an Ogamm inscription as *Ercias*
(MacNeill 1909, p. 355). The Irish name of the Clyde,
*Clōth, appearing in the genitive *Cloithe*, was derived from the
Britannic nominative *Clōta*. (See p. 159 ; cf. Jackson 1953,
pp. 306, 309.) The Old-Irish genitive of a collective in -*acht*
occurs in *Ceannachte*. A genitive plural occurs in *vadum clied*
55b, from the nominative singular *cléth > *clíath*. *Lathreg* may
have been an A-stem ; see 26a. The genitive *Cainle*, denoting
a mountain and a district, could be a genitive of Old-Irish
caindel ' candle ' or ' torch ', with loss of *d* between *n* and *l* ;
cf. the Irish name *Cnoc na Caindle* (Hogan 1910, p. 276).

A woman's-name (presumably *Rōd* (δ), and an A-stem),
in the genitive case, has been postulated in *mocu fir-Roide* 132a.
(See MacNeill 1911, p. 81.)

In turning Irish A-stems into Latin, Adomnan generally
added to the Irish nominative singular the Latin nominative
ending -*a*, and inflected the word as a noun of the Latin first
declension. The Irish river Moy is named in a Latin accusative
case *Modam*, which stands for the Irish nominative *Mód* >
Múad. The Latin accusative *Muadam*, and Irish genitive
Muaide, occur in the Book of Armagh, 14c6, 15a1. The

Old-Irish nominative plural *Connachta* is implied by Adomnan's Latin genitive plural *Connachtarum*, although that is based upon the Irish nominative singular *Connacht*. From Adomnan's Latin island-names, *Elena* and *Oidecha*, we infer Irish A-stems **Elen* and **Oidech*. (See below.)

Some monosyllabic A-stems that have short *e* in their nominative change *e* to *i* in the genitive (cf. p. 135). The river Ness is named by Adomnan probably in Latin only : accusative *Nesam* (twice), and genitive *Nisae* (twice). These forms stand in apposition to *fluium* and *fluminis* respectively. They represent the nominative and genitive stems of an Old-Irish **Nes*, genitive *Nise*. The B manuscripts read *-e-* instead of *-i-* in the Latin genitive, perhaps through levelling.

A similar change, of stressed short *o* to *u*, occurs in *lunge*, the genitive of *long* ' ship ', an A-stem.

The Old-Irish change of stressed short *i* to *e* before a syllable containing *a* or *o* did not normally occur before *nd* ; e.g. *find*, not *fend*, is the derivative of **windos*, **winda*, ' white '. But *fend* does occur, perhaps dialectally, in Adomnan. The compositional form *fend-* (for **windo-*) is seen in the Irish river-name *Fendæ* ' white goddess ' (see below). That name is in the genitive case. Probably this river was the Finn, in Donegal, Adomnan's own country. The alternative possibility, that *Fendæ* could have been his Latin genitive of *Fenda*, a latinized form of an Irish nominative feminine *fend*, may be dismissed, in view of his *Lōchdae*, for which see below, p. 142.

It can be inferred from the manuscript readings that Adomnan's name of the river Boyne was *Bo fend* (59a). Reeves gave the reading of B3 wrongly as *bofind*, and that rendering was repeated in Thesaurus 1903, p. xxxi. If in Adomnan's form of the name the second element was stressed, the meaning would be ' white cow ' ; but if the stress was on the first element, the name would have been a composite adjective, ' cow-white ', an attribute of the river goddess. (See p. 150.) The *e* of *fend* would then be explained as a lowering of *i* in an unstressed syllable, before a neutral consonant. The further stage of that lowering was reached in the later form *Bo'and* (accusative *Bo'aind*). With this, compare *cenand* ' white-headed ' (Thurneysen 1946, p. 75). Ptolemy's form of this river-name, seven centuries earlier, appears to have been *bououinda*. None of the variant spellings quoted in Ptolemy 1883, p. 79, includes the *s* that was the nominative ending of *bous (Thurneysen 1946, p. 40). We may therefore assume that *bou* in Ptolemy's spelling was the compositional form of *bous, and that the name meant ' cow-white ', as in Adomnan.

In all other instances of *find*, A uses the normal form *find*, compositionally or as an epithet. But the B manuscripts consistently use the forms Fennio, Fendbarr, Fenten, which are formations from *fend*.

In A-stems whose nominative case had more than one syllable, a short *e* in the final syllable of the nominative became short *i* in the genitive case, except when it was followed by a neutral consonant-group. (Cf. Thurneysen 1946, § 103.) Adomnan's Irish genitives *Gruthriche* and perhaps *draigniche* may be A-stems, with nominatives *Gruthrech* and *draignech*.

In three nouns that occur in Adomnan the stem-suffix *a* was formerly preceded by *w* : these are more conveniently described as WA-stems. They are *dea* ; *nau* ; and *Io* or *Iou*, for which see below under island-names. (See the history of *w* in Old Irish, in Thurneysen 1946, §§ 201–06 and p. 37.)

The Old-Irish *dēa* ' goddess ' is derived from *deiwa > *dēwa > *dēaw > *dēa*. Its genitive was *deiwias > *dēwe > *dēe > *dē*. Both these cases appear in the Book of Armagh, in the nominative *Bandea* 11c21, for the river Shannon, and genitive *Bandæ* 15b30, for the river Bann.

Adomnan mentions two compound river-names, in the genitive case, that have *dē* as their second element : (1) *Fendæ* 132a ' white goddess ' ; cf. *fend* above. (2) *Lōchdae* 5b ' black goddess '. That meaning is confirmed by Adomnan's Latin *nigra dea* 85a, the modern Lochy, in Inverness-shire. *Nigra dea* was translated in Reeves 1857, p. 155, as *Dubh bandea* ; and in Thesaurus 1903, p. 279, as *Dubdea*, which Marstrander, in R.I.A. Dictionary, under *2. Dea*, erroneously accepted as a place-name, and wrongly identified with the Dee of Aberdeenshire. The genitive *Loogdae* (γ, δ), in which *oo* stands for long *o*, occurs in A.U. 728 = 729, as the name of another river. (See Watson 1926, p. 50.)

The forms *-de*, *-dæ*, *-dae*, are spelling variations of the genitive *dē*. The B spellings, (1) *-dé* and (2) *-dëe*, suggest that the *e* was doubled or otherwise marked for length in their common source. The genitive *-de* occurs in *au inde* 78a, perhaps for *áu'finde* ' of the white-eared goddess '. The implication may be that that divinity also was a river.

Nau 'ship', a feminine WA-stem, occurs in the genitive singular *naue* 4a. (See Thurneysen 1946, § 69.)

Irish IA-stems (declension IV) are feminine. They have nominative and genitive alike, both ending in *-e*, preceded by a palatal consonant ; or in *-e > -(a)e > -ae > -a*, preceded by a neutral consonant-group.

A nominative of this declension is *Ailbine* 55b (genitive *Ailbine*, in the Book of Armagh, 9c15–16). *Eilne* 38a, and *Slane* 21a, may be genitives in this declension. *Cēt(t)e* and *Ceate* (19a, 49b, 58ab) are genitives either of an IA-stem or of an A-stem.

Adomnan shows two spellings of an unsyncopated genitive, *drebene* and *drebinæ* (17b, 4a), which may be of an IA-stem (or possibly an A-stem), and which after syncope would have become *dreibne* (β) or possibly *dreimne* (μ). (Cf. O'Rahilly 1946, pp. 464–5.)

Aethneam 4a is a latinized accusative of Irish *Ethne*, an IA-stem. Several island-names in *-ea* may have been formed from Irish IA-stems with nominatives in *-e*. (See below.)

Irish JA-stems (declension V ; see Thurneysen 1946, pp. 184 ff.) are feminine. They have nominatives singular ending in a palatal consonant, but in the other cases resemble IA-stems.

Mōne, in *Onde-mmone* 17b, is the genitive of *móin*, ' moor ' or ' bog ', inflected as a JA-stem. The *m* was doubled in A, to show that it was unlenited.

Maugina 57b may be assumed to represent an Irish woman's-name *Maugin*, a JA-stem. Cf. *Mugain*, a later form of the name (Oengus 1905, p. 258, commentary).

In *monasteriolum quod scotice Trioit vocitatur* 41a, *Trioit* may be feminine, the nominative of a JA-stem ; or it may be the genitive of an O-stem, with the word *monasteriolum* not repeated, but implied. B1 B3 read here *Triota*, and that is also the Latin ablative in A's contents-list, 6a. If *Triota* was Adomnan's spelling, it should imply an Irish feminine nominative, *Triot*, an A-stem. An A-stem is also implied by for example an Irish genitive, *Treoiti*, in A.U. 1004 = 1005. But between A.D. 738 and 911, the genitive in A.U. is, nine times, *Treoit*, which suggests that A's *Trioit* was thought to be the genitive of an O-stem, *Triot*.

Kailli 78a is the nominative plural of the Irish *caill* ' wood ', a JA-stem (M.I. genitive singular *caille*).

Old-Irish I-stems (declension VI) were masculine, feminine, and neuter. Their nominatives normally ended in a palatal (*i*-tonal) consonant. The genitive case ended in -*o* (later -*a*) ; in Ogamm, -*ōs* > -*ō*. The -*o* neutralized a preceding single consonant, and was changed by a preceding palatal consonant-group to -*eo* (later -*ea* and -*e*).

The name of the island called *Airthrago* 100b is in the Irish genitive case (' of the foreshore '), from a nominative *airthráig*, a compound of *tráig* ' shore ', which is an I-stem, genitive *trágo* > *trága*. (See below.)

The masculine I-stem *clóin* ' meadow ' occurs in the Irish plural nominative *Cloni* 130b. The Latin adjective *Clonoensis* 14a, 15b appears to have been formed from the Irish genitive *clóno*.

The obscure noun *nin* (meaning something like ' wave ') is used by Adomnan as a masculine or neuter I-stem (62b). The context of the phrase *hinin glas* (for *i nin nglas*) requires that *nin* should be in the accusative case after the preposition *i* in the sense of ' into '. An A-stem or a feminine I-stem would have been followed by *nglais*, not *nglas* ; an O-stem would have become *nen*. Adomnan's evidence tends to dissociate *nin* from *en* (' water '), with which it has been entangled.

Muir-, ' sea ', in *Muirbolc* and *Muirchol*, is the Irish compositional form of an I-stem. The compositional *dair-*, ' oak ', in *Dairmag* 14a, may be an I-stem or a guttural stem ; but *daur-*, ' oak ', in the Appendix, is a U-stem, and the earlier form of the word.

Very few I-stems are turned into Latin by Adomnan. Latin adjectives are formed by adding *-us* to the nominatives of two Irish I-stem adjectives : *coilriginus* 111ab (*cóil + rigin* is a dvandva, or coordinate, compound, ' thin and tough ') ; and *laitirus* 86a (apparently meaning ' strong ').

The Latin ending *-ius* is added to the Irish nominative in *Dermitius* in 18a, 20b, 21a, and in later pages regularly *Diormitius*. The genitives are *Dermiti* and *Diormiti*. The name appears in the Book of Armagh, 18b, as *Diarmuit*. It is an Irish I-stem (formed from the phrase *dí formut* ' without envying ' ; see Thurneysen 1946, § 345). The form *Dermit* results, according to Meyer, Wortkunde § 155 (1918), from regular syncope, and has short *e*.

Old-Irish U-stems (declension VII) were masculine and neuter. Their nominatives normally ended in a *u*-tonal consonant, if the consonant could receive *u*-tone ; otherwise, in a neutral consonant. The genitive case, as in I-stem inflexion, ended in *-o* (later *-a*) ; in Ogamm, *-ōs*.

Nominatives of Irish U-stems are *Forcus* (gg), 18a ; and *snám*, a masculine verbal noun. A U-stem in composition is *maug-*, in *Maugdornorum* (A). *Maug* is an early form of *mug* (see Thurneysen 1946, p. 50.)

Three Irish U-stem nouns are latinized by adding *-us* to the Irish nominative, and inflecting in the Latin second declension. Archaic Irish *Āid* is given by Adomnan seven times in its Irish genitive *Aido*. (The name is later *Áed*, genitive *Áeda*.) Adomnan latinizes the name as *Aidus*, genitive *Aidi*, accusative *Aidum*, and an ablative *Aido* 37a. *Emchatus* 115a, inflected in Latin as an O-stem, is probably a partly-Irish form of a British name *Ambicatus*, a U-stem. (See p. 160.) *Fedilmithum* 4a is the Latin accusative of the Irish nominative *Fedilmid* (*Fedelmith* in the Appendix). This was probably a U-stem. The Irish forms in the Book of Armagh 16cd are :

nom. *Fedelmid*, and gen. *Fedelmedo*, *Fedelmtheo*, beside a Latin nominative *Fedelmidius*.

The Irish name *Fergus* (γ), a U-stem, appears in the Irish genitive, *Ferguso*, 4a and Appendix. The kindred U-stem, archaic Irish *Oingus* (γ), later *Aengus*, is latinized by adding *-ius* to the Irish nominative : *Oingussius* 21a (with single *-s-* in B1 B3), and the ablative *Oingusio* 21a.

It may perhaps be assumed that Adomnan had met the names Diormitius and Oingusius in some earlier Latin writing.

Old-Irish consonantal stems had lost their final stem-consonant in the nominative and suffixless dative singular. Adomnan's latinizations are based upon these cases, and therefore do not show the stem-consonant.

Three Irish guttural stems (Thurneysen's declension VIII) are latinized by Adomnan. Two of them belong to the type in which the Irish nominative ends in a palatal consonant. Adomnan adds to that consonant the Latin ending *-ius*, and inflects the word accordingly. He does not include a glide-vowel before the consonant. The Irish man's-name *Echoid*, so spelt in the Appendix, (*Echuid* in the Book of Armagh, 191a11) is rendered in Latin *Echodius* by Adomnan ; its Latin genitive is *Echudi* in 98a. The Irish genitive was *Echdach* (cf. Thurneysen 1946, p. 203). The nominative became later *Echaid*, and lastly *Eochaid* with stressed short *o*, originally a glide-vowel (between *e* and *u*-tonal *ch*). (See Bergin 1932, pp. 142, 143, etc. ; Thurneysen 1946, p. 57.) The name tended to be inflected as an I-stem, with genitive *Eochada*. Adomnan's Latin nominative *Lugudius* and ablative *Lugidio* represent the Irish guttural stem *Luguid* (so spelt in the Appendix), or *Lugid*. This name became *Lugaid* later, but it must not be confused with Adomnan's *Lugaidus*, below.

The third Irish guttural stem latinized by Adomnan was of the type whose nominative ended in a vowel. The Irish name *Ainmu(i)re* (later *Ainmire*) is rendered in the nominative case *Ainmorius* 18a (*Anmorius* in B1 B3). Here, as in *Colgius* below, the final vowel of the Irish nominative was dropped before the Latin -*ius* was added. Adomnan's *Ainmurech* 49b and the *Ainmuireg* of 108a are Irish genitives of *Ainmu(i)re*.

An Irish feminine guttural stem *brí* ' hill ' occurs in the genitive plural *Breg*, after the Latin *campum* 40a, 92b, translating the Irish district name Mag-breg.

The Irish nominative *Féchre* (for the later *Fíachra*) is implied by Adomnan's Irish genitives *Fechureg* 22b, and *Fechreg* 121a (*Fechrech* B1 B3). MacNeill 1909, p. 360, thought that -*chu*- stood here for ' an aspirate *q* rather than a distinct syllable '. The vowel that separated *ch* from *r* in this word had already been syncopated in an Ogamm inscription (ibid.). (Cf. O'Rahilly 1946, p. 464 ; 1950, p. 396 ; Jackson 1953, p. 141.)

The compositional *dair* 14a may be a guttural stem (gen. *darach*). (See above, p. 145.)

One lenited-dental stem (Thurneysen's declension IX) is latinized by Adomnan, in the island-name *Scia* ; see below. The Irish disyllabic noun *nie, nia*, ' sister's son ', of the same declension, occurs in the Irish genitives (probably singular) *neth* 13b, and *niath* 25b (see Thurneysen 1946, p. 207). In Adomnan the word might have its alternative or transferred meaning, of ' champion '. The genitive (singular or plural) *nieth* in A.U. 692 = 693 is an archaic form, showing that here A.U. used a nearly contemporary source. In Adomnan's *niath, ia* is not a breaking of long *e*. The words *niath* and *nieth* were disyllabic.

N-stems and ION-stems (Thurneysen's declension XI). An N-stem whose nominative ended in a non-palatal consonant is latinized by Adomnan by adding -*us* to the Irish nominative : *Lugaidus* 27a, 58a, 86ab, with non-palatal *d* (δ). He never confuses this name with the guttural stem *Luguid*, with palatal *d* (δ), above. The genitive of *Lugaid* is *Lugadon* and *Lugedon* in A.U. 780, 789, 799 = 781, 790, 800. See Thesaurus 1903, p. 288, line 35 (genitive *Luguaedon*). So also Adomnan's *Nemaidon* is an Irish genitive of *Nemaid*, an N-stem, with non-palatal *d* (δ).

An ION-stem with Irish nominative ending in -*u* was latinized by dropping the final -*u* and adding -*ius* : the Irish nominative *Colgu* 58b, 115a, becomes in Latin *Colcius* and *Colgius*, with Latin inflexion for accusative dative and ablative cases ; but the genitive case is given in the Old-Irish forms *Colcen, Colgen*, and the archaic Old-Irish form *Colgion*. (See Thurneysen 1946, p. 212.)

Rechru 16b is the Irish nominative of an ION-stem ; its suffix-less dative *Rechre* is implied in the Latin ablative *Rechrea* 93b. (See below.) The Irish dative *Teilte* is the suffix-less dative of **Teiltiu*, an ION-stem. (See under 106b.)

Adomnan's *Abæ* 32b is to be read *Abe*, the Old-Irish genitive of the feminine N-stem *aub* (β), the accusative of which was *abinn* in the Book of Armagh, 18c2. The inflexion is irregular for a feminine noun ; *abe* is formed like the genitive of a neuter N-stem (Thurneysen 1946, § 333). The final vowel of the neuter genitive of an N-stem stood for the termination **-ens* (ibid. § 332), before which the *b* would normally have been palatal. Since Adomnan does not insert *a*-glides, his spelling does not show that the *b* of *Abæ* had non-palatal quality (see p. 130). The spelling of the genitive *abae* in a Milan gloss had no doubt the same phonetic significance (Thesaurus 1901, p. 266, line 30 ; cf. the genitive *dáe*, ibid. p. 377, line 23).

A neuter N-stem with nominative ending in a palatal consonant, and with genitive in *-e*, occurs in A's genitive *tómme* 132a (apparently *tome* in the source of the B manuscripts), implying the nominative **tóimm* (later *túaimm*).

In Irish neuter S-stems (Thurneysen's declension XIII) the stem-consonant, *s*, being between vowels, has entirely disappeared. Instances in Adomnan are : the genitive *onde* 17b of *ond*, in the language called ' iarnbélre ' (cf. O'Davoren 1904, p. 430 ; Cormac 1862, p. 9 ; O'Rahilly 1946, p. 88); *mag* 14a, dative *maig* in the Appendix ; and probably *áu* ' ear ', in compositional form, in *au inde* 78a.

An Old-Irish noun of heteroclite declension, with stems **bóu-* and **bow-* ' cow ', occurs in Adomnan's nominative *bó* 59a, 67b, and archaic genitive *bóu* (63a ; also in Bede, H.E. IV 4). (See Thurneysen 1946, pp. 40, 45, 125, 216–17 ;

Pokorny, pp. 482–3.) The compositional form occurs in *Bo'end* (see pp. 141-2).

When settlers brought Goidelic speech into Ireland and south-western Scotland, it was a fully inflected language, comparable with Latin and Greek. Strong stress-accent developed on the first syllables of words ; and the final syllables were weakened or lost. Somewhat later, in words of three or more syllables, the vowel of the second syllable was lost, by syncope. The period of this syncope spread over a considerable space of time. It reached its climax about the time when Columba entered upon his pilgrimage in Britain, four generations before Adomnan.

Nevertheless, Adomnan retained some memory of the unsyncopated forms of names. He wrote a genitive *Colgion* 35b, as well as the later forms *Colcen* and *Colgen* ; and the genitive *drebene* 17b and *drebinæ* 4a, instead of *dreibne* (see p. 143). Bede wrote *Meilochon*, for the genitive of king Brude's father's name, in a spelling that is partly Irish, and is unsyncopated. He may have heard this name from the messengers of king Nechtan.

Knowledge of the older forms of names would not have been confined to Adomnan. Some of the Ogamm funerary inscriptions in which names appear in forms earlier than the syncopated forms were probably written after the period of syncope, in continuance of an early funerary convention. (Cf. Jackson 1953, p. 141, note 1.)

In Adomnan's text, there are several instances of composite nouns, and composite adjectives, formed according to the principles that were followed in Old Irish (and that are still found in Scottish Gaelic, according to John Fraser in *R.C.* XLI (1924), pp. 250–1).[1]

In close compounds, a noun or adjective is preceded by a noun or adjective which qualifies it ; and which takes the word-stress, and causes lenition of an initial letter of the second

---

[1] This was in accordance with the teaching of Donald Mackinnon. There are exceptions, arising from different causes, in modern speech ; and Thurneysen did not accept the rule as invariable in Old Irish. A. O. A.

element. Noun + noun : *Brōn'bachal* (β) ' sorrow staff ', an
epithet ; *Dair'mag* (μ, γ) ' oak plain ' ; *Delc'ros* (ρ) ' thorn
promontory ' ; *Fáil'be* (β) ' wolf-killer ' ; *Muir'bolc* (β, gg)
' sea bay ' ; *Muir'chol* ' sea hazel '. Adjective + noun : *Aith'-
chambas* ' sharp bay ' ; *Lōch'dae* (δ) ' black goddess ' ; *Fen'dæ*
' white goddess ' (here *d* is delenited after *nd*) ; *Glas'derc*
' grey-eye ', an epithet used as a personal name (here *d* is
delenited after the *s*).

Close compounds of noun + adjective : *Bō'[f]end* ' cow-
white ', see pp. 141-2 ; *Bran'dub* ' raven-black ' (with delenited
d), in the Appendix. Compare similar compounds in Pedersen
1913, p. 5.

Loose compound nouns are formed of a noun followed by
a qualifying adjective, or by a noun in the genitive case. The
second element takes the word-stress, and an initial consonant
of the second element is lenited or not according to its grammatical synthesis. Noun with adjective : Adomnan's translation of the name *Lam dess* (μ, δ) as *manus dextera* ' right hand '
shows that that name was a normal grammatical synthesis of
a feminine noun and a following stressed adjective. *Cen[n]
calad* (δ) is an epithet ' hard head ' (if the epithet had been
Cen'chalad, it would have meant ' hard-headed ', but there is
no established instance of *c* written for *ch* in A, except in the
group *ct* for *cht* in *Maucteus*). Noun with genitive : *Ached-bóu*,
translated ' cow's meadow ' ; *Daire-Calcig*, translated ' oakwood of Calgach ' ; *Ard-Cēannachte* ; *Eirros-domno* (μ).

In some compounds (of dvandva composition), neither
element qualifies the other, but an initial consonant of the
second element is commonly lenited, probably showing that
in those words the main stress was on the first element : *Coilrigin* ' thin and tough ' ; *Artchain* ' high and smooth ', a place-
name ; *Finten*, apparently ' white and old ', from *find + sen*.

Compounds that begin with a particle or proclitic prefix
vary in their accentuation. (Cf. *Der'mitius* and *Dior'mitius*,
above.)

LATIN ADJECTIVES FROM IRISH NAMES

From Irish tribal and territorial names, certain O-stem adjectives were made, ending in -*ech* preceded by a palatal consonant. They were used also as nouns, and their plurals became tribal names. Instances of these adjectives are : *Muimnech, Laignech, Cruithnech,* based upon *Mumu* (an N-stem), *Lagin,* and *Cruthen.* These adjectives are not latinized by Adomnan, who substitutes for them Latin adjectives (used also as nouns) which are formed by adding to the Irish tribal and territorial names the Latin adjective terminations -*icus*, -*ica*, and -*ensis*, -*enses*. Thus the genitive plural *Laginensium* 13b takes the place of the Irish *Laignech*. In this instance, the basis is the Irish plural *Lagin* (as in *Laginorum* 59b).

If these Latin adjectives, formed from Irish tribal or territorial names, were given in Adomnan's own spelling-system, his *Lagenensis* 113b, *Lagenensium* 73a (-*gin*- in the source of the B manuscripts), and *Lagenica* 113b, would probably show that he knew an Irish singular **Lagen* ; and his *Muminensium* 45b, and *Cruthinicum* 36a, would probably show that he knew Irish plurals **Mumin* and **Cruthin*. (This last form was also the genitive singular of the eponym *Cruthen,* latinized as *Cru'thini* 50a). But these are not safe inferences. Irish monks would have formed Latin substitutes for the principal Irish tribal and territorial names before the time when Adomnan wrote, and their writings might have influenced his spellings.

In *stagni Aporici* 83b ' lake of Apor(s) ', the adjective-ending -*icus* has been added to *apor* (see p. 158). The Latin genitive plural of *apor* occurs in *stagno Aporum* 67b, which can be explained as a Latin second-declension genitive in -*um* : *apor-um* (cf. Lindsay 1894, pp. 401–02 ; Sommer 1914, § 200).

Ethica terra and *insula*, and genitive *Aethici pilagi*, are Latin formations upon the island-name *Eth* (or *Heth*) ; see below.

In the Latin ablative *Clonoensi,* 14a 15b, the basis is *Clóno,* genitive of the Irish *Clóin,* an I-stem, the name of a large Irish monastery. This seems to be an exceptional Latin formation, adopted by Adomnan.

ISLAND-NAMES

A dozen island-names present a special problem. They are given as Latin A-stems or IA-stems, beside the word *insula*. It has been customary to think that these are adjectives qualifying *insula*. But according to Latin usage the names would be substantives, in apposition to *insula*. Those that are known to contain the Irish name followed by the Latin ending -*a* must be regarded as nouns, since our analysis of Adomnan's methods of latinization has shown no instance in which he has formed a Latin adjective by adding the Latin adjectival case-endings to an Irish noun.

In one island-name the Latin form is a substantival O-stem, differing in gender from the *insula* that is in apposition to it. This appears in 42a : *in Coloso insula*, and *de insula Coloso* ; and in 70b : *inter Maleam et Colosum insulas*, where Malea as well as Colosus is a noun. These instances confirm the presumption that Adomnan's island-names are normally intended to be nouns.

From the inflected Latin island-names in -*ea* we must infer, according to Adomnan's usual latinization, Irish feminine nouns ending in -*e*, namely the IA-stems (declension IV) : *Ile*, *Male, *Ege, *Saine ; and an ION-stem *Rechre.

Adomnan's *Ilea insula* represents a feminine noun *Ile* ' Islay '. In a verse that is included in T. 9d17 (cf. E.S. 1, p. 148), *daraile* rhymes with *i cind tire*. The spelling *daraile* is therefore corrupt. It should perhaps be emended to *dar íle* ' across Islay ', as in C.S. p. 78 ; and *ile* in this verse would then be the accusative of an Old-Irish masculine stem. (Cf. p. 60.)

*Male may have been the Old-Irish form of the name that is given by Ptolemy (1883, p. 81) as *Malaios*. The modern *Muile* ' Mull ' can have been derived from *Male. (See Watson 1926, p. 38.)

In *Ege from Adomnan's *Egea* the g should be spirant (γ). The Old-Irish genitive *Ego* in A.U. 724 = 725, 751 = 752, should also have spirant g (γ) ; but it has the inflexion of an

I-stem, nominative perhaps *Eig* (γ). *Ega*, the genitive occurring in A.U. 616 = 617, is a later spelling of *Ego*. ' Donnan of Eigg ' is called *Donnán Ega* (γ), in Oengus 1905, p. 107 (*Eca*, with *c* for non-spirant *g*, in L.B. version). The Scottish-Gaelic name of Eigg is *Eige* (Dieckhoff) or *Eilean Eige* (Watson 1926, p. 85), with non-spirant *g*. This *Eige* might have been an IA-stem, but is explained as *eige*, genitive of *eag* ' a notch ' (an A-stem), because the island is conspicuously divided by a valley. If Adomnan's **Ege* was the island of Eigg, its name must later have been changed by attraction to *eige*, through false etymology. The early Irish annotators give contradictory accounts of the place of Donnan's martyrdom, and it might possibly not have been the island now called Eigg.

*Saine is a probable inference from *Sainea*, but it does not occur elsewhere, and has not been identified.

Rechrea (93b) is based upon **Rechre*, clearly the suffix-less dative (or locative) of *Rechru* (16b) ' Rathlin ', a feminine ION-stem. The suffix-less dative of Irish consonantal stems very often took the place of their nominative (as *Ére* > *Éire* took the place of *Ériu*).

Similar inferences from Adomnan's island-names ending in -*a* preceded by a consonant are rather less secure.

An Irish nominative **Elen*, an A-stem, is perhaps implied by Adomnan's *in monasterio Elenae insulae* (67a). No corresponding island-name has been found. **Elen* might be expected to have had a genitive **E(i)lne*. (This name has nothing to do with the modern Scottish Gaelic *Eilean* ' island ', which is a word borrowed from Old Norse *eyland* long after Adomnan's time.)

Ad Hinbinam insulam, in 26b, and in later pages *in hinba insula*, six times, probably refer to one island. Adomnan's *Hinba* (serving as a Latin ablative) should stand for an Irish nominative, **Inb* (β), which would not have been a Goidelic O-stem or A-stem, or a Britannic A-stem, unless possibly the *i* was a long vowel ; but which could have been an Irish feminine N-stem. Adomnan's *Hinbinam* looks like a Latin adjective formed from the Latin *Hinba*, but it could have been

M

formed, contrary to Adomnan's custom, from the accusative (*inbin*) of an Irish N-stem. The initial *h* was doubtless silent.

The proposed explanation given by Watson (1926, p. 84) is that *Hinba* stands for the Irish verbal noun *inbe* ' incision '. He appears to have thought that it might denote the cleft between the Paps of Jura. They are the distinctive feature of that island, and are visible from a great distance. Against this very plausible theory it may be said that *inbe* was a neuter noun, an IO-stem, which should have become (*h*)*Inbeum* in Adomnan's Latin ; conversely, if *Hinba* stood for *inbe*, it would suggest that *inbe* was feminine, an IA-stem ; and that should have become (*h*)*Inbea*. Watson's suggestion would involve a departure from Adomnan's usual procedure.

A possible alternative is that *Hinba* might be an Irish noun, or a non-Celtic noun taken into Irish, used in apposition to *insula*. There is so much doubt about the name that we have thought it necessary to retain the Latin form ' Hinba ' in speaking of this island.

Hinba may have been Colonsay or Jura. It cannot have been in the Garvelloch Islands (see Watson 1926, p. 81). There was a ' place of anchorites ' in the island, on a bay called Muirbolc Mar. If in Jura, this place might have been near Loch Tarbert ; if in Colonsay, beside Kiloran Bay, near the north end of the island, where there is land suitable for a monastery.

Iova, in the Latin accusative, genitive, and ablative, cases (*Iovam insulam, Iovae insulae, Iovā insulā*), should represent an Irish feminine WA-stem noun (see above, p. 142) ; **iwowa* > **Io* or **Iou*, in which a final *w* was perhaps still audible, as in *nau* (genitive *naue*), and *bou*, above. With *Iova* we have to compare Adomnan's *Iogenanus* and *Eugenani*, for one person in 60a ; and *Iogenanum*, 107a. In all these names, *Io*- may stand for **iwo*- > *eó* ' yew-tree '. The island-name appears as *Eo* in Walafridus Strabo ; and in Irish annals at A.D. 716, where it is identified with the *civitas* or community of the monks (*in Eo civitate*, T. 12c38–9, *in Eoa civitate*, A.U. 715 = 716).

There was also a synonymous form *Í*, with genitive *Ie*. This nominative *Í*, was according to Watson (1926, pp. 89–90) originally the dative of a shortened stem, **Iwia*. The form *Í* survived the Scandinavian occupation ; but it cannot be of Scandinavian origin, since it appears already in Bede, who spells it *Hii*, with silent *H* and doubled *i* for *ī*. The modern name is *I Chalumchille* (Dieckhoff). The English name ' Iona ' was derived from Adomnan's *Iova*, through a textual error, the reading of *u* as *n*, and was (we believe) not current before the fourteenth century.

Oidecham insulam (64a) has an Irish genitive case *Aíthche* in the same column. It must be assumed that *Oidecha* was a latinization of a noun, *Oídech* (or *Aídech*), with spirant *d*. This variation of vowels, and the unvoicing of spirant *d* before *ch*, are not unusual. The island was on the route from Iona to Ireland. Perhaps the same name appears in the Senchus fer nAlban, as *Odeich*, a place of twenty houses, in Islay. If *Odeich* were the correct spelling, it could have been a JA-stem ; but *Oídech* would have been an A-stem. The genitive of *Oídech*, in A, is marked with an accent, as though to distinguish it from *aithche*, genitive of *adaig* ' night ', a JA-stem. Instead of *Oi-* and *Aí-* in this word, the B manuscripts have *Ovi-*, suggesting *oí* ' sheep '. This island-name is still unexplained.

In Scia insula (5a, 34b, 74a) implies an Irish nominative *Sci*, a feminine noun, for ' Skye '. An early note in A.U. 667 = 668 has the genitive *Sceth*, which could be an inflexion of *Sci* in the lenited-dental declension IX. The name is certainly older than the Irish settlement in that district. Most manuscripts of Ptolemy (1883, p. 104) give the island-name as *Skitis*.

The terms *Ethica terra* and *Ethica insula* (24b etc. ; Ae-64b) refer without doubt to the island of Tiree. (See Watson 1926, pp. 85–6.) They are artificial Latin developments of the name that is met in Latin Lives as *Heth* (with long vowel). (See p. 151.) *Etheticam terram*, 65a, if not a textual error in A, is an arbitrary variation.

The identity of *Colosus insula* with Coll depends not on

language but on Adomnan's narrative. From the southern coast of Ardnamurchan a ship was seen sinking between *Colosus* and Mull (70b). It is clear from the account of Erc's funeral, if not from Erc's poaching expedition, (42ab) that *Colosus* was near Tiree. The modern name *Collasa* for ' Colonsay ' was derived, according to Watson 1926, p. 84, not from *Coloss + ey*, but from *Kolbeins-ey* ; and the sea between Colonsay and Mull would not have been visible from Ardnamurchan.

The word *Colosus*, with Adomnan's unvoiced -*s*-, could have represented an Irish masculine noun *Colos(s) ; but the modern Gaelic name of Coll, *Cola* (Watson 1926, p. 84), is perhaps sufficient evidence that *Colos(s) was not the Old-Irish form. Adomnan's *Colosus*, with unvoiced -*s*-, is formally identical with the Latin *colossus* ' gigantic figure '. We know of no special reason why Adomnan should have given the island that epithet. He may have given it fancifully, basing it on the Irish name, somewhat as he gave to Tiree the fanciful Latin name of *Ethica terra*.

The island *quae scotice vocitatur airthrago* may have been called in Old Irish *inis airthrago* ' island of the foreshore ' (see p. 144) ; a description, rather than a name. The locality suggests Shona, off Moidart, although that is not a tidal island.

The island *quae Ommon nuncupatur*, 37b, has not been identified. The name is as yet unexplained.

In *Geonae cohortis*, 34b, there is nothing to show whether *Geona* was an island, and not much sign that it was a place. The basis might have been *Geon, very probably not an Irish word.

The island ' that may in Latin be called long ' (72b) seems to be described rather than named. It is possible that ' long island ' might have been a name for the island of Lewis and Harris, or even for the whole string of Outer Hebrides that are called ' the Long Island ' now (*An Innis Fhada*).

British Names

In or near the island of Skye, and in the ' district of the Picts ', Columba is represented as having spoken to inhabitants of North Britain ' through an interpreter ' (35a, 78a).

Adomnan's renderings of North-British names show mixture of Irish and British phonetics. This may have resulted from their reaching him through Irish settlers who had not entirely assimilated the North-British names, or through a district in which the two languages were mixed. It has also to be kept in mind that the North-British area was large and scattered, and we must not *a priori* assume that only one North-British language pervaded it.

Lenition of consonants differed in Irish and British. Irish lenited *c*, *t*, became *ch*, *th* ; British lenited *p*, *c*, *t*, became *b*, *g*, *d* (frequently written *p*, *c*, *t*). Irish and British lenited *b*, *g*, *d*, became β, γ, δ, (written *b*, *g*, *d*) and British lenited *g* later disappeared.

In Old-Irish writing, the mediae *b*, *g*, *d*, of various origins, in medial or final position are often written *p*, *c*, *t*.

When Adomnan quotes names that contain a British, or North-British, lenited sound, he often substitutes for it the Irish lenited sound of the same letter. British *t > d* is written *t* (in *Catlon*, *Emchat*, *Miati*) ; and *th* (in *Emchath*, *Miathi*, *Cloithe*, *Reth*). British *c > g* is written *ch* in ?*Broichanus*, *Emchat*(*h*) ; and *g* in ?*Crog*.

British spirantized tenues (in certain positions, *p*, *c*, *t > ph*, *ch*, *th*) have not been proved to occur in North British. (See Jackson 1955, p. 164, and Jackson 1953, pp. 565–73.)

The name of Urquhart, *Airchartdan* 114b, is a complete transmutation to Irish form of a North-British *arcarden'*, ' forewood ' ; with the Irish *air* for North-British *are > ar*, Irish *ch* for North-British *c > g*, manuscript A's *rtd* for *rd* (*d* being here unlenited in North British, see Jackson 1955, p. 164), and Irish -*an* following a neutral consonant-group. The same Irish form is the origin of the modern name in Scottish Gaelic,

Urchardan (Watson 1926, p. 95), and of the English ' Urquhart '.

A word *apor* occurs in two Latin derivatives, 67b and 83b. (See p. 151.) It occurs also in the name *Apor-crosan* (see p. 107), and later in *Abbor-doboir* (Aberdour in north Aberdeenshire ; Book of Deer, f. 3a). This *apor* (bb) may be a North-British variant of British *aper* (bb), and mean ' river mouth ' ; although *aper* points to the root *bher, while *apor* suggests the sound-grade *bhor. (Cf. O'Rahilly 1946, p. 356 ; Jackson 1953, p. 427.)

Artbrananus 34b, 35a, is a latinized form of an Irish or a North-British man's-name. In Irish, and perhaps in North British, *Art* was the equivalent of British *arth* ' bear '. *Branan* appears to be a diminutive of *bran* ' raven ', either in Irish or in North British. (For British names in *-*agn-* > -*an*, see Jackson 1953, p. 461.)

The name of Arturius, Aidan's son, 18b, 19a, is a latinization of British *Arthūr*, with Irish or North-British *rt* for *rth* (cf. Irish *Artuir* in T. 9d15, where *ui* perhaps represents the sound of British *ū'*).

For *Broichanus* see p. 84. There is no sufficient evidence to show that -*oi*- would have survived, or how it would have developed, in North British of Adomnan's time.

Adomnan's Latin *Bru(i)deus* represents an Irish form *Bru(i)de* (δ), derived from *Brudjos or *Brodjos. If *Brodjos was the Goidelic form, and was derived from Britannic, the borrowing could not have been much later than A.D. 500 (Jackson 1953, p. 143). If *Brodjos were the source also of the North-British form of the name, that might help to explain Bede's *Bridius* and some of the later variations of spelling, e.g. *Bred*, and *Bre(i)dei* and *Bridei*, in the lists of Pictish kings ; since in South British *Brodjos would be expected to become *Bre(i)d* (δ) or *Bryd* (δ).

Catlon 8a–9a seems to stand for a primitive-Welsh *Cadwallon* the third syllable of which contained the long *o* that later became *aw* (cf. E. Zupitza, in *Z.C.P.* III, p. 594 ; Jackson 1953, p. 287). This name appears in the genitive case, as *Cathloen*, in A.U. 631 = 632.

Cloithe 21b is the genitive of **Clōth*, an Irish derivative of South-British *Clōta*, from **Cloutā*. This borrowing must have been made before the Britannic change of *ō* > *ū* ; i.e. before the end of the third century, according to Jackson 1953, p. 321.

Crogreth is traceable to two parent-Celtic words : **croucā* ('hump' or 'heap'), an A-stem ; and **ratis* ('fern'), an I-stem. (See 47a, and note.) In its context, each of its elements is in the genitive case. There are two alternative interpretations.

(1) In O.I., **croucā* became *crōch* (> *cruach*), and *crog* could be explained as a manner of writing the Irish *crōch* ; *croch* is the reading of the B manuscripts. (See p. 126) The genitive of O.I. *crōch* would have been *crōiche*. **Ratis* became in O.I. *raith*, the genitive of which was *ratho* > *ratha*. *Raith* was the basis of the district-name of Rannoch. The substitution of nominative for genitive cases would be contrary to Adomnan's custom (cf. *bellum Cule-drebene* and *bellum quod scotice dicitur Onde-mmōne* in 17b).

(2) In S.B., **croucā* became **crōc-* > **crūc-* > *crūg*. (These British sound-changes, and their dates, are discussed in Jackson 1953, §§ 22, 142.) If *crogreth* was an Irish attempt to spell a North-British name, it would show that N.B. *crōg* then retained the long *o* that before Adomnan's time had in South British changed to long *ū* (cf. Jackson 1955, p. 165) ; and that the second *c* of *crōc-* had become a voiced stop (*g*) through normal British lenition. This would be the only instance in Adomnan of a non-spirant *g* preceded by a vowel. The spelling with *g* instead of *c* is unusual (Thurneysen 1946, p. 22), and might result from the attempt to write a foreign sound. *Reth*, from **ratis*, would be an instance of *i*-affected *a* in North British ; cf. *Emchat*(*h*) below. The final *th* would be explained as a substitution of Irish lenited *t* for British *t* > *d* (see above).

The second interpretation, rather than the first, seems to be justified by the evidence. If *Crogreth* was a spelling of a North-British name, the absence of genitive forms would create no difficulty, since there was no case-inflexion in North-British speech.

Emchat 115a, or *Emchath* 114b, is a hibernicization of a North-British derivative of a name identical with the Gallic *Ambicatus*, a U-stem. In South British, the prefix *ambi-* lost its final vowel, and became *am-* without *i-* affection (Jackson 1953, pp. 580–1). The same prefix in Irish was *embi-*, and that had become *imbi-* two centuries before the time when Adomnan wrote (Jackson 1953, pp. 132, 143). *Imbi-* became *imb-* > *imm,-* and *imm* did not later become *emm*. (See Thurneysen 1946, § 841). It seems to follow that the *Em-* of *Emchat(h)* was derived from North-British speech ; that the final vowel of *ambi-* had remained in North British long enough to affect the *a* ; and that the *e* of *Emchat(h)* is an instance of the *i*-affection of *a* in the North-British language.

Geonae cohortis 34b. See p. 156.

The name that Adomnan latinizes as Miathi (*Miat(h)orum*, 18a, 19a) may have been, and therefore probably was, a survival of Dio's Maiatai, one of the tribal groups with which the Romans negotiated in the beginning of the third century. If *Miathi* represents a survival of the word *Maiatai*, *th* would be the Irish lenition of *t*.

Nes is the Irish river-name implied by Adomnan's Latin forms, for the river Ness in the ' province of the Picts '. (See p. 141.) We must assume that there was a similar name in North British for that river.

Roderc 21b, 22a, is a name given by Adomnan probably in its Irish form, with stress on the first syllable. The *rc* (not *rch*) is either Irish, or North British. This man was a king of Dumbarton, and his language would presumably have been Cumbrian. The name in South British appears as *Riderch'*.

Tarain 71a is a North-British man's-name ; cf. the Gallic Taranis, a thunder-god. But the alternative spelling *Tarachin* (for *Taraïn*) in the source of A.U. and T. suggests that the *i* was syllabic, and not merely a palatal glide.

Tothail 21b is an Irish genitive of *Tōthal* > *Túathal*. A South-British form of the name was *Tutagual*. The B manuscripts read *Totail*, and that might have been Adomnan's spelling.

Virolec 115a appears to be a compound of **wīro-* ' true ' (Welsh *gwir*) and **liccā* > N.B. *lecc* (Welsh *llech*) ' flat stone ' (an A-stem). The retention of a compositional form *Viro-* is noteworthy. Initial *V-* in Adomnan regularly indicates a British or North-British name.

If *Vigeno* is the true reading in the story added in the B manuscripts (see under 68a), it would point to a North-British name *Vigen*.

ADOMNAN'S LATIN COMPOSITION

When the text of A is supported by the B manuscripts, there is a strong presumption that it represents the actual words of Adomnan. His Latin has some pronounced characteristics. He creates difficulty for his readers or hearers by his trick of showing the grammatical connexion between words through their endings, or grammatical forms, somewhat in the manner of Latin verse, instead of through the natural order of the words in prose. His sentences are often rather intricate, but never unintelligible ; and with familiarity the intricacy becomes less disconcerting.

Adomnan has also a habit of avoiding the repetition of a word by substituting for it another word of similar meaning, and in some cases a diminutive. This creates real ambiguity, since a word used as a synonym may not retain its own proper meaning. He uses many words for ' ship ', perhaps four times as many as the types of ship that they denote.

In general, Adomnan's writing shows that his knowledge of Latin was wide and scholarly. Occasionally, he uses words that are unfamiliar to us, either because they were taken from a foreign source (e.g. *parasticia*), or because they had become distorted in monastic use (e.g. *genucla*).

There are occasional instances of confusion between the uses of pluperfect and preterite or imperfect tenses (cf. also Geyer 1898, p. 472). In relation to past time, as well as to present time, Adomnan uses the Latin present participle freely, in the sense of a subordinate clause, or of a co-ordinate sentence. There are instances of this usage in 128a and 131b. Adomnan's historic present tenses are synonymous with past tenses, and to render them, as Fowler does, by present tenses, is mistranslation. So for example in 78b, . . . *videns, confirmans . . . conpellat . . . ut nullo modo . . . dubitarent*, the participles, like the principal verb, are in the historic present ; and *confirmans* is construed with a sequent past subjunctive ; the meaning is ' . . . addressed them . . . encouraging them not to doubt '.

Some Irish idioms affected Adomnan, as well as other Irish writers of Latin. Thus we find *nobīscum* 100b, for O.I. *linn* ; *belligeratio* 112b, 114ab, for *cath* ' battalion ' ; *erat Columbanus qui* 98a ; *inesse*, frequently, for *bith and* (cf. Geyer 1898, p. 467) ; *apud* 19b, 20a, for *la* ; *alius*, in the sense of O.I. *alaile* (cf. Geyer 1898, p. 238).

ACCENTS

In Irish manuscripts of the Old-Irish period, accents were occasionally placed above long vowels, under the main word-stress ; and above half-long vowels, under secondary stress. Very few accents were written above Irish words, by the text hand of A : *cúle* 4a, *sétni* 18a, *coire salcháin* 46b, *aithche* 64a, *librán* 91b, *snám luthir* 98a, *tómme* 132a. Above Latin words, an accent in A indicates length of vowel or a corresponding quality of sound. It occurs most often above monosyllables that were originally long ; e.g. *me, te, se, nos, vos, mi, hic, sic, o, os, re* ; and above the unstressed *-is* of datives and ablatives plural, but never above *-iis*, and never in the contracted form *sc~is* for *sanctis*. In the Latin dative *brendeno* 29b an accent has been written by the text hand above *r*, because there was not enough room for it above the *en*-ligature. This appears to be the only accent in the text hand of A that may be intended to indicate stress : the first syllable was stressed, because the second syllable was short (p. 134). In some later Irish manuscripts an accent was occasionally written over the *e* of the

Irish form of the name, *Brenann*, but the length of that vowel seems to need confirmation. In *cór* 94b, and the *án* of *ánnon* 95b, the text hand seems to have marked with an accent a short monosyllable.

B1 and B2 occasionally use accents that may be length-accents derived from an Irish exemplar ; e.g. the Irish genitive *fendé*. Both manuscripts mark with an accent some Latin vocalic monosyllables (*á*, *ó*). In B1 an accent is very often placed above the vowel of a stressed syllable in a Latin word, to indicate word-stress ; and also on some vowels of Irish names, apparently at random, without regard to the Irish pronunciation. These stress-accents were very probably supplied by the scribe of B1. The accents of B1 and B2 are of little significance, except where they show survival of Irish influence. B1 and B2 frequently mark doubled vowels with a double accent, which ought to indicate diaeresis ; since Anglo-Norman manuscripts of the twelfth century and later marked diaeresis in that way. But instances of this in Irish names were more probably derived ultimately from an Irish manuscript, in which the doubled vowel would have indicated length.

In this edition, accents that we believe were intended by the writers to indicate length of vowel are printed over the vowel (e.g. *Cúle*, *dictís*, in A) ; those that we believe were intended (rightly or wrongly) to mark stress are printed after the vowel (e.g. *Bre'ndeno* in A ; *onde'mone*, *occe'ani*, in B1). Double accents over double vowels are printed as a mark of diaeresis above the first vowel (e.g. from B1 B2, *filü* for Latin *filii* ; and *böo*, *mäar*, for Irish *bó*, *már*. Cf. from B2, *locdëe* for *Locdé*, and *conrü* for *Conrí* in Appendix).

All accents that were written in A by the text hand are retained in our text. Accents that were added in A by later hands are given in our notes. The presence or absence of accents in the B manuscripts is noted only (1) where the word has to be noted for some other reason ; (2) very occasionally, where e.g. a stress-accent in one of the B manuscripts affects the sense of a Latin word ; (3) in all proper names.

In transcribing or directly quoting from any manuscript we

retain the accents that occur in the manuscript, and do not add any accents. When we think it necessary to show that a vowel was long, although it has no mark of length in the manuscript, we place above it the conventional macron ($^-$) : e.g. *Nēllis* for A's *nellis*.

Except when we are transcribing or directly quoting from a manuscript, we use an acute accent, placed above, to mark long vowels in Irish words, and leave half-long vowels unaccented. Thus in the translation and elsewhere we write ' Néll ' or ' Níall ' ; and ' Adomnan ', not ' Adomnán '.

THE WRITING OF MANUSCRIPT A

Manuscript A is described in Lowe 1956, p. 45 ; cf. ibid. p. 61. Full-size facsimiles of the handwriting are given in Lowe 1935, facing p. xii (6ab) ; Lowe 1956, no. 998 (part of 17ab) ; Lindsay 1910, plate II (upper part of 108ab). In order to show how the insertion in 108a was made, we have given a facsimile of the whole page on a reduced scale. We give also nearly full-size facsimiles of parts of 14a, 55a, and 93a.

When we describe as ' parchment ' the material on which the manuscript was written, we use that term in its wider sense, not intending to specify the nature of the prepared skin. Reeves said that it was ' young goat-skin ' ; Lowe says that it is ' vellum ', or calf-skin.

The manuscript consists of 69 folios, of which the first 60 (pp. 1 to 120) form five quires of twelve folios. Quire-numbers *i* to *v* have been added in long shapeless letters, in the bottom margins of pages 24, 48, 72, 96, and 120. Punctures, and lines impressed with a hard point, were used to define the columns and to guide the lines of writing. The pages were normally ruled for 28 lines. The last three folios of the fourth quire (pp. 91–6) have 30 lines, closely spaced. In the fifth quire, the four central folios (pp. 105–12) have 27 lines ; so also do pages 121–6, but their lines are more widely spaced. Pages 127–34 have only 26 lines. The following folio (pp. 135, 136) has 27 lines.

Ornamental initials at the beginnings of chapters, and minor decorated initials within the chapters, were illumined with red or yellow colours. Accents and other signs were sometimes duplicated in red ink. The ornamental and decorated letters were drawn or written by the writer of manuscript A. The decorated *Q* at the top of 24b was made before the word *demoraretur* was written in the third line. The initial letters of chapters extend through two or three lines, or more, and the writing is adjusted to fit them.

Titles, or chapter-headings, above the chapters, were written in red ink, and so were often postponed until it was convenient to use red ink. Thus, for instance, in 54b, a space of three lines had been left for a title that actually occupied four ; and in 122b, a title of five lines was squeezed into the space of four. In 68a, a space of $3\frac{1}{2}$ lines was left for the title, and would have been enough for its first sentence. Actually five lines were needed, and the title spread into the lower margin, and into the upper margin of 68b. In 116a, three lines at the top of the column had been left blank. The title completely filled that space, and its last four letters were written between the first and second lines of the chapter.

In Lindsay 1910, pp. 1–4, A is described as a majuscule manuscript ('insular half-uncial', Lindsay 1915, p. 487). The lettering is, on a larger scale, identical with that of the insertion in 108a, and of *plaustro vectus* in 124b ; and if that is an early Irish minuscule (cf. Lindsay 1910, pp. 2–3), it is reasonable to regard the text of A as written in large-scale early Irish minuscule. Compare Lowe 1956, p. 45, and 1935, pp. xi–xii.

The *et*-sign (7), universal in later Irish minuscule manuscripts, is not used in A.

The Irish minuscule letters are in general derived from Latin demi-uncials ; and not directly from uncials. But the round forms of *d* and *s* that occur in manuscript A are uncial in origin. Some forms of *m*, *n*, *r*, and probably of *a*, that are derived from uncial forms, are occasionally written at the beginnings of words, or after a decorated initial. Two medial letters *r* resembling uncial *r* may have resulted from alteration (25a15, 116a16).

The letters *f* and straight *s*, occasionally *p*, *r* (106a5, 122a9), *m* and *n*, have, in addition to their usual Irish forms, also cursive forms, in which the writer, after making a down-stroke, makes an up-stroke without lifting the pen. The letter *z* also appears to have been written cursively, or without lifting the pen. A cursive final *m*, in an *em*-ligature, occurs in 93a17. A cursive *s* sometimes becomes the basis of a decorative initial letter.

The writing varies in its relation to the ruled lines, which are so faint as to be seldom seen in facsimiles. When we speak of ' upper ' and ' lower ' lines, we mean the upper and lower levels of the letters *m* and *n*, as normally written.

Down-strokes that begin letters, on or above the upper line, and also the second down-stroke of *u*, are embellished with a ' triangular top ', a thickening formed on the left side in an upward direction, before the downward stroke. This characteristic feature of early Irish writing will be seen in any of the facsimiles. In some large initial letters, the triangular top is artificially drawn in outline.

Words are as a rule separated by spaces ; but prepositions are apt to be attached to the words that follow them, and prefixes are often separated from the verbs to which they belong. No real confusion appears to have resulted from these and other dislocations, and in our text we have substituted the normal divisions of words.

Within words or parts of words, letters make contact or do not make contact with one another, according to a system that results primarily from their shapes. The letters *a c l r x*, and *z*, have a projecting toe which permits contact with a following letter, sometimes even with the initial letter of the following word, over a blank space. The letters *i h m n u* and straight *d* have no such forward-pointing toe, and normally do not touch the following letter. Thus *cl* is distinguished from straight *d*, since *cl* is joined to a following letter, and *d* is not (cf. *tudicla* 93b12). Similarly *r* is joined to a following letter, while *n* is not. In 55a, *xu* cannot stand for *duodecim* (xii), as Reeves thought, but must stand for *quindecim* (xv). The letters *g* and *t* have cross-bars that may make contact with letters on either side. The contacts of letters are not to be regarded as cursive features. In the group *lb*, the *l* does not touch the *b* in 116b22 and 134b15; and in 127a26, *bb* has apparently been written in error for *lb*, and corrected at the time of writing. These instances suggest that *lb* and *bb* were then already liable to be confused.

The most usual form of *a* in the manuscript is derived from demi-uncial script. Among the several forms of *a* used initially, some have the oblique stroke projecting above the loop, and retain in this closer resemblance to the uncial *a* (e.g. 108a4, 7a3); in other cases, the projection is vertical (e.g. 14a11; 67b3).

The variations of the letter include some instances of an open *a* (as in 115b14). These hardly ever occur except in subscript position, and in the group *ae*. There is an instance of subscript *a* in 93a15.

Monosyllabic *ae* is written *ae* (as in 93a18); ligature of *a* with *e* (29a26, 39a22, 91b23, 111b27, 131b13); open *a* attached to *e* (as in 93a16); half of open *a*, a mere hook, attached before *e* (as in 93a19); or a hook or loop below *e* (as in 14a4). In the Irish river-name *loch dae* 5b, an open *a* is attached to *e* (see pp. 130, 142). Disyllabic *ae* is not written with any ligature (see 104b, note). In *eneus* 49b, 99a, the initial syllable *a* has been lost in speech.

The letters *e* and *f* have projecting tongues. The tongue of *f* is normally a little above the lower line of writing, and may touch a following letter, but does not form a ligature with it. The tongue of *e* is normally a little lower than the upper line of writing, and touches the following letter. But when the following letter is *m*, *n*, *p*, *r*, or straight *s*, a ligature is commonly formed: instead of the tongue of the *e* and the triangular top of the following letter, there is only a quite short serif. In these ligatures the *e* has its elongated form. When the *e* is followed by *t* or *g*, the *e* is rounder, and the tongue and cross-bar coalesce. More frequently, in the group *et* the tongue coalesces with the lower stroke of the *t*, and the bar of the *t* becomes a stroke often running obliquely upwards : this was a traditional cursive form. Ligatures of *e* with *i* and *u* are not found in this manuscript.

The letter *i* varies in length, shape and position, mainly for calligraphic reasons. No distinction is made between its phonetic values. Subscript *i*, usually curved, is written to save space, at the ends of lines (e.g. in *revelationi|bus*, 6a10). Superscript *i* over *q* stands for *ui* (e.g. *qui* 6a4, *inquiens* 25a17) ; over *p*, it stands for *ri* in *pri|mis*, 80b6, and *pri|mo*, 82b13.

The letter *u* occurs in the normal position very seldom in its *v* form (48a17). In superscript position it is regularly written *v* (e.g. 108a14). Written above *q*, the form is always *v*. The *u* and *v* shapes do not indicate any difference in pronunciation. In a space-saving ligature of *-us*, straight *s* is written in place of the second stroke of *u* ; e.g. *cujus* in 51a17, and *testatus* in 57a16. This ligature was misunderstood by Reeves. It is distinguishable from *is*, since *i* does not protrude, and should not touch a following *s*. (Cf. carefully *primordiis* in 6a16 ; Lowe 1935, facing p. xii.)

The bow of *p* springs from the shaft, and curves downward from the upper almost to the lower line, where it is met, or nearly met, by a short third stroke from the left. The loop is not closed. Substituted for this third stroke of the pen, a transverse or oblique line across the shaft, meeting or continuing the second stroke, changed the *p* to the Irish symbol for *pro*.

The writer of A punctuated the text with medial points, which marked pauses of various lengths, and answered the purpose of our comma, semi-colon, and full stop. Many pauses were left unmarked. The medial point was frequently lowered after the tongue of *e*, and after straight *s*.

These punctuation marks show the characteristic cutting of the text hand's pens. The marks are usually somewhat diamond-shaped, and tend to project at the lower corner where the pen was lifted. Occasionally they are shaped like a very small 7 (e.g. 121b27). The writer did not use the larger and more angular 7-sign that is sometimes found in Irish manuscripts at the ends of sections. In a demi-uncial Irish copy of the Gospels, written in the seventh century, the end of one section is marked by a whole line of 7-shaped signs, graduated in size, the smallest of which closely resemble those in manuscript A (T.C.D. 55 (A.IV.15) ; Lowe 1935, no. 271).

In manuscript A, the end of a chapter, or of a section, and sometimes of a chapter-heading, was marked with two points, the second of which was commonly elongated, and finished with a rising line. (At the time when A was written, the up-turned final stroke had no tonal significance.) The writer sometimes varied this two-point sign, usually by repeating it, or doubling its first point. When two or more points are used in this way, we represent them in our transcript by two full stops.

In A, words that run on from one line to the next are not connected by any hyphen. The double hyphen in *defu=isset* 7ab, if it were attributable to the text hand, would be a unique exception.

Marks of transposition by the text hand appear in 128b. The writer made corrections by erasure, or without erasure (as in 49a12), and not by *puncta delentia*.

Irish words quoted in manuscript A are commonly marked by roughly-horizontal short strokes or over-dashes, approximately one over every syllable. These have sometimes been misread as accents or as abbreviation-marks. These over-dashes have no bearing upon the spelling of the words over which they stand, but merely serve the same purpose as italicization in modern type. In the Book of Armagh acute accents answer the same purpose. (Compare Lindsay 1923, p. 19.)

The abbreviation-sign, or ' bar ', in manuscript A is sometimes confusable with the over-dash, but as a rule it is more carefully made. It is a curved horizontal stroke, is heaviest at the left, and tapers upwards to the right. It thus differs from the accent, which is thin at the left, mounts in a curve

N

opposite to the curve of the bar, and is heaviest at the right.
In A, the bar stands for *n* in *i* ~ only. It never stands for *m*.
When the bar needs to be shown, we represent it by a con-
ventional tilde (~) after the letter over which it is written.

The *m*-sign stands for *m* after the vowel over which it is
written. It is a space-saving sign, not a contraction. It is a
cursive *m*, in a horizontal position ; but was derived from the
space-saving *m* written downwards, at the end of a line.
(Compare Lindsay 1915, pp. 342–5.) In *sanctus* and *sancti*,
4a12, 108a3 and 4, the *m*-sign is used arbitrarily as a substitute
for an abbreviation bar.

Accents, bars, and *m*-signs, are frequently repeated in red
ink, in manuscript A.

The *nomina sacra* are written in the usual contractions :
ds ~ ' Deus ', inflected *di* ~ , *do* ~ , *dm* ~ ; but *deum* for a well-
god is written in full, 61b. *ih* ~ *s* ' Jesus ', inflected *ih* ~ *u*
(genitive and ablative). *xp* ~ *s* ' Christus ', inflected *xp* ~ *i*,
xp ~ *o*, *xp* ~ *m*. *dn* ~ *s* ' Dominus ', inflected *dn* ~ *i*, *dn* ~ *m*, *dn* ~ *o* ;
but *dominus* for a secular lord is written in full, 88ab. *sp* ~ *s*
' Spiritus ', inflected *sp* ~ *ui*, *sp* ~ *m*, *sp* ~ *u* ; the same contraction is used for the human spirit. *sc* ~ *s* ' Sanctus ', fully
inflected.

In certain words, abbreviations by suspension occur : *apo* ~ *s*
' apostolum ' 45a9; *et ce* ~ *t* ' et cetera ' 8b14; *co* ~ *l* ' Columbae'
14a17 ; *epi* ~ *s* ' episcopus ' 53b12, 113b21, ' episcopi ' 113a11 ;
fi ~ ' filius ' 20a28 ; *n* ~ *o* ' nomen ' 71a19, 132a7, ' nomine '
22a27 ; *pa* ~ *s* ' passus ' 39b6 ; *te* ~ *m* ' tempore '.

The other abbreviations used in A are given below. We
have been able to add only a few that are not included in
Lindsay 1910, pp. 3–4. We give references to column and line
for symbols that occur seldom in A, or that are difficult to
describe without the help of our facsimile pages.

a ~ ' aut ' 61b19 ; *b* ~ ' bene- ' 68a28 ; *b* : ' -bus ' ;
d ~ *r* ' dicitur ' ; *dc* ~ *s* ' dicens ' 108a6 ; *e* ~ *e* ' esse ' ; *h* ~
' haec ' ; *h·* ' hoc ' (see 108a24, and cf. 65a footnote) ; *h* with
a tag to the right, ' autem ' (see 108a24) ; *i* ~ ' in, in- ' ; *l* ~
' vel ' 80b27 ; *n* ~ ' non ' ; *n* ~ *c* ' nunc ' ; *no* ~ *e* ' nomine ' ;

n : ' nus ' 5a22, 81b3 ; *p* ~ ' prae, prae-, pre- ' (cf. *p* ~ *tium*
91b22, *p* ~ *spit* ~ *o* 6a4 ,*dep* ~ *catio* 113b12. The preposition and
prefix are most commonly written in full. In 27b4, *p* ~ stands
for the adverb. *p* ~ *ter* stands for ' praeter-') ; *p* with a tag to
the right, ' per, per- ' (see 108a13, 15, 19, 20, 23. The same
symbol occurs in *super* 119b13) ; *p* in a modified form, with a
line through the shaft, ' pro, pro- ' (see p. 168, and 93a27,
108a5, 117a footnote. In three instances in which the transverse line is horizontal, a downward hook was later added to
its left end by an emender, as if to avoid confusion with the
continental symbol for *per* : 45b, 87b, 91b. In 9b6, a hooked
transverse stroke across the shaft of *p* was written perhaps by
the text hand); *p*ⁱ 'pri-'; *p*ᵒ 'post'; *p*ᵒ*ea* 'postea' 119b12;
q ~ 'quae'; *q* : '-que'; *q* :. 'quae'; *q*; '-que' (120b19;
the tail of the ; touches the shaft of the *q* in 110a13, 113a4,
114b20, 125a21) ; *q* with a hooked down-stroke springing
from the right of the shaft near the lower line and passing to
the left downwards through the middle of the shaft, ' quod '
(see 108a18, 30. The same symbol occurs in *aliquod* 125b24) ;
q with a double-hooked transverse line across the middle of
the shaft (down, across, and down), ' quam ' (the same symbol
occurs in *quamlibet* 104a17) ; *q* with a transverse horizontal
line across the middle of the shaft, tending to rise on the right-
hand side, ' quia ' ; *q*ⁱ ' qui ' ; *q* ~ *m* ' quoniam ' 108a7 ;
q ~ *q* ' quoque ' ; *qs* ~ *i* ' quasi ' 88a1, 122b14 ; *r* ~ ' -rum ' ;
r ~ *t* '-runt ' ; *s* ~ ' sed ' ; *s* ~ *t* ' sunt ' ; *t* with a heavy hook
attached to the right end of the cross-bar, ' -tur ' (see 108a24.
This is a peculiarly Irish symbol) ; *t* ~ *n* ' tamen ' 103a8,
126a4 ; *tm* ~ ' tantum ' ; *v*ₒ ' vero '.

Conventional symbols occur for *autem* (above) ; for *con-*,
an inverted *c* (see 108a25) ; for *ejus*, an open *e* upside-down ;
for *enim*, two minims joined through their middles by a bar ;
for *est*, a colon crossed by a bar (see 108a25).

The Irish symbol for *et* and *ocus*, resembling the figure 7,
is not used in A. The symbols for *quia*, *vel*, and *sed*, in later
Irish writing represented *ar*, *no*, and *acht*, respectively.

Later Additions in Manuscript A

Alterations, mainly of spelling, were entered in the first four quires of manuscript A (1a–96b), in Caroline minuscule writing of the ninth century, in some 'continental centre' (Lowe 1956, p. 45). They were made with very finely cut pens, in ink less black than the ink used by the text hand. The general uniformity of method and lettering suggests that these alterations were made nearly at one time, and in one district. We have designated them as 'm.h.', for 'minuscule hand', without intending to imply that they were all entered by one man. The 2-shaped -*ur* symbol used by m.h. (47a bottom line) probably shows that the writing was later than A.D. 820 (see Lindsay 1915, § 471).

Similar pens and ink were used for corrections and additions in A, that are not letters. These include pointed circumflex accents, usually indicating a long vowel ; and acute accents that often indicate stress. These acute accents have sometimes been mistaken for accents written by the text hand (e.g. *Ernánus* in Thesaurus 1903, p. 274 line 25). Many of the added acute accents are more heavily made at the lower end, and are then easily distinguishable from accents made by the text hand.

Added punctuation in A includes many medial points, used in the manner of modern commas and semi-colons. High points are entered several times in 93a–95a, and with one exception (94a5) appear to mark a major pause between sentences. At the end of a sentence or clause, a medial point, whether added or original, is very often associated with certain added signs, that in similar position occasionally stand alone. These we denominate ' up-signs ' and ' down-signs '.

The rising signs resemble acute accents, placed above and to the right of the point. The down-signs are either (1) an angular virgule, made like a small 7, usually placed below the point, or to the right of it (above it, four times in 86ab) ; or (2) a curved comma-like sign, of varying length, beginning on or just above the lower line of writing, and tapering downward towards the left. Frequently a punctuator formed a down-sign by attaching a downward line to a point made by the text hand.

A few of the curved comma-like signs in A could possibly have been made by the text hand's pen (e.g. 9a26, 37b1). The text hand wrote a similar form in some of the abbreviations of -*que* (see above). It seems probable, however, that all the comma-like signs used in punctuation were later additions. The colour of the ink used might be decisive, but facsimiles are inadequate evidence for difference of colour.

The down-sign is used by the punctuator to mark the end of a sentence ; sometimes it is added to the text hand's end-of-section sign. It is regularly added before a speech or quotation. No distinction seems to be made in use between the virgule and the curved comma, except that the virgule is sometimes preferred at the end of a line. The up-sign marks a lesser stop. It is often used where we might write a semicolon. It is also used to mark off a parenthesis ; or at the end of a sentence that leads up in sense to the sentence that follows ; or merely to introduce emphatically a principal clause. The distinction between down-signs and up-signs seems to have been less grammatical than rhetorical. Further evidence is needed to show whether there is any connexion between these signs and signs used in early Byzantine musical notation. (Compare the comma-like *apostrophos* and the *oxeia*, like an acute accent, illustrated in the *New Oxford History of Music*, II, pp. 36–7 ; those were used to indicate fall and rise in pitch, in the intoning of the Lessons.) Whatever their origin and precise significance may have been, the signs are not used in A with strict consistency.

Up-signs do not appear to have been commonly used in punctuation before the ninth century. They were used by the text hands of some eight-century manuscripts written in the region of St Gall, and in the north of Italy (e.g. in Lowe 1956, no. 909.) Punctuation in the up-and-down system was often added by ninth-century revisers to earlier manuscripts, including many in the St Gall collection (ibid. nos. 893–997).

A number of ninth-century emendations interestingly similar to those in A were made at St Gall in an eighth-century manuscript containing Lives of Saints (ibid. no. 940). The emendations include *u* changed to *o* by bridging (see 14a10), a long vertical *i* drawn through original *e* (a frequent alteration in A, as in Lowe 1956, no. 998), up-signs, virgules, and comma-like down-signs.

There is no evidence that the alterations in A were made in connexion with the making of the shortened continental version of Adomnan (× 872). That version includes parts of the work that the emender did not touch, and omits some parts (including chapter-headings) that received alterations. We have seen (p. 18) that a single copy of A may have been the basis both of the shortened version and of the version represented by P. There is very little evidence that when that copy was made the alterations had already been entered in A. Two texts of the shortened version, L and C (Reeves is silent about S, F, D), read *virtutibus* for Adomnan's *virtutis* in 69a, as does the emender, but their reading could have resulted from independent misunderstandings of Adomnan's text. (Cf. our note on various readings of *de volatus* 85b.) P reads *quod*, not the emender's *quodque*, in 7a. On the whole it seems probable that the alterations were later than the copy.

There are a few early alterations in A that cannot be attributed to m.h. Among these are some instances of a loop made with an exceedingly fine pen, attached to the text hand's *e* to make an *ae* symbol. M.h.'s own loop occurs in a complete *ae* symbol in 29a, and probably, as an addition to the text hand's *e*, in 76a, 62b, 86b, and more doubtfully in 95b : it is an elongated, somewhat pointed, loop, nearly straight on the left side and curved on the right. Three of the possibly-earlier loops are of symmetrical hair-pin shape, touching the *e* at two slightly separated points : 49b14, where the ink seems paler, and the pen finer, than in an alteration by m.h. of *i* to *e* a few lines further on ; 90a8, where the ink seems paler than in an alteration of *e* to *i* in the same word ; and 2a13, where a more rounded hair-pin loop is attached, exceptionally, to the upper part of the *e*. The loop in 90a8 might be by the same pen that added some long faint rising marks of punctuation, later superseded by shorter and firmer up-signs, in 90a1, 4, 6, 9. A closed loop of rounded form, very fine and faint, is attached to the *e* by a short stalk in 80a6. Most of these forms of loop could be paralleled from continental manuscripts written in pre-Caroline minuscule of the eighth or early ninth century : the hair-pin shape in e.g. Lowe 1956, no. 1021 ; the stalked loop, in the subscript *a* used by a writer of the Laon az- script, in *Palaeographia Latina*, ɪɪ, facsimile I.

Some corrections by erasure may have been later than m.h. ; see notes on *filii* under 56a, and on *reliquiis* under 85b. There are a few alterations of *e* to *i* by erasure in *ebernia* (24a3, 10).

The early-eighth-century date attributed to the writing of A rests on historical grounds (see pp. 103-05). The alterations in A are palaeographical evidence that the manuscript was taken to the continent not later than the early years of the ninth century, perhaps before 800. Where, and exactly when, the alterations were made are problems for palaeographers. The later presence of the manuscript in Reichenau suggests that it may have been taken by the pilgrim road that led to Rome by lake Constance and St Gall (see Lowe 1956, p. v). Why it was taken is a matter for conjecture.

Alio intempore uir beatus.
In mediterranea ebrianie
pante monaſteriodnu quod ſco
tice dici daim maz diuino ſum
danſ nutu pſhi aliquot dṁnona
tur mćhireſ liburt animo uiſi
tane ſnatnſ qui inclonoſhiſ
ſci cenani cćnabio commane
bant Audito q: eiuſ accessu
uniuſhſi undiq: ab ageſluliſ mo
naſteſtio uicinis Cum hiſ qui
ibidṁ in uſhtiſunt congnſħa
ti Cum omni alacritate ſu
um conſequbiſcſ abbaṁn ali
thṁnum ſſco col quaſi ange
lo dṁi obuia ṁnſſi ualum
monaſteſtiu uis animſ pſhi
gunt humiliatiſq: intṁnam

 me
ba
din
tai
ua
bra
dur
In c
tai
uel
qu
occ
ip s
te
pen
con
ac
ppi
ſub

Schaffhausen, Generalia 1, page 14, lines 2–20

ṙeminata contra huius
naturā tᵭᵐ proficia-
ma ṗrᵗa econtra fac at
secundum ᵱᶜ mandatum;
cui cluṙ clonabᵗ quod cū
q: ab eo poꝛtulaueᵗ; ṗed
& qui misi sunt simul hoc
ad cliclénunt dicendo; ṗᶜ
columba qui noꝛ adᵗ̄ cum
hoc miꝗt munᵭᵉ · hoc man
clatū ṗᵭ̄noꝛ clᵗᵘa commͭ̄
claurt ṛᵉᵗᵗᵉ dicenꝛ; homo
illᵉ In omni potᵗᵗᵗa dī con
fidat · Seᵗᵉs eius quamuiꝛ
de mᵭᵗᵉ iunio xu ṗᵗᵗnisiꝛ
dieb: ṙeminata In princi
piꝛ aᵗᵗꝛti mᵭ̄siꝛ mᵗᵗun;
Obsequtuꝛ plebeuꝛ anan
do & ṙᵭninando · & meᵗᵗn
auam ruꝛnaclicto Intᵗ̄ nzo

Schaffhausen, Generalia 1, page 55, lines 7–26

...ationis dificillima contra
...unctionib: & ideo p̄ime
d̄no de angustia ab solu
...tionem dari tibi ... at
...ia & mihi est cogitatio...
... de meus matris pan...
...a ... habebit pro
...tum · hæc dicebat ... il
...ut mulierculis motus mi
...tatione ad ecclesiam cun
... plexit q: ... b: pro ea
...pm de homine natu... exo
at; & post pncationem
...tonum ...sur. ad pria
...pro ... occurrit
... in quibus nunc propter
...· dns ihs de muliere ...
...tus opportune mis...
...ubi ... eam de angus
...liberauit. & pro...

De quo d...
...udicla...
habuent...
qui in ...
...un...

A... yo...
In ...
...un in...
ad eum ...
batur ...
dicebat...
manital...
tebat co...
quibus d...
ad uocan...
eam hac...
...hi tuam...
cans con...
...hunt d...

ruptu caput eius ordinant
benedixerit :· Commeneus in libro
quo derrirtatib: sci columbe ȩpt
sic dixit quod scs columba de aidano
& de posteris eius & de regno suo pfe
tane cecinit dr. In dubitantib.
nieele O aidane qm nullus aduer
tanionu tuonu tibi poterit neq̇ te
ne donec prius enaudulcitiā a
zar inme & inposterior meor pprieu
ergo tu filii commenda utẜipti
filiu & nepotib: & posteris tuis cō
mibdbit ne p̄ consilia mala cono
receptnū regni huis dsnanib: puis
p̄dant In quo cū q̇ bini tempore
malū aduersu me aut adurstuis
cognator meos qui rtunt in hibr
nia geccunt flagillū q causa
tui ab angelo purtuiuī pma
nuū dr rup eos inmagnū plagi
tium uenerunt & con uinon
aure tui ab eis & inimici eo
num uel purtuis eos confor
tabuit :· hr uaticinuū tenpori
b: nortuir opletū = Inbello noth
domnallo brecco nepote aidani
fine causa uastante puincia
domnail nepotis ainmure & ̇
adie illa urq̇ hodie adhuc inpcl
uo rt ab ex tranei q purpinia do
lonir speioni = In curte :·
De angelonū apparatio
ne alicuiup beati buit
uim pēuir

Algo in tempore cum
uir psr in ioua com
monaretur insula qui
dam clepuir monacus bni
to bonis actibus intertur
molgtia connstuir corpo
ris ad extrena psi ductur
ert. quem cum uir usitian
etur in hona sui uistante
extuis paulispsi adlectu
lum eius ad pistus & ei be
neeliceir ocius clomū egne
ditur nolens uielthe mo
ribrem. qui ecele momb
to port sci deelomu recē
rū uiri pnir brten finir
urtam. tū uir pnedicabi
lir inplateola rui deambu
lanr monartui ponnbous
ad cȩlū oculis clurtiur ual
cle obrtu per cetis ammina
batur. qui dam ucro psia
thi aidanus nomine filiu
libin bone in dolir & ne
legiorur homo. qui prolur
cle fnatrub: eapstu ad pur

Schaffhausen, Generalia 1, page 108

Adomnan's Life of Columba

In nomine Jesu Christi
Orditur praefatio [1]

BEATI nostri patroni [2] Christo sufragante vitam
discripturus,[3] fratrum flagitationibus obsecundare volens,
in primís eandem lecturos quosque ammonere procurabo
ut fidem dictís adhibeant conpertís et res magis quam
verba perpendant, quae ut estimo inculta et vilia esse
videntur. Meminerintque regnum dei non in elo-
quentiae exuberantia sed in fidei florulentia constare.
Et nec ob [4] aliqua scoticae [5] vilis videlicet ling[u]ae [6]
aut humana onomata aut gentium obscura locorumve
vocabula, quae ut puto inter alias exterarum [7] gentium
diversas vilescunt linguas, utilium et non sine divina
opitu|latione gestarum dispiciant [8] rerum pronuntia-
tionem.

1b

Sed et hoc lectorem ammonendum putavimus quod
de beatae memoriae viro plura studio brevitatis etiam
memoria digna a nobís sint praetermisa,[9] et quasi pauca
de plurimís ob evitandum fastidium lecturorum sint [10]
craxata.[11] Et hoc ut arbitror quisque haec lecturus forte
annotabit quod minima de maximís per populos [12] fama

---

[1] Instead of this title, B1 reads : *Incipit prologus in vita sancti columbe abbatis* ; and B2, *Incipit prefatio in* [ ] *columbe episcopi.* About eight folios, presumably a quire, are missing from the beginning of B3. Its text begins in the middle of I 3 ; see 15a.

[2] In A, rising punctuation-signs have been added (not in the text hand and not by m.h.) after *patroni, discripturus, volens, procurabo, videntur, exuberantia, constare, lingae, vocabula, linguas* ; and a dot and falling sign after *perpendant.*

[3] discripturus A ; des- B1 B2

[4] ob A B2 ; ab B1

[5] scoticae A ; scottice B1 ; scocie B2

[6] lingae A ; lingue B1 B2

[7] exterarum A B2 ; exterrarum B1

[8] dispiciant A ; des- B1. Missing in B2.

178

In the name of Jesus Christ,
the Preface begins

Wishing to respond to the importunity of the
brothers, with Christ's favour I shall describe the life of
our blessed patron ; and I shall in the first place
endeavour to persuade all who may read it to have faith
in the established facts that I relate, and to regard the
substance rather than the words, which appear, I think,
crude and of little worth. Let them remember that the
kingdom of God inheres not in exuberance of rhetoric,
but in the blossoming of faith. Let them not despise the
publication of deeds that are profitable, and that have
not been accomplished without the help of God, on
account of some unfamiliar words of the Irish tongue, a
poor language, designations of men, or names of tribes
and places ; words that, I suppose, are held to be of no
value, among other different tongues of foreign peoples.

We have thought that the reader should be warned
of this also, that for the sake of brevity, we have left out
many things concerning the man of blessed memory,
even things that were worthy of remembrance ; and that
to avoid cloying the appetite of those who shall read, only
a few things out of very many have been written down.
And every future reader of these things will, I think,
perhaps observe that rumour has spread widely among

---

9 praetermisa A ; s has later been added above the line, before s (m.h.).
pretermissa B1 B2
10 sint A B2 ; sunt B1
11 craxata A ; carraxa'ta B1 ; caraxata B2
12 populos A B1 ; plurimos B2

de eodem beato [1] viro devulgata [2] disperserit ad horum
etiam paucorum conparationem quae nunc breviter
craxare [3] disponimus.

Hinc [4] post hanc primam praefatiunculam de nostri
vocamine praesulis in exordio secunde [5] deo auxiliante
intimare exordiar. .[6] |

2a   In nomine Jesu Christi
                        Secunda [7] praefatio

VIR ERAT vitae venerabilis et beatae memoriae
monasteriorum pater et fundator, cum Jona [8] profeta
omonimon sortitus nomen.[9]   Nam licet diverso trium
diversarum sono linguarum unam tamen eandemque
rem significat hoc quod ebreice [10] dicitur *jona*,[11] grecitas
vero *peristera* [12] vocitat, et latina lingua *columba* nuncupatur.   Tale tantumque vocabulum homini dei non sine
divina inditum [13] providentia creditur.   Nam et juxta
evangeliorum fidem spiritus sanctus super unigenitum
aeterni patris discendisse [14] monstratur in forma illius
aviculae quae columba dicitur.   Unde plerumque [in
2b s]acrosanctis [15] librís co|lumba mistice spiritum sanctum

    [1] beato A. Omitted in B1 B2.
    [2] devulgata A ; div- B1 B2
    [3] craxare A ; caraxa're B1 ; caraxare B2
    [4] hinc A B2 ; hinc etiam B1
    [5] secunde A B1 B2
    [6] *exordiar*, in A, is followed by the double dot that marks the end of a
section. The last two lines of 1b are left blank.
    [7] secunda A ; secunda o'ritur B1 ; secunda orditur B2
    [8] iona A B2 ; ioná B1
    [9] nomen A B1 ; nomine B2
    [10] ebreice A ; the second *e* has been altered later to *ae*, with a very fine
pen. ebra'ice B1 ; hebraice B2
    [11] iona A B2 ; ioná B1
    [12] πηριστηρα A B1, glossed *peristera* in B1 ; περυστη B2. This is for
περιστερά 'pigeon'. See pp. 309, 462.

the peoples only very little of the very great matters concerning this blessed man, in comparison with even these few things that we propose now briefly to set down.

After this first slight preface I pass on, with God's help, to tell of our superior's name, in the beginning of the second.

In the name of Jesus Christ, the second Preface

There was a man of venerable life and blessed memory, the father and founder of monasteries, who received the same name as the prophet Jonah. For although sounding differently in the three different languages, yet what is pronounced *iona* in Hebrew, and what Greek calls *peristera*, and what in the Latin language is named *columba*, means one and the same thing. So good and great a name is believed not to have been put upon the man of God without divine dispensation. According to the truth of the gospels, moreover, the Holy Spirit is shown to have descended upon the only-begotten son of the eternal Father in the form of that little bird that is called a dove. Hence often in sacred books a dove is understood to signify mystically the Holy Spirit.

---

[13] inditum A ; i'nditum B1 ; indutum B2
[14] discendisse A ; des- B1 B2
[15]]acrosanctis A (*in s* at the beginning of the line in the bottom corner have been obliterated as if by the washing-out of a stain) ; in sacro sanctis B1 ; in sanctis B2

significare dinoscitur. Proinde et salvator in evangelio [1]
suís praecipit [2] discipulís, ut columbarum in corde puro
insertam semplicitatem [3] contenerent.[4] Columba etenim
semplex [5] et innocens est avis. Hoc itaque vocamine et
homo semplex [6] innocensque nuncupari debuit, qui in
sé columbinís moribus spiritui sancto hospitium praebuit.
Cui nomini non inconvenienter congruit illud quod in
proverbiis [7] scriptum est : Melius est nomen bonum
quam divitiae multae. Hic igitur noster praesul non
inmerito non solum a diebus infantiae hoc vocabulo deo
donante adornatus proprio ditatus est, sed etiam
3a praemisís [8] multorum cyclís annorum ante suae nati|vi-
tatis diem cuidam Christi militi spiritu revelante sancto [9]
quasi filius repromisionis [10] mirabili profetatione nominatus est. Nam quidam proselytus brito [11] homo sanctus
sancti Patricii episcopi discipulus Maucteus [12] nomine ita
de nostro profetizavit patrono sicuti nobís ab antiquís
traditum expertís conpertum habetur. ' In novissimís '
ait ' saeculi temporibus filius nasciturus est cujus nomen
Columba per omnes insularum ociani [13] provincias devulgabitur [14] notum, novissimaque orbis tempora clare
inlustrabit. Mei et ipsius duorum monasteriolorum
agelluli unius sepisculae [15] intervallo disterminabuntur.
Homo [16] valde deo carus et grandis coram ipso meriti '.[17]

1 *evangelio*. Vulgate, Matt. x. 16
2 praecipit A ; pre'cipit B1 ; precepit B2
3 semplicitatem A ; simplicitatem B1 ; simplicitate B2
4 contenerent A ; contine'rent B1 ; continerent B2
5 6 semplex A ; simplex B1 B2
7 *proverbiis*. Vulgate, Prov. xxii. 1
8 praemisís A, with a minuscule *s* later added above the line, before the
first *s*. premissis B1 B2
9 spiritu revelante sancto A B2 ; the same in B1, but with transposition
signs, probably entered by the text hand, before *spiritu* and above *sancto*,
so as to read : *sancto spiritu revelante.*
10 repromisionis A ; a faint round *s* has been added later above the line,
before the first *s*, with a fine pen. repromissionis B1 B2

Similarly in the gospel, the Saviour himself bade his disciples to have within them the simplicity implanted in the pure heart of doves. For indeed the dove is a simple and innocent bird. Therefore a simple and innocent person also was rightly called by this name, since he with dovelike disposition offered to the Holy Spirit a dwelling in himself. This name aptly fits what is written in the Book of Proverbs, ' Better is a good name than many riches '. Not only was this our superior by God's gift worthily enriched from the days of his infancy with the adornment of this proper name, but also, many revolving years before the day of his birth, by revelation of the Holy Spirit to a soldier of Christ, he was named as a son of promise in a miraculous prophecy. For it is an accepted fact passed down to us from ancient men who knew of it that a certain British stranger, a holy man, a disciple of the holy bishop Patrick, called Maucte, prophesied thus of our patron, saying : ' In the last years of the world a son will be born, whose name Columba will become famous through all the provinces of the islands of Ocean, and will brightly illumine the latest years of the earth. The fields of our two monasteries, mine and his, will be separated by the width of one small hedge : a man very dear to God, and of high merit in his sight.'

---

[11] brito A ; bri'tto B1 ; britto B2
[12] maucteus A ; ma'cteus B1 ; macteus B2. This was Móchta, the abbot of Louth, whose death is entered in A.U. 534=535.
[13] ociani A ; the first i has been altered later to e, by a minuscule hand with a fine pen. occe'ani B1 ; occeani B2
[14] devulgabitur A ; the e has been altered later to i with a fine pen. di- B1 B2
[15] sepisculae A ; epi'scule B1 ; sepiscule B2
[16] Homo A ; homo B1 ; et ille homo B2
[17] meriti A B1 ; erit B2

3b   Hujus [1] igitur nostri Columbae | vitam et mores
discribens [2] in primís brevi sermonis textu in quantum
valuero strictim conpraehendam et ante lectoris oculos
sanctam ejus conversationem pariter exponam ; sed et
de miraculís ejus succincte quaedam quasi legentibus
avide praegustanda [3] ponam, quae tamen inferius per
tris [4] divisa libros plenius explicabuntur ; quorum
primus profeticas revelationes, secundus vero divinas per
ipsum virtutes effectas, tertius angelicas apparationes [5]
contenebit [6] et quasdam super hominem dei caelestis
claritudinis manifestation[e]s. [7] Nemo itaque me de hoc
tam praedicabili viro aut mentitum estimet aut quasi
quaedam dubia vel incerta scripturum ; sed ea quae
majorum [8] fideliumque virorum tradita expertorum
4a   cognovi [9] | relatione narraturum et sine ulla ambiguitate
craxaturum [10] sciat, et vel ex hís quae ante nos in-
serta paginís repperire potuimus, vel ex hís quae
auditu ab expertís quibusdam fidelibus antiquís sine
ulla dubitatione narrantibus diligentius sciscitantes
didicimus.

[1] *Hujus* begins a new section in A B1 B2.
[2] discribens A ; des- B1 B2
[3] praegustanda A ; pregustando B1 ; pregustanda B2
[4] tris A ; an *e* has been written later by a m.h. above the *i.*   tres B1 B2
[5] apparationes A ; apparitiones B1 B2
[6] contenebit A ; -tin- B1 B2
[7] manifestationis A ; the last *i* has later been altered to *e* (m.h.).
manifestationes B1 B2. A's reading is a scribal error.
[8] *majorum.* Here *majores*, like O.I. *sruithi*, may mean either ' predecessors ' or ' elders '.
[9] cognovi A B1 B2. Reeves 1857, p. 8, rendered this *congrua*, and noted
that it was not legible in A. The bottom corner of this folio (3b, 4a) has been
stained, and is slightly reinforced, perhaps with injury to some letters. The
first *a* of *tra/dita* (3b27), and the *gnovi* of *cognovi* (3b28), and the *qu*
of *quaedam* (3b24), have apparently been written later, and certainly not
by the text hand, but very possibly over traces of letters written by the text
hand. The shortened version (derived from A) in L, C, F, S, reads *cognovi* ;
so also P. D reads *congruo.* Stephen White transcribed *congrua.*
[10] craxaturum A ; caraxaturum B1 B2

In describing the life and character of this our Columba, I shall first in brief language condense in as small space as I can, and at the same time bring before the eyes of the reader, his holy way of life ; and shall also set before those that read, as morsels to be eagerly savoured, some instances of his miracles. These things will be more fully disclosed below, divided into three books, of which the first will contain prophetic revelations ; the second, divine miracles effected through him ; the third, appearances of angels, and certain manifestations of heavenly brightness above the man of God. Let not any one suppose that I will write concerning this so memorable man either falsehood, or things that might be doubtful or unsure ; but let him understand that I shall relate what has come to my knowledge through the tradition passed on by our predecessors, and by trustworthy men who knew the facts ; and that I shall set it down unequivocally, and either from among those things that we have been able to find put into writing before our time, or else from among those that we have learned, after diligent inquiry, by hearing them from the lips of certain informed and trustworthy aged men who related them without any hesitation.

o

Sanctus igitur Columba nobilibus fuerat oriundus genitalibus, patrem habens Fedilmithum [1] filium Ferguso,[2] matrem Aethneam [3] nomine, cujus pater latine filius navis dici potest, scotica [4] vero lingua mac naue.[5] Hic anno secundo post Cule-drebinæ [6] bellum, aetatis vero suae xlii,[7] de Scotia ad Brittanniam pro Christo perigrinari volens enavigavit.

4b   Qui et a puero | christiano deditus tirocinio et sapientiae studiis, integritatem corporis et animae puritatem deo donante custodiens, quamvis in terra positus caelestibus sé aptum moribus ostendebat. Erat enim aspectu angelicus sermone nitidus opere sanctus ingenio optimus consilio magnus.[8] Per annos xxxiiii.[9] insulanus miles conversatus [10] nullum etiam unius horae intervallum transire poterat quo non aut orationi aut lectioni [11] vel [12] scriptioni vel etiam alicui operationi incumberet. Jejunationum quoque et vigiliarum indefesís laborationibus sine ulla intermisione [13] die noctuque ita occupatus ut supra humanam possibilitatem unius cujusque pondus specialis videretur operis. Et

5a inter haec omnibus carus | hilarem semper faciem ostendens sanctam, spiritus sancti gaudio in intimís laetificabatur praecordiis. .

[1] fedilmithum A, with five over-dashes ; fedilmithun B1 ; fedilmithum B2.
[2] ferguso A ; fergo's B1 ; fergosi B2
[3] aethneam A ; e'thneam B1 ; ethneam B2
[4] scotica A ; sco'ttica B1 ; scotia B2
[5] mac naue A ; mac naue' B1 ; macnaue B2. The O.I. *nau* means 'boat' (see p. 143).
[6] cúle drebi|næ A, with an accent and four over-dashes ; culedredine B1 ; culedrebine B2. See pp. 71, 140, 143.
[7] xlii A ; quadragesimo secundo B1 B2
[8] *magnus.* The text, in *integritatem corporis* above, and from *in terra* to *magnus*, is verbally derived from the Actus Silvestri ; see Brüning 1917, p. 253, and Colgrave 1940, p. 316.
[9] xxxiiii. A ; triginta iiiior B1 ; triginta quattuor B2

The holy Columba was born of noble parents, having as his father Fedelmith, Fergus's son, and his mother, Ethne by name, whose father may be called in Latin ' son of a ship ', and in the Irish tongue *Mac-naue*. In the second year after the battle of Cul-drebene, the forty-second year of his age, Columba sailed away from Ireland to Britain, wishing to be a pilgrim for Christ.

Devoted even from boyhood to the Christian noviciate and the study of philosophy, preserving by God's favour integrity of body and purity of soul, he showed himself, though placed on earth, ready for the life of heaven ; for he was angelic in aspect, refined in speech, holy in work, excellent in ability, great in counsel. Living as an island soldier for thirty-four years, he could not pass even the space of a single hour without applying himself to prayer, or to reading, or to writing or some kind of work. Also by day and by night, without any inter-mission, he was so occupied with unwearying labours of fasts and vigils that the burden of each several work seemed beyond the strength of man. And with all this he was loving to every one, his holy face ever showed gladness, and he was happy in his inmost heart with the joy of the Holy Spirit.

---

[10] *conversatus.* A punctuation mark (up-sign) after this word is added later (probably in the ninth century), but is intended to show that the sentence does not end here, as Reeves wrongly supposed.

[11] *lectioni.* From *nullum* to *lectioni*, with *incumberet* below, the text is based upon the Life of Martin (Sulpicius Severus, p. 136 ; see Brüning 1917, p. 248).

[12] vel A B1 ; aut B2

[13] intermi|sione A; an *s* has been added by m.h. after the second *i*. intermissione B1 B2

Nunc [1] primi libri kapitulationes ordiuntur.

[6a]   De virtutum miraculís brevis narratio.

[11a]   De sancto Finteno abbate [2] Tailchani [3] filio,
        quomodo de ipso sanctus Columba profetavit.

[14a]   De Erneneo filio Craseni [4] profetia ejus.

[16a]   De adventu Cainnichi [5] quomodo praenuntiavit.

[16b]   De periculo sancti Colmani [6] gente mocu-Sailni
        sancto Columbe revelato.

[17a]   De Cormaco nepote Letha[ni].[7]

[17b–18b]   Profetationes ejus de bellís :

[18b–22a]   De regibus.[8]

[22a]   De duobus puerís [quorum] secundum verbum
        ejus in fine septimanae unus [9] mortuus est.

[22b]   De Colcio filio Aido Draigniche, et de quodam
        occulto matris ipsius peccato.

[23a]   De signo mortis ejusdem viri.[10]

[23b]   Profetia sancti Columbae de Laisrano hortulano.|

5b [24a]   De ceto magno quomodo profetavit.[11]

[25b]   De quodam Baitano qui cum ceterís ad mariti-
        mum remigavit desertum.

---

[1] *Nunc.* From here to *brevis narratio* (6a12), the writing of A is in colour.
B1 omits from *Nunc* to *profetia sancti* (6a8). B2 omits from *Nunc* to *narratio*
(5a8). The items are written continuously in A, and every item begins in
a new line in B2.

[2] abbate A. Omitted in B2.

[3] tailchani A ; talcani B2

[4] craseni A ; crasseni B2

[5] cainnichi A ; cainnechi B2

[6] Colmani A ; columbani B2

[7] letha| A, with three over-dashes ; lethani B2, as in A 17a.

[8] *regibus.* B2 writes [P]*rophetationes* to *regibus* as one item.

[9] *unus,* in A, has been added by the text hand above the line, with a dot
to place it after *septimanae* ; but the missing *quorum* has not been supplied.
A mark above the end of *septimanae* is unintelligible. B2 reads correctly :
De duobus pueris quorum unus secundum verbum ejus in fine septimane mortuus est.
The chapter-heading in A 22a contains *quorum,* but omits *unus.*

[10] *de signo* to *viri.* This item is here entered as a chapter-heading in
A B2 ; but below (23a) the manuscripts (A B1 B3) do not give it as a
separate chapter.

Now the chapter-headings of the first book begin.

[I 1] Summary of miracles of power.

[I 2] Of the abbot Saint Finten, Tailchan's son ; how Saint Columba prophesied concerning him.

[I 3] His prophecy concerning Ernene, Crasen's son.

[I 4] How he foretold the coming of Cainnech.

[I 5] Of the peril of Saint Colman, of the family mocu-Sailni, revealed to Saint Columba.

[I 6] Of Cormac, grandson of Léthan.

[I 7–8] His prophecies concerning battles :

[I 9–15] Concerning kings.

[I 16] Of two boys [of whom], according to his word, one died at the end of a week.

[I 17] Of Colcu, Aid Draigniche's son, and of his mother's hidden sin.

[I 17] Of a portent of the same man's death.

[I 18] Prophecy of Saint Columba concerning Laisran the gardener.

[I 19] How he prophesied concerning a great whale.

[I 20] Of Baitan, who with the others rowed to a desert in the sea.

---

[11] p[ro]|fetavit A ; prophetavit B2. In the facsimiles of A, there is no trace of the tail of the *pro*-sign. It may have been obscured by a small hole in the parchment, before *p*. The hole penetrates thirteen folios, from 1b to 26a. Another small hole, in the upper margin, pierces 1b to 38a.

[26b]   De quodam Nemano ficto penetente [1] qui postea secundum [2] verbum sancti carnem equae furtivae [3] comedit.

[27a]   De illo infelici viro qui cum sua genitrice peccavit.

[28a]   De *.I.* vocali littera quae una in salterio defuit.

[28b]   De libro in ydriam cadente.

[29a]   De corniculo atramenti inclinato.

[29a]   De adventu alicujus Aidani [4] qui jejunium solvit.

[29b]   De aliquo misero viro qui ad fretum clamitabat mox morituro. .

[30a]   De civitate Romaniae partis super quam ignis de celo cicidit.[5]

[31a]   De Laisrano [6] filio Feradaig [7] quomodo manacos[8] probavit in labore.

[31b]   De Fechno Binc.[9]

[32b]   De Cailtano monaco.

[33a]   De duobus perigrinís.[10]

[34b]   De Artbranano sene quem in Scia insula babtizavit.

[35a]   De naviculae transmotatione [11] juxta stagnum Lochdae.[12] |

---

[1] pe|netente A ; the first *e* is not quite visible in the facsimiles. penitente B2

[2] secundum| A ; *-um* is not visible in the facsimiles. secundum B2

[3] furtivae A ; future B2

[4] *Aidani.* In A, some faint letters near the right margin, in this word, and in *jejunium*, have been touched up in modern times ; but there seems to be no reasonable doubt about the readings.

[5] cicidit A ; cecidit B2

[6] laisrano A ; laistrano B2

[7] feradaig A ; feradachi B2

[8] manacos A ;]chus B2

[9] binc A, with one over-dash. The reading of B2 is given in Reeves 1857, p. 456, as *bivi.* In our facsimile of B2, folio 193, the letters *biu* are clearly visible. The fourth letter does not seem to be *i.* It might be the lower part of a *c*, but the upper part is not visible. Fechno's epithet in the text of the chapter, 31b–32b is *sapiens.*

---

10 perigrinís A ; peregrinis sancti viri prophetia B2
11 transmotatione A ; -mut- B2
12 loch dae A, with two over-dashes ; the *a* is open, rather small, and slightly raised. locdëe B2. This place-name is not in the text of 35a. The open *a* caused Reeves to read *diæ*, wrongly. His false reading has misled later writers, including Watson 1926, pp. 50, 438, but Watson gave the correct spelling in MacBain 1922, pp. 42, 147, 194. In Thesaurus 1903, p. 272, the word was spelt correctly, but one of the over-dashes was mis-rendered as a macron above the *a*. With *lōchdae* ' of the black goddess ' as a river-name, cf. *fendæ* ' of the white goddess ', 132a ; see pp. 141-2.

6a [35b] De Gallano filio Fachtni [1] quem daemones rapuere.

[40a] De Lugidio claudo.

[40b] De Enano [2] filio Gruthriche. [3]

[41a] De prespitero qui erat in Triota. [4]

[42a] De Erco furunculo.

[43a] De Cronano poeta.

[43b] De Ronano filio Aido filii Colcen, [5] et Colmano cane [6] filio Aileni, profetia sancti. .

[1] fachtni A ; fachni B2
[2] enano A B2 ; but the name is Nemanus in 40b–41a.
[3] gruthriche A B2, with three over-dashes in A.
[4] triota A ; troita B2, apparently, in a scorched line. Reeves read *trioita* in B2.
[5] colcen A ; colgen B2
[6] colmano cane A ; columbano B2

Incipit primi libri textus
de profeticís revelationibus [1]

De virtutum miraculís brevis narratio

VIR itaque venerandus qualia virtutum documenta
dederit in hujus libelli primordiis secundum nostram
promisam [2] superius promisiunculam [3] breviter sunt
demonstranda.

Diversorum namque infestationes morborum homines in nomine domini Jesu Christi virtute orationum
perpessos sanavit. Daemonumque infestas ipse unus
homo et innumeras contra sé belligerantes catervas
6b occulís corporalibus visas | et incipientes mortiferos super
ejus cenubialem [4] coetum inferre morbos hac nostra de
insula retrotrusas [5] primaria deo auxiliante repulit.
Bestiarum furiosam rabiem partim mortificatione partim
forti repulsione Christo adjuvante conpiscuit.[6] Tumores
quoque fluctuum [7] instar montium aliquando in magna
tempestate consurgentium ipso ocius orante sedati
humiliati [8] sunt. Navisque ipsius in qua et ipse cassu [9]
navigabat tunc temporis facta tranquilitate portum
adpulsa est optatum.[10] In regione [11] Pictorum aliquantís

---

[1] *Incipit* to *revelationibus*, A. Instead of this title, B1 reads : *Hic primus
ordi'tur liber de vita ac mira'culis sanctissimi patris nostri columbe abba'tis ac
sacerdotis.* B2 reads : *Incipit liber de vita et miraculis [beati pa]tris columbe.*
The letters within brackets are given by Reeves 1857, p. 456, but are not
quite visible in our facsimile.

[2] promisam A ; an *s* has been added above, by m.h., before *s.* -miss-
B1 B2

[3] promisiunculam A ; an *s* has been added above by m.h., before *s.*
-miss- B1 B2

[4] cenubialem A ; the *u* has been altered later to *o*, by bridging with a
very faint line. cenobialem B1 B2

[5] retrotrusas A ; retrotrusos B1 ; illegible in our facsimile of B2.

The text of the first book begins :
Of prophetic revelations

[I 1] A summary of miracles of power

What proofs of his powers the venerable man dis-
played must briefly be shown in the beginning of this
book, according to our promise given above.

By virtue of prayers and in the name of the Lord
Jesus Christ he healed people who endured the attacks
of various diseases.

He, one man alone, with God's aid repulsed innumerable hostile bands of demons making war against
him, visible to his bodily eyes, and preparing to inflict
deadly diseases upon his community of monks ; and
they were thrust back from this our principal island.

With Christ's help, he checked the raging fury of
wild beasts, by killing some and strongly repelling
others. Swelling waves also, that once in a great storm
rose like mountains, quickly subsided at his prayer, and
were stilled. And his ship, in which he himself chanced
to be sailing, was at that time, when the calm fell,
carried to the desired haven. On his return from a

---

[6] conpiscuit A ; the first *i* has been altered by m.h. to *e*. *conpe'scuit*
B1 ;]ompescuit B2
[7] fluctuum A ; flu'ctuum maris B1 ; fluctuum [? maris] B2
[8] humiliati A ; m.h. has added *que* above the line. et humiliati B1 B2
[9] cassu A ; the first *s* has later been erased. casu B1 B2
[10] *optatum.* In A, the *p* is abnormally formed, resulting from an alteration, presumably of *b*. The clause is taken from 82a, although it fits better
the sense of 62b.
[11] regione A B1 ; religione B2

diebus manens, inde reversus, ut magos confunderet contra flatus contrarios venti erexit velum ; et ita veloci
7a cursu ejus navicula enatans [1] festinabat | acsi secundum habuisset ventum. Aliis quoque [2] temporibus venti navigantibus contrarii in secundos ipso orante conversi sunt. In eadem supra memorata regione lapidem de flumine candidum detulit quem ad aliquas profuturum benedixit sanitates ; qui lapis contra naturam in aqua intinctus [3] quasi pomum supernatavit. Hoc divinum miraculum coram Brudeo [4] rege et familiaribus ejus factum est. In eadem itidem provincia cujusdam plebei credentis mortuum puerum suscitavit, quod [5] est majoris miraculi, vivumque et incolumem patri et matri adsignavit. Alio in tempore idem vir beatus juvenis diaconus in Ebernia [6] apud Findbarrum [7] sanctum episcopum commanens, cum ad sacrosancta misteria
7b necessarium defu|isset vinum, virtute orationis aquam puram in verum vertit vinum. . Sed et caelestis ingens claritudinis lumen et in noctis tenebrís et in luce diei super eum aliquando quibusdam ex fratribus diversís et separatís vicibus apparuit effussum. . [8] Sanctorum quoque angelorum dulces [9] et suavissimas frequentationes luminosas habere meruit. Quorumdam justorum animas crebro ab angelís ad summa caelorum vehi sancto revelante spiritu videbat. Sed et reproborum alias ad inferna a

[1] enatans A B2 ; in A, an accent has later been added with a fine pen above *e*, to indicate stress. e'natans B1
[2] Aliis quoque A ; Aliisque B1 ?B2
[3] intinctus A ; inti'nctus B1 ; instinctus B2
[4] brudeo A B2 ; bru'deo B1
[5] quod A ; m.h. has added *que*. B1 and B2 omit *quod* to *miraculi*. See 78a–79a.
[6] ebernia A ; an *i* has been written by m.h. above the first *e*. hibernia B1 B2
[7] findbarrum A ; fendbarrum B1 B2. The *e* in B1 has been altered from *i*, perhaps by the text hand.

visit of some days to the district of the Picts, he raised his sail against the blasts of contrary wind, in order to confound the magicians, and so his boat put out and sped on a rapid course as though it had had a following wind.

At other times also, through his prayers, winds unfavourable to voyagers were changed to favourable ones.

In the same district mentioned above, he took a white stone from the river, and blessed it, so that it should effect some cures. Contrary to nature, that stone, when immersed in water, floated like an apple. This divine miracle was performed in the presence of king Brude and his household.

In the same province, he restored to life—and this is a major miracle—the dead son of a believing layman, and gave him back alive and unharmed to his father and mother.

At another time, in his youth, when the blessed man was in Ireland, living as a deacon with the holy bishop Findbarr, and the necessary wine for the most holy mysteries was lacking, by virtue of prayer he changed pure water into true wine.

Sometimes also there appeared to certain of the brothers, on various different occasions, a great light of heavenly brightness poured out upon him, either in the darkness of night or in the light of day.

He was held worthy to receive in shining light the sweet and most pleasant visitations of holy angels.

---

[8] effussum A ; the first *s* has later been erased.   effusum B1 B2
[9] dulces A B2 ; duces B1

daemonibus ferri [1] sepe numero aspiciebat. Plurimorum in carne mortali adhuc conversantium futura plerumque praenuntiabat [2] merita, aliorum laeta, aliorum tristia.[3] In bellorumque terrificís fragoribus hoc a deo virtute

8a orationum inpetravit,[4] ut alii | reges victi et alii regnatores efficerentur victores. Hoc tale praevilegium [5] non tantum in hac praesenti [6] vita conversanti, sed etiam post ejus de carne transitum, quasi cuidam victoriali et fortissimo propugnatori a deo omnium sanctorum condonatum est honorificatore.

Hujus talis honorificantiae [7] viro honorabili ab omnipotente [8] caelitus conlatae etiam unum proferemus exemplum, quod Ossualdo [9] regnatori saxonico pridie quam contra Catlonem [10] Britonum regem fortissimum proeliaretur ostensum erat. Nam cum idem Ossualdus [11] rex esset in procinctu belli castrametatus quadam die in sua papillione supra pulvillum dormiens sanctum Columbam in visu videt forma coruscantem [12] angelica cujus alta proceritas vertice nubes tangere videbatur.

8b Qui scilicet | vir beatus suum regi proprium revelans nomen in medio castrorum stans eadem castra, excepta quadam parva extremitate, sui protegebat fulgida veste. Et haec confirmatoria contulit verba, eadem scilicet quae dominus ad Jesue bén Nun [13] ante transitum Jordanis

---

[1] ferri A ; ferre B1 B2

[2] praenuntiabat A ; pronunciabat B1 ; prenuntiabat B2

[3] aliorum tristitia A ; the first *ti* has later been rubbed out with moisture. et aliorum tristia B1 B2

[4] inpetravit A ; impetravit B1 ; imprecavit B2

[5] praevilegium A ; the *ae* symbol has been altered later to *i*, by a perpendicular line drawn with a fine pen. pri- B1 B2

[6] hac praesenti A ; presenti hac B1 ; hac presenti B2

[7] honorificantiae A ; honorificentie B1 B2

[8] *omnipotente*. In A, there is an apparently meaningless dot above the tongue of the final *e* ; and so also in the loop of the *b* of *nubes*, at the end of the column.

[9] ossualdo A ; oswaldo B1 B2

Often, by revelation of the Holy Spirit, he saw the souls of just men borne by angels to the height of heaven ; and time and again he beheld other souls of the wicked being carried to hell by demons.

Very often he foretold the future rewards of many who still lived in mortal flesh, of some happy, of others sad.

And in the terrible crashings of battles, by virtue of prayer he obtained from God that some kings were conquered, and other rulers were conquerors. This special favour was bestowed by God, who honours all saints, on him, not only while he continued in this present life, but also after his departure from the flesh, as on a triumphant and powerful champion.

Of this special honour, conferred by the Almighty from on high upon the honourable man, we shall offer one more example, that was shown to Oswald, the English ruler, on the day before he fought against Catlon, a mighty king of the Britons. One day when king Oswald was encamped in readiness for battle, sleeping on his pillow in his tent he saw in a vision Saint Columba, radiant in angelic form, whose lofty height seemed with its head to touch the clouds. The blessed man revealed his own name to the king, and standing in the midst of the camp he covered it with his shining raiment, all but a small remote part ; and gave him these words of encouragement, the same that the Lord spoke to Joshua ben-Nun before the crossing of

---

10 catlonem A B2 ; cathlo'nem B1
11 ossualdus A ; osuualdus B1 B2
12 coruscantem A ; choruscante B1 ; choruscantem B2
13 jesue bén nun A ; jo'sué bennún B1 ; josu[e ben] num B2. See Joshua i.

mortuo Moyse proloqutus est, dicens : ' Confortare et age viriliter. Ecce ero [1] tecum ', et cetera. Sanctus itaque Columba haec ad regem in visu loquens addit : ' Hac sequenti nocte de castrís ad bellum procede. Hac enim vice mihi dominus donavit ut hostes in fugam vertantur tui, et tuus Catlon [2] inimicus in manus tradatur tuas, et post bellum victor revertaris et feliciter regnes.'

Post haec verba expergitus [3] rex senatui congregato 9a hanc enarrat visionem ; | qua confortati omnes totus populus promittit sé post reversionem de bello crediturum et babtismum suscepturum. Nam usque in id temporis tota illa Saxonia [4] gentilitatis et ignorantiae tenebrís obscurata erat, excepto ipso rege Ossualdo [5] cum xii.[6] virís qui cum eo Scotos inter exsolante [7] babtizati sunt. Quid plura ? Eadem subsequta nocte Ossualdus [8] rex sicuti in visu edoctus [9] fuerat de castrís ad bellum cum admodum pauciore exercitu contra milia numerosa progreditur. Cui a domino sicut ei promisum est felix et facilis est concessa victoria, et rege trucidato Catlone [10] victor post bellum reversus postea totius Brittanniae imperator a deo ordinatus [11] est.

9b   Hanc mihi Adomnano [12] narrationem meus de|cessor noster abbas [13] Failbeus [14] indubitanter enarravit. Qui

[1] ero A B2 ; ego ero B1
[2] catlon A B2 ; cathlon B1
[3] exper|gitus A ; a line has later been drawn through *gitus,* and *rectus* has been added after *exper,* in a late hand. expergefactus B1, on an erasure ; experrectus B2
[4] saxonia A B2 ; saxo'nia B1
[5] ossualdo A ; osuualdo B1 B2
[6] xii A ; duo'decim B1 ; duodecim B2
[7] exsolante A ; exulante B1 B2
[8] ossualdus A ; osuualdus B1 ; os[B2
[9] *edoctus.* In A, there is a meaningless dot immediately above, between *d* and *o.*
[10] catlone A B2 ; cathlo'ne B1

the Jordan, after the death of Moses, saying : ' Be strong, and act manfully ; behold I will be with you ', and so on. Thus in the vision Saint Columba spoke to the king, and added : ' This coming night, go forth from the camp to battle ; for the Lord has granted to me that at this time your enemies shall be turned to flight, and your adversary Catlon shall be delivered into your hands. And after the battle you shall return victorious and reign happily '.

The king, awakened after these words, related this vision to the assembled council. All were thereby strengthened, and the whole people promised that after returning from the battle they would believe, and accept baptism. For up to that time all that land of the English was shadowed by the darkness of heathenism and ignorance, excepting the king Oswald himself, and twelve men who had been baptized with him, while he was in exile among the Irish. Why should I say more ? On that same following night, as he had been instructed in the vision, king Oswald advanced from the camp, with a much smaller army, to battle against many thousands. And as had been promised to him, a happy and easy victory was granted to him by the Lord. King Catlon was slaughtered ; and the victor, returning from the battle, was afterwards ordained by God as emperor of the whole of Britain.

This was confidently narrated to me, Adomnan, by my predecessor, our abbot Failbe. He asserted that he

---

[11] *a deo ordinatus.* Cf. the Irish high-king Diormit *deo auctore ordinatum*, 36b ; and the ordination of Aidan, 107a–108a.

[12] adomnano A ; adamna'no B1 ; á damnano B2

[13] noster abbas A B2 ; abbas noster B1

[14] failbeus A B2 ; failbe'us B1

P

sé ab ore ipsius Ossualdi [1] regis Segineo [2] abbati eandem enuntiantis visionem audisse protestatus [3] est.

Sed et hoc etiam non praetereundum videtur, quod ejusdem beati viri per quaedam scoticae [4] lingae [5] laudum ipsius carmina et nominis commemorationem quidam quamlibet scelerati laicae conversationis homines et sanguinarii, ea nocte qua eadem [6] decantaverant cantica, de manibus inimicorum qui eandem eorumdem cantorum domum circumsteterant sint liberati ; qui flammas inter et gladios et lanceas incolomes [7] evassere.[8] Mirumque in modum pauci [9] ex ipsís, qui easdem sancti viri commemorationis quasi parvipendentes canere noluerant decantationes, in illo emulorum impetu soli 10a disperierant.   Hujus miraculi testes non | duo aut tres juxta legem [10] sed etiam centeni aut eo amplius adhiberi potuere.[11]   Non enim [12] in uno aut loco aut tempore hoc idem contegisse [13] conprobatur ; sed etiam diversís locís et temporibus in Scotia et Brittannia simili tamen et modo et causa liberationis factum fuisse sine ulla ambiguitate exploratum est.   Haec ab expertís unius cujusque regionis ubicumque [14] res eadem simili contegit [15] miraculo indubitanter didicimus.[16]

[1] ossualdi A ; osuualdi B1 B2

[2] segineo A B2 ; segi'neo B1

[3] *protestatus*.   In A, the *pro* symbol is a *p* with horizontal cross-stroke through the shaft, finished with a downward hook ; this may have been an alteration made by the text hand at the time of writing.

[4] scoticae A ; sco'ttice B1; scottie B2. See p. 89.

[5] lingae A ; lingue B1 B2

[6] eadem A B2 ; in A, a stress accent has later been added above the first *e*. e'adem B1

[7] incolomes A ; inco'lumes B1; incolumes B2

[8] evassere A ; the first *s* has later been erased. evase're B1 ; evasere B2. Adomnan describes here an episode that must have been regarded as supreme evidence of Saint Columba's miraculous power ; and he designedly expresses it in a single sentence that is a superlative example of his more intricate literary style.

[9] pauci A B1 ; paucis B2

had heard the vision from the mouth of king Oswald himself, relating it to abbot Segene.

This also seems to be a thing that should not be passed unnoticed : that certain lay people of the same blessed man, though they were guilty men and blood-stained, were through certain songs of his praises in the Irish tongue, and the commemoration of his name, delivered, on the night in which they had chanted those songs, from the hands of their enemies who had surrounded the house of the singers ; and they escaped unhurt, through flames, and swords, and spears. A few of them had refused to sing, as if valuing little the chantings of the holy man's commemoration, and miraculously those few alone had perished in the enemies' assault.

Of this miracle it has been possible to produce not two witnesses or three, as law requires, but a hundred or more. For not in one place or time only is the same thing proved to have happened, but it has been established beyond any doubt as having happened at various places and times, in Ireland and Britain, but in like manner and with the like cause of deliverance. We have learned these things, without room for doubt, from people who knew the facts in every district, wherever the same thing happened, with the same miracle.

---

[10] *legem.* This is based upon the Vulgate, Deut. xix. 15.

[11] potuere A B2 ; in A, a circumflex accent has been added by m.h., above the first *e.* potue're B1

[12] *enim.* In A, this is the Irish symbol (the H symbol, see Lindsay 1915, pp. 63–5), here misrendered by Reeves as *tantum.*

[13] contegisse A ; the first *e* has later been altered to *i*, with a vertical line. -tig- B1 B2

[14] *ubicumque.* In A, a meaningless dot stands immediately above *bi.*

[15] contegit A ; the *e* has later been altered to *i*, with a down-stroke. -tig- B1 B2

[16] didicimus A B2 ; didiscimus B1

Sed ut ad propossitum [1] redeamus : inter ea miracula quae idem vir domini in carne mortali conversans deo donante perficerat,[2] ab annís juvenilibus coepit etiam profetiae spiritu pollere,[3] ventura praedicere, praesentibus absentia nuntiare, quia quamvis absens corpore praesens tamen spiritu longe acta pervidere [4] poterat.

10b Nam juxta Pauli [5] | vocem, ' qui adheret domino unus spiritus est '. Unde et idem vir domini sanctus Columba, sicut et ipse quibusdam paucís fratribus [6] de re eadem [7] aliquando percunctantibus non negavit, in aliquantís dialis gratiae speculationibus totum etiam mundum veluti uno solis radio collectum sinu mentis mirabiliter laxato manifestatum perspiciens speculabatur.[8]

Haec de sancti viri híc [9] ideo enarrata sunt virtutibus ut avidior lector breviter perscripta quasi dulciores quasdam praegustet dapes ; quae tamen plenius in tribus inferius librís domino auxiliante enarrabuntur. Nunc mihi non indecenter videtur beati viri licet praepostero [10] ordine profetationes effari quas de sanctis quibusdam et inlustribus virís diversís prolocutus est temporibus. . |

[1] propossitum A ; the first *s* has later been erased. propositum B1 B2
[2] perficerat A ; the *i* has been altered by m.h. to *e*. -fe′c- B1 ; -fec-B2. In A, m.h. has inserted its down-sign for the end of a sentence, after this word, erroneously.
[3] pollere A B2 ; in A, an acute accent has later been added with a fine pen above the first *e*. polle′re B1
[4] pervidere A ; previdere B1 B2
[5] *Pauli*. Vulgate, 1 Cor. vi. 17.
[6] *paucís fratribus*. This is a significant deviation from the passage to which it refers, 44b and 45 a, where the communication is said to have been made to Lugbe mocu-Blai alone.
[7] eadem A ; an acute accent has later been added with a fine pen above *a*. ea′dem B1 B2
[8] *speculabatur*. This passage (from *totum etiam*), like the account to which it refers, is based upon passages of Pope Gregory I's Dialogues. See p. 20.
[9] híc A ; huc B1 ?B2
[10] prae posterero A (-*t˜ero*); prepo′stero B1 ; prepostero B2

But to return to our subject : along with the miracles that, by the gift of God, this man of the Lord performed while he lived in mortal flesh, he began from his youthful years to be strong also in the spirit of prophecy ; to foretell future events ; to declare absent things to those present, because although absent in the body he was present in spirit, and able to observe what took place far away. For according to the words of Paul, ' he who clings to the Lord is one spirit '. So too, as this holy man of the Lord, Columba, himself admitted to a few brothers who once questioned him closely about this very thing, in some speculations made with divine favour the scope of his mind was miraculously enlarged, and he saw plainly, and contemplated, even the whole world as it were caught up in one ray of the sun.

These things have here been related concerning the powers of the holy man, so that the more avid reader may savour, as a foretaste of a sweeter feast, what has been written in brief and, with the Lord's help, will be more fully related below, in three books. It seems to me not improper to tell now, though in inverted order, of the prophecies of the blessed man, which at various times he uttered concerning certain holy and eminent men.

11a
De sancto Finteno [1] abbate
filio Tailchani [2]

SANCTUS FINTENUS [3] qui postea per universas Scotorum eclesias valde noscibilis habetus [4] est, a puerili
aetate integritatem carnis et animae deo adjuvante
custodiens studiis dialis sofias [5] deditus, hoc propossitum [6] in annís juventatis [7] conversatus in corde habuit,
ut nostrum sanctum Columbam Heverniam [8] deserens
perigrinaturus [9] adiret. Eodem aestuans desiderio, ad
quendam vadit seniorem sibi amicum in sua gente [10]
prudentissimum venerandumque clericum qui scotice
vocitabatur [11] Colum Crag,[12] ut ab eo quasi prudente
aliquod audiret consilium. Cui cum suos tales de-
nudaret cogitatus hoc ab eo responsum accipit [13]:
'Tuum [14] ut estimo a deo inspiratum devotumque
11b desiderium quis prohibere potest, ne ad | sanctum
Columbam transnavigare debeas?' Eadem [15] hora
cassu [16] duo adveniunt monaci [17] sancti Columbae qui de
sua interrogati ambulatione, 'Nuper' aiunt, 'de Brittannia remigantes hodie a roboreto Calgachi [18] venimus'.

---

¹ finteno A ; fente'no B1. Not legible in B2. The death of ' Fintan,
son of Telchan ', is entered in A.U. under 634=635. His death was
commemorated on 21 October (Oengus 1905, p. 217 ; cf the commentary
ibid. p. 226). Finten is better known by the derived name Munnu (cf.
Meyer, Wortkunde, § 33). A late life of Munnu is edited in Plummer
1910, ii, pp. 226–39 ; cf. ibid., i, pp. lxxxiv ff. See above, pp. 101-02.
² tailchani A ; talca'ni B1 ; talchani B2. B1 adds to the title : *quomodo
de ipso sanctus columba prophetavit.*
³ fintenus A ; fentenus B1 B2
⁴ habetus A ; the *e* has later been altered to *i* by a vertical line drawn
by a fine pen. -bit- B1 B2
⁵ sofias A ; soph'ie B1 ; sophias B2
⁶ propossitum A ; the first *s* has later been erased. propo'situm B1;
propositum B2
⁷ juventatis A ; juventutis B1 B2
⁸ heverniam A ; hibe'rniam B1 ; hyberniam B2
⁹ perigrinaturus A ; the first *i* has been altered by m.h. to *e*. pereg-
B1 B2

[I 2] Of the abbot Saint Finten, son of Tailchan

Saint Finten, who was afterwards held in high repute among all the churches of the Irish, with God's help preserving from the age of boyhood integrity of body and soul, and being devoted to studies of divine wisdom, had in his heart, while still in the years of his youth, the purpose of leaving Ireland and going to our holy Columba, in order to live in pilgrimage. Burning with that desire, he went to a friend of his, a certain elder in his own tribe, a very wise and venerable priest, who was called in Irish *Colum Crag* ; to obtain from him, as from a wise man, some advice. When he had exposed to him these things that were in his mind, he received from him this answer : ' Who can forbid your desire inspired, as I think, by God, and devout ; and say that you ought not to sail over to the holy Columba ? '

In the same hour it happened that two monks of Saint Columba arrived. On being asked about their journey, they said : ' We have recently rowed from Britain, and today have come from the oakwood of

---

[10] *gente.* Finten's family is said to be the mocu-Moie, in 13a. In the Life of Munnu, he is said to belong to the cenel-Conaill (Plummer 1910, ii, p. 226).

[11] vocitabatur A B1 ; vocabatur B2

[12] colum crag A, with over-dashes above *um* and *ra* (not as in Thesaurus 1903, p. 272) ; columcrach B1 B2. Meyer, Contributions, enters *crach* ' harsh, rough ? ', an epithet.

[13] accipit A ; the first *i* has been altered by m.h. to *e*. a'ccipit B1 ; accepit B2

[14] Tuum A ; Tuum est B1 B2. In B1 B2, a new sentence begins at *quis* below, with a point and capital letter.

[15] Eadem A B2 ; in A, an acute accent has been added later, above *a*. Ea'dem B1

[16] cassu A ; the first *s* has later been erased. casu B1 B2

[17] monaci A ; an *h* has been added by m.h. above *ci*. monachi B1 B2

[18] calgachi A ; ca'lcagi B1 ; calga[B2

'Suspes anne [1] est' ait Columb Crag,[2] 'vester Columba
sanctus pater?'[3]   Qui valde inlacrimati cum magno
dixerunt merore : 'Vere salvus est noster ille patronus
qui hís diebus nuper ad Christum commigravit'.
Quibus auditís Finten et Columb [4] et omnes qui ibidem
inerant prostratís in terram vultibus amare flevere.[5]
Fintenus [6] consequenter percunctatur dicens : 'Quem
post sé successorem reliquit?'[7] 'Baitheneum'[8] aiunt,
'suum alumnum'.[9]   Omnibusque clamitantibus, 'dig-
num et debetum,'[10] Columb [11] ad Fintenum [12] inquit :
'Quid ad haec Fintene [13] facies?'[14]   Qui respondens ait :
12a 'Si dominus permiserit[15] | ad Baitheneum [16] virum
sanctum et sapientem enavigabo, et si me susciperit,[17]
ipsum abbatem habebo'.

Tum deinde supra memoratum Columbum [18] osculatus et ei valedicens navigationem praeparat et sine
morula ulla [19] transnavigans Iovam [20] devenit insulam.
Et nec dum in id temporis usque nomen ejus in hís locís
erat notum ; unde et in primís quasi quidam ignotus
hospes hospitaliter susceptus, alia die internuntium [21] ad
Baitheneum [22] mittit ejus allocutionem facie ad faciem

---

[1] Suspes anne A ; the *u* has later been altered to *o*, by bridging. Sospes
ne B1 B2
[2] columb crag A, with three over-dashes ; columcra'ch B1 B2
[3] *pater.* An interrogation sign follows this word in B1 B2, and has been
added by m.h. in A.
[4] finten et columb A ; fentenus et columcr' B1 ; fenten et columba B2
[5] flevere A ; an acute accent has later been added with a fine pen
above the second *e.* fleve're B1 ?B2
[6] Fintenus A ; Fentenus B1 ?B2
[7] *reliquit.* An interrogation sign follows this word in B1 B2, and has
been added by m.h. in A.
[8] Baitheneum A ; Baithe'num B1.   Not legible in B2.
[9] *alumnum,* 'foster-son' or 'pupil', is equivalent with O.I. *daltae.*
[10] debetum A ; de'bitum B1 ; debitum B2
[11] Columb A ; Columcr' B1 ; Columba B2
[12] fintenum A ; fentenum B1 B2
[13] fintene A ; fentene B1 B2

Calcach [Derry] '. ' Is all well with your father, the holy Columba ? ' said Columb Crag. With many tears, and very sorrowfully, they said : ' Truly he is well, our patron ; since within the last few days he has departed to Christ '. When they heard this, Finten and Columb, and all who were present there, with faces prostrate to the ground, wept bitterly. Thereupon Finten inquired, saying : ' Whom has he left as his successor ? ' ' Baithene, his foster-son ', they said. And while all exclaimed, ' A worthy and fitting successor ', Columb said to Finten : ' What in this case, Finten, will you do ? ' He answered : ' If the Lord permits, I shall sail out to Baithene, who is a wise and holy man ; and if he receive me, I shall have him as my abbot '.

Thereafter he kissed and bade farewell to Columb, prepared his voyage, and crossing without any delay, reached the island of Io [Iona]. Up to that time his name was not yet known in these parts, and so he was at first received with the hospitality given to an unknown guest ; and next day he sent an intermediary to Baithene, desiring speech with him face to face. He,

[14] *facies.* An interrogation sign follows this word in B1 and B2, and has been added by m.h. in A.

[15] *permiserit.* After this word, in A, *ad baitheneum* (repeated in 12a) has been written and partly erased.

[16] baitheneum A ; baithe'num B1 ; baithenum B2

[17] susciperit A ; the *i* has been altered by m.h. to *e*. susce'perit B1 ; sus[B2

[18] columbum A ; columcr' B1 ; columbam B2

[19] morula ulla A, with transposition signs, probably added later, not by the text hand. ulla mo'rula B1 ; ulla morula B2

[20] *Iovam.* The island is consistently called *ioua insula* in A B1 B2. See pp. 1, 154.

[21] internuntium A ; *inter* has later been erased, apparently after the shortened version, and the version represented by P, had been copied from A. internuncium B1 ; internuntium B2

[22] baitheneum A ; baithe'num B1 ; baithenum B2

habere volens. Qui ut erat affabilis et perigrinís[1]
appetibilis jubet ad se adduci. Qui statim adductus
primo ut conveniebat flexís genibus in terra[2] sé prostravit. Jususque a sancto seniore surgit, et resedens[3]
interrogatur a Baitheneo[4] adhuc inscio de gente et
12b provincia nomineque et | conversatione, et pro qua
causa inierit navigationis laborem. Qui ita interrogatus
omnia per ordinem[5] enarrans ut susciperetur humiliter
expostulat. Cui sanctus senior hís ab hospite auditís,
simulque hunc esse virum cognoscens de quo pridem
aliquando sanctus Columba profetice vaticinatus est,
' Gratias ' ait, ' deo meo[6] agere debeo quidem in tuo
adventu filii.[7] Sed hoc indubitanter scito quod noster
monacus non eris '. Hoc audiens hospes valde con-
tristatus infit : ' Forsitan ego indignus tuus non mereor
fieri monacus '. Senior consequenter inquit : ' Non
quod ut dicis indignus esses hoc dixi, sed quamvis
maluissem[8] té apud me retenere[9] mandatum tamen
sancti Columbae mei decessoris profanare non possum,
13a per quem spiritus sanctus de té profetavit. | Alia namque
die mihi soli seorsum síc profetico profatus ore inter
cetera dixit : ' Haec mea ó Baithenee[10] intentius debes
audire verba. Statim namque post meum de hoc ad
Christum saeculo[11] exspectatum et valde desideratum
transitum, quidam de Scotia frater qui nunc bene

[1] perigrinís A ; peregrinis B1 B2
[2] terra A ; terram B1 B2
[3] resedens A ; re'sidens B1 ; residens B2
[4] baitheneo A ; baitheno B1 B2
[5] ordinem A B1 B2. In A, the letters before d have been written over an erasure, by a late hand. The shortened version and P, which are derived from A, read ordinem.
[6] meo A B1 ; nostro B2
[7] filii A ; the third i has later been erased. fili B1 B2
[8] maluissem A B1 B2. In A, ll was written, and the first l was deleted with a dot below, by the text hand at the time of writing.

being approachable, and accessible to strangers, bade him be brought in. He was brought at once, and first, as was fitting, bowed his knees and prostrated himself upon the ground ; and arose when bidden by the older saint. He sat down, and was questioned by Baithene, who did not as yet know his tribe and province, name and manner of life, and for what reason he had undertaken the labour of voyaging. Thus questioned, he related everything in order, and begged humbly to be received.

The elder saint, hearing this from his guest, and at the same time recognizing that this was the man of whom Saint Columba had once prophetically foretold, said to him : ' I ought indeed, my son, to give thanks to my God at your coming ; but this you must know for certain, you shall not be our monk '. When he heard this, the guest was much saddened, and said : ' Perhaps because I am undeserving I am not thought worthy to become your monk '. Thereupon the elder replied : ' I said this not because you were unworthy, as you say. But although I should have preferred to keep you with me, I cannot profane the command of Saint Columba, my predecessor, through whom the Holy Spirit prophesied of you. For, speaking with prophetic lips, privately to me alone one day, he said this, among other things : " You must now, Baithene, give close attention to my words. Immediately after my expected and much wished-for passing from this world to Christ, there will come to you a brother from Ireland, who, directing rightly his youth in virtuous

---

⁹ retenere A ; the second e has later been altered to i with a fine pen. retine're B1. Not visible in B2.

¹⁰ baithenee A ; baithe'ne B1 ; baithene B2

¹¹ ad christum saeculo A ; seculo ad christum B1 B2

juvenilem bonis moribus regens aetatem sacrae lectionis
studiis satis inbuitur, nomine Fintenus,[1] gente mocu-
Moie,[2] cujus pater Tailchanus [3] vocitatur, ad té inquam
perveniens humiliter expostulabit, ut ipsum suscipiens
inter ceteros adnumeres monacos.[4] Sed hoc ei in dei
praescientia praedistinatum [5] non est, ut ipse alicujus
abbatis monacus [6] fieret, sed ut monacorum abbas et
animarum dux ad caeleste regnum ollim electus a deo
est.   Noles itaque hunc memoratum virum in hís
13b nostrís apud | té retenere [7] insulís, ne et dei voluntati
contraire videaris.   Sed haec ei intimans verba ad
Scotiam in pace remittas ; ut in Laginensium [8] vicinís
mari finibus monasterium [9] construat, et ibidem Christi
ovinum [10] pascens gregem innumeras ad patriam animas
caelestem perducat.'   Haec audiens sanctus junior
Christo [11] lacrimas fundens agit gratias,[12] inquiens :
' Secundum sancti Columbae profeticam fiat mihi et
mirabilem praescientiam '.   Hísdemque [13] diebus verbís
sanctorum obtemperans et a Baitheneo [14] accipiens benedictionem in pace ad Scotiam transnavigat.[15]

Haec mihi quodam narrante relegioso [16] sene praespitero [17] Christi milite Oisseneo [18] nomine Ernani [19] filio

---

[1] fintenus A ; fentenus B1 B2
[2] mocumoie A, with four over-dashes; mocumo'ie' B1 ; mocumoye B2
[3] tailchanus A ; ta'lcanus B1 ; talcanus B2
[4] monacos A ; a small *h* has been written by m.h. above *co*. monachos
B1 B2
[5] praedistinatum A ; predestinatum B1 B2
[6] monacus A B1 ; *h* is added in A, as above. monachus B2
[7] retenere A ; the second *e* has later been altered to *i* by a down-stroke
with a fine pen. -tin- B1 B2
[8] *Laginensium*. The Lagin were a tribe whose name was given to the
province of Leinster.
[9] *monasterium*. This is said to be Tech-Munnu, now Taghmon, county
Wexford.
[10] ovinum A B2 ; in A, a circumflex accent has later been added above *i*.
ovinum B1, altered by erasure to *ovium*.
[11] christo A B2 ; christi B1

ways, is now being well instructed in studies of sacred literature. His name is Finten, of the family mocu-Moie, and his father is called Tailchan ; and he will humbly request you to receive and include him among the other monks. But in God's prescience it is not predestined for him to become a monk of any abbot, but he has long since been chosen by God as an abbot of monks, and a leader of souls to the heavenly kingdom. You will therefore refuse to keep this man with you in these islands of ours, lest you should even seem to oppose the will of God. But tell him these words, and send him back in peace to Ireland ; so that he may construct a monastery in the coastal territories of the Lagin, and there feed a flock of Christ's sheep, and lead unnumbered souls to the heavenly country ".'

Hearing this, the younger saint with a shower of tears gave thanks to Christ, and said : ' May it happen to me according to the prophetic and miraculous foreknowledge of Saint Columba '. Within a few days, in obedience to the words of the saints, and receiving Baithene's blessing, he sailed over to Ireland in peace.

This I have learned with certainty ; it was told to me by a religious old man, a priest, and soldier of Christ, by name Oissene, Ernan's son, of the family

---

¹² agit gratias A ; ait, gra˜s B1 B2
¹³ *Hisdemque*. After this word, three folios of B2 are missing. See under 27b.
¹⁴ baitheneo A ; baitheno B1
¹⁵ transnavigat A ; transnavigavit B1
¹⁶ relegioso A ; the second *e* has later been altered to *i*, by a down-stroke with a fine pen. religioso B1
¹⁷ praespitero A; presb''ro B1
¹⁸ oisseneo A ; oissene'o B1
¹⁹ ernani A ; erna'ni B1

gente mocu Neth-corb[1] indubitanter didici ; qui sé
eadem omnia supra memorata verba ejusdem ab ore
sancti Finteni[2] filii Tailchani[3] audisse testatus est ipsius
monacus. |

14a   De Erneneo[4] filio Craseni
                        sancti Columbae profetia

ALIO IN TEMPORE vir beatus in mediterranea[5]
Eberniae[6] parte monasterio[l]um[7] quod scotice dicitur
Dairmag[8] divino fundans nutu per aliquot demoratus
menses, libuit animo visitare fratres qui in Clonoensi
sancti Cerani[9] cenubio[10] commanebant. Auditoque
ejus accessu universi undique ab agellulís monasterio
vicinís, cum hís qui ibidem inventi sunt congregati, cum
omni alacritate suum consequentes abbatem Alitherum[11]
sancto Columbae[12] quasi angelo domini obviam, egresi
valum monasterii, unanimes[13] pergunt ; humiliatísque
in terram vultibus eo viso[14] cum omni reverentia
exosculatus ab eis est[15] ; ymnísque et laudibus resonantes
honorifice ad eclesiam perducunt. Quandamque de

[1] mocu neth corb A, with four over-dashes, above *mo*, *cu*, *e*, and *o*.
mocu netcorb B1, with an erasure between *o* and *c*. This was the family of
Dal neth-Corb, the principal tribe of the Lagin (cf. MacNeill 1911, pp. 79,
83).
[2] finteni A ; fente'ni B1
[3] tailchani A; talcani B1
[4] *Erneneo.* ' The repose of Ernaine, Cresene's son ' is placed by A.U.
under 634=635. On 18 August, ' Cresséne's son, my Ernóc, exalted to the
company of the Lord ', according to Oengus 1905, p. 177 (cf. the commentary ibid., p. 186). His churches are believed to have been in the
counties of Wicklow and Carlow.
[5] *mediterranea.* This district was Mide, the inland territory now partly
represented by county Westmeath.
[6] eberniae A ; a small *i* has been written later above the first *e*. hibe'rnie
B1
[7] monasteriorum A ; *rum* has later been deleted by underlining, and a
small *u*~ has been written by m.h. above *o*. monasterium B1, and the
shortened version. The form *monasteriolum* occurs in 3a, for a monastery
of Columba, and in 41a, for the monastery of Trevet.

mocu Neth-corb. He attested that he had heard all the same words reported above, from the mouth of the same Saint Finten, Tailchan's son, whose monk he was.

[I 3] Saint Columba's prophecy concerning Ernene, Crasen's son

At one time, when for some months the blessed man remained in the midland district of Ireland, while by God's will founding the monastery that is called in Irish *Dairmag* [Durrow], it pleased him to visit the brothers who lived in the monastery of Clóin of Saint Ceran [Clonmacnoise].

When they heard of his approach, all those that were in the fields near the monastery came from every side, and joined those that were within it, and with the utmost eagerness accompanying their abbot Alither they passed outside the boundary-wall of the monastery, and with one accord went to meet Saint Columba, as if he had been an angel of the Lord. On seeing him they bowed their faces to the earth, and he was kissed by them with all reverence, and singing hymns and praises they led him with honour to the church. They

---

[8] dairmag A ; darmag B1. The *g* has been altered in A by m.h., to resemble a continental form of *g*. (The *d* in the Zürich photograph has been distorted by a photographic flaw that is not present in Mr Koch's facsimile.)

[9] cerani A ; cera'ni B1

[10] cenubio A ; the *u* has later been altered to *o* by bridging. ceno'bio B1. The monasteries of Clonmacnoise and Durrow were upon the great road from Dublin to the west. See Colm Ó Lochlainn, in Féil-sgríbhinn, 1940, p. 471, and map.

[11] alitherum A, with three over-dashes ; alithe'rum B1. See p. 88.

[12] co~l A, an exceptional instance of suspension ; columbe B1

[13] un animes A ; una'nimes B1

[14] viso A ; visu B1

[15] ab eis est A ; est ab eis B1

lignís piramidem [1] erga sanctum deambulantem con-
14b stringentes a quatuor virís eque ambulan|tibus sub-
portari fecerunt, ne videlicet sanctus senior Columba
ejusdem fratrum multitudinis constipatione molestaretur.

Eadem hora quidam valde dispectus [2] vultu et habitu
puer familiaris, et necdum senioribus placens, retro in
quantum valuit sé occultans accessit, ut videlicet vel
illius anfibali fimbriam quo vir beatus induebatur
occulte, et si fieri possit [3] ipso nesciente et non sentiente,
tangeret. Sed hoc tamen sanctum non latuit ; nam
quod corporalibus occulís retro se actum intueri non
potuit spiritalibus [4] perspexit. Unde subito restitit et
post sé extendens manum cervicem pueri tenet ; ipsumque trahens, ante faciem suam statuit. Omnibusque
qui ibidem circumstabant dicentibus, ' Dimitte, dimitte ;
quare hunc infelicem et injuriosum retenes [5] puerum ? ',
15a sanctus econtra haec | puro [6] pectore verba depromit
profetica : ' Sinete [7] fratres, sinete [8] modo '. Ad puerum
vero valde tremefactum dicit : ' Ó filii,[9] aperi ós tuum
et porrege [10] linguam '. Jusus tum puer cum ingenti
tremore aperiens ós linguam porrexit, quam sanctus
sanctam extendens manum deligenter [11] benedicens ita
profetice profatur dicens : ' Hic puer quamvis vobís
nunc dispicabilis [12] et valde vilis videatur nemo tamen

---

[1] *piramidem* This probably means a square or diamond-shaped frame
made of four branches tied together at the ends. Adomnan used the
expression *lapidea pyramis* to describe low walls round two tombs, in *De
Locis*, pp. 257, 259.　　　　　　　　　　[2] dispectus A ; despectus B1
[3] possit A ; posset B1, correctly.
[4] spiritalibus A; spiritualibus B1
[5] retenes A ; a small *i* has later been written above the second *e*.
re'tines B1　　　　　　　　　　　[6] *puro*. With *-ro* B3 begins.
[7] sinete A ; a small *i* has later been written above the first *e*. Sinite
B1 B3
[8] sinete A; the first *e* has later been altered to *i* by a down-stroke with
a fine pen. -nit- B1 B3
[9] filii A ; the third *i* has later been erased. fili B1 B3

bound together a kind of barrier of branches, and
caused it to be carried about the saint as he walked,
by four men keeping pace with him ; lest the elder
Saint Columba should be troubled by the thronging of
that crowd of brothers.

Meanwhile, a boy of the congregation, much looked
down upon for his countenance and bearing, and not
yet approved by the elders, came up behind, keeping
out of sight as much as he could, intending to touch,
secretly and if possible without the blessed man's
knowledge or perception, were it but the hem of the
cloak in which the blessed man was wrapped. But this
was not concealed from the saint. For what he could
not with bodily eyes observe, done behind his back,
he discerned with spiritual sight. So he suddenly
stopped ; and putting out his hand behind him he
took hold of the boy's neck, pulled him forward, and
made him stand before his face. When all those that
stood by said, ' Send him away ! Send him away !
Why do you keep hold of this unlucky and mischievous
boy ? ', on the contrary the saint drew from his pure
breast these prophetic words : ' Let be, brothers, let
be '. And to the boy, who was trembling greatly, he
said : ' My son, open your mouth, and put out your
tongue '. In great trepidation the boy then opened
his mouth as he was bidden, and put out his tongue,
which the saint, extending his holy hand, earnestly
blessed. And the saint spoke thus prophetically, saying :
' Although this boy appears to you now contemptible

[10] porrege A ; a small *i* has later been written above the first *e*. -rig-
B1 B3
[11] deligenter A ; the first *e* has later been altered to *i*, with a short
down-stroke. dil- B1 B3
[12] dispicabilis A ; des- B1 B3

Q

218 ADOMNAN'S

ipsum ob id dispiciat.[1] Ab hac enim hora non solum
vobís non displicebit sed valde placebit ; bonísque
moribus et animae virtutibus paulatim de die in diem
crescet. Sapientia quoque et prudentia magis ac magis
in eo ab hac die [2] adaugebitur, et in hac vestra congregatione grandis est futurus profectus ; lingua quoque
15b ejus, salubri et doctrina,[3] eloquentia | a deo donabitur '.

Hic erat Erneneus [4] filius Craseni,[5] postea per omnes
Scotiae eclesias famosus et valde notissimus ; qui haec
omnia supra scripta verba Segeneo [6] abbati de sé profetata enarraverat, meo decessore Failbeo [7] intentius
audiente, qui et ipse cum Segeneo [8] praesens inerat.
Cujus revelatione [9] et ego ipse cognovi haec eadem quae
enarravi.

Sed et multa alia hisdem diebus quibus in Clonoensi [10]
cenubio [11] sanctus hospitabatur revelante profetavit
sancto spiritu : hoc est de illa quae post dies multos ob
diversitatem paschalis festi orta est inter Scotiae eclesias
discordia ; et de quibusdam angelicís [12] frequentationibus
sibi manifestatís, quibus quaedam intra ejusdem cenubii[13]
septa ab angelís [14] tunc temporis frequentabantur loca. . |

---

[1] dispiciat A ; des- Bı B3
[2] *ab hac die.* In A, the same words have been written again, in error ;
and were later deleted by a horizontal line drawn through the letters with
a fine pen.
[3] et doctrina A ; et doctrinali Bı B3. After *doctrina*, in A, *et* has been
inserted above the line, by a later, non-Irish hand, with a rather broad pen
(making ' with both salutary doctrine and salutary eloquence ', an improbable meaning). This change was made before the shortened version
was written. It was wrongly accepted by Reeves. The reading of Bı
B3 would give ' salutary and doctrinal eloquence ', also an unsatisfactory
meaning. Their reading shows that the added *et* was not present in the
common source. We have punctuated *salubri et doctrina* as a parenthesis,
which Adomnan's style would permit.
[4] erneneus A ; ernene'us Bı B3
[5] craseni A ; crase'ni Bı B3
[6] Segeneo A ; segine'o Bı ; segineo B3
[7] failbeo A B3 ; failbe'o Bı

and of very little worth, yet let no man despise him on that account.   For from this hour not only will he not displease you, but he will greatly please you.   And he will grow by degrees from day to day in good ways, and virtues of the soul ;   wisdom also with discretion will be increased in him more and more, from this day ; and in this community of yours he will be a man of great eminence.   His tongue also will receive from God eloquence, with healthful doctrine '.

This was Ernene, Crasen's son, famous afterwards among all the churches of Ireland, and very widely known.   He related to abbot Segene all these words that I have written above, of the prophecy concerning himself.   My predecessor Failbe also was present along with Segene, and listened intently ;   and from his disclosure I too have myself learned these same words that I have related.

During those days in which the saint was a guest in the monastery of Clóin, he prophesied also many other things, by revelation of the Holy Spirit :   that is to say, concerning the great dispute that after many days arose among the churches of Ireland over the diversity in time of the Easter festival ;   and concerning some angelic visitations revealed to him, in which certain places within the enclosure of that monastery were frequented by angels, at that time.

---

[8] segeneo A ; segine'o B1 B3
[9] revelatione A ; relatione B1; relacione B3
[10] clonoensi A B3 ; clonoe'nsi B1
[11] cenubio A ; the u has later been altered to o, by bridging. ceno'bio B1 ; cenobio B3
[12] angelicís A ; angelicis B1 ; anglicis B3
[13] cenubii A ; the u has later been altered to o, by bridging. cenobii B1 B3
[14] ab angelís A. Omitted in B1. ab anglicis B3

16a   De adventu sancti Cainnichi abbatis [1] de quo
           sanctus Columba profetaliter [2] prenuntiavit

ALIO IN TEMPORE, cum in Iova [3] insula die fragosae
tempestatis et intollerabilis undarum magnitudinis
sedens in domu [4] sanctus, et fratribus praecipiens,
diceret, ' Praeparate ocius hospitium, aquamque ad
lavandos hospitum pedes exaurite ', [5] quidam ex ipsís
frater consequenter, ' Quis ' ait, ' hac die valde ventosa
et nimis periculosa licet breve fretum prospere transnavigare potest ? ' Quo audito sanctus síc profatur :
' Cuidam sancto et electo homini, qui ad nos ante
vesperam perveniet, [6] omnipotens tranquillitatem quamlibet in tempestate donavit'. Et ecce eadem [7] die
aliquandiu a fratribus exspectata navis, in qua sanctus
inerat Cainnechus, [8] juxta sancti profetationem pervenit. |
16b Cui sanctus cum fratribus obviam venit, et ab eo
honorifice et hospitaliter susceptus est. Illi vero nautae
qui cum Cainnecho [9] inerant, interrogati a fratribus de
qualitate navigationis, síc retulerunt sicuti sanctus
Columba prius de tempestate et tranquillitate pariter
deo donante in eodem mari et hisdem horís mirabili
divisione praedixerat ; et tempestatem eminus visam
non sensise [10] professi sunt. .

    [1] cainnichi abbatis A ; abbatis cainne'thi B1 ; cainnechi abbatis B3.
Cainnech of Aghaboe died probably in A.D. 603 ; see E.S., 1, p. 55. His
death was commemorated on 11 October (Oengus 1905, p. 215). Cf. 63a.
He was of the family of mocu-Dalon or corcu-Dalan of Ciannachta in the
county of Derry, whose name survives in the name of Keenaght (Plummer
1910, 1, p. 152).
    [2] profetaliter A ; prophetaliter B1 ; prophetabiliter B3
    [3] iova A B1 (as always in A B1 B2) ; iona B3 (as always in B3). We
do not henceforth note this spelling variation in B3.
    [4] domu A ; the u has later been altered to o, by bridging. domo B1 B3
    [5] exaurite A ; a small h has later been added by m.h. above, before a.
exhaur- B1 B3
    [6] perveniet A B3 ; adve'niet B1

[I 4] Of the arrival of the abbot Saint Cainnech, which Saint Columba had prophetically foretold

At another time, in the island of Io, on a day of crashing storm and unendurably high waves, when the saint, sitting in the house and giving orders to the brothers, said : ' Prepare the guest-house quickly, and draw water for washing the feet of guests ', one of the brothers then said : ' On this very windy and too-perilous day, who can cross in safety even the narrow strait ? ' Hearing him, the saint spoke thus : ' To one holy and chosen man, who will reach us before the evening, the Omnipotent has granted calm, though in the midst of storm '.

And behold, on the same day, a ship that the brothers had for some time awaited and in which Saint Cainnech was, arrived according to the saint's prophecy. The saint with the brothers went to meet him, and honourably and hospitably received him. And the sailors who were in the ship with Cainnech, when asked by the brothers what kind of voyage they had had, replied in exact agreement with what Saint Columba had earlier foretold of storm and calm together, by God's dispensation, in the same sea and at the same hours, but miraculously separated ; and they declared that they had not felt the storm, which they had seen far off.

---

7 eadem A ; an acute accent has later been added with a fine pen above *a*. e'adem B1 ; ea'dem B3
8 cainnechus A ; canne'tus B1 ; cannechus B3
9 cainnecho A ; canne'co B1 ; cannecho B3
10 sensise A ; sensisse se B1 B3. With A's reading cf. *profetentur . . . sensise*, in 38b.

De periculo sancti Colmani [1] episcopi
mocu-Sailni [2] in mari juxta insulam quae
vocitatur Rechru. .

ALIA ITIDEM die sanctus Columba in sua commanens
matrice eclesia repente in hanc subridens erupit vocem,
dicens : ' Columbanus filius Beognai [3] ad nos trans-
17a navigare incipiens nunc in un|dosís carubdis [4] Brecani
aestibus valde periclitatur ; ambasque ad caelum in
prora sedens palmas elevat, turbatum quoque et tam
formidabile pilagus [5] benedicit. Quem tamen dominus
síc terret, non ut navis naufragio in qua ipse resedet [6]
undís obruatur, sed potius ad orandum intentius
suscitetur, ut ad nos deo propitio post transvadatum
perveniat periculum '. .

De Cormaco [7]

ALIO QUOQUE IN TEMPORE de Cormacco [8] nepote
Lethani,[9] viro utique sancto, qui tribus non minus

---

[1] colmani A ; columbani B1 B3. This was apparently Colman Elo,
' Colman of Lynally ' (in Offaly, not far from Durrow), whose death was
entered in A.U. from Cuanu's Book, under 610=611. He is called
Colman Ela mocu (sic lege) *Seilli* in T. 9b28-9. The Latin Life of Colman Elo
in Plummer 1910, I, p. 258, says that he was a son of Beogne. The Irish
tract *Apgitir crábaid* (' Alphabet of devotion ') was attributed to this Colman
Beogna's son, not to Colman maccu Béognae, as in Kuno Meyer's title
(*Z.C.P.*, III, p. 447). The date of its composition was actually later ;
and according to Kenney 1929, not earlier than the eighth century.
Colman Elo's death was commemorated on 26 September (Oengus 1905,
p. 196 ; cf. the commentary ibid., p. 212). He is called ' priest ' by
Adomnan (64a–65a) in the year before Columba's death, and was presumably not yet bishop at the time spoken of in 16b.
[2] mocusailni A B3 ; mocusai'lni B1
[3] beognai A B3 ; beognay B1
[4] carubdis A ; a small *y* has later been written, probably by m.h.,
above *u*. caribdis B1 B3. This is the *coire Brecain* in Cormac 1862, p. 13 ;
a part of the strait between Rathlin and Antrim. See Watson 1926,
pp. 63, 94.

[I 5] Of the peril of the bishop Saint Colman mocu-Sailni in the sea near the island that is called Rechru [Rathlin]

In like manner on another day, Saint Columba, while he was living in his mother church, suddenly exclaimed, with a smile : ' Colman, Beogna's son, has begun to sail over to us, and is now in great danger in the surging tides of the whirlpool of Brecan ; and sitting in the prow he raises both hands to heaven, and blesses the troubled and very terrible sea. But the Lord terrifies him thus, not in order that the ship in which he sits may be overwhelmed by the waves in shipwreck, but rather to rouse him to more fervent prayer that with God's favour he may reach us after passing through the danger '.

[I 6] Concerning Cormac

Also at another time, Saint Columba prophesied and spoke thus concerning Cormac, Léthan's grandson, a

---

[5] et tam formidabile pilagus A ; the *i* of *pilagus* has been altered by m.h. to *e.* fretum et tam formida'bile B1 ; et tam formidabile pelagus B3

[6] resedet A ; the second *e* has later been altered to *i*, by a long downstroke. -sid- B1 B3

[7] cormaco A ; sancto Cormacco B1 ; cormacco B3. Cormac, grandson of Léthan, is called the founder of a monastery, in 118a. He was a monk of Columba (95a, 97a), probably at Durrow, where he was buried (Oengus 1905, p. 156 ; Reeves 1857, p. 267) ; but Oengus calls him *clérech* ' cleric' only, not abbot.

[8] cormacco A B3 ; corma'cco B1

[9] lethani A ; letha'ni B1 ; le'thani B3

vicibus [1] herimum [2] in ociano [3] laboriose [4] quaesivit, nec tamen invenit, sanctus Columba ita profetizans ait : ' Hodie iterum Cormac [5] desertum reperire cupiens enavigare incipit, ab illa regione quae,[6] ultra Modam [7] 17b fluium sita, Eirros-domno [8] dicitur. | Nec tamen etiam hac vice quod quaerit inveniet ; et non ob aliam ejus culpam nisi quod alicujus relegiosi [9] abbatis monacum ipso non permittente discessorem secum non recte comitari navigio susciperit ' [10]. .

De bellorum fragoribus longe
comisorum [11] beati profetia viri. .

Post BELLUM Cule-drebene [12] sicuti nobis traditum est duobus transactís annís, quo tempore vir beatus de Scotia perigrinaturus [13] primitus enavigavit, quadam die, hoc est eadem hora qua in Scotia comisum [14] est bellum quod scotice dicitur Ondemmone,[15] idem homo dei coram Conallo rege filio Comgill [16] in Brittannia [17] conversatus per omnia enarravit, tam de bello comisso

---

[1] *tribus . . . vicibus.* Two of Cormac's voyages (the ' second ' and ' third ') are mentioned by Adomnan (94b–97b), who there appears to count this one as the first. But it is implied below (*iterum incipit*) that Cormac had made a false start before.

[2] herimum A ; the *i* has been altered by m.h. to *e.* -rem- B1 B3

[3] ociano A ; the *i* has been altered by m.h. to *e.* occe'ano B1 ; occeano B3

[4] laboriosae A ; laboriose B1 B3

[5] cormac A B1 ; cormaccus B3

[6] quae A ; qui B1; que B3

[7] modam A ; a circumflex accent has later been added with a fine pen above *a.* modan B1 B3. This river is now the Moy, between Sligo and Mayo counties.

[8] eirros domno A, with four over-dashes ; eirrosdomno B1 B3. This was part of Mayo (see Reeves 1857, p. 31 ; Hogan 1910, p. 472).

[9] relegiosi A ; -lig- B1 B3

[10] susciperit A ; the *i* has been altered by m.h. to *e.* susce'perit B1 ; susceperit B3

holy man who sought with great labour not less than three times a desert in the ocean, and yet found none : ' Today again Cormac, desiring to find a desert, begins his voyage from the district that is called Eirros-domno, lying beyond the river Mód [Moy]. But this time also he will not find what he seeks ; and for no other fault on his part than that he has improperly taken with him as a companion of his voyage a man who, being the monk of a religious abbot, has departed without the abbot's consent '.

[I 7] A prophecy of the blessed man concerning the crash of battles fought far away

At the time when the blessed man first sailed away from Ireland, to be a pilgrim, two years after the battle of Cul-drebene, as we have been told, on a certain day, that is at the very hour when the battle that is in Irish called ' of Ond-móne ' was fought in Ireland, the same man of God, while living in Britain, gave a complete account in the presence of king Conall, Comgells' son, not only of the fighting of the battle, but also of those

---

[11] comisorum A ; a small *s* has later been written in black ink above *is*. commissorum B1 B3

[12] cule drebene A ; culedredi'ne B1 ; culedrebene B3

[13] perigrinaturus A ; pereg- B1 B3

[14] comisum A ; a small *s* has been added by m.h. above *i*. commissum B1 B3

[15] ondemmone A, without over-dashes ; the first *m* is superscript. onde'mone B1 ; ondemone B3. *Onde* is the genitive of *ond*, a ' rock ' or ' stone ' ; *mōne* is genitive of *móin* ' swamp '. The battle-place is called Móin Daire-lothair in the Irish annals. See pp. 74, 143, 148.

[16] comgill A ; comgil B1 B3

[17] brittannia A ; britta'nnia B1 ; bryttannia B3

quam etiam de illís regibus quibus dominus de inimicís
18a victoriam | condonavit, quorum propria vocabula Ain-
morius ¹ filius Sétni,² et ii. filii maic-Erce,³ Domnallus
et Forcus.⁴ Sed et de rege Cruithniorum qui Echodius
Laib ⁵ vocitabatur, quemadmodum victus currui insedens ⁶ evaserit, similiter sanctus profetizavit.⁷ .

De bello Miathoru[m] ⁸

ALIO IN TEMPORE, hoc est post multos a supra
memorato bello annorum transcursus, cum esset vir
sanctus in Iova insula, subito ad suum dicit ministratorem Dermitium ⁹ : ' Clocam pulsa '. Cujus sonitu
fratres incitati ad eclesiam ipso sancto praesule praeeunte
ocius currunt. Ad quos ibidem flexís genibus infit :
' Nunc intente pro hoc populo et Aidano rege dominum
oremus. Hac enim hora ineunt bellum '. Et post
18b modicum intervallum egresus ¹⁰ | oratorium respiciens in
caelum inquit : ' Nunc barbari ¹¹ in fugam vertuntur ;
Aidanoque quamlibet infelix tamen concessa victoria
est '. Sed et de numero de exercitu Aidani interfectorum
ccctorum et iii.¹² virorum vir beatus profetice narravit. .

---

¹ ainmorius A ; anmo'rius B1 ; anmorius B3
² sétni A ; scethni B1 ; scetni B3. Perhaps *ce* is an error for *ee*, indicating long *e*.
³ maic erce A ; maice'rce B1 ; maicerce B3. Mac-Erce, or Muirchertach, was a son of Muiredach, son of Eogan, son of Néll. See 20a.
The descendants of this Mac-Erce formed a branch of the cenel-nEogain
(cf. A.U., 628=629 and 629=630).
⁴ forcus A B3 ; fergus B1, altered from ?*forcus*. He was the ancestor
of the cenel-Forcuso ; see MacNeill 1911, p. 86.
⁵ echodius laib A ; echuius laib B1 ; echuiuslaid B3. See p. 66. The
death of his son Eugan is entered in A.U. under 610=611.
⁶ insedens A ; insidens B1 B3
⁷ similiter sanctus profetizavit A ; prophetizavit similiter sanctus vir
B1 ; prophetizavit similiter sanctus B3
⁸ miathoru A ; maithorum B1 ; miathorum B3
⁹ dermitium A ; diormi'cium B1 ; vermicium B3

kings to whom the Lord granted victory over their enemies ; and whose proper names were Ainmure, Sétne's son, and two sons of Mac-erce, Domnall and Forcus ; and similarly the saint prophesied of a king of the Cruithni, who was called Echoid Laib, how he was defeated, and escaped, sitting in a chariot.

[I 8] Concerning the battle of the Miathi

At another time, when the holy man was in the island of Io, after many years had gone by since the above-mentioned battle, he suddenly said to his attend- ant Diormit : ' Strike the bell '. Summoned by its clang, the brothers ran quickly to the church, the holy superior going before them. He knelt down and addressed them there : ' Now let us pray earnestly to the Lord for this people, and for the king Aidan. For in this hour they are going into battle '. And after a short time he left the oratory, and looking into the sky he said : ' Now the barbarians are turned to flight ; and the victory is yielded to Aidan, unhappy though it is '. And also the blessed man told prophetically the number of the dead in Aidan's army, three hundred and three men.

---

[10] egresus A ; a small *s* has been added by m.h. above *es*. egressus B1 B3

[11] *barbari*. Adomnan's use of this word implies that the Miathi were not speakers of Irish, and at the same time seems to show that they were not the southern people of the Picti who had accepted Ninian's teaching of Christianity.

[12] ccctorum et iii A ; a small *u~* has been added by m.h. after *iii*, to read *trium*. trecentorum et trium B1 B3

De filiis Aidani regis
sancti Columbae profetia

ALIO IN TEMPORE ante supradictum bellum sanctus
Aidanum regem interrogat de regni successore. Illo sé
respondente nescire, quis esset de tribus filiis suís
regnaturus, Arturius [1] an Echodius Find an Domingartus,[2] sanctus consequenter hoc profatur modo :
' Nullus ex hís tribus erit regnator ; nam in bellís
cadent, ab inimicís trucidandi. Sed nunc si alios
19a juniores habes ad me veniant ; et quem ex eís ele|gerit
dominus regem subito super meum inruet gremium '.
Quibus accitís secundum verbum sancti Echodius [3]
Buide adveniens in sinu ejus recubuit. Statimque
sanctus eum osculatus benedixit ; et ad patrem ait :
' Hic est superstes, et rex post té regnaturus, et filii ejus
post eum regnabunt '. Sic omnia post suís temporibus
plene adinpleta sunt. Nam Arturius [4] et Echodius Fint [5]
non longo post temporis intervallo Miatorum [6] superius
memorato in bello trucidati sunt. Domingartus vero in
Saxonia bellica in strage [7] interfectus est. Echodius [8]
autem Buide [9] post patrem in regnum successit. .

[1] arturius A B1 ; arcu'rius B3
[2] domingartus A B3 ; dominga'rtus B1
[3] echodius A B3 ; echo'dius B1
[4] arturius A B3 ; artu'rius B1
[5] fint A ; find B1 B3
[6] miatorum A ; Mitithorum B1 ; micitorum B3. Here the source of
B1 B3 has had an open Irish *a*, copied as *ci*.
[7] in strage A B3 ; strage B1. See p. 41.
[8] Echodius A B3 ; Eco'dius B1
[9] buide A B1 ; biude B3

[I 9] A prophecy of Saint Columba
concerning king Aidan's sons

At another time, before the above-mentioned battle, the saint questioned king Aidan about a successor to the kingdom. When he answered that he did not know which of his three sons should reign, Artuir, or Echoid Find, or Domingart, the saint then spoke in this manner : ' None of these three will be king ; for they will fall in battles, slain by enemies. But now, if you have others that are younger, let them come to me, and the one whom the Lord has chosen from among them to be king will run at once to my knee '.

They were called, according to the saint's word ; and when Echoid Buide came in, he leaned on Columba's bosom. Immediately the saint kissed and blessed him, and said to the father : ' This is the survivor, and he will reign after you as king ; and his sons will reign after him '.

All these things were completely fulfilled afterwards, in their time. For Artuir and Echoid Find were slain a little while later, in the battle of the Miathi mentioned above. Domingart was killed in a rout of battle in England. And Echoid Buide succeeded to the kingdom after his father.

De Domnallo filio Aido. .

DOMNALLUS FILIUS Aido [1] adhuc puer ad sanctum Columbam in dorso Cete [2] per nutritores adductus [3] est. 19b Quem intuens per|cunctatur inquiens : ' Cujus est filius hic quem adduxistis ? ' [4] Illís respondentibus, ' Hic est Domnallus filius Aido,[5] qui ad te ideo perductus est ut tua redeat benedictione ditatus ',[6] quem cum sanctus benedixisset, contenuo [7] ait : ' Hic post super [8] omnes suos fratres superstes erit, et rex valde famosus. Nec umquam in manus inimicorum tradetur, sed morte placida in senectute, et intra domum suam, coram amicorum familiarium turba super suum morietur lectum '. Quae omnia secundum beati vaticinium viri de eo vere adimpleta sunt. .

De Scandlano filio Colmani. . [9]

EODEM TEMPORE sanctus et in eodem loco ad Scandlanum [10] fili[um] [11] Colmani [12] apud Aidum [13] regem in vinculís retentum visitare eum cupiens pergit ; ipsumque

---

[1] filius aido A B3 ; filius aido' B1. Here, and in the title above, *aido* is the Irish genitive case.

[2] cete A, with two over-dashes ; cete B1 B3. The place was Druimm-céte, where Columba attended the famous council of A.D. 575. See 49b, and p. 40.

[3] *adductus*. In A, a small *u* has been written by m.h. above the text-hand's ligature for *us*.

[4] *adduxistis*. In A, there was no punctuation sign after this word: a down-sign and an interrogation sign have been added by m.h. in A ; B1 has a point with question-mark ; and B3, a down-sign with question-mark.

[5] aido A B3 ; aido' B1

[6] ditatus A B1 B3 ; in A, a small *u* has been added by m.h. above the text-hand's ligature for *us*. In A, there was no punctuation sign after *ditatus* : a point and down-sign have been added by m.h. in A ; B1 has a point, and B3 a down-sign.

[7] contenuo A ; the *e* has later been altered to *i* by a long down-stroke with a fine pen. conti'nuo B1 ; continuo B3

[I 10] Concerning Domnall, Aid's son

Domnall, Aid's son, while still a boy, was brought by his foster-parents to Saint Columba in the ridge of Céte. And he, looking upon him, asked : ' Whose son is this, whom you have brought ? ' When they replied, ' This is Domnall, Aid's son, who has been brought to you in order that he may return enriched with your benediction ', and when he had blessed him, the saint said immediately : ' This boy will in the end outlive all his brothers, and will be a very famous king. He will never be delivered into the hands of enemies ; but will die on his bed by a peaceful death, in old age, and within his own house, surrounded by a crowd of his intimate friends '. All these things were truly fulfilled according to the blessed man's prophecy concerning him.

[I 11] Concerning Scandlan, Colman's son

At the same time and in the same place, while Scandlan, Colman's son, was held in chains by king Aid, the saint went to him, desiring to see him ; and after

---

⁸ super A. Omitted in B1 B3.   ⁹ colmani A B3 ; colmanni B1

¹⁰ scandlanum A B3 ; scandla'num B1. Later accounts name this hostage Scandlan Mór, and say that his father was Cennfaelad, king of Osraige (cf. E.S., 1, pp. 81–3, cxlv). In Tigernach, Scandlan Mór is called ' king of Osraige ' at his death, about A.D. 644 ; but his father is not there named (T. 10b10). Adomnan is evidence of a tradition that Scandlan's father was Colman, the king of Osraige who died about 607 (T. 9b2). Colman was perhaps for a time deprived of the kingship (cf. Plummer 1910, 1, pp. 166–7) ; and according to regnal lists, he was immediately succeeded not by Scandlan but by Cennfaelad. Apparently Cennfaelad, who was succeeded by Scandlan, was erroneously represented in some king-list to have been Scandlan's father. Scandlan was a child in 575.

¹¹ fili A ; a small u~ has been added after this by m.h., to read *filium*. filium B1 B3

¹² colmani A B3 ; colmanni B1   ¹³ aidum A B3 ; a'idum B1

232   ADOMNAN'S

20a cum benedixisset confortans | ait : ' Filii ¹ noles ² contri-
stari sed potius laetare et confortare.   Aidus ³ enim rex
apud ⁴ quem vinculatus es de hoc mundo té praecedet,
et post aliqua exilii tempora xxx. annís in gente tua rex
regnaturus es.⁵   Iterumque de regno effugaberis, et per
aliquot exsolabis ⁶ dies, post quos a populo reinvitatus
per tria regnabis brevia tempora '.

Quae cuncta juxta vaticinationem sancti pleni
expleta sunt.   Nam post xxx. annos de regno expulsus
per aliquod ⁷ exsolavit ⁸ spatium temporis, sed post a
populo reinvitatus non ut putabat tribus annís sed ternís
regnavit mensibus ; post quos contenuo ⁹ obiit. .

De duobus aliis regnatoribus qui duo nepotes
Muiredachi¹⁰ vocitabantur Baitanus filius maic-
Erce ¹¹ et Echodius ¹² filius Domnail ¹³ beati
profetatio viri |

20b   ALIO IN TEMPORE per asperam et saxosam regionem
iter faciens quae dicitur Artda-muirchol,¹⁴ et suos audiens
comites Laisranum utique filium Feradachi et Dermitium ¹⁵ ministratorem de duobus supra memoratís
regibus in via sermocinari, haec ad eos verba depromit :

¹ filii A ; the third *i* has later been deleted by a point below with a
fine pen.   Fili B1 B3
² noles A ; noli B1 B3
³ Aidus A B3 ; A'idus B1
⁴ *apud* is used here for the Irish preposition *la*, as it is in 19b25, and
often by other Irish writers.
⁵ es A B3 ; in A, a small minuscule *t* added later after *s*.   e's B1
⁶ exsolabis A ; m.h. has inserted *er* above, after *b*, with placing dots.
exula'bis B1 ; exulabis B3
⁷ aliquod A ; a'liquod B1 ; aliquot B3
⁸ exsolavit A ; m.h. has written *tus* in small letters in the margin, to
read *exsolatus*.   exulavit B1 B3
⁹ contenuo A ; the *e* has later been altered to *i* by a long down-stroke
with a fine pen.   conti'nuo B1 ; continuo B3
¹⁰ muiredachi A ; muiretha'chi B1 ; muirethachi B3

blessing him, said, to encourage him : ' My son, do
not be sad, but rather be joyful, and of good heart.
For king Aid by whom you have been chained will leave
this world before you ; and after some seasons in exile,
you will reign as king among your own people for
thirty years. And again you will be a fugitive from
the kingdom ; and will be in exile for a number of days
after which, recalled by the people, you will reign for
three short seasons '.

All these things were entirely fulfilled according to
the saint's prophecy. For after thirty years he was driven
from the kingdom, and was in exile for some period of
time ; but afterwards, recalled by the people, he
reigned, not for three years, as he supposed he should,
but for three months, immediately after which he died.

[I 12] Prophecy of the blessed man concerning
two other kings, who were called two grandsons
of Muiredach, Baitan, son of Mac-erce,
and Echoid, Domnall's son

At another time, when he was making a journey
through the rough and rocky district that is called
Artda-muirchol [Ardnamurchan], and heard his companions, namely Laisran Feradach's son, and the attendant Diormit, talking on the way about the two kings
mentioned above, he addressed them in these words :

---

11 maic erce A ; maicerke B1 ; maicerce B3. Cf. 18a.
12 echodius A ; ecu'dius B1 ; euchudius B3
13 domnail A; damnail B1 B3
14 artda muirchol A (with *t* not quite joining *d*) ; ardamuircol B1 B3.
The ' heights of Muirchol ' are the hills of Ardnamurchan. See p. 150.
There is a pass through the border of Ardnamurchan from Loch Sunart to
Loch Shiel.
15 dermitium A ; dermi'cium B1 ; dermicium B3

R

'Ó filioli, quare inaniter de hís síc confabulamini?
Nam illi ambo reges de quibus nunc sermocinamini
nuper ab inimicís decapitati disperierunt.[1]   In hac
quoque die aliqui de Scotia adventantes nautae haec
eadem vobís de illís indicabunt regibus'.

Quod venerabilis viri vaticinium eadem die de
Evernia [2] navigatores, ad locum qui dicitur Muirbolc
paradisi [3] pervenientes, supra scriptís ejus binís comitibus
et in eadem navi cum sancto navigantibus de hísdem
21a in|terfectís regibus expletum retulerunt. .

De Oingusio [4] filio Aido Commani [5]
sancti profetia viri

HIC NAMQUE de patria cum aliis duobus fratribus
effugatus ad sanctum in Britanniam [6] perigrinantem [7]
exsul [8] venit. Cuique benedicens haec de eo profetizans
sancto promit de pectore verba : ' Hic juvenis defunctís
ejus ceterís fratribus superstes remanens multo est
regnaturus in patria tempore, et inimici ejus coram ipso
cadent, nec tamen ipse umquam in manus tradetur
inimicorum ; sed morte placida senex inter amicos
morietur '. Quae omnia juxta sancti verbum plene sunt
adinpleta. Hic est Oingussius [9] cujus cognomentum
Bronbachal. .[10]

---

[1] disperierunt A ; disperie′runt B1 ; disperiere B3
[2] evernia A ; the first *e* has later been changed to *i* by a short down-
stroke with a fine pen. hibe′rnia B1 ; hybernia B3. The name is here
synonymous with *Scotia* above, and Scotland is not included in either name.
[3] paradisi A B3 ; paradi′si B1. See Watson 1926, p. 79. *Muirbolc*
meant ' sea-bay ', and its place must have been on the Ardnamurchan
side of Loch Sunart, or more probably on the north side of the headland,
near the mouth of the river Shiel, perhaps Kentra Bay.
[4] oingusio A B3 ; oingu′sio B1
[5] Commani A B1 B3. Before this name, *filii* may have been omitted.
Cf. Reeves 1857, p. 41.
[6] britanniam A ; brittannia B1 B3

' My children, why do you thus idly converse about these things, seeing that both the kings of whom you are now talking have recently perished, beheaded by their enemies ? On this day, too, sailors arriving from Ireland will tell you the same, about these kings '.

On the same day, mariners arriving from Ireland at the place that is called Muirbolc of paradise, related to his two companions named above, who sailed with the saint in the same ship, that this prophecy of the venerable man concerning the slaying of these kings had been fulfilled.

[I 13] Prophecy of the holy man concerning Oingus, son of Aid Comman

This man, driven out from his country with two of his brothers, came as an exile to Britain, to the saint living in pilgrimage there ; who, blessing him, drew from his holy breast these words in prophecy concerning him : ' This young man, surviving after the rest of his brothers are dead, will reign in his country for a long time ; and his enemies will fall in his presence. He himself will never be delivered into the hands of enemies, but will die by a peaceful death, an old man, among friends '.

All this was completely fulfilled according to the saint's word. This was the Oingus whose epithet was Bronbachal.

---

7 perigrinantem A ; pereg- B1 B3
8 exsul A ; exul B1 B3
9 oingussius A ; oingu'sius B1 ; omgusius B3
10 bronbachal A B1 B3 ; in A, an acute accent has been added later, above *o*. The death of Oingus Bronbachal, king of the cenel-Coirpri, is entered in A.U. under 648=649.

Profetia [1] beati viri de filio
Dermiti [2] regis qui Aidus Slane [3]
lingua nominatus est scotica |

21b ALIO IN TEMPORE cum vir beatus in Scotia per
aliquot demoraretur dies ad supradictum Aidum [4] ad sé
venientem síc profetice locutus ait: ' Praecavere debes
filii [5] ne tibi a deo totius Everniae [6] regni praerogativam
monarchiae praedistinatam [7] parricidali faciente peccato
amittas. Nam si quandoque illud commiseris, non toto
patris [8] regno sed ejus aliqua parte in gente tua brevi
frueris [9] tempore '.

Quae verba sancti síc sunt expleta secundum ejus
vaticinationem. Nam post Suibneum [10] filium Columbani dolo ab eo interfectum, non plus ut fertur quam
iiii. annís et tribus mensibus regni concessa potitus [11] est
parte. .[12]

[1] Profetia A ; prophetiam B1 ; prophecia B3. The first three words
are transferred in B1 B3 from the beginning to the end of this chapter-
heading.

[2] dermiti A B3 ; dermi'ti B1. This was Diormit, Cerball's son, king of
the southern Ui-Néill, and high-king of Ireland. See pp. 75-6.

[3] aidus slane A B3 ; aidusslane B1

[4] aidum A B3 ; a'idum B1

[5] filii A ; the third i has later been deleted with a point below. fili B1 B3

[6] everniae A ; hibe'rnie B1 ; hibernie B3

[7] praedistinatam A ; predestinatam B1 B3

[8] *patris*. In A, a point made with a fine pen below i is unexplained.
A still finer dot seems to have been placed below the second stroke of r in
tribus below.

[9] frueris A ; an acute accent has later been added above *e*. finie'ris B1 ;
finieris B3 : here the Irish letters *ru* have been misread as *ini*.

[10] suibneum A B3 ; suibne'um B1

[11] potitus A ; poti'tus B1 ; pocius B3

[12] parte A B1 ; parce B3

[I 14] Prophecy of the blessed man concerning king Diormit's son who was called Aid Slane in the Irish tongue

At another time, when the blessed man was staying for some days in Ireland, and Aid (mentioned above) came to him, he spoke to him prophetically thus, saying : ' My son, you must take heed lest by reason of the sin of parricide you lose the prerogative of monarchy over the kingdom of all Ireland, predestined for you by God. For if ever you commit that sin, you will enjoy not the whole kingdom of your father, but only some part of it, in your own tribe, and for but a short time '.

These words of the saint were fulfilled exactly according to his prediction. For after Aid had treacherously killed Suibne, Colman's son, he had dominion over the part of the kingdom that had been yielded to him for no more, as it is told, than four years and three months.

De rege Roderco [1] filio Tothail [2]
qui in [3] petra Cloithe [4] regnavit
beati viri profetia

ALIO IDEM IN TEMPORE, ut [5] erat sancti viri amicus,
22a aliquam ad eum occultam | per Lugbeum [6] mocu-Min [7]
legationem misit, scire volens si ab inimicís esset trucidandus an non. At vero Lugbeus a sancto interrogatus [8]
de eodem rege et regno et populo ejus [9] respondens quasi
misertus dicit : ' Quid de illo inquiris misero, qui qua
hora ab inimicís occidatur nullo modo scire [10] potest ?'
Sanctus tum deinde profatur : ' Numquam in manus
tradetur inimicorum ; sed in sua super suam pluma-
tiunculam morietur domu '.[11]   Quod sancti de rege
Roderco [12] vaticinium plene adimpletum est.   Nam
juxta verbum ejus in domu [13] sua morte placida obiit. .

De duobus puerís, quorum [unus] [14] juxta
verbum sancti in fine ebdomadis obiit,
profetia sancti [15]

ALIO IN TEMPORE duo quidam plebei ad sanctum in
Iova commorantem insula deveniunt.   Quorum unus
Meldanus nomine de filio suo qui praesens erat sanctum
22b inter|rogat, quid ei esset futurum.   Cui sanctus síc

---

[1] roderco A B3 ; rode'rco B1. This Roderc, Tóthal's son, was evidently
the Riderch, Tutagual's son, of Welsh pedigrees ; and the Riderch Hen
who fought against king Hussa of the Bernicians, about the beginning of the
seventh century. See E.S., 1, p. 13.
[2] tothail A ; totai'l B1 ; totail B3   [3] in A. Omitted in B1 B3
[4] petra cloithe A B3 ; petraclo'ithe B1. This is a translation of the
O.I. *Ail* (an I-stem ; genitive *Aloo*, in Book of Armagh 20c2), or *Ail-
Clóithe* 'rock of Clyde ', i.e. Dumbarton. It may be inferred from this
prophecy that the siege of Dumbarton, which was the subject of an Irish
tale, and in which the Irish settlers presumably gained the fortress, did
not occur before Roderc's death.
[5] ut A B1 B3. Reeves read *hic ut*, erroneously.

[I 15] The blessed man's prophecy concerning the king Roderc, Tóthal's son, who reigned in the rock of Clóth [Clyde]

At one time this king, since he was a friend of the holy man, sent Lugbe mocu-Min to him with a kind of secret commission, desiring to know whether he should be slain by enemies, or not. So Lugbe, when he was questioned by the saint about the king, and his kingdom and people, answered as if in pity, and said : ' Why do you ask about that afflicted man, who can never know at what hour he is to be killed by enemies ? ' Then the saint spoke : ' He shall never be delivered into the hands of enemies ; but he shall die on his own feather pillow, in his own house '.

This prediction of the saint concerning king Roderc was fully fulfilled. For according to the saint's word he died in his own house, a peaceful death.

[I 16] Prophecy of the saint concerning two boys of whom [one], according to the saint's word, died at the end of a week

At another time two laymen came to the saint, then living in the island of Io. One of them, named Meldan, questioned the saint about his son, who was present, as to what would happen to him. To him the saint

---

6 lugbeum A B3 ; lugbe'um B1. This chapter implies that Lugbe mocu-Min knew the Cumbrian language.

7 mocumin A B1 B3 ; with three over-dashes in A.

8 interrogatus A B1 ; intergatus B3

9 *ejus.* In A, this is the symbol resembling an inverted *e* ; in Reeves's text, wrongly *et.*   10 scire A ; sciri B1 B3

11 domu A ; domo B1 B3   12 roderco A B3 ; rode'rco B1

13 domu A ; domo B3. From *Nam* to *obiit* is omitted in B1.

14 unus B1 B3. Omitted in A.   15 sancti A B3 ; sancti viri B1

profatur : ' Nonne sabbati dies [1] hodierna est ? Filius tuus sexta feria in fine morietur septimanae ; octavaque [2] die, hoc est sabbato, huc [3] sepelietur '.

Alter proinde plebeus nomine Glasdercus [4] et ipse de filio quem ibidem secum habuit nihilominus [5] inter- rogans talem sancti audit responsionem : ' Filius tuus Ernanus [6] suos videbit nepotes, et in hac insula senex sepelietur '. Quae omnia secundum verbum sancti de puerís ambobus suís plene temporibus sunt expleta. .

De Colcio,[7] Aido [8] Draigniche [9] filio, a nepotibus Fechureg [10] orto, et de quodam occulto matris ejus peccato, profetia sancti. .

ALIO IN TEMPORE supra memoratum Colgium,[11] apud sé in Iova commo|rantem insula, sanctus de sua inter- rogat genitrice, si esset relegiosa [12] an non. Cui ipse inquiens ait : ' Bene moratam et bonae famae [13] meam novi matrem '. Sanctus tum síc profetice profatur : ' Mox deo volente ad Scotiam profectus, matrem dili- gentius de quodam suo pergrandi peccato interroga occulto,[14] quod nulli hominum confiteri vult '. Qui haec

[1] *sabbati dies*, Saturday. Cf. 126a.
[2] octavaque A B3 ; octavoque B1
[3] huc A ; hic B1 B3. In A, the word has been altered later by erasure to *hic*. Presumably in the ninth century, a minuscule hand has apparently joined the toe of the *i* to the *c*, and added a cirumflex accent, subsequently erased, above the *i*. The shortened version (in L, and apparently in C D F S) reads *hic*.
[4] glasdercus A ; glasdercis B1 B3, perhaps through the misreading of an Irish *us* ligature.
[5] nihilominus A ; nichil- B1 B3
[6] ernanus A B3 ; in A, an acute accent has later been added above *a*. erna'nus B1
[7] colcio A ; co'lgio B1 ; colgio B3
[8] aido A, with two over-dashes ; a'ido B1 ; aido B3
[9] *draigniche*. This is apparently ' of the blackthorn-brake ', a genitive of *draignech*. Cf. p. 142.

23a

spoke thus : ' Is not this the day of Sabbath ? At the end of a week, on the Friday, your son will die, and on the eighth day from now, that is on the Sabbath, will be brought here for burial '.

Likewise the other layman, named Glasderc, also asked a similar question about the son whom he had with him there, and he received from the saint this reply : ' Your son Ernan shall see his grandsons, and shall be buried on this island in old age '.

All these things were entirely fulfilled in their times, in accordance with the saint's words concerning the two boys.

[I 17] Prophecy of the saint concerning Colcu, Aid Draigniche's son, one of the descendants of Féchre ; and concerning a hidden sin of his mother

At another time the saint questioned Colcu (named above) who was living with him in the island of Io, about his mother, whether she were a religious woman, or no. Colcu replying said : ' That my mother is of good character and good repute, I know '. Then the saint spoke thus prophetically : ' Set out soon, God willing, for Ireland, and question your mother very earnestly about a very grave sin that she has hidden, and that she is not willing to confess to any man '.

---

[10] fechureg A B3 ; fe'gurech B1. For the consonantal group involved, see p. 147. The ' grandsons ' or ' descendants of Féchre ' were said by Reeves to have been the ui-Fiachrach of Galway ; but there was another family of the same name in the north of Connaught (cf. Hogan 1910, p. 671).

[11] colgium A B3 ; co'lgium B1

[12] relegiosa A ; -lig- B1 B3

[13] bene moratam et bonae famae A ; bone fame et bene moratam B1 ; bene moratam et bone fame B3

[14] occulto A ; occulte B1 B3

audiens obsequtus ad Eberniam [1] emigravit. Proinde mater ab eo studiose interrogata, quamlibet primule infitians, tamen suum confessa est peccatum ; et juxta sancti judicationem [2] penitudinem [3] agens sanata, de sé quod sancto manifestatum [4] est valde mirata est.

Colgius [5] vero ad sanctum reversus per aliquot dies apud eum commoratus, de fine sui interrogans temporis, hoc a sancto audit responsum : ' In tua quam amas | 23b patria primarius alicujus eclesiae per multos eris annos. Et si forte aliquando tuum videris pincernam in cena amicorum ludentem, auritoriumque [6] in giro per collum torquentem, scito té mox in brevi moriturum '. Quid plura ? Haec eadem beati viri profetatio síc per omnia est adimpleta, quemadmodum de Colgio [7] eodem est profetata. .

De Laisrano [8] hortulano [9] homine sancto

VIR BEATUS quendam de suís monacum nomine Trenanum gente mocu-Runtir legatum ad Scotiam exire quadam praecipit [10] die. Qui hominis dei obsequtus jusioni [11] navigationem parat festinus ; unumque sibi deesse navigatorem coram sancto queritur. Sanctus haec consequenter eidem respondens sacro promit de pectore verba dicens : ' Nauta[m] [12] quem tibi non

[1] eberniam A ; hibe'rniam B1 ; hyberniam B3
[2] judicationem A ; indicationem B1 (the first *n* written on an erasure) ; judicacionem B3
[3] penitudinem A B3 ; plenitudinem B1 (*ple* written on an erasure).
[4] manifestatum A B3 ; manifestum B1. Adomnan does not explain what this sin was, and later writers are not evidence of what he had in mind.
[5] Colgius A B3 ; Co'lgius B1
[6] *auritorium* (derived from a supine of *haurire*) was a vessel for drawing water or wine. The story implies that the pitcher, containing liquid, flew from the butler's hand and killed Colcu.
[7] colgio A B3 ; co'lgio B1

Hearing this, he complied and departed for Ireland. His mother, assiduously questioned by him, at first denied, but yet confessed, her sin ; and by doing penance according to the saint's decision she was restored. And she marvelled greatly at what had been revealed to the saint concerning her.

Colcu returned to the saint, and remaining with him for some days questioned him about the end of his own time on earth ; and obtained from the saint this reply : ' You will be for many years the head of a church within your native country that you love. And if at any time you chance to see your butler amusing himself at a supper-party of friends, and swinging a pitcher in a circle by its neck, know that you shall very soon die '.

Why say more ? This same prophecy of the blessed man was fulfilled in all things precisely as it had been prophesied, of this Colcu.

[I 18] Concerning Laisran the gardener, a holy man

On a certain day the blessed man ordered one of his monks, called Trenan, of the family mocu-Runtir, to go to Ireland as an emissary. He, obeying the order of the man of God, prepared for his voyage quickly ; and he complained to the saint that he lacked one mariner. Thereupon the saint in reply drew from his holy breast these words, saying : ' The sailor who, you

---

[8] laisrano A B3 ; laisra'no B1
[9] hortulano A ; ortolano B1 ; ortholano B3
[10] praecipit A ; m.h. has altered the first *i* to *e*. -cip- B1 B3
[11] jusioni A ; a small *s* has been added by m.h. above *si*. jussio'ni B1 ; jussioni B3
[12] Nauta A B1 B3

24a adhuc | suppetisse dicis nunc invenire non possum.
Vade in pace. Usque quo ad Eberniam[1] pervenias
prosperos et secundos habebis flatus. Quendamque
obvium videbis hominem eminus occursurum, qui
primus prae ceterís navis proram tuae tenebit in Scotia.
Hic erit comes tui iteris[2] per aliquot in Ebernia dies.[3]
Teque inde revertentem ad nos usque comitabitur vir a
deo electus ; qui in hoc meo monasterio per omne
reliquum tempus bene conversabitur '.

Quid plura ? Trenanus accipiens a sancto benedictionem plenís velís per omnia transmeavit maria. Et
ecce appropinquanti ad portum naviculae Laisranus
mocu-Moie citior ceterís occurrit, tenetque proram.
Nautae recognoscunt ipsum esse de quo sanctus praedixerat. .

De ceto magno quomodo
sanctus praesciens dixerat. . |

24b   QUADAM DIE, cum vir venerabilis[4] in Iova demoraretur insula, quidam frater Berachus[5] nomine ad Ethicam[6]
proponens insulam navigare ad sanctum mane accedens
ab eo benedici postulat. Quem sanctus intuitus[7]
inquit[8] : ' Ó filii,[9] hodie intentius praecaveto ne
Ethicam cursu ad terram directo per latius coneris
transmeare pilagus,[10] sed potius circumiens[11] minores

---

[1] eberniam A ; the first e has later been partly erased, to form i.
hibe'rniam B1 ; hiberniam B3
[2] iteris A ; iti'neris B1 ; itineris B3
[3] in ebernia dies A ; the first e has later been erased, and an i formed
upon it. dies in hibe'rnia B1 ; dies in hibernia B3
[4] venerabilis A B1 ; verabilis B3
[5] berachus A ; be'rachus B1 ; barachus B3
[6] ethicam A B3 ; e'thicham B1. See p. 155.
[7] intuitus A ; intu'itus B1 ; intuitur B3
[8] inquit A B3 ; ait B1

tell me, has not yet come forward, I cannot at present find. Go in peace : until you reach Ireland, you will have fair and favourable breezes. And you will see a little way off a man approaching, who will run to you and, in advance of the others, be the first to grasp the prow of your ship in Ireland. This man will be the companion of your journey in Ireland for some days, and when you return he will accompany you to us. A man chosen by God, he will live a good life in this my monastery throughout the rest of his time '.

Why say more ? Trenan received a blessing from the saint, and crossed with full sails through all the seas. And behold, as the ship neared the harbour, Laisran mocu-Moie ran faster than the others and took hold of the prow. The sailors perceived that he was the man of whom the saint had spoken before.

[I 19] How the saint spoke with foreknowledge concerning a great whale

On a certain day, while the venerable man was in the island of Io, a brother named Berach, intending to sail to the island of Eth [Tiree], went in the morning to the saint, and desired his blessing. The saint looked upon him and said : ' My son, be very careful not to attempt to take the direct route across the open sea to the land of Eth this day, but instead to sail round about,

---

⁹ filii A ; the third i was deleted later with a point above, and a note O file was written by m.h. in the blank space between columns a and b (below an O which was apparently a false start) ; still later, the last i was erased. fili B1 B3
¹⁰ pilagus A ; the i has been altered by m.h. to e. pe′lagus B1 ; pelagus B3
¹¹ circumiens A ; circu′iens B1 ; circuiens B3

secus naviges insulas,[1] ne videlicet aliquo monstruoso
perterritus prodigio vix inde possis evadere'. Qui a
sancto accepta benedictione secessit ; et navim conscen-
dens sancti verbum quasi parvipendens transgreditur.
Majora proinde Aethici [2] transmeans spatia pilagi,[3] ipse
25a　et qui ibi inerant nautae vident ; et ecce | cetus [4] mirae
et inmensae magnitudinis, se instar montis eregens,[5] ora
aperit patula nimis dentosa supernatans. Tum proinde
remiges deposito velo valde perterriti retro reversi illam
abortam [6] ex beluino motu fluctuationem vix evadere
potuerunt. Sanctique verbum recognoscentes profeticum ammirabantur.[7]

Eadem [8] quoque die sanctus Baitheneo [9] ad supra
memoratam insulam navigaturo mane de eodem intimavit ceto, inquiens : ' Hac praeterita nocte media
cetus magnus de profundo maris sé sublevavit,[10] et inter
Iovam et Ethicam insulam sé hodie in superficiem
ereget [11] equoris '. Cui Baitheneus [12] respondens [13] infit :
' Ego et [14] illa bilua [15] sub dei potestate sumus '. Sanctus
25b　' Vade ' ait, ' in pace. Fides tua in Christo | té ab hoc
defendet periculo '. Baitheneus [16] tum deinde a sancto
benedictione accepta a portu enavigat, transcursísque

---

[1] *minores insulas :* i.e. the Treshnish Islands, between Staffa and Coll.

[2] aethici A ; ethici B1 ; ethnici B3

[3] pilagi A ; the first *i* has been altered by m.h. to *e*. pe'lagi B1 ;
pelagi B3

[4] *cetus.* This ' whale ' is here assimilated to the traditional idea of the
sea-monster of Jonah.

[5] eregens A ; a small *i* has been written by m.h. above the second *e*.
-rig- B1 B3

[6] abortam A ; obortam B1 B3

[7] ammirabantur A B3 ; in A, a small *d* has been written by m.h. above
the first *m*. admirabantur B1

[8] Eadem A B3 ; in A, a circumflex accent has later been added with a
fine pen above the *a*. Ea'dem B1

[9] baitheneo A ; baithe'neo B1 ; baitheno B3

[10] sublevavit A ; the third *u* has later been bridged, and given a down-
stroke, to make *b*, erroneously. sullevavit B1 ; sullivavit B3

by the small islands ; lest you be terrified by a pro-
digious monster, and be scarcely able to escape '.

After receiving the saint's blessing, he went away,
and entered his ship ; and as though making light of
the saint's command, transgressed it.   And so, while
crossing the wide stretch of the sea of Eth, he and the
sailors that were with him there looked up, and behold,
a whale, of marvellous and enormous size, swimming
on the surface, rose up like a mountain, and opened
gaping jaws, with many teeth.   So then the rowers
dropped the sail, and in great terror reversed their
course, and were with difficulty able to escape from
the wash raised by the motion of the beast.   Remem-
bering the saint's prophetic words, they marvelled.

Also on the same day, in the morning, the saint
gave news of the same whale to Baithene, who was
about to sail to the above-mentioned island ; and he
said : ' In the middle of last night, a great whale rose
from the depths of the ocean, and today it will rise to
the surface of the sea between the islands of Io and Eth '.
Baithene said to him in reply : ' I and that beast are
in God's power '.   ' Go in peace ', said the saint ; ' your
faith in Christ will protect you from this danger '.

Thereupon Baithene received the saint's blessing
and sailed from the harbour.   And after covering a

---

[11] ereget A ; a small *i* has been written by m.h. above the second *e*.
e'riget B1 ; erigit B3

[12] baitheneus A B3 ; baitene'us B1

[13] respondens A B3. Omitted in B1.

[14] *et*. Below this word, in A, *et* has been written with a fine pen, and
smudged out.   In the bottom margin, *fertur* has been written by m.h.,
and smudged out.

[15] bilua A ; the *i* has been altered by m.h. to *e*.   be'lua B1 ; bellua B3

[16] Baitheneus A B3 ; Baithe'neus B1

non parvís ponti spatiis ipse et socii cetum aspiciunt ;
perterritísque omnibus, ipse solus equor et cetum ambís [1]
manibus elevatís benedicit intrepidus. Eodemque momento bilua [2] magna sé sub fluctus inmergens nusquam
deinceps eís apparuit. .

De quodam Baitano, qui cum ceterís
desertum marinum appetens enavigaverat,
sancti profetia viri. .

ALIO IN TEMPORE quidam [3] Baitanus, gente [4] nepos
niath Taloirc,[5] benedici á sancto petivit, cum ceterís in
mari herimum [6] quaesiturus. Cui valedicens [7] sanctus
hoc de ipso profeticum protulit verbum [8] : ' Hic homo,
qui ad quaerendum in ociano [9] desertum pergit, non in
26a deserto conditus jacebit, sed illo in loco sepelietur | ubi
oves femina trans sepulchrum ejus minabit '.

Idem itaque Baitanus post longos per ventosa circuitus equora herimo [10] non reperta ad patriam reversus
multís ibidem annís cujusdam cellulae dominus permansit [11] quae scotice Lathreg-inden [12] dicitur. Hísdemque diebus accedit quibus [13] post aliqua mortuus tempora
sepultus est in roboreto Calcagi,[14] ut propter hostilitatis

---

[1] ambís A ; ambis B1 ; ambabus B3
[2] bilua A ; the *i* has been altered by m.h. to *e*. belua B1 B3
[3] quidam A B1 ; quida B3
[4] gente A B3. Omitted in B1.
[5] niath taloirc A ; niathaloirc B1 ; mathaloirc B3. Baitan was a
grandson, or descendant, ' of Talorc's nephew ' (sister's son) ; see p. 147.
Grammatically, *niath* could also be genitive plural.
[6] herimum A ; the *i* has been altered by m.h. to *e*. -rem- B1 B3
[7] *valedicens*. In A, the letter between *l* and *d* has been obliterated,
possibly by a blot afterwards erased. The letter *e* (not in the text hand)
was written above *i*, and placing-dots, after the *e* and below the erasure,
mark where it should stand.
[8] *verbum*. Adomnan does not say whether this prophecy was made
before or after Columba had left Ireland.

great stretch of the ocean he and his companions saw
the whale ; and while they all were terrified, he alone
undaunted, raising both his hands, blessed the sea and
the whale. In the same instant the great beast plunged
beneath the waves, and appeared to them no more.

[I 20] Prophecy of the holy man concerning one
Baitan, who with the others had sailed
out looking for a desert place in the sea

At another time, a man Baitan, by family a descendant of nia-Taloirc, asked to be blessed by the saint on
going to seek with the others a desert place in the sea.
Bidding him farewell, the saint pronounced the following prophecy concerning him : ' This man, who goes
to seek a desert in the ocean, will not lie buried in a
desert place, but will be buried in that place in which
a woman will drive sheep across his grave '.

The same Baitan, after long circuitous voyaging
through windy seas, having found no desert place,
returned to his country ; and for many years he continued there as the head of a small church, which in
Irish is called *Lathreg-inden*. After some seasons in the
oakwood of Calcach [Derry] he died and was buried

---

[9] ociano A ; the *i* has been altered by m.h. to *e*. occe'ano B1 ;
occeano B3
[10] herimo A ; the *i* has been altered by m.h. to *e*. -rem- B1 B3
[11] permansit A ; remansit B1 B3
[12] lathreg inden A, with four over-dashes ; lathreginden B1 B3. The
meaning seems to be ' house-site of Finden '. Here Adomnan may be
admitted as evidence that *lathrech* could be a feminine noun ; it is elsewhere
inflected as a masculine or neuter O-stem. Since the *f* of *finden* is lenited,
synthesis requires that *lathreg* should be either nominative feminine, or
genitive masculine or neuter.
[13] Hísdemque diebus accedit quibus A ; Qui B1 B3, reducing to
nonsense the intricate sentence of A.
[14] calcagi A : ca'lgagi B1 ; calgachi B3

S

incursum vicina ad ejusdem loci eclesiam plebicula [1]
cum mulieribus et parvulís confugeret. Unde contigit
ut quadam die mulier depraehenderetur aliqua quae
suas per ejusdem viri sepulchrum nuper sepulti oviculas
minabat. Et unus ex hís qui viderant sanctus sacerdos
dixit : ' Nunc profetia sancti Columbae expleta est
multís prius devulgata [2] annís '. Qui utique supra
26b memoratus prespiter mihi haec | de Baitano enarrans
retulit, Mailodranus [3] nomine, Christi miles, gente
mocu-[Cu]rin. .[4]

De Nemano [5] quodam ficto penetente [6]
sancti profetatio [7] viri

ALIO IN TEMPORE sanctus ad Hinbinam [8] insulam
pervenit [9] ; eademque die ut etiam penitentibus aliqua
praecipit [10] cibi consulatio [11] indulgeretur. Erat autem
ibi inter penetentes [12] quidam Nemanus [13] filius Cathir [14]
qui a sancto jusus [15] rennuit [16] oblatam accipere con-
sulatiunculam.[17] Quem sanctus hís conpellat verbís :
' Ó Nemane,[18] a me et Baitheneo [19] indultam non recipis
aliquam refectionis indulgentiam.[20] Erit tempus quo

[1] plebicula A ; plebe'cula B1 ; plebecula B3
[2] devulgata A ; a small *i* has been written by m.h. above *e*. div- B1 B3
[3] mailodranus A B3 ; mailrodanus B1. This is a latinized form of
Mailodran, a derivative of *Mailodar* or *-odur*. Cf. Maud Joynt, in R.I.A.
Contributions, under *mael* and *odran*.
[4] mo | curin A ; mocucuri'n B1 ; mocu|curin B3. In A, there is a
gap, probably through erasure of two letters, after *mo* ; and *curin* is centred
in the next line. The presumption is that the text hand had written
mocu|curin.
[5] nemano A B3 ; nema'no B1
[6] penetente A ; penitente B1 ; penitenti B3
[7] profetatio A ; propheti'a B1 ; prophecia B3
[8] hinbinam A B3 ; hinbi'nam B1
[9] insulam pervenit A ; perve'nit i'nsulam B1 ; pervenit insulam B3
[10] praecipit A ; precepit B1 ; precipit B3
[11] consulatio A ; the *u* later altered to *o* by bridging. -sol- B1 B3

there. And about the same time, it happened that because of an attack by enemies the neighbouring lay-people, with their women and children, took refuge in the church of that place. And so it came about that one day a woman was observed driving her sheep through the burial-place of that man, who had recently been buried there. And one of those that saw it, a holy priest, said : ' Now the prophecy of Saint Columba has been fulfilled, that was made known many years ago '. He, that is to say the above-mentioned priest, related these things to me, in telling me about Baitan. His name was Mailodran, a soldier of Christ, of the family mocu-[Cu]rin.

[I 21] Prophecy of the holy man
concerning Neman, a false penitent

At another time, the saint came to the island of Hinba. And on that day he ordered that some indulgence in food should be allowed, even to the penitents. There was among the penitents there one Neman, Cather's son, who refused to take at the saint's bidding the proffered consolation. Him the saint addressed in these words : ' Neman, you do not accept an indulgence in diet that I and Baithene have granted. The

---

¹² penetentes A ; a small *i* has later been written with a fine pen above the second *e*. -nit- B1 B3
¹³ nemanus A B3 ; ne'manus B1, altered by the text hand from *nema'nus*.
¹⁴ cathir A B3 ; cathi'r B1
¹⁵ jusus A ; m.h. has written *s* above the first *us*. jussus B1 B3
¹⁶ rennuit A ; the first *n* has later been erased. re'nuit B1 ; renuit B3
¹⁷ consulatiunculam A ; the first *u* has later been altered to *o* by bridging. -sol- B1 B3
¹⁸ nemane A B3 ; ne'mane B1
¹⁹ baitheneo A B3 ; baithe'neo B1
²⁰ *indulgentiam*. After this word B3 has a question mark.

cum furacibus [1] furtivae [2] carnem in silva manducabis
equae '.   Hic idem itaque postea ad seculum reversus in
27a saltu cum furibus talem comedens carnem juxta | verbum
sancti de graticula [3] sumtam [4] lignea inventus est.

De infelici quodam qui
cum sua dormivit genitrice

ALIO IN TEMPORE fratres intempesta nocte suscitat
sanctus ; ad quos in eclesia congregatos dicit : ' Nunc
dominum intentius precemur.   Nam hac in hora aliquod [5] inauditum in mundo peccatum perpetratum est,
pro quo valde timenda judicialis vindicta '.[6]   De quo
peccato crastino [7] die aliquibus paucís percunctantibus
intimavit, inquiens : ' Post paucos menses cum Lugaido [8]
nesciente infelix ille homuncio ad Iovam perveniet
insulam '.

Alia itaque die sanctus ad Diormitium [9] interjectís
quibusdam mensibus praecipiens profatur [10] : ' Surge
citius.   Ecce Lugaidus [11] appropinquat, dicque [12] ei ut
miserum quem secum in navi habet in Maleam [13] pro-
27b pellat | insulam, ne hujus insulae cispitem [14] calcet '.
Qui praecepto sancti obsequutus ad mare pergit,
Lugaidoque [15] adventanti omnia sancti prosequitur de

---

[1] furacibus A ; furantibus B1 B3
[2] furtivae A, with a deletion point above the Irish *ae*-symbol ; furtive
B1 B3. If the deletion point in A was a correction by the text hand, the
reading intended was *furtive* ' stealthily ', as in Reeves's text, and we may
compare *laboriosae* for *laboriose* in 17a. But it seems to us probable that what
Adomnan wrote was *furtivae*, which makes the better sense. Compare the
Life of Enda, in Plummer 1910, II, p. 73, where a stolen horse appears in a
similar story. In B1 B3, the *e* would stand for either *e* or *ae*.
[3] graticula A ; crat- B1 B3
[4] sumtam A ; a small *p* has later been written with a fine pen above *mt*,
and afterwards smeared out. sumptam B1 B3
[5] aliquod A B1 ; aliquot B3
[6] vindicta A ; est vindicta B1 B3

time will come when in a wood, with thieves, you will chew the flesh of a stolen mare '.

And so afterwards, when he had returned to the world, this same man was discovered, according to the saint's word, in a forest pasture with thieves, consuming such flesh taken from a wooden griddle.

[I 22] Concerning an unhappy man who slept with his mother

At another time, the saint roused the brothers in the dead of night ; and when they had assembled in the church he said to them : ' Now let us pray earnestly to the Lord, because in this hour a sin unheard-of in this world has been committed, for which the judicial penalty must be very terrible '. And on the following day, in answer to a few of the brothers who asked him about that sin, he said : ' After a few months, that unhappy fellow will arrive in the island of Io, accompanying Lugaid, who will know nothing of the matter '.

So one day, after some months had passed, the saint gave an order to Diormit, and said : ' Rise quickly : see, Lugaid is approaching. Tell him that he must cast out upon the island of Male [Mull] the wretch that he has with him in the ship, so that he may not set foot upon the sod of this island '. Obeying the saint's

---

7 crastino A ; crastina B1 B3
8 lugaido A B3 ; luga'ido B1
9 diormitium A ; diormi'tium B1 ; diormicium B3
10 profatur A B3 ; prefatur B1
11 lugaidus A B3 ; luga'dius B1
12 dicque A ; Dic B1 ; Dicque B3
13 maleam A B3 ; ma'leam B1
14 cispitem A ; the first *i* has been altered by m.h. to *e*. ces- B1 B3. The top lines of 27b and 26a in A are badly stained.
15 lugaidoque A B3 ; luga'idoque B1

infelici viro verba. Quibus auditís ille infelix juravit numquam se cibum cum aliis accepturum nisi prius sanctum [1] videret Columbam eumque alloqueretur. Quae infelicis verba Diormitius [2] ad sanctum reversus retulit. Quibus conpertís sanctus ad portum perrexit. Baitheneoque [3] prolatís sacrae scripturae testimoniis suggerenti ut miseri penitudo susciperetur sanctus consequenter inquit : ' Ó Baithenee,[4] hic homo fratricidium in modum perpetravit Caín,[5] et cum sua matre mechatus est '. Tum deinde miser in litore flexís genibus [6] leges penetentiae [7] expleturum sé promisit, juxta sancti judicationem. Cui sanctus ait : ' Si xii.[8] annís inter Brittones [9] cum fletu et lacrimís penetentiam [10] egeris, nec ad Scotiam | usque ad mortem reversus fueris, forsan deus peccato ignoscat tuo '. Haec dicens sanctus ad suos conversus [11] dicit [12] : ' Hic homo filius est perditionis, qui quam promisit penetentiam [13] non explebit sed mox ad Scotiam revertetur, ibique in brevi ab inimicís interficiendus peribit '. Quae omnia secundum [14] sancti profetiam ita contigerunt. Nam miser hísdem diebus ad Eberniam [15] reversus in regione quae vocitatur Lea [16]

28a

---

[1] sanctum A B3. Omitted in B1

[2] diormitius A ; diormi'cius B1 ; dormitius B3

[3] Baitheneoque A B3 ; Baithe'neoque B1

[4] baithenee A B3 ; baithe'nëe B1

[5] caín A B1 ; cham B3

[6] *genibus*. With this word, after three lost folios, B2 begins again (see under 13b and 37a).

[7] penetentiae A ; the second *e* has later been altered to *i* with a long down-stroke made by a fine pen. -nit- B1 B2 B3

[8] xii A ; duo'decim B1 ; duodecim B2 B3

[9] brittones A B2 B3 ; bri'ttones B1

[10] penetentiam A ; the second *e* has been altered as above. -nit- B1 B2 B3

[11] conversus A B1 B3 ; reversus B2

[12] dicit A B2 B3 ; dixit B1

[13] penetentiam A ; the second *e* has later been altered to *i*, with a very fine down-stroke. -nit- B1 B2 B3

command, Diormit went down to the sea and, when
Lugaid came near, repeated to him all that the saint
had said about the unhappy man. That unfortunate,
hearing these things, swore that he would never take
food with others until he had first seen Saint Columba,
and spoken with him.

Diormit returned to the saint and reported to him
these words of the unfortunate man. On learning them,
the saint went down to the harbour ; and when Baithene
suggested, quoting as evidence passages of holy scripture,
that the wretch's penitence should be accepted, the
saint said in reply : ' Baithene, this man has perpetrated
fratricide, in the manner of Cain, and incest with his
mother '.

Thereupon the wretch, kneeling on the shore, vowed
that he would perform what the laws of penance
required, according to the decision of the saint. And
to him the saint replied : ' If you do penance among
the Britons with wailing and weeping for twelve years,
and do not return to Ireland until your death, perhaps
God will condone your sin '. Saying this, the saint
turned to his people and said : ' This man is a son
of perdition ; he will not fulfil the penance that he has
promised, but in a little while will return to Ireland,
and will there shortly perish, killed by his enemies '.

All these things happened thus, in accordance with
the saint's prophecy. For the wretch returned to
Ireland about the same time, and in the district that

---

14 secundum A B1 B2 ; secumdum B3
15 eberniam A ; a small *i* has later been written above the first *e*.
hibe'rniam B1 ; hiberniam B2 B3
16 lea A, with a long over-dash ; lea' B1 ; léa B2 B3. There may have
been a mark of length in the source of the B manuscripts.

in manus incedens [1] inimicorum trucidatus est. Hic de nepotibus Turtrei [2] erat. .

De .I. vocali
littera

QUADAM DIE BAITHENEUS [3] ad sanctum accedens ait : ' Necesse habeo ut aliquis de fratribus mecum psalterium quod scripsi percurrens emendet '.[4] Quo audito sanctus síc profatur : ' Cur hanc super nos infers sine causa molestiam ? [5] Nam in tuo hoc de quo dicis psalterio | nec una superflua repperietur littera nec alia deesse excepta .I. vocali quae sola deest '. Et síc [6] toto perlecto psalterio sicuti sanctus praedixerat repertum exploratum est.

28b

De libro in aquarium [7] vas sanctus
sicuti [8] praedixerat cadente

QUADAM ITIDEM die ad focum in monasterio [9] sedens videt Lugbeum [10] gente mocu-Min [11] eminus librum legentem. Cui repente ait : ' Praecave filii,[12] praecave. Estimo enim quod quem lectitas liber in aquae plenum sit cassurus[13] vasculum'. Quod mox ita contigit. Nam[14]

---

[1] incedens A ; -cid- B1 B2 B3
[2] turtrei A B2 B3, with three over-dashes in A ; turtre'i B1. The ui-Thuirtri were to the south of Lé ; to the west, and later to the north, of Lough Neagh. They were a branch of the mocu-Uais ; see Walsh 1921.
[3] baitheneus A B1 B3 ; baithenus B2
[4] emendet A B3 ; eme'ndet B1 ; emendat B2
[5] *molestiam.* After this word and above a medial point in the text hand, A has an added question-mark (not m.h.). B1 B2 B3 have question-marks.
[6] síc A ; sic B1 B3 ; sit B2
[7] aquarium A ; aqua'rium B1 ; aquarum B3 ?B2
[8] sanctus sicuti A B2 B3 ; sicuti sanctus B1
[9] *monasterio.* In this chapter, *monasterium* means the common house of the monastery. See p. 113.
[10] lugbeum A B2 B3 ; lugre'um B1

is called Lé he fell into the hands of his enemies, and was put to death.   He was of the grandsons of Turtre.

[I 23] Of the
vowel *I*

One day, Baithene went to the saint and said : ' I have need of one of the brothers, to run through and emend with me the psalter that I have written '.   Hearing this, the saint spoke thus : ' Why do you impose this trouble upon us, without cause ?   Since in this psalter of yours, of which you speak, neither will one letter be found to be superfluous, nor another to have been left out ; except a vowel *I*, which alone is missing '. And so, when the whole psalter had been read through, exactly what the saint had foretold was found to be confirmed.

[I 24] Concerning a book that fell into a
ewer, as the saint had foretold

Similarly one day, while he sat beside the hearth in the monastery, he saw at a little distance Lugbe, of the family mocu-Min, reading a book.   To him he suddenly said : ' Take care, my son, take care !   For I believe that the book you are studying is going to fall into a vessel full of water '.

---

¹¹ mocumin A B2, with three over-dashes in A ; mocumi′n B1 ; mocu-minn B3
¹² filii A B2 ; in A, the last *i* has later been erased.   fili B1 B3
¹³ cassurus A ; the first *s* has later been deleted, with a point above, and a point below.   casurus B1 B2 B3
¹⁴ Nam A B1 B2 ; Nam dum B3

ille supra memoratus juvenis post aliquod breve intervallum ad aliquam consurgens in monasterio mini-
strationem verbi oblitus beati viri, libellus quem sub
ascella¹ neglegentius² inclusit subito in ydriam³ aqua
repletam cicidit. .⁴ |

29a   De corniculo atramenti
                       inaniter defusso⁵

ALIA INTER HAEC die ultra fretum Iovae insulae
clamatum est.   Quem sanctus sedens in tegoriolo⁶
tabulís subfulto audiens clamorem dicit : ' Homo qui
ultra clamitat fretum non est subtilis sensus ; nam hodie
mei corniculum atramenti inclinans effundet '.   Quod
verbum ejus ministrator Diormitius⁷ audiens paulisper
ante januam stans gravem⁸ exspectabat superventurum
hospitem, ut corniculum defenderet.   Sed alia mox
faciente causa inde recessit ; et post ejus recessum hospes
molestus supervenit,⁹ sanctumque osculandum appetens¹⁰
ora vestimenti inclinatum effudit atramenti corniculum. .

                De alicujus adventu hospitis
                quem sanctus praenuntiavit. .¹¹

29b   ALIO ITIDEM TEMPORE sanctus die iii.¹² feriae fra|tribus
síc profatus est : ' Crastina quarta feria jejunare pro-

¹ ascella A B2 B3 ; acella B1   ² neglegentius A ; -lig- B1 B2 B3
³ ydriam A ; fossam B1 B2 B3
⁴ cicidit A ; the first *i* has been altered by m.h. to *e*. ce'cidit B1 ;
cecidit B2 B3
⁵ defusso A ; difuso B1 ; diffuso B2 ; defuso B3
⁶ tegoriolo A ; a small *u* has been written by m.h. above *e*, and also
above the first *o*. tuguri'olo B1 ; tuguriolo B2 ; tugurriolo B3. This
was Columba's writing-hut, not his sleeping-place (*hospitium* or *hospitiolum*).
See pp. 109-13.
⁷ diormitius A ; diormi'cius B1 ; diormicius B2 B3
⁸ gravem A B1 B2 ; gravamen B3

And that presently happened. For the above-named youth, rising after a short time to perform some task in the monastery, forgot what the blessed man had said, and the book, which he had carelessly put under his arm, suddenly fell into a ewer full of water.

[I 25] Of a little ink-horn foolishly spilt

Further, on another day there was a shouting, beyond the strait of the island of Io. The saint, sitting in the hut that was supported on planks, heard the shouting, and said : ' The man who is shouting beyond the strait is not a man of delicate perceptions. Now today he will upset and empty the horn that holds my ink '. His attendant Diormit, hearing him say this, stood for a little while in front of the door, and awaited the arrival of the cumbersome guest, so as to protect the ink-horn ; but presently some other matter caused him to withdraw from there, and after he had withdrawn the disturbing guest arrived. And, eagerly advancing to kiss the saint, he upset and emptied the horn of ink with the border of his garment.

[I 26] Concerning a guest's arrival that the saint foretold

Similarly at another time, on a third day of the week, the saint thus addressed the brothers : ' On the

⁹ supervenit A B2 B3 ; in A, a circumflex accent has later been added with a fine pen above the second *e*. superve'nit B1

¹⁰ appetens A B2 B3 ; in A, an acute accent has later been added with a fine pen above the *a*. a'ppetens B1

¹¹ praenuntiavit A ; -avit B1, altered to -*avit ita* ; -avit B2 B3

¹² .iii. A (for *tertiae*) ; an *ae*-symbol has been added by m.h. below the third *i*. tercie B1 B3. Missing in B2.

ponimus, sed tamen superveniente quodam molesto
hospite consuetudinarium [1] solvetur jejunium '. Quod
ita ut sancto [2] praeostensum est accedit.[3] Nam mane
eadem iiii.[4] feria alius ultra fretum clamitabat [5] proselytus
Aidanus nomine, filius Fergnoi ; [6] qui ut fertur xii.[7]
annís [8] Bre'ndeno [9] ministravit mocu-Alti [10] : vir valde
relegiosus,[11] qui ut advenit ejusdem diei juxta verbum
sancti jejunationem solvit.

De aliquo miserabili viro qui ultra
supradictum clamitabat fretum

QUADAM QUOQUE DIE, quendam ultra fretum audiens
clamitantem sanctus hoc profatur modo : ' Valde mise-
randus est ille clamitans homo, qui aliqua ad carnalia
medicamenta petiturus pertenentia [12] ad nos venit. Cui
oportunius erat veram de peccatís hodie penitudinem
30a gerere, nam in hujus fine ebdomadis | morietur '. Quod
verbum qui inerant praesentes advenienti [13] misero in-
timavere, sed ille parvipendens acceptís quae poposcerat
citius recessit ; et secundum sancti profeticum verbum
ante finem ejusdem septimanae [14] mortuus est.

---

[1] consuetudinarium A B2 ; consuetudina'rium B1 ; cos- B3. Wednesday was observed as a weekly fast in the Irish church.
  [2] sancto A B2 B3 ; á sancto B1
  [3] accedit A (for *accidit*) ; a small *i* has later been written with a fine
pen above the *e*. a'ccidit B1 ; accidit B2 B3
  [4] iiii A ; a small *a* has been added (probably by m.h.). die .iiii.ta B1 ;
quarta B2 B3   [5] clamitabat A B1 B3 ; clamabat B2
  [6] Fergnoi A B2 B3 ; Fergnoi' B1
  [7] xii A ; duodecim B1 B3 ; duodecm B2
  [8] annís A ; annis B1 B3 ; anni B2
  [9] b'rendeno A ; brendeno B1 B2 B3. See 118a, and p. 162.
  [10] mocualti A B1 B3 ; mucuanti B2   [11] relegiosus A ; -lig- B1 B2 B3
  [12] pertenentia A ; a small *i* has been written by m.h. above the second
e. -tin- B1 B2 B3   [13] advenienti A B2 B3 ; adventanti B1
  [14] *septimanae*. This probably means ' six days later ' ; cf. 22b, and
p. 119.

fourth day of the week, tomorrow, we propose to fast ; but nevertheless a disturbing guest will arrive, and the customary fast will be relaxed '.

This befell as it had been revealed to the saint beforehand. For on the same fourth day of the week, in the morning, another stranger shouted across the strait : a very religious man, by name Aidan, Fergno's son, who (it is said) for twelve years attended upon Brenden mocu-Alti. He, when he arrived, relaxed that day's fast, as the saint had said.

[I 27] Concerning a pitiable man who
shouted beyond the above-mentioned strait

Also on a certain day the saint, hearing some one shouting beyond the strait, spoke in this manner : ' Much to be pitied is that man who is shouting and who has come to us to seek things suitable for physical remedies, when today the fitter thing for him was to occupy himself with true repentance for his sins. For in the end of this week he will die '.

Those who were there present made this saying known to the unfortunate man when he arrived ; but, thinking little of it, he took what he had asked for, and went away at once. And in accordance with the prophetic words of the saint, before the end of the same week he died.

De romani juris civitate igni sulfureo celitus prolapso conbusta sancti viri profetia

ALIO ITIDEM IN TEMPORE Lugbeus gente moccu-Min,[1] cujus supra mentionem fecimus, quadam ad sanctum die [2] post frugum veniens triturationem [3] nullo modo ejus faciem intueri potuit miro superfussam [4] rubore ; valdeque pertimescens cito aufugit. Quem sanctus conplosís paulum [5] manibus revocat. Qui reversus a sancto statim interrogatus cur ocius aufugisset, hoc dedit responsum : ' Ideo fugi quia nimis pertimui '. Et post aliquod modicum intervallum fiducialius | agens audet sanctum interrogare, inquiens : ' Num quid hac in hora tibi aliqua formidabilis ostensa visio est ? ' Cui sanctus talem dedit responsionem : ' Tam terrifica ultio nunc in remota orbis parte peracta est '. ' Qualis ' ait juvenis, ' vindicta et in qua regione facta ? ' Sanctus tum sic profatur : ' Sulfurea de caelo flamma super romani juris civitatem [6] intra [7] Italiae terminos sitam hac hora [8] effusa est, triaque ferme milia virorum excepto matrum puerorumque numero disperierunt. Et antequam praesens finiatur annus gallici [9] nautae de Galliarum provinciis adventantes haec eadem tibi enarrabunt '.

Quae verba post aliquot menses veridica fuisse sunt conprobata. Nam idem Lugbeus [10] simul cum [11] sancto

30b (margin)

---

[1] moc|cumin A ; mocumi'n B1 ; mocumin B2 B3

[2] *quadam . . . die.* Cf. *quadam die . . . autumnali tempore,* 54a.

[3] *triturationem.* The time of this story appears to be after the yearly threshing of the grain and before the end of the calendar year.

[4] superfussam A ; the first s has later been deleted with a point above. superfusam B1 B2 B3   [5] paulum A ; paululum B1 B2 B3

[6] *civitatem.* Adomnan gives no indication by which this city can be identified. With regard to the assumption of Notker Balbulus that the place was Citta Nuova in Istria, see Brüning 1917, p. 290.

[7] intra A B1 B3 ; in terra B2

[8] hac hora A B1 B3 ; hora hac B2

[I 28] The holy man's prophecy concerning a
city of the Roman dominion, consumed by
sulphurous fire that had fallen from heaven

Similarly at another time, on a day after the threshing of the grain, Lugbe, of the family mocu-Min, whom
we have mentioned above, going to the saint was quite
unable to look upon his face, which was flushed with
marvellous redness ; and becoming greatly afraid he
quickly fled away. But the saint called him back by
slight clapping of his hands. Returning, he was at
once asked why he had run away so quickly, and he
made this reply : ' I fled because I was much afraid '.
And proceeding with greater confidence, after a slight
pause, he took courage to question the saint, saying :
' No fearful vision has been shown to you, has it, in
this hour ? ' The saint gave him this answer : ' Very
terrible retribution has just now been made, in a distant
part of the world '. ' What kind of retribution ', said
the youth, ' and in what country has it been made ? '
Then the saint spoke thus : ' In this hour, sulphurous
flame has been poured down from heaven upon a city
of the Roman dominion within the borders of Italy ;
close upon three thousand men, not counting the
number of women and children, have perished, and
before the present year is ended the Gallic sailors
arriving from the provinces of Gaul will tell you the
same '.

After some months, these words were proved to
have been correct. For this Lugbe went, along with

---

⁹ gallici A B2 ; ga'llici B1 ; gallice B3
¹⁰ lugbeus A B2 B3 ; lugbe'us B1
¹¹ *cum.* Before this word in A, there is a blank space of about seven
letters. No sign of an erasure can be seen in the facsimiles.

31a viro ad | caput regionis [1] pergens, nauclerum et nautas adventantis [2] barcae interrogans, síc omnia illa [3] de civitate cum civibus ab eís audit [4] enarrata quemadmodum a praedicabili viro sunt praedicta. .

De Laisrano filio Feradachi [5]
beati visio viri. .

QUADAM BRUMALI et valde frigida die sanctus magno molestatus merore flevit. Quem suus ministrator Diormitius [6] de causa interrogans mestitiae hoc ab eo responsum accipit [7] : ' Non inmerito Ó filiole ego hac in hora contristor, meos videns monacos [8] quos Laisranus nunc gravi fatigatos labore in alicujus majoris domus [9] fabrica molestat. Quae mihi valde displicet '.[10] Mirum dictu, eodem momento horae Laisranus habitans in 31b monasterio roboreti | campi quodam modo coactus, et quasi quadam pira intrinsecus succensus, jubet monacos [11] a labore cessare, aliquamque cibationum consulationem [12] praeparari ; et non solum in eadem die otiari, sed et in ceterís asperae tempestatis diebus requiescere. Quae verba ad fratres consulatoria [13] a Laisrano dicta sanctus in spiritu audiens flere cessavit, et mirabiliter

---

[1] *caput regionis.* This is not the equivalent of O.I. *cenn tíre* ' land's end '. But George Buchanan equated it with ' Kintyre ', and the error was followed by other writers ; cf. Watson 1926, p. 92. The *caput* of Argyll was probably Dun Add, in the times of Columba and of Adomnan. See pp. 39, 124.

[2] adventantis A B1 B3 ; -tes B2. After this word in A there is a blank space of two or three letters, with no sign in the facsimiles of erasure.

[3] illa A. Omitted in B1 B2 B3

[4] audit A B3 ; audivit B1 B2

[5] feradachi A B2 B3 ; ferdachi B1

[6] diormitius A B2 ; diormi'cius B1 ; diormicius B3

[7] accipit A ; accepit B1 B2 B3

[8] monacos A ; a small *h* has been added by m.h. above *co*. monachos B1 B2 B3

the holy man, to the chief place of the district ; and he questioned the master and sailors of a ship that arrived, and heard those things about the city and its inhabitants related by them, all precisely as the memorable man had said before.

[I 29] Vision of the blessed man concerning Laisran, Feradach's son

On a very cold winter day the holy man was afflicted with great sorrow, and wept. His attendant, Diormit, questioned him about the cause of his sadness, and received from him this answer : ' Not without good cause, my son, do I grieve at this hour, when I see that Laisran is now harassing my monks in the construction of a large building, although they are exhausted with heavy labour ; and it vexes me greatly '.

Strange to tell, at the same moment of time Laisran, whose abode was in the monastery of the plain of the oakwood [Durrow], being in some way impelled, and as if kindled with an inward fire, ordered that the monks should cease work ; that some consolation of food should be prepared ; and that they should not only take leisure on that day, but also rest on the remaining days of rough weather. The saint, hearing in the spirit these consolatory words spoken by Laisran to the brothers, ceased to weep ; and wonderfully gladdened

---

9 *domus*. This is not certainly the same building that is called *monasterium rotundum* and *magna domus* in 115ab.

10 displicet A ; -ent B1 B2 B3. If A's reading is right, *res* or *molestatio* must be understood.

11 monacos A ; monachos B1 B2 ; monochos B3

12 consulationem A ; -sol- B1 B2 B3

13 consulatoria A ; -sol- B1 B3. Missing in B2.

T

gavisus ipse in Iova insula commanens [1] fratribus qui ad
praesens inerant per omnia enarravit ; et Laisranum
monacorum [2] benedixit consulatorem. . [3]

De Fechno [4] sapiente [5] quomodo penitens
ad sanctum Columbam, ab eodem
praenuntiatus, venit

ALIO IN TEMPORE sanctus in cacumine sedens montis [6]
qui nostro huic monasterio eminus supereminet ad suum
ministratorem Diormitium [7] conversus profatus est,[8]
32a dicens : ' Miror [9] quare tardius | appropinquat quaedam
de Scotia navis, quae quendam advehit sapientem virum
qui in quodam facinore lapsus lacrimosam gerens
penitudinem mox adveniet'. Post proinde haut [10]
grande intervallum ad austrum prospiciens minister
velum navis videt ad portum propinquantis. Quam cum
sancto adventantem demonstraret cito surgit,[11] inquiens :
' Eamus proselyto obviam cujus veram Christus suscipit
penetentiam '.[12]

At vero Feachnaus [13] de navi discendens [14] sancto ad
portum pervenienti obvius occurrit. Cum fletu et
lamento ante pedes ejus ingeniculans flexís genibus
amarissime ingemuit ; et coram omnibus qui ibidem
inerant peccantias [15] confitetur suas. Sanctus tum cum
eo pariter inlacrimatus ad eum ait : ' Surge filii [16] et

---

[1] commanens A B2 ; co'mmanens B1 ; commonens B3
[2] monacorum A ; monachorum B1 B3 ; monachum B2
[3] consulatorem A ; -sol- B1 B2 B3   [4] fechno A B1 B3 ; fectno B2
[5] sapiente A ; sapiente viro B1 B2 B3
[6] *montis.* This was probably the hill called Cnoc Mòr, which overlooks
the village and modern harbours of Iona, and is visible from almost the
whole of the monastic enclosure, at a distance of less than half a mile.
[7] diormitium A B2 ; diormi'tium B1 ; diormicium B3
[8] profatus est A B1 B2 ; profatur B3
[9] miror A ; Miror B1 B3 ; Miro B2

he, being in the island of Io, repeated them in full to
the brothers who were with him at the time. And he
blessed Laisran as the consoler of the monks.

[I 30] Concerning Féchna, a wise man ; how
he came as a penitent to Saint Columba, by
whom his coming was foretold

At another time, the saint was sitting on the top of
the hill that at a little distance overlooks this monastery
of ours ; and turning to his attendant Diormit he spoke,
saying : ' I wonder why a certain ship from Ireland
approaches so slowly. It brings a wise man who has
become guilty of a misdeed, and who will soon arrive,
in tearful repentance '.

After a short interval the attendant, looking out to
the south, saw the sail of a ship that was approaching
the harbour. When he pointed out to the saint that
the ship was coming in, Columba rose quickly, saying :
' Let us go to meet the new-comer, whose true repentance Christ accepts '.

When the saint reached the harbour, Féchna stepped
down from the ship and ran to meet him. Kneeling
before his feet, he groaned bitterly, with weeping and
lamentation, on bended knees ; and confessed his sins
before all those that were present. Then the saint, as
much in tears as he, said to him : ' Rise, my son, and

---

10 haut A ; aut B1 ; haud B2 B3
11 surgit A ; surge B1 B2 B3
12 penetentiam A ; penit- B1 B2 B3
13 feachnaus A ; fechna'nus B1 ; fechnaus B2 B3
14 discendens A ; the *i* has been altered by m.h. to *e*. des- B1 B2 B3
15 peccantias A ; culpas B1 B2 B3
16 filii A ; the third *i* has later been deleted with a point below made
with a fine pen. fili B1 B2 B3

consulare.[1] Dimisa sunt tua quae commisisti pecca-
32b mina. Quia sicut scriptum est : | " Cor contritum et
humiliatum deus non spernit ".' [2] Qui surgens gaudenter
a sancto susceptus ad Baitheneum [3] tunc temporis in
campo Lunge [4] praepossitum [5] commorantem post aliquot est emisus [6] dies, in pace commigrans. .[7]

De Cailtano ejus monaco
sancti [8] profetatio viri. .

ALIO IN TEMPORE binos mittens [9] monacos ad suum
alium monacum nomine Cailtanum,[10] qui eodem tempore
praepossitus [11] erat in cella quae hodieque ejus fratris
Diuni [12] vocabulo vocitatur, stagno adherens Abæ [13]
fluminis, haec per eosdem nuntios sanctus commendat
verba : ' Cito euntes ad Cailtanum properate, dicitote-
que ei ut ad me sine ulla veniat morula '. Qui verbo [14]
sancti obsequuti exeuntes et ad cellam Diuni [15] per-
33a venientes suae legatiunculae qualitatem | Cailtano
intimaverunt. Qui eadem hora nullo demoratus modo
sancti prosequutus legatos ad eum in Iova insula [16] commorantem eorum iteneris [17] comes celeriter pervenit.

[1] consulare A ; -sol- B1 B2 B3
[2] *Cor* to *spernit*, in A, is based upon the Vulgate, Ps. l. 19. B1 B3 have :
deus contritum non spernit et humiliatum cor ; and similarly B2, with *aspernit*
for *spernit*. The reading of the B version is in Adomnan's style, and the
reading of A may have been assimilated to the text of the Vulgate.
[3] baitheneum A B2 B3 ; baithe'neum B1
[4] *campus lunge*, for Irish *mag lunge* ' field of ship ', was the place in Tiree
of a monastery (subject to Iona) to which penitents were sent ; cf. 88b
and p. 141.
[5] praepos|situm A ; the first *s* has later been erased. prepo'situm B1 ;
prepositum B2 B3
[6] emisus A ; a small *s* has been written by m.h. above the first *s*.
emissus B1 B2 B3
[7] *commigrans*. Cf. *ad dominum commigravit*, 115a.
[8] sancti A B1 B3. Omitted in B2.
[9] mittens A B1 B3. Omitted in B2.

be comforted. Your sins that you have committed have been forgiven, because as it is written : " A contrite and a humbled heart God does not despise ".' And Féchna rising was joyfully received by the saint. After some days he was sent to Baithene, who lived at that time as prior in the plain of Long ; and he went in peace.

[I 31] The holy man's prophecy
concerning his monk Cailtan

At another time the holy man sent two monks to another of his monks, by name Cailtan, who was at that time prior in the monastery that even today is called by the name of his brother, Diún, beside the lake of the river Aub [Awe] ; and by the same messengers he sent these words : ' Go quickly, hasten to Cailtan, and bid him come to me without any delay '. Obeying the saint's word they set out, and arrived at the monastery of Diún, and communicated to Cailtan the nature of their mission. In the same hour, without lingering in any way, he accompanied the envoys of the saint, and as companion of their journey speedily reached

---

[10] cailtanum A B3 ; cailta'num B1 ;]num B2

[11] praepossitus A ; the first s has later been erased. prepositus B1 B3. Missing in B2.

[12] diuni A B3, with two over-dashes in A ; divini B1 ; dium B2. The over-dashes in A show that the writer believed this to be an Irish name, not the Latin Divinus. See p. 136. The place of *cella Diuni* is unknown.

[13] abæ A, with two over-dashes ; abae B1 B3 ; ab áe B2. See p. 148. *Aub*, ' river ' or ' water ', is here the name given to the notable river that flows from Loch Awe to Loch Etive and the sea.

[14] verbo A ; verba B1 B2 B3

[15] diuni A B3 ; di'uni B1 ;]ini B2 (Reeves read in B2 *ionunini*).

[16] iova insula A B2 ; iovam insulam B1 ; iona insula B3

[17] iteneris A ; iti'neris B1 ; itineris B2 B3

Quo viso sanctus ad eum taliter loquutus hís conpellat
verbís : ' Ó Cailtane, bene fecisti ad me oboedienter
festinando ; requiesce paulisper.   Idcirco ad te in-
vitandum misi, amans amicum, ut híc mecum in vera
finias oboedientia vitae cursum tuae.   Nam ante hujus
ebdomadis finem ad dominum [1] in pace transibis '.
Quibus auditís gratias agens deo sanctumque lacrimans
exosculatus ad hospitium accepta ab eo benedictione
pergit.   Eademque subsequta infirmatus nocte juxta
verbum sancti in eadem septimana ad Christum dominum emigravit.

De duobus perigrinís [2] fratribus
sancti provida [3] profetatio viri |

33b   QUADAM DOMINICA die ultra sepe memoratum clamatum est fretum.   Quem audiens sanctus clamorem ad
fratres qui ibidem inerant, ' Ite ' ait, ' celeriter ;
perigrinosque [4] de lonquinqua [5] venientes regione ad nos
ocius adducite '.   Qui continuo obsequuti transfretantes
adduxerunt hospites.   Quos sanctus exosculatos [6] consequenter de causa percunctatur iteris.[7]   Qui respondentes
aiunt : ' Ut hoc etiam anno apud té perigrinemur [8]
venimus '.[9]   Quibus sanctus hanc dedit responsionem :
' Apud me ut dicitis anni unius spatio perigrinari [10] non

---

[1] dominum A B1 B2.   Omitted in B3.
[2] perigrinís A ; peregrinis B1 B2 B3
[3] provida A B3 ; pro'vida B1.   Omitted in B2.
[4] perigrinosque A ; -reg- B1 B3.   Missing in B2.
[5] lonquinqua A ; longinqua B1 B2 B3
[6] exosculatos A ; exosculatus B1 B2 B3
[7] iteris A ; iti'neris B1 ; itineris B2 B3
[8] perigrinemur A ; -reg- B1 B3 ?B2
[9] venimus A B2 B3 ; in A, an acute accent has later been added with a
fine pen above the *e*.   ve'nimus B1
[10] perigrinari A ; -reg- B1 B2 B3

him in the island of Io. The saint, when he saw him,
thus addressed him, speaking to him in these words :
' You have done well, Cailtan, in hastening to me
obediently. Rest for a little. As one that loves his
friend, I have sent to invite you, so that here with me
in true obedience you may end the course of your life ;
for before the end of this week you will pass to the
Lord in peace '.

Cailtan, hearing this, rendered thanks to God ; and
weeping he kissed the saint, and after he had received
his blessing went to the guest-house. He fell ill on that
same following night, and in accordance with the saint's
word he departed to Christ the Lord within the same
week.

[I 32] The holy man's prophetic foresight,
concerning two brothers who were pilgrims

On one Lord's-day, there was a shout on the other
side of the often-mentioned strait. The saint heard the
cry, and said to the brothers that were present with
him : ' Make haste, and bring to us quickly the pilgrims,
who come from a district far away '. They obeyed at
once, crossed over, and brought the guests. After
kissing the guests, the saint then questioned them about
the motive of their journey. They said in reply : ' We
have come, to be pilgrims in your monastery for this
year '. To them the saint gave this answer : ' You
cannot remain in pilgrimage with me for the space of

poteritis, nisi prius monacicum [1] promiseritis votum '.[2]
Quod qui inerant praesentes valde mirati sunt ad
hospites eadem hora adventantes [3] dici. Ad quae sancti
verba senior respondens frater ait : ' Hoc in mente
34a propossitum [4] licet | in hanc horam usque nullatenus
habuerimus, tamen tuum sequemur consilium divinitus
ut credimus inspiratum '.

Quid plura ? Eodem horae momento oratorium
cum sancto ingressi devote flexís genibus votum
monachiale [5] voverunt. Sanctus tum deinde ad fratres
conversus ait : ' Hi duo proselyti vivam deo sé ipsos
exhibentes hostiam, longaque in brevi christianae tempora militiae conplentes,[6] hoc mox eodem mense ad
Christum dominum in pace [7] transibunt '. Quibus
auditís ambo fratres gratias deo agentes ad hospitium
deducti sunt. Interjectísque diebus septem senior frater
coepit infirmari. Et eadem peracta septimana ad
dominum emigravit. Similiter et alter post septem alios
dies infirmatus, ejusdem in fine ebdomadis ad dominum
34b feliciter transit.[8] Et | síc secundum sancti veridicam
profetiam intra ejudsem mensis terminum ambo praesentem finiunt vitam. .

[1] monacicum A ; a small *ch* has been written by m.h. above the *i*.
-na'ch- B1 ; -nach- B2 B3

[2] *votum.* See p. 118. Opposite this word, in the outer margin of A, a
plus-sign with four dots has been written, apparently in modern times.

[3] adventantes A B1 B2 ; adventates B3

[4] propossitum A ; the first *s* has later been erased. propositum B1
B2 B3

[5] monachiale A ; monachi'le B1 ; monachile B2 B3

[6] *conplentes.* There is some doubt here whether the meaning is ' crown-
ing in a short space long years of Christian service ', or ' comprising in
a short space the equivalent of many years of Christian service '.

[7] in pace A. Omitted in B1 B2 B3.

[8] transit A ; tra'nsiit B1 ; transiit B2 B3

one year, as you say, unless first you take the monastic vow '. Those that were present there marvelled greatly that this was said to guests who had arrived in that very hour. The elder brother, in answer to these words of the saint, said : ' Although until this hour we have not at all had this purpose in mind, yet we shall follow your counsel which, we believe, is divinely inspired '.

Why say more ? At that same moment they entered the oratory with the saint, and on bended knees devoutly took the monastic vow. Thereupon the saint turned to his monks and said : ' These two strangers, offering themselves as a living sacrifice to God, and consummating in a short space long years of service as soldiers of Christ, presently within this same month will depart in peace to Christ the Lord '.

When they heard this, the two brothers gave thanks to God, and were conducted to the guest-house. After an interval of seven days, the elder brother fell ill, and after that week was completed he departed to the Lord. Similarly also the other fell ill after another seven days, and in the end of that week passed happily to the Lord. And so according to the saint's true prophecy, they both ended this life within the space of that same month.

De quodam Artbranano [1]
sancti profetia viri

CUM [2] PER ALIQUOT dies in insula demoraretur Scia,[3]
vir beatus alicujus loci [4] terrulam mari vicinam baculo
percutiens ad comites síc ait : ' Mirum dictu Ó filioli
hodie in hac hujus loci terrula quidam gentilis senex,
naturale per totam bonum custodiens vitam, et babti-
zabitur et morietur et sepelietur '. Et ecce quasi post
unius intervallum horae navicula ad eundem supervenit [5] portum, cujus in prora quidam advectus est
decrepitus senex, Geonae primarius [6] cohortis ; quem
bini juvenes de navi sublevantes ante beati conspectum
35a viri deponunt. | Qui statim verbo dei a sancto per inter-
praetem recepto credens ab eodem babtizatus est. Et
post expleta babtizationis ministeria [7] sicuti sanctus
profetizavit eodem in loco consequenter obiit, ibidemque
socii congesto [8] lapidum acervo sepeliunt. Qui hodieque
in ora cernitur maritima. Fluiusque [9] ejusdem loci in
quo idem baptisma acciperat [10] ex nomine ejus dobur [11]
Artbranani [12] usque in hodiernum nominatus est [13] diem
ab acculís [14] vocitatur. .

[1] artbranano A B2 B3 ; artbrana'no B1.
[2] Cum A B1 B3 ; Aum B2, a mistake of the decorator.
[3] scia A B2 B3 ; sci'a B1. See p. 155.
[4] *loci*. Here and below, *locus* is probably used in the sense of O.I. *bale*
' place ', later very often found as the first element in the name of a dwelling
among cultivated lands.
[5] supervenit A B2 B3 ; in A, a circumflex accent has later been added
with a fine pen above the second *e*. superpe'rvenit B1
[6] geonae primarius A ; primarius ge'one B1 ; primarius geone B2 B3.
This ' cohort ' seems to have been some defensive band or military con-
fraternity. Its place (?Geon), perhaps an island, is unknown.
[7] ministeria A ; misteria B1 B2 B3
[8] congesto A B1 B2 ; congestu B3
[9] Fluiusque A B2 ; Fluvius B1 ; Fluviusque B3
[10] acciperat A ; the *i* has been altered by m.h. to *e*. acce'perat B1 ;
acceperat B2 B3

[I 33] The holy man's prophecy
concerning a certain Artbranan

When the blessed man was spending some days in
the island of Sci [Skye], in a certain place he struck with
his staff a plot of ground beside the sea, and spoke
thus to those that accompanied him : ' My children,
strange to tell, today in this place, on this plot of ground,
a certain pagan old man, who has preserved natural
goodness throughout his whole life, will be baptized,
and will die, and will be buried '. And behold, after
the space of about one hour, a little ship came to land
at that harbourage, and in its prow was carried a feeble
old man, the leader of the cohort of Geon (?). Two
young men lifted him from the ship, and set him
down in front of the blessed man. And as soon as he
had, through an interpreter, received the word of God
from the saint, he believed, and was baptized by him.
And after the rites of baptism had been performed, he
presently died in that place, as the saint had prophesied,
and there his companions buried him, building a cairn
of stones. It can still be seen today upon the sea-coast.
And the stream of that place, in which he received
baptism, down to the present day named after his
name, is called by the people of the district ' *dobur* of
Artbranan '.

---

[11] dobur A, with two over-dashes ; dobur B1 B2 B3. This was an O.I.
word for ' water '.

[12] artbranani A B2 B3 ; artbrana'ni B1. His name was not originally
Irish, since Columba needed to speak to him through an interpreter.
See p. 158.

[13] nominatus est A ; nominatus B1 B2 B3. The *est* in A has later been
deleted, with three dots above, and with a horizontal line through, the
letters ; both deletions are made with a very fine pen. The word may
not have been in A's exemplar. It is redundant.

[14] acculís A ; the *u* has later been altered to *o* by bridging. -col- B1
B2 B3

De navicula [1] noctu [2] transmotata [3]
sancto praecipiente

ALIO IN TEMPORE trans Britanniae [4] dorsum iter agens aliquo in desertís viculo agellís reperto ibidem juxta alicujus marginem rivoli [5] stagnum [6] intrantis sanctus
35b mansionem faciens, eadem nocte dormientes semi|sopore degustato suscitat comites, dicens : ' Nunc nunc celerius [7] foras exeuntes nostram quam ultra rivum naviculam possuistis [8] in domu [9] huc citius advehite, et in viciniore domucula [10] ponite '. Qui contenuo [11] oboedientes sicut eís [12] praeceptum est fecerunt. Ipsísque iterum quiescentibus sanctus post quoddam intervallum silenter Diormitium [13] pulsat, inquiens : ' Nunc stans extra domum aspice quid in illo agitur viculo, ubi prius vestram possuistis naviculam '. Qui sancti praecepto obsequutus domum egreditur, et respiciens videt [14] vicum flamma vastante totum concremari ; reversusque ad sanctum quod ibidem agebatur retulit. Sanctus proinde fratribus de quodam narravit [15] emulo persequutore, qui easdem domus [16] eadem incenderat [17] nocte. .

[1] navicula A B3 ; navi'cula B1 ; naviculi B2
[2] noctu A B2 B3. Omitted in B1.
[3] transmotata A ; -mut- B1 B2 B3
[4] britanniae A ; britta'nnie B1 ; brittannie B2 ; britannie B3. *Dorsum Brittanniae* was a Latin rendering of O.I. *druimm nAlpan* ' spine of Britain ', strictly the watershed. See p. 59.
[5] rivoli A ; rivuli B1 B2 B3
[6] *stagnum.* This was Loch Lochy, the lake of the river Lochy (*stagnum lŏch dae*, 5b). See 85a and pp. 142, 150.
[7] celerius A B1 B3 ; scelerrus B2
[8] possuistis A ; the first *s* has later been erased. posu- B1 B2 B3
[9] domu A ; a bar-sign (tilde) has been added by m.h. above *u.* domo B1 B2 B3. Reeves read *domum*, but the tilde is never used by the writer of A for *m.*
[10] domucula A ; domu'ncula B1 ; domuncula B2 B3
[11] contenuo A ; the *e* has later been altered to *i*, with a long down stroke made with a fine pen. -tin- B1 B2 B3

[I 34] Concerning a boat transferred from one place to another by night, at the command of the saint

At another time, the saint, on a journey across the spine of Britain, finding a hamlet among deserted fields, made his lodging there beside the bank of a stream that flowed into a lake. In the same night, when his companions were slumbering, and had tasted their first sleep, he roused them, saying : ' Go out now, go quickly, and bring hither at once our boat that you left in a house beyond the stream ; and place it in a nearer hut '. They obeyed at once, and did as they were bidden. And when they were again at rest, after some little time the saint silently touched Diormit, saying : ' Now stand outside the house, and see what is happening in the hamlet where first you put your boat '. Obeying the saint's command, he left the house, looked back, and saw that the whole village was being consumed with devastating flame. He returned to the saint, and reported what was happening there. Thereupon the saint gave the brothers an account of a certain hostile pursuer who had set fire to those houses on that night.

---

[12] eís A.   Omitted in B1 B2 B3.
[13] diormitium A B2 ; diormi'cium B1 ; diormicium B3
[14] videt A B1 B2 ; vidit B3
[15] narravit A B2 B3 ; narrante B1
[16] domus A ; domos B1 B2 B3
[17] incenderat A B2 ; ince'nderat B1 ; incenderet B3

De Gallano filio Fachtni [1] qui erat
in diocisi [2] Colgion [3] filii Cellaig [4]|

36a   QUADAM ITIDEM die sanctus in suo sedens tegoriolo [5]
Colcio [6] eidem lectitanti juxta sé profetizans ait : ' Nunc
unum tenacem primarium de tuae praepossitís [7] diociseos [8] daemones ad inferna rapiunt '.   At vero hoc
audiens Colcius [9] tempus et horam in tabula discribens,[10]
post aliquot menses ad patriam reversus Gallanum [11]
filium Fachtni [12] eodem horae momento [13] obiisse [14] ab
acculís [15] ejusdem regionis percunctatus invenit, quo vir
beatus eidem [16] a demonibus raptum enarravit. .

[17] Beati profetatio viri [18] de Findchano [19]
prespitero illius monasterii fundatore quod
scotice Artchain [20] nuncupatur in Ethica [21]
terra. .

ALIO IN TEMPORE supra memoratus prespiter Findchanus, Christi miles, Aidum [22] cognomento Nigrum,
36b   regio genere ortum, Cruthinicum [23] gente, de | Scotia ad

---

[1] fachtni A B1 B3 ; fachni B2.   This Fachtne could have been, but is
not known to have been, the same man as the Fachtna, Coilbath's son,
who was, according to the list in L.L. 41e, king of Dal-nAridi, and whose
successor, his nephew Eochu, Conlaid's son, died in A.D. 553. Eochu̧was
king also of the Ulaid, and was the eponym of the ui-Echach of Ulaid. He
was followed (according to the same list) as king of Dal-nAridi by Aid
Brecc, who was killed in 563 ; see p. 74. Adomnan's story implies that
Gallan was a notable layman, and that his district was well known.
[2] diocisi A ; dio'cesi B1 ; diocesi B2 B3.   This is the Greek dioikēsis,
' administration ' or province.   Its synonym below is regio ; it was Colcu's
home-land (patria).   The chapter implies that Colcu was still a student
(lectitans, 36a).   Cf. 115a, 58b.
[3] Colgion.   See p. 148.   The death of ' Colgu Cellach's son ' is placed
by A.U. under 621=622.   [4] cellaig A ; kallachi B1 ; cellachi B2 B3
[5] tegoriolo A ; a small u has been written by m.h. above e, and also
above the first o.   tuguri'olo B1 ; tuguriolo B2 B3
[6] colcio A ; colgi'o B1 ; colgio B2 B3
[7] praepossitís A ; the first s has later been erased.   prepositis B1 B2 B3

[I 35] Concerning Gallan, Fachtne's son, who was in the disctrict of Colcu, Cellach's son

On a certain day the saint, sitting in his hut, said prophetically to this Colcu, who was studying beside him : ' Now demons are dragging to hell one grasping leader from among the chief men of your district '. When he heard this, Colcu wrote down the date and hour, on a tablet. And returning to his country after some months, he learned by questioning, from people of the district, that Gallan, Fachtne's son, had died in the same hour in which the blessed man had told him of the seizure by demons.

[I 36] The blessed man's prophecy concerning the priest Findchan, founder of the monastery that is in Irish called *Artchain*, in the land of Eth [Tiree]

At another time, the above-mentioned priest Findchan, a soldier of Christ, brought with him in clerical garb, from Ireland to Britain, Aid, surnamed the Black,

---

8 diociseos A ; a small *e* has been written faintly by m.h. over the second *i*.   dioce′seós B1 ; diocese′os B2 ; dioceseos B3
9 colcius A ; co′lgius B1 ; colgius B3.   Missing in B2.
10 discribens A ; des- B1 B3.   Missing in B2.
11 gallanum A B2 B3 ; galla′num B1
12 fachtni A, with two over-dashes ; fachtni B1 ; factni B2 B3
13 *horae momento*.   See p. 123.   14 obiisse A ; obisse B1 B2 B3
15 acculís A ; the *u* has later been altered to *o* by bridging. accolis B1 B2 B3
16 *eidem*. In B1 this has been altered to *eisdem* but not by the text hand.
17 This chapter (I 36) is not mentioned in the contents list, 6a.
18 Beati profetatio viri A. Omitted in B1 B2 B3.
19 findchano A B2 B3 ; findca′no B1
20 artchain A, with two over-dashes ; ardicaïin B1 ; ardehaiin B2 ; ardcaiin B3
21 ethica A B2 B3 ; e′thica B1   22 aidum A B3 ; a′idum B1 B2
23 cruthinicum A B3 ; cruithi′nicum B1 ; crutinium B2.   See p. 63.

Brittanniam [1] sub clericatus [2] habitu secum adduxit, ut
in suo apud sé monasterio per aliquot perigrinaretur [3]
annos. Qui scilicet Aidus [4] Niger valde sanguinarius
homo et multorum fuerat trucidator. Qui et Diormitium [5] filium Cerbulis [6] totius Scotiae regnatorem deo
auctore ordinatum interficerat.[7] Hic itaque idem
Aidus [8] post aliquantum in perigrinatione [9] transactum
tempus accito episcopo quamvis non recte apud supradictum Findchanum [10] prespiter ordinatus est. Episcopus tamen non est ausus super caput ejus manum
inponere, nisi prius idem Findchanus [11] Aidum carnaliter
amans suam [12] capiti ejus pro confirmatione inponeret
37a dexteram. Quae talis ordi|natio cum postea sancto
intimaretur [13] viro egre tulit. Tum proinde hanc de illo
Findchano et de Aido ordinato formidabilem profatur
sententiam, inquiens : ' Illa manus dextera, quam Findchanus contra fas et jus eclesiasticum [14] super caput filii
perditionis inpossuit,[15] mox conputrescet et post magnos
dolorum cruciatus ipsum in terram sepelienda [16] praecedet.[17] Et ipse post suam humatam manum per multos
superstes victurus est annos. Ordinatus vero indebete [18]
Aidus [19] sicuti canis ad vomitum revertetur suum. Et
ipse rursum sanguilentus [20] trucidator existet, et ad

---

[1] brittanniam A B1 B2 ; britanniam B3
[2] clericatus A B1 B2 ; claricatus B3
[3] perigrinaretur A ; pegrinaretur B1 ; peregrinaretur B2 B3
[4] aidus A B2 B3 ; a′idus B1
[5] diormitium A B1 B2 ; diormicium B3
[6] cerbulis A B1 B3 ; cerbubulis B2. See p. 136.
[7] interficerat A ; the second *i* has been altered by m.h. to *e*. -fe′c- B1 ;
-fec- B2 B3
[8] aidus A B2 B3 ; a′idus B1   [9] perigrinatione A ; -reg- B1 B2 B3
[10] findchanum A B3 ; findca′num B1 ; findcanum B2
[11] findchanus A B2 B3 ; findcha′nus B1
[12] suam A B1 B3 ; suas B2
[13] *intimaretur.* After this word, three folios of B2 are missing. See under
13b, 50b.

Cruithnian by race, and of royal lineage ; intending that he should for some years be a pilgrim with him in his monastery.   This Aid the Black had been a very bloody man, and a slayer of many men ; he had also killed Diormit, Cerball's son, who had been ordained, by God's will, as the ruler of all Ireland.   This same Aid, then, after passing some time in pilgrimage, was ordained as priest, although not rightly, in the above-mentioned Findchan's monastery, a bishop being summoned for the purpose.   But the bishop dared not lay his hand upon Aid's head, until first Findchan (whose love for Aid was earthly) laid his right hand upon Aid's head, for confirmation.

When the ordination thus made was afterwards reported to the holy man, he was much displeased. Thereupon he pronounced the following terrible sentence upon that Findchan, and upon the Aid who had been ordained, saying :   ' That right hand which, contrary to divine law and the law of the church, Findchan has laid upon the head of a son of perdition will presently rot, and after torments of great pain will precede him into the earth in burial ; and surviving after his hand has been buried he will live for many years.   And Aid, unworthily ordained, will return like a dog to his vomit, and he will again be a bloody killer,

---

¹⁴ *eclesiasticum.*   In A, the letters *um* are superscript, above a vacant space, from which apparently *a* has been erased.

¹⁵ inpossuit A ;   the first *s* has later been deleted with a point below made with a fine pen.   impo′suit B1 ;   imposuit B3

¹⁶ *sepelienda.*   In A, a bar-sign has been added later above *a*, probably by m.h., wrongly supplying *m.*

¹⁷ praecedet A ;   a small *i* has been written by m.h. above the second *e.* precedet B1, altered by the text-hand to *preci′det* ;   precedet B3

¹⁸ indebete A ;   -ite B1 B3

¹⁹ aidus A B3 ;   a′idus B1

²⁰ sanguilentus A B3 ;   sangui′nolentus B1

U

ultimum lancea jugul[a]tus [1] de ligno in aquam cadens
submersus morietur. Talem multo prius terminum
37b promeruit vitae, qui totius | regem trucidavit Scotiae '.
Quae beati viri profetia de utroque adimpleta est.
Nam prespiteri Findchani dexter prae pugnus [2] putre-
factus in terram eum praecessit, in illa sepultus insula
quae Ommon [3] nuncupatur. Ipse vero juxta verbum
sancti Columbae per multos post vixit annos. Aidus [4]
vero Niger, solummodo nomine prespiter, ad sua priora
reversus scelera dolo lancea transfixus de prora ratis [5]
in aquam lapsus stagneam disperiit. .

[6] De quodam sancti solamine spiritus
monacís in via laboriosís miso [7]

INTER HAS praedicabiles profetici spiritus profetationes non ab re [8] videtur etiam de quadam spiritali [9]
consulatione [10] nostrís commemorare literulís quam aliquando sancti Columbae monaci [11] spiritu ejus ipsís in
via obviante sentiebant. .

38a   Alio namque in tempore | fratres post mesionis [12]
opera vespere ad monasterium redeuntes, et ad illum
pervenientes [13] locum qui scotice nuncupatur Cuul Eilne, [14]

[1] jugulentus A ; a small *a* has been written by m.h. above *e*, and *n* has been deleted with a dot below. -latus B1 B3
[2] p˜pugnus A B1 ; prepugnus B3. Here *p˜* is wrongly rendered as *per* by Reeves and in Thesaurus 1903, p. 276. It was the regular Irish symbol for *prae*.
[3] ommon A, with two over-dashes ; omon B1 B3. This island is unidentified.   [4] Aidus A B3 ; A'idus B1
[5] *ratis*, primarily a raft of logs, is here used metonymically for a ship, with a wooden stem (cf. *ligno*, 37a). In A.U., 587=588, Aid is said to have been killed ' in a ship ' (*i luing*). See p. 75. Cf. Kenneth Jackson, in Féilsgríbhinn 1940, p. 536.
[6] This double chapter (I 37) is not mentioned in the contents-list, 6a.
[7] miso A ; misso B3. Omitted in B1.
[8] abre A B1 ; in A, a circumflex accent has later been added with a fine pen above *e*. ab re B3

and at last, pierced with a spear, will fall from wood into water, and die by drowning. He has deserved such an end much sooner, who has slaughtered the king of all Ireland '.

This prophecy of the blessed man was fulfilled in regard to them both. For the right hand of the priest Findchan decayed first, and preceded him into the earth, being buried in the island that is called Ommon. But he himself, according to the word of Saint Columba, lived for many years afterwards. And Aid the Black, priest only in name, returned to his former evil deeds, and, pierced with a spear by treachery, fell from the prow of a ship, into the water of a lake, and perished.

[I 37] Concerning a certain relief by the holy man's spirit, sent to labouring monks upon the way

Among these memorable revelations of the prophetic spirit, it seems not out of place to record also in our pages a certain spiritual refreshment once felt by monks of Saint Columba when his spirit met them on the way.

For at one time, returning towards the monastery in the evening after their work on the harvest, when they came to the place that is in Irish called *Cuul-Eilne*

---

⁹ spiritali A ; spirituali B1 B3
¹⁰ consulatione A ; -sol- B1 B3
¹¹ monaci A ; a small *h* has been added by m.h. above *ci*. monachi B1 B3
¹² mesionis A ; the *o* has been altered from a round *s* by erasure of the lower part of the *s*, apparently by the text-hand at the time of writing ; a small *s* has been written by m.h. above *si*. messionis B1 B3. After this word, in A, three or four letters, probably *tem*, have been written and erased by the text-hand, at the end of the line.
¹³ pervenientes A B1 ; perve|venientes B3
¹⁴ cuul eilne A, with three over-dashes ; cuuleilne B1 B3. See pp. 140, 143.

qui utique locus inter occidentalem Iovae insulae
campulum et nostrum monasterium medius esse dicitur,[1]
mirum quid et inconsuetum singuli sibi sentire [2] videbantur ; quod tamen alius alio [3] intimare nullo modo
audebat.[4] Et sic per aliquot dies eodem in [5] loco
eademque vespertina sentiebant hora. Fuit autem
hisdem [6] in [7] diebus sanctus Baitheneus [8] inter eos operum
dispensator, qui síc ad ipsos [9] alia die [10] est proloquutus,
inquiens : ' Nunc fratres confiteri [11] debetis singuli si
aliquod in hoc medio loco inter mesem [12] et monasterium
inconsuetum et inopinatum sentitis miraculum '. Unus
38b tum ex eís senior, ' Juxta tuam ' ait, ' ju|sionem, [13] quod
mihi hoc in loco ostensum est dicam. Nam et in hís
praetereuntibus dieculís et nunc etiam quandam miri
odoris flagrantiam [14] acsi universorum florum in unum
sentio collectorum ; quendam quoque quasi ignis
ardorem, non penalem sed quodam modo suavem ; sed
et quandam in corde insuetam et inconparabilem [15]
infusam laetificationem quae me subito mirabiliter consulatur,[16] et in tantum laetificat, ut nullius meroris,
nullius laboris, meminisse possim. Sed et onus quod
meo quamvis grave porto in dorso ab hoc loco usquequo

---

[1] *dicitur.* A possible alternative interpretation is : ' which is said to be
the place half-way between '.
   [2] sentire A B1 ; sentiri B3   [3] alio A ; alïi B1 ; alii B3
   [4] audebat A ; aude′bat B1 ; audiebat B3
   [5] in A B3. Omitted in B1, in a line that has been erased and rewritten
on a smaller scale.
   [6] *hisdem.* In A, a deletion dot has later been added with a fine pen
below *h*.
   [7] in A. Omitted in B1 B3.
   [8] baitheneus A B3 ; baithe′neus B1
   [9] ipsos A B3 ; eos B1
   [10] *alia die.* In A, the down-stroke of the second *a*, and the loop of *d*,
have spread, as though re-written on a surface that had been abraded or
damped.
   [11] *confiteri.* In A, an acute accent has later been added with a fine pen
above *e*.

(which place is said to be half way between the little western plain of the island of Io, and our monastery), the brothers severally seemed to themselves to feel something marvellous and strange. But they did not by any means venture to speak of it, one to another. And for several days they had this feeling, in the same place, and at the same vesper hour.

During these days Saint Baithene was the controller of work among them ; and on one day he spoke thus to them, saying : ' Now, brothers, you must confess, each of you, whether you feel any strange and un-expected miracle in this place half-way between the harvest-field and the monastery '. Then one of them, a senior, said : ' According to your command, I shall tell what has been revealed to me in this place. For both in these last few days, and also now, I perceive a fragrant smell, of marvellous sweetness, as of all flowers combined into one ; and also a heat as of fire, not painful, but in some manner pleasant ; and in addition a kind of inspired joyousness of heart, strange and incomparable, which in a moment miraculously revives me, and so greatly gladdens me that all grief and all labour are forgotten. Moreover, the load that I bear upon my back, however heavy it may be, is so greatly

---

¹² mesem A ; a small *s* has been added by m.h. above *se*.   messem B1 B3

¹³ jusionem A ;   visionem B1, altered later to *jussionem*, not by the text hand ;   visionem B3

¹⁴ flagrantiam A ; fragla'nciam B1 (with *r* written above *l*, by a reviser) ; flagranciam B3

¹⁵ *inconparabilem*.   In A, two deletion points have later been added below *n*, and a tilde has been added above the *o*, to read *-com-*, by m.h. using a very fine pen. B1 has *ɔ*, and B3 has *co~*, both reading either *con* or *com*.

¹⁶ consulatur A ; -sol- B1 B3

ad monasterium perveniatur, quomodo nescio, in tantum relevatur, ut me oneratum non sentiam '.

Quid plura ? Síc omnes illi mesores [1] operarii de sé 39a singillatim profetentur [2] per omnia sensise,[3] sicuti | unus ex eís coram enarraverat.[4] Singulique simul flexís genibus a sancto postularunt Baitheneo,[5] ut ejusdem miri solaminis [6] causam et originem quod et ipse sicut et ceteri sentiebat [7] illís ignorantibus intimare procuraret. Quibus consequenter hoc dedit responsum, ' Scitis ' inquiens, ' quod noster senior Columba de nobís anxie cogitet, et nos ad sé tardius pervenientes egre ferat, nostri memor laboris. Et idcirco quia corporaliter obviam nobís non venit spiritus ejus nostrís obviat gresibus.[8] Qui taliter nos consulans [9] laetificat '. Quibus auditís verbís ingeniculantes cum ingenti gratulatione expansís ad caelum manibus Christum in sancto venerantur et beato [10] viro.[11] .

Sed et hoc silere non debemus quod nobís ab expertís quibusdam de voce beati psalmodiae [12] viri 39b indubi|tanter traditum est. Quae scilicet vox venerabilis viri in eclesia [13] cum fratribus decantantis aliquando per iiii.[14] stadia, hoc est d.[15] passus, aliquando vero per octo, hoc est mille passus,[16] inconparabili elevata modo audiebatur. Mirum dictu, nec in auribus eorum qui secum

---

[1] mesores A ; a small s has been added by m.h. above so. messores B1 B3   [2] profetentur A ; -fit- B1 B3
[3] sensise A ; a small s has been written by m.h. above the final se. sensisse B1 B3   [4] enarraverat A ; enarra'verat B1 ; enarravit B3
[5] baitheneo A B3 ; baithene'o B1
[6] solaminis A B1 ; salaminis B3
[7] sentiebant A, with a deletion point, apparently by the text-hand, above the second n. senciebat B1 B3
[8] gresibus A ; a small s has been written by m.h. above si. gressibus B1 B3
[9] consulans A ; the u has later been altered to o by bridging. -so'l- B1 ; -sol- B3   [10] beato A B3 ; beto B1
[11] et beato viro. These words are centred in A, and followed by a three-

lightened (how, I do not know), from this place until we reach the monastery, that I feel no burden '.

Why say more ? All those harvest-workers confessed, each on his own behalf, that they had felt in all respects exactly as one of them had openly described. All as one man bowed their knees, and begged of Saint Baithene that he would endeavour to explain to them in their ignorance the cause and origin of the marvellous relief, which he felt as well as the others. Thereupon he gave them this answer, saying : ' You know that our senior, Columba, thinks of us with solicitude and, mindful of our labour, is much distressed when we are late in reaching him. And for the reason that he does not come in the body to meet us, his spirit meets us as we walk, and in this fashion refreshes and gladdens us '. Hearing these words, they knelt down, raising their hands toward heaven with expressions of great joy, and worshipped Christ in the holy and blessed man.

And this too we ought not to pass over in silence that has been told us without question by certain men who knew of it, concerning the voice of the blessed man in singing psalms. This voice of the venerable man, when he sang in the church with the brothers, was raised in an incomparable manner, and was heard at a distance sometimes of four furlongs, that is, five hundred paces, sometimes even of eight, that is, a thousand paces. Strange to say, in the ears of those

---

point stop, marking the end of a chapter (see p. 169). *Sed et hoc* begins a chapter, with a large initial letter extending through two lines, in A B1 B3.

[12] psalmodiae A ; salmodi'e B1 ; psalmodie B3

[13] e|clesia A ; a *c* has later been written, not in the text hand, before *c*. ecclesiam B1 ; ecclesia B3

[14] iiii A ; quatuor B1 B3   [15] d. A ; quingentos B1 B3

[16] pa~s A, for *passus*, or possibly *passuum* as below ; passus B1 B3. The Roman stadium contained 125 passus, and was considerably less than a furlong.

in eclesia stabant vox ejus modum humanae vocis in clamoris granditate excedebat. Sed tamen eadem[1] hora qui ultra mille passuum lonquinquitatem[2] stabant síc clare eandem audiebant vocem, ut illos quos canebat[3] versiculos etiam per[4] singulas possent distingere[5] syllabas. Similiter enim ejus vox in auribus prope et longe audientium personabat. Sed[6] hoc de voce miraculum beati viri non semper sed raro accedisse[7] conprobatur, quod tamen sine divini spiritus gratia nullo modo fieri potuisset.

40a   [8] Sed et illud non est tacendum quod aliquando | de tali et inconparabili vocis ejus sublevatione juxta Brudei[9] regis munitionem accedisse[10] traditur. Nam ipse sanctus cum paucís fratribus extra regis munitionem dum vespertinales dei laudes ex more celebraret, quidam magi ad eos propius accedentes in quantum poterant prohibere conabantur, ne de ore ipsorum divinae laudis sonus inter gentiles audiretur populos. Quo conperto sanctus xl. et iiii.[11] psalmum decantare coepit. Mirumque in modum ita vox ejus in aere eodem momento instar alicujus formidabilis tonitrui elevata est, ut et rex et populus intolerabili essent pavore perterriti. .

---

[1] eadem A B3 ; in A, a circumflex accent has later been written with a fine pen above *a*. ea'dem B1

[2] lonquinquitatem A ; a deletion dot has later been added below, and a *g* written by m.h. above, the first *q*. longin- B1 B3

[3] *canebat*. In A, a cursive *n* has been inserted above *at*, wrongly, perhaps by a modern hand.

[4] *per*. In A, deletion points before and after the Irish symbol for *per* have been added later with a fine pen.

[5] distingere A ; a *u* (probably m.h.) has been added above *e*, and dots have been placed below the *e* and above the *r*. distinguere B1 B3

[6] Above the medial point before *Sed*, in A, there is a half-inch pen-mark, unexplained.

[7] accedisse A ; the first *e* has later been altered to *i*, with a long downstroke with fine pen. accid -B1 B3

[8] A large initial *S* extends through two lines of writing in A B1 B3, and begins the lines, as a new chapter, in B1 B3.

that stood with him in the church, his voice did not exceed the volume of a human voice in magnitude of sound ; and yet at the same time those that stood at a distance of more than a mile heard the same voice so clearly that they could distinguish every syllable in the verses that he sang. For his voice sounded alike in the ears of those that heard it, near or far. This miracle of the blessed man's voice is proved to have happened only rarely, not always ; but yet it could not have happened at all, without the grace of the Divine Spirit.

This too should not remain untold, which, as an instance of this incomparable uplifting of his voice, is said to have happened once beside the fortress of king Brude. While the saint himself with a few brothers was celebrating according to custom the praises of God, at vespers, outside the king's fortress, certain magicians came close to them, and tried to prohibit it to the best of their power, lest the sound of divine praise from their lips should be heard among the heathen peoples. Understanding this, the saint began to sing the forty-fourth psalm. And in the same moment his voice was, in a marvellous manner, so raised in the air like a terrible peal of thunder, that both the king and the people were filled with intolerable dread.

---

[9] brudei A B3 ; bru'dei B1

[10] accedisse A ; a small *i* has been written by m.h. above the first *e*, and a deletion dot below the *e*. accid- B1 B3

[11] xl et iiii A ; quadragesimum et quartum B1 B3. Ps. xliv of the Vulgate (*Eructavit cor meum*) is Ps. xlv in the English version.

De quodam divite qui
Lugudius [1] Clodus vocitabatur

ALIO IN TEMPORE cum in Scotia per aliquot sanctus
demoraretur dies, alium currui insedentem [2] videns
40b clericum, qui gaudenter per|agrabat campum Breg, [3]
primo interrogans de eo quis esset, hoc ab amicís
ejusdem viri de eo accipit responsum : ' Hic est Lugudius
Clodus, homo dives et honoratus in plebe '. Sanctus
consequenter respondens inquit : ' Non ita video : sed
homuncio miser et pauper in die qua morietur tria apud
sé vicinorum praetersoria in una retentabit maceria ;
unamque electam de vaccís praetersoriorum [4] occidi
jubebit [5] sibi. [6] De cujus [7] cocta carne postulabit aliquam sibi partem dari cum meritrice [8] in eodem lectulo
cubanti. De qua utique particula mursum [9] accipiens
statim ibidem strangulabitur et morietur '. Quae omnia
sicuti ab expertís traditur juxta sancti profeticum [10]
adinpleta sunt verbum. . [11]

De Nemano [12] filio Gruthriche [13]
sancti profetia [14] |

41a   HUNC ENIM cum sanctus de malís suís corriperet
parvipendens sanctum subsannabat. Cui respondens
vir beatus ait : ' In nomine domini Nemane [15] aliqua de

---

[1] lugudius A B3 ; lugu'dius B1   [2] insedentem A ; insid- B1 B3
[3] *campum Breg.* This was Mag-breg, ' plain of Brega ' ; see p. 147. The
district called Brega (or ' Bregia ') extended from north of the Boyne to
south of the Liffey. Mag-breg seems to have included Teilte (105b, 106b).
Through Mag-breg, Libran reached Durrow, from the sea or a navigable
river (92b).
[4] praetersoriorum A ; -soriorum B1 ; -sorium B3. *Praetersoria* was
possibly a monastic abbreviation of **praetercursoria.*
[5] jubebit A B3 ; videbit B1.
[6] sibi A. Omitted in B1 B3.   [7] cujus A ; unius B1 B3

[I 38] Concerning a certain rich man, who was called Luguid the Lame

At another time, while the saint was for some days in Ireland, he saw a cleric sitting in a car and gaily driving over the plain of Brega. He first asked about him, who he was, and received from that man's friends this answer concerning him : ' That is Luguid the Lame, a wealthy man, and respected among the people '. Then the saint said in reply : ' It is not thus that I see him. But on the day on which he dies, a poor and wretched man, he will have in his possession three stray beasts belonging to his neighbours, retained in one stone enclosure. And he will order one cow, chosen from the stray beasts, to be killed for him, and will ask that a portion of its cooked flesh should be given to him, as he reclines on the same couch with a harlot. So taking a mouthful of that portion, he will then and there be choked, and die '.

All these things, as is said by men who know, were completely fulfilled, according to the saint's prophetic word.

[I 39] The saint's prophecy concerning Neman, Gruthrech's son

This man, when the saint rebuked him for his bad deeds, mocked him, with disdain. The blessed man said to him in reply : ' In the name of the Lord, I will

---

8 meritrice A ; mere- B1 B3   9 mursum A ; morsum B1 B3
10 profeticum A ; prophetiam B1 ; propheciam B3
11 verbum A. Omitted in B1 B3.   12 nemano A B3 ; nema'no B1
13 gruthriche A (so also A B2 in 6a) ; grutheriche B1 ; gluteriche B3. See p. 142.
14 profetia A ; prophetie verbum B1 ; prophecie verbum B3
15 nemane A B3 ; nema'ne B1

té veridica loquar verba. Inimici tui repperient [1] té in eodem cum meritrice [2] cubantem cubiculo, ibidemque trucidaberis ; daemones quoque ad loca penarum tuam rapient animam '. Hic idem Nemanus [3] post aliquot annos in uno cum meritrice [4] lectulo repertus in regione Cainle [5] juxta verbum sancti [6] ab inimicís decapitatus disperiit..

De quodam prespitero sancti viri profetatio [7]

Alio in tempore sanctus cum in Scotiensium [8] paulo superius moraretur memorata regione, casu dominica die ad quoddam devenit vicinum monasteriolum quod
41b scotice Trioit [9] vocitatur. Eadem [10] pro|inde die quendam audiens prespiterum sacra eucaristiae misteria conficientem, quem ideo fratres qui ibidem commanebant ad misarum [11] elegerant peragenda sollemnia quia valde relegiosum [12] aestimabant, repente hanc formidabilem de ore profert vocem : ' Munda et inmunda pariter nunc permisceri [13] cernuntur ; hoc est munda sacrae oblationis ministeria [14] per inmundum hominem ministrata, qui in sua interim [15] conscientia aliquod grande occultat facinus '. Haec qui inerant audientes

[1] repperient A ; pe'riment B1 ; periment B3

[2] meritrice A ; mere- B1 B3

[3] nemanus A B3 ; nema'nus B1

[4] meritrice A ; mere- B1 B3

[5] cainle A B1 B3, with two over-dashes in A. The place is unidentified, but see p. 140.

[6] verbum sancti A ; sancti vaticinium B1 B3 (-ci'n- B1)

[7] sancti viri profetatio A ; qui erat in triota (-o'- B1) sancti prophetia (-cia B3) viri B1 B3. Cf. the contents-list in 6a.

[8] scotiensium A ; scote'nsium B1 ; scottensium B3. The district referred to (40b) is Mag-breg.

[9] trioit A, with two over-dashes ; trio'ta B1 ; triota B3. The place was Trevet, in the barony of Skreen, county Meath.

tell some words of truth, Neman, concerning you. Your enemies will discover you, lying in the same bed-chamber with a harlot, and there you will be slain ; and demons will drag your soul to the place of torments '.

After some years, this same Neman, discovered in one couch with a harlot, in the district of Cainle, perished, beheaded by enemies, according to the saint's word.

[I 40] The holy man's prophecy concerning a certain priest

On one occasion, when the saint was for a time in the district of the Irish, that was mentioned a little above, he happened to come on a Lord's-day to a neighbouring small monastery that is called in Irish *Trioit* [Trevet]. So on the same day, when he heard a certain priest consecrating the sacred elements of the Eucharist, a priest whom the brothers residing there had chosen to perform the ceremony of the Mass because they thought him very religious, the saint suddenly let pass from his lips this terrible saying : ' Now we see clean and unclean intermingled together : the clean rite of the sacred offering administered by an unclean man, who at the same time keeps hidden in his own conscience a great sin '. Those that were present, and heard this, trembled

---

[10] eadem A ; a circumflex accent has later been added with a fine pen above *a*. Eodem B1 B3

[11] misarum A ; a small *s* has been written by m.h. above *is*. missarum B1 B3

[12] relegiosum A ; a small *i* has been written by m.h. above the second *e*. -lig- B1 B3

[13] permisceri A ; misceri B1 B3

[14] ministeria A ; misteria B1 B3

[15] *interim*. A possible alternative translation is ' as yet '.

tremefacti nimis obstupuere.[1] Ille vero de quo haec dicebantur verba coram omnibus peccantiam [2] conpulsus est suam [3] confiteri. Christique [4] commilitones qui in eclesia sanctum circumstantes occulta cordis audierant manifestantem divinam in eo scientiam cum magna ammiratione glorificarunt.[5] |

42a   De Erco [6] fure mocu-Druidi [7] qui in Coloso [8] insula commanebat sancti profetizatio [9] viri

ALIO IN TEMPORE sanctus in Iova commanens insula accitís ad se binís de fratribus virís, quorum vocabula Lugbeus[10] et Silnanus,[11] eisdem praecipiens dicit : 'Nunc ad Maleam [12] transfretate insulam, et in campulís mari vicinís Ercum [13] quaerite furacem ; qui nocte praeterita solus occulte de insula Coloso perveniens sub sua [14] feno tecta navicula inter arenarum cumulos per diem sé occultare conatur, ut noctu ad parvam [15] transnaviget insulam ubi marini nostri juris vituli [16] generantur et generant, ut de illís furanter [17] occisís edax valde furax [18] suam replens naviculam ad suum repedet[19] habitaculum.'

Qui haec audientes obsequuti emigrant, furemque in 42b locís a sancto praesignatís absconsum | reperiunt, et ad

---

[1] obstupuere A ; a circumflex accent has later been added with a fine pen above the first *e*. -e're B1 B3
[2] peccantiam A ; peccatum B1 B3
[3] suam A ; suum B1 B3
[4] que A. Omitted in B1 B3.
[5] glorificarunt A ; -cave'runt B1 ; -caverunt B3
[6] erco A B1 ; ereo B3
[7] mocu druidi A ; mocudru'idi B1 ; mocudruidi B3 (or possibly -*driudi* ; the three minims are written without apices, although in B3 an apex is habitually written over *i*).
[8] coloso A B3 ; colo'so B1. Cf. 70b and p. 155.
[9] profetizatio A ; prophetatio B1 ; prophetacio B3
[10] lugbeus A ; lugbe'us B1 ; lubbeus B3
[11] silnanus A ; selnanus B1 B3. See 55b–57a.
[12] maleam A B3 ; male'am B1

and were much astounded. And he about whom these words were said was compelled to confess his sinfulness before them all. And the fellow-soldiers of Christ who, standing about the saint in the church, had heard him expose the secrets of the heart, marvelling greatly glorified the divine knowledge that was in him.

[I 41] The holy man's prophecy concerning
a thief, Erc, mocu-Druidi, who lived in
the island Colossus [Coll]

At another time, while the saint was living in the island of Io, he called to him two of the brothers, men whose names were Lugbe and Silnan, and gave them an order, saying : ' Now cross the strait to the island of Male [Mull], and look for the thief Erc, in the little plains beside the sea. He came last night secretly, alone, from the island Colossus, and he is trying to conceal himself during the day among sand-hills, under his boat which he has covered with grass ; so that by night he may sail across to the small island where the sea-calves that pertain to us breed and are bred ; in order that the greedy robber may fill his boat with those that he thievishly kills, and make his way back to his dwelling '.

Hearing this, they obediently set out ; and they found the thief hidden in the place indicated beforehand

---

[13] ercum A B1 B3, with two over-dashes in A.
[14] *sua.* In A, a small *o* has been written by m.h. above the *a*.
[15] parvam A B3 ; puram B1
[16] *marini vituli,* i.e. Atlantic seals.
[17] furanter A ; furenter B1 B3
[18] furax A B3 ; et furax B1
[19] repedet A ; an acute accent has later been added with a fine pen first above the *e.* re'pedet B1 B3

sanctum sicuti illís praeciperat [1] perduxerunt. Quo viso
sanctus ad eum dicit : ' Quare tu res alienas divinum
transgressus mandatum sepe furaris ? [2] Quando necesse
habueris, ad nos veniens necessaria accipies postulata '.
Et haec dicens praecipit [3] berbices [4] occidi et pro focís
dari misero furaci, ne vacuus ad sua remearet.

Et [5] post aliquantum tempus sanctus in spiritu
vicinam furis praevidens mortem ad Baitheneum, [6] eo in
tempore praepossitum [7] commorantem in campo Lunge, [8]
mittit ut eidem furi quoddam pingue pecus et vi.
modios [9] novissima mittat [10] munera. Quibus a Baitheneo sicut sanctus commendaverat transmisís [11] ea die
inventus est morte subita praeventus furax misellus ; et
in exequiis ejus transmisa [12] expensa sunt xenia. .[13] |

43a   De Cronano poeta sancti
                         profetia [14] viri

ALIO IN TEMPORE sanctus cum juxta stagnum Cei, [15]
prope hostium fluminis quod latine Bos [16] dicitur, die
aliqua cum fratribus sederet, [17] quidam ad eos scoticus

[1] praeciperat A ; the *i* has been altered by m.h. to *e*. -ce′p- B1 ;
-cep- B3
[2] *furaris*. After this word, in A, a question-mark has been added by
m.h. ; B1 B3 have question-marks.
[3] praecipit A ; -cep- B1 B3
[4] berbices A ; a circumflex accent has later been added with a fine pen
above *i*. berbi′ces B1 ; verveces B3
[5] Et A B1 ; Q' B3
[6] baitheneum A B3 ; baithe′neum B1
[7] praepossitum A ; the first *s* has later been deleted with a dot below.
-posi- B1 B3
[8] lunge A B1 B3, with two over-dashes in A.
[9] *modios*. The Roman modius was rather less than a peck ; cf. 54b,
and Vulgate, Ruth iii. 15, 17.
[10] mittat A B1. Omitted in B3.
[11] transmisís A ; a small *s* has been added by m.h. above the first *i*.
-missis B1 B3

by the saint. And they brought him to the saint, who had so ordered them. Seeing him, the saint said to him : ' Why do you repeatedly steal other people's property, transgressing the divine commandment? When you have need, come to us, and you will receive the necessary things that you ask for '. And saying this, he ordered wethers to be killed, and given instead of seals to the miserable thief ; so that he should not return home empty.

After some time, the saint, foreseeing in the spirit the thief's imminent death, sent to Baithene, then living as prior in the plain of Long, and bade him send to that thief a fat beast and six measures of grain, as last gifts. When Baithene had dispatched these as the saint had asked him to do, the pitiful thief was found overtaken by sudden death on that day ; and the gifts that had been sent were used at his funeral.

[I 42] The holy man's prophecy concerning the poet Cronan

One day, at another time, while the saint was sitting with some brothers beside the lake Cei [Lough Key], near the mouth of the river that is called in Latin ' cow ' [the Boyle], a certain Irish poet came to them.

---

[12] transmi|sa A ; a minuscule *s* has later been added after *i*. -missa B1 B3
[13] xenia A ; exenia B1 B3
[14] profetia A ; propheta'tio B1 ; prophecia B3
[15] cei A B3, with one over-dash in A ; ce'i B1. Cf. 67b. The name *Cei* is in the genitive case ; the nominative does not occur in Adomnan.
[16] *bos*. The O.I. name of the river, Bó, ' cow ', is given in 67b. This is the river Boyle that flows into Lough Key. Near where the outlet of Lough Key joins the Shannon was the *cella magna Deathrib*, 52a.
[17] sederet A B3 ; in A, a small *i* has been written by m.h. above the second *e*, wrongly, perhaps intending *sideret*. sede'ret B1

X

poeta [1] devenit.[2] Qui cum post aliquam recessiset sermocinationem, fratres ad sanctum, 'Cur' aiunt, 'a nobís regrediente Cronano poeta aliquod ex more [3] suae artis canticum non postulasti modolabiliter [4] decantari?' Quibus sanctus : 'Quare et vos nunc inutilia profertis verba? Quomodo ab illo misero homuncione carmen postularem laetitiae, qui nunc ab inimicís trucidatus [5] finem adusque ocius pervenit [6] vitae?' Hís a sancto dictís, et ecce ultra flumen aliquis clamitat homo, 43b dicens : 'Ille poeta qui a vobís nuper sospes | rediit hora in hác ab inimicís in via interfectus est'. Omnes tum qui praesentes inerant valde mirati sé invicem intuentes obstipuere. .[7]

De duobus tigernís [8] sancti vaticinatio viri, qui ambo motuís [9] vulneribus [10] disperierant

ALIO ITIDEM IN TEMPORE sanctus in Iova conversans insula repente inter legendum summo cum ingenti ammiratione gemitu ingemuit mesto. Quod videns qui praesens inerat Lugbeus mocu-Blai coepit ab eo percunctari subiti causam meroris. Cui sanctus valde mestificatus hanc dedit responsionem : 'Duo quidam nunc regii generis viri in Scotia motuís[11] inter sé vulneribus transfixi disperierunt, haut procul a monasterio quod

---

[1] *scoticus poeta :* i.e., a composer of verses in the Irish language.
[2] devenit A B3 ; in A, a circumflex accent has later been added with a fine pen above the second *e*. deve'nit Bi
[3] *ex more.* Cf. 45 b, 118a.
[4] modolabiliter A ; a small *u* has been added by m.h. above the second *o*. modu- Bi B3
[5] trucidatus A ; trucidandus Bi B3
[6] pervenit A B3 ; perve'nit Bi
[7] obstipuere A ; a small *u* has been added by m.h. above the *i*, and a circumflex accent above the first *e*. obstupue're Bi ; obstupuere B3
[8] *tigernís.* This is a Latin formation from Irish *tigern* 'lord'. See p. 134.
[9] motuís A ; mu'tuis Bi ; mutuis B3

When, after some conversation, he had gone away, the brothers said to the saint : ' When the poet Cronan was leaving us, why did you not according to the custom ask for a song of his own composition, sung to a tune ? ' And the saint replied : ' Why do you too now utter idle words ? How would I ask a song of gladness from that unhappy fellow, who has now suddenly reached the end of his life, slaughtered by enemies ? '

After the saint had said this, behold a man on the other side of the river shouted, saying : ' That poet who recently came safely back from you has in this hour been killed upon the way, by enemies '. All who were then present greatly marvelled, and looked at one another in amazement.

[I 43] The holy man's prophecy concerning two lords who had both perished by mutually inflicted wounds

Similarly at another time, while the holy man lived in the island of Io, when he was reading he suddenly groaned with a deep sorrowful sigh, in great wonder. Perceiving this, the man who was with him, Lugbe mocu-Blai, began to question him about the cause of his sudden grief ; and to him the saint, greatly sorrowing, gave this reply : ' Two men of royal birth in Ireland have now perished, pierced each by the other with mutual wounds, not far from the monastery that

---

[10] *vulneribus.* In the facsimiles of A, the *b* only of the *-bus* symbol (b:) is here visible.
[11] *motuís* A ; a small *u* has been written by m.h. above the *o*. *mutuis* B1 B3

dicitur Cell-rois ¹ in provincia Maugdornorum.² Octavaque die hac peracta ebdomade ³ ultra fretum alius
44a clamitabit, qui haec de Evernia ⁴ veniens ita taliter |
facta enarrabit. Sed hoc Ó filiole quandiu vixero
nemini indices '.

Octava proinde ultra fretum clamatum est die.
Sanctus tum supra memoratum ad se Lugbeum ⁵ vocans
silenter ad eum ait : ' Qui nunc clamitat ultra fretum
ipse est de quo tibi prius dixeram longeus ⁶ viator. Vade
et ⁷ adduc eum ad nos '. Qui celeriter ⁸ adductus inter
cetera hoc etiam retulit : ' Duo ' inquiens, ' in parte
Maugdornorum ⁹ nobiles viri se motuo ¹⁰ vulnerantes
mortui sunt, hoc est Colman Canis ¹¹ filius Aileni,¹² et
Ronanus filius Aido ¹³ filii Colgen de Anteriorum ¹⁴
genere, prope fines illorum locorum ubi illud monasterium cernitur quod dicitur Cell-roiss '.¹⁵

Post haec illius verba narratoris idem Lugbeus,¹⁶
Christi miles, sanctum seorsum coepit interrogare,
dicens : ' Quaesso ¹⁷ mihi de hís talibus narres profeticís
revelationibus, quomodo si per visum tibi an auditum
44b an alio homi|nibus incognito manifestantur modo '. Ad

¹ cell rois A, with an over-dash above *rois* ; ceilrois B1 ; cellros B3.
The name in A B1 means ' monastery of the forest '.
² maugdornorum A ; maugdorneo'rum B1 ; maugdorneorum B3.
See p. 137. The ' province ' or ' part ' of the Maugdorni was in county
Monaghan. See Hogan 1910, p. 544 ; Reeves 1857, pp. 81–2.
³ ebdomade A ; ebdomada B1 B3
⁴ evernia A ; hibe'rnia B1 ; hibernia B3
⁵ lugbeum A B3 ; lugbe'um B1
⁶ longeus A ; longus B1 B3. In 61a, A has *longeus* for *longaevus*. Cf.
Plummer 1910, II, p. 189, where a Life of Mochua describes him as *longaevus
viator*, at an implied age of 59 years.
⁷ vade et A ; valde, et B1 B3, erroneously.
⁸ celeriter A B3 ; sceleriter B1
⁹ maugdornorum A ; -neorum B1 B3
¹⁰ motuo A ; a small *u* has been written by m.h. above the first *o*.
mutuo B1 B3
¹¹ canis A ; cognomento canis B1 B3. This renders the Irish *cú* ' dog '.

is called Cell-rois, in the province of the Maugdorni. And on the eighth day, after this week has ended, a man will shout beyond the strait, who, coming from Ireland, will tell that these things have happened as I have said. But, my son, so long as I live do not reveal this to any one '.

On the eighth day, there was a shouting beyond the strait. Then the saint called Lugbe to him, and said to him quietly : ' The man who is now shouting beyond the strait is that old traveller of whom I spoke to you before. Go, and bring him to us '. He was speedily brought in, and with the rest of his news he related this also, saying : ' In the region of the Maugdorni, two men of noble birth have died, each wounding the other ; namely, Colman Dog, Ailen's son, and Ronan, the son of Aid, son of Colcu, of the race of the Easterners ; near the boundaries of the region where the monastery that is called Cell-rois can be seen '.

After these words of the narrator, the same Lugbe, soldier of Christ, began to question the saint when they were alone, saying : ' Tell me, I beg you, about such prophetic revelations, how they are made to you ; by seeing or hearing, or in some way unknown to

His brother, 'Maelduin Alene's son' (†611), is called ' king of the Mogdornai ' in A.U. 22b16.

[12] aileni A B1 B3, with two over-dashes in A.

[13] aido A B3 ; a'ido B1. This Aid was king of the Airthir, and his death is entered in A.U. under 609=610.

[14] *anteriorum*. These were the Airthir of eastern Airgialla. Cf. 109 b. Adomnan may mean that both Colman and Ronan were of the Airthir, since that group included the Maugdorni. See James Hogan, in Féilsgríbhinn 1940, p. 408.

[15] cell roiss A, with two over-dashes; celrois B1 ; cellrois B3

[16] lugbeus A B3 ; lugbe'us B1

[17] quaesso A ; the first *s* has later been deleted with a point beneath made by a fine pen. queso B1 B3

haec sanctus : 'De qua nunc' ait, 'inquiris valde subtili ré nullatenus tibi quamlibet aliquam intimare particulam potero, nisi prius flexís genibus per nomen excelsi dei mihi firmiter promittas hoc té obscurissimum sacramentum nulli umquam hominum cunctís diebus vitae meae enarraturum'. Qui haec audiens flexit contenuo [1] genua et prostrato in terram vultu juxta sancti praeceptionem plene omnia promisit. Qua statim perfecta promisione [2] sanctus ad surgentem síc locutus inquit : 'Sunt nonnulli quamlibet pauci admodum quibus divina hoc contulit gratia, ut etiam totum [3] totius terrae orbem, cum ambitu ociani [4] et caeli, uno eodemque momento quasi [5] sub uno solis radio mira-
45a biliter | laxato mentis sinu clare et manifestissime speculentur'.[6]

Hoc miraculum sanctus quamvís de aliis electís dicere videatur, vanam utique fugiens gloriam, de sé ipso tamen dixisse, per oblicum licet, nullus dubitare debet qui Paulum legit apostolum vas electionis [7] de talibus nar-rantem sibi revelatís visionibus. Non enim ita scripsit, 'scio me', sed 'scio hominem [8] raptum usque ad tertium caelum'. Quod quamlibet de alio dicere videatur, nemo tamen dubitat síc de propria humilitatem cus-todiens enarrare persona. Quem etiam et noster Columba in spiritalium [9] visionum narratione sequtus est superius memorata, quam ab eo supradictus vir,

---

[1] contenuo A ; a small *i* has been written by m.h. above the *e*. -ti'n-
Bɪ ; -tin- B3

[2] promisione A ; a small *s* has been written by m.h. above *is*. -issi-
Bɪ B3

[3] totum A ; totum licet non semper Bɪ B3. The reading of Bɪ B3 seems to be required ; cf. 10b.

[4] ociani A ; the first *i* has been altered by m.h. to *e*. occe'ani Bɪ ; occeani B3   [5] quasi A B3 ; quas Bɪ

[6] *speculentur*. This passage, from *etiam totum*, is verbally reconstructed from Dialogue II or IV of pope Gregory I. See 10b and p. 20. It is

men ? ' To this the saint said : ' Of the very subtle matter about which you now ask, I shall not be able to tell you anything at all, even the least particle, unless you first kneel and firmly promise me in the name of God on high that you will never, during all the days of my life, tell of this darkest mystery to any person '. Hearing this, Lugbe immediately knelt, and with his face downcast to the ground he fully promised everything, according to the saint's command. Rising as soon as the promise had been completed, he was thus addressed by the saint, who said : ' There are some, although few indeed, on whom divine favour has bestowed the gift of contemplating, clearly and very distinctly, with scope of mind miraculously enlarged, in one and the same moment, as though under one ray of the sun, even the whole circle of the whole earth, with the ocean and sky about it '.

Although the saint, as one that shuns vain-glory, seems to tell this miracle of others of the elect, yet that he has spoken of himself, albeit indirectly, should be doubted by none who has read the apostle Paul, a vessel of election, telling of such visions revealed to himself : for Paul has thus written, not ' I know myself ', but ' I know a man, caught up to the third heaven ' ; and although he seems to tell this of another, none doubts that he speaks in this way of his own person, preserving his humility. Likewise our Columba also has followed him in the account given above of visions of the spirit ; which account the above-mentioned man,

doubtful which of the Dialogues was uppermost in Adomnan's recollection.

[7] *vas electionis :* derived from the Vulgate, Acts ix. 15.

[8] *scio hominem :* derived from Vulgate, 2 Cor. xii, 2. Bede quotes the same verse in connexion with Cuthbert. See Colgrave 1940, p. 178.

[9] spiritalium A ; -tua'l- B1 ; -tual- B3

quem plurimum sanctus amabat, magnís precibus praemisís [1] vir potuit extorquere, sicut ipse [2] coram aliorum
45b personís [3] sanctorum | post sancti Columbae transitum
testatus est. A quibus haec quae de sancto supra
narravimus indubitanter didicimus. .

[4] De Cronano [5] episcopo

ALIO IN TEMPORE quidam de Muminensium [6] provincia proselytus ad sanctum venit qui se in quantum
potuit occultabat humiliter, ut nullus sciret quod esset
episcopus. Sed tamen sanctum hoc non poterat latere.
Nam alia die dominica a sancto jusus Christi corpus [7] ex
more conficere sanctum advocat, ut simul quasi duo
prespiteri dominicum panem frangerent. Sanctus
proinde [8] ad altarium accedens repente intuitus faciem
ejus síc eum conpellat : ' Benedicat té Christus, frater.
Hunc solus episcopali ritu frange panem. Nunc scimus
quod sis episcopus : quare hucusque te occultare conatus
es, ut tibi a nobís debeta [9] non redderetur veneratio ? '
46a Quo audito | sancti verbo humilis perigrinus [10] valde
stupefactus Christum in sancto veneratus est. Et qui
inerant praesentes nimis ammirati glorificarunt[11] deum. .

---

[1] praemisís A ; a small *s* has been added by m.h. above the first *i*.
premissis B1 B3
[2] ipse A. Omitted in B1 B3.
[3] aliorum personís A ; personis aliorum B1 B3
[4] This and the remaining chapters of Book I are not included in the
contents list, 6a.
[5] cronano A B3 ; sancto cronano B1
[6] muminensium A B3 ; mugine'nsium B1. A district called Mumu
gave its name to the province of Munster.
[7] *Christi corpus.* The appointment of a stranger as celebrant, by courtesy,
took place in accordance with decrees of councils (see Reeves 1857, p. 85).
The present passage is evidence of the practice at Iona, in the seventh
century.
[8] *proinde.* In A, the Irish symbol for *pro* has been altered by m.h. to
the continental symbol.

whom the saint very greatly loved, was hardly able to extort from him, after making great supplication ; as Lugbe himself attested, in the personal presence of other saints, after Saint Columba's death. And from them we have learned of the saint, without any doubt, these things that we have related above.

[I 44] Concerning the bishop Cronan

At another time, there came to the saint from the province of the men of Mumu a stranger who humbly kept himself out of sight, as much as he could, so that none knew that he was a bishop. But yet that could not remain hidden from the saint. For on the next Lord's-day, when he was bidden by the saint to prepare, according to custom, the body of Christ, he called the saint to assist him, so that they should as two presbyters together break the Lord's bread. Thereupon the saint, going to the altar, suddenly looked upon his face, and thus addressed him : ' Christ bless you, brother ; break this bread alone, according to the episcopal rite. Now we know you are a bishop : why until now have you tried to conceal yourself, so that the reverence due to you was not paid by us ? ' Hearing the saint say this, the humble pilgrim was much astonished, and reverenced Christ in the saint. And those that were present there, greatly marvelling, glorified God.

---

⁹ debeta A ; a small *i* has been written by m.h. above the second *e*. debita B1 B3
¹⁰ perigrinus A ; the first *i* has been altered by m.h. to *e*. -reg- B1 B3
¹¹ glorificarunt A ; -cave'runt B1 ; -caverunt B3

De Ernano prespitero
sancti profetia viri

ALIO ITIDEM[1] in tempore vir venerandus Ernanum prespiterum senem suum aunculum[2] ad praepossituram[3] illius monasterii transmisit quod in Hinba[4] insula ante plures fundaverat annos. Itaque cum ipsum sanctus emigrantem exosculatus benediceret hoc de eo intulit vaticinium, dicens : 'Hunc meum nunc egredientem amicum non me spero iterum in hoc saeculo viventem visurum'.

Itaque idem Ernanus post non multos dies quadam molestatus egrimonia ad sanctum volens reportatus est. Cujus in perventione valde gavisus ire obvius ad portum coepit. | Ipse vero Ernanus quamlibet infirmis[5] propriis tamen vestigiis a portu obviare sancto conabatur valde alacer. Sed cum esset inter ambos quasi xxiiii.[6] pasuum[7] intervallum subita morte praeventus, priusquam sanctus faciem ejus videret viventis, exspirans in terram cicidit[8] ; ne verbum sancti ullo frustraretur modo. Unde in eodem loco ante januam canabae[9] crux infixa est ; et altera ubi sanctus restitit illo exspirante similiter crux hodieque[10] infixa stat. .

46b

---

[1] itidem A B3. Omitted in B1.

[2] aunculum A ; avunc- B1 B3. Ernan, Columba's uncle, is named among the twelve original monks of Columba in Britain. See the Appendix.

[3] praepossituram A ; the first s has later been deleted with a point below made by a fine pen. -osi- B1 B3

[4] hinba A B3 ; himba B1

[5] infirmis A ; -mus B1 B3

[6] xxiiii A ; viginti quatuor B1 B3

[7] pasuum A ; -ss- B1 B3. 24 Roman paces were 48 steps, or 120 Roman feet. That was an estimate of the distance between the two crosses mentioned below ; and it is implied that from the one cross the other was out of sight. See p. 21.

[8] cicidit A ; ce'c- B1 ; cec- B3   [9] *canabae*. See p. 115.

[10] similiter crux hodieque A : similiterque crux hodie B1 B3 (si'm- B1)

[I 45] The holy man's prophecy concerning the priest Ernan

Also at another time, the venerable man sent the priest Ernan, his aged uncle, to be prior of the monastery that, many years before, he had founded in the island of Hinba. The saint kissed him at his departure, and blessed him ; and uttered this prophecy concerning him : ' This friend of mine, now setting out, I do not expect that I shall see again, while he lives in this world '.

So, before many days had passed, the same Ernan was attacked by an illness, and by his own wish was carried back to the saint. And he, greatly rejoicing in his arrival, set out to meet him at the harbour. And Ernan himself, although feeble, yet on his own feet, very eagerly endeavoured to go from the harbour to meet the saint. But when there was between the two a distance of some twenty-four paces, he was overtaken by sudden death, and fell to the ground dying, before the saint could see his face in life ; so that the saint's word should not be rendered vain in any way. And therefore the cross was set up in that place before the doorway of the shed ; and likewise the other cross, set up where the saint stood when Ernan died, stands even today.

De alicujus plebei familiola [1]
sancti profetia [2] viri. .

ALIO QUOQUE IN TEMPORE quidam inter ceteros ad
sanctum plebeus venit in loco hospitantem qui scotice
vocitatur Coire-salcháin.[3] Quem cum sanctus ad sé
vespere venientem vidisset, ' Ubi ' ait, ' habitas ? ' [4]
47a Ille inquit : | ' In regione quae litoribus stagni Crog-
reth [5] est contermina ego inhabito '. ' Illam quam dicis
provinciolam ' ait sanctus, ' nunc barbari populantur
vastatores '. Quo audito miser plebeus maritam et
filios deplangere coepit. Quem sanctus valde merentem
videns consulans [6] inquit : ' Vade homuncule vade.
Tua familiola tota in montem fugiens evassit [7] ; tua
vero omnia pecuscula secum invasores abigerunt,[8]
omnemque domus suppellectilem similiter saevi raptores
cum praeda rapuere '. Haec audiens plebeus ad patriam
regresus cuncta sicuti a sancto praedicta síc invenit
expleta. .

De quodam plebeo Goreo [9] nomine filio
Aidani sancti profetia [10] viri

ALIO ITIDEM IN TEMPORE quidam plebeus omnium
illius aetatis in populo Korkureti [11] fortissimus [12] virorum

[1] *familiola*. In this chapter, Columba is represented as using diminutives
throughout his conversation with his visitor from beyond the Spine, as if
he were talking to a child.
[2] profetia A ; propheta'tio B1 ; proph'ia B3
[3] coire salcháin A, with two over-dashes above *coire* ; co'ire salcani'
B1 ; coire salcani B3. See p. 87.
[4] *habitas*. After this word, in A, m.h. has added a question-mark.
B1 B3 have question-marks.
[5] crog reth A, with two over-dashes ; crochcret B1 ; crochreth B3.
The name is of North-British origin (see p. 159). Crog-reth is almost
certainly the Cruach on the boundary of Argyllshire (Watson 1926, p. 78).
The lake near the Cruach is Loch Rannoch ; and the region mentioned by
Adomnan was within the modern district of Rannoch.

[I 46] The holy man's prophecy concerning the family of a certain layman

Also at another time, when the saint was a guest at the place that is in Irish called *Coire-salcháin*, there came to him among the rest a certain layman ; and when the saint saw him coming to him in the evening, ' Where ' he said, ' do you live ? ' He replied : ' In the district bordering upon the shores of the lake of Crog-reth is my home '. ' The district that you speak of ' said the saint, ' is now being plundered by barbarian marauders '. When he heard this, the unhappy layman began to bewail his wife and children. The saint, seeing that he was greatly grieved, comforted him, saying : ' Go, little man, go ! Your whole family has escaped, fleeing to the mountain. But the invaders have driven away with them all your little cattle ; and the cruel robbers have likewise carried off with the prey all your house-hold furniture '. Hearing this, the layman returned to his district, and found that everything had happened exactly as the saint had foretold.

[I 47] The holy man's prophecy concerning a certain layman, by name Góre, Aidan's son

Similarly at another time, a certain layman, the strongest of all the men of that time among the people

---

[6] consulans A ; *u* later altered to *o* by bridging. -so'l- B1 ; -sol B3
[7] evassit A ; the first *s* later deleted with a dot below. evasit B1 B3
[8] abigerunt A B1 ; ambi- B3   [9] goreo A B3 ; gore'o B1
[10] profetia A ; prophetatio B1 ; prophecia B3
[11] korkureti A, with four over-dashes ; the letters *k r t* are of the Greek type of alphabet used in p. 137 of A, and the inference is that Adomnan's writing of this name was ostensibly Greek. cope'upeti B1 ; corforepti B3. The family-name Corcu-reti appears to be synonymous with Dal-Réti, and Góre may have been regarded as a son of king Aidan. See pp. 22, 35.
[12] *fortissimus*, perhaps ' most valiant '.

47b a sancto percuncta[tur] [1] | viro qua morte esset prae-
veniendus.[2] Cui sanctus : ' Nec in bello ' ait, ' nec in
mari, morieris. Comes tui iteneris [3] a quo non suspicaris
causa erit tuae mortis '. ' Fortassis ' inquit Goreus,[4]
' aliquis de meís comitantibus amicís me trucidare
cogitet ; aut marita ob alicujus junioris viri amorem me
maleficio [5] mortificare '. Sanctus : ' Non ita ' ait,
' continget '. ' Quare ' Goreus inquit, ' de meo inter-
fectore mihi nunc intimare non vis ? ' Sanctus : ' Idcirco ' ait, ' nolo tibi de illo tuo comite nocuo [6] nunc
manifestius aliquid edicere,[7] ne te ejus crebra recogniti
recordatio nimis mestificet, donec illa veniat dies qua
ejusdem rei veritatem probabis '.

Quid inmoramur verbís ? Post aliquot annorum
excursus idem supra memoratus Goreus [8] casu alia die
sub navi [9] resedens [10] cultello proprio cristiliam [11] de
48a astili | eradebat. Tum deinde alios prope inter sé
belligerantes audiens citius surgit, ut eos a belligeratione
separaret ; eodemque cultello illa subitatione neglegentius [12] in terra dimiso ejus genucla [13] offenso graviter
vulnerata est. Et tali faciente comite causa ei [14] morti-
ficationis aborta [15] est ; quam ipse continuo secundum
sancti vaticinationem viri mente perculsus recognovit.
Postque aliquantos menses eodem aggravatus dolore
moritur.

---

[1] percuncta A ; an abbreviated *tur* has been added, probably by m.h.,
at the end of the line. -atur B1 B3
[2] praeveniendus A ; perimendus B1 ; preveniendus B3
[3] iteneris A ; itin- B1 B3   [4] goreus A B3 ; gore'us B1
[5] *maleficio,* ' sorcery ' or possibly ' poison '.
[6] nocuo A ; no'cuo B1 ; nucuo B3
[7] edicere A ; edi'cere B1 ; edicece B3
[8] goreus A B3 ; gore'us B1
[9] *sub navi.* An inverted curach provided convenient shelter. Cf. 42a.
[10] resedens A ; a small *i* has been written by m.h. above the second *e*.
-sid- B1 B3

of the corcu-Réti, asked the holy man by what death
he should be cut off.   The saint said to him : ' You
will die neither in battle, nor in the sea.   A companion
of your journey, from whom you suspect nothing, will
be the cause of your death '.   ' Perhaps ' said Góre,
' one of the friends that accompany me may have it in
mind to kill me ; or my wife, to contrive my death by
magic art, for love of a younger man '.   The saint said :
' It will not happen so '.   ' Why ' said Góre, ' will you
not tell me now about my slayer ? '   The saint replied :
' I will not disclose anything to you more plainly now,
about that baneful companion of yours, lest you be too
greatly troubled by frequent remembrance of what you
know, before the day comes on which you will learn
the truth of this matter '.

Why linger over words ?   After some years had
passed, it chanced one day that the same Góre was
sitting under a ship, and with his own knife was scraping
the bark (?) from a spear-shaft.   Then he heard some
men near by fighting among themselves, and he rose
quickly, to part the fighters ; and his knee, striking
against that knife, which in the sudden movement he
had carelessly dropped on the ground, was severely
wounded.   And by this companion's doing, the cause
of his death arose.   Directly, with consternation of mind,
he remembered that it was in accordance with the
prophecy of the holy man.   And after some months,
oppressed by this evil, he died.

---

[11] *cristiliam.* This may perhaps have been a corruption, in speech, of
crustulam. At the same time, *is* could have been a textual error for the
Irish ligature of *us.*

[12] neglegentius A ; neglig- B1 ; neclig- B3

[13] genucla A ; geni'cula B1 ; genicula B3

[14] ei A B3 ; ejus B1

[15] aborta A ; oborta B1 B3

De alia etiam ré quamlibet minore puto non esse tacenda sancti jucunda praescientia et profetizatio [1] viri

ALIO NAMQUE IN TEMPORE cum sanctus in Iova inhabitaret insula, unum de fratribus advocans síc conpellat : ' Tertia ab hac inlucescente [2] die exspectare debebis in occidentali hujus insulae parte, super maris oram sedens. Nam de aquilonali Everniae [3] regione 48b quaedam hospita grus [4] | ventís per longos aeris agitata circuitus post nonam diei horam valde fessa et fatigata superveniet, et pene consumptís viribus coram té in litore cadens recumbet. Quam misericorditer sublevare curabis, et ad propinquam deportabis domum, ibidemque hospitaliter receptam per tres dies et noctes ei ministrans sollicite cibabis. Et post, expleto recreata triduo, nolens ultra apud nos perigrinari,[5] ad priorem Scotiae dulcem unde orta [6] remeabit regionem plene resumtís viribus. Quam ideo tibi síc deligenter [7] commendo, quia de nostrae paternitatis regione [8] est oriunda '.

Obsecundat frater, tertiaque die [9] post horam nonam ut jusus [10] praescitae [11] adventum prestulatur [12] hospitae ; 49a adventantemque [13] de litore | levat lapsam, ad hospitium

---

[1] profetizatio A ; prophetia B1 ; prophetica B3
[2] *inlucescente.* If this is to be taken with *hac*, the suggestion is that the conversation occurred after the office of prime. Cf. p. 122.
[3] everniae A ; hibernie B1 B3
[4] grus A B3 ; crus B1
[5] perigrinari A ; -reg- B1 B3
[6] orta A B3 ; orta est B1
[7] deligenter A ; dil- B1 B3
[8] *regione.* The ancestral land of Columba (and of Adomnan) was the land of the cenel-Conaill, in north-western Ireland.
[9] *tertia die* would normally mean ' two days later ' ; but above, 48a, the meaning seems to be ' three days after ' the time of speaking, and the same is implied by *post ternos soles*, 49a.

[I 48] In another matter also, though it be a
lesser one, yet I think that the holy man's
pleasant foreknowledge and prophecy
should not be passed over in silence

At one time, while the saint was living in the island
of Io, he called in one of the brothers, and thus addressed him : ' On the third day from this that dawns,
you must watch in the western part of this island, sitting
above the sea-shore ; for after the ninth hour of the
day a guest will arrive from the northern region of
Ireland, very tired and weary, a crane that has been
tossed by winds through long circuits of the air. And
with its strength almost exhausted it will fall near you
and lie upon the shore. You will take heed to lift it
tenderly, and carry it to the house near by ; and,
having taken it in as a guest there for three days and
nights, you will wait upon it, and feed it with anxious
care. And afterwards, at the end of the three days,
revived and not wishing to be longer in pilgrimage
with us, it will return with fully recovered strength to
the sweet district of Ireland from which at first it came.
I commend it to you thus earnestly, for this reason, that
it comes from the district of our fathers '.

The brother obeyed ; and on the third day, after
the ninth hour, as he had been bidden, he awaited the
coming of the foreknown guest. When it arrived, he
lifted it from the shore where it had fallen ; in its

---

[10] ut jusus A. Omitted in B1 B3.
[11] praescitae A ; a circumflex accent has later been added with a fine
pen above *i*. presci'te B1 ; prescite B3
[12] prestulatur A ; the first *u* has later been altered to *o* by bridging.
-stol- B1 B3
[13] adventantemque A B1 ; -tatem- B3

Y

portat infirmam, essurientem [1] cibat. Cui ad monasterium vespere reverso sanctus non interrogans sed narrans ait : ' Benedicat te deus, mi filii,[2] quia perigrinae [3] bene ministrasti hospitae ; quae in perigrinatione [4] non demorabitur, sed post ternos soles ad patriam repeda[b]it '.[5] Quod ita ut sanctus praedixit et [6] rés etiam probavit. Nam trinalibus hospitata diebus, coram hospite ministro [7] de terra sé primum volando elevans in sublime, paulisperque [8] in aere viam speculata, ociani [9] transvadato equore ad Everniam [10] recto volatus cursu die repedavit tranquillo. .

De bello quod in munitione Cethirni [11] post multa commisum est tempora, et de quodam fonticulo ejusdem terrulae proximo, beati [12] praescientia viri. . |

49b   ALIO IN TEMPORE vir beatus cum post regum in dorso Cette [13] condictum, Aidi [14] videlicet filii Ainmurech,[15] et Aidani [16] filii Gabrani,[17] ad campos reverteretur equore[o]s,[18] ipse et Comgellus abbas [19] quadam serena aestei [20] temporis die haut procul a supra memorata

[1] essurientem A ; the first s has later been deleted with a dot below made by a fine pen. esu- B1 B3
[2] filii A ; the third i has later been deleted with a dot below made by a fine pen. fili B1 B3
[3] perigrinae A ; peregrine B1 B3   [4] perigrinatione ; pere- B1 B3
[5] repedavit A ; a small b (?text hand) has been written above v. -abit B1 B3   [6] et A. Omitted in B1 B3.
[7] ministro. In A, a medial punctuation point is wrongly placed, by the text-hand, after this word. The point stands before coram in B1 B3.
[8] paulisperque A B3 ; paulisper B1
[9] ociani A ; the first i has been altered by m.h. to e. occeano B1 ; occeani B3
[10] everniam A ; hiberniam B1 B3
[11] munitio cethirni is a translation of dún Cethirn. The place intended was almost certainly the hill-fort on Sconce Hill, about five miles west of Coleraine. See Reeves 1857, pp. 95–6.

weakness, he carried it to the lodging ; in its hunger, he fed it. When he returned to the monastery in the evening, the saint, not questioning but affirming, said to him : ' God bless you, my son, because you have tended well the pilgrim guest ; which will not remain in pilgrimage, but after three days will return home '.

This, precisely as the saint foretold, the event also proved to be true. After being a guest for three days, it first rose from the ground in the presence of its host that had cared for it, and flew to a height ; and then, after studying the way for a while in the air, crossed the expanse of ocean, and in calm weather took its way back to Ireland, in a straight line of flight.

[I 49] The blessed man's foreknowledge regarding a battle that was fought many years later in the fortress of Cethern ; and regarding a well close to the land of that fortress

At one time, after the conference of kings in the ridge of Cete (namely of Aid, Ainmure's son, and Aidan, Gabran's son), when the blessed man was returning to the plains of the sea-coast, he and the abbot Comgell sat down not far from the above-mentioned fortress, on

[12] beati A ; sancti B1 B3
[13] cette A, with two over-dashes; cete B1 B3. The council of Druimm-céte was held perhaps at the Mullach, near Newtown Limavady, on the river Roe, in county Londonderry, about A.D. 575. See p. 40.
[14] aidi A B3, with two over-dashes in A ; a'idi B1
[15] ainmurech A B1, with three over-dashes in A ; ammurech B3
[16] aidani A ; aida'ni B1 ; aidam B3
[17] gabrani A B3, with three over-dashes in A ; gabra'ni B1
[18] equoreas A ; a very fine dot has later been added above a. -eos B1 B3
[19] abbas. Comgell was the founder of the abbey of Bangor, county Down. His death is entered in A.U. under A.D. 601=602.
[20] aestei A ; estivi B1 B3

munitione resedent.[1] Tum proinde aqua de quodam proximo ad manus lavandas fonticulo ad sanctos in eneo [2] defertur vasculo. Quam cum sanctus Columba accipisset [3] ad abbatem Comgellum a latere sedentem síc profatur : ' Ille fonticulus, Ó Comgelle, de quo haec effussa nobís allata est aqua veniet dies quando nullís ussibus [4] humanís aptus erit '. ' Qua causa ' ait Comgellus,[5] ' ejus fontana corrumpetur unda ? [6] ' Sanctus tum [7] Columba : ' Quia humano ' inquit, ' cruore replebitur. Nam mei cognitionales [8] | amici, et tui secundum carnem cognati, (hoc est Nellis [9] nepotes, et Cruthini [10] populi) in hac vicina munitione Cethirni [11] belligerantes committent bellum. Unde in supra memorato fonte aliquis de mea cognitione trucidabitur homuncio ; cujus cum ceterís interfecti sanguine ejusdem fonticuli locus replebitur '.

50a

Quae ejus veridica suo tempore post multos vaticinatio expleta est annos. In quo bello ut multi norunt populi Domnallus Aidi filius victor sublimatus est [12] ; et in eodem secundum sancti vaticinium viri fonticulo quidam de parantella [13] ejus interfectus est homo. Alius

---

[1] resedent A[^];[^] the second *e* has later been altered to *i* with a downstroke by a fine pen. resideret B1 ; resident B3

[2] eneo A B3 ; in A, an acute accent has later been added with a fine pen above the first *e*, and a hairpin loop has been added below, with a very fine pen, changing *e* to *ae*. e'neo B1

[3] accipisset A ; the first *i* has been altered by m.h. to *e*. -cep- B1 B3

[4] ussibus A ; the first *s* has later been deleted with a dot below. usibus B1 B3

[5] comgellus A B3 ; cogellus B1

[6] unda A B3 ; vena B1

[7] tum A B1 ; tunc B3

[8] cognitionales A ; cogniciales B1 ; cognicionales B3

[9] nellis A B3 ; nellus B1. Columba's people were the northern Ui-Néill. See pp. 67, 136.

[10] cruthini A B3 ; cruithi'ni B1. See p. 134. Here, the *Cru'thini populi* are placed in antithesis to *Néllis nepotes*. The construction is parallel with that of *genus Loerni* 101b. It is noteworthy that Adomnan makes Cruthen the eponym of the Cruithni, and not an individual Cruithnian. The

a fine day of summer. Then water for washing their hands was brought to the saints in a bronze vessel, from a well close by. When Saint Columba had received it, he spoke thus to abbot Comgell, who was sitting by his side : ' Comgell, the day will come when that well, from which this water, poured out for us, has been brought, will be fit for no human use '. ' How ' said Comgell, ' will its springing water be defiled ? ' Saint Columba then replied : ' Because it will be filled with human blood. For my friends by kinship, and your kinsmen according to the flesh (that is to say the descendants of Néll, and the peoples of Cruthen), being at war will fight a battle in this near-by fortress of Cethern. And so one of my kindred will be slaughtered in the above-mentioned well, and with the blood of that poor fellow, killed among the rest, the place of that well will be filled '.

This true prophecy of his was fulfilled in its time, after many years, in the battle in which, as many people know, Domnall Aid's son was raised up as victor ; and in the same well, in accordance with the holy man's prophecy, a certain man of his kindred was killed.

---

words *Cruthini populi* represent the Irish *Cruthen-tuatha* (literally ' Cruthen-tribes '). If *Cruthini* had been a nominative plural, it would, according to Adomnan's normal usage, have been a noun in apposition, not an adjective. Comgell (called *mocu-Aridi*, 118a) was a member of the tribe Dal-nAridi, which held the principal kingdom of Cruithni in northern Ireland.

[11] cethirni A ; cethi'rni B1 ; cechirni B3

[12] *sublimatus est.* This may mean that Domnall Aid's son became the king of Ireland after the battle. In the battle of Dun-Cethirn (A.U. 628=629), Comgell's kinsman, Congal Caich, the king of Dal-nAridi and of Ulaid, was defeated. He was killed in a battle fought against Domnall Aid's son at Roth ; see pp. 47-8.

[13] parantella A ; a small *e* has been written by m.h. above the second *a*, and the first *l* has been erased but not by the text-hand. parentela B1 B3

mihi Adomnano [1] Christi miles Finanus nomine, qui
vitam multís anchoriticam [2] annís juxta roboreti monas-
50b terium campi inrepraehensibi|liter ducebat, de eodem
bello sé praesente commiso [3] aliqua enarrans, protestatus
est in supradicto fonte truncum cadaverinum vidisse ;
eademque die ad monasterium sancti Comgil [4] quod
scotice dicitur Cambas [5] commiso [6] reversum bello, quia
inde prius venerat ; ibidemque duos sancti Comgilli [7]
senes [8] monacos [9] repperisse, quibus cum de bello coram
sé acto et de fonticulo humano cruore corrupto aliquanta
enarraret, illi consequenter : ' Verus profeta Columba '
aiunt, ' qui haec omnia, quae hodie [10] de bello et de
fonticulo expleta enarras, ante multos annos futura nobís
audientibus coram sancto Comgello juxta Cethirni [11]
sedens munitionem praenuntiaverat ' [12]. .

De diversorum discretione xeniorum
sancto revelata [13] viro diali gratia. . |

51a   EODEM IN TEMPORE Conallus episcopus Cule-rathin,[14]
collectís a populo campi Eilni [15] pene innumerabilibus
xeniis,[16] beato viro hospitium praeparavit post condictum

[1] adomnano A ; á domnano B1 ; adamnano B3
[2] anchoriticam A ; the first *i* has been altered by m.h. to *e*. anacore'-
ticam B1 ; anachoreticam B3
[3] commiso A ; a small *s* has been added by m.h. above *is*. -isso B1 B3
[4] comgil A ; comgelli B1 B3
[5] cambas A B1 B3, with two over-dashes in A. This monastery is said
to have been on the west side of the Bann. Cf. Reeves 1857, p. 96.
[6] commi|so A ; an *s* has been added by m.h. after *i*. -isso B1 B3
[7] comgilli A ; comgelli B1 B3
[8] senes A. Omitted in B1 B3.
[9] monacos A ; a small *h* has been written by m.h. above *co*. -chos
B1 B3
[10] *quae hodie.* Here B2 begins again ; see 37a.
[11] cethirni A ; ce'thirni B1 ; with *-in* changed to *-ni* by an apex added
above the last stroke by the text-hand ; cethirin B2 B3
[12] praenuntiaverat A ; -at B1 B3 ; -ant B2

Another soldier of Christ, Finan by name, who for many years lived irreproachably the life of an anchorite beside the monastery of the plain of the oakwood [Durrow], described to me, Adomnan, some things concerning that battle, fought in his presence, and bore witness that he had seen a dismembered corpse in the above-mentioned well ; and that returning on the same day, after the battle was fought, to the monastery of Saint Comgell that is in Irish called *Cambas*, since it was from there that he had come before, he had found there two old men, monks of Saint Comgell. And when he had related to them something concerning the battle that had been fought in his sight, and the well defiled with human blood, they immediately said : ' A true prophet was Columba who, in our hearing, foretold as happening in the future all these things concerning the battle, and the well, that you tell us have been fulfilled today, when, many years ago, he sat with Saint Comgell beside the fortress of Cethern '.

[I 50] Concerning the distinction, revealed to the holy man by the grace of God, between different gifts

At the same time, Conall, the bishop of Cul-rathin [Coleraine], collected from the people of the plain of Eilne almost innumerable gifts, and prepared a lodging

---

13 *revelata*. In A, the *ve* has been inserted above, by the text-hand.
14 culerathin A B2 B3, with four over-dashes in A ; culerathi 'n B1. The bishop of Coleraine appears also to have been head of the monastery.
15 eilni A, with two over-dashes ; elni' B1 ; elni B2 B3. Eilne lay between the rivers Bann and Bush.
16 xeniis A B1 B2 ; exeniis B3

supra memoratorum regum turba prosequente multa
revertenti. Proinde sancto advenienti [1] viro xenia [2]
populi multa in platea monasterii strata [3] benedicenda
adsignantur. Quae cum benedicens aspiceret, xenium
alicujus opulenti viri specialiter demonstrans : ' Virum '
ait, ' cujus est hoc xenium [4] pro misericordiis pauperum
et ejus largitione dei [5] comitatur misericordia '.

Itemque aliud discernit inter alia multa xenium,[6]
inquiens : ' De hoc ego xenio viri sapientis et avari nullo
modo gustare possum nisi prius veram de peccato
51b avaritiae penitudinem egerit '. Quod verbum | cito in
turba devulgatum [7] audiens adcurrit [8] Columbus filius
Aidi [9] conscius, et coram sancto flexís genibus penitentiam agit, et de cetero avaritiae abrenuntiaturum sé
promittit, et largitatem cum morum emendatione conse-
quuturum. Et jusus [10] a sancto surgere ex illa hora est
sanatus de vitio tenacitatis. Erat enim vir sapiens sicuti
sancto in ejus revelatum erat xenio.

Ille vero dives largus, Brendenus [11] nomine, de cujus
xenio paulo superius dictum est, audiens et ipse sancti
verba de sé dicta ingeniculans ad pedes sancti precatur,
ut pro eo ad dominum sanctus fundat precem. Qui ab
eo primum pro quibusdam suís objurgatus peccatís
penitudinem gerens, de cetero sé emendaturum pro-
missit. Et [12] síc uterque de propriis emendatus et sanatus
est vitiis. . |

---

[1] *advenienti.* Before this word, in A, *et* has been added by m.h. above
the line, unnecessarily.
[2] xenia A B1 B2 ; exenia B3
[3] *in platea strata.* Cf. p. 114. Another possible translation is : ' in the
paved courtyard '.
[4] xenium A B1 B3 ; exenium B2
[5] dei A ; diu B1 B2 B3 (perhaps an error for *dn˜i*, domini).
[6] xenium A B1 B2 ; exenium B3
[7] devulgatum A ; the *e* has later been altered to *i* with a long down-
stroke made by a fine pen. div- B1 B2 B3

for the blessed man, when, with a large crowd accompanying him, he was returning after the conference of the above-named kings. So when the holy man arrived, the many gifts of the people were presented to him for benediction, laid out in the courtyard of the monastery. While he was blessing and examining them, he pointed especially to the gift of a rich man, saying : ' God's mercy goes with the man whose gift this is, for his mercies to the poor, and his generosity '.

Again, he distinguished one gift among many others, saying : ' I can taste nothing of this, the gift of a wise but avaricious man, unless he first shows true repentance for the sin of avarice '. This saying was quickly made known among the crowd, and hearing it Columb, Aid's son, conscience-stricken, ran up, and on bended knees expressed penitence in the presence of the saint, and promised that he would thenceforward renounce avarice, mend his ways, and practise liberality. And when he was bidden by the saint to rise, from that hour he was cured of the vice of meanness. For he was a wise man, as had been revealed to the saint in his gift.

That generous rich man, by name Brenden, of whose gift mention was made a little above, also heard the saint's words spoken concerning himself ; and kneeling at the saint's feet, he prayed that the saint would raise a prayer for him to the Lord. First he was chidden by him for certain sins, and professing repentance he promised that he would thenceforth amend. And so each was corrected and healed of his particular faults.

---

[8] adcurrit A ; cucurrit B1 ; accurrit B2 B3
[9] aidi A B2 B3, with two over-dashes in A ; a'idi B1
[10] jusus A ; a small *s* has been written by m.h. above the first *us*. jussus B1 B2 B3
[11] brendenus A B2 B3 ; brede'nus B1   [12] et A ; Et B1 B2 ; Q' B3

52a   Simili scientia sanctus et alio tempore xenium
alicujus tenacis viri inter multa cognovit xenia, Diormiti [1]
nomine, ad cellam magnam Deathrib [2] in ejus adventu
collecta.

Haec de beati viri profetica gratia, quasi de plurimís
pauca, in hujus libelli textu primi craxasse [3] sufficiat.
' Pauca ' dixi, nam hoc de venerabili viro non est dubi-
tandum, quod valde numerosiora fuerint quae in
notitiam hominum sacramenta interius celata [4] venire
nullo modo poterant quam ea quae quasi quaedam
parva aliquando stillicidia veluti per quasdam rimulas
alicujus pleni vassis [5] ferventissimo novo distillabant [6]
vino. Nam sancti et apostolici viri vanam evitantes
gloriam plerumque in quantum possunt interna quaedam
52b   arcana [7] sibi intrinsecus | a deo manifestata celare
festinant. Sed deus nonnulla ex eís, vellint nollint [8] ipsi,
devulgat [9] et in medium quoquo profert modo ; videlicet glorificare volens glorificantes sé sanctos, hoc est
ipsum dominum, cui gloria in saecula saeculorum. . [10]

Huic [11] primo libro híc [12] inponitur terminus. .[13]

[1] diormiti A B3 ; diormi'thi B1 ;]ti B2
[2] deathrib A, with three over-dashes ; dethirid B1 ; dethrib B3.
Missing in B2. This place was below Lough Key, near the Shannon. See
43a, 67b, and p. 70.
[3] craxasse A ; caraxasse B1 B3. Missing in B2.
[4] celata A B2 B3 ; scelata B1
[5] vassis A ; the first s has later been deleted with a dot below made by
a fine pen. vasis B1 B2 B3
[6] distillabant A B1 B2 ; des- B3
[7] arcana A ; a small h has been written by m.h. above ca. archana
B1 B2 B3
[8] vellint nollint A ; the first l in each word has later been deleted with
a dot below made by a fine pen. velint nolint B1 B2 B3
[9] devulgat A ; the e has later been altered to i with a down-stroke
made by a fine pen. div- B1 B2 B3
[10] saeculorum A ; seculorum amen B1 B2 B3
[11] Huic A ; Hic B1 ; De B3. Missing in B2.

At another time, with similar knowledge, the saint recognized the gift of a certain niggardly man, Diormit by name, among many gifts that were brought to the great church of Deathrib at the coming of the saint.

Let it suffice to have written down these things, as a few instances out of very many of the blessed man's prophetic gift, in the text of this first book. I say ' few ', because it cannot be doubted, in the case of the venerable man, that the instances which, inwardly concealed as holy mysteries, could never come to the knowledge of men, were far more numerous than those that from time to time dripped, as it were, like small drops through the cracks of a vessel filled with new strongly-fermenting wine. For holy and apostolic men, shunning vainglory, very often hasten to conceal, as well as they can, such inner secrets as are manifested to them inwardly by God. But, whether they will or no, God makes known, and in one way or another publicly exposes, some of these things ; inasmuch as he wishes to glorify the saints that glorify him, namely the Lord himself, to whom be glory, through the ages of the ages.

Here an end is put to this first book.

---

¹² híc A. Omitted in B₁ B₂ B₃.

¹³ *terminus.* After this word, a contents-list of Book II is given by B₂ B₃, beginning : *Capitula secundi libri incipiunt de virtutum miraculis* ; and ending : *Expliciunt capitula secundi libri* (B₃ ; B₂ partly illegible). In general, the list copies the chapter-headings that appear in B₁ B₂ B₃. Deviations of the list from the chapter-headings are noted below, in the footnotes. See p. 9. The contents-list was included in the editions of Reeves and Fowler, who placed it after *comitatur* below.

Nunc sequens orditur [1] liber de virtutum miraculís
quae plerumque etiam profetalis praescientia [2] comitatur. .

53a   De vino quod de aqua factum est [3] |

ALIO IN TEMPORE [4] cum vir venerandus [5] in Scotia
apud sanctum Findbarrum [6] episcopum adhuc juvenis
sapientiam sacrae scripturae addiscens commaneret,
quadam sollemni die vinum ad sacrificiale misterium [7]
cassu [8] aliquo minime inveniebatur. De cujus defectu
cum ministros altaris inter sé conquirentes [9] audiret, ad
fontem sumpto pergit [10] urceo, ut ad sacra eucharistiae
ministeria aquam quasi diacon [11] fontanam auriret.[12] Ipse
quippe illís in diebus erat in diaconatus gradu amministrans.[13] Vir itaque beatus aquaticum quod de latice
ausit [14] elimentum [15] invocato nomine domini Jesu Christi
fideliter benedixit, qui in Cana [16] Galileae [17] aquam [18]
convertit ; quo [19] etiam in hoc operante miraculo in-
53b ferior hoc est aquatica | natura in gratiorem videlicet
vinalem per manus praedicabilis viri conversa est
speciem.

Vir itaque sanctus a fonte reversus et eclesiam intrans
talem juxta altare urceum intra se habentem deponit

[1] Nunc sequens orditur A ; Incipit secundus B1 B3. Instead of *Nunc*
to *comitatur*, B2 read : *Incipit liber [secundus].*

[2] plerumque etiam profetalis praescientia A ; plerumque et prescientia
propheta'lis B1 ; plenissime plerumque eciam presciencia prophetalis B3

[3] *De* to *est.* So also in B1 and contents-list of B3 ; omitted here by B3.
B2 and contents-list of B2 read : *De vino quod factum est de aqua.* A's heading
is written in the third and fourth of eleven lines that had been left blank
at the foot of 52b. In the bottom of the column, 6 or 7 letters (?m.h.)
have been written, with the page upside-down, perhaps beginning *Colum* ;
and smeared out, while the ink was wet.

[4] Alio in tempore A B1 B3. Omitted in B2.

[5] vir venerandus A ; venerandus vir B1 B3; vir sanctus columba B2

[6] findbarrum A ; fendbarrum B1 B2 B3. See p. 68.

[7] misterium A B1 B3 ; ministerium B2

Now begins the next book, concerning miracles of power, which are often accompanied by prophetic foreknowledge.

[II 1] Of wine that was made from water

At one time, when the venerable man, while still a youth, was living in Ireland with the holy bishop Findbarr, acquiring knowledge of sacred scripture, it chanced on a certain festival that no wine was found for the sacrificial rite. When he heard the attendants of the altar lamenting among themselves over the lack of it, he took a pitcher and went to the well, so that he as a deacon might draw spring water for the sacred purposes of the Eucharist ; for at that time he was serving in the order of deacon. So the blessed man blessed in faith the watery element that he drew from the spring, calling on the name of the Lord Jesus Christ, who transmuted water in Cana of Galilee ; by whose power in this miracle also the baser, that is the watery, substance was changed into the more desirable form, that is to say of wine, through the hands of the memorable man. The holy man returned from the well and entered the church, and put down beside the altar the

---

[8] cassu A ; the first *s* has later been erased. casu B1 B2 B3

[9] conquirentes A ; -quer- B1 B2 B3

[10] pergit A. Omitted in B1 B2 B3.

[11] diacon| A ; a *us* symbol has been written by m.h. above *n*. diaconus B1 B2 B3. Cf. *diacon* in 73a2.

[12] auriret A ; an *h* has been written by m.h. before *a*. haur- B1 B2 B3

[13] *amministrans*. In A, the first *m* has been underlined, and *d* has been written by m.h. above it.

[14] ausit A ; hausit B1 B2 B3   [15] elimentum A ; ele- B1 B2 B3

[16] cana A ; a small *h* has been written by m.h. above *ca*. chana B1 B2 B3   [17] galileae A ; galilëe B1 ; galëe B2 ; galilee B3

[18] aquam A ; aquam in vinum B1 B2 B3

[19] quo A ; Quod B1 ; Quo B2 B3

liquorem, et ad ministros : ' Habetis ' ait, ' vinum quod
dominus Jesus ad sua misit peragenda misteria '. Quo
cognito sanctus cum [1] ministrís episcopus [2] eximias deo
referunt [3] grates. Sanctus vero juvenis hoc non sibimet
sed sancto Vinniavo [4] adscribebat episcopo. Hoc itaque
protum [5] virtutis documentum Christus dominus per
suum declaravit discipulum, quod in eadem [6] ré initium
ponens signorum in Cana [7] Galileae [8] operatus est per
semet ipsum.

Hujus [9] inquam libelli quasi quaedam lucerna in-
lustret exordium, quod per nostrum Columbam diale
manifestatum est miraculum, ut deinceps transeamus
54a ad caetera quae per ipsum | ostensa sunt virtutum
miracula. .

De alicujus arboris fructu amaro per sancti
benedictionem in dulcidinem [10] verso [11]

QUAEDAM ERAT arbor valde pomosa prope monasterium roboris campi in australi ejus parte ; de qua cum
incolae loci quoddam haberent [12] pro nimia fructus
amaritudine querimonium, quadam die sanctus [13] ad
eam [14] accessit autumnali tempore. Vidensque lignum
incassum abundos [15] habere fructus, qui ex eís gustantes
plus lederent quam dilectarent,[16] sancta elevata manu

---

[1] cum A B2 B3. Omitted in B1.
[2] epi˜s A ; episcopus B2 ; episcopis B1 B3. In B1, the final *s* of
ministris and of *episcopis* has been erased, and a marginal note by the reviser
emends *sanctus* to *sancti*.
[3] referunt A B3 ; re'ferunt B1 ; refert B2, correcting the grammar.
[4] vinniavo A B2 ; vinniano B1 B3
[5] protum A ; promptum B1 B2 B3
[6] eadem A B2 B3 ; in A, a circumflex accent has later been added with
a fine pen above *a*. ea'dem B1
[7] cana A ; chana B1 B2 B3
[8] galileae A ; galilee B1 B3; galëe B2
[9] *Hujus* has a large coloured initial letter in A B1 B2 B3.

pitcher containing this fluid. And he said to the attendants : ' Here is wine, which the Lord Jesus has sent for the performance of his rite '. Learning this, the holy bishop with the attendants returned great thanks to God. But the holy youth attributed it not to himself, but to the holy bishop Findbarr. And so Christ the Lord manifested through his disciple, as a first evidence of power, this that he had performed through himself in Cana of Galilee, when he made the same thing the beginning of his signs.

Let this miracle of God that was shown through our Columba illumine like a lantern the opening of this book, so that we may pass forward to the other miracles of power that were shown through him.

[II 2] Concerning the bitter fruit of a tree, turned to sweetness by the saint's blessing

Near the monastery of the plain of the oak [Durrow], on its southern side, there was a tree that bore much fruit. Since the inhabitants of the place made a complaint against it because of the too great bitterness of the fruit, the saint went to it one day in the autumn season. And seeing that the tree vainly produced abundant fruit, more hurtful than pleasing to those that tasted it, he raised his holy hand, blessed the tree, and

---

[10] dulcidinem A ; -ced- B1 B3. Illegible in B2.
[11] The contents-list of B2 and of B3 reads : *De amarissimis alicujus arboris pomis in dulcedinem per sancti benedictionem versis* (B2 partly illegible).
[12] haberent A B1 B3 ; -entur B2
[13] sanctus A B1 B3. Omitted in B2.
[14] eam A B1 B3 ; eandem B2
[15] abundos A ; habundos B1 B3. Missing in B2.
[16] dilectarent A ; the *i* has been altered by m.h. to *e*. del- B1 B2 B3

benedicens ait : 'In nomine omnipotentis dei, omnis
tua amaritudo Ó arbor amara a té recedat, tuaque huc
usque amarissima nunc in dulcissima vertantur poma '.
Mirum dictu, dicto citius eodemque momento ejusdem
54b arboris | omnia poma amisa[1] amaritudine in miram
secundum verbum sancti versa sunt dulcidinem. .[2]

De segite[3] post medium aestatis tempus
seminata, et in exordio agusti mens[is][4]
sancto orante mesa in Iova conversante
insula.[5] .

ALIO IN TEMPORE sanctus suos misit monacos,[6] ut de
alicujus plebei agellulo virgarum fasciculos ad hospitium
afferent[7] construendum. Qui cum ad sanctum oneraria
repleta navi de supradictís virgularum materiis reversi
venirent, dicerentque plebeum ejusdem causa dispendii
valde contristatum, sanctus consequenter precipiens
dicit : ' Ne ergo illum scandalizemus virum, ad ipsum a
nobís bis terni deferantur ordei modii[8] ; eosdemque hís
in[9] diebus arata ipse seminet in terra '. Quibus ad
55a plebeum Findchanum[10] | nomine juxta sancti jusionem
misís,[11] et coram eo cum tali commendatione adsignatís,
gratanter accipiens ait : 'Quomodo post medium
esteum[12] tempus seges seminata contra hujus naturam
terrae proficiet ? '[13] Marita econtra : ' Fac ' ait, ' secun-

---

[1] amisa A ; a small *s* has been written by m.h. above *i*. amissa B1
B2 B3
[2] dulcidinem A ; -ced- B1 B2 B3   [3] segite A ; segete B1 B2 B3
[4] agusti mense A ; mensis augusti B1 ; augusti mensis B2 B3
[5] The contents-list of B2 and of B3 reads : *De terra post medium estatis
tempus arata et seminata mensis augusti incipientis exordio maturam messem proferente.*
[6] monacos A ; a small *h* has been written by m.h. above *co*. -chos
B1 B2 B3
[7] afferent A B3 ; in A, a small *r* has been written by m.h. above *r*.
afferrent B1 B2

said : ' In the name of almighty God, thou bitter tree, may all thy bitterness leave thee, and thy fruit, hitherto most bitter, now become most sweet '. Marvellous to say, more quickly than words, and in the same moment, all the fruit of that tree lost its bitterness, and was changed, according to the saint's word, into wonderful sweetness.

[II 3] Concerning a crop of grain sown after the middle of summer, and reaped in the beginning of the month of August, at the prayer of the saint, while he was living in the island of Io

At one time, the saint sent his monks to bring bundles of wattle from the field of a certain layman, for the building of a guest-house. When, having filled a freight-ship with the aforesaid materials of wattle, they returned and came to the saint, and said that the layman was much distressed on account of this loss, the saint immediately gave instructions, saying : ' Therefore, lest we offend the man, let twice three measures of barley be taken to him from us ; and let him sow the same at this time, in ploughed land '.

When, according to the saint's command, the grain had been sent to the layman, Findchan by name, and delivered to him with this instruction, he, while receiving it gladly, said : ' How shall a crop sown after midsummer succeed, against the nature of this land ? ' His wife on the contrary said : ' Do according to the bidding

---

[8] *modii.* Cf. 42b.   [9] in A B1 B3. Omitted in B2.

[10] findchanum A ; findcha'num B1 ; findcanum B2 B3

[11] misís A ; a small *s* has been added by m.h. above the first *is.* missis B1 B2 B3   [12] esteum A ; esti'vum B1 ; estivum B2 B3

[13] *proficiet.* After this word, in A, a question-mark has been added by m.h. ; B1 B2 B3 have question-marks.

z

dum sancti mandatum, cui dominus donabit quod-
cumque ab eo postulaverit'. Sed et qui misi[1] sunt simul
hoc addiderunt, dicendo : ' Sanctus Columba, qui nos
ad té cum hoc misit munere, hoc mandatum per nos de
tua commendavit segite,[2] dicens : " Homo ille in omnipotentia dei confidat. Seges ejus quamvis de mense
junio xv.[3] premisís[4] diebus seminata in principiis agusti[5]
mensis metetur ".' Obsequitur plebeus arando[6] et
seminando ; et mesem[7] quam supradicto in tempore
contra spem seminavit cum omnium ammiratione[8] |
55b vicinorum in exordio agusti[9] mensis maturam juxta
verbum sancti mesuit,[10] in loco terrae quae dicitur
Delcros. .[11]

De morbifera[12] nube et
plurimorum[13] sanitate. .

ALIO ITIDEM[14] IN TEMPORE cum sanctus in Iova
commoraretur insula, sedens in monticulo qui latine
munitio[15] magna dicitur, videt ab aquilone nubem
densam et pluialem[16] de mari die serena abortam.[17] Qua
ascendente visa sanctus ad quendam de suís juxta se
monacum[18] sedentem, nomine Silnanum filium Nemai-

---

[1] misi A ; a small *s* has been written by m.h. above *is*. missi B1 B2 B3
[2] segite A ; the *i* has been altered by m.h. to *e*. -get- B1 B2 B3
[3] xu A ; quindecim B1 B3 ; qui[B2. Reeves misread *xu* as *xii*. See
p. 167.
[4] premisís A ; a small *s* has been added by m.h. above the first *i*.
premissis B1 B3 ;]sis B2
[5] agusti A ; augusti B1 B2 B3
[6] arando A B1 ; orando B3. Illegible in B2.
[7] mesem A ; a small *s* has been written by m.h. above *es*. messem
B1 B2 B3
[8] *ammiratione*. In A, a small *d* has later been written above the first *m*.
[9] agusti A ; augusti B1 B2 B3
[10] mesuit A ; a small *s* has been written by m.h. above *es*. messuit
B1 B2 B3
[11] delcros A B3 ; delcors B1 ; d[e]lcros B2. In A, the *c* does not join
the *r*. The name is a compound of *delc* and *ros*.

of the saint, to whom the Lord will grant whatever he may ask of him '. And likewise the messengers also added this, and said : ' Saint Columba, who has sent us to you with this gift, gave this injunction through us in regard to your crop, saying : " Let that man trust in the omnipotence of God. His crop, although sown after fifteen days of the month of June have passed, will be reaped in the beginning of the month of August ".'

The layman obeyed, in ploughing and sowing. And the harvest that, at the time spoken of above, he had sown without hope, he reaped, to the astonishment of all the neighbours, in the beginning of the month of August, fully ripe, according to the saint's word ; in a piece of the land that is called Delcros.

[II 4] Of a pestiferous cloud, and the healing of very many people

Also at another time, while the saint was living in the island of Io, as he sat on the little hill that is in Latin called ' great fortress ', he saw a heavy rain-cloud that had risen from the sea in the north, on a clear day. Watching it as it rose, the saint said to one of his monks, sitting beside him, by name Silnan, Nemaid's son,

---

[12] morbifera A B3 ; morbi'fera B1 ; mortifera B2

[13] *plurimorum.* The contents-list of B2 reads *languentium* ; that of B3, -*cium*.

[14] itidem A B2 ; i'tidem B1. Omitted in B3.

[15] munitio A ; muni'tio B1 ; munitio mun B2 ; municio B3. This word is a translation of Irish *dún* ' fortress ' (a neuter O-stem which in Iona has become feminine, and appears there to mean ' hill '); The *munitio magna* is Dun-Í, which has a clear view to the north, and no fortification.

[16] plu|ialem A ; a *v* has been added by m.h. before *i*. pluvialem B1 B2 B3

[17] abortam A ; ob- B1 B2 B3

[18] monacum A ; a small *h* has been written by m.h. above *c*. -chum B1 B2 B3

don,[1] mocu-Sogin[2] : ' Haec nubes ' ait, ' valde nocua
hominibus et pecoribus erit. Hacque die velocius trans-
volans super aliquantam Scotiae partem, hoc est ab illo
rivulo qui dicitur Ailbine[3] usque ad vadum Clied,[4]
pluiam vespere distillabit morbiferam, quae gravia et
purulenta humanís in corporibus et in pecorum uberibus|
56a nasci faciet ulcera. Quibus homines morbidi et pecodes[5]
illa veninosa[6] gravitudine usque ad mortem molestati
laborabunt. Sed nos eorum miserati subvenire langori-
bus domino miserante debemus. Tu ergo Silnane[7] nunc
mecum discendens[8] de monte navigationem praepara
crastina[9] die, vita comite et deo volente, a me pane
accepto dei invocato nomine benedicto ; quo in aqua[10]
intincto homines ea consparsi[11] et pecora celerem re-
cuperabunt salutem '.

Quid moramur ? Die crastina hís quae necessaria
erant citius praeparatís Silnanus accepto de manu sancti
pane benedicto in pace enavigavit. Cui sanctus a sé
eadem[12] emigranti hora addit hoc consulatorium[13]
verbum, dicens : ' Confide filii,[14] ventos habebis secundos
et prosperos die noctuque usque[15] ad illam pervenias

[1] nemai|don A, with three over-dashes ; nemaidon B1 B3 ; nemaido
B2. See p. 147. Reeves 1857, p. 108, read this as *Nemani-don*, wrongly
interpreting the heavy dash over *ma* as an *n* symbol (which A does not use).

[2] mocusogin A B2 B3, with four over-dashes in A ; mocusogi'n B1.
The mocu-Sogin appear to have been regarded as Cruithnians. See
MacNeill 1911, pp. 62, 90 ; O'Rahilly 1946, pp. 465-6.

[3] ailbine A B2 B3, with three over-dashes in A ; ailbi'ne B1. This
river is identified with the Delvin, on the north boundary of county Dublin.

[4] clied A, with two over-dashes ; clëeth B1 (the *th* was entered by the
text-hand in accordance with a marginal alteration by the reviser) ; dëeth
B2 ; cleeth B3. The *vadum Clied* or *Cleeth* became later *Áth clíath*, 'ford of
hurdles', over the Liffey at Dublin.

[5] pecodes A ; a small *u* has been written by m.h. above *o*. pecudes
B1 B2 B3

[6] veninosa A ; the *i* has been altered by m.h. to *e*. venenosa B1 B2 B3

[7] silnane A B2 B3; silna'ne B1

[8] discendens A ; the *i* has been altered by m.h. to *e*. des- B1 B2 B3

[9] Crastina A B1 B2 B3

---

mocu-Sogin : ' This cloud will be very hurtful to men and beasts ; and on this day it will quickly move across, and in the evening drop pestiferous rain upon some part of Ireland, that is to say from the stream that is called Ailbine to Ath-clíath [Dublin] ; and it will cause severe and festering sores to form on human bodies and the udders of animals. Men and cattle who suffer from them, afflicted with that poisonous disease, will be sick even to death. But we must take pity upon them and help them in their illness, by the mercy of God. You, Silnan, therefore now go down with me from the hill, and prepare to make a voyage tomorrow, if life continue and God will, after receiving from me bread that has been blessed with invocation of the name of God. When it is dipped in water, men and beasts sprinkled with that water will speedily recover health '.

Why do we linger ? On the next day, all the necessary things having been quickly made ready, Silnan received from the saint's hand the bread that had been blessed ; and he sailed away in peace. The saint gave him this additional word of encouragement in the hour of his departure, saying : ' Be confident, my son ; you will have favourable and prosperous winds, by day and night, until you arrive at the district that is called

---

[10] aqua A ; aquam B1 B3. Illegible in B2.

[11] consparsi A ; the loop of the *a* has been deleted by underpointing, and the second part of the *a* has been altered by m.h. to *e*. -sper- B1 B3. Illegible in B2.

[12] eadem A B3 ; in A, a circumflex accent has been written by m.h. above *a*. ea'dem B1. Illegible in B2.

[13] consulatorium A ; -sol- B1 B3. Illegible in B2.

[14] filii A ; the third *i* has been erased, later than the time when a medial point (?m.h.) was inserted as punctuation after this word. fili B1 B3. Illegible in B2.

[15] usque A ; usque quo B1 B2 B3

56b regionem quae dicitur Ard-ceannachte,[1] ut languen|tibus ibidem celerius cum salubri subvenias pane '.

Quid plura ? Silnanus verbo obsequutus sancti, prospera et celeri [2] navigatione auxiliante domino ad supra memoratam perveniens partem, illius regionis [3] plebem de qua sanctus praedixerat devastatam nubis praedictae morbifera reperiit pluia superpluente citius praecurrentis. In primísque bis terni viri in eadem [4] mari vicina domu [5] reperti in extrimís [6] morte positi appropinquante [7] ab eodem Silnano aqua benedictionis aspersi in eadem praesenti [8] die oportunius sanati sunt. Cujus subitae sanationis rumor [9] per totam illam morbo pestilentiore [10] vastatam regionem cito devulgatus [11] omnem morbidum ad sancti Columbae legatum invitavit populum ; qui juxta sancti mandatum homines [12] et pecora pane intincta benedicto aqua consparsit.[13] Et

57a continuo | plenam recuperantes salutem homines cum pecodibus [14] salvati Christum in sancto Columba cum eximia [15] gratiarum actione laudarunt.

In hac itaque suprascripta narratione ut estimo duo haec manifeste pariter comitantur,[16] hoc est gratia profetationis de nube, et virtutis miraculum in egrotantium

---

[1] ard ceannachte A ; ardcenachte B1 ; ardcenacte B2 B3. This was a district in Brega, to the north of Dublin.
[2] celeri A ; ce'leri B1 ; sceleri B2 B3
[3] *regionis*. After this word, there is no mark of punctuation in A B1 B2 B3. But one of the ninth-century or later punctuators has added a low point in A, and that was wrongly accepted by Reeves. After *partem* above, A B3 have no stop, but there is a correct punctuation mark in B1 B2.
[4] eadem A B3 ; ei'dem B1 (altered, apparently from *eadem*) ; eodem B2
[5] domu A ; domo B1 B2 B3
[6] extrimís A ; the first *i* has been altered by m.h. to *e*. -rem- B1 B2 B3
[7] appropinquante A B1 B2 ; -ti B3
[8] praesenti A. Omitted in B1 B2 B3.
[9] rumor A B1 B2 ; rumur B3
[10] pestilentiore A B1 B2 ; pestilencie B3
[11] devulgatus A ; di- B1 B2 B3
[12] homines A B1 B3 ; homine B2

Ard-ceannachte, so that you may quickly cure the sick in that place, with the healing bread '.

Why say more ? Following the saint's instruction, after a prosperous and speedy voyage Silnan arrived, with the Lord's help, at the place aforesaid ; and found the people of that district, of whom the saint had fore-told, devastated by the pestiferous rain falling upon them from the cloud, which had gone more quickly before him. In the first place six men, in extremity and with death approaching, found in one house near the sea, were sprinkled by Silnan with water of the blessing, and were opportunely restored to health on that same day. The fame of that sudden cure was spread swiftly through the whole of that district, wasted by very pestilent disease, and drew all the sick people to Saint Columba's messenger, who according to the saint's command sprinkled men and beasts with water in which the blessed bread had been dipped. And immediately recovering full health the men, saved with their cattle, praised Christ in Saint Columba, with very great rendering of thanks.

In the story written above, these two things are, as I think, clearly associated together : that is to say, the grace of prophecy concerning the cloud, and the miracle of power in the curing of the sick. That these things

---

[13] consparsit A ; the *a* has been altered by m.h. to *e* (as in *consparsi*, 56a). -spe'r- B1 ; -sper- B2 B3

[14] pecodibus A ; a small *u* has been written by m.h. above *o*. -cud- B1 B2 B3

[15] eximia A B2 B3 ; maxima B1

[16] comitantur A B1 B2 ; comittantur B3, with the *a* altered from *u*.

sanitate. Haec per omnia esse verissima supradictus Silnanus Christi miles sancti legatus Columbae coram Segineo [1] abbate et ceterís testatus est senioribus. .[2]

De Maugina [3] sancta virgine Daimeni filia quae inhabitaverat hi Clochur [4] filiorum Daimeni [5]

ALIO IN TEMPORE sanctus, cum in [6] Iova demoraretur insula, prima diei hora quendam advocans fratrem Lugaidum [7] nomine, cujus cognomentum scotice Lathir [8] dicitur ; et taliter eum | conpellat, dicens [9] : ' Praepara cito ad Scotiam celerem navigationem, nam mihi valde est necesse té usque ad Clocherum [10] filiorum [11] Daimeni distinare [12] legatum. In hac enim praeterita nocte cassu [13] aliquo Maugina [14] sancta virgo filia Daimeni [15] ab oratorio post misam [16] domum reversa titubavit, coxaque ejus in duas confracta est partes.[17] Haec sepius meum inclamitans nomen commemorat, a domino sperans sé accepturam per me consulationem '.[18]

Quid plura ? Lugaido [19] obsecundanti et consequenter emigranti sanctus pineam tradit cum benedictione

57b

[1] segineo A B2 B3 ; segine'o B1

[2] *senioribus.* After this, B1 B2 add : *Transeamus ad alia* ' Let us pass to other things '.

[3] maugina A ; maugu'ina B1 ; mauguina B2 B3

[4] hi clochur A ; in loco qui scottice dicitur clocher B1 B3 (clochcher B1) ; in loco q[ui sco]tie dicitur clocher B2. A's reading is O.I. for ' in Clocher '. The place was Clogher in Tyrone, later the head of an ecclesiastical district to the west of Armagh.

[5] The contents-list of B2 and of B3 reads : *De mauguina sancta virgine et fracture coxe ejus sanata.*

[6] in A B1 B2. Omitted in B3.

[7] lugaidum A B2 ; luga'idum B1 ; lugaidium B3

[8] lathir A B2 B3, with two over-dashes in A ; lathi'r B1. *Lathir* here, and *laitirus* in 86a, are equally well attested as Adomnan's spellings. They are epithets of the same man, and should express the same attribute. But they are inconsistent forms. *Láitir* ' strong ' would make sense, but it is difficult to decide that *lathir* is wrong.

[9] *dicens.* The construction is : *advocans et taliter dicens . . . conpellat.*

are in all respects perfectly true the aforesaid soldier of
Christ, Silnan, Saint Columba's messenger, testified in
presence of the abbot Segene and the other elders.

[II 5] Concerning Maugin, a holy virgin, Daimen's daughter, who lived in Clocher of the sons of Daimen

At another time while the saint resided in the island
of Io, in the first hour of the day he summoned a brother,
Lugaid by name, whose epithet in Irish speech is *Lathir*,
and addressed him in these words : ' Prepare at once
a speedy voyage to Ireland, for it is very needful that I
should send you as an emissary to Clocher of the sons
of Daimen. In this past night by some mischance the
holy virgin Maugin, daughter of Daimen, returning
after the office from the oratory to her house, stumbled ;
and her hip was broken into two pieces. Crying aloud
she constantly repeats my name, hoping that she will
obtain relief through me from the Lord '.
Why say more ? Lugaid obeyed, and was presently
setting out, when the saint handed to him a little box

---

[10] clocherum A B2 B3 ; clo'cherum B1
[11] filiorum A ; filium B1 B2 B3
[12] distinare A ; des- B1 B2 B3
[13] cassu A ; the first *s* has later been deleted with a dot below made
with a fine pen. casu B1 B3. Omitted in B2.
[14] ma|ugina A, with an over-dash above *ma* ; maugu'ina B1 ; mauguina
B2 B3
[15] daime|ni A, with two over-dashes above *daime* ; daime'ni B1 ;
daimeni B2 B3
[16] misam, A ; missam B1 B2 B3. *Missa* means here the office of midnight. See p. 122.
[17] *partes*. In *De Locis* (Geyer 1898, p. 290), Adomnan described the
death of a horse, *cujus coxa in duas confracta est partes*.
[18] consulationem A ; the *u* has later been altered to *o* by bridging.
-sol- B1 B2 B3
[19] lugaido A B2 B3 ; luga'ido B1

capsellam, dicens : ' Benedictio [1] quae in hac capsel-
lula contenetur [2] quando ad Mauginam [3] pervenies
visitandam in aquae vasculum intinguatur ; eademque
benedictionis aqua super ejus infundatur coxam.   Et
58a statim invocato dei nomine coxale conjungetur | os et
densebitur [4] ;   et sancta virgo plenam recuperabit
salutem '.   Et hoc sanctus addit : ' En ego coram [5] in
hujus [6] capsae operculo numerum xxiii. [7] annorum
[describo], [8] quibus sacra virgo in hac presenti post
eandem salutem victura est vita '.

Quae omnia síc plene expleta sunt, sicuti a sancto
praedicta.   Nam statim ut Lugaidus [9] ad sanctam pervenit virginem aqua benedicta sicut sanctus commendavit perfussa coxa sine ulla morula condensato osse
plene sanata est.   Et in adventu legati sancti Columbae
cum ingenti gratiarum actione gavisa xxiii. [10] annís
secundum [11] sancti profetiam post sanitatem in bonís
actibus permanens vixit. .

De hís quae [12] in dorso Ceate [13] peractae [14] sunt
diversorum sanitatibus morborum. . [15]

VIR VITAE praedicabilis, sicuti nobis ab expertís
58b traditum est, diver|sorum langores infirmorum invocato

---

[1] *benedictio*, an object that has been blessed ; but here possibly a
written prayer. Cf. 58b, 59a, 80b.

[2] contenetur A ; the first *e* has later been altered to *i* with a long
down-stroke. -tin- B1 B2 B3

[3] mau|ginam A, with an over-dash above *mau* ; maugui'nam B1 ;
mauguinam B2 B3

[4] coxale conjungetur os et densebitur A ; coxalis (coxa'lis B1) con-
junctura solidabitur B1 B2 B3

[5] *coram*. With this word, Columba is made to take Lugaid as a witness ;
but its meaning is ambiguous, either ' in your presence ' or ' with my
own hand '.   [6] hujus A ; ejus B1 B2 B3

[7] xxiii A ; viginti trium B1 B2 B3

[8] describo B1 B2 B3. Omitted in A.

of pine-wood with a blessing, saying : ' When you arrive to visit Maugin, let the blessing that is contained in this little box be dipped into a vessel of water, and let the same water of the blessing be poured over her hip ; and as soon as the name of God has been invoked, the hip-bone will join and be knit togther, and the holy virgin will regain complete health '. And the saint added this : ' See, in your presence I [write] on the lid of this box the number of the years, twenty-three, that the holy virgin will live in this present life, after this cure '.

All these things were entirely so fulfilled, just as they had been foretold by the saint. For as soon as Lugaid came to the holy virgin, and her hip was sprinkled, as the saint instructed, with the blessed water, the bone joined firmly with no delay at all, and the hip was completely healed. And with great rendering of thanks she rejoiced over the coming of Saint Columba's emissary, and according to the saint's prophecy, continuing in good works, she lived after her healing for twenty-three years.

[II 6] Concerning the cures of various
diseases, performed in the ridge of Céte

As has been told us by men that knew of it, the man of memorable life cured the ailments of various sick

---

9 lugaidus A B2 B3 ; luga'idus B1
10 xxiii A ; viginti tribus B1 B2 B3
11 secundum A B1 ; secumdum B3. Omitted in B2.
12 quae A ; que B1 B2 ; qui B3   13 ceate A ; cete B1 B2 B3
14 peractae A ; peracta B1 B2 B3
15 The contents-list of B2 and of B3 reads : *De multorum morbis fimbrie vestimenti ejus tactu in dorso cete sanatis* ' Of many people's diseases that were cured, in the ridge of Céte, by their touching the hem of his garment '.

Christi nomine illís in diebus sanavit, quibus ad regum
pergens condictum in dorso Cette [1] brevi commoratus
est tempore.   Nam aut sanctae manus protensione aut
aqua ab eo benedicta egroti plures aspersi, aut etiam
fimbriae ejus tactu anfibali, aut alicujus rei salis videlicet
vel panis benedictione accepta et limfís [2] intincta, plenam
credentes recuperarunt salutem. .

De petra salis a sancto benedicta
quam ignis absumere non potuit

ALIO ITIDEM IN TEMPORE Colgu [3] filius Cellachi [4]
postulatam a sancto petram salis benedictam accipit [5]
sorori et suae nutrici profuturam ;   quae ofthalmiae [6]
laborabat valde gravi langore.   Talem eulogiam eadem [7]
59a soror et nutricia de manu | fratris accipiens in pariete
super lectum suspendit ;   cassuque [8] post aliquantos
contegit [9] dies ut idem viculus cum supradictae domucula [10] feminae flamma vastante totus concremaretur.
Mirum dictu illius parietis particula, ne beati viri in ea
deperiret suspensa benedictio, post totam ambustam [11]
domum stans inlessa [12] permansit, nec ignis ausus est
attingere binales in quibus talis pendebat salis petra
sudes. .[13]

---

[1] cette A, with two over-dashes ; cete B1 B3.   Illegible in B2.
[2] limfís A ; limphis B1 B2 ; limfis B3
[3] colgu A ; colgius B1 ; colgiu B2 B3.   Cf. 35b.
[4] cellachi A B2 B3 ; ce'llachi B1
[5] accipit A B3 ; a'ccipit B1 ; accepit B2
[6] ofthalmiae A ; ofchalmie B1 ; ofthalmie B2 ; ofthamie B3
[7] eadem A B2 B3 ; in A, an acute accent has later been added with a
fine pen above the first *e*.   e'adem B1
[8] cassuque A ; the first *s* has later been deleted with a dot below made
by a fine pen.   Casuque B1 B2 B3
[9] contegit A ; the *e* has later been altered to *i*, with a very faint down-
stroke. -tig- B1 B2 B3
[10] domucula A ; -u'nc- B1 ; -unc- B2 B3

people, by invocation of the name of Christ, during those days in which, when he went to the conference of kings, he remained for a short time in the ridge of Céte. By the extending of his holy hand, or when they were sprinkled with water blessed by him, or even by touching the hem of his cloak, or by receiving a blessing of any thing, such as salt, or bread, and dipping it in water, very many sick people, believing, regained full health.

[II 7] Of rock-salt, blessed by the saint, which fire could not consume

So at another time, Colcu, Cellach's son, requested and received from the saint a piece of rock-salt, blessed for the benefit of his sister and foster-mother, who was suffering from a very severe inflammation of the eyes. That sister and foster-mother received this blessing from her brother's hand, and hung it on the wall above her bed. It happened by a mischance, after some days, that the village was entirely burned down with devastating flame, including that woman's cottage. Strange to say, a small part of that wall remained, standing undamaged, after the whole house had been burned about it, so that the blessed man's blessing, hung up on it, should not perish. And the fire did not dare to touch the two pegs on which this rock-salt hung.

---

[11] ambustam A B1 B3 ; combustam B2
[12] inlessa A ; the first *s* has later been deleted with a dot below made by a fine pen. illesa B1 B3. Illegible in B2.
[13] *sudes.* In A, a small *i* has been written by m.h. above the *e*.

De librario folio sancti manu discripto [1]
quod aqua corrumpi non potuit. . [2]

ALIUD MIRACULUM estimo non [3] tacendum quod aliquando factum est per contrarium elimentum.[4] Multorum namque transcursís annorum circulís [5] post [6] beati
ad dominum transitum viri, quidam juvenis de equo
lapsus, in flumine quod scotice [7] Boend [8] voci|tatur
mersus et mortuus, xx.[9] sub aqua diebus permansit.
Qui, sicuti sub ascella [10] cadens libros in pellicio [11] re-
conditos sacculo habebat, ita etiam post supra memoratum dierum numerum est repertus sacculum[12] cum librís
inter brachium et latus contenens.[13]   Cujus etiam ad
aridam reportato cadavere, et aperto sacculo, folium
sancti Columbae sanctis scriptum degitulís[14] inter aliorum
folia librorum non tantum corrupta sed et putrefacta
inventum est siccum et nullo modo corruptum, acsi in
scriniolo [15] esset reconditum.[16]

De alio miraculo in
ré simili gesto

ALIO IN TEMPORE ymnorum liber septimaniorum [17]
sancti Columbae manu discriptus [18] de cujusdam pueri de

[II 8] Concerning a page that was written by the saint's hand, and that could not be injured by water

I think that another miracle should not be omitted, that was once performed in connexion with the contrary element. The cycles of many years had run by after the blessed man's departure to the Lord, when a certain young man falling from a horse sank and was drowned in the river that is in Irish called *Boend* [Boyne], and remained under the water for twenty days. And just as when he fell he had had books enclosed in a skin satchel under his arm, so also he was found after the said number of days holding fast between his arm and side the satchel with the books. When his body was brought back to dry land, and the satchel was opened, among the pages of other books which were not merely damaged, but even rotten, the page written by the holy fingers of Saint Columba was found dry, and not at all injured, as though it had been kept in a coffer.

[II 9] Concerning another miracle performed in a similar matter

At another time a book of hymns for the week, written in the hand of Saint Columba, fell from the

---

[11] pellicio A B2 B3 ; pelli′ceo B1, with *ceo* written small over an erasure.
[12] sacculum A B3 ; in A, a small *s* has been written by m.h. above *m*, wrongly. sa′cculum B1. Illegible in B2.
[13] contenens A ; the first *e* has later been altered to *i* with a down-stroke of a fine pen. -tin- B1 B2 B3   [14] degitulís A ; dig- B1 B2 B3
[15] scriniolo A B2 B3 ; in A, a stress-accent has been added later with a fine pen above the second *i*. scrini′olo B1
[16] *reconditum*. In A, a stress-accent has later been added with a fine pen above the *o*.   [17] septimaniorum A ; septimanariorum B1 B2 B3
[18] discriptus A ; des- B1 B2 B3

ponte elapsi humerís cum pellicio [1] in quo inerat [2] sac-
culo in quodam partis Laginorum fluio submersus |
60a cicidit.[3] Qui videlicet libellus, a natalicio domini usque
ad pascalium consummationem [4] dierum in aquís permanens, postea in ripa fluminis a feminís quibusdam
ibidem deambulantibus repertus, ad quendam Iogenanum [5] prespiterum gente Pictum [6] cujus prius juris
erat in eodem non solum madefacto sed etiam putrefacto
portatur sacculo. Quem scilicet sacculum idem Iogenanus aperiens suum incorruptum libellum invenit, et
ita nitidum et siccum acsi in scrinio tanto permansiset
tempore et numquam in aquas [7] cicidisset.[8]

Sed et alia de librís manu sancti Columbae craxatís [9]
similia ab expertís indubitanter didicimus in diversís
acta locís. Qui scilicet libri in aquís [10] mersi nullo modo
corrumpi potuere.[11] De supra memorati vero Eugenani [12]
60b libro a virís quibusdam veracibus [13] | et perfectís bonique
testimonii sine ulla [14] ambiguitate relationem accipimus,[15]
qui eundem libellum post tot supradictos submersionis
dies candidissimum et lucidissimum considerarunt.[16]

Haec [17] duo quamlibet in rebus parvís peracta et per
contraria ostensa elimenta,[18] ignem scilicet et aquam,

---

[1] pellicio A B2 ; pelli'cio Bı ; pelliceo B3
[2] inerat A B2 B3 ; i'nerant Bı
[3] cicidit A ; the first *i* has been altered by m.h. to *e*. ce'c- Bı ; cec-
B2 B3
[4] *consummationem*. See p. 123.
[5] iogenanum A B3 ; iogena'num Bı ; ioienanum B2
[6] *Pictum*. A priest in Ireland who had been born in the provinces
beyond the Spine of Britain, and who possessed a book alleged to have
been transcribed by Columba, had very probably gone to Ireland from
Iona, and may have been educated there.
[7] aquas A Bı B3 ; aquam B2
[8] cicidisset A ; cec- Bı B2 B3
[9] craxatís A ; caraxa'tis Bı ; caraxatis B2 B3
[10] aquís A ; aquas Bı B2 B3
[11] potuere A B2 B3 ; in A, a circumflex accent has later been written
with a fine pen above the first *e*. potue're Bı

shoulders of a boy who had slipped from a bridge, and, with the skin satchel that contained it, was submerged in a certain river of the region of the Lagin. This book remained in the water from the Lord's nativity until the days of Easter were concluded, and after that, found on the river bank by some women who were walking there, it was carried to a certain priest Iogenan, a Pict by race, to whom it formerly belonged ; in the same satchel, which was not only sodden, but even rotten. When Iogenan opened the satchel, he found his book undamaged, and as clean and dry as if it had remained all that time in a coffer, and had never fallen into the water.

Other similar things too, that occurred in different places, we have heard without question, from those who knew of them, concerning books written by the hand of Saint Columba ; which (that is to say the books), lying in water, have been able to remain entirely unharmed. But in the case of the above-named Iogenan's book, we have received an account of the facts, without any possible doubt, from certain truthful and blameless men of good testimony, who found the same book to be, after so many days of immersion, extraordinarily white and clear.

These two things, although performed in small matters, and shown in contrary elements, namely fire

---

[12] eugenani A ; iogenani B1 B2 B3. There is a slight presumption that the B texts have here preserved Adomnan's spelling.

[13] veracibus A B3 ; vera'cibus B1. Omitted in B2.

[14] ulla A B2 B3. Omitted in B1.

[15] accipimus A ; the first i has been altered by m.h. to e. -ce'p- B1ᵣ; -cep- B2 B3

[16] considerarunt A ; -averunt B1 B2 B3

[17] *Haec* has a bold h in A ; a larger and more decorative H, beginning a new paragraph, in B1 B2 B3.

[18] elimenta A ; the i has been altered by m.h. to e. ele- B1 B2 B3

2A

beati testantur honorem viri et quanti et qualis meriti
apud habeatur deum.[1]

De aqua quae sancto orante
ex dura producta est petr[a]. [2] .

ET QUIA PAULO superius aquatici facta est mentio
elimenti,[3] silere non debemus etiam alia miracula quae
per sanctum dominus ejusdem in re licet diversis temporibus et locís creaturae peregit. [4] .

    Alio namque in tempore, cum sanctus in sua con-
61a versaretur perigrinati|one,[5] infans ei per parentes ad
babtizandum offertur iter agenti. Et quia in vicinís
aqua non inveniebatur locís, sanctus ad proximam
declinans rupem flexís genibus paulisper oravit ; et post
orationem surgens ejusdem rupis frontem benedixit. De
qua consequenter aqua abundanter ebulliens fluxit, in
qua continuo infantulum babtizavit. De quo etiam
babtizato haec vaticinans intulit verba, inquiens : ' Hic
puerulus usque in extremam longeus [6] vivet aetatem.
In annís juvenilibus carnalibus desideriis satis serviturus,
et deinceps cristianae [7] usque in [8] exitum militiae manci-
pandus, in bona senectute ad dominum [9] emigrabit '.
    Quae omnia eidem viro juxta sancti contigerunt [10]

---

[1] habeatur deum A ; deum habeatur B1 B2 B3
[2] petro A ; petra B1 B2 B3, and the contents-list of B2 and of B3.
[3] elimenti A ; ele- B1 B3 ?B2
[4] *peregit.* This sentence is written as a separate paragraph in A, beginning with a decorative *Et.* In B1 B2 B3, it continues the chapter-heading,
written in coloured ink ; but it is not included in the contents-list of B2 B3.
[5] perigrinatione A ; pereg- B1 B3. Illegible in B2.
[6] longeus A ; a small *v* has been written by m.h. above *eu.* longevus
B1 B2 B3. Cf. 44a.
[7] cristianae A ; a small *h* has later been added above *cr.* christiane
B1 B2 B3, in abbreviated form.
[8] in A ; ad B1 B2 B3   [9] dominum A B2 B3 ; deum B1
[10] *contigerunt.* In A, a circumflex accent has later been written with a
fine pen above *e.*

and water, bear witness to the honour of the blessed man, and prove how greatly and how highly he is esteemed by God.

[II 10] Of water that, at the prayer of the saint, was produced from hard rock

And because just above reference has been made to the element of water, we ought to mention also other miracles, which the Lord performed through the saint in connexion with the same substance, although in different times and places.

At one time during the saint's life in pilgrimage, while he was making a journey, an infant was brought to him by its parents for baptism. And because water was not to be found anywhere near, the saint turned aside to a rock close by, bowed his knees, and prayed for a little while. And rising after his prayer, he blessed the face of the rock, from which thereupon water flowed in an abundant cascade ; and in it he immediately baptized the infant. And also, concerning the baptized child, he pronounced these prophetic words, saying : ' This little boy will live long, to extreme age. In the years of his youth he will sufficiently obey the desires of the flesh, and afterwards, devoted until his death to service as a soldier of Christ, will depart to the Lord in good old age '.

All these things happened to that man according to

vaticinium. Hic erat Ligu Cen-calad,[1] cujus parentes
61b fuerant in Artdaib -muirchol,[2] | ubi hodieque fonticulus
sancti nomine [3] Columbae pollens cernitur. .

De alia maligna fontana aqua quam vir beatus in Pictorum regione benedixit [4]

ALIO IN TEMPORE vir beatus, cum in Pictorum provincia per aliquo[t] [5] demoraretur dies, audiens in plebe
gentili de alio fonte devulgari [6] famam, quem quasi
deum stolidi homines diabulo [7] eorum obcaecante sensus
venerabantur. Nam de eodem fonticulo bibentes aut in
eo manus vel pedes de industria lavantes,[8] daemonica [9]
deo permittente percussi arte aut lepri [10] aut lusci aut
etiam debiles aut quibuscumque aliis infestati infirmi-
tatibus revertebantur. Ob quae omnia seducti gentiles
divinum fonti deferebant honorem. Quibus conpertís
sanctus alia die intrepidus accessit ad fontem. Quod
videntes magi, quos sepe ipse confussos [11] et victos a sé
62a repellebat, | valde gavisi sunt, scilicet putantes eum
similia illius nocuae tactu aquae passurum. Ille vero
inprimís elevata manu sancta cum invocatione Christi
nominis manus lavat et pedes. Tum deinde cum sociis
de eadem a sé benedicta bibit.[12] Ex illaque [13] die

---

[1] ligu cenca|lad A ; ligucencalath B1 B2 ; ligucen calath B3. Reeves
misread B3 as *lugucen calath*, and his reading was quoted by Thesaurus
1903, p. 277.
[2] artdaib muirchol A (with the *t* not joined to the *d*) ; ardaib muircol
B1 B2 B3 (with a dot separating the words in B3). See pp. 133, 150. The
preposition *in* should perhaps here be regarded as Irish.
[3] nomine A B1 B2. Omitted in B3.
[4] The contents-list of B2 and of B3 reads : *De aqua fontana quam sanctus
ultra brittannicum benedixit dorsum et sanavit* (B2 partly missing).
[5] aliquod A ; a small *t* has been written by m.h. above *d*. aliquot
B1 B2 B3   [6] devulgari A ; div- B1 B2 B3
[7] diabulo A ; the *u* has later been altered to *o* by bridging. -bolo
B1 B2 B3

the saint's prophecy. This was Ligu Cen-calad, whose parents were in Artda-muirchol [Ardnamurchan]. And there even today a spring is seen, that is potent in the name of Saint Columba.

[II 11] Concerning the malignant water of another well, which the holy man blessed, in the land of the Picts

At one time, when the blessed man passed some days in the province of the Picts, he heard that the fame of another well was wide-spread among the heathen populace, and that the insensate people venerated it as a god, the devil deluding their understanding. For those that drank from this well, or deliberately washed their hands or feet in it, were struck, by devilish art, God permitting it, and returned leprous, or half blind, or even crippled, or suffering from some other infirmity. Led astray by all this, the heathen gave honour to the well as to a god. When he learned of that, the saint went boldly to the well one day. The magicians, whom he often repelled from himself in confusion and defeat, rejoiced greatly when they saw this, since they imagined that he would suffer the like ills, from touching that noxious water. But he, first raising his holy hand in invocation of the name of Christ, washed his hands and feet ; and after that, with those that accompanied him, drank of the same water, which he had blessed. And

---

[8] lavantes A B1 B3 ; levantes B2
[9] daemonica A ; demoni'aca B1 ; demonica B2 B3
[10] lepri A ; leprosi B1 B3 ; leproso B2
[11] confussos A ; the first *s* has later been deleted with a dot above. -usos B1 B2 B3
[12] bibit A ; bibit aqua B1 B3 ; bibit a'[B2
[13] ex illaque A B3 ; et ex illa B1. Illegible in B2.

daemones ab eodem recesserunt fonte ; et non solum
nulli nocere permisus est, sed etiam post sancti benedictionem et in eo lavationem multae in populo in-
firmitates per eundem sanatae sunt fontem. .

De beati viri in mari periculo et
tempestatis ¹ eo ² orante subita sedatione ³

ALIO IN TEMPORE vir sanctus in mari periclitari cepit ;
totum namque vas navis valde concussum magnís
undarum cumulís fortiter feriebatur, grandi undique
insistente ventorum tempestate. Nautae ⁴ tum forte
62b sancto sentinam ⁵ cum illís exaurire | conanti ⁶ aiunt :
' Quod nunc agis non magnopere nobis proficit periclitantibus ; exorare potius debes pro pereuntibus '. Quo
audito aquam cessat amaram ex inani ré ⁷ *hi nin glas,*⁸
dulcem vero et intentam precem ⁹ coepit ad dominum
fundere. Mirum dictu, eodem horae momento quo
sanctus in prora stans extensís ad caelum palmís omni-
potentem exoravit, tota aeris tempestas et maris sevitia ¹⁰
dicto citius sedata cessavit, et statim serenissima tran-

---

¹ tempestatis A B1 ; tep- B3. Illegible in B2.

² eo A B1. Illegible in B2 ; omitted in B3.

³ The contents-list of B2 and of B3 reads : *De sancti periculo in mari, et de magna tempestate in tranquillitatem continuo orante ipso conversa* (B2 partly illegible).

⁴ *nautae,* in A, follows a punctuation dot (text-hand), and has a bold initial ; *Naute* in B1 B2 B3 begins a new sentence.

⁵ *sentinam.* In A, two dots were added later with a fine pen over *s* ; a similar pair of dots in the margin stands above this added note (m.h.) : *sentina est fervida aqua navis* ' sentina is surging water in a ship '.

⁶ conanti A B1 B2 ; conati B3

⁷ ex| in ani ré A ; exinanire B1 B2 B3 (-ni′re B1). If the words are read *ex inani re,* they would mean ' to no advantage ', and *fundere* would govern both *aquam* and *precem.* But if they were read *exinanire,* ' to empty ', the object would be *aquam,* and the object of *fundere* would be *precem* only. Adomnan seems to have intended his words to be a pun, with two possible interpretations.

from that day, the demons withdrew from that well, and not only was it not permitted to harm any one, but after the saint's blessing, and washing in it, many infirmities among the people were in fact cured by the same well.

[II 12] Concerning the blessed man's danger on the sea, and the sudden calming of the storm at his prayer

At another time, the holy man began to be in danger on the sea. For the whole body of the ship was violently shaken, and heavily struck by great masses of waves, with a mighty storm of winds that pressed on all sides. Then it happened that the sailors said to him, as he tried with them to bail the water out of the ship : ' What you are doing now does not very greatly profit us in our danger. You should rather pray for us who are perishing '. Hearing this, he ceased to pour out vainly bitter water into the green wave [?], and began to pour out sweet and fervent prayer to the Lord. Marvellously, in the same moment of time in which the saint, standing in the prow, extended his palms to heaven and prayed to the Almighty, the whole tempest of the air and wildness of the sea in less time than it takes to tell subsided and became still ; and immediately

---

[8] hinin glas A, with three over-dashes ; hini'nglas B1 ; hi'ninglas B2 ; hininglas B3. With *ex inani re*, the Irish phrase would have the meaning ' into deep sea ' ; with *exinanire*, the phrase would have a double meaning, ' into deep sea ', and ' without effect '. We must suppose that ' to pour water into the sea ' was an Irish proverb of futility. (Cf. *in mare fundat aquas*, in Ovid, *Tristia*, v ; Eleg. 6, line 44.) See p. 144.

[9] precem A B1 B3 ; parcem B2

[10] sevitia A B1 B2 ; in A, the *e* has been altered by m.h. to the *ae* symbol. sevicia B3

quilitas subsequuta est. Qui vero navi inerant obstupe-
facti cum magna ammiratione referentes gratias glorificaverunt deum in sancto et praedicabili viro. .

De alio ejus in mari
simili periculo [1]

ALIO QUOQUE IN TEMPORE seva nimis insistente et
63a periculosa tempestate | sociis ut pro eís sanctus dominum
exoraret inclamitantibus, hoc eís dedit responsum,
dicens : ' Hac in die non est meum pro vobís in hoc
periculo constitutís orare, sed est abbatis Cainnichi [2]
sancti viri '. Mira dicturus sum. Eadem [3] hora sanctus
Cainnechus [4] in suo conversans monasterio, quod latine
campulus bovis dicitur, scotice vero Ached-bou,[5] spiritu
revelante sancto supradictam sancti Columbae interiore
cordis aure vocem audierat. Et cum forte post nonam
coepisset horam [6] in refectorio eulogiam [7] frangere, ocius
deserit mensulam, unoque in [8] pede inherente calceo et
altero pro nimia festinatione relicto festinanter pergit hac
cum voce ad eclesiam : ' Non est nobís nunc temporis
prandere [9] quando in mari periclitatur navis sancti
63b Columbae. Hoc enim momento ipse hujus [10] | nomen
Cainnichi [11] ingeminans commemorat, ut pro eo et sociis
periclitantibus Christum exoret '. Post haec illius verba

---

[1] *periculo.* After this, B1 B2 B3 add : *in vortice brecain* (altered to *brecani*,
by an apex above the last stroke, in B1 ; *bercaynni* in B2). The contents-list
of B2 and of B3 reads : *De altero ejus periculo et de sancto cainnecho pro ipso et
sociis ejus orante* (B2 partly illegible).
[2] cainnichi A B3 ; cainnichi' B1 (with faint apices on the first and
second *i*). Illegible in B2.
[3] eadem A ; a circumflex accent has later been written with a fine pen
above *a*. Ea'dem B1 ; Eadem B3. Illegible in B2.
[4] cainnechus A B2 ; cainnichus B1 B3 (faint apices above the *i*'s, B1).
[5] ached bou A, with three over-dashes (one above *ou*) ; acheth bou
B1 ; acheth bou˜ B2 (as if for *boum*) ; achetbbou B3
[6] *post nonam horam,* the time for dinner. See p. 122.

there followed the fairest calm. Those who were in the ship were amazed, and returning thanks, with great wonder glorified God in the holy and memorable man.

[II 13] Of another similar danger to him on the sea

Also at another time, when a very fierce and dangerous storm was blowing, and his companions importuned the saint to pray to the Lord for them, he gave them this answer, and said : ' On this day it is not for me to pray for you in this danger that you are in ; it is for the holy man, the abbot Cainnech '.

I have marvellous things to tell. In the same hour, Saint Cainnech, being in his own monastery, which is in Latin called ' field of the cow ', and in Irish, *Ached-bou* [Aghaboe], by revelation of the Holy Spirit heard in the inner ear of his heart those words of Saint Columba. And since it chanced that he had begun after the ninth hour to break the holy bread in the refectory, he suddenly abandoned the small table, and with one shoe on his foot, and the other left behind through the excess of his haste, he went hurriedly to the church, with these words : ' We cannot have dinner at this time, when Saint Columba's ship is in danger on the sea. For at this moment he repeatedly calls upon the name of this Cainnech, to pray to Christ for him, and his companions in peril '. After saying these words he entered

---

[7] *eulogiam* here means bread that has been prepared for use in the Eucharist, but not consecrated.

[8] in A B1 B2. Omitted in B3.

[9] prandere A B2 B3 ; in A, a circumflex accent has later been written with a fine pen above the first *e*. prande're B1

[10] hujus A ; ejus B1 B2 B3

[11] cainnichi A B2 B3 ; cai'nnichi B1

oratorium ingressus flexís genibus paulisper [1] oravit.
Ejusque orationem exaudiente domino ilico tempestas
cessavit, et mare valde tranquillum factum est. Tum
deinde sanctus Columba, Cainnichi [2] ad eclesiam pro-
perationem in spiritu videns quamlibet longe conver-
santis, mirabiliter hoc de puro pectore profert verbum,[3]
dicens : ' Nunc cognovi, Ó Cainneche,[4] quod deus tuam
exaudierit precem. Nunc valde nobís proficit tuus ad
eclesiam velox cum uno calciamento cursus '. In hoc
itaque tali miraculo amborum ut credimus oratio
cooperata est sanctorum. .

De baculo in portu sancti
Cainnichi [5] neglecto [6]

ALIO IN TEMPORE idem supra memoratus Cainnechus[7]
64a suum a portu Iovae | insulae ad Scotiam navigare
incipiens baculum secum portare oblitus est.[8] Qui
scilicet ejus baculus post ipsius egresum in litore repertus
sancti in manum traditus est Columbae. Quemque [9]
domum reversus in oratorium portat, et ibidem solus in
oratione diutius demoratur.

Cainnechus[10] proinde ad Oidecham[11] appropinquans
insulam subito de sua oblivione conpunctus interius
perculsus est. Sed post modicum intervallum de navi
discendens [12] et in terra cum oratione genua [13] flectens
baculum quem in portu Iovae insulae [14] oblitus post sé

---

[1] paulisper A B1 B2 ; palisper B3
[2] cainnichi A B2 B3 ; cai'nnichi B1   [3] verbum A ; verba B1 B2 B3
[4] cainneche A B2 ; cai'nniche B1 ; cainni'che B3
[5] cainnichi A ; cai'nnichi B1 ; cainnechi B2 and contents-list of B3
and ? of B2 ; cainechi B3
[6] neglecto A B1 B2 ; neclecto B3
[7] cainnechus A B2 ; cainnichus B1 B3
[8] est A. Omitted in B1 B2 B3.

the oratory, bowed his knees, and prayed for a little while. The Lord heard his prayer, and at once the storm ceased, and the sea became perfectly calm.

Then Saint Columba, miraculously seeing in the spirit the hastening of Cainnech to the church, although Cainnech was far away, pronounced these words from his pure heart, saying : ' Now, Cainnech, I know that God has heard your prayer. Now your swift running to the church, wearing one shoe, greatly helps us '.

In this so great miracle, the prayers of both the saints worked, we believe, together.

[II 14] Concerning Saint Cainnech's staff, left behind at the harbour

At another time the same Cainnech, mentioned above, forgot to take with him his staff, when he began to sail for Ireland from the harbour of the island of Io. After his departure, this staff of his was found on the shore, and put into Saint Columba's hand ; and when he had returned home, he carried it into the oratory, and there for a long time remained alone, in prayer.

So Cainnech, approaching the island of Oídech, suddenly conscious of his forgetfulness, was struck with inward dismay. But after a little while, leaving the ship, and kneeling on the ground in prayer, he discovered, there before him on the turf of the land of Oídech, the staff that he had forgotten and left behind

---

⁹ quemque A ; quem B1 B3. Missing in B2.
¹⁰ Cainnechus A B2 B3 ; Cai'nnichus B1, altered from -ech-.
¹¹ oidecham A ; ovide'tham B1, with the th erased ; ovidecham B3. Illegible in B2.
¹² discendens A ; des- B1 B2 B3
¹³ genua A B1 B2 ; ganua B3
¹⁴ insulae A ; insule B2 B3. Omitted in B1.

reliquit super cispitem [1] terrulae Aíthche[2] ante sé
invenit.[3] De cujus etiam effecta divinitus evectione
valde est miratus cum gratiarum in deo actione. .

De Baitheneo [4] et Columbano filio Beogni [5]
sanctis prespiterís eadem sibi die ventum
prosperum a deo per beati viri orationem
donari postulantibus, sed diversa
navigantibus via [6] |

64b   ALIO QUOQUE IN TEMPORE superius [7] memorati sancti
viri ad sanctum venientes ab eo simul unianimes [8]
postulant ut ipse a domino postulans inpetraret prosperum crastina die ventum sibi dari, diversa emigraturís [9]
via. Quibus sanctus respondens hoc dedit responsum :
' Mane [10] crastina die Baitheneus [11] a portu Iovae
enavigans insulae flatum habebit [12] secundum usquequo
ad portum perveniat campi Lunge '.[13] Quod ita juxta
sancti verbum dominus donavit. Nam Baitheneus plenís
eadem [14] die velís magnum totum [15] pilagus [16] usque ad
Aethicam [17] transmeavit terram.

[1] cispitem A ; ces- B1 B3. Illegible in B2.
[2] aíthche A ; a hook has later been attached below the e, with a very
fine pen, to make an ae symbol. ovide'the B1, with the h erased ; ovidchae
B2 B3. See p. 155.
[3] invenit A ; invenit positum B1 B2 B3 (-ve'n- B1)
[4] baitheneo A B3 ; baithe'neo B1. Illegible in B2.
[5] beogni A ; beo'gnoi B1, with ?i erased between n and o ; beog[B2 ;
beognoi B3. Here the reading beognoi or beognai is to be preferred. Cf.
16b, and see p. 139.
[6] The contents-list of B2 and of B3 reads : De baitheneo et columbano filio
beognoi qui a (á B2) sancto secundum eadem die sed diversa via ventum sibi dari
postularunt (postulaverunt B2). According to legends of uncertain value,
Baithene and Colman were cousins, nephews of Columba.
[7] superius A B1 B2 ; supernis B3
[8] unianimes A ; the first i has later been deleted with a point below
made by a fine pen. unanimes B1 B2 B3 (-a'- B1)
[9] emigraturís A ; -ris B1 B2 ; -rus B3
[10] Mane A. Omitted in B1 B2 B3.

him at the harbour of the island of Io. And he marvelled greatly, with thanksgiving to God, because of its transference divinely effected.

[II 15] Concerning the holy priests Baithene, and Colman, son of Beogna, when they asked through the blessed man's prayer from God, for wind to be granted favourable to themselves, on the same day, although they were sailing in different directions

Once also the above-named holy men came to the saint and at the same time, with one accord, asked him to ask and obtain from the Lord that favourable wind should be given to them on the following day, when they were to set out in different directions. In reply, the saint gave them this answer : ' Early tomorrow Baithene, sailing from the harbour of the island of Io, will have a favourable breeze until he reaches the harbour of the plain of Long '. And this the Lord granted, according to the saint's word. For Baithene with full sails on that day crossed the whole great sea to the land of Eth [Tiree].

---

[11] baitheneus A B2 B3 ; baithe'neus B1. So also thrice below, in 64b–65a.

[12] habebit A B1 B2 ; -bat B3

[13] lunge A B2 B3 ; lu'nge B1. Cf. 32b.

[14] eadem A B2 B3 ; in A, a circumflex accent has later been added with a fine pen above *a*. ea'dem B1

[15] *totum*. In A, a -*que* symbol has been added by m.h.

[16] pilagus A ; the *i* has been altered by m.h. to *e*. pelagus B1 B2 B3

[17] aethicam A ; e'thicam B1 ; ethicam B2 B3

Hora vero ejusdem diei tertia vir venerandus Columbanum advocat [1] prespiterum, dicens : ' Nunc Baitheneus
prospere obtatum pervenit ad portum. Ad navigandum
té hodie praepara.[2] Mox dominus ventum convertet
65a aquilonem '. Cui síc prolato | beati viri verbo eadem [3]
hora auster [4] obsecundans ventus sé in aquiloneum convertit flatum. Et ita in eadem die uterque vir [5] sanctus
alter ab altero in pace aversus, Baitheneus mane ad
Etheticam [6] terram, Columbanus post meridiem Everniam [7] incipiens appetere, plenís enavigavit velís et
flatibus secundís. Hoc [8] inlustris viri virtute orationum
domino donante effectum est miraculum, quia sicut
scriptum est : ' Omnia possibilia sunt credenti '.[9] Post
illa in die sancti Columbani egresum sanctus hoc de illo[10]
profeticum Columba protulit verbum : ' Vir sanctus
Columbanus cui emigranti benediximus nusquam in hoc
saeculo faciem videbit meam '. Quod ita post expletum
est, nam eodem anno sanctus Columba ad dominum
transiit. .

De repulsione daemonis qui in
lactario latitabat vasculo. .[11] |

65b ALIO IN TEMPORE quidam juvenis Columbanus
nomine nepos Briuni [12] ad januam tegorioli [13] subito

---

[1] advocat A B2 B3 ; in A, an acute accent has later been written with
a fine pen above the first a. a'dvocat B1
[2] praepara A ; pre'- B1 ; pre- B3 ; propera B2
[3] eadem A B2 B3 ; a circumflex accent has later been added with a
fine pen above a. e'adem B1
[4] auster, ' south wind '. This implies that Tiree was to the north of
Iona ; but it is to the north-west.   [5] vir A. Omitted in B1 B2 B3.
[6] etheticam A ; e'thicam B1 ; ethicam B2 B3
[7] everniam A ; hibe'rniam B1 ; hiberniam B2 B3
[8] hoc A (the Irish symbol, h with a dot above the bow ; the dot was
later altered with a fine pen to an apostrophe, possibly intending to read
hujus. Cf. Lindsay 1915, pp. 100, 35). Hoc B1 B2 B3

And at the third hour of the same day the venerable man called to him the priest Colman, saying : ' Now Baithene has safely reached his desired harbour. Make ready to sail today ; the Lord will presently change the wind to north '. The south wind, complying with the blessed man's word thus uttered, in the same hour changed into a northerly breeze.

And so in one day the two holy men, parting each from the other in peace, put to sea with full sails and favourable breezes ; Baithene in the morning to the land of Eth, Colman after mid-day beginning his voyage to Ireland. This miracle, the Lord granting it, was performed by virtue of the prayers of the celebrated man ; because, as it is written, all things are possible to him who believes.

After the departure of Saint Colman on that day, Saint Columba pronounced this prophetic saying concerning him : ' The holy man Colman, whom we have blessed on his departure, will never in this world see my face again '. And that was afterwards fulfilled. For in the same year Saint Columba departed to the Lord.

[II 16] Concerning the expulsion of a demon
who lurked in a milk-vessel

At another time, a certain youth, by name Colman, descendant of Briún, reaching the door of the hut in

---

⁹ *credenti.* Vulg. Mark ix. 22
¹⁰ hoc de illo A ; de illo hoc B1 B2 B3
¹¹ The contents-list of B2 and of B3 reads : *De demonis repulsione qui in lactis vasculo latitabat.*
¹² briuni A B2, with three over-dashes in A ; briuni′ B1 ; briɪɪni B3
¹³ tegorioli A ; tuguri′oli B1 ;]rioli B2 ; tugurioli B3

perveniens restitit, in quo vir beatus scribebat. Hic idem
post vaccarum reversus mulsionem in dorso portans
vasculum novo plenum lacte dicit ad sanctum ut juxta
morem tale benediceret onus. Sanctus tum ex adverso
eminus in aere signum salutare manu elevata depinxit
[et invocato dei nomine vas benedixit],[1] quod ilico valde
concusum est ; gergennaque[2] operculi per sua bina
foramina retrusa longius projecta est. Operculum terra
tenus cicidit.[3] Lac ex majore mensura in solum defusum[4] est. Juvenculus vas cum parvo quod remanserat
lactis super fundum in terra deponit. Genua supliciter
flectit. Ad quem sanctus : ' Surge ' ait, ' Columbane.
Hodie in tua operatione neglegenter[5] egisti. Dae-
monem enim in fundo vacui latitantem vasculi inpresso
66a dominicae crucis signo ante infus|sionem[6] lactis non
effugasti. Cujus videlicet signi nunc[7] virtutem non
sustenens[8] tremefactus toto pariter turbato vasse[9] velo-
citer cum lactis effussione aufugit. Huc ergo ad me
propius vasculum ut illud benedicam approxima '. Quo
facto sanctus semivacuum quod benedixerat vas eodem
momento divinitus repletum repertum est, parvumque
quod prius in fundo vassis[10] remanserat sub sanctae
manus benedictione usque ad summum citius excre-
verat. .

[1] *et* to *benedixit* in B1 B2 B3 ; omitted in A, through homoioteleuton.
[2] *gergenna.* This word is explained by its context as a wedge, passing
through holes (*foramina*) in two lugs that projected from the rim of the
milk-vessel, and holding down a lid. The word could hardly have been
derived from *gerrchenn* ' short-head ' ; *gerrcend* ' lock ' (Meyer 1892, p. 87)
was more probably derived from *gergenna.*
[3] cicidit A ; the first *i* has been altered by m.h. to *e.* ce'c- B1 ; cec-
B2 B3   [4] defusum A ; diffusum B1 B2 B3
[5] neglegenter A ; negli- B1 B2 ; necli- B3
[6] infus|sionem A ; the first *s* has later been erased. -usi- B1 B2 B3
[7] nunc A B1 B3. Omitted in B2.
[8] sustenens A ; the first *e* has later been altered to *i* with a down-
stroke of a fine pen. -tin- B1 B2 B3

which the blessed man was writing, suddenly stopped. This youth had returned after the milking of the cows, carrying on his back a vessel full of new milk ; and he said to the saint that he should bless this burden, according to the custom. Then the saint, being at a little distance, with upraised hand made in the air the saving sign towards it, [and with invocation of the name of God blessed the vessel,] which was at once violently shaken. The fastening-peg of the lid was thrust back through its two holes, and thrown far off ; the lid fell to the ground ; the greater part of the milk was spilt upon the earth. The boy put down the vessel on its base, upon the ground, with the little that remained of the milk. He bowed his knees in supplication. The saint said to him : ‘ Rise, Colman. You have been careless in your work today. Before the milk was poured in, you did not, by imprinting the sign of the Lord’s cross, expel a demon that lurked in the bottom of the empty vessel. Now, unable to endure the power of that sign, by his trembling he has shaken the whole vessel, and has spilt the milk in his sudden flight. Bring hither therefore the vessel, nearer to me, so that I may bless it.’

When this was done, the half-empty vessel that the saint had blessed was found in the same moment to have been divinely filled again ; and the little that had remained before in the bottom of the vessel had, under the blessing of his holy hand, instantly swelled up to the brim.

---

[9] vasse A ; a deletion point has later been added above the first *s*. va'se B1 ; vase B2 B3

[10] vassis A ; a deletion point has later been added above the first *s*. vasis B1 B2 B3

2B

De vasculo quod quidam maleficus nomine
Silnanus lacte de masculo bove expreso
repleverat [1]

Hoc in domu [2] alicujus plebei divitis, qui in monte
Cainle [3] commorabatur Foirtgirni [4] nomine factum
traditur. Ubi cum sanctus hospitaretur, inter rusticanos
contendentes duos quorum prius adventum prescivit
recta judicatione judicavit. Unusque ex eís qui maleficus
erat a sancto ju|sus de bove masculo qui prope erat lac
arte diabulica [5] expressit. Quod sanctus non ut illa
confirmaret maleficia fieri jusit, quod absit, sed ut ea
coram multitudine distrueret.[6] Vir itaque beatus vas
ut videbatur tali plenum lacte sibi ocius dari poposcit ;
et hac cum sententia benedixit, dicens : ' Modo pro-
babitur non esse hoc verum quod putatur lac, sed
daemonum fraude ad decipiendos homines decoloratus
sanguis '. Et continuo lacteus ille color in naturam
versus est [7] propriam, hoc est in sanguinem. Bos quoque,
qui per unius horae momentum turpi macie tabidus et
maceratus erat morti proximus, benedicta a sancto aqua
superfusus mira sub celeritate [8] sanatus est. .

66b (margin)

---

[1] The contents-list of B2 and of B3 reads : *De vasculo quod quidam*
maleficus lacte de masculo bove expresso diabolica replevit arte ; sed sancto orante
ipsum quod videbatur lac in sanguinem hoc est in naturam propriam versum est (B2
partly illegible).

[2] domu A ; domo B1 B3. Illegible in B2.

[3] cainle A B3 ; cai'nle B1. Illegible in B2. Cf. 41a.

[4] foirtgirni A B3, with one over-dash above *oi* in A ; foirtgi'rni B1.
Illegible in B2.

[5] diabulica A ; the *u* has later been altered to *o* by bridging. -bo'l-
B1 ; -bol- B2 B3.

[6] distrueret A ; the *i* has been altered by m.h. to *e*. des- B1 B3.
Illegible in B2.

[7] est A B1 B2. Omitted in B3.

[8] celeritate A B1 B2 ; scel- B3

[II 17] Concerning a vessel that a certain
sorcerer, called Silnan, had filled with
milk drawn from a bull

This is said to have happened in the house of a rich
layman called Foirtgern, who lived on the mountain
Cainle. While the saint was a guest there, he judged
with a true judgement between two rustics who were
disputing, and whose arrival he had foreseen. One of
them, who was a sorcerer, at the saint's command by
diabolic art drew milk from a bull, which was near
by. This the saint commanded to be done, not in order
to confirm those sorceries (let it not be thought), but
in order to confound them before the crowd. So the
blessed man asked that the vessel, full, as it seemed, of
this milk, should at once be given to him ; and blessed
it with this pronouncement, saying : ' Now this will
be shown not to be the true milk that it is thought to
be, but blood bleached by the imposture of demons, to
deceive mankind '. And immediately that milky colour
was changed to its proper nature, that is into blood.
The bull also, which for the space of an hour, shrunk
with hideous leanness and wasted, was at the point of
death, was sprinkled with water that had been blessed
by the saint ; and it was cured with marvellous rapidity.

De Lugneo [1] mocu-Min [2]

QUADAM DIE quidam bonae [3] indolis juvenis Lug-
67a neus [4] | nomine, qui postea senex in monasterio Elenae [5]
insulae praepossitus [6] erat, ad sanctum veniens queritur
de profluio [7] sanguinis qui crebro per multos menses de
naribus ejus inmoderate profluebat. Quo propius [8]
accito [9] sanctus ambas ipsius nares binís manus dexterae
digitulís constringens benedixit. Ex qua hora benedictionis numquam sanguis de nasso [10] ejus usque ad
extremum distillavit diem. .

De piscibus beato viro specialiter
a deo praeparatís [11]

ALIO IN TEMPORE cum praedicabilis viri sociales
strenui piscatores quinos [12] in rete pisces coepissent [13] in
fluio Sale [14] piscoso, sanctus ad eos : ' Iterato ' ait, ' rete
in flumen mittite, et statim invenietis grandem quem
mihi dominus praeparavit piscem '. Qui verbo sancti
67b obtemperantes mirae magnitudinis | traxerunt in retia-
culo essocem a deo sibi praeparatum. .

[1] lugneo A B2 B3 ; lugne'o B1
[2] mocumin A B2 B3 ; mocumi'n B1. The contents-list of B2 and of
B3 reads : *De lugneo mocumin* (*mocumi'n* B2) *quem sanctus de profluvio sanguinis
qui crebro ex naribus ejus profluebat oracione et digitorum tactu sanavit.* After
sanguinis, B2 adds *lattitabat,* in error.
[3] bonae A ; bone B1 B3 ; bove B2
[4] lugneus A B2 B3 ; lugne'us B1
[5] elenae A B2 B3 ; he'lene B1. This island is unidentified.
[6] praepossitus A ; a deletion point has later been added with a fine
pen above the first *s.* prepositus B1 B3 ; propositus B2
[7] profluio A ; proflu'vio B1 ; profluo B2 ; profluvio B3
[8] propius A B1 B3 ; prius B2
[9] accito A B2 B3 ; in A, a circumflex accent has later been added with
a fine pen above *i.* acci'to B1
[10] nasso A ; deletion points have later been added with a fine pen above
and below the first *s.* naso B1 B3. Illegible in B2.

[II 18] Concerning Lugne mocu-Min

One day, a young man of good ability, called Lugne, (who afterwards, when he was an old man, was the prior of a monastery in the island of Elen) came to the saint and complained of a discharge of blood that at frequent intervals during many months had flowed immoderately from his nostrils. The saint bade him come nearer ; and blessed him, pressing together both his nostrils with two fingers of the right hand. And from the hour of that blessing until his last day, blood never fell from his nose.

[II 19] Concerning fishes that were specially provided by God for the blessed man

At another time, when the memorable man's companions, active fishers, had caught five fishes in a net, in the river Sale, which abounds with fish, the saint said to them : ' Cast the net once more into the river ; and immediately you shall find a great fish, which the Lord has provided for me '. They followed the saint's instruction, and drew in with the net a salmon of marvellous size, provided for them by God.

---

[11] The heading of this chapter is illegible in B2. In B1 B3, and in the contents-list of B2 and of B3, it is : *De esoce (eso'ce* B1) *magno in fluvio sale* (*sale* is omitted in contents-list) *juxta verbum sancti invento.*

[12] quinos A B3 ; in A, a circumflex accent has later been added above *i.* qui'nos B1 ; qui[B2

[13] coepissent A ; cep- B1 B3. Illegible in B2. Read : *cepissent.*

[14] *Sale.* Perhaps the Blackwater, in county Meath. See p. 70.

Alio [1] quoque in tempore cum sanctus juxta Cei [2] stagnum aliquantís demoraretur diebus comites ire ad piscandum cupientes retardavit, dicens : ' Hodie et cras nullus in flumine reperietur piscis ; tertia mittam vos die, et invenietis binos grandes in rete retentos fluminales essoces '. Quos, ita post duas dieculas rete mittentes, duos rarissimae magnitudinis in fluio qui dicitur Bo [3] reperientes ad terram traxerunt.

In hís duabus memoratís piscationibus miraculi apparet virtus et profetica simul praescientia comitata. Pro quibus sanctus et socii deo grates eximias reddiderunt. .[4]

De Nesano curvo qui in ea regione conversabatur quae stagno Aporum [5] est contermina. . [6] |

68a HIC [7] NESANUS [8] cum esset valde inops sanctum alio tempore gaudenter hospitio recipit [9] virum. Cui cum hospitaliter secundum vires unius noctis spatio ministrasset, sanctus ab eo inquirit, cujus boculas [10] numeri haberet. Ille ait : ' Quinque '. Sanctus consequenter :

[1] *Alio* is written in A as though it began a chapter. The two half-chapters are separated by a line left blank, but both halves are included in A's chapter-heading. Reeves numbered the two halves as one chapter. Each half has a separate title in B1 B2 B3. The title of the second half, in B1, B2 (partly missing), B3, and in the contents-list of B2 and of B3, is : *De duobus piscibus illo prophetante in flumine quod vocitatur böo (boo B3) repertis.*

[2] *Cei.* In A, there is one over-dash, resembling the bar abbreviation-sign. Cf. 43a. Here also *cei* is probably genitive.

[3] bo A, with an over-dash, somewhat resembling an accent ; böo B1 B2 ; bo.o. B3

[4] *Pro* to *reddiderunt.* This sentence seems to have been misplaced in the common source of A B1 B2 B3 ; it should have followed *traxerunt*, and we have placed it there in the translation. It is to be noted however that *pro* does not begin a new sentence in any of the manuscripts, and that in A no original punctuation mark follows *traxerunt* or *comitata.*

[5] *stagno aporum.* Here *aporum* is a Latin genitive plural of *apor*, derived from North-British speech. The ' lake of river mouths ' was upper Loch

Also at another time, while the saint was staying for some days beside the lake Cei [Lough Key], his companions wished to go fishing ; and he delayed them, saying : ' Today and tomorrow not one fish will be found in the river. On the third day I will send you, and you shall find two great river salmon caught in the net '. So after two days they cast their net and found in the river that is called Bo [Boyle], and drew to land, those two salmon of most exceptional size. And for them the saint and his companions rendered very great thanks to God.

In these two above-mentioned catches of fish there appears the power of miracle, with prophetic fore-knowledge also accompanying it.

[II 20] Concerning Nesan the Crooked, who lived in the district [Lochaber] that borders upon the lake of river-mouths

This Nesan, when he was very poor, once joyfully received the holy man as a guest. After Nesan had provided for him hospitably according to his means for the space of one night, the saint inquired of him how many cows he had. He said : ' Five '. Thereupon

---

Linnhe, *an Linne Dhubh*, and the district named by Adomnan extended to that arm of the sea ; as does the modern district of Lochaber. Cf. Watson 1926, pp. 78–9.
[6] The contents-list of B2 and of B3 reads : *De quodam plebeo qui nesanus (ne's-* B2) *curvus dicebatur.*
[7] Hic A B1 B3 ; Sic B2
[8] nesanus A B2 B3 ; nesa'nus B1
[9] recipit A ; recepit B1 B2 B3
[10] boculas A B1 B2 B3 (bo'c- B1) ; in A, *u*, and apparently a deletion dot, have been written by m.h. above *o*.

'Ad me' ait, 'adduc, ut eas ¹ benedicam'. Quibus
adductís et elevata manu sancta benedictís : ' Ab hac
die tuae pauculae quinque vacculae ² crescent' ait
sanctus, 'usque ad centum et quinque vaccarum
numerum'.   Et quia idem ³ Nesanus ⁴ homo plebeus
erat cum uxore et filiis hoc etiam ei vir beatus benedictionis augmentum intulit, dicens : ' Erit semen tuum
in filiis et nepotibus benedictum'. Quae omnia plene
juxta verbum sancti sine ulla expleta sunt inminutione. .⁵

De quodam vero di'vite tenacissimo nomine Vi'geno ⁶ qui
sanctum Columbam despe'xerat, nec eum hospicio recepit, hanc
econtrario pro'tulit prophetalem sentenciam, i'nquiens : ' Illius
autem avari divitie, qui Christum in peregrinis hospi'tibus
sprevit, ab hac die paulatim imminuentur, et ad ni'chilum
redigentur ; et ipse mendicabit, et filius ejus cum semivacua
de domo in domum pe'rula discurret ; et ab aliquo ejus e'mulo
securi in fossula excusso'rii percussus morietur'. Que omnia
de utroque juxta sancti propheti'am viri plene sunt expleta.

De Columbano eque plebeo ⁷ viro cujus pecora
admodum pauca vir sanctus benedixit ; sed
post illius benedictionem usque ad
centenarium | creverunt numerum. .⁸

68b

ALIO QUOQUE TEMPORE,⁹ vir beatus quadam nocte
cum apud supra memoratum Columbanum tunc tem-

¹ eas A B1 B2 ; eis B3
² vacculae A ; -le B2 B3 ; vacce B1. Adomnan's use of diminutives
in the talk of Columba to this man, and to Columbanus, below, suggests
that they were not of Irish origin, although their names are Irish in form.
Cf. 46b.
³ idem. In A, a circumflex accent has later been added with a fine
pen above i.   ⁴ nesanus A B2 B3 ; nesa'nus B1
⁵ inminutione. The chapter is continued, without a break, in B1 B2 B3.
This continuation was perhaps made by Adomnan (see p. 8). It receives
a separate chapter-heading in the contents-list of B2 and of B3 : De quodam
divite tenacissimo nomine vigeno (vi'geno B2). We take the continuation from

the saint said : ' Bring them to me, so that I may bless them '. They were brought, and the saint raising his holy hand blessed them, and said : ' From this day, your small number of five little cows will increase up to one hundred and five cows '. And because this Nesan was a layman, with wife and children, the blessed man gave him this further benediction also, saying : ' Your seed will be blessed in your sons and grandsons '. All these things were completely fulfilled in accordance with the saint's word, without any diminution.

But concerning a certain very niggardly rich man, Vigenus by name, who had slighted Saint Columba, and did not receive him as a guest, he pronounced on the contrary this prophetic doom : ' The riches of that greedy man, who has spurned Christ in pilgrim guests, will from this day be gradually diminished, and will be reduced to nothing. And he himself will be a beggar, and his son will run from house to house with a half-empty bag. And he will die, struck with an axe by one of his enemies, in the trench of a threshing-floor '.

All these things concerning each were completely fulfilled according to the prophecy of the holy man.

[II 21] Of Colman, another layman ; whose cattle, very few in number, the holy man blessed. And after blessing they increased to a hundred

At another time, when the blessed man was well entertained one night at the house of the above-named

B1. Much of it is illegible in B2. B2 and B3 give no accents, and there are some insignificant variations of spelling that we have not noted.

6 vi'geno B1 ; ingenio B3. Illegible in B2.

7 *eque plebeo.* This refers to the subject of the previous chapter in A, Nesan, called *plebeus.* Vigenus, the subject of the preceding chapter in B1 B2 B3, is not explicitly called *plebeus.* It seems, therefore, that the Vigenus chapter was not in Adomnan's original version.

8 *creverunt numerum* is, in A, written in the upper margin.

9 tempore A ; in tempore B1 B2 B3

poris inopem bene hospitaretur, mane primo sanctus
sicuti superius de Naesano [1] commemoratum est de
quantitate [2] et qualitate substantiae plebeum hospitem
interrogat. Qui interrogatus : ' Quinque ' ait, ' tan-
tummodo habeo vacculas ; quae si eas benedixeris [3] in
majus crescent '. Quas ilico a sancto jusus [4] adduxit ;
similique modo ut supra de Nesani [5] quinís dictum est
vacculís, et hujus Columbani boculas [6] quinales equaliter
benedicens, inquit : ' Centenas et quinque deo donante
habebis vaccas. Et erit in filiis et nepotibus tuís florida
benedictio '.

Quae omnia juxta beati viri profetationem in agrís
et pecoribus ejus et prole plenissime adinpleta sunt.
69a Mirumque in modum numerus a sancto | praefinitus
supra memoratís [7] ambobus virís in centinario [8] vaccarum et quinario expletus numero nullo modo superaddi
potuit ; nam illa quae supra praefinitum excedebant [9]
numerum diversís praerepta cassibus [10] nusquam con-
paruerant, excepto eo quod aut in usus proprios familiae
aut etiam in opus elimoysinae [11] expendi poterat.

In hac itaque narratione, ut in ceterís, virtutis [12]
miraculum et profetia simul aperte ostenditur. Nam in
magna vaccarum ampliatione [13] benedictionis pariter et
orationis virtus apparet, et in praefinitione numeri
profetalis praescientia. .

---

[1] naesano A ; the first *a* has later been erased (see p. 130). nesa'no B1 ;
nesano B2 B3
[2] quantitate A B1 B2 ; quantite B3
[3] benedixeris A B1 B2 (-di'x- B1) ; benedixieris B3
[4] jusus A ; a small *s* has been added by m.h. above *us*. jussus B1 B2 B3
[5] nesani A B1 B3 ; nasani B2
[6] boculas A B2 B3 ; in A, a small *u* has been written by m.h. above *o*.
bo'culas B1
[7] memoratís A ; -tus B1 ; -tis B2 B3
[8] centinario A ; the first *i* has been altered by m.h. to *e*. -ten- B1 B2 B3
[9] excedebant A ; -bat B1 B2 B3

Colman, then a poor man, the saint (as has been related above in the case of Nesan) questioned his lay host in the early morning about the nature and amount of his property. Thus questioned, he replied : ' I have but five little cows ; if you bless them, they will become more '. He brought them immediately at the command of the saint, who, just as has been told above of the five little cows of Nesan, blessed likewise the five little cows of this Colman also, and said : ' God granting it, you shall have a hundred and five cows. And there will be a blessing of fruitfulness upon your sons and grandsons '.

All these things were very completely fulfilled according to the prophecy of the blessed man, in Colman's fields and cattle, and in his descendants. And in a strange manner, when the number fixed by the saint for either of those men had reached the total of a hundred and five cows, it could not be increased by any means. For those beasts that surpassed the above predetermined number were carried off by various mischances and nowhere seen again ; except any one that could be devoted either to the own needs of the household, or else to the use of charity.

In this story, as in the others, a miracle of power, together with prophecy, is clearly shown. For in the great increase of cows, the power of blessing appears equally with that of prayer ; and in the predetermination of the number, prophetic foreknowledge.

---

[10] cassibus A ; the first *s* has later been deleted with dots above and below made by a fine pen. casibus B1 B2 B3
[11] elimoysinae A ; elemo′sine B1 ; elemosine B2 B3
[12] virtutis A B1 B3 ; in A, small letters *bu* have been added by m.h. above *is*, and marked with dots for insertion between *i* and *s*. Illegible in B2.
[13] ampliatione A ; amplifica- B1 B3. Illegible in B2.

De malefactorum interitu qui
sanctum dispexerant [1]

VIR VENERANDUS supra memoratum Columbanum,[2]
69b quem de paupere virtus benedictionis ejus [3] ditem | fecit,
valde deligebat,[4] quia ei multa pietatis officia praebebat.
Erat autem illo in tempore quidam malefactor homo
bonorum persecutor [5] nomine Ioan [6] filius Conallis filii [7]
Domnallis [8] de regio Gabrani ortus genere.[9] Hic supradictum Colum [10] sancti amicum Columbae perseque-
batur, domumque ejus omnibus in ea inventís devasta-
verat ereptís non semel sed bis inimiciter agens. Unde
forte non inmerito eidem maligno accedit[11] viro, ut tertia
vice post ejusdem domus tertiam depredationem [12]
beatum virum quem quasi longius possitum[13] dispexerat[14]
propius appropinquantem ad navem [15] revertens preda
onustus cum sociis obvium haberet. Quem cum sanctus
de suís corriperet malís predamque deponere rogans
suaderet ille inmitis et insuadibilis permanens sanctum
dispexit,[16] navimque cum praeda ascendens beatum
70a virum subsannabat [17] et diridebat.[18] | Quem sanctus ad
mare usque prosequutus est, vitreasque intrans aquas

---

[1] The chapter-heading in B1 is : *De i'nteritu Johannis filii conallis, die ea'dem qua sanctum spernens dehonoravit.* So also (without accents, and reading *eadem die*) in B3 and in contents-list of B2 and of B3. B2 reads :] *filii conallis ea*[ ] *dehonoravit.*   [2] columbanum A B2 B3 ; colmanum B1
[3] ejus A. Omitted in B1 B3 ; missing in B2.
[4] deligebat A ; a small *i* has later been written above the first *e*. dil- B1 B2 B3
[5] persecutor A B1 B3 ; in A, a small *q* has been written (by ?m.h.) above *c*. Illegible in B2.
[6] io|an A, with two over-dashes ; johannes B1 B2 B3. Cf. 72a.
[7] filii A ; filius B1 B3. Missing in B2.
[8] domnal|lis A ; domnalli B1 B3 ;]nalli B2. See p. 136.
[9] gabrani ortus genere A ; genere gabrani ortus B1 B3 ; genere gab[B2. Ioan's grandfather was a son of Gabran (E.S., 1, p. cl). In A, a later curved line, made with at least two strokes, connects the end of *regio* with the *g* of *gabrani*.

[II 22] Concerning the destruction of evil-doers who had scorned the saint

The venerable man greatly loved the above-named Colman, whom the power of his blessing raised from poverty to wealth ; for Colman rendered him many pious services. There was at that time a certain man, sprung from the royal family of Gabran ; an evil-doer, an oppressor of good men, by name Ioan, son of Conall, son of Domnall. He oppressed the aforesaid Colman, Saint Columba's friend, and acting as an enemy had sacked his house, carrying off all that he found there, not once, but twice. So it happened not undeservedly to this evil man that on the third occasion, after his third plundering of the same house, when, with his associates, he was returning, laden with booty, to his ship, he encountered the blessed man, whom he had scorned as being very far away, approaching very near. When the saint rebuked him for his misdeeds, and entreated him to put down the booty, he remained unyielding and obstinate, and scorned the saint ; and entering his ship with the booty he scoffed at the blessed man, and mocked him. The saint followed him down to the sea, and entering knee-deep the glassy waters of the ocean

---

[10] colum| A, with an over-dash above *ol* (see p. 127) ; colmanum B1 ; columbanum B2 B3

[11] accedit A ; accidit B1 B2 B3

[12] depredationem A B1 B2 ; deprecacionem B3

[13] possitum A ; the first *s* has later been deleted with a dot above made by a fine pen. positum B1 B2 B3

[14] dispexerat A ; des- B1 B2 B3

[15] *navem.* In A, the *e* has later been altered to *i* with a down-stroke of a fine pen.

[16] dispexit A ; des- B1 B2 B3

[17] subsannabat A ; -a′vit B1 ; -avit B2 B3

[18] diridebat A ; der- B1 B2 B3

usque ad genua equoreas levatís ad caelum ambís [1]
manibus Christum intente precatur, qui suos glorificantes sé glorificat electos.

Est vero ille portus in quo post egresum per-
sequutoris stans paulisper dominum exorabat [2] in loco qui
scotice vocitatur [3] Aithchambas [4] Art-muirchol. [5] Tum
proinde sanctus expleta oratione ad aridam reversus in
eminentiore cum comitibus sedet [6] loco. Ad quos illa in
hora formidabilia valde profert verba, dicens : ' Hic
miserabilis homuncio qui Christum in suís dispexit [7]
servís ad portum a quo nuper coram vobís emigravit
numquam revertetur, sed nec ad alias [8] quas appetit [9]
terras subita praeventus morte cum suís perveniet malís
cooperatoribus. Hodie quam mox videbitis de nube a
borea orta [10] in|mitis inmisa [11] procella eum cum sociis
submerget, nec de eís etiam unus remanebit fabulator '.

Post aliquantum paucularum interventum morarum
die serenissima, et ecce de mari aborta [12] sicut sanctus
dixerat [13] nubes cum magno [14] fragore venti emisa [15]
raptorem cum praeda inter Maleam [16] et Colosum [17]
insulas [18] inveniens subito turbato submersit medio mari.
Nec ex eís juxta verbum sancti qui navi inerant etiam
unus evassit. [19] Mirumque in modum toto circumquaque

70b

[1] ambís A ; ambabus B1 B2 B3

[2] paulisper dominum exorabat A ; dominum exorabat paulisper B1
B2 B3   [3] vocitatur A ; vocatur B1 B2 B3

[4] aithchambas A, with three over-dashes ; aidcambas B1 B2 ; ad
cambasi B3. The place intended was probably known to Adomnan, but
it has not been identified. See p. 150.

[5] art muirchol A, with three over-dashes ; ardmuircol B1 ; ardmuircoll
B2 B3. See 20b.   [6] sedet A B1 ; sedit B2 B3

[7] dispexit A ; des- B1 B2 B3

[8] alias A B3 ; illas B1. Missing in B2.

[9] appetit A B3 ; in A, an acute accent has later been added with a fine
pen above *a*. a'ppetit B1. Missing in B2.

[10] orta A ; ortam B1 B3. Missing in B2.

[11] inmisa A ; a small *s* has been added by m.h. above *is*. immensa B2
B3 ; et inmensa B1   [12] aborta A ; oborta B1 B3. Illegible in B2.

he raised both hands to heaven, and earnestly prayed
to Christ, who glorifies his chosen ones that glorify him.

That harbour in which for a little while he stood
praying to the Lord, after the persecutor's departure,
is in the place that is called in Irish *Aithchambas Art-
muirchol.* Then after finishing his prayer the saint
returned to dry land, and sat with his companions on
higher ground ; and in that hour he spoke to them
very terrible words, saying : ' This wretched mortal,
who has despised Christ in his servants, will never
return to the harbour from which as you saw he has
lately departed ; and neither will he reach with his
fellow evil-doers the other lands for which he makes
his course, for he will be overtaken by sudden death.
This day very soon, you shall see, a violent squall,
hurled from a cloud that rises in the north, will sink
him with his company ; and not even one of them
will survive to tell the story '.

After an interval of some little time, the day being
very calm, behold, as the saint had said, a cloud arose
from the sea, and was released with great clamour of
wind ; and finding the robber with his booty between
the islands Male [Mull] and Colossus [Coll], it suddenly
raised a storm in the middle of the sea and sank him.
And in accordance with the saint's word not even one
escaped of those that were in the vessel. And in a
marvellous manner, while all the sea remained calm

---

13 dixerat A ; predixerat B1 B2 B3
14 magno A B1 B2 ; altered in B1 from *magna.* magna B3
15 emisa A ; a small *s* has been added by m.h. above *is.* emissa B1 B2 B3
16 maleam A B2 B3 ; ma'leam B1
17 colosum A B1 B2 ; colosam B3
18 insulas A B1 ; insulam B3. Illegible in B2.
19 evassit A ; the first *s* has later been deleted, with points above and
below. evasit B1 B2 B3

manente [1] tranquillo equore, talis una rapaces ad inferna submersos prostravit procella, misere quidem sed digne. .

De quodam Feradacho subita
morte subtract[o] [2]

ALIO QUOQUE IN TEMPORE vir sanctus quendam de
71a nobili Pictorum genere [3] | exsulem [4] Tarainum [5] nomine
in manum alicujus Feradachi [6] ditis viri qui in Ilea [7]
insula habitabat deligenter [8] adsignans commendavit, ut
in ejus comitatu quasi unus de amicís per aliquot menses
conversaretur. Quem cum tali commendatione de
sancti manu viri suscipisset [9] commendatum, post paucos
dies dolose agens crudili [10] eum jusione [11] trucidavit.
Quod inmane [12] scelus cum sancto a comeantibus esset
nuntiatum, síc respondens profatus est : ' Non mihi [13]
sed deo ille infelix homunculus mentitus est, cujus nomen
de libro vitae delebitur. Haec verba aesteo [14] nunc
mediante proloquimur tempore ; sed autumnali antequam de suilla degustet carne arboreo [15] saginata fructu
subita praeventus morte ad infernalia rapietur loca '.
71b Haec sancti profetia | viri cum misello nuntiaretur [16]
homuncioni,[17] dispiciens [18] inrissit [19] sanctum. Et post

[1] toto circumquaque manente A ; circumquaque manente toto B1
B2 B3
[2] The chapter-heading reads, in B1 B2 B3, and the contents-list of
B2 and of B3 : *De alicujus (ali'cujus B1) feradachi morte fraudulenti viri,
a sancto prenunciata* (partly missing or illegible in B2 and the contents-list of
B2).
[3] Below this column, with the page upside-down, m.h. has written,
and smeared out, *M Milium*, a trial of the pen.
[4] exsulem A ; e'xulem B1 ; exulem B2 B3
[5] tarainum A B2 B3 ; tharainum B1
[6] feradachi A B2 B3 ; ferada'chi B1
[7] ilea A ; i'lia B1 ; ilia B2 B3
[8] deligenter A ; the first *e* has later been changed to *i* with a down-
stroke of a fine pen. dil- B1 B2 B3
[9] suscipisset A ; the first *i* has been altered by m.h. to *e*. -cep- B1 B2 B3

round about, this one squall drowned the plunderers and
cast them down to hell, a wretched but a worthy fate.

[II 23] Of a certain Feradach, carried off by sudden death

Also at another time, the holy man committed an
exile, Tarain by name, of a noble family of the Picts, to
the protection of a certain Feradach, a rich man, who
lived in the island of Ile [Islay] ; earnestly requiring
that Tarain should for some months live in Feradach's
retinue, as one of his friends. When he had received
him from the hand of the holy man, commended with
this commendation, after a few days Feradach acted
treacherously and, by a cruel order, caused him to be
slain. When this monstrous crime was reported to the
saint by travellers, he thus declared in reply : ' That
unhappy being has lied not to me, but to God ; his
name will be removed from the book of life. Now in
the midsummer season we pronounce these words, but
in the autumn season, before he can taste pigs' flesh
fattened on the fruit of trees, he will be overtaken by
sudden death and carried off to the infernal regions '.

When this prophecy of the holy man was reported to
the wretched mortal, he scorned the saint and mocked

---

10 crudili A ; the first *i* has been altered by m.h. to *e*. crudeli B1 B2 B3
11 jusione A ; a small *s* has been added by m.h. above *us*. juss- B1 B2 B3
12 Quod inmane A B1 ; Qui in-mane B2 ; Qui i˜mane B3
13 mihi A ; nobis B1 B2 B3
14 aesteo A ; estivo B1 B2 B3
15 arboreo A ; a'rborum B1 ; arborum B2 B3
16 *nuntiaretur.* In A, the end of the Irish *tur* symbol is faint. Reeves
misread the word as *nuntiaret.*
17 homuncioni A B2 B3 ; homutioni B1
18 dispiciens A ; des- B1 B3. Illegible in B2.
19 inrissit A ; a small *r* has been written by m.h. above *n*, and deletion
points entered below *n* and the first *s*. irrisit B1 B3. Illegible in B2.

2C

dies aliquot autumnalium mens[i]um [1] eo jubente scrofa
nucum inpinguata nucleís jugulatur, necdum aliis ejusdem viri [2] jugulatís suibus. De qua celeriter exinterata [3]
partem sibi in veru celerius assari [4] praecipit,[5] ut de ea
inpatiens homo praegustans beati viri profetationem
distrueret.[6] Qua videlicet [7] assata dari sibi poposcit
aliquam praegustandam mursus [8] particulam ; ad quam
percipiendam extensam manum priusquam ad ós con-
verteret exspirans mortuus retro in dorsum cicidit.[9] Et
qui viderant et qui audierant valde tremefacti ammi-
rantes Christum in sancto profeta honorificantes glorificarunt. . [10]

De alio quodam nefario homine eclesiarum [11] persecutore, cujus nomen latine manus dextera dicitur. .[12] |

72a   ALIO IN TEMPORE vir beatus cum alios eclesiarum
persequutores in Hinba [13] commoratus insula excommonicare [14] coepisset, filios videlicet Conallis filii Domnaill,[15] quorum unus erat Ioan [16] de quo supra retulimus,
quidam ex eorundem malefactoribus sociis diabuli [17]
instinctu cum hasta inruit,[18] ut sanctum interficeret.

[1] mensum A ; a subscript *i* has been added by m.h. after *s*, in lighter ink. mensium B1 B3. Illegible in B2.
[2] *jugulatur* to *viri* in A B1 B3 ; omitted in B2 through homoioteleuton.
[3] exinterata A ; exent- B1 B2 B3
[4] *assari.* In A, a circumflex accent has later been added with a fine pen above the second *a*.
[5] praecipit A ; precepit B1 B2 B3
[6] distrueret A ; the *i* has been altered by m.h. to *e.* des- B1 B2 B3
[7] *videlicet.* After this word, *parte* appears to have been omitted, in the common source of A B1 B2 B3.
[8] mursus A ; morsus B1 B2 B3
[9] cicidit A ; the first *i* has been altered by m.h. to *e.* ce'c- B1 ; cec- B2 B3   [10] glorificarunt A ; -averunt B1 B2 B3
[11] *quodam* to *eclesiarum* in A ; omitted in B1 B2 B3, and in the contents-list of B2 and of B3.

him. After some days of the autumn months, a sow
fattened on kernels of nuts was slaughtered by his
command, before any of his other pigs had been killed.
And he ordered that the sow should be quickly dis-
embowelled, and that part of it should at once be
broiled for him on a spit ; so that the rash fellow, by
tasting of it in advance, might confound the blessed
man's prophecy. When the part had been broiled, he
asked for a morsel to be given him to taste. Before he
could bring to his mouth the hand that he had stretched
out to receive the morsel, he expired, and fell dead on
his back. And those that saw, and those that heard,
trembled greatly, marvelled, and glorified Christ, hon-
ouring him in his holy prophet.

[II 24] Concerning another impious man, a
persecutor of churches, whose name is called
' Right Hand ' in Latin

At another time, when the blessed man was in the
island of Hinba, and had begun to excommunicate other
persecutors of churches, namely the sons of Conall
Domnall's son, (of whom one was Ioan, whose story
we told above) one of their company of evil-doers,
prompted by the devil, rushed in with a spear, intending

---

[12] manus dextera dicitur A B3, and the contents-list of B2 and of B3 ;
dicitur manus dextera B1 ; manus dextra [B2

[13] hinba A ; hi'mba B1 ;]ba B2 ; himba B3

[14] excommonicare A ; a small *u* has been written by m.h. above the
second *o*. -muni- B1 B2 B3

[15] domnaill A B2 B3 ; domnai'l B1

[16] ioan A, with two over-dashes ; johannes B1 B2 B3

[17] diabuli A ; the *u* has later been altered to *o* by bridging. -boli
B1 B2 B3

[18] inruit A ; a small *r* has been written by m.h. above *n*. i'rruit B1 ;
irruit B2 B3

Quod praecavens [1] unus ex fratribus, Findluganus [2] nomine, mori paratus pro sancto viro cucula [3] ejus indutus intercessit. Sed mirum in modum, beati viri tale vestimentum quasi quaedam munitissima et inpenetrabilis lurica,[4] quamlibet fortis viri forti inpulsione acutioris hastae, transfigi [5] non potuit, sed inlessum [6] permansit. Et qui eo indutus erat intactus et incolomis [7] tali protectus est munimento. Ille vero sceleratus, qui

72b manus dextera [8] [dicebatur],[9] retro repedavit, | estimans quod sanctum hasta transfixisset virum.

Post ex [10] ea die conpletum [11] annum, cum sanctus in Iova commoraretur insula : ' Usque in hanc diem ' ait, ' intigratus [12] est annus, ex qua die Lam Dess [13] in quantum potuit Findluganum [14] mea jugulavit vice ; sed et ipse ut estimo hac in [15] hora jugulatur '. Quod juxta sancti revelationem eodem momento in illa insula factum est quae [16] latine longa [17] vocitari potest, ubi ipse solus Lam Des [18] in aliqua virorum utrimque acta belligeratione Cronani [19] filii Baitani [20] jaculo transfixus, in nomine ut fertur sancti Columbae emiso,[21] interierat ; et post ejus interitum belligerare viri cessarunt. .

[1] praecavens A ; an acute accent has later been added with a fine pen above $p̃$. pre'- B1 ; pre- B2 B3
[2] findluganus A B1 B2 ; finducanus B3
[3] cucula A ; a small l has been written by m.h. above ul. -ulla B1 B2 B3
[4] lurica A ; the u has later been altered to o by bridging ; and a circumflex accent has been added with a fine pen above i. lori'ca B1 ; lorica B2 B3. (Cf. O.I. *lúrech*, S.G. *lùireach*, 'shirt of mail', applied to a charm against mischance.)
[5] transfigi A B2 B3 ; in A, a circumflex accent has later been added with a fine pen above the first i. transfi'gi B1
[6] inlessum A ; the first s has later been deleted with points above and below made by a fine pen. illessum B1 B2 B3
[7] incolomis A ; inco'lumis B1 ; incolumis B2 B3
[8] dextera A B1 ; dextra B2 B3   [9] dicebatur B1 B2 B3. Omitted in A.
[10] ex A B3 ; hec B1. Omitted in B2.
[11] conpletum A B2 ; copletum B1 ; co̰pletum B3
[12] intigratus A ; the second i has been altered by m.h. to e. -teg-B1 B2 B3

to kill the˙ saint. In order to prevent this, one of the monks, by name Findlugan, wearing the holy man's cowl, came between, ready to die for him. But miraculously that garment of the blessed man, like a coat of well-fortified and impenetrable armour, could not be pierced even by a strong man's powerful thrust of a very sharp spear, but remained uninjured ; and the man that was clad in it was shielded by that covering from hurt or harm. But the miscreant, who [was called] Right Hand, withdrew, believing that the spear had transfixed the holy man.

When a whole year had passed from that day, and the saint was in the island of Io, he said : ' A year has been completed to this day from the day on which Lám Dess did his best to kill Findlugan in my place. But in this hour, as I believe, he is himself being killed '. And in accordance with the revelation of the saint, at the same moment this happened in the island that in Latin may be called ' long '. In a fight that took place there this Lám Dess alone of the men on either side perished, pierced by the javelin of Cronan, Baitan's son (thrown, it is said, in the name of Saint Columba). And after his death, the men stopped fighting.

---

[13] lam dess A, with one over-dash (above *lam* ; misread *Lám* in Thesaurus 1903, p. 278) ; lamdhes B1 ; laudes B2 ; lamdes B3. In A, a later hand has written above *lam*, with a very fine pen, a sign that, so far as it can be seen in the facsimiles, seems to be the continental symbol for *quaere*. The name is ' right hand ' in O.I., but was probably not understood by the annotator. It had previously been given in a Latin translation only, *manus dextera*.

[14] findluganum A B3 ; findlucanum B1. Illegible in B2.
[15] in A. Omitted in B1 B2 B3.
[16] quae A ; quod B1 ; que B3. Illegible in B2.
[17] *longa*. See p. 156.
[18] lam des A, with two over-dashes ; lamdhes B1 ; lamdes B2 B3
[19] cronani A B3 ; crona'ni B1 ; croma'ni B2. See p. 79.
[20] baitani A ; baeta'ni B1 ; baetani B2 B3
[21] emiso A ; a small *s* has been added by m.h. above *is*. emisso B1 B2 B3

De alio itidem innocentium
73a   persequutore [1] |

CUM VIR BEATUS adhuc juvenis diacon [2] in parte
Lagenensium [3] divinam addiscens sapientiam conversaretur, quadam accedit [4] die ut homo quidam in-
nocuorum inmitis persequutor crudilis [5] quandam in
campi planitie [6] filiolam fugientem persequeretur. Quae
cum forte Gemmanum [7] senem supra memorati juvenis [8] |
diaconi magistrum in campo legentem vidisset, ad eum
recto cursu quanta valuit velocitate confugit. Qui tali
perturbatus subitatione Columbam eminus legentem
advocat, ut ambo in quantum valuissent filiam a per-
sequente defenderent. Qui statim superveniens, nulla eís
ab eo data reverentia, filiam sub vestimentís eorum
lancea jugulavit, et relinquens jacentem mortuam super
73b pedes eorum aversus | abire coepit.

Senex tum valde tristificatus conversus ad Columbam [9] : ' Quanto,' ait, ' sancte puer Columba, hoc scelus
cum nostra dehonoratione temporis spatio inultum fieri
judex justus [10] patietur deus ? ' Sanctus consequenter hanc in ipsum sceleratorem protulit sententiam,[11]
dicens : ' Eadem hora qua interfectae ab eo filiae anima
ascendit ad caelos, anima ipsius interfectoris discendat [12]

---

[1] The chapter-heading in B1, B3, and B2 so far as it is legible, and in the
contents-list of B2 and of B3, reads : *De alio* (*alia* B1) *innocencium persecutore,
qui in laginensium* (*langin-* B1) *provincia* (*provintia* contents-list of B2) *sicut
ananias* (*annani'as* B1, *annanias* contents-list of B3) *coram petro eodem momento
a sancto terribiliter objurgatus cecidit* (*ce'c-* B1) *mortuus.*
[2] diacon| A ; a *us* symbol has been written by m.h. above *n*, with a
very fine pen. dia'conus B1 ; diaconus B2 B3
[3] lagenensium A ; the first *e* has later been altered to *i*, by erasure.
laginensium B1 B3 (-ne'n- B1) ; lagiensium B2
[4] accedit A ; the *e* has later been altered to *i*, by erasure (cf. above).
a'ccidit B1 ; accidit B2 B3
[5] crudilis A ; the first *i* has been altered by m.h., very faintly, to *e*. et
crudilis B1 ; crudelis B3. Illegible in B2.

[II 25] Concerning yet another oppressor of innocents

While the blessed man, still a young deacon, was living in the region of the Lagin, studying divine wisdom, it happened one day that a certain cruel man, a pitiless oppressor of the innocent, was pursuing a young girl, who fled upon the level surface of the plain. When by chance she saw the aforesaid young deacon's master, the aged Gemman, reading on the plain, she ran straight to him for protection with all the speed she could. Alarmed by this sudden happening he called to him Columba, who was reading at a little distance, so that together they might to the extent of their power defend the girl from her pursuer. But as soon as the man came near, showing them no reverence he killed the girl with a spear, under their robes. And he left her lying dead upon their feet, and turning away began to depart.

Then the old man in great distress of mind turned to Columba, and said : ' For how long, holy boy, Columba, will God, the just judge, suffer this crime, and our dishonour, to go unavenged ? ' Thereupon the saint pronounced this sentence upon the miscreant : ' In the same hour in which the soul of the girl whom he has slain ascends to heaven, let the soul of the slayer

---

[6] *campi planitie*. This plain, in the district of the Lagin, was presumably Mag-lagen, to the south of the Liffey.

[7] gemmanum A B2 B3 ; gemma'num B1

[8] juvenis A ; juvenilis B1 B2 B3

[9] columbam A ; sanctum columbam B1 B2 B3

[10] judex justus A ; justus judex B1 B2 B3

[11] sententiam A B2 ; sentenciam B1 ; setenciam B3

[12] discendat A ; desc- B1 B3 and ?B2

ad inferos '. Et [1] dicto citius, cum verbo, sicut Annanias [2] coram Petro,[3] sic et ille innocentium jugulator coram oculís sancti juvenis in eadem mortuus [4] cicidit [5] terrula. Cujus rumor subitae et formidabilis vindictae continuo per multas Scotiae provincias cum mira sancti diaconi fama devulgatus [6] est. .

Hucusque de adversariorum terrificís ultionibus dixisse susficiat.[7] Nunc de bestiis aliqua narrabimus pauca. |

74a   [8] ALIO IN TEMPORE vir beatus cum in Scia [9] insula aliquantís demoraretur diebus, paulo longius solus orationis intuitu separatus a fratribus silvam ingressus densam, mirae magnitudinis aprum quem forte venatici canes persequebantur [10] obvium habuit. Quo viso eminus sanctus aspiciens eum [11] restitit. Tum [12] deinde invocato dei nomine sancta elevata manu cum intenta dicit ad eum oratione : ' Ulterius huc procedere noles [13] ; in loco [14] ad quem nunc devenisti morire '.[15] Quo sancti in silvís personante verbo non solum ultra accedere non valuit, sed ante faciem ipsius [16] terribilis ferus verbi ejus virtute mortificatus cito conruit. .[17]

[1] et A ; Et B1 B2 ; Quo B3
[2] annanias A B2 B3 ; ananias B1
[3] *Petro.* Cf. Vulgate, Acts v. 5.
[4] mortuus A B1. Omitted in B3 ; illegible in B2.
[5] cicidit A ; cec- B1 B3. Illegible in B2.
[6] devulgatus A ; div- B1 B3. Missing in B2.
[7] susficiat A ; suff- B1 B2 B3
[8] This chapter has no heading in A. The heading in B1 is : *De apri mortificatione qui á sancto eminus cecidit, signo prostratus dominice crucis.* The heading is verbally the same in B2 (as far as it is legible), B3, and the contents-list of B2 and of B3.
[9] scia A ; sua B1 B3. Illegible in B2.
[10] *quem* to *persequebantur.* In place of this clause, B1 B2 B3 read *tunc.*
[11] eum A ; tunc B1 ; tum B2 B3
[12] Tum A B1 B2 ; Tunc B3
[13] *noles.* Cf. 75a.

descend to hell '. And more quickly than speech, with that word, like Ananias before Peter, so also before the eyes of the holy youth that killer of innocents fell dead on the spot. The fame of this sudden and dreadful vengeance was immediately spread abroad throughout many provinces of Ireland, with wonderful renown of the holy deacon.

Let it suffice to have told so much of terrible vengeance upon enemies. Now we shall tell some few things about animals.

[II 26]

At another time, when the blessed man was for some days in the island of Sci [Skye], being alone for the sake of prayer, and separated from the brothers by a considerable distance, he entered a dense wood, and encountered a boar of remarkable size, which was being pursued by hunting-dogs. The saint saw it a little way off, and stood still, regarding it. Then he raised his holy hand, with invocation of the name of God, and praying intently said to the boar : ' You will approach no further ; in the place to which you have now come, die '. When these words of the saint rang out in the wood, not only was the wild beast unable to advance further, but before Columba's face it immediately fell, slain by the power of his terrible word.

---

[14] loco A ; loco hoc B1 B2 B3
[15] morire A ; the *i* has been altered by m.h. to *e*. quanto'cius mo'rere B1 ; q[ ]totius mo'rere B2 ; quantocius morere B3
[16] ipsius A B2 B3 ; ejus B1
[17] conruit A ; a small *r* has been written by m.h. above *n*. co'rruit B1 ; corruit B2 B3

De cujusdam aquatilis bestiae virtute
orationis beati viri repulsione. . [1]

74b   ALIO QUOQUE IN TEMPORE, | cum vir beatus in Pic-
torum provincia per aliquot moraretur dies, necesse
habuit fluium [2] transire Nesam.[3]   Ad cujus cum acces-
sisset ripam alios ex acculís [4] aspicit misellum humantes
homunculum, quem ut ipsi sepultores ferebant quaedam
paulo ante nantem aquatilis praeripiens [5] bestia mursu [6]
momordit sevissimo.   Cujus miserum cadaver [7] sero
licet quidam in alno [8] subvenientes porrectís praeripuere
uncinís.   Vir econtra beatus haec audiens praecipit ut [9]
aliquis ex comitibus enatans [10] caupallum [11] in altera
stantem ripa ad se navigando reducat.   Quo sancti
audito praedicabilis viri praecepto, Lugneus [12] mocu-
Min [13] nihil moratus obsecundans,[14] depositís excepta
vestimentís tunica, inmittit sé in aquas.   Sed bilua,[15]
75a   quae prius non tam satiata quam | in praedam accensa,
in profundo fluminis latitabat.   Sentiens eo nante [16]
turbatam supra aquam, subito emergens natatilis ad
hominem in medio natantem alveo cum ingenti fremitu
aperto cucurrit ore.   Vir tum [17] beatus videns, omnibus

---

[1] The chapter-heading in B1 is : *De alia aquatili bestia que eo orante et
manum é contra levante retro repulsa est, ne lugne'o natanti vicino noce'ret.* So also
(without accents) B2 B3 and the contents-list of B2 and of B3.

[2] fluium A ; a small *v* has been written by m.h. above *ui.* fluvium
B1 B2 B3

[3] nesam A ; nessa'mi: B1 ; nessamius B2 ; nessamus B3

[4] acculís A ; a'ccolis B1 ; accolis B2 B3

[5] praeripiens A ; p˜ri'piens B1 ; p˜ripiens B3.   Omitted by B2.

[6] mursu A ; the first *u* has later been altered to *o* by bridging. raptu
B1 B2 B3

[7] *cadaver.* In A, a circumflex accent has later been written with a fine
pen above the second *a.*

[8] *alno.* In Latin usage, *alnus* was a wooden boat ; and the context
favours that meaning here.   [9] ut A B2 B3 ; aut B1

[10] enatans A B3 ; in A, an acute accent has later been written above *e.*
e'natans B1.   Illegible in B2.

[II 27] Concerning a certain water beast driven away by the power of the blessed man's prayer

Also at another time, when the blessed man was for a number of days in the province of the Picts, he had to cross the river Nes [Ness]. When he reached its bank, he saw a poor fellow being buried by other inhabitants ; and the buriers said that, while swimming not long before, he had been seized and most savagely bitten by a water beast. Some men, going to his rescue in a wooden boat, though too late, had put out hooks and caught hold of his wretched corpse. When the blessed man heard this, he ordered notwithstanding that one of his companions should swim out and bring back to him, by sailing, a boat that stood on the opposite bank. Hearing this order of the holy and memorable man, Lugne mocu-Min obeyed without delay, and putting off his clothes, excepting his tunic, plunged into the water. But the monster, whose appetite had earlier been not so much sated as whetted for prey, lurked in the depth of the river. Feeling the water above disturbed by Lugne's swimming, it suddenly swam up to the surface, and with gaping mouth and with great roaring rushed towards the man swimming in the middle of the stream. While all that were there,

---

[11] caupallum A B2 B3 ; caballum B1
[12] lugneus A B3 ; lugne'us B1. Illegible in B2.
[13] mocumin A B1 B3 and ?B2, with three over-dashes in A.
[14] obsecundans A B3 ; obsecu'ndas B1. Missing in B2.
[15] bilua A ; the *i* has been altered by m.h. to *e*. be'lua B1 ; be[B2 ; belua B3
[16] nante A ; natante B1 B2 B3
[17] Vir tum A ; Tum vir B1 B3 ;]vir B2

qui inerant [1] tam barbarís quam etiam fratribus nimio
terrore perculsís, cum salutare sancta elevata manu in
vacuo aere crucis pincxisset signum invocato dei nomine
feroci imperavit bestiae, dicens : ' Noles [2] ultra progredi,[3]
nec hominem tangas. Retro citius revertere '. Tum
vero bestia hac sancti audita voce retrorsum acsi funibus
retraheretur velociore recursu fugit tremefacta,[4] quae
prius Lugneo [5] nanti eo usque appropinquavit ut
hominem inter et [6] bestiam non amplius esset quam
75b unius contuli [7] longitudo. Fratres tum | recessise [8]
videntes bestiam,[9] Lugneumque [10] commilitonem ad eos
intactum et incolomem [11] in navicula [12] reversum, cum
ingenti ammiratione glorificaverunt deum [13] in beato
viro. Sed et gentiles barbari qui ad praesens inerant
ejusdem miraculi magnitudine quod [14] et ipsi viderant
conpulsi deum magnificarunt [15] christianorum. .

De benedicta a sancto hujus insulae terrula
ne deinceps in ea viperarum alicui
nocerent venina [16]

QUADAM DIE EJUSDEM aestei [17] temporis quo ad
dominum[18] transiit, ad visitandos fratres sanctus plaustro

---

[1] inerant A B2 B3 ; in A, a later mark above the first *n* may be intended
for a stress-accent. i'nerant B1
[2] noles A B1 B2 B3. This must be the future indicative, notwithstanding
that it is followed by *tangas* in the present subjunctive.
[3] progredi A B2 B3 ; in A, an acute accent has later been written with
a fine pen above *o*. pro'gredi B1
[4] tremefacta · quae A ; retracioneque facta B1 ; retractione factaque
B2 B3   [5] lugneo A B2 B3 ; lugne'o B1
[6] hominem inter et A ; inter hominem et inter B1 B2 B3
[7] contuli A B3 ; co'ntuli B1. Omitted in B2.
[8] recessise A ; -isse B1 B2 ; -isset B3
[9] videntes bestiam A ; bestiam videntes B1 B2 B3
[10] lugneumque A B1 B2 ; lugneum B3
[11] incolomem A ; -lum- B1 B2 B3
[12] navicula A B1 B2 ; -lam B3

barbarians and even the brothers, were struck down
with extreme terror, the blessed man, who was watching, raised his holy hand and drew the saving sign of
the cross in the empty air ; and then, invoking the
name of God, he commanded the savage beast, and
said : ' You will go no further. Do not touch the man ;
turn backward speedily '. Then, hearing this command
of the saint, the beast, as if pulled back with ropes, fled
terrified in swift retreat ; although it had before
approached so close to Lugne as he swam that there
was no more than the length of one short pole between
man and beast.

Then, seeing that the beast had withdrawn and that
their fellow-soldier Lugne had returned to them unharmed and safe, in the boat, the brothers with great
amazement glorified God in the blessed man. And also
the pagan barbarians who were there at the time,
impelled by the magnitude of this miracle that they
themselves had seen, magnified the God of the Christians.

[II 28] Concerning the saint's blessing of the
soil of this island, so that thenceforward the
poison of snakes should hurt no one in it

On a certain day of that summer season in which he
passed to the Lord, the saint went, drawn in a wagon,

---

¹³ deum A B1 B3 ; christum B2
¹⁴ quod A ; qui B1 B2 B3
¹⁵ magnificarunt A ; -caverunt B1 B2 B3
¹⁶ The chapter-heading in B1 : *De insule Iove viperinis serpentibus, qui ex qua die sanctus eam benedixit, nulli hominum nec etiam pecoribus nocere po'terint.* Verbally the same in B2 B3 and their contents-lists, except that they read *potuere*, and that B3 and its contents-list have, as usual, *Ione* for *Iove*. The title of A alone shows that its source was composed in Iona ; see pp. 8-9.
¹⁷ aestei A ; estivi B1 B3. Illegible in B2. This was in May, [597], according to 124b. ¹⁸ dominum A B1 B2 ; omitted by B3.

vectus pergit qui in campulo occidentali Iovae insulae
opus maceriale ¹ exercebant. Post quorum consulatoria ² a sancto prolata alloquia, in eminentiore stans
loco sic vaticinatur, dicens : ' Ex hac filioli die scio
76a quod in hujus campuli locís numquam | poteritis in
futurum videre faciem meam.' Quos hoc audito verbo
valde tristificatos videns, consulari ³ eos in quantum
fieri possit conatus ambas manus elevat sanctas, et totam
hanc nostram benedicens insulam ait : ' Ex hoc hujus
horulae momento omnia viperarum venina ⁴ nullo modo
in hujus insulae terrulís ⁵ aut hominibus aut pecoribus
nocere poterunt, quandiu Christi mandata ejusdem
commorationis incolae observaverint '. .

<h3 style="text-align:center">De pugione a sancto cum dominicae
crucis signaculo benedicta ⁶</h3>

ALIO IN TEMPORE, quidam frater nomine Molua ⁷
nepos Briuni,⁸ ad sanctum eadem ⁹ scribentem hora
veniens, dicit ad eum : ' Hoc quod in manu habeo
ferrum quesso ¹⁰ benedicas '. Qui paululum extensa
76b manu sancta cum calamo¹¹ signans benedixit, ad | librum
de quo scribebat facie conversa. Quo videlicet supradicto fratre cum ferro benedicto recedente sanctus per-

¹ maceriale A ; materiale B1 B2 B3, wrongly accepted by Reeves.
Opus maceriale should mean the building of dry-stone walls. Cf. *maceria*, in
40b, and *lapidum maceria* in Adomnan's *De Locis*, p. 243 (but *maceriola*,
p. 229, is a partition cut out of rock).
² consulatoria A ; conlatoria B1 ; consolatoria B2 B3
³ consulari A ; the *u* has later been altered to *o* by bridging. -sol-
B1 B2 B3
⁴ venina A ; the *i* has been altered to *e*, by a fine pen (not m.h.).
venena B1 B2 B3
⁵ terrulís A ; -lis B1 B2 ; -lus B3
⁶ The contents-list of B2 and of B3 reads : *De hasta ab eo signata, que
deinceps nullo modo quamlibet fortiter impulsa, alicui potuit nocere animanti.*
⁷ molua A B1 B2 B3, with two over-dashes in A. See p. 107.

to visit the brothers who were engaged upon the building
of stone enclosures in the little western plain of the
island of Io. After addressing some words of comfort
to them, the saint, standing on higher ground, prophesied thus, saying : ' My sons, I know that from
this day forward you will never more be able to see my
face within this little plain '. When he saw that they
were greatly saddened by hearing this, he tried to comfort them as far as might be, and raising both his holy
hands he blessed all this island of ours, and said :
' From this moment of this hour, all poisons of snakes
shall be powerless to harm men or cattle in the lands
of this island, so long as the inhabitants of that dwelling-
place shall observe the commandments of Christ '.

[II 29] Concerning a dagger blessed by the
saint with the sign of the Lord's cross

At another time, a brother, by name Mo-lua descendant of Briún, came to the saint at a time when he
was writing, and said to him : ' Please bless this
implement that I have in my hand '. Columba held
out his holy hand a little way, made with his pen a
sign of the cross, and gave the blessing, while his face
was turned towards the book from which he was copying.
And when the aforesaid brother went away with the
implement that had been blessed, the saint asked :

⁸ briuni A B2 B3 ; briu'ni B1
⁹ eadem A B2 B3 ; in A, a circumflex accent has later been written by
a fine pen above *a*. ea'dem B1
¹⁰ ques|so A ; later, a subscript *a* has been written before *e*, and the
first *s* has been deleted with dots above and below made by a fine pen.
queso B1 B2 B3
¹¹ *cum calamo*. Columba's pen might literally have been a reed.

cunctatur, dicens : ' Quod fratri ferrum [1] benedixi ? ' [2]
Diormitius [3] pius ejus ministrator : ' Pugionem ' ait,
' ad jugulandos tauros vel boves benedixisti '. Qui
econtra respondens infit : ' Ferrum quod benedixi con-
fido in domino meo quia [4] nec homini nec pecori
nocebit '.

Quod sancti firmissimum eadem hora conprobatum
est verbum. Nam idem frater valum [5] egresus monasterii bovem jugulare volens tribus firmís vicibus et forti
inpulsione conatus, nec [6] tamen potuit etiam ejus trans-
figere pellem. Quod monaci [7] scientes experti ejusdem
pugionis ferrum ignis resolutum calore per omnia
monasterii ferramenta liquefactum diviserunt inlinitum,[8]
77a nec postea ullam | potuere carnem vulnerare, illius
sancti manente benedictionis fortitudine. .

<h3 style="text-align:center">De Diormiti [9] egrotantis
sanitate</h3>

ALIO IN TEMPORE Diormitius [10] sancti pius minister
usque ad mortem egrotavit. Ad quem in extremís
constitutum sanctus visitans accessit, Christique invocato
nomine infirmis [11] ad lectulum stans et pro eo exorans
dixit : ' Exorabilis mihi fias precor domine mí, et
animam mei ministratoris pii de hujus carnis habitaculo
me non auferas superstite.' [12] Et hoc dicto aliquantisper
conticuit.[13] Tum proinde hanc de sacro ore profert

---

[1] fratri ferrum A ; ferrum fratri B1 B2 B3
[2] *benedixi.* After this word, a question-mark has been added later with
a fine pen, in A ; and there is a question-mark in B1 B2 B3.
[3] diormitius A ; Diormi'cius B1 ; Diormitius B2 ; Diormicius B3
[4] quia A ; quod B1 B2 B3
[5] *valum.* See p. 109.
[6] nec A B1 ; nec non B2 ; non B3
[7] monaci A ; a small *h* has been written by m.h. above *ci.* mo'nachi
B1 ; monachi B3. Missing in B2.

' What implement have I blessed for the brother ? '
Diormit, his devoted attendant, said : ' You have
blessed a dagger for the killing of bulls or cows '. But
he said in reply : ' I trust in my Lord that the implement I have blessed will not hurt either man or beast '.

This word of the saint was proved in that same hour
to be very well founded. For the brother went outside
the rampart of the monastery, intending to kill a cow,
and thrusting strongly made three serious attempts, yet
was unable even to pierce its skin. When they knew
of this, skilled monks softened the metal of that dagger
in a hot fire, and distributed it, melted, by overlaying
it upon all the iron tools of the monastery ; and after
that, the tools were not able to wound any flesh, because
the efficacy of that blessing of the saint continued.

[II 30] Of the healing of
Diormit, when he was sick

At another time, Diormit, the saint's devoted attendant, was mortally sick. The saint went to visit him
when he was at the point of death, invoked the name
of Christ, and, standing by the bedside of the sick man,
prayed for him, and said : ' My Lord, I beseech thee,
hear my prayer ; and while I live take not away from
the habitation of this flesh the soul of my devoted
servant '. After saying this, he was silent for a space.
Thereafter he let fall these words from his holy lips,

---

[8] inlinitum A ; a circumflex accent has later been written with a fine
pen above the third *i*. illini'tum B1 ; illinitum B2 B3

[9] diormiti A ; -micïi B1 ; -itïi B2 ; -icii B3

[10] diormitius A B2 ; -i'cius B1 ; -icius B3

[11] infirmis A ; the *s* has later been erased. infirmi B1 B2 B3

[12] superstite A B2 B3 ; in A, a faint acute accent has later been written
with a fine pen above the first *e*. supe'rstite B1

[13] aliquantisper conticuit A B1 B2 (-ti'c- B1) ; aliquantis perconticuit B3

2D

vocem, dicens : 'Hic meus non solum hac vice nunc
non morietur puer, sed etiam post meum annís vivet
multís obitum '. Cujus haec exoratio [1] est exaudita.
77b Nam Diormitius [2] statim post sancti exau|dibilem [3]
precem plenam recupera[v]it [4] salutem. Per multos
quoque annos post sancti ad dominum emigrationem
supervixit.

De Finteni [5] filii Aido [6] in
extremís positi sanitate

ALIO QUOQUE IN TEMPORE, sanctus cum trans Brittannicum [7] iter ageret dorsum, quidam juvenis unus
comitum subita molestatus egrimonia ad extrema usque
perductus est,[8] nomine Fintenus [9] ; pro quo com-
militones sanctum mesti rogitant ut oraret. Qui statim
eís conpatiens sanctas cum intenta oratione expandit ad
caelum manus, egrotumque [10] benedicens ait : 'Hic pro
quo interpellatis juvenculus vita vivet longa, et post
omnium nostrorum [11] qui híc adsumus exitum superstes
remanebit, in bona moriturus senecta '.

Quod beati viri vaticinium plene per omnia expletum
78a est. Nam idem juvenis, illius postea | monasterii
fundator quod dicitur Kailli au inde,[12] in bona senectute
praesentem terminavit vitam. .

[1] exoratio A ; oratio B1 B2 ; oracio B3
[2] diormitius A B2 ; -icius B1 B3
[3] exaudi|dibilem A ; exaudibilem B1 B2 B3 (-di′b- B1)
[4] recuperabit A ; a small *v* has been written by m.h. above *b*. -a′vit
B1 ; -avit B2 B3
[5] finteni A ; fente′ni B1 ; fen[B2 ; fenteni B3 and the contents-list
of B2 and of B3.
[6] aido A B3 and the contents-list of B2 and of B3 ; a′ido B1 ;]do B2
[7] brittannicum A B1 B2 (-a′- B1) ; britannicum B3
[8] est A B1 B2. Omitted in B3.
[9] fintenus A ; fente′nus B1 ; fentenus B2 B3
[10] egrotumque A B1 B2 ; egroque B3

saying : ' Now not only will this servant of mine not die on this occasion, but he will even live for many years after my death '.

This supplication of the saint was heard ; for immediately after his acceptable prayer, Diormit recovered his full health. Also he survived for many years after the saint's departure to the Lord.

[II 31] Concerning the healing of Finten,
Aid's son, at the point of death

Also at another time, when the saint was making a journey across the spine of Britain, one of his companions, a young man, by name Finten, was attacked by sudden illness and brought to the point of death. His fellow-soldiers sorrowfully implored the saint to pray for him. The saint at once took pity upon them, and spread his holy hands to heaven, with earnest prayer, blessed the sick youth, and said : ' This boy for whom you plead will live a long life ; and after the death of all of us who are here, will survive us, dying in good old age '.

This prophecy of the blessed man was entirely fulfilled in all things. For the same youth, afterwards the founder of the monastery that is called Cailli áufinde, ended this life in good old age.

---

11 nostro|rum A ; nostrum B1 B2 B3
12 kailli au inde A, with five over-dashes ; kailli anfinde B1 B2 ; kailli anfind B3. The common source probably had *kailli aufinde*. Adomnan's *kailli* is apparently the nominative plural of a noun, *caill* ' wood '. It is qualified by *au inde*, which is a feminine compound, either *aufinde* ' of the White-eared ', or perhaps *aufind+dē*, with the usual reduction of *ndd* to *nd*, ' of the white-eared goddess '. See pp. 143, 144, 148.

De puero quem mortuum vir venerandus
in Christi domini [1] nomine suscitavit.[2] .

ILLO IN TEMPORE [3] quo sanctus Columba in Pictorum provincia per aliquot demorabatur dies, quidam cum tota plebeus familia verbum vitae per interpretatorem [4] sancto predicante viro audiens credidit, credensque babtizatus est maritus cum marita liberísque et familiaribus. Et post aliquantum diecularum intervallum paucarum unus filiorum [5] patris familias gravi correptus egritudine usque ad confinia mortis et vitae perductus est. Quem cum magi morientem vidissent parentibus cum magna exprobratione coeperunt inludere, suosque 78b quasi fortiores magnificare deos, | christianorum vero tamquam infirmiori deo derogare.

Quae omnia cum beato intimarentur viro zelo suscitatus dei ad domum cum suís comitibus amici pergit plebei, ubi parentes nuper defunctae [6] prolis mestas celebrabant [7] exequias. Quos sanctus valde tristificatos videns confirmans dictís [8] conpellat consulatoriis,[9] ut nullo modo de divina omnipotentia dubitarent. Consequenterque percunctatur, dicens : 'In quo hospitiolo corpus defuncti jacet pueri?' [10] Pater tum [11] orbatus sanctum sub mestum deducit [12] culmen. Qui statim omnem foris exclusam relinquens catervam solus mestificatum intrat habitaculum ; ubi ilico flexís genibus

---

[1] domini A B3. Omitted in B1 B2.
[2] The contents-list of B2 and of B3 reads: *De puero quem mortuum in nomine domini Jesu Christi in regione pictorum suscitavit.*
[3] Illo in tempore A B2 B3 ; In tempore illo B1. See p. 81.
[4] *per interpretatorem.* This implies that the Irish language was not understood by the people living to the east of the Spine. See p. 157.
[5] filiorum A B1 B3 ; filius B2
[6] defunctae A ; -te B1 B3 ; deflere B2
[7] celebrabant A B1 B2 ; celebrant B3
[8] confirmans dictís A ; dictis confirmans B1 B2 B3

[II 32] Concerning a boy whom the venerable man raised from death, in the name of Christ the Lord

At the time when Saint Columba passed some days in the province of the Picts, a certain layman with his whole household heard and believed the word of life, through an interpreter, at the preaching of the holy man ; and believing, was baptized, the husband, with his wife and children, and his servants. And after the interval of a few short days, a son of the head of the household was seized by a severe illness, and brought to the boundary of death and life. When the magicians saw that he was dying, they began to taunt his parents, with great reproach, and to magnify their own gods as the stronger, and to belittle the Christians' God as the weaker.

When all this was reported to the blessed man, he was roused with zeal for God, and went with his companions to the house of the layman, his friend ; where the parents were performing the sad funeral rites for the child that had lately died. Seeing that they were in great grief, the saint addressed them with heartening words, encouraging them to have no doubt at all of the divine omnipotence. Thereafter he questioned them, saying : ' In what lodging lies the body of the dead boy ? ' Then the bereaved father led the saint under the sad roof. And he, leaving all the company outside, immediately entered the sorrowful habitation alone ; and there at once he knelt, and, his face suffused

---

⁹ consulatoriis A ; -sol- B1 B2 B3
¹⁰ *pueri*. After this word, a question-mark (?m.h.) has been added in A ; and there are question-marks in B1 B2 B3.
¹¹ tum A B2 B3 ; cum B1   ¹² deducit A B2 B3 ; ducit B1

faciem ubertim lacrimís inrigans Christum precatur
dominum. Et post ingeniculationem surgens oculos
convertit ad mortuum, dicens : ' In nomine domini |
79a Jesu Christi resuscitare, et sta super pedes tuos '. Cum
hac sancti honorabili voce anima ad corpus [1] rediit,
defunctusque apertís revixit oculís ; cujus manum tenens
apostolicus homo erexit, et in statione [2] stabiliens secum
domum egresus deducit, et parentibus redivivum
adsignavit. Clamor tum [3] populi attollitur, plangor [4] in
laetationem [5] convertitur, deus christianorum glori-
ficatur.

Hoc noster Columba cum Elia [6] et Eliseo [7] profetís
habeat [8] sibi commone [9] virtutis miraculum, et cum
Petro et Paulo et Joanne [10] apostolís partem honoris
similem in defunctorum resuscitatione, et inter utrosque,
hoc est profetarum et apostolorum coetus, honorificam
caelestis patriae sedem homo profeticus et apostolicus
aeternalem, cum Christo qui regnat cum patre in unitate
spiritus sancti per omnia saecula saeculorum. . [11] |

79b   De Broichano [12] mago ob ancellae [13]
retentionem [14] infirmato, et pro ejus
liberatione sanato [15]

EODEM IN TEMPORE vir venerandus quandam a
Broichano [16] mago scoticam postulavit servam humani-
tatis miseratione liberandam. Quam cum ille duro

[1] anima ad corpus A B1 ; anima et corpus B2 ; ad corpus anima B3
[2] statione A B1 B3 ; statione et B2   [3] tum A B1 B3 ; tunc B2
[4] plangor A ; planctus B1 B2 B3
[5] laetationem A ; leticiam B1 B2 B3   [6] elia A ; helia B1 B2 B3
[7] eliseo A ; helise'o B1 ; heliseo B2 B3
[8] habeat A B1 B2; habebat B3
[9] commone A ; commune B1 B2 B3
[10] joanne A ; johanne B1 B3. Illegible in B2.
[11] *amen* is added in B1 B2 B3.
[12] broichano A B1 B3 (-a'no B1) ; bricano B2

with tears, prayed to Christ the Lord. Rising from his
knees he turned his eyes to the dead boy, and said :
' In the name of the Lord Jesus Christ be restored to
life, and stand upon thy feet '. With these glorious
words of the saint, the soul returned to the body ; and
the dead boy opened his eyes, and lived again. The
apostolic man took his hand and raised him, and
steadying him on his feet led him out from the house,
and committed him, alive again, to his parents. Then
a shout of the people arose, mourning was turned into
rejoicing, the God of the Christians was glorified.

Let this miracle of power, in the raising of the dead,
be attributed to our Columba, in common with the
prophets Elijah and Elisha ; and a like share of honour
with the apostles Peter and Paul and John ; and a
glorious eternal place in the heavenly land, among
both the companies, namely of prophets and apostles,
as a man prophetic and apostolic : with Christ, who
reigns with the Father in the unity of the Holy Spirit,
through all the ages of the ages.

[II 33] Concerning the magician Broichan,
who was smitten with illness because he
retained a female slave ; and was cured,
when he released her

At the same time, the venerable man asked of the
magician Broichan that a certain slave, an Irish woman,
should be released as an act of human kindness. And

---

[13] ancellae A ; ancille B1 B3. Illegible in B2.

[14] retentionem A B1 ; Jonem B2 ; -ionis B3

[15] The contents-list of B2 and of B3 reads : *De conflictu ejus contra magum
broichanum ob ancille retentionem, et de lapide quem sanctus benedixit qui in aqua
quasi (sicut B2) pomum supernatavit.*

[16] abroichano A, with four over-dashes (a spelling error) ; á broichano
B1 ; á broicano B2 ; a broichano B3

valde et stolido retentaret animo,[1] sanctus ad eum
loquutus hoc profatur modo : ' Scito Broichane [2] scito
quia si mihi hanc perigrinam [3] libe[ra]re [4] captivam [5]
nolueris priusquam de hac revertar provincia, citius
morieris '.[6] Et hoc coram Bruideo [7] rege dicens domum
egresus regiam ad Nesam [8] venit fluium. De quo videlicet fluio lapidem attollens candidum, ad comites :
' Signate ' ait, ' hunc candidum lapidem, per quem
dominus in hoc gentili populo multas egrotorum perficiet
sanitates '. Et hoc effatus verbum consequenter intulit,
inquiens : ' Nunc Broichanus [9] fortiter concussus est ;
80a nam angelus de | caelo misus[10] graviter illum[11] percutiens
vitream in manu ejus de qua bibebat confregit in multa
biberam fragmenta, ipsum vero anchellantem [12] egra [13]
reliquit suspiria morti vicinum. Hoc in loco paululum
exspectemus binos regis nuntios ad nós celeriter misos,[14]
ut Broichano [15] morienti citius subveniamus. Nunc
Broichanus formidabiliter correptus ancellulam [16] libe-
rare est paratus '.

Adhuc sancto haec loquente verba, ecce sicuti praedixit duo a rege misi [17] equites adveniunt ; omnia quae
in regis munitione de Froichano[18] juxta sancti vaticinium
sunt acta [19] enarrantes ; et de poculi confractione et de

---

[1] duro valde et stolido retentaret animo A ; latro valde et fortiter
retentaret B1 B2 B3
[2] broichane A B1 B3 ; broicane B2
[3] perigrinam A ; the first *i* altered by m.h. to *e*. -reg- B1 B2 B3
[4] libe|re A ; *ra* added by m.h. at end of line. liberare B1 B2 B3
[5] captivam A B1 B2. Omitted in B3.
[6] morieris A B1 B3 ; in A, a circumflex accent has later been added
with a fine pen above *e*. Illegible in B2.
[7] bruideo A ; bru'deo B1 ; brudeno B2 ; brudeo B3
[8] nesam A B2 B3 ; nessam B1
[9] broichanus A B1 B3 ; broicanus B2
[10] misus A ; a small *s* written by m.h. above *is*. missus B1 B2 B3
[11] *graviter illum*. These two words were written twice in A ; the first
pair was later partly erased, probably not by the text hand.

when Broichan, with unyielding and obstinate heart, retained her, the saint addressing him spoke in this manner : ' Know this, Broichan, know that if you will not release for me this pilgrim captive before I depart from this province, you shall presently die '. This he said before king Brude ; and he left the king's house, and came to the river Nes [Ness]. From that river he took a white stone, and said to his companions : ' Mark this white stone. Through it the Lord will work many cures of the sick among this heathen people '. And after pronouncing these words he continued : ' Now Broichan has received a hard blow. For an angel sent from heaven has struck him heavily, and broken into many pieces in his hand the glass vessel from which he was drinking, and has left him breathing with difficulty, and near to death. Let us wait a little in this place for two messengers of the king, sent to us in haste, to obtain our immediate help for the dying Broichan. Now Broichan, terribly stricken, is ready to release the slave-girl '.

While the saint was still speaking these words, behold, as he had predicted, two men on horse-back, sent by the king, arrived, and told all that had happened concerning Broichan, in the king's fortress, in accordance with the prophecy of the saint : the breaking of

---

[12] anchellantem A ; anhelantem B1 B3 ; anelantem B2
[13] egra A B1 B2 B3. In A, a very fine loop has later been attached below *e*, to make the *ae* symbol. See p. 175.
[14] mi|sos A ; an *s* has been added by m.h. after *i*. missos B1 B2 B3
[15] broichano A B1 B3 ; braichano B2
[16] ancellulam A ; a very small *i* has been written (? by m.h.) above *e*. -ci'll- B1 ; -cill- B2 B3
[17] misi A ; a small *s* has been written by m.h. above *is*. missi B1 B2 B3
[18] froichano A ; broichano B1 B3 ; briochano B2. See p. 84.
[19] acta A B1 B3 ; facta B2

magi correptione et de servulae parata absolutione.[1]
Hocque [2] intulerunt dicentes : ' Rex et ejus familiares
80b nos ad té miserunt, ut nutricio [3] ejus | Broichano [4]
subvenias mox morituro '. Quibus auditís legatorum
verbís sanctus binos de comitum numero ad regem cum
lapide a sé benedicto mittit, dicens : ' Si in primís
promiserit sé Broichanus famulam liberaturam, tum
deinde hic lapillus intinguatur in aqua et síc eo [5] bibat,
et continuo salutem recuperabit. Si vero renuerit
refragans absolvi servam, statim morietur '.

Duo misi [6] verbo sancti obsequentes ad aulam deveniunt regiam, verba viri venerabilis regi enarrantes.
Quibus intimatis [7] regi et nutricio ejus Broichano valde
expaverunt. Eademque hora liberata famula sancti
legatis viri adsignatur ; lapis in aqua [8] intingitur,
mirumque in modum contra naturam lithus [9] in aquís
supernat [10] quasi pomum vel nux, nec potuit sancti
81a benedictio viri | submergi. De quo Broichanus [11] natante
bibens lapide statim a vicina rediit morte, intigramque[12]
carnis recuperavit salutem. Talis vero lapis postea in
thesaurís regis reconditus multas[13] in populo egritudinum
sanitates, similiter in aqua natans intinctus, domino
miserante efficit.[14]   Mirum dictu, ab hís egrotís quorum

---

[1] absolutione A B1 B2 ; obsolucione B3
[2] hocque A ; Hecque B1 ; Hocque B2 B3
[3] *nutricio* is the equivalent of O.I. *aite* ' foster-father '. It does not imply
that Brude was of immature age. See p. 38.
[4] broichano A B1 ; braichano B2 ; baichano B3
[5] eo A ; de ea B1 B2 B3. Reeves read *de eo*, unnecessarily.
[6] misi A ; a small *s* has been written by m.h. above *is*. missi, B1 B2 B3
[7] intimatis A B1 ;]timatis B2 ; auditus B3
[8] aqua A B1 B3 ; qua B2
[9] lithus A ; lapis B1 B3. Illegible in B2.
[10] supernat| A ; after this, m.h. has added *at*. supernatat B1 B2 B3
(-per- B1)   [11] broichanus A B1 B3 ; briochanus B2
[12] intigramque A ; the second *i* has been altered by m.h. to *e*. -teg-
B1 B2 B3
[13] multas A B1 B3 ; multa B2   [14] efficit A ; effecit B1 B2 B3

the cup, the magician's seizure, the intended release of the slave-girl. And they added this : ' The king and the persons of his household have sent us to you, to obtain your help for his foster-father Broichan, who is near death '.

When he heard these words of the envoys, the saint sent two out of the number of his companions to the king, with the stone that he had blessed, and said : ' If first Broichan promises that he will release the slave-girl, then let this small stone be dipped in water, and let him drink thereof, and he will at once recover health. But if he refuses, and opposes the slave-girl's release, he will immediately die '.

The two emissaries went to the king's castle, in obedience to the saint's instructions, and repeated to the king the words of the venerable man. When these things had been made known to the king and to Broichan his foster-father, they were very much afraid. And in the same hour the slave-girl, set free, was handed over to the envoys of the holy man. The stone was dipped in water ; and, in a marvellous manner, contrary to nature the stone floated in the water, as though it had been an apple or a nut. And the blessing of the holy man could not be submerged. After he had drunk of the floating stone, Broichan immediately returned from the brink of death, and recovered full bodily health.

This stone was afterwards kept among the king's treasures. When it was dipped thus in water, and floated, it effected by the Lord's mercy many cures of diseases among the people. Strange to say, when it

vitae terminus supervenerat requisitus idem lapis nullo
modo reperiri poterat. Síc et in die obitus Brudei [1] regis
quaerebatur, nec tamen in eodem loco ubi [2] fuerat prius
reconditus inveniebatur. .

De beati viri contra Broichanum magum refragatione, et [3] venti contrarietate

POST SUPRA memorata peracta quadam die Broichanus [4] ad sanctum proloquens [5] virum infit : ' Dicito
mihi Columba, quo tempore proponis enavigare ? '
81b Sanctus : | ' Tertia' ait, ' die, deo volente et vita comite,
navigationem proponimus incipere '. Broichanus [6]
econtra : ' Non poteris ' ait, ' nam ego ventum tibi
contrarium facere caliginemque umbrosam super-
inducere possum '. Sanctus : ' Omnipotentia dei ' ait,
' omnium dominatur, in cujus nomine nostri omnes
motus ipso gubernante deriguntur '.[7] Quid plura ?
Sanctus die eadem [8] sicut corde proposuit ad lacum
Nisae [9] fluminis longum multa prosequente caterva
venit. Magi vero gaudere tum coepere,[10] magnam
videntes superinductam caliginem et contrarium cum
tempestate flatum.

Nec mirum haec interdum arte daemonum posse fieri,
deo permittente, ut etiam venti et equora in asperius

---

[1] brudei A B2 B3 ; bru'dei B1
[2] ubi A B1 B3. Omitted in B2.
[3] et|et A ; et B1 B2 B3
[4] broichanus A B1 B3 ; broicanus B2
[5] proloquens A B3 ?B2 ; in A, a stress accent has later been written with a fine pen above the first o. pro'- B1
[6] Broichanus A B1 B3 ; Broicanus B2
[7] deriguntur A ; the e has later been altered to i with a down-stroke of a fine pen. dir- B1 B2 B3
[8] eadem A B3 ; in A, a circumflex accent has later been written with a fine pen above a. ea'dem B1 ; eodem B2

was sought by sick people whose time had come, the stone could by no means be found. So also it was looked for on the day of king Brude's death, and it was not found in the place where it had formerly been kept.

[II 34] Of the blessed man's resistance to the magician Broichan ; and of contrary wind

After the events recorded above, one day Broichan, addressing the holy man, said : ' Tell me, Columba, when do you intend to sail ? ' The saint said : ' We propose, God willing and life lasting, to begin our voyage on the day after tomorrow '. Broichan, on the contrary, said : ' You will not have the power ; for I have power to raise an adverse wind against you, and to bring up a mist of darkness '. The saint said : ' The omnipotence of God rules all things, and in his name, under his guidance, all our movements are directed '. Why say more ? On the appointed day as he had intended the saint came to the long lake of the river Nes [Ness], followed by a large crowd. Then the magicians began to exult, because they saw a great mist brought up, and a stormy adverse wind.

It is not strange that, with God's permission, these things can at times be done by the art of demons, so that even winds and waves can be roused to violence.

---

⁹ nisae A ; nesse B1 ; nesae B2 B3. A's *nisae* (with ligatured *ae*) would spell the genitive either of Adomnan's latinized **Nesa*, or of the O.I. **Nes*. See pp. 130, 141.

¹⁰ coepere A ; a circumflex accent has later been written with a fine pen above the second *e*. cé|pe're B1 ; cepe're B2 ; cepere B3

concitentur. Síc enim aliquando daemoniorum legiones[1] sancto Germano episcopo de sinu gallico[2] causa humanae salutis ad Brittanniam naviganti medio in equore occur- 82a rerant, et oponentes | pericula procellas concitabant ; caelum diemque tenebrarum caligine obducebant. Quae tamen omnia sancto orante Germano dicto citius sedata detersa cessarunt caligine.

Noster itaque Columba videns contra se elimenta[3] concitari furentia Christum invocat dominum ; cimbulamque ascendens nautís esitantibus[4] ipse constantior factus velum contra ventum jubet subregi.[5] Quo facto omni inspectante turba navigium flatus contra adversos mira vectum[6] occurrit velocitate. Et post haut grande intervallum venti contrarii ad iteneris[7] ministeria cum omnium ammiratione revertuntur. Et síc per totam illam diem flabrís lenibus secundís flantibus beati cimba viri obtatum provecta[8] ad portum pulsa[9] est.

Perpendat itaque lector quantus[10] et qualis idem vir 82b venerandus in quo deus | omnipotens talibus praescriptís miraculorum virtutibus coram plebe gentilica inlustre suum manifestavit nomen. .

[1] *legiones.* In A, below and to the left of *le*, another hand has later written with a fine pen *legio* as a suggested emendation, afterwards wiped out. The passage in Constantius's Life of Germanus from which this paragraph of Adomnan is partly taken has *legionis* (or *relegionis, religioni*) *inimica vis daemonum.* In Adomnan's preceding account of Broichan's threat of storm, and in the following account of Columba's voyage, Adomnan uses a few words (e.g. *caligo*) taken from, or suggested by, Constantius. The relevant passage of Constantius is quoted in Reeves 1857, p. 149, and partly in Brüning 1917, p. 252.

[2] *sinu gallico,* Constantius's name of some bay in France.

[3] elimenta A ; the *i* has been altered by m.h. to *e.* elem- B1 B2 B3

[4] esitantibus A ; a small *h* has been added by m.h. above, before *e.* hes- B1 B2 B3

[5] subregi A ; a small *i* has been written by m.h. above *e.* su′brigi B1 B2 B3   [6] vectum A ; factum B1 B2 B3

[7] iteneris A ; a small *i* has been written by m.h. above the first *e.* itin- B1 B2 B3   [8] provecta A ; profecta B1 B3 and ?B2

[9] pulsa A ; appulsa B1 B2 B3   [10] quantus A ; quantus sit B1 B2 B3

Thus did hosts of evil spirits once attack the holy bishop Germanus in the midst of the sea, when he was sailing from the bay of Gaul to Britain, in the cause of man's salvation. They put perils in his way, and stirred up storms ; they covered sky and daylight with a mist of darkness. But more quickly than speech, at the prayer of Saint Germanus all these things were calmed, and ceased. And the mist was cleared away.

So our Columba, seeing that the elements were being roused to fury against him, called upon Christ the Lord. He entered the boat, and while the sailors hesitated, he himself, more steadfast, ordered the sail to be raised against the wind. When this was done, and with the whole crowd looking on, the ship moved with extraordinary speed, sailing against the contrary wind. And after but a short space of time, to the astonishment of all, the adverse winds were turned about, to serve the voyage. So throughout that day, driven by gentle breezes blowing favourably, the blessed man's boat was carried to the desired harbour.

Let the reader reflect how great and of what nature was the venerable man, in whom almighty God made manifest to the heathen people the glory of his name through those signs of miraculous power described above.

De spontanea regiae [1] munitionis
portae subita apertione [2]

ALIO IN TEMPORE, hoc est in prima sancti fatigatione
iteneris [3] ad regem Brudeum, cassu [4] contegit [5] ut idem
rex, fastu elatus regio, suae munitionis superbe agens in
primo beati adventu viri non aperiret portas.[6] Quod ut
cognovit homo dei cum comitibus ad valvas portarum
accedens primum dominicae crucis inprimens signum,
tum deinde manum pulsans contra ostia ponit ; quae
continuo sponte retro retrusís fortiter serrís cum omni
celeritate aperta sunt. Quibus statim apertís sanctus
consequenter cum sociis intrat. Quo cognito rex cum
83a   senatu valde pertimescens domum | egresus obviam cum
veneratione beato pergit viro, pacificísque verbís blande
admodum conpellat. Et ex ea in posterum die sanctum
et venerabilem virum idem regnator suae omnibus vitae
reliquís diebus valde magna honoravit ut decuit honorificantia. .[7]

De eclesiae duorum [8] agri rivorum [9]
simili reclusione. .

ALIO ITIDEM in tempore vir beatus aliquantís in
Scotia diebus conversatus ad visitandos fratres qui in
monasterio duum [10] ruris commanebant rivulorum ab

---

[1] regiae A ; rege B1 ;]gie B2 ; regie B3 and contents-list of B2 ;
regis contents-list of B3, with the s erased.

[2] portae subita apertione A B1 B2 (porte B1 ?B2). Omitted in B3.

[3] iteneris A ; itin- B1 B2 B3. See p. 82.

[4] cassu A ; the first s has later been deleted with points above and
below made with a fine pen. casu B1 B2 B3

[5] contegit A ; a small i has been written by m.h. above e. -tig- B1 B3.
Illegible in B2.

[6] portas. This act is attributed to royal pride, rather than to the king's
antagonism to Christianity (cf. p. 85). It belongs to the legend that was
expanded in the Life of Comgell (see p. 22).

[II 35] Concerning the sudden spontaneous
opening of the gate of the royal fortress

At another time, that is on the saint's first tiring
expedition to king Brude, it happened that the king,
uplifted with royal pride, acted haughtily, and did not
open the gate of his fortress at the first arrival of the
blessed man. When the man of God learned this, he
went with his companions up to the doors of the gate,
and first imprinting the sign of the Lord's cross upon
the doors, he then knocked, and laid his hand upon
them. And immediately the bars were forcibly drawn
back, and the doors opened of themselves with all
speed. As soon as they were open, the saint entered
with his associates.

Learning this, the king with his council was much
alarmed, and left the house, and went to meet the blessed
man with reverence ; and addressed him very pleas-
antly, with words of peace. And from that day onwards,
throughout the rest of his life, that ruler greatly honoured
the holy and venerable man, as was fitting, with high
esteem.

[II 36] Concerning a similar opening of the
church of the land of two streams [Terryglass]

Again at another time the blessed man, while living
for some days in Ireland, went to visit the brothers who
occupied the monastery of the land of two streams, and

---

7 honorificantia A B1 ; -cen- B2 B3
8 duorum A B1 B2. Omitted in B3.
9 rivorum A and contents-list of B2 and of B3 ; rivulorum B1 B2 B3
10 duum A B2 B3 ; duorum B1

eís invitatus perrexit. Sed cassu [1] aliquo accedit [2] ut eo ad eclesiam accedente claves non repperirentur oratorii. Cum vero sanctus de non repertís adhuc clavibus et de obserratís [3] foribus inter sé conquirentes [4] alios audisset, 83b ipse ad hostium appropinquans : ' Potens est | dominus ' ait, ' domum suam servís etiam sine clavibus aperire suís '. Cum hac tum voce subito retro retrusís forti motu pissulís [5] sponte aperta janua sanctus cum omnium ammiratione eclesiam ante omnes ingreditur. Et hospitaliter a fratribus susceptus honorabiliter ab omnibus veneratur. .

De quodam plebeo mendico cui sanctus sudem faciens ad jugulandas benedixit feras. . [6]

ALIO IN TEMPORE quidam ad sanctum plebeus venit pauperrimus qui in ea habitabat regione quae stagni litoribus aporici [7] est contermina.[8] Huic ergo miserabili viro, qui unde maritam et parvulos cibaret non habebat, vir beatus petenti miseratus ut potuit quandam largitus elimoysinam [9] ait : ' Miselle homuncio, tolle de silva 84a contulum vicina et ad me ocius [10] | defer '. Obsecundans miser juxta sancti jusionem [11] detulit materiam. Quam sanctus excipiens in veru exacuit. Quodque propria

---

[1] cassu A ; the first *s* has later been deleted with dots above and below made by a fine pen. casu B1 B2 B3

[2] accedit A ; a small *i* has been written by m.h. above *e*. accidit B1 B2 B3 (a'cc- B1)

[3] obserratís A ; the first *r* has later been deleted with dots above and below made by a fine pen. obserratis B1, with the first *r* erased ; observatis B2, with the *v* deleted by two dots below ; obseratis B3

[4] conquirentes A ; -quer- B1 B2 B3

[5] pissulís A ; pessulis B1 B2 B3

[6] The contents-list of B2 and of B3 reads : *De alio paupere plebeo mendico (medico B2) cui sanctus sudem faciens benedixit ad ferarum jugulacionem silvestrium.*

[7] aporici A B2 B3 ; apo'rici B1. See 67b.

[8] contermina A B3 ?B2 ; conterminata B1

who had invited him. But it happened by some chance that when he came to the church its keys were not found. The saint heard the others lamenting among themselves that the keys were still missing, and that the doors were barred ; and he himself, going to the doorway, said : ' The Lord has power to open his house for his servants, even without keys '.

Then at this saying, with a vigorous motion the bolts were suddenly drawn back, the door opened of its own accord, and, while every one marvelled, the saint entered the church, first of them all. And he was hospitably entertained by the brothers, and was revered by them all with honour.

[II 37] Of a certain beggarly layman, for whom the saint made a stake and blessed it for the killing of wild animals

At another time, a certain layman came to the saint, a very poor man, who dwelt in that district [Lochaber] that borders upon the shores of the lake of river-mouths. Pitying this wretched man, who had not the means to feed his wife and children, the blessed man bestowed upon him, when he asked, such alms as he could give, and said : ' My poor fellow, take from the forest near by a stick of wood, and bring it to me quickly '. The poor man obeyed, and fetched the wood according to the saint's command. The saint took it, and shaped it into a spike. Sharpening this with his own hands, and

---

⁹ elimoysinam A ; elemosinam B1 B2 B3
¹⁰ ocius A B3 ; o'cius B1 ; otius B2
¹¹ jusionem A ; a small s has been written by m.h. above us. jussi-B1 B2 B3

exacuminans manu benedicens et illi adsignans inopi
dixit : ' Hoc veru deligenter [1] custodi ; quod ut credo
nec homini nec alicui pecori nocere potuit, exceptís ferís
bestiis quoque et piscibus. Et quandiu talem habueris
sudem numquam in domu [2] tua cervinae carnis cibatio
abundans deerit'. Quod audiens miser mendiculus [3]
valde gavisus domum revertitur, veruque in remotís
infixit terrulae locís, quae [4] silvestres frequentabant
ferae. Et vicina transacta nocte mane primo [5] pergit
revisitare volens veru, in quo mirae magnitudinis cervum
cicidisse [6] reperit [7] transfixum.

Quid plura ? Nulla ut nobis traditum est transire
84b po|terat dies qua non aut cervum aut cervam aut
aliquam repperiret in veru infixo [8] cicidisse [9] bestiam.
Repleta quoque tota de ferinís carnibus domu,[10] vicinís
superflua vendebat quae hospitium suae domus capere
non poterat. Sed tamen diabuli [11] invidia per sociam ut
Adam et hunc etiam miserum invenit, quae non quasi
prudens sed fatua taliter ad maritum [12] locuta est :
' Tolle de terra veru. Nam si in eo homines aut etiam
pecora perierint, tu ipse et ego cum nostrís liberís aut
occidemur aut captivi [13] ducemur '. Ad haec maritus
inquit : ' Non ita fiet, nam sanctus vir mihi benedicens
sudem dixit quod numquam hominibus aut etiam pecoribus nocebit '.

[1] deligenter A ; a small i has been written by m.h. above the first e.
dil- B1 B2 B3
[2] domu A ; domo B1 B2 B3
[3] mendiculus A B2 ; mendi'cus B1 ; mendicus B3
[4] quae A ; que B1 B2 B3, altered to quo in B1.
[5] primo A B1 B3. Omitted in B2.
[6] cicidisse A ; the first i has been altered by m.h. to e. cec- B1 B2 B3
[7] reperit A B2 ; repe'riit B1, with the first i erased ; reperiit B3
[8] infixo A B1 B2 ; fixo B3
[9] cicidisse A ; the first i has been altered by m.h. to e. cec- B1 B2 B3
[10] domu A ; domo B1 B2 B3

blessing it, he bestowed it upon the needy man, and said : ' Keep this spike carefully. It will, I believe, have power to hurt neither man nor any cattle, but only wild animals, and also fish. And so long as you have this stake, there will never be wanting in your house an abundant supply of venison to eat '.

Hearing this, the wretched beggar returned home, rejoicing greatly. He set up the spike in an out-of-the-way part of the district, frequented by wild creatures. And when the next night had passed, in the early morning he went to visit the spike again, and found that a stag of marvellous size had fallen transfixed upon it.

Why say more ? As we are told, no day could pass without his finding that a stag or a hind, or some other creature, had fallen upon the spike he had fixed up. Also when the house was completely filled with the carcasses of wild animals, he sold to neighbours the excess that the hospitality of his house could not use. But the malice of the devil reached this wretched man, as it did Adam, through his wife. She, not like a wise woman but as a fool, spoke to her husband thus : ' Take up the spike from the ground. For if people, or if cattle, should perish upon it, you yourself and I, with our children, will either be put to death, or be led into slavery '. To this the husband replied : ' That will not happen ; for the holy man said, when he blessed the stake for me, that it will never hurt people, or cattle '.

---

[11] diabuli A ; the *u* has later been altered to *o* by bridging. diaboli B1 B3. Illegible in B2.

[12] maritum A B1 B2 B3. In A, a circumflex accent has later been written with a fine pen above *i*.

[13] *captivi*. Cf. the instance of slavery substituted for death, under Irish law, in 88a.

Post haec verba mendicus uxori consentiens pergit,
85a et tollens de terra veru intra domum | quasi amans illud [1]
secus parietem possuit ; in quo mox domisticus [2] ejus
incedens [3] canis disperiit.[4] Quo pereunte rursum marita:
' Unus ' ait, ' filiorum tuorum incedet [5] in sudem et
peribit '. Quo audito ejus verbo maritus veru de pariete
removens ad silvam reportat, et in densioribus [6] infixit
dumís, ut putabat ubi a nullo posset animante offendi.
Sed postera reversus die capream in eo cicidisse [7] et
periisse [8] reperiit.[9] Inde quoque illud removens in
fluio [10] qui latine dici potest nigra dea [11] juxta ripam sub
aquís abscondens infixit. Quod alia revisitans die
esocem in eo mirae magnitudinis transfixum et retentum
invenit ; quem de flumine elevans vix solus ad domum
portare poterat. Veruque secum de aqua simul re-
85b portans extrin|secus in superiore tecti adfixit loco ; in
quo et corbus [12] de volatus [13] impetu lapsus disperiit
jugulatus. Quo facto miser fatuae cojugis [14] consilio
depravatus veru tollens de tecto adsumpta securi in
plures concidens [15] particulas in ignem proicit. Et post

---

[1] amans illud A B1 B2 B3 ; in B2, a punctuation sign follows *illud*.
Reeves substituted *amens, illud* in his text, without justification. Cf. *amans
amicum* in 33a.
[2] domisticus A ; the first *i* was altered by m.h. to *e* ; the second *i* had
been similarly altered, and the alteration wiped out. -me's- B1 ; -mes-
B2 B3
[3] incedens A B1 B2 B3. In A, the first *e* has later been altered to *i*,
(1) with a vertical down-stroke of a fine pen, and (2) with a small *i* written
by m.h. above *e*. Cf. 28a.
[4] disperiit A B1 B2 B3 (-pe'r- B1) ; in A, the last *i* has later been
deleted with a point above made by a fine pen.
[5] incedent A ; the second *n* has later been deleted with points above and
below made by a fine pen. incedet B1 B2 B3 (-ce'd- B1)
[6] densioribus A B1 B2 ; densoribus B3
[7] cicidisse A ; the first *i* has been altered by m.h. to *e*. cec- B1 B2 B3
[8] periisse A ; perisse B1 B2 B3
[9] reperiit A B1 B3, with the first *i* erased in B1 ; reperit B2
[10] fluio A ; fluvium B1 B2 B3
[11] *nigra dea*. This is the river Lochy that flows from Loch Lochy to
Loch Linnhe. See 5b, and p. 142.

After these words the beggar, yielding to his wife, went, and lifting the spike from the ground placed it, as if he loved the thing, inside the house, beside the wall. And before long his house-dog fell on it and was killed. When the dog died, the wife said again : ' One of your children will fall upon the stake, and be killed '. Hearing her say this, the husband removed the spike from the wall, and carried it back to the forest, fixing it in a very dense thorn-brake, where, as he thought, no living thing could stumble upon it. But returning on the following day, he found that a she-goat had fallen upon it and been killed. He removed the spike again from there, and fixed it in the river that in Latin may be called ' black goddess ' [Lochy], hiding it near the bank, under the water. When he went back to it next day, he found a salmon of marvellous size impaled and held fast upon it. When he lifted the salmon out of the river he was hardly able to carry it home by himself. He carried the spike back with him from the water at the same time, and fixed it in a high place on the outside of the roof. And on it a raven also, falling from rapid flight, was pierced through, and perished. After that, the wretched man, led astray by the advice of his foolish wife, lifted the spike down from the roof, took an axe, chopped the spike into many small pieces, and threw them into a fire. And afterwards he began

---

[12] corbus A ; corvus B1 B2 B3
[13] de volatus A B2 (with very slight space after *de*) ; devolatus B1 B3, followed by Reeves. In A, a small *u* has been added by m.h. above *a*, construing *devolutus* as a participle and *lapsus* as the genitive of a noun. The shortened version, derived from A, apparently read *devolutus* (L and Reeves's F ; but *de volatus* in C).
[14] cojugis A ; a small *n* has been written by m.h. above *o*. conjugis B1 B2 B3
[15] concidens A B1 B2 B3. In A, a circumflex accent has later been placed above *i*.

quasi suae paupertatis amisso non mediocri solacio,[1] re-
mendicare ut meretus [2] coepit. Quod videlicet penuriae
rerum solamen sepe superius in veru [3] memorato de-
pendebat ; quod pro pedicís [4] et retibus et omni
venationis et piscationis genere servatum posset sufficere,
beati viri donatum benedictione ; quodque amisum [5]
miser plebeus eo ditatus pro tempore ipse cum tota
familiola sero licet omnibus de cetero deplanxit reliquiis [6]
diebus vitae.

86a

De lactario utre quem salacia [7] abstulit
unda, | et venilia [8] iterum representavit
in priore loco [9]

ALIO IN TEMPORE beati legatus viri, Lugaidus nomine
cognomento Laitirus,[10] ad Scotiam jusus [11] navigare proponens, inter navalia navis sancti instrumenta utrem
lactarium quaesitum inveniens sub mari congestís super
eum non parvís lapidibus madefaciendum posuit.[12]
Veniensque ad sanctum quod de utre fecit intimavit.
Qui subridens inquit : ' Uter quem ut dicis sub undís
possuisti [13] hac vice ut estimo non té ad Everniam [14]

[1] solacio A B3 ; solatio B1 B2
[2] meretus A ; the second *e* has later been altered to *i*, with a down-
stroke of a fine pen. meritus B1 B2 B3
[3] in veru A B1 B3 ; invenru B2
[4] pro pedicís A ; a stress accent made with a fine pen has later been
placed above *e*. pro pe'dicis B1 ; pro peditis B2 ; propedicis B3
[5] amisum A ; small *s* written by m.h. above *is*. amissum B1 B2 B3
[6] reliquiis A ; the third *i* was later deleted by a dot below made with a
fine pen, and still later the second *i* was erased. re'liquis B1 ; reliquias B2,
with *a* deleted by a dot below ; reliquis B3
[7] salacia A ; salatia B1 B2 B3
[8] *venilia.* The use of these expressions (*salacia* and *venilia*) was described
by Augustine. See Reeves 1857, p. 156.
[9] The contents-list of B2 and of B3 reads : *De utre lactario quem unda
maris abduxit et reduxit ad terram.*
[10] laitirus A B2 B3 ; laiti'rus B1. This appears to be an early instance
of the modern *láidir* ' strong '. In 57a, the epithet, in Irish, is spelt *lathir*.

again to beg, as a deserving person, on the plea that a great alleviation of his poverty had been lost. But that alleviation, the relief of his want, was dependent upon the spike often mentioned above ; which if it had been preserved could have supplied the place of snares and nets, and every kind of hunting and fishing, since it was endowed with the blessing of the holy man ; but which, when lost, the wretched layman who had for a time been enriched by it bewailed thenceforward, although too late, himself with his whole family, during all the remaining days of his life.

[II 38] Concerning a milk-skin which the
ebb-tide carried away, and the flood-tide
brought back again in the same place

At another time, the blessed man's emissary, by name Lugaid, surnamed Laitir, planning to sail to Ireland as he was bidden, looked for and found among the sea-going equipment of the saint's ship a milk-skin, and placed it in the sea, to soften, heaping some fairly large stones upon it. And he went to the saint, and told him what he had done with the skin. The saint said with a smile : ' The skin that you say you have put under the water will not, I think, accompany you this time to Ireland '. ' Why ' said Lugaid, ' shall I

---

[11] jusus A ; a small *s* has been written by m.h. above the first *s*. missus B1 ; jussus B2 B3

[12] posu|it A, *uit* written in margin in the text hand ; posuit B1 B2 B3

[13] possuisti A ; the first *s* has later been deleted with points above and below. posuisti B1 B2 B3

[14] everniam A ; the first *e* was later altered to *i*, with a down-stroke of a fine pen, and a small *b* was written by m.h. above *v*. hiberniam B1 B3. Illegible in B2.

comitabitur '. ' Cur ' ait, ' non mecum in navi comitem
eum habere potero ? ' [1]   Sanctus :   ' Altera ' inquit,
' die quod res probabit scies '.

Itaque Lugaidus [2] mane postera die ad retrahendum
de mari utrem pergit ; quem tamen salacia [3] noctu
subtraxit [4] unda. Quo non reperto ad sanctum reversus
86b tristis flexís in terram [5] | genibus suam confessus est
neglegentiam.[6] Cui sanctus illum consulatus [7] ait :
' Noli frater pro fragilibus contristari rebus. Uter quem
salacia [8] sustulit unda ad suum locum post tuum
egresum [9] reportabit venilia '.

Eadem die, post Lugaidi de Iova insula emigrationem, hora transacta nona,[10] sanctus circumstantibus
síc profatus ait :   ' Nunc ex vobis unus ad [11] equor [12]
pergat. Utrem de quo Lugaidus [13] querebatur, et quem
salacia [14] sustulerat unda, nunc venilia retrahens in loco
unde subtractus est repraesentavit '. Quo sancti audito
verbo quidam alacer juvenis ad oram [15] cucurrit maris ;
repertumque utrem sicut praedixerat sanctus cursu
reversus concito [16] reportans valde gavisus coram sancto
87a cum omnium qui ibidem in|erant ammiratione ad-
signavit.

In hís ut sepe dictum est binís narrationibus superius
discriptís,[17] quamlibet in parvís rebus, sude videlicet et

---

[1] *potero*. After this, above a point in text hand, a question-mark has
been added by m.h. in A ; and there are question-marks in B1 B2 B3.
     [2] lugaidus A B2 B3 ; luga'idus B1   [3] salacia A B3 ; salatia B1 B2
     [4] subtraxit A B2 B3 ; subtra'xerat B1
     [5] in|terram A, added by the text hand, at the end of, and below, the
last line. Omitted in B1 B2 B3. The words are included in the shortened
version.
     [6] neglegentiam A ; -lige'n- B1 ; necligenciam B3. Illegible in B2.
     [7] consulatus A ; the first *u* has later been altered to *o* by bridging.
-sol- B1 B3. Illegible in B2.
     [8] salacia A B3 ; salatia B1 B2
     [9] egresum A ; a small *s* has been written by m.h. above *es*. -ss- B1
B2 B3

not be able to have it as my companion in the ship ? '
The saint said : ' Tomorrow you shall know what the
event will disclose '.

So Lugaid went early on the following day to recover
the skin from the sea.   But the ebb-tide had carried it
off in the night.   Not finding it, he returned sadly to
the saint.   He knelt upon the ground and confessed his
negligence.   The saint said to him reassuringly : ' Do
not grieve, brother, over things that perish.   The skin
that the ebbing tide has carried away, the flowing tide
will bring back to its place after you have gone '.

On the same day, after Lugaid's departure from the
island of Io, and when the hour of none was ended, the
saint spoke thus to those that stood about him, and said :
' Now one of you go to the sea : the skin that Lugaid
lamented, and that the ebb-tide had removed, the flood-
tide has now brought back and restored to the place
from which it had been taken away '.   Hearing these
words of the saint, one active lad ran to the sea-shore,
and raced back carrying the skin, which he had found
as the saint had foretold ; and he joyfully handed it
over in the presence of the saint, while all who were
there marvelled.

In these two stories told above, (although they concern small matters, namely a spike and a skin) prophecy,

---

[10] *nona*.   This episode suggests that there was a period of leisure after
dinner.   See p. 122.   [11] ad A B1 B3 ; ex B2
[12] *equor*.   In A, the *e* has been altered to the *ae* symbol by the addition
of a fine subscript closed loop.   See p. 174.
[13] lugaidus A B2 B3 ; luga'idus B1
[14] salacia A B3 ; salatia B1 B2
[15] oram A B1 B3 ; in A, a small *h* has been written (? by m.h.) above,
before *o*.   horam B2
[16] concito A B2 B3 ; in A, a stress accent was later added with a fine
pen above the first *o*.   co'ncito B1
[17] discriptís A ; des- B1 B2 B3

utre, profetia simul et virtutis miraculum comitari
cernuntur. Nunc ad alia tendamus.[1]

De Librano harundineti
profetatio sancti [2] viri. .

ALIO IN TEMPORE, cum vir sanctus in Iova conversaretur insula, homo quidam plebeus nuper sumpto
clericatus habitu de Scotia transnavigans ad insulanum
beati monasterium viri devenit. Quem cum alia die
sanctus in hospitio resedem [3] hospitantem invenisset
solum, primum de patria de gente et causa iteneris [4] a
sancto interrogatus, de Connachtarum [5] regione oriun-
dum sé professus est, et ad delenda in perigrinatione [6]
87b peccamina longo fatigatum | itenere.[7] Cui cum sanctus,
ut de suae penitudinis exploraret qualitate, dura et
laboriosa ante oculos monasterialia [8] propossuisset [9]
imperia, ipse consequenter ad sanctum respondens
inquit : ' Paratus sum ad omnia quaecumque mihi
jubere volueris, quamlibet durissima quamlibet indigna'.

Quid plura ? Eadem [10] hora omnia sua confessus
peccata leges penitentiae flexís in terram genibus se
impleturum promisit.[11] Cui sanctus : ' Surge ' ait, ' et
resede '.[12] Tum deinde resedentem [13] síc conpellat :

---

[1] nunc ad alia tendamus A B1 B2. Omitted in B3.

[2] profetatio sancti A ; propheta'tio sancti B1 ;]sancti B2 ; prophetacio
sancti B3 ; sancti prophetatio contents-list of B2 and of B3 (-acio B3)

[3] resedem A ; the second e has later been altered to i, with a down-
stroke of a fine pen. residere B1 ; residens B2 ; residenti B3

[4] iteneris A ; -tin- B1 B2 B3

[5] connachtarum, A ; conactarum B1 B3 ;]starum B2

[6] perigrinatione A ; the first i altered by m.h. to e. -reg- B1 B2 B3

[7] itenere A ; the first e altered to i, with a down-stroke of a fine pen.
itinere B1 B2 B3

[8] monasterialia A B2 B3 ; monasteriola B1

[9] propossuisset A ; the first s has later been deleted with dots above
and below. -osu- B1 B2 B3

and at the same time a miracle of power, as often re-
marked, are seen to go together.   Now let us turn to
other things.

[II 39] Prophecy of the holy man
concerning Libran of the reed-plot

At another time when the holy man lived in the
island of Io, a certain layman who had recently put on
clerical dress sailed across from Ireland, and came to
the island monastery of the blessed man.   Next day
the saint found him sitting alone as a guest in the hospice.
The saint first asked him about his country, his family,
and the cause of his journey ;   and he declared that he
was a native of the district of the Connachta, and that
he had made the long laborious journey on purpose to
expiate his sins in pilgrimage.

When, in order to make trial of the nature of his
penitence, the saint had exposed to his view the hard
and heavy discipline of monastic life, he then said to
the saint in reply :   ' I am ready for any commands
that you may wish to impose upon me, though they be
very hard, though they be humiliating '.

To be brief, in that hour he confessed all his sins ;
and promised, kneeling on the ground, that he would
perform all that the laws of penance required.   The
saint said to him :   ' Rise, and sit ' ;   and when he was
seated, then addressed him thus :   ' You are required

---

¹⁰ eadem A ; a circumflex accent has later been written with a fine pen
above *a*.   Ea'dem B1 B2 ;   Eadem B3
¹¹ promisit A B2 B3 ;   promi'sit B1.   In A, the Irish sign for *pro* has later
been altered to the continental symbol (m.h.).   Cf. 91b20.
¹² resede A ;   the second *e* has later been altered to *i*, with a down-stroke
of a fine pen.   -sid- B1 B2 B3
¹³ resedentem A ;   altered as above.   -sid- B1 B2 B3

'Septennem debebis in Ethica[1] penitentiam explere terra. Ego et tu usque quo numerum expleas septinalium[2] annorum deo donante victuri sumus'.

Quibus sancti confortatus dictís grates deo agens ad sanctum : 'Quid me' ait, 'agere oportet de quodam meo falso juramento?[3] Nam ego quendam in patria 88a commanens trucidavi homuncionem.[4] | Post cujus trucidationem quasi reus in vinculís retentus sum. Sed mihi quidam cognitionalis homo ejusdem parentellae[5] valde opibus opulentus subveniens me oportune et de vinculís vinculatum absolvit, et de morte reum eripuit. Cui post absolutionem cum firma juratione promiseram me eidem omnibus meae diebus vitae[6] serviturum. Sed post aliquot dies in servitute peractos, servire homini dedignatus et deo potius obsecundare mallens, desertor illius carnalis domini juramentum infringens decessi[7] ; et ad te domino meum prosperante iter perveni'.

Ad haec sanctus virum[8] pro talibus valde angi videns sicuti prius profetans profatur, inquiens : 'Post septenorum sicut tibi dictum est expletionem annorum, diebus ad me huc quadragensimalibus[9] venies, ut in pascali 88b sollemnitate ad altarium accedas, | et eucharistiam sumas'.

Quid verbís immoramur? Sancti viri imperiis per omnia penitens obsequitur perigrinus[10] ; hisdemque[11]

---

[1] ethica A B2 B3 ; e'thica B1

[2] septinalium A ; the first *i* has been altered by m.h. to *e*. septenna'lium B1 ; septennalium B2 B3

[3] *quodam meo falso juramento.* This question, and the explanation that follows it, should not have been put into direct speech ; since according to Adomnan's previous statement the penitent had confessed *omnia sua peccata* before Columba imposed upon him the seven-years' penance for manslaughter.

[4] homuncionem A B3 ; homunitionem B1 ; homuntionem B2

[5] parentellae A ; the first *l* has later been deleted with dots above and below made with a fine pen. -tele B1 B2 B3. Here, 'the same kindred' probably means the dead man's kindred.

to complete a penance of seven years, in the land of
Eth [Tiree]. We shall live, I and you, God granting it,
until you complete the number of seven years '.

Encouraged by these words of the saint, he rendered
thanks to God, and said to the saint : ' What must I
do with regard to a false oath that I gave ? For while
I lived in my native land I killed a man. After he was
killed, I was held in chains, as one condemned. But a
very wealthy relative, of the same kindred, coming to
my assistance, opportunely released me, a prisoner, from
chains, and rescued me, a condemned man, from death.
After my release I promised to him with a binding oath
that I would serve him during all the days of my life.
But after some days passed in servitude, disdaining to
be a servant of man, and choosing rather to obey God,
I broke my oath, and departed, deserting that earthly
master. And with the Lord's favour on my journey, I
have come to you '.

Seeing that the man was greatly distressed about
these things, the saint, as before, spoke prophetically in
reply, saying : ' After the completion of the seven years
of which you have been told, you will come to me here,
throughout the days of Lent, so that in the celebration
of Easter you may approach the altar, and receive the
Eucharist '.

Why linger over words ? The pilgrim penitent
obeyed the orders of the holy man in everything. He

---

[6] meae diebus vitae A ; mee diebus vite B1 B2 (mëe B2) ; diebus vite
mee B3
[7] decessi A B2 B3 ; dicessi B1
[8] virum A B1 ; mirum B3. Illegible in B2.
[9] quadragensimalibus A ; -gesi- B1 B2 B3
[10] perigrinus A ; pereg- B1 B2 B3
[11] hisdemque A ; Hisdem B1 B2 B3

diebus ad monasterium campi misus [1] Lunge [2] ibidem
plene expletís in penitentia septem annís ad sanctum
diebus quadragensimae [3] juxta ejus priorem profeticam
jusionem [4] revertitur. Et post peractam pascae sollempnitatem [5] in qua jusus [6] ad altare accessit, ad sanctum de
supra interrogans memorato venit juramento. Cui
sanctus interroganti talia vaticinans responsa profatur :
' Tuus de quo mihi aliquando dixeras carnalis superest
dominus ; paterque et mater et fratres adhuc vivunt.
Nunc ergo praeparare té debes ad navigationem '. Et
inter haec verba macheram beluinís ornatam dolatís
89a protulit dentibus,[7] dicens : ' Hoc accipe | tecum por-
tandum munus quod domino pro tua redemptione
offeres ; sed tamen nullo modo accipiet. Habet enim
bene moratam cojugem,[8] cujus salubri obtemperans
consilio té eadem [9] die gratis sine pretio libertate [10]
donabit, cingulum ex more captivi de tuís resolvens
lumbís. Sed hac ancxietate solutus aliam e latere
surgentem non effugies sollicitudinem. Nam tui fratres
undique coartabunt[11] té, ut tanto tempore patri debetam[12]
sed neglectam redintigres [13] pietatem. Tu tamen sine
ulla esitatione voluntati eorum obsecundans patrem [14]
senem pie excipias confovendum. Quod onus quamlibet

[1] misus A ; a small *s* has been written by m.h. above *is*. missus B1
B2 B3
[2] lunge A B1 B2 ; longe B3
[3] quadragensimae A ; the *n* has later been partly erased (not by text
hand). -gesime B1 B2 B3
[4] jusionem A ; a small *s* has been written by m.h. above *us*. jussi-
B1 B2 B3
[5] sollempnitatem A ; solempni- B1 ; sollemni- B2 ; solenni- B3
[6] jusus A ; a small *s* has been written by m.h. above *us*. jussus B1 B2 B3
[7] *beluinís dentibus*. Literally ' teeth of a great [sea]-animal '. Walrus
ivory was used for decorated hilts of Irish swords ; see Solinus XXII,
quoted in Fowler 1894, p. 110 ; and above, p. 21.
[8] cojugem A ; a small *n* has been written by m.h. above *oj*. conjugem
B1 B2 B3 (co'n- B1)

was sent within those days to the monastery of the plain
of Long ; and completed there seven full years of
penance. In accordance with the saint's former prophetic command, he returned to him for the days of
Lent ; and after the celebration of Easter had been
completed, in which as he was bidden he had approached
the altar, he went to the saint, and questioned him about
the above-mentioned oath. To his question the saint
prophesying made this reply : ' Your earthly lord, of
whom you once told me, is alive ; and your father, and
mother, and brothers, still live. Now therefore you
must prepare yourself for a voyage '. With these words
he held out a sword decorated with shaped pieces of
ivory, saying : ' Take this, to carry with you as a gift
that you will offer to your lord for your redemption ;
but yet he will by no means accept it. For he has a
virtuous wife, and yielding to her sound advice he will
on that day grant you liberty, freely and without
recompense, unloosing according to custom the captive's
belt from your loins. But when your mind has been
relieved from this anxiety, you will not escape another
responsibility arising at your side ; for your brothers
will together constrain you to make good the filial
service that you have for so long owed to your father,
and have neglected. But obey their will without
hesitation, and receive your aged father into your dutiful
care. And although that charge may seem to you

---

⁹ eadem A B2 B3 ; in A, a circumflex accent has later been added with
a fine pen above *a*. ea′dem B1
¹⁰ libertate A B3 ; -tatem B1, with *m* erased ; -tati B2
¹¹ coartabunt A B1 B2 ; -bant B3
¹² debetam A ; the second *e* has later been partly erased. -bit- B1 B2 B3
¹³ redintigres A ; the second *i* has been altered by m.h. to *e*. -teg-
B1 B2 B3
¹⁴ patrem A B1 ; patrem tuum B3. Illegible in B2.

2F

tibi videatur grave contristari non debes, quia mox
depones. Nam ex qua die incipies patri ministrare alia [1]

89b in fine ejusdem septimane mortuum sepelies. | Sed post
patris sepultionem iterum fratres té acriter conpellent,
ut matri etiam debita pietatis inpendas obsequia. De
qua profecto conpulsione tuus junior té absolvet frater
qui tua vice paratus omne pietatis opus quod debes pro
té matri serviens reddet '.

Post haec verba supra memoratus frater, Libranus
nomine, accepto munere sancti ditatus benedictione
perrexit ; et ad patriam perveniens omnia secundum
sancti vaticinium invenit vere probata. Nam statim ut
pretium suae offerens libertatis ostendit domino accipere
volenti, refragans uxor : ' Ut quid nobís ' ait, ' hoc
accipere quod sanctus pretium misit Columba ? Hoc
non sumus digni. Liberetur ei pius hic gratis ministrator. Magis nobis sancti viri benedictio proficiet quam
hoc quod offertur pretium '. Audiens itaque maritus |

90a hoc maritae salubre consilium continuo gratis liberavit
servum.

Qui post [2] juxta profetiam sancti conpulsus a fratribus patrem cui ministrare coepit septima die mortuum
sepelivit. Quo sepulto ut et matri debete [3] deserviret
conpellitur. Sed subveniente juniore fratre sicuti sanctus
praedixerat vicem ejus adinplente absolvitur ; qui [4] ad
fratres síc dicebat : ' Nullo modo nos oportet [5] fratrem in

---

[1] *alia.* Below, 90a, the interval is six days.

[2] post A B2 B3 ; postea B1

[3] debete A ; the second *e* has later been altered to *i*, with a down-stroke
of a fine pen, and the third *e* has been altered erroneously to the *ae* symbol,
by a fine loop (cf. 86b14), perhaps of the eighth century (see p. 175). debite
B1 B2 B3

[4] qui A ; Qui B1 B2 ; Sed junior qui B3

[5] *oportet.* In B1 B2 B3, this word is placed after *retentare.*

burdensome, you need not be disheartened, since you will lay it down soon. For on one day you will begin to wait upon your father, and on another at the end of the same week he will have died, and you will bury him. After your father's burial, your brothers will again urge you sharply to pay also the services of filial duty that are owed to your mother. But from that obligation your younger brother will in fact release you, for he will be ready to render in your place all the labour of filial duty that you owe, serving your mother on your behalf'.

After these words, the aforesaid brother, namely Libran, went away, taking the gift and enriched with the saint's blessing. And arriving in his native land, he found everything confirmed as the saint had prophesied. As soon as he showed the price of his liberty, offering it to his master, who was willing to receive it, the master's wife refused, saying : ' How can we take this price that Saint Columba has sent ? We are not worthy of this. Let this pious servant be released for him without payment. The holy man's blessing will profit us more than this price that is offered '. When the husband heard this salutary counsel of his wife, he immediately released his slave without payment.

Then Libran, in accordance with the prophecy of the saint, was compelled by his brothers and began to serve his father ; and on the seventh day, his father being dead, he buried him. After his father was buried, Libran was compelled duly to devote himself to his mother also ; but he was released, because his younger brother came to his assistance, as the saint had foretold, and took his place, speaking to the brothers thus : ' We ought by no means to detain our brother in this

patria retentare qui per vii.[1] annos apud sanctum
Columbam in Brittannia salutem exercuit animae '.

Postque ab omnibus quibus molestabatur absolutus
matri et fratribus valedicens, liber reversus, ad locum qui
scotice vocitatur Daire-Calcig [2] pervenit ; ibidemque
navem [3] sub velo a portu emigrantem inveniens clamitans de litore rogitat ut ipsum nautae cum eís susciperent
90b navigaturum | ad [4] Britanniam.[5] Sed ipsi non sus-
cipientes refutaverunt eum quia non erant de monacís [6]
sancti Columbae. Tum deinde ad eundem venerabilem
loquens virum (quamlibet longe absentem tamen spiritu
presentem, ut mox res probavit) : ' Placetne tibi ' ait,
' sancte Columba, ut hí nautae qui me tuum non
suscipiunt socium plenís velís et secundís enavigent
ventís ? ' In hac voce ventus qui ante illís erat secundus
dicto citius versus est contrarius. Inter haec videntes
virum eundem e regione secus flumen [7] cursitantem
subito inter sé inito [8] consilio ad ipsum de navi inclami-
tantes dicunt nautici : ' Fortassis idcirco citius in
contrarium nobís conversus est ventus, quia [9] té suscipere
rennuerimus. Quod si etiam nunc té ad nos in navem [10]
91a invitaverimus, con|trarios nunc nobís flatus in secundos
convertere poteris '. Hís auditís viator ad eos dixit :
' Sanctus Columba ad quem vado, et cui hucusque per
vii.[11] annos obsecundavi, si me susciperitis [12] prosperum

---

[1] vii A ; septem B1 B2 B3
[2] daire calcig A ; daire' calgai'ch B1 ; daire calgaich B2 B3
[3] navem A ; the e has later been altered to i, with a down-stroke of a
fine pen. navim B1 B2 B3
[4] ad A B1 B2 ; in B3
[5] britanniam A ; britt- B1 B2 B3
[6] monacís A ; a small h has been written by m.h. above ci. mo'nachis
B1 ; monachis B2 B3
[7] flumen. The Foyle, between Derry and Lough Foyle.
[8] inito. In A, a stress accent has later been added with a fine pen
above the first i.

country, considering that he has for seven years, in Britain with Saint Columba, laboured for the salvation of his soul '.

After that, relieved from all his troubles, he bade farewell to his mother, and his brothers, and returned a free man, coming to the place that is called in Irish *Daire-Calcig* [Derry]. There he found a ship under sail, setting out from the harbour, and called from the shore, begging the sailors to take him with them, as a voyager to Britain. But they repelled him, and would not receive him, because they were not of the monks of Saint Columba. Thereupon he spoke to that venerable man, (who although far distant was yet present in spirit, as the event soon showed) and said : ' Does it please you, holy Columba, that these sailors who will not receive me, your associate, are sailing away with full sails and with favourable winds ? ' As he said this, the wind that had before been in their favour was changed, more quickly than speech, to a contrary wind. Meanwhile, the sailors saw that the same man was running alongside of them, by the river ; and suddenly taking counsel together they shouted to him from the ship, saying : ' Perhaps the wind has turned so suddenly against us because we refused to take you with us. And if now we do invite you to join us in the ship, you will be able to change winds that are now against us into winds that are favourable '. Hearing this, the traveller said to them : ' Saint Columba, to whom I am going, and whom I have obeyed for the last seven years, will,

---

⁹ quia A ; quod B1 B2 B3

¹⁰ navem A ; the *e* has later been altered to *i*, with a down-stroke of a fine pen. navim B1 B2 B3   ¹¹ vii A ; septem B1 B2 B3

¹² susciperitis A ; the first *i* has been altered by m.h. to *e*. -cep- B1 B2 B3

vobís ventum a domino suo virtute orationum inpetrare poterit'. Quibus auditís navem[1] terrae approximant ipsumque ad eos in eam invitant.[2] Qui statim rate ascensa : ' In nomine omnipotentis '[3] ait, ' cui sanctus Columba inculpabiliter servit, tensís rudentibus[4] levate velum '. Quo facto, continuo contraria venti flamina in secunda vertuntur, prosperaque usque ad Britanniam[5] plenís successit navigatio velís.

Libranusque postquam ad loca perventum est brittannica illam deserens navem[6] et nautís benedicens ad sanctum devenit Columbam in Iova commorantem insula. Qui videlicet vir beatus gaudenter suscipiens |

91b eum omnia quae de eo[7] in itenere[8] acta sunt nullo alio intimante plene narravit : et de domino, et uxoris ejus salubri consilio, quomodo ejusdem suassu[9] liberatus est ; de fratribus quoque ; de morte[10] patris et ejus finita septimana sepultione ; de matre, et de fratris oportuna junioris subventione ; de hís quae in regresu[11] acta sunt ; de vento contrario et secundo ; de verbís nautarum qui primo eum suscipere recusarunt ; de promisione prosperi flatus, et de prospera eo suscepto in navi venti conversione. Quid plura, omnia quae sanctus adinplenda profetavit[12] expleta enarravit. Post haec

[1] navem A ; the e has later been altered to i, with a down-stroke of a fine pen. navim B1 B2 B3

[2] invitant A B1 B3 ; in A, a circumflex accent has later been written with a fine pen above the second i. -vi't- B1

[3] nomine omnipotentis A B3 ; nomine omnipotentis dei B1 ; omnipotentis nomine B2

[4] tensís rudentibus. Cf. the apparently synonymous protensís rudentibu s in 101a, and see p. 117.

[5] britanniam A ; britt- B1 B2 B3

[6] navem A ; a small i written by m.h. above e. navim B1 B2 B3

[7] eo. After this, in the extreme top margin of A, m.h. has written mem.

[8] itenere A ; a small i has been written by m.h. above the first e. -ti'n- B1 ; -tin- B2 B3

[9] suassu A ; the second s has later been deleted with dots above and below made with a fine pen. suasu B1 B2 B3

if you take me with you, be able to obtain from his Lord by the power of prayer a wind that will favour you'. When they heard this, they brought the ship to the land, and invited him to join them in it. Immediately on entering the ship, he said : ' In the name of the Almighty whom Saint Columba blamelessly serves, hoist the sail, making taut the ropes '. They did this, and the contrary winds were at once changed to favourable ones, and a prosperous voyage to Britain followed, with full sails.

After their arrival in British land, Libran left that ship, and blessing the sailors made his way to Saint Columba, who was living in the island of Io. The blessed man received him joyfully, and related in full, without being told by any one, all that had happened to Libran on his journey : of the lord, and his wife's salutary counsel ; how Libran had been set free, by her persuasion ; also of his brothers ; of his father's death, and burial after the end of seven days ; of his mother, and of the timely help of his younger brother ; of the things that happened on his way back ; of the wind, contrary and favourable ; of the words of the sailors who at first refused to receive him ; of the promise of prosperous winds, and the favourable change of wind after he had been received in the ship. To be brief, all that the saint had prophesied would happen, he repeated as having been fulfilled. After this narra-

---

[10] de morte A B2 B3 ; ac de morte B1
[11] in regresu A ; in regressu B1 B2 ; ingressu B3
[12] profetavit A ; proph- B1 B2 B3. In A, the Irish symbol for *pro* has been altered to the continental symbol, by m.h.; cf. 87b14.

verba viator pretium suae quod a sancto accipit[1]
redemptionis adsignavit. Cui sanctus eadem[2] hora
vocabulum indidit, inquiens : ' Tu Libranus vocaberis,
eo quod sis liber '.

Qui videlicet Librán[3] hísdem in diebus votum mona-
92a cicum[4] devotus vovit. Et cum a sancto viro | ad mona-
sterium in quo prius vii.[5] annís penitens domino serviit[6]
remitteretur, haec ab eo profetica de se prolata accipit[7]
verba valedicente : ' Vita vives longa, et in bona
senectute vitam terminabis praesentem. At tamen non
in Brittannia sed in Scotia resurges '. Quod verbum
audiens flexís genibus amare flevit. Quem sanctus valde
mestum videns consulari[8] coepit, dicens : ' Surge et
noles tristificari. In uno meorum morieris[9] monasteriorum, et cum electís erit pars tua meís in regno
monacís,[10] cum quibus in resurrectionem vitae de somno
mortis evigelabis '.[11] Qu[a][12] a sancto accepta non
mediocri consulatione[13] valde laetatus et sancti benedictione ditatus in pace perrexit.

Quae sancti de eodem viro verax postea est adinpleta
profetatio. Nam cum per multos annales cyclos in
monasterio campi Lunge post sancti Columbae de mundo
92b transitum oboedienter domino | deserviret monacus,[14]
pro quadam monasteriali utilitate ad Scotiam misus[15]

---

[1] accipit A ; -cep- B1 B2 B3
[2] eadem A B2 B3 ; in A, a circumflex accent has later been written
with a fine pen above *a*. e'adem B1
[3] librán A ; libranus B1 B2 B3
[4] monacicum A ; a small *h* has been added by m.h. above *ci*. -chi-
B1 B2 B3
[5] vii. A ; septem B1 B2 B3
[6] serviit A ; servivit B1 B2 B3
[7] accipit A ; -cep- B1 B2 B3
[8] consulari A ; the *u* later altered to *o* by bridging. -sol-B1 B2 B3
[9] morieris A B2 B3 ; in A, a circumflex accent has later been written
with a fine pen above *e*. morie'ris B1
[10] monacís A ; a small *h* written by m.h. above *ci*. -chis B1 B2 B3

tion, the traveller handed over the price of his ransom, which he had received from the saint. In the same hour the saint gave him a name, saying : ' You shall be called Libran, because you are free. '

In those same days this Libran devoutly vowed the monastic vow. And when he was sent back by the holy man to the monastery in which he had formerly served the Lord as a penitent for seven years, he received these prophetic words concerning him, spoken by Columba in farewell : ' You will live for a long life-time, and end this present life in good old age. Nevertheless your resurrection will be not in Britain, but in Ireland '. Hearing these words, Libran bowed his knees and wept bitterly. Seeing that he was very sad, the saint began to comfort him, saying : ' Rise, and do not be grieved. You will die in one of my monasteries ; and your part in the Kingdom will be with my elect monks, and with them you will awake from the sleep of death into the resurrection of life '. Much cheered by the great comfort that he had received from the saint, and enriched with the saint's benediction, he went away in peace.

This truthful prophecy of the saint concerning that man was afterwards fulfilled. For when he had served the Lord obediently as a monk in the monastery of the plain of Long for many years after the passing of Saint Columba from the world, he was sent, a very old man, to Ireland, on some monastic business ; and as soon as

---

[11] evigelabis A ; the second e has later been altered to i, with a downstroke of a fine pen. -gil- B1 B2 B3

[12] qui A, altered by erasure from *quia* ; Qua B1 B2 B3

[13] consulatione A ; the u later altered to o by bridging. -sol- B1 B2 B3

[14] monacus A ; a small h has been written by m.h. above cu. -chis B1 B3 ; -chus B2

[15] misus A ; a small s written by m.h. above is. missus B1 B2 B3

valde senex, statim ut de navi discendit [1] pergens per
campum Breg ad monasterium devenit roborei [2] campi.
Ibidemque hospes receptus hospitio quadam molestatus
infirmitate septima egrotationis die [3] in pace ad dominum perrexit ; et inter sancti Columbae electos humatus
est monacos,[4] secundum ejus vaticinium in vitam
resurrecturus aeternam.

Has de Librano harundineti sancti veridicas Columbae vaticinationes scripsise sufficiat. Qui videlicet
Libranus ideo harundineti est vocitatus [5] quia in harun-
dineto multís annís harundines collegendo [6] laboraverat. .

De quadam muliercula magnas et valde [7]
dificiliores parturitionis ut Evae filia
tortiones passa [8] |

93a   QUADAM DIE SANCTUS in Iova commanens insula cito
a lectione surgit et subridens dicit : ' Nunc ad oratorium
mihi properandum, ut pro quadam misellula deum
deprecer [9] femina, quae nunc in Evernia [10] nomen hujus
inclamitans commemorat Columbae, in magnís parturitionis dificillimae torta punitionibus. Et ideo per
me a domino de angustia absolutionem dari sibi sperat,
quia et mihi est cognitionalis de meae matris parentella [11]
genitorem habens progenitum '. Haec dicens sanctus
illius mulierculae motus miseratione ad eclesiam currit,
flexísque genibus pro ea Christum de homine natum

---

[1] discendit A ; the first *i* has been altered by m.h. to *e*. des- B1 B2 B3
[2] devenit roborei A ; roboreti deve'nit B1 ; roborei devenit B2 B3
[3] *septima die.* I.e. after six days.
[4] monacos A ; a small *h* has been written by m.h. above *co*. -chos
B1 B2 B3
[5] vocitatus A B1 ; vocatus B2 B3
[6] collegendo A ; a small *i* has been written by m.h. above the first *e*.
colligendo B1 B3 ; colli[B2

he landed from the ship he went through the plain of
Brega, and came to the monastery of the oak plain
[Durrow]. There, hospitably received as a guest, he
fell ill of a malady ; and on the seventh day of his
illness he went to the Lord in peace. And he was
buried among the elect monks of Saint Columba,
according to his prophecy, to rise again into eternal life.

Let it suffice to have written these true prophecies
of Saint Columba concerning Libran of the reed-plot.
This Libran is called ' of the reed-plot ', because for
many years he worked in a reed-plot, gathering reeds.

[II 40] Of a certain young woman who was suffering, as a daughter of Eve, great and very hard pangs of childbirth

One day, while the saint was in the island of Io, he
rose quickly from reading, and said with a smile : ' Now
I must go in haste to the oratory, to plead with God for
a certain woman in distress, who now in Ireland cries
out, calling the name of this Columba, while racked by
the pangs of a very difficult birth ; and hopes that relief
from her distress may be granted to her by the Lord
through me, for the reason that she is related to me,
and has a father born of my mother's kindred '. Saying
this, the saint, moved by pity for that young woman,
ran to the church, and bending his knees prayed for

---

[7] valde A B1 B2. Omitted in B3.

[8] *parturitionis* to *passa*. Instead of these words, the contents-list of B2
and of B3 reads : *parturitiones* (-*ici*- B3) *tortiones passa et sanata.*

[9] deprecer A B2 B3 ; in A, a stress accent has later been written with
a fine pen above the first *e.* de'precer B1

[10] evernia A ; hibernia B1 B3 ; ybernia B2

[11] parentella A ; the second *l* has later been partly erased. -e'la B1 ;
-ela, B2 B3

exorat.[1] Et post precationem oratorium egresus [2] ad fratres profatur occurrentes, inquiens : ' Nunc propitius dominus Jesus de muliere progenitus oportune miserae subveniens eam de angustiis liberavit ; et prospere |
93b prolem peperiit,[3] nec hac morietur vice '. Eadem [4] hora, sicuti sanctus profetizavit, misella femina nomen ejus invocans absoluta salutem recuperavit. Ita ab aliquibus postea de Scotia et de eadem regione ubi mulier inhabitabat transmeantibus intimatum est.

De quodam Lugneo [5] guberneta,[6] cognomento Tudicla,[7] quem sua cojux [8] odio habuerat valde deformem, qui in Rechrea [9] commorabatur insula. .[10]

ALIO IN TEMPORE cum vir sanctus in Rechrea [11] hospitaretur [12] insula quidam plebeus ad eum veniens de sua querebatur uxore, quae ut ipse dicebat odio habens eum ad maritalem [13] nullo modo ammitebat concubitum accedere. Quibus auditís sanctus maritam advocans in quantum potuit eam hac de causa corripere coepit, inquiens : ' Quare mulier tuam a te carnem abdicare conaris ; domino dicente, " Erunt duo in carne una " ? [14]

___

[1] exorat A B3 ; in A, a circumflex accent has later been written with a fine pen above *a*. exo′rat B1 ; e′xorat B2

[2] egresus A ; a small *s* has been written by m.h. above *su*. -essus B1 B2 B3

[3] peperiit A ; pe′perit B1 ; pe[ ]rit B2 ; peperit B3

[4] Eadem A B2 B3 ; in A, a circumflex accent has later been written with a fine pen above *a*. Ea′dem B1 [5] lugneo A B2 B3 ; lugne′o B1

[6] guberneta A ; gubernatore B1 B3. Illegible in B2. The word *guberneta* is a latinized form of the Greek *kybernētēs* ' steersman ' or ' pilot '.

[7] tudicla A ; tutlida B1 (or possibly *tutlicla*) ; tudica (?) B2 ; tutida B3. Reeves, and Thesaurus 1903 p. 279, read in A, falsely, *Tudida* (cf. p. 166). The Latin word *tudicula*, a diminutive formation from *tudes* ' hammer ', was used by Columella for an olive-crusher. With the form and gender of Adomnan's *tudicla*, compare his *genucla*, 48a, for *genucula*, from *genu*.

her to Christ, the son of man. After praying he left
the oratory, and spoke to brothers who met him, and
said : ' Now the Lord Jesus, born of woman, shows
favour, and giving timely help to the sufferer has
released her from her distress. And she has safely borne
a child, and will not die at this time '.

In the same hour, exactly as the saint had prophesied, the poor woman who called upon his name
was relieved, and was restored to health. It was so
reported afterwards by some people who crossed the
sea from Ireland, from the same district in which the
woman lived.

[II 41] Concerning a certain Lugne, a pilot, surnamed Tudicla, who lived in the island of Rechru, and whom his wife held in aversion because he was very ugly

At another time, when the holy man was a guest
in the island of Rechru [Rathlin], a certain layman
came to him and complained regarding his wife, who,
as he said, had an aversion to him, and would not allow
him to enter into marital relations. Hearing this, the
saint bade the wife approach, and began to chide her
as well as he could on that account, saying : ' Why,
woman, do you attempt to put from you your own
flesh ? The Lord says, ' 'Two shall be in one flesh ''.

---

⁸ cojux A ; conjux B1 ; conjunx B3. Illegible in B2.
⁹ rechrea A B2 B3 ; re'chrea B1. See p. 153.
¹⁰ The contents-list of B2 and of B3 reads: *De conjuge lugnei odiosi gubernatoris.*
¹¹ rechrea A B2 B3 ; re'chrea B1
¹² *hospitaretur.* The monastery in Rathlin was not founded until 635×. See p. 91.
¹³ odio habens eum ad maritalem A B1 B2. Omitted in B3.
¹⁴ *una.* Vulgate, Matt. xix. 5 ; Mark x. 8

94a Itaque | caro tui cojugis [1] tua caro est'. Quae respondens [2] : 'Omnia' inquit, 'quaecumque mihi praeciperis [3] sum parata quamlibet sint valde laboriosa adinplere,[4] excepto uno, ut me nullo conpellas modo in uno lecto dormire cum Lugneo.[5] Omnem domus curam exercere non recusso,[6] aut si jubeas etiam maria transire, et in aliquo[7] puellarum monasterio permanere'. Sanctus tum ait : 'Non potest recte fieri quod dicis. Nam adhuc viro vivente, alligata es a lege viri.[8] Quod enim deus licite conjunxit nefas est separari'. Et hís dictís consequenter intulit : 'Hac in die tres, hoc est ego et maritus cum cojuge,[9] jejunantes dominum precemur'. Illa dehinc : 'Scio' ait, 'quia tibi inpossibile non erit, ut ea quae vel dificilia vel etiam inpossibilia videntur a deo inpetrata donentur'.

Quid plura, marita eadem die cum sancto jejunare consentit, et maritus similiter. Nocteque subsequente
94b sanctus in | somnís [10] pro eís deprecatus est. Posteraque die sanctus maritam praesente [11] síc conpellat marito : 'Ó femina, si ut hesterna dicebas die parata hodie es ad feminarum emigrare monasteriolum?' Illa : 'Nunc' inquit, 'cognovi quia tua a deo de me est audita oratio. Nam quem heri oderam hodie amo. Cór [12] enim meum

¹ cojugis A ; co'nj- B1 ; conj- B2 B3
² respondens A ; respondit B1 B2 B3
³ praeciperis A ; the first *i* has been altered by m.h. to *e*. -ce'p- B1 ; -cep- B2 B3
⁴ adinplere A ; the *n* has later been altered clumsily to *m* not by the text hand. adimp- B1 B2 B3
⁵ lugneo A B2 B3 ; lugne'o B1
⁶ recusso A ; the first *s* has later been deleted with points above and below made by a fine pen. recu'so B1 ; recuso B2 B3
⁷ *aliquo*. In A, the small final *o* has been formed (? by the text hand) out of a partly-erased *a*.
⁸ *lege viri*. This differs somewhat from the sentence of Paul's Epistle to the Romans (vii. 2) upon which it is based : see the Vulgate version and the Greek New Testament.
⁹ cojuge A ; co'nj- B1 conj- B2 B3

Therefore the flesh of your husband is your flesh '. She replied : ' I am ready to perform all things whatsoever that you may enjoin on me, however burdensome : save one thing, that you do not constrain me to sleep in one bed with Lugne. I do not refuse to carry on the whole management of the house ; or, if you command it, even to cross the seas, and remain in some monastery of nuns '. Then the saint said : ' What you suggest cannot rightly be done. Since your husband is still alive, you are bound by the law of the husband ; for it is forbidden that that should be separated, which God has lawfully joined '. After saying this, he continued : ' On this day let us three, myself, and the husband with his wife, pray to the Lord, fasting '. Then she said : ' I know it will not be impossible that things appearing difficult or even impossible may be granted by God to you, when you ask for them '.

In short, the wife agreed to fast on the same day, and the husband also, with the saint. And on the night following, in sleep, the saint prayed for them. On the next day the saint thus addressed the wife, in the presence of her husband : ' Woman, are you today, as you said yesterday, ready to depart to a monastery of nuns ? ' She said : ' I know now that your prayer concerning me has been heard by God. For him whom I loathed yesterday I love today. In this past night,

---

10 in | somnís A ; in sompnis B1 B3. Missing in B2. Reeves's reading *insomnis* (' awake ') is not in the texts, but may have been Adomnan's meaning.

11 praesente A ; presentem B1 ; presen[B2 ; presente B3

12 Cór A ; Cor B1 B2 B3. See p. 163.

hac nocte praeterita quomodo ignoro in me [1] inmotatum [2] est de odio in amorem '.

Quid moramur ? Ab eadem [3] die usque ad diem
obitus anima ejusdem maritae indesociabiliter [4] in amore
conglutinata est mariti, ut illa maritalis concubitus
debita quae prius reddere rennuebat nullo modo
deinceps recussaret. .

De navigatione Cormaci [5] nepotis
Lethani [6] profetatio beati viri [7]

ALIO IN TEMPORE Cormacus,[8] Christi miles, de quo
in primo hujus opusculi libello breviter aliqua com-
95a memoravimus pauca,[9] etiam | secunda vice conatus est
herimum [10] in ociano [11] quaerere. Qui postquam a terrís
per infinitum ocianum [12] plenís enavigavit velís, hisdem
diebus sanctus Columba, cum ultra dorsum moraretur
Brittanniae, Brudeo [13] regi [14] praesente Orcadum [15] regulo
commendavit, dicens : ' Aliqui ex nostrís nuper emigra-
verunt, desertum in pilago [16] intransmeabili invenire
obtantes. Qui si forte post longos circuitus Orcadas [17]
devenerint insulas, huic regulo cujus obsedes [18] in manu
tua sunt deligenter [19] commenda, ne aliquid adversi intra
terminos ejus contra eos fiat '. Hoc vero sanctus ita
dicebat quia in spiritu praecognovit [20] quod post aliquot

---

[1] in me A. Omitted in B1 B2 B3.
[2] inmotatum A, divided by a flaw in the parchment ; a small u has
been written by m.h. above o. -mut- B1 B2 B3
[3] eadem A B2 B3 ; in A, a circumflex accent has later been added by
a fine pen above a. ea'dem B1   [4] indesociabiliter A ; indiss- B1 B2 B3
[5] cormaci A B2 B3 ; Cormacci B1   [6] lethani A B2 B3 ; letha'ni B1
[7] The contents-list of B2 and of B3 reads: De cormaco (chormacho B2)
nepote lethani (letani B2) et ejus navigationibus sancti columbe prophetacio (-tio B2).
[8] cormacus A B3 ; -ma'ccus B1 ; -maccus B2   [9] pauca. See 17ab.
[10] herimum A ; the i has been altered by m.h. to e. heremum B1 B2 B3
[11] ociano A ; the i altered by m.h. to e. occe'ano B1 ; occeano B2 B3

(how, I do not know) my heart has been changed in me from hate to love '.

Let us pass on. From that day until the day of her death, that wife's affections were indissolubly set in love of her husband ; so that the dues of the marriage-bed, which she had formerly refused to grant, she never again denied.

[II 42] The blessed man's prophecy concerning the voyage of Cormac, grandson of Léthan

At another time, Cormac, a soldier of Christ, of whom we have briefly related some few things in the first book of this work, attempted for the second time to seek a desert place in the ocean. After he had sailed away from the land, with full sails, over the limitless ocean, in those same days Saint Columba, while he was beyond the spine of Britain, charged king Brude, in the presence of the subject-king of the Orcades, saying : ' Some of our people have recently gone out desiring to find a desert place in the sea that cannot be crossed. Earnestly charge this king, whose hostages are in your hand, that, if after long wanderings our people chance to land in the islands of the Orcades, nothing untoward shall happen to them within his territories '. The saint spoke thus because he foreknew

---

[12] ocianum A ; the *i* has been altered by m.h. to *e*. occeanum B1 B3. Illegible in B2.

[13] brudeo A B3 ; bru'deo B1 ; bru[B2

[14] regi A ; rege B1 B2 B3 (wrongly)

[15] orcadum A B2 B3 ; o'rcadum B1

[16] pilago A ; the *i* has been altered by m.h. to *e*. pe'l- B1 ; pel- B2 B3

[17] orcadas A B2 B3 ; o'rcadas B1

[18] obsedes A ; a small *i* has been written by m.h. above the first *e*. -sid- B1 B2 B3   [19] deligenter A ; dil- B1 B2 B3

[20] praecognovit A ; cognovit B1 ; precog- B2 B3

2G

menses idem Cormaccus [1] esset ad Orcadas [2] venturus. Quod ita postea evenit.[3] Et propter supradictam sancti viri commendationem de morte in Orcadibus liberatus est vicina.

95b   Post aliquantum paucorum intervallum men|sium, cum sanctus in Iova commoraretur insula, quadam die coram eo ejusdem Cormaci [4] mentio ab aliquibus subito aboritur [5] sermocinantibus et taliter dicentibus : ' Quomodo Cormaci [6] navigatio prosperane án non provenit adhuc nescitur '. Quo audito verbo sanctus hac profatur voce,[7] dicens : ' Cormacum [8] de quo nunc loquemini [9] hodie mox pervenientem videbitis '. Et post quasi unius horae interventum, mirum dictu et [10] ecce inopinato Cormacus [11] superveniens oratorium cum omnium ammiratione et gratiarum ingreditur actione. .

     Et quia de hujus Cormaci [12] secunda navigatione beati profetationem breviter intulerimus viri, nunc et de tertia eque[13] profeticae ejus scientiae aliqua discribenda[14] sunt verba.

     Cum idem Cormacus [15] tertia in ociano [16] mari fatigaretur vice, prope usque ad mortem periclitari coepit. Nam cum ejus navis a terrís per xiiii.[17] aestei[18] temporis |

96a dies totidemque noctes[19] plenís velís austro[20] flante vento ad septemtrionalis plagam caeli directo excurreret cursu,

[1] cormaccus A B2 ; corma'ccus B1 ; cormacus B3
[2] orcadas A B2 B3 ; o'rcadas B1
[3] evenit A B2 B3 ; in A, a circumflex accent has later been written with a fine pen above the second *e*. eve'nit B1
[4] cormaci A B2 B3 ; cormacci B1
[5] aboritur A ; oritur B1 ; oboritur B2 B3
[6] cormaci A B2 B3 ; cormacci B1
[7] hac profatur voce A B1 B2 ; hec profatur B3
[8] Cormacum A B3 ; Cormaccum B1. Illegible in B2.
[9] loquemini A ; the *e* has later been altered to *i*, with a down-stroke of a fine pen. -qui'm- B1 ; -quim- B2 B3
[10] et A. Omitted in B1 B3 ; illegible in B2.
[11] cormacus A B2 B3 ; cormaccus B1

in the spirit that after some months this Cormac would come to the Orcades. And it did afterwards so happen. And because of the aforesaid commendation of the holy man, Cormac was delivered from imminent death in the Orcades.

After an interval of a few months, when the saint was living in the island of Io, one day in his presence men who were conversing together suddenly made mention of Cormac, and spoke in this manner : ' How Cormac's voyage has fared, whether it is successful or not, is still unknown '. Hearing them talk thus, the saint uttered these words, saying : ' You speak of Cormac ; today quite soon you will see him arrive '. And after the interval of about one hour, strange to tell, behold, Cormac appearing unexpectedly entered the oratory ; and all were amazed and rendered thanks.

Since we have briefly inserted the prophecy of the blessed man concerning the second voyage of this Cormac, we must now write down also some words showing his prophetic knowledge likewise of the third.

While Cormac was labouring for the third time in the sea of Ocean, he came into dangers that nearly caused his death. When his ship, blown by the south wind, had driven with full sails in a straight course from land towards the region of the northern sky, for fourteen summer days and as many nights, such a voyage

---

[12] cormaci A B2 B3 ; cormacci B1
[13] *eque*. In A, the first *e* has later been altered to the *ae* symbol by a fine loop, perhaps of the eighth century (see p. 174).
[14] discribenda A ; des- B1 B2 B3
[15] cormacus A B2 B3 ; cormaccus B1
[16] ociano A ; occeano B1 B2 B3 (-e′a- B1)
[17] xiiii A B2 ; quatuordecim B1 B3 (-o′r- B1)
[18] aestei A ; estivi B1 B2 B3
[19] totidemque noctes A B3 ; totidemque noctem B2. Omitted in B1.
[20] austro A B1 B2 ; astro B3

ejusmodi navigatio ultra humani excursus modum et
inremeabilis videbatur. Unde contigit ut post decimam
ejusdem quarti et decimi horam diei, quidam pene
insustentabiles undique et valde formidabiles consur-
gerent terrores. Quaedam quippe usque in id temporis
invisae mare [1] obtegentes occurrerant tetrae et infestae
nimis bestiolae, quae horribili impetu carinam et latera
pupimque et proram ita forti feriebant percusura, ut
pellicium tectum navis penetrales putarentur penetrare
posse. Quae, ut hí qui inerant ibidem postea narrarunt,
prope magnitudine ranarum aculeís [2] permolestae non
tamen volatiles sed natatiles erant ; sed et remorum |
96b infestabant palmulas. Quibus visís inter cetera monstra,
quae non hujus est temporis enarrare,[3] Cormaccus [4] cum
nautís comitibus, valde turbati [5] et pertimescentes,[6] deum
qui est in angustís [7] pius et oportunus auxiliator inlacrimati precantur.[8]

Eadem hora et sanctus noster Columba quamlibet
longe absens corpore spiritu tamen praesens in navi cum
Cormaco [9] erat. Unde eodem momento personante
signo[10] fratres ad oratorium convocans et eclesiam intrans
adstantibus síc more sibi consueto profetizans profatur,
dicens : 'Fratres, tota intentione pro Cormaco [11] orate,
qui nunc humanae discursionis limitem inmoderate
navigando excessit. Nunc quasdam monstruosas ante
non visas et pene indicibiles patitur horrificas perturba-
97a tiones. Itaque | nostrís [12] commembribus in periculo

[1] mare A B2 B3 ; maris B1

[2] *aculei* usually means ' stings ', but here the context suggests that they
were in front, and resembled beaks of birds.

[3] *enarrare*. A point with up-sign added in A after this word is the last
alteration made by m.h. or the fine pen in A.

[4] Cormaccus A ; cormaccus B1 ; cormacus B2 B3

[5] turbati A ; turbatis B1 B2 B3   [6] pertimescentes A ; -tibus B1 B2 B3

[7] angustís A ; -tïis B1 B2 ; -tiis, B3.   The B version substitutes *angustiae*
' a strait ' for A's *angusta* ' cases of difficulty '. Cf. A's *angustiae* in 93a.

appeared to be beyond the range of human exploration, and one from which there could be no return. And so it happened, after the tenth hour of the fourteenth day, that there arose all around them almost over-whelming and very dreadful objects of terror ; for they were met by loathsome and exceedingly dangerous small creatures covering the sea, such as had never been seen before that time ; and these struck with terrible impact the bottom and sides, the stern and prow, with so strong a thrust that they were thought able to pierce and penetrate the skin-covering of the ship. As those that were present there related aferwards, these creatures were about the size of frogs, very injurious by reason of their stings, but they did not fly, they swam. And moreover they damaged the blades of the oars. Seeing these with the other prodigies, which this is not the time to recount, Cormac and his fellow-sailors were in great alarm and terror, and with tears prayed to God, who is a true and ready helper in times of need.

At that same hour, our Saint Columba also, though far distant in body, was nevertheless in spirit present with Cormac in the ship. So in that moment, calling the brothers together to the oratory with the sound of the bell, and entering the church, he spoke thus pro-phetically according to his custom to those that were standing by, and said : ' Brothers, pray with your whole might for Cormac, who now in his voyage has far exceeded the bounds of human travel. Now he endures the terrors of certain horrible and monstrous things never before seen, and almost indescribable. In our

---

[8] inlacrimati precantur A ; illacrimatus precatur B1 B2 B3
[9] cormaco A B2 B3 ; corma'cco B1   [10] signo A B1 B3. Omitted in B2.
[11] cormaco A B2 B3 ; corma'cco B1
[12] itaque nostrís A ; Nostris itaque B1 B2 B3

intollerabili constitutís mente conpati debemus fratribus,
et dominum exorare cum eís. Ecce enim nunc Cormacus ¹ cum suís nautís faciem lacrimís ubertim inrigans
Christum intentius ² precatur, et nos ipsum orando
adjuvemus, ut austrum flantem ventum usque hodie per
xiiii.³ dies nostri ⁴ miseratus in aquilonem convertat.
Qui videlicet aquiloneus ventus navem ⁵ Cormaci ⁶ de
periculís retrahat '.

Et haec dicens flebili cum voce flexís genibus ante
altarium omnipotentiam dei ventorum et cunctarum
gubernatricem precatur rerum ; et post orationem cito
surgit, et abstergens lacrimas gaudenter grates deo agit,
dicens : ' Nunc, fratres, nostrís congratulemur pro
quibus oramus carís, quia dominus austrum nunc in
97b [aquilonem] ⁷ | convertet flatum nostros ⁸ de periculís
commembres retrahentem, quos huc ad nos iterum
reducet '. Et continuo cum ejus voce auster cessavit
ventus, et inspiravit aquiloneus per multos post dies, et
navis Cormaci ⁹ ad terras reducta est, et pervenit
Cormac ¹⁰ ad sanctum Columbam, et sé donante deo ¹¹
facie ad faciem cum ingenti omnium ammiratione
viderant et non mediocri laetatione.

Perpendat itaque lector quantus et qualis idem vir
beatus,¹² qui talem profeticam habens scientiam ventís
et ociano ¹³ Christi invocato nomine potuit imperare. .

¹ cormacus A B2 B3 ; cormaccus B1
² intentius A B2 ; intencius B1 ; intentus B3
³ xiiii A B2 ; quatuordecim B1 B3 (-o'r- B1)
⁴ nostri A ; nos B1 B2 B3   ⁵ navem A ; navim B1 B2 B3
⁶ cormaci A B2 B3 ; corma'cci B1
⁷ aquilonem B1 B2 B3. In A, over a blank space or erasure, an italic
hand (? seventeenth century) has written *aquilonarem*, which is followed by
Reeves. Manuscript L of the shortened version reads *aquilonem* ; Reeves
cites no readings from C, D, F, S. The reading of P is : *dominus austrum
nunc convertit flatum.*
⁸ *nostros.* After this word, in A, a comma-sign has wrongly been added,
perhaps by the writer of *aquilonarem.*

minds, therefore, we must share the sufferings of our brothers, our fellow-members, who are placed in unendurable danger ; and we must pray to the Lord with them. For now behold Cormac, copiously watering his face with tears, prays earnestly with his sailors to Christ, and let us help him in praying, that Christ may take pity upon us, and may turn into a north wind the south wind that has blown for fourteen days, until today ; so that this northerly wind may bring Cormac's ship out of its dangers '.

After saying this, he bent his knees before the altar, and in a tearful voice prayed to the omnipotence of God, which controls the winds and all things. After praying, he rose quickly, and wiping away the tears joyfully rendered thanks to God, saying : ' Now, brothers, we may congratulate our friends for whom we are praying, because the Lord will now change the south into a [north] wind bringing our fellow-members back from their dangers, and will lead them here to us again '. And simultaneously with his words, the south wind ceased, and the north wind blew for many days afterwards. Cormac's ship was brought back to land, and Cormac came to Saint Columba ; and God granting it they saw each other face to face, to the great wonder of all, and with uncommon rejoicing.

Let the reader therefore consider how great and of what nature was this blessed man, who had such prophetic knowledge, and by invoking the name of Christ was able to command the winds and the ocean.

---

[9] cormaci A B2 B3 ; corma'cci B1
[10] cormac A ; cormaccus B1 ; cormacus B2 B3
[11] deo A ; domino B1 B2 B3
[12] beatus A ; beatus fu'erit B1 ; beatus fuerit B2 B3
[13] ociano A ; occe'ano B1 ; oceano B2 ; occeano B3

De venerabilis viri in curru evectione absque currilium obicum communitione. .

ALIO IN TEMPORE, cum in Scotia per aliquot dies
sanctus conversaretur, aliquibus eclesiasticís utilitatibus
98a coactus, currum ab eo | prius benedictum ascendit
junctum, sed non insertís primo qua neglegentia [1]
accedente nescitur necessariis obicibus per axionum [2]
extrema foramina. Erat autem eadem diecula Columbanus filius Echudi,[3] vir sanctus, illius monasterii fundator quod scotica vocitatur lingua Snám luthir,[4] qui
operam aurigae in eodem curriculo cum sancto exercebat
Columba. Fuit itaque talis ejusdem agitatio diei per
longa viarum spatia sine ulla rotarum humerulorumque
separatione sive [5] labefactatione,[6] nulla ut supra dictum
est obicum retentione vel communitione [7] retenente,[8] sed
sola diali síc venerando prestante gratia viro, ut currus
cui insederat salubriter absque ulla inpeditione recta
incederet orbita.

98b   Huc usque de virtutum miraculís quae | per prae-
dicabilem virum in praesenti conversantem vita divina
operata est omnipotentia scripsise suficiat. . Nunc etiam
quaedam [9] de hís quae post ejus de carne transitum ei a
domino donata conprobantur pauca sunt commemo-
randa. .

---

[1] neglegentia A ; negligentia B1 B2 ; necligencia B3
[2] axionum A ; axium B1 B2 B3. These *axiones* (or *axes*) seem to be the
ends of an axle-tree (*axis*, Greek *axōn*) that did not revolve.
[3] echudi A B2 B3 ; echudi' B1. Cf. Bergin 1932, p. 145.
[4] snám luthir A, with one over-dash, above *lu* ; snamluthir B1 ?B2 ;
snam luthir B3. See Reeves 1857, pp. 173-174. *Snám* was a swimming-
ford ; *luthir* is unexplained.
[5] sive A B2 B3 ; sine B1
[6] labefactatione A B1 B2 ; labefactione B3
[7] communitione A B1 B2 (-ici- B1) ; communione B3

[II 43] Concerning the venerable man's riding in a carriage without the security of linch-pins

At another time, when the saint was living for some days in Ireland, compelled by ecclesiastical affairs he entered a carriage that had previously been blessed by him, and that had been yoked, but by some unknown negligence without the necessary bolts having first been inserted through holes in the ends of the axle-tree. It was Colman, Echuid's son, a holy man, the founder of the monastery that is called in the Irish language *Snám luthir* [Slanore], who on that day acted as driver in the carriage with Saint Columba. The day's driving over the long distances they travelled did not cause any separation of the wheels from the axle-shoulders, or any slackening, although, as has been said above, the wheels were held on by no retaining or securing bolts ; God's grace alone so preserving the venerable man that the carriage in which he sat followed a true course, safely and without any hindrance.

Let it suffice to have written thus far about the miracles of power which the divine omnipotence performed through the memorable man, while he continued in the present life. Now a few must also be recorded of those that are proved to have been granted by the Lord to him, after his passing from the flesh.

---

[8] retenente A ; -tin- B1 B2 B3
[9] quaedam A ; quidam B1 ; quedam B2 B3

De pluia post aliquot siccitatis menses beati
ob honorem viri super [1] sitientem domino
donante terram effussa [2]

ANTE ANNOS namque ferme xvii.[3] in hís torpentibus
terrís valde grandis verno tempore facta est siccitas jugis
et dura, in tantum ut illa domini in levitico [4] libro
transgresoribus coaptata populís comminatio videretur
inminere, qua dicit : ' Dabo [5] caelum vobís desuper
99a sicut ferrum, | et terram eneam. Consummetur incassum
labor vester, nec proferet terra germen nec arbores poma
praebebunt ', et cetera.

Nos itaque haec legentes, et inminentem plagam
pertimescentes, hoc inito consilio fieri consiliati sumus,
ut aliqui ex nostrís senioribus nuper aratum et seminatum
campum cum sancti Columbae candida circumirent [6]
tunica, et librís stilo ipsius discriptís,[7] levarentque [8] in
aere et excuterent eandem per ter tunicam qua etiam
hora exitus ejus de carne indutus erat, et ejus aperirent
libros et legerent in colliculo angelorum, ubi aliquando
caelestis patriae cives ad beati viri condictum [9] visi sunt
discendere.[10]

Quae postquam omnia juxta initum sunt peracta
99b consilium, mirum dictu, | eadem die caelum in prae-
teritís mensibus, martio videlicet et apreli,[11] nudatum

---

[1] super A B1 B2 and c.l. of B2 and of B3. Omitted in B3.
[2] After this title, a line is left blank in A. In B1 the title is continued :
*Miraculum quod nunc deo propi'tio describere incipimus, nostris temporibus factum
proprïis inspeximus oculis.* Verbally the same in B2, B3 and contents-list of
B2 and of B3 ; in the contents-list the sentence is written as if it were the
title of a separate chapter. See p. 8.
[3] xuii A ; quatuordecim B1 B2 B3 (-o'r- B1). See p. 167. Reeves read
A wrongly, as *quatuordecim.*
[4] levitico A B3 ; levi'tico B1 ; levi[B2. Cf. Vulgate, Lev. xxvi. 19–20.
[5] *dabo.* In A, *da* is just visible through a stain that penetrates to pp. 97
and 100, and is deepest on 98b and 99a.

[II 44] Concerning rain that fell upon thirsty land after some months of drought, the Lord granting it in honour of the blessed man. [The miracle that now with God's favour we are about to describe was performed in our time, and we have seen it with our own eyes.]

For indeed about seventeen years ago, in the season of spring, there was a very great drought, persistent and severe, in these lifeless fields ; to such an extent that the peoples seemed to be threatened by the Lord's curse laid upon transgressors, where he says, in the book of Leviticus : ' I will give to you a sky above like iron, and earth like bronze. Your labour shall be spent in vain. The earth shall yield no produce, nor shall the trees give fruit ', and so forth.

Reading this, and in dread of the impending stroke, we formed a plan, and decided upon this course : that some of our elders should go round the plain that had been lately ploughed and sown, taking with them the white tunic of Saint Columba, and books in his own handwriting ; and should three times raise and shake in the air that tunic, which he wore in the hour of his departure from the flesh ; and should open his books and read from them, on the hill of the angels, where at one time the citizens of the heavenly country were seen descending to confer with the holy man.

After all these things had been performed according to the adopted plan, strange to tell, on the same day the sky, which had been bare of clouds during the

---

[6] circumirent A ; circuirent B1 B2 B3 (-i'rent B1)
[7] discriptís A ; descriptis B1 B2 B3
[8] levarentque A B1 ?B2 ; lav- B3
[9] condictum A B1 B2 ; condittum B3. See 117b.
[10] discendere A ; des- B1 B2 B3   [11] apreli A ; aprili B1 B2 B3

nubibus mira sub celeritate ipsis de ponto ascendentibus ilico opertum est, et pluia facta est magna die noctuque discendens.[1]   Et sitiens prius terra satis satiata oportune germina produxit sua, et valde laetas eodem anno segites.[2]   Unius itaque beati commemoratio nominis viri, in tunica et librís commemorata, multís regionibus eadem vice et populís salubri subvenit oportunitate. .[3]

De ventorum flatibus contrariis venerabilis viri virtute orationum in secundos conversís ventos

PRAETERITORUM NOBÍS quae non vidimus talium miraculorum [4] praesentia quae ipsi perspeximus fidem indubitanter confirmant.   Ventorum namque flamina contrariorum tribus nos ipsi vicibus in secunda vidimus |
100a   conversa.   Prima vice, cum dolatae per terram pineae [5] et roboreae traherentur longae navis [6] et magnae navium pariter materiae eveherentur domus,[7] beati viri vestimenta et libros inito consilio super altare cum salmís [8] et jejunatione et ejus nominis invocatione possuimus, ut a domino ventorum prosperitatem nobís profuturam inpetraret.   Quod ita eidem sancto viro deo donante factum est.   Nam ea die qua nostri nautae omnibus

---

[1] discendens A ; des- B1 B2 B3   [2] segites A ; -get- B1 B2 B3
[3] oportunitate A B3 ; oportunitate.   Ad alia veniamus B1 B2
[4] *talium miraculorum.*   Here Adomnan refers back to the words of the chapter-heading, i.e. miracles of wind-changing.
[5] per terram pineae A.   Omitted in B1 B2 B3.
[6] navis A ; naves B1 B2 B3.   See p. 131.   Reeves silently altered *navis* to *naves,* thus completely changing the meaning of A's sentence.   The change of *navis* to *naves* in the B texts belongs to the class of grammatical emendations, true or false, that are automatically made by medieval scribes.   The translation in E.S., 1, p. 187, was made from Reeves's ʹext.   But A's reading is grammatical, and gives good sense.   It eliminates the former implication that dug-out boats were conveyed to Iona.   The expression *longa navis* was not used to mean a dug-out canoe, but meant a sea-going ship built of wood.

previous months, namely March and April, was with
marvellous rapidity instantly covered with clouds
that rose from the sea ; and there was great rain,
falling by day and by night. And the earth, previously
parched, was well watered, and produced its crop in
season, and a very plentiful harvest in that same year.
Thus the commemoration of the name of one blessed
man, made with his tunic and books, on that occasion
brought saving and timely help to many districts and
peoples.

[II 45] Concerning winds that were contrary
and that by the virtue of the venerable man's
prayers were changed to favourable winds

The credibility of miracles of this kind, that happened in past times and that we have not seen, is
confirmed for us beyond doubt by those of the present
day, that we ourselves have observed. For indeed we
ourselves have thrice seen contrary winds turned into
favourable ones.

On the first occasion when dressed timbers of pine
and oak for a long ship were being drawn over land, and
timbers were being conveyed for the great house, as
well as for ships, we adopted the plan of laying garments
and books of the blessed man upon the altar, with
psalms and fasting, and invocation of his name ; in
order that he might obtain from the Lord prosperous
winds in our favour. And so it happened, God granting
it to that holy man. For on the day on which our

---

7 *domus*. See 31a, 115ab, and p. 113.
8 salmís A ; palmis B1 ; psalmis B2 B3

praeparatís supra memoratarum ligna materiarum pro-
possuere scafís per mare et curucis trahere, venti
praeteritís contrarii diebus subito in secundos conversi
sunt. Tum deinde per longas et oblicas [1] vias tota die
prosperís flatibus [2] deo propitio famulantibus et plenís
sine ulla retardatione velís ad Iovam insulam omnis illa |
100b navalis emigratio prospere pervenit.

Secunda vero vice, cum post aliquantos inter-
venientes annos aliae nobiscum [3] roboreae ab hostio
fluminis Sale [4] xii.[5] curucís congregatís materiae ad
nostrum renovandum traherentur monasterium,[6] alia [7]
die tranquillo nautís mare palmulís verrentibus subito
nobís contrarius insurgit fabonius [8] qui et zefirus [9] ventus.
In proximam tum declinamus insulam quae scotice
vocitatur Airthrago,[10] in ea portum ad manendum
quaerentes. Sed inter haec de illa inportuna venti
contrarietate querimur,[11] et quodam modo quasi accus-
sare nostrum Columbam coepimus, dicentes : ' Placetne
tibi sancte haec nobis adversa retardatio ? Huc usque
101a a té deo propitio | aliquod nostrorum [12] laborum praestari
speravimus consulatorium [13] adjumentum,[14] té videlicet
estimantes [15] alicujus esse grandis apud deum honoris '.

Hís dictís, post modicum quasi unius momenti intervallulum,[16] mirum dictu ecce fabonius [17] ventus cessat

---

[1] oblicas A ; obliquas B1 B2 B3   [2] flatibus A B1 B3 ; ventis B2
[3] *nobiscum*. The Latin *cum* is used (as the Irish *la* could be used) for ' by'.
[4] sale A B2 B3 ; sale' B1. This was probably the Shiel, between the
counties of Argyll and Inverness.   [5] xii A ; duodecim B1 B2 B3
[6] *monasterium*. Here, as in 28b and 115a, the common house of the
monastery appears to be meant. See p. 113.
[7] Alia A B1 B2 B3, after a punctuation point that does not here mark
the end of a sentence. Reeves changed the word to *alio*, altering the
construction and meaning.
[8] fabonius A ; favonius B1 B2 B3 (-vo'n- B1)
[9] zefirus A B3 ; zephirus B1 ?B2
[10] airthrago A ; airtrago B1 B3 ; airtago B2. Perhaps this island was
Shona ; see p. 156.

sailors had made all ready and intended with boats and curachs to tow the pieces of timber through the sea, the winds that had been contrary on previous days were suddenly changed to propitious ones. Then with God's favour, attended during the whole day by prosperous breezes, without slackening speed and with full sails throughout the long and devious route, that whole sea-transport came safely to the island of Io.

On the second occasion, some years later, when twelve curachs had been collected, and other oak timbers were being towed by us from the mouth of the river Sale, for the restoration of our monastery, one day, while in still weather the sailors were sweeping the sea with their oars, suddenly the wind Favonius, which is also called Zephyrus, arose against us. We turned aside then to the nearest island, which is called in Irish ' of Airthraig ', seeking in it a harbour in which we could remain. But meanwhile we complained about the inconvenience of this contrary wind, and began in a manner as it were to upbraid our Columba, saying : ' Is this hindrance that opposes us pleasing to you, holy one ? Till now, we have expected some consolation of help in our labours to be given by you, with God's favour, since we imagined that you were in somewhat high honour with God '.

A short space, as it were of one moment, after we had spoken, behold, the contrary wind Favonius mar-

---

[11] querimur A, altered by erasure from *quaerimur* ; querimur B1 B2 B3
[12] nostrorum A B1 B3.   Omitted in B2.
[13] consulatorium A ; -sol- B1 B2 B3
[14] adjumentum A B1 B2 ; adjuventum B3
[15] estimantes A B1 B2 ; estimentes B3
[16] intervallulum A ; intervallum B1 B2 B3
[17] fabonius A B3 ; favonius B1 B2 (-vo'n- B1)

contrarius, ulturnusque [1] flat dicto citius secundus. Jusi
tum nautae antemnas crucis instar et vela protensís
sublevant rudentibus [2] ; prosperísque et lenibus flabrís
eadem die nostram appetentes insulam sine ulla laboratione cum illís omnibus qui navibus inerant nostrís [3]
cooperatoribus in lignorum evectione gaudentes de-
vehimur.

Non mediocriter quamlibet levis illa querula nobís
sancti accussatio viri profuit. Quantique et qualis est
101b apud dominum meriti sanctus ap|paret, quem [4] in
ventorum ipse tam celeri conversione audierat.

Tertia proinde vice, cum nos aesteo [5] tempore post
everniensis [6] sinodi [7] condictum in plebe generis Loerni [8]
per aliquot venti contrarietate retardaremur dies, ad
Saineam [9] devenimus insulam ; ibidemque demoratos
festivae [10] sancti Columbae nox et sollemnis diei [11] nos
invenit valde tristificatos videlicet desiderantes eandem
diem in Iova facere [12] laetificam insula. Unde sicut prius
alia querebamur vice, dicentes : ' Placetne tibi sancte
crastinam tuae festivitatis inter plebeos et non in tua
eclesia transigere diem ? [13] Facile tibi est talis in exordio
diei a domino inpetrare, ut contrarii in secundos ver-

---

[1] ulturnusque A ; vult- B1 B2 B3. Favonius was the west wind.
Vulturnus usually meant a wind blowing from 30° (more or less) east of
south ; a wind that in modern sailing might have served to take a boat
from Shona to Iona, but hardly in Adomnan's time, and with logs in tow.
Adomnan used the word Vulturnus differently. Cf. his *De Locis* (Geyer
1898, p. 228, and the diagram on p. 231) : *quattuor ... ad Vulturnum spectant,
qui et Caecias* [sic lege ; the MSS have *lc* and *lt*, misread presumably from
an Irish *ec*] *dicitur ventus, alii vero quattuor ad Eurum respiciunt.* Here Eurus is
30° (more or less) east of south, and Vulturnus is made 30° (more or less)
north of east. A wind from that direction would have been entirely
favourable for the voyage from Shona.

[2] *rudentibus.* Cf. 91a, and see p. 117.

[3] inerant nostrís A ; in nostris i'nerant B1 ; inerant nostris B2 B3

[4] quem A B2 B3 ; que B1

[5] aesteo A ; estivo B1 B2 B3

[6] everniensis A ; hiberniensis B1 B3 ?B2

vellously fell, and more quickly than speech the favourable Vulturnus blew. Then at our bidding the sailors
raised the yards up cross-wise, and the sails, stretching
tight the ropes ; and rejoicing we were carried by fair
and gentle breezes, without any effort, until we reached
our island on the same day, and with us all those that
had been in the ships, helping us to fetch the wood.

That querulous complaint, light though it was,
against the holy man profited us in no small measure.
It is clear of how great and high merit in the sight of
the Lord is the saint whom he heard in so swift changing
of the winds.

So too on the third occasion, in the summer season,
after the meeting of the Irish synod, when for several
days we were delayed by contrary wind among the
people of the tribe of Loern, we came to the island of
Saine, and there the night of the festive and solemn
day of Saint Columba found us waiting, much saddened,
because we desired to spend that joyful day in the island
of Io. Therefore again, as before, we complained,
saying : ' Does it please you, holy one, that we should
pass the day of your festivity tomorrow among laymen
and not in your church ? In the beginning of such a
day it is an easy thing for you to obtain of the Lord
that the contrary winds should be turned to favourable

---

[7] *sinodi.* Adomnan seems to have attended this synod as abbot of Iona.

[8] loerni A B2 ; loerni′ B1 ; lorrni B3 (with two small-capital *r*'s).
Cf. pp. 37, 79.

[9] saineam A B2 B3 ; saine′am B1. This island has not been identified.

[10] festivae A ; festiva B1 B2 B3

[11] diei A ; dies B1 B3. Illegible in B2. See p. 120.

[12] *facere.* In A, an *et* ligature was begun, instead of *a*, and neither
finished nor corrected.

[13] *nos* must be supplied, perhaps before *crastinam.*

2H

tantur venti, et in tua celebremus eclesia tui natalis
102a misa|rum sollemnia.

Post eandem transactam noctem diluculo mane con-
surgimus, et videntes cessasse [1] contrarios flatus con-
scensís navibus nullo flante vento in mare progredimur.
Et ecce statim post nos auster cardinalis qui et nothus
inflat. Tum proinde ovantes nautae vela subregunt.[2]
Sícque ea die talis sine labore nostra tam festina navigatio
et tam prospera beato viro donante deo fuit, ut sicuti
prius exobtavimus post horam diei tertiam ad Iovae
portum pervenientes insulae, postea manuum et pedum
peracta lavatione hora sexta eclesiam cum fratribus
intrantes sacra misarum sollempnia pariter celebrare-
mus ; in die festo inquam natalis [3] sanctorum Columbae
et Baithenei,[4] cujus diluculo ut supra dictum est de
102b Sainea [5] insula longius | sita emigravimus.

Hujus ergo praemisae narrationis testes non bini
tantum vel terni secundum legem sed centeni et amplius
adhuc exstant. .[6]

De mortalitate

ET HOC ETIAM ut estimo non inter minora virtutum
miracula connumerandum videtur, de mortalitate quae
nostrís temporibus terrarum orbem bis ex parte vasta-
verat majore. Nam ut de ceteris taceam latioribus
Eoropae [7] regionibus, hoc est Italia et ipsa romana
civitate et cisalpinis [8] Galliarum provinciis,[9] hispanís [10]

[1] cessasse A ; cessare B1 B2 B3   [2] subregunt A ; -rig- B1 B2 B3
[3] natalis A B2 B3 ; natale B1
[4] baithenei A B2 ; baithe'nei B1 ; baitheni B3
[5] sainea A B2 B3 ; saine'a B1
[6] exstant A ; extant. Veniamus ad alia B1 B2 ; extant B3
[7] eoropae A ; europe B1 B3 ?B2
[8] cisalpinis A ; cis alpinas B1 B3 (-pi'n- B1) ; eis alpinas B2

ones, and that we should celebrate in your church the
solemn rites of masses, on your natal day '.

After that night had passed, we arose in the morning
twilight, and seeing that the contrary winds had ceased
we entered the ships, and, with no wind blowing, put
out to sea ; and immediately the due south wind, which
is also called Notus, rose behind us.   Then the sailors
exulting raised the sails, and thus with no labour this
journey of ours was on that day so rapid and so prosperous, God granting it to the blessed man, that just
as we had before desired we arrived at the harbour of
the island of Io, after the third hour of the day ; and
later, after the washing of hands and feet, we entered
the church with the brothers, and at the sixth hour we
celebrated with them the holy ceremonies of the Mass ;
on the festival, I repeat, of the Natal day of the saints
Columba and Baithene, in the dawn of which, as was
said above, we had sailed out from the island of Saine,
a long distance away.

To the truth of the foregoing narrative there are
still living not two witnesses only, or three, as law
requires, but a hundred, and more.

[II 46] Of the plague

This also I consider should not be reckoned among
lesser miracles of power, in connexion with the plague
that twice in our times ravaged the greater part of the
surface of the earth.   Not to speak of the other wider
regions of Europe (that is to say, of Italy and the city
of Rome itself, and the provinces of Gaul on this side

---

⁹ provinciis A ; provincias B1 B3 (-vi'nc- B1) ; provintiam B2
¹⁰ hispanís A ; hispanias B1 B2 B3 (-pa'n- B1)

quoque Pirinei [1] montis interjectu disterminatís,[2] ociani [3] insulae per totum, videlicet Scotia et Brittannia, binís vicibus [4] vastatae sunt dira pestilentia, exceptís duobus populís, hoc est Pictorum plebe et Scotorum Brit|tanniae inter [5] quos utrosque dorsi montes brittannici disterminant.[6] Et quamvis utrorumque populorum non desint [7] grandia peccata, quibus plerumque ad iracondiam [8] aeternus provocatur judex, utrísque tamen huc usque patienter ferens ipse pepercit. Cui alio itaque haec tribuitur gratia a deo conlata nisi sancto Columbae, cujus monasteria intra utrorumque populorum terminos fundata ab utrísque usque ad praesens tempus valde sunt honorificata? Sed [9] hoc quod nunc dicturi sumus ut arbitramur non sine gemitu audiendum est, quia sunt plerique in utrísque populís valde stolidi qui sé sanctorum orationibus a morbís [10] defensos nescientes ingrati dei patientia male abutuntur. Nos vero deo agimus crebras grates qui nós et in hís nostrís insulís orante pro nobís nostro venerabili pa|trono a mortalitatum invassionibus defendit, et in Saxonia regem Aldfridum [11] visitantes amicum adhuc non cessante pestilentia et multos hinc inde vicos devastante. Ita tamen nos [12] dominus et in prima post bellum Ecfridi [13] visitatione, et

103a (margin)
103b (margin)

[1] pirinei A B1 ; pirenei B2 B3
[2] disterminatís A ; -natas B1 B2 B3
[3] ociani A ; occe'ani B1 ; oceani B2 ; occeani B3
[4] *binis vicibus.* The earlier plague may have been that mentioned in connexion with the solar eclipse of A.D. 664, by Bede and Irish annals.
[5] inter A B1 B2. Omitted in B3.
[6] *disterminant.* In A, the second *n* has been inserted, by the text hand, above *at.*
[7] desint A B2 B3 ; de'sunt B1
[8] iracondiam A ; -cun- B1 B2 B3
[9] *sed.* In A, this abbreviated word (*s~*) has later been erased, possibly because it was thought to have been a repetition of *sunt.* P reads *Sed* ; this chapter was not included in the shortened version.
[10] morbís A ; morbis B1 B2 ; moribus B3
[11] aldfridum A B2 ; eldfridi B1 ; alfridum B3. See p. 54.

of the Alps, and the Spanish provinces, separated by the barrier of the Pyrenean mountain), the islands of the Ocean, namely Ireland and Britain, were twice ravaged throughout by a terrible pestilence, excepting two peoples only, that is the population of Picts, and of Irish in Britain, between which peoples the mountains of the spine of Britain are the boundary. And although neither people is without great sins, by which the Eternal Judge is often provoked to anger, yet until now he has spared both of them, enduring patiently. To whom else can this favour conferred by God be attributed, but to Saint Columba, whose monasteries, placed within the boundaries of both peoples, are down to the present time held in great honour by them both ?

But what we are now going to tell is, as we judge, not to be heard without sorrow, that there are in both nations many very foolish people who, not knowing that they have been protected from disease by the prayers of saints, ungratefully abuse God's patience. We, however, give frequent thanks to God, who, through the prayers of our venerable patron on our behalf, has protected us from the invasion of plagues, both in these our islands, and in England, when we visited our friend king Aldfrith, while the pestilence still continued and devastated many villages on all sides. But both in our first visit, after the battle of Ecfrith, and in our second

---

[12] nos A B1 B3. Omitted in B2.
[13] ecfridi A ; egfridi B1 B3. Missing in B2. The battle of Dunnichen was fought in A.D. 685, and Adomnan's visits are placed in 686 and 688.

in secunda interjectís duobus annís, in tali mortalitatis medio deambulantes periculo liberavit, ut ne unus etiam de nostrís comitibus moriretur,[1] nec aliquis ex eís aliquo molestaretur morbo. .

Híc secundus de virtutum miraculís finiendus est liber, in quo animadvertere lector debet quod etiam de conpertís in eo multa propter legentium evitandum praetermisa sint [2] fastidium. .

Finitur secundus liber. .[3]

[1] moriretur A ; moreretur B1 B2 B3
[3] sint A B2 B3 ; sunt B1
[3] Phinityr sekyndys liber A, in ostensibly Greek characters of contemporary uncial type (with eta for short *e* in *secundus*) ; see p. 180. Explicit liber secundus B1 B2 B3. After this, B2 B3 insert a contents-list of book III, beginning : *Incipiunt capitula tercii libri* ; and ending : *Expliciunt capitula tercii libri.* We give variant readings from this list, in the same manner as from the contents-list of book II ; see under 52b.

visit, two years later, although we walked in the midst of this danger of plague, the Lord so delivered us that not even one of our companions died, nor was any of them smitten by any disease.

Here must end the second book, of miracles of power ; in which the reader should observe that even of the known instances many have been omitted in it, in order to avoid cloying the appetite of those that read.

The second book ends.

Híc tertius liber orditur de angelicís visionibus. .[1] |

104a   [2] In primo ex hís tribus libellís libro, ut [3] superius [4] commemoratum est, de profeticís revelationibus quaedam breviter succincteque domino navante [5] discripta [6] sunt. . In secundo superiore, de virtutum miraculís quae per beatum declarata sunt virum, et quae ut sepe dictum est [7] plerumque profetationis comitatur gratia. In hoc vero tertio, de angelicís apparationibus [8] quae vel aliis de beato viro, vel ipsi de aliis, revelatae sunt ; et de hís quae utroque quamlibet disparili modo, hoc est ipsi proprie et plenius, aliis vero [9] inproprie et ex quadam parte, sunt manifestatae,[10] hoc est extrinsecus et explorative, in hísdem tamen vel angelorum vel caelestis visionibus lucis. Quae utique talium discrepantiae visionum suís craxatae [11] locís inferius clarebunt. |

104b   Sed nunc ut a primordiis beati nativitatis viri easdem discribere [12] angelicas apparationes [13] incipiamus.

Angelus domini in somniis [14] genitrici venerabilis viri quadam nocte inter conceptum ejus et partum apparuit ; eique quasi quoddam mirae pulchritudinis peplum adsistens detulit, in quo veluti universorum decorosi

---

[1] *Híc* to *visionibus.* Instead of this title, B1 reads : *Incipit textus libri tercii de angelicis visionibus vel apparitionibus, que vel aliis de beato viro, vel eidem de aliis revelate sunt.* B2 has no title of book III. B3 reads : *Incipit textus tercii libri de angelicis visionibus.* The title given by B1 seems to have been in the common original of the B texts, for the greater part of it (*De angelicis apparicionibus que* to *sunt*) appears, written as if it were the first item of book III, in the contents-list of B2 and of B3.
[2] There is no heading of the first chapter in A B3. B1 has : *De angelo domini qui ejus genitrici in sompnis post ipsius in utero conceptionem appa'ruit.* Verbally the same heading is in B2, and in contents-list of B2 and of B3.
[3] ut A B2 B3. Omitted in B1.
[4] *superius.* See 3b.
[5] navante A ; juvante B1 B2 B3
[6] discripta A ; des- B1 B2 B3
[7] est A B1. Omitted in B2 B3.
[8] apparationibus A ; -rici- B1 B3 ; -riti- B2

Here begins the third book, of angelic visions.

In the first of these three books, as has been indicated above, some things have with the Lord's assistance been described briefly and in few words concerning prophetic revelations ; in the second book above, concerning miracles of power, which have been manifested through the blessed man, and which, as has been said many times, the grace of prophecy often accompanies ; and in this third book, concerning angelic apparitions, that were revealed to others in relation to the blessed man, or to him in relation to others, and concerning those that were made visible to both, though in unequal measure (that is, to him directly and more fully, and to others indirectly and only in part, that is to say from without and by stealth), but in the same visions, either of angels, or of heavenly light. These disparities of the visions will appear clearly below, written in their places.

Now let us begin to describe these angelic apparitions from the time before the birth of the blessed man.

[III 1]

An angel of the Lord appeared to the mother of the venerable man in a dream, one night between his conception and his birth ; and standing there, gave her, as it seemed, a robe of marvellous beauty, in which there appeared embroidered splendid colours, as it were of

---

⁹ vero A. Omitted in B1 B2 B3.
¹⁰ manifestatae A ; -state B1 B2 ; -ste B3
¹¹ craxatae A ; caraxate B1 B2 B3 (-a'te B1)
¹² discribere A ; des- B1 B2 B3
¹³ apparationes A ; -rici- B1 B3. Illegible in B2.
¹⁴ somniis A ; sompnis B1 B3. Illegible in B2.

colores florum depicti videbantur. Quodque post aliquod breve intervallum ejus de manibus reposcens
abstulit ; elevansque et expandens in aere [1] dimisit
vacuo. Illa vero de illo tristificata sublato síc ad illum
venerandi habitus virum : ' Cur a me ' ait, ' hoc laeti-
ficum tam cito abstrahis [2] pallium ? ' Ille consequenter :
' Idcirco ' inquit, ' quia hoc sagum alicujus est tam
magnifici honoris, apud te diutius retenere [3] non poteris.'

105a   Hís dictís supra memoratum peplum | mulier
paulatim a sé elongari volando videbat, camporumque
latitudinem in majus crescendo excedere, montesque et
saltus majore sui mensura superare. Vocemque hujuscemodi [4] subsecutam audierat : ' Mulier, noles tristificari. Viro enim cui matrimoniali [copula] [5] es juncta
talem filium editura es [6] floridum qui quasi unus
profetarum dei inter ipsos connumerabitur ; innumera-
biliumque animarum dux ad caelestem a deo patriam
est praedistinatus '.[7] In hac audita voce mulier expergescitur. .[8]

De radio luminoso super dormientis
ipsius pueri faciem viso

ALIA [9] IN NOCTE ejusdem beati pueri nutritor,[10] specta-
bilis vitae vir, prespiter Cruithnechanus,[11] post misam [12]

---

[1] *aere.* In A, the *ae* symbol has been altered to a small *a* followed by *e*, by the text hand, probably at the time of writing.
[2] abstrahis A B1 B2 (a'b- B1); abstahis B3
[3] diutius retenere A ; retinere diutius B1 B2 B3 (-cius B3)
[4] hujuscemodi A ; hujusmodi B1 B2 B3
[5] copula B1 B2 B3. Omitted in A. In A, *federe* has been added above, after *juncta*, in letters imitating the text hand, but in modern times, with a modern caret. Different texts of the shortened version, derived from A, appear to have supplied here different words : L and C read *foedere* after *juncta* ; and D, according to Reeves, reads *jure* before *juncta*. P reads *cui matrimonio juncta es.*

all kinds of flowers. And after some little space, asking
it back, he took it from her hands. And raising it, and
spreading it out, he let it go in the empty air. Grieved
by losing it, she spoke thus to that man of reverend
aspect : ' Why do you so quickly take from me this
joyous mantle ? ' Then he said : ' For the reason that
this cloak is of very glorious honour, you will not be
able to keep it longer with you '.

After these words, the woman saw that robe gradually recede from her in flight, grow greater, and surpass
the breadth of the plains, and excel in its greater measure
the mountains and woods. And she heard a voice that
followed, speaking thus : ' Woman, do not grieve, for
you will bear to the man to whom you are joined by
[the bond] of marriage a son, of such grace that he, as
though one of the prophets of God, shall be counted in
their number ; and he has been predestined by God to
be a leader of innumerable souls to the heavenly
country '. While she heard this voice, the woman
awoke.

]III 2] Concerning a ray of light seen above
the face of that boy while he slept

One night, this blessed boy's foster-father, a man of
admirable life, the priest Cruithnechan, returning to his

---

[6] *es* was altered, in A, from *est*, by erasure, before the following word
was written.

[7] praedistinatus A ; predest- B1 B2 B3

[8] expergescitur A ; -gi's- B1 ; -gis- B2 B3

[9] Alia A B1 B2 ; Alio B3

[10] *nutritor*, and *alumnus* below, stand for the Irish *aite* and *dalte*, ' foster-
father ' and ' foster-son ', or ' tutor ' and ' pupil'.

[11] cruithnechanus A B2 ; -neca'nus B1 ; -necanus B3

[12] *misam.* Here probably the Eucharist is not meant. See p. 122.

105b ab eclesia ad hospitiolum re|vertens totam invenit
domum suam clara inradiatam ¹ luce ; globum quippe
igneum super pueruli dormientis faciem ² stantem vidit.
Quo viso statim intremuit, et prostrato in terram vultu
valde miratus spiritus sancti gratiam super suum intel-
lexit alumnum caelitus effussam. .

De angelorum apparatione ³ sanctorum
quos sanctus Brendenus ⁴ beati comites
viri per campum viderat commeantes

Post namque multorum intervalla temporum, cum
a⁵ quadam sinodo pro quibusdam veniabilibus ⁶ et tam ⁷
excusabilibus causís non recte ut post in fine claruit
sanctus excommonicaretur ⁸ Columba, ad eandem contra
ipsum collectam venit congregationem. Quem cum
eminus appropinquantem sanctus vidisset Brendenus, |
106a illius monasterii fundator quod scotice Birra nuncupatur,
citius surgit, et inclinata facie eum veneratus exosculatur.
Quem ⁹ cum aliqui ¹⁰ illius seniores coetus ¹¹ seorsum
ceterís¹² redarguerent semotís,¹³ dicentes : ' Quare coram
excommonicato ¹⁴ surgere et eum exosculari non ren-
nueris ? ' ; taliter ad eos inquiens : ' Si vós ' ait,
' videretis ¹⁵ ea quae mihi dominus hac in die de hoc suo
quem dehonoratis electo manifestare non dedignatus

¹ inradiantam A ; a short stroke has later been added (not by text hand)
as a mark of deletion, above the second n. irradiatam B1 B3 ;]atam B2
² *faciem* is repeated in B3.
³ apparatione A ; -riti- B1 B2 and contents-list of B2 ; -rici- B3 and
contents-list of B3
⁴ sanctus brendenus A B1 and contents-list of B2 and of B3 ; brendenus
sanctus B2 B3
⁵ a A B3 ; á B2. Omitted in B1.
⁶ veniabilibus A B1 B3 (-bi'l- B1) ; venerabilibus B2
⁷ tam A ; tamen L. Omitted in B1 B2 B3 and C.
⁸ excommonicaretur A ; -mmunc- B1 ; -mmunic- B2 B3
⁹ Quem A B2 B3 ; Que B1

lodging from the church after the office, found his whole
house illumined with clear light ; for he saw a ball of
fire standing above the place of the sleeping child.
Seeing this, he began at once to tremble ; and marvelling greatly bowed his face to the ground, and understood that the grace of the Holy Spirit had been poured
from heaven upon his foster-son.

[III 3] Concerning an apparition of holy angels
whom Saint Brenden saw going through the
plain in company with the blessed man

After many years had passed, when, on a charge of
offences that were trivial and very pardonable, Saint
Columba was excommunicated by a certain synod (improperly, as afterwards became known in the end), he
came to the assembly that had been convoked against
him.

When Saint Brenden (the founder of the monastery
that is in Irish called *Birra* [Birr]) saw him approaching
at a little distance, he rose quickly and bowed his face,
and he kissed Columba reverently. Some of the elders of
that assembly, putting the others aside, remonstrated
with Brenden apart, saying : ' Why do you not refuse
to rise in the presence of an excommunicated person,
and to kiss him ? ' Then he addressed them thus : ' If
you had seen what the Lord has deigned to reveal to
me this day, concerning this his chosen one, whom you

---

[10] aliqui A B1 B2 ; alicui B3
[11] coetus A ; cetus B1 B2 ; fetus B3
[12] ceterís A. Omitted in B1 B2 B3.
[13] semotís A ; semotis B2 B3 ; semotim B1
[14] excommonicato A ; excomun- B1 ; excommun- B2 B3
[15] videretis A B1 B2 (in B2, altered from -*rit*-) ; -rit- B3

est, numquam excommonicasetis [1] quem deus non solum
secundum vestram non rectam sententiam nullo excommonicat [2] modo, sed etiam magis ac magis magnificat '.
Illi econtra : ' Quomodo ' aiunt, ' ut dicis ipsum glorificat deus quem nos non sine causa excommonicavimus,[3]
scire cupimus '. ' Ignicomam et valde luminosam ' ait
106b Brendenus, | ' columnam vidi eundem quem vos di-
spicitis [4] antecedentem dei hominem, angelos quoque
sanctos per campum ejus iteris [5] comites. Hunc itaque
spernere non audeo quem populorum ducem ad vitam
a deo praeordinatum video '. Hís ab eo dictís non
tantum ultra sanctum excommonicare non ausi cessarunt, sed etiam valde venerati honorarunt.

Hoc famen [6] factum est *hi Teilte.* .[7]

De angelo domini quem sanctus Finnio [8]
beati viri socium iteneris [9] vidit

ALIO IN TEMPORE vir sanctus venerandum episcopum
Finnionem,[10] suum videlicet magistrum, juvenis senem
adiit. Quem cum sanctus Finnio [11] ad sé appropinquantem vidisset, angelum domini pariter ejus comitem

---

[1] excommonicasetis A ; excomunicassetis B1 B3 ; excommunicassetis
B2
[2] excommonicat A ; excomu'n- B1 ; excommun- B2 ; excomun- B3
[3] excommonicavimus A ; excommun- B1 B2 ; excomun- B3
[4] dispicitis A ; des- B1 B2 B3
[5] iteris A ; itineris B1 B2 B3 (-ti'n- B1)
[6] *famen.* Reeves 1857, pp. 444, 194, wrongly thought that this was an
error for *tamen.* Cf. *famen* in 115b.
[7] hiteilte A, with four over-dashes. This is O.I. for ' in Teiltiu ', Teltown, county Meath. See p. 73, and cf. R.I.A. Contributions, under
Tailtiu. The sentence *Hoc* to *teilte* is not in B1 B2 B3. It was probably an
addition by Adomnan to the exemplar of A. A continuation of the chapter,
by Adomnan, appears to have been misplaced, and stands at the end of
the following chapter, in A B1 B2 B3. In our translation we have restored
it to its proper position.

deprive of honour, you would never have excommunicated him whom God not only does by no means excommunicate, according to your unjust decree, but even more and more greatly magnifies'. They said, on the other hand : ' How, we should like to know, does God exalt, as you say, him whom we have excommunicated, not without cause ? ' ' I have seen a pillar ' Brenden said, ' fiery and very bright, going before that man of God, whom you despise ; and holy angels accompanying him on his way, through the plain. Therefore I dare not humiliate this man, whom I see to have been predestined by God to be a leader of nations into life '.

When he had spoken thus, not only did they desist, daring to proceed no farther with the excommunication of the saint, but they even honoured him with great reverence.

This utterance was made in Teiltiu [Teltown].

In those same days, the saint sailed over to Britain, with twelve disciples as his fellow-soldiers.

[III 4] Concerning an angel of the Lord, whom
Saint Finnio saw attending the journey of
the blessed man

At one time the holy man, a youth, went to the aged man, the venerable bishop Finnio, his master. When Saint Finnio saw him coming towards him, he saw likewise an angel of the Lord, accompanying him upon

---

⁸ finnio A ; fe′nnio B1 ; fennio B2 B3 and contents-list of B2 and of B3. This bishop Finnio was probably the Findbarr, or Vinniavus, of 53ab. See pp. 68-70.
⁹ iteneris A ; -ti′n- B1 ; -tin- B2 B3 and contents-list of B2 and of B3
¹⁰ finnionem A ; fennionem B1 B2 B3
¹¹ finnio A ; fennio B1 B2 B3

iteris [1] vidit ; et ut nobís ab expertís traditur quibusdam
asstantibus intimavit fratribus, inquiens : ' Ecce [2] nunc |
107a videatis sanctum advenientem Columbam, qui sui com-
meatus meruit habere socium angelum caelicolam '.

Hísdem diebus sanctus cum xii.[3] commilitonibus
discipulís ad Brittanniam transnavigavit. .[4]

De angelo domini qui ad sanctum Columbam
in Hinba [5] commorantem [6] insula per visum
apparuit, misus ut Aidanum in regem
ordinaret [7]

ALIO IN TEMPORE, cum vir praedicabilis in Hinba [8]
commoraretur insula, quadam nocte in extasi mentis
angelum domini ad sé misum vidit, qui in manu vitreum
ordinationis regum habebat librum. Quem cum vir
venerandus de manu angeli accipisset [9] ab eo jusus legere
coepit. Qui cum secundum quod ei in libro erat
commendatum Aidanum in regem ordinare recussaret,
quia magis Iogenanum [10] fratrem ejus dilegeret,[11] subito
107b angelus extendens ma|num sanctum percussit flagillo,[12]
cujus livorosum [13] in ejus latere vestigium omnibus suae
diebus permansit vitae. Hocque intulit verbum : ' Pro
certo scias ' inquiens, ' quia ad té a deo misus sum cum
vitreo libro, ut juxta verba quae in eo legisti Aidanum in

---

[1] iteris A ; itineris B1 B2 B3
[2] Ecce A ; En B1 B3 ; Et B2
[3] xii A ; duodecim B1 B2 B3. See the list of Columba's companions,
in the Appendix, below.
[4] *Hísdem* to *transnavigavit*. This sentence is clearly out of place here,
since the chapter describes an episode of Columba's youth, and Adomnan
says that Columba was in his forty-second year when he went to Britain
(4a). The sentence fits perfectly the end of the preceding chapter, and no
other place in the Life.
[5] hinba A ; himba B1 B3 and contents-list of B2 and of B3 ; hymba B2
[6] commorantem A B1 and contents-list of B2 and of B3 ; -tem B2,
altered from -*tes* ; -te B3

his way. And as we are told by men with knowledge of it, Finnio exclaimed to some brothers who were standing by : ' Look, behold now the holy Columba comes, who has deserved to have as his travelling-companion an angel of heaven '.

[III 5] Concerning an angel of the Lord, who appeared in a vision to Saint Columba, then living in the island of Hinba ; and who was sent to bid him ordain Aidan as king

At one time, while the memorable man was living in the island of Hinba, he saw one night, in a trance of the mind, an angel of the Lord, who had been sent to him, and who had in his hand a glass book of the ordination of kings. And when the venerable man had received it from the hand of the angel, by the angel's command he began to read it. But when he refused to ordain Aidan as king, according to what was commanded him in the book, because he loved Iogenan, Aidan's brother, more, the angel suddenly stretched out his hand and struck the holy man with a scourge, the livid scar from which remained on his side all the days of his life. And the angel added these words, saying : ' Know surely that I am sent to you by God, with the book of glass, in order that, according to what you have read in it, you shall ordain Aidan to the kingship. But

---

7 ordinaret A B1 B2 B3 ; -ent contents-list of B3. Illegible in contents-list of B2.
8 hinba A ; himba B1 B3 ; imba B2
9 accipisset A ; -cep- B1 B2 B3
10 iogenanum A B3 ; ioiena'num B1. The words *quia* to *dilegeret* are omitted in B2.
11 dilegeret A ; -li'g- B1 ; -lig- B3
12 flagillo A ; flagello B1 B2 B3
13 livorosum A ; livosum B1 B2 B3 (-vo's- B1)

21

regnum ordines. Quod si obsecundare huic nolueris jusioni, percutiam te [1] iterato '.

Hic itaque angelus domini cum per tris [2] contenuas [3] noctes eundem in manu [4] vitreum habens codicem apparuisset, eademque domini jusa de regis ejusdem ordinatione commendasset, sanctus verbo obsequtus domini ad Iovam transnavigavit insulam, ibidemque Aidanum hísdem adventantem [5] diebus in regem sicut erat jusus ordinavit. Et inter ordinationis verba de filiis et nepotibus pronepotibusque ejus futura profetizavit, 108a inponensque manum | super caput ejus ordinans benedixit. .

[6] Cummeneus albus [7] in libro quem de virtutibus sancti Columbae scripsit síc dixit, quod sanctus Columba de Aidano et de posterís ejus et de regno suo profetare coepit, dicens : ' Indubitanter crede, Ó Aidane, quoniam nullus adversariorum tuorum tibi poterit resistere, donec prius fraudulentiam agas in me et in posteros meos. Propterea ergo tú filiis commenda, ut et ipsi filiis et nepotibus et posterís suís commendent, ne per consilia mala eorum sceptrum regni hujus de manibus suís perdant. In quocumque enim tempore malum adversum me aut adversus cognatos meos qui sunt in Hibernia fecerint, flagillum quod causa tui ab angelo sustenui per manum dei super eos in magnum flagitium vertetur ; et cor virorum auferetur ab eís, et inimici eorum vehimenter super eos confortabuntur '. .

Hoc autem vaticinium temporibus nostrís conpletum est in bello Roth, Domnallo Brecco nepot[e] [8] Aidani sine causa

---

[1] te A B2 B3. Omitted in B1.   [2] tris A ; tres B1 B2 B3
[3] contenuas A ; -tin- B1 B2 B3   [4] manu A B1 B2 ; navi B3
[5] adventantem diebus A ; diebus adventantem B1 B2 B3
[6] *Cummeneus* to *incutit.* This passage is not in B1 B2 B3. It was inserted, in smaller lettering, by the writer of A, almost certainly not on the authority of Adomnan. It contains the only fragment of Cummene's work that is known to exist. See pp. 13, 91, 103.
[7] *albus* is written by the text hand above *mene.*
[8] In *nepot[e]*, the last letter is formed like the first part of *o.*

if you refuse to obey this command, I shall strike you again '.

So when this angel of the Lord had appeared on three successive nights with the same book of glass in his hand, and had charged him with the same commands of the Lord, for the ordaining of the same king, the holy man submitted to the word of the Lord. He sailed over to the island of Io, and there, as he had been bidden, he ordained as king Aidan, who arrived about that time. And among the words of the ordination he prophesied future things of Aidan's sons, and grandsons, and great-grandsons. And laying his hand upon Aidan's head he ordained and blessed him.

Cummene the White, in a book that he wrote on the miraculous powers of Saint Columba, spoke to this effect, that Saint Columba began to prophesy of Aidan, and of his descendants, and of their kingdom, saying : ' Believe, O Aidan, and doubt not, that none of your opponents will be able to stand against you until first you practise deceit against me, and against my successors. For this reason therefore do you charge your sons that they also shall charge their sons and grandsons and descendants, not through evil counsels to lose their sceptre of this kingdom from their hands. For at whatever time they shall do evil to me, or to my kindred who are in Ireland, the scourge that I have endured from an angel on your account will be turned by the hand of God to a great disgrace upon them. And the heart of men will be taken from them ; and their enemies will be strongly heartened against them.'

This prophecy has been fulfilled in our times, in the battle of Roth, when Domnall Brecc, Aidan's grandson, without cause

vastante provinciam Domnail nepotis Ainmuireg. Et a die
illa usque hodie adhuc in proclivo sunt ab extraneís : quod
suspiria doloris pectori incutit.[1] .

De angelorum apparatione [2] alicujus beati
108b   Brittonis [3] | animam ad caelum vehentium

ALIO IN TEMPORE, cum vir sanctus in Iova commoraretur insula, quidam de suís monacus [4] Brito bonís
actibus intentus molestia correptus corporis [5] ad extrema
perductus est. Quem cum vir venerandus in hora
sui visitaret exitus, paulisper ad lectulum ejus adsistens
et ei benedicens ocius domum egreditur nolens videre
morientem [6] ; qui eodem momento post sancti de domu
secessum viri praesentem finiit vitam.

Tum vir praedicabilis in plateola sui deambulans
monasterii porrectís ad caelum oculís diutius valde
obstupescens ammirabatur. Quidam vero frater Aidanus
nomine filius Libir,[7] bonae indolis et relegiosus [8] homo,
109a qui solus de fratribus eadem adfuit | hora, flexís genibus
rogare coepit, ut sanctus eidem tantae ammirationis
causam intimaret. Cui sanctus : ' Nunc sanctos angelos
in aere contra adversarias potestates belligerare vidi.
Christoque agonithetae [9] gratias ago, quia victores angeli
animam hujus perigrini,[10] qui primus [11] apud nos in hac

---

[1] See pp. 47-8, 51, for historical implications of this paragraph.
[2] apparatione A ; -riti- B1 and contents-list of B2 ; -rici- B3 and
contents-list of B3. Illegible in B2.
[3] brittonis A and contents-list of B3 ; bri'tonis B1 ; britonis B3 and
contents-list of B2 ;]tonis B2
[4] monacus A B1 ; -chus B2 ; -chis B3
[5] correptus corporis A ; corporis correptus B1 B2 B3
[6] *morientem.* Here it is implied that Columba avoided being present at
a death, which would have caused pollution, and prevented him as a priest
from celebrating Mass. See the Tallaght Discourse § 65, where Leviticus
is named as the authority. Reconsecration by a bishop would have been
needed to remove the pollution, and Adomnan seems to assume that there

wasted the province of Domnall, Ainmuire's grandson. And they are from that day to this still held down by strangers ; which fills the breast with sighs of grief.

[III 6] Concerning an apparition of angels carrying the soul of a holy Briton to heaven

At another time, when the holy man was living in the island of Io, one of his monks, a Briton, devoted to good works, was attacked by a bodily affliction, and brought to the point of death. When the venerable man visited him in the hour of his decease, after standing for a little while beside his couch, and blessing him, he quickly left the house, being unwilling to see him die. And immediately after the holy man had gone away from the house, the monk ended the present life.

Then while the memorable man was walking in the court of his monastery, he turned his eyes to the sky, and was much amazed, and marvelled for a long time. A brother, called Aidan, Liber's son, a man of good ability, and religious, who alone of the brothers was present at that hour, bending his knees began to ask the saint to tell him the cause of so great marvelling. To him the saint replied : ' Now I have seen holy angels at war in the air against the adversary powers. And I render thanks to Christ the arbiter, because the angels have victoriously carried off to the joys of the heavenly

---

was no bishop in the community of Iona in Columba's time (cf. the episode of bishop Cronan, 45b).

[7] libir A B1 B2 ; liber B3

[8] relegiosus A ; -lig- B1 B2 B3

[9] agonithetae A ; -te B2 B3 ; agoni'tice B1, altered from -tece.

[10] perigrini A ; -reg- B1 B2 B3

[11] primus. This chapter differs greatly from the legend of the death of Odran in the Irish Life of Columba (cf. E.S., 1, p. 45) ; and it may have been written on purpose to contradict an early form of that legend.

insula mortuus est, ad caelestis patriae gaudia evexerunt.
Sed hoc quesso sacramentum nemini in vita mea
reveles '. .

De angelorum revelata eidem sancto viro
visione, qui animam alicujus Diormiti [1]
ad caelum ducebant. .

ALIO IN TEMPORE quidam everniensis [2] perigrinus [3]
ad sanctum perveniens per aliquot apud eum menses [4]
in Iova commanebat insula. Cui vir beatus alia die :
' Nunc ' ait, ' quidam de conprovincialibus [5] tuís clericus

109b ad caelum ab angelís portatur, | cujus adhuc ignoro
nomen '. Frater vero hoc audiens coepit secum de
provincia [6] perscrutari anteriorum, qui scotice ind
Airthir [7] nuncupantur,[8] et de illius beati hominis vocabulo. Hocque consequenter intulit verbum, inquiens :
' Alium Christi scio militonem qui sibi in eodem terri-
torio in quo et ego commanebam [9] monasteriolum con-
struxit, nomine Diormitium '.[10] Cui sanctus ait : ' Ipse
est [11] de quo dicis qui nunc ab angelís dei in paradisum
deductus est '.

Sed hoc etiam non neglegenter [12] annotandum est,
quod idem vir venerabilis multa sibi a deo arcana [13] ab
aliis celata sacramenta nullo modo in hominum notitiam
prodi passus sit : duabus, ut ipse aliquando paucís

[1] diormiti A ; -mi'tïi B1 ; -micïi B2 ; -mitii contents-list of B2 ;
-micii B3 and contents-list of B3
[2] everniensis A ; hiberniensis B1 B3 ; hyberni[B2
[3] perigrinus A ; -reg- B1 B2 B3
[4] apud eum menses A B1 B3 ; dies apud eum B2
[5] conprovincialibus A ; between *de* and *provincialibus*, a small *con*
symbol has been added above the line, and a small placing point inserted
beneath it, both probably by the text hand. com- (*or* con-) B1 B2 B3.
The shortened version and P, both derived from A, omitted *con*. So also
did Reeves.   [6] provincia A ; vita B1 B2 B3

country the soul of this pilgrim, who first among us has died in this island. But I beg, do not reveal this mystery to any one, in my life-time '.

[III 7] Concerning a vision, revealed to the holy man, of angels who were leading to heaven the soul of one Diormit

At another time, an Irish pilgrim, coming to the saint, remained for some months with him in the island of Io. One day, the blessed man said to him : ' Now a cleric, a man of your own province, is being carried to heaven by angels. As yet, I do not know his name '. The brother, hearing this, began to search his memory regarding the province of the easterners, who are in Irish called *ind Airthir*, and for the name of that holy man. Then he added these words : ' I know another soldier of Christ, named Diormit, who has constructed for himself a little monastery in the same region in which I also lived '. The saint said to him : ' He of whom you speak is the man who has now been led to paradise by angels of God '.

But this also is to be observed with care, that many secret mysteries, hidden from others, but imparted to him by God, were never allowed by this venerable man to reach the knowledge of men. There were for this

[7] indairthir A, with four over-dashes ; ondairtir B1 B3 ?B2 (-ti'r B1). See 44a, and p. 134.

[8] nuncupantur A B3 ; -atur B1. Missing in B2.

[9] commanebam A ; -e'bat B1 (-*t* altered to -*m*, ?not by text hand) ; -ebat B2 B3

[10] diormitium A B2 ; -mi'ti- B1 ; -mici- B3

[11] ait ipse est A ; ipse est ait B1 B2 B3

[12] neglegenter A ; neglig- B1 ; neclig- B3. Illegible in B2.

[13] arcana A ; archana B1 B2 B3. The meaning ' secrets imparted ' needs a passive participle, which Adomnan has apparently not supplied.

intimaverat fratribus, causís existentibus, hoc est ut
110a jactantiam devitaret, et ad [1] semet ipsum [2] | inter-
rogandum insustentabiles turbas de se aliqua interrogare
volentes devulgata [3] revelationum fama non invitaret.

De angelorum contra daemones forti
belligeratione sancto in eodem bello
oportune subvenientium. .[4]

ALIA DIE VIR sanctus in Iova conversans insula
remotiorem ab hominibus [5] locum aptumque [6] ad orationem in saltibus [7] quaesivit. Ibidemque cum orare
coepisset subito, ut ipse postea paucís intimaverat fratribus, videt contra sé tetram et nigerrimam daemonum
cum ferreís veribus aciem proeliari ; qui sicuti sancto
viro per spiritum revelatum erat monasterium ejus
invadere et multos ex fratribus hísdem volebant jugulare
sudibus. Ipse vero contra tales emulos unus homo
innumeros accepta Pauli armatura apostoli forti con-
110b flictu dimicabat. Et | ita ex majore diei parte utrimque
dimicatum est ; nec innumerabiles unum vincere [8]
poterant, nec eos unus de sua valebat insula repellere,
donec angeli dei, ut sanctus post quibusdam non multís
retulerat, in am[mi]niculum [9] adfuere ; quorum [10] timore
proturbati daemones loco cessere.

---

[1] ad A B1 B3 ; ab B2   [2] ipsum in | A ; ipsum B1 B2 B3, correctly.
[3] devulgata A ; div- B1 B2 B3
[4] subvenientium A B1 B2 and contents-list of B2 and of B3 (-ie'nt- B1) ;
-ientis B3
[5] hominibus A B1 (on an erasure in B1) ; omnibus B2 B3
[6] aptumque A B1 B3 ; apertumque B2
[7] *saltibus.* These *saltus* were, doubtless, the valleys and rocky corridors
that characterize central Iona to the south-west of Dun-Í.
[8] vincere A B2 B3 ; evi'ncere B1
[9] am|niculum A ; *mi* : has been added at the end of the line, in a
modern hand. adminiculum B1 B2 B3 (-ni'c- B1)
[10] quorum A ; quo B1 B2 B3

two reasons, as he at one time told a few of the brothers ;
namely, to avoid boasting ; and not, through wide-
spread reports of his revelations, to invite questioning
of himself by intolerable crowds of people who wished
to ask some question of him.

[III 8] Concerning a strong combat against
demons by angels who in that battle brought
timely help to the saint

One day, while the holy man was living his life in
the island of Io, he sought in wild places a spot more
remote from mankind, and suitable for prayer. And
when he had begun to pray there, suddenly, as he afterwards informed a few brothers, he saw a foul and very
black array of demons making war against him with
iron spits. They, as was revealed by the Spirit to the
holy man, wished to assail his monastery, and with
these same spikes to slaughter many of the brothers.
But he, one man against these innumerable enemies,
fought a strong fight, taking to himself the armour of
the apostle Paul.

So for the greater part of the day the battle continued
on both sides, and neither could the numberless enemies
defeat the one man, nor was the one strong enough to
drive them from his island ; until, as the saint afterwards related to a few men, angels of God came to his
support. Through fear of them the demons were
repelled, and withdrew.

Eademque die sanctus ad monasterium post dae-
moniorum reversus de sua insula effugationem, hoc de
eisdem turmís hostilibus verbum profatur, inquiens :
' Illi exitiabiles emuli, qui hac die de hujus terrulae
deo propitio regione angelís nobís subvenientibus ad
Ethicam [1] effugati sunt terram, ibidem [2] saevi invasores
fratrum monasteria [3] invadent, et pestilentes [4] inferent
morbos ; quorum molestia infestati multi morientur '.

111a   Quod [5] hísdem diebus juxta beati prae|scientiam viri
ita et [6] factum est.   Et post interveniente biduo ei
revelante spiritu : ' Bene ' ait, ' Baitheneus [7] auxiliante
deo dispensavit, ut ejusdem eclesiae cui deo auctore
praeest in [8] campo Lunge [9] jejuniis et orationibus col-
lectio a daemonum defendatur [10] invasione ; ubi nemo,
excepto uno qui mortuus est, hac vice morietur '.   Quod
ita juxta vaticinium ejus expletum est.   Nam cum multi
in ceterís ejusdem insulae monasteriis eodem morbo
morirentur,[11] nemo nisi unus de quo sanctus dixit apud
Baitheneum [12] in sua est mortuus congregatione. .

[1] ethicam A B2 B3 ; e'thicam B1
[2] ibidem A B1 ; ibidemque B2 B3
[3] monasteria A B1 B3 ; monasteriola B2
[4] pestilentes A ?B2 ; -tos B1 B3
[5] quod A ; Quos B1 ; Quod B2 B3
[6] ita et A ; ita B1 B2 B3
[7] Baitheneus A ; baithe'neus B1, later altered to -nus ; baitheneus
B2 B3
[8] in A B2 B3 ; ut in B1
[9] lunge A B1 B2 B3, with two over-dashes in A.
[10] defendatur A B1 ; -antur B2 B3
[11] morirentur A ; morrer- B1 ; morer- B3.   Illegible in B2.
[12] baitheneum A B2 B3 ; baithe'neum B1

On the same day, when the saint returned to the monastery, after the repulse of the demons from his island, he pronounced these words about those hostile forces, saying : ' The deadly foes who have today, by God's favour, angels helping us, been driven away from the region of this little land, to the land of Eth [Tiree], will cruelly invade the monasteries of brothers there, and will bring upon them pestilential diseases ; and many that suffer from the affliction of those diseases will die '.

In accordance with the foreknowledge of the blessed man, that happened in the days that followed. After two days' interval, by the revelation of the Spirit, he said : ' With the help of God, Baithene has contrived well, so that the community of the church over which, by God's disposition, he rules, in the plain of Long, is defended by fasts and prayers from the assault of demons ; and no one there, excepting one man who has died, will die on this occasion '.

This was fulfilled according to his prophecy. For while many in the other monasteries of the same island died of that disease, only the one man of whom the saint had spoken died in Baithene's community.

De angelorum apparatione [1] quos vir dei
viderat alicujus animam nomine [2] Columbi
fabri ferrarii Coilrigini [3] cognomento ad
caelos evehere

QUIDAM FABER ferrarius in mediterranea Scotiae
111b habitabat parte [4] elimoysinarum [5] operibus satis | in-
tentus et ceterís justitiae actibus plenus. Hic cum ad
extrema in bona senectute perduceretur supra memoratus Columbus cognominatus Coilriginus,[6] eadem hora
qua de corpore eductus est sanctus Columba in Iova
commanens insula paucís quibusdam sé circumstantibus
síc profatus senioribus : ' Columbus Coilriginus ' [7] ait,
' faber ferrarius non incassum laboravit, qui de propria
manuum laboratione suarum praemia emax felix con-
par[a]vit [8] aeterna. Ecce enim nunc anima ejus a sanctis
vehitur angelís ad caelestis patriae gaudia. Nam quod-
cumque de suae artis negotiatione adquirere potuit in
egenorum elimoysinas [9] expendit '. . .

De angelorum simili visione [10] quos vir beatus [11]
aspexerat alicujus bene moratae feminae
animam ad caelum ferre |

112a   ALIO ITIDEM IN TEMPORE vir sanctus in Iova conversans insula quadam die subito oculos ad caelum
diregens [12] haec profatus est verba : ' Felix mulier felix
bene morata, cujus animam nunc angeli dei ad para-

---

[1] apparatione A ; -riti- B1 and contents-list of B2 ; -rici- B3 and
contents-list of B3. Illegible in B2.
[2] nomine A B2 B3 and contents-list of B2 and of B3 ; ejus B1
[3] coil rigini A ; coilrigini B1 B2 B3   [4] mediterranea . . . parte. Cf. 14a.
[5] elimoysinarum A ; elemos- B1 B2 B3
[6-7] coil riginus A, with very slight separation ; coilriginus B1 B2 B3
(-ri'g- B1)   [8] conparuit A ; -ravit B1 B2 B3

[III 9] Concerning an apparition of angels, whom the man of God saw carrying to the heavens the soul of a certain iron-smith, named Columb, surnamed Coilrigin

In the midland part of Ireland dwelt a certain iron-smith, much devoted to works of charity, and full of the other acts of righteousness. When this man, the above-named Columb, surnamed Coilrigin, came in good old age to the end of his life, in the same hour in which he was taken from the body, Saint Columba living in the island of Io spoke to some few of the elders who were standing beside him, and said : ' Columb Coilrigin the iron-smith has not laboured in vain. He has been fortunate in procuring with the labour of his own hands the eternal rewards that he desired to buy. See now, his soul is being carried by holy angels to the joys of the heavenly country. For whatever he was able to gain by practising his craft he laid out in alms to the needy '.

[III 10] Concerning a similar vision of angels whom the blessed man beheld carrying to heaven the soul of a certain virtuous woman

At another time also, while the holy man lived in the island of Io, one day he suddenly turned his eyes to the sky, and uttered these words : ' Happy woman, happy and virtuous, whose soul the angels of God are now carrying to paradise '.

9 elimoysinas A ; elemo's- B1 ; elemos- B2 B3
10 visione A B2 B3 and contents-list of B2 and of B3. Omitted in B1.
11 beatus A B1 B2 B3 and contents-list of B3 ; sanctus contents-list of B2
12 diregens A ; -rig- B1 B3. Illegible in B2.

disum evehunt '. Erat autem quidam relegiosus [1] frater
Genereus nomine Saxo, pistor, opus pistorium [2] exercens,
qui hoc audierat verbum ex ore sancti prolatum.
Eademque die mensis eodem terminato anno sanctus
eidem Genereo Saxoni : ' Miram rem video ', ait.
' Ecce mulier de qua té praesente praeterito dixeram
anno nunc mariti sui relegiosi [3] cujusdam plebei in aere
obviat animae, et cum sanctis angelís contra emulas pro
ea belligerat potestates ; quorum amminiculo ejusdem
112b homuncionis [4] justitia suf|fragante a daemonum belli-
gerationibus erepta ad aeternae refrigerationis locum
anima ipsius est perducta '. .

De angelorum apparatione [5] sanctorum quos
sanctus Columba obvios in transitu viderat
beati Brendini [6] animae, illius monasterii
fundatoris quod scotice Birra nuncupatur

ALIA ITIDEM DIE, dum vir venerandus in Iova conversaretur insula, mane primo suum advocat sepe memoratum ministratorem, Diormitium [7] nomine, eique praecipit,[8] inquiens : ' Sacra celeriter eucharistiae ministeria
praeparentur. Hodie enim natalis beati Brendini [9]
dies '.[10] ' Quare ' ait minister, ' talia misarum sollempnia hodierna praeparari praecipis ? Nullus enim ad nos
de Scotia sancti illius viri obitus pervenit nuntius '.

[1] relegiosus A ; -lig- B1 B2 B3
[2] pistorium A B2 ; -rum B1 B3
[3] relegiosi A ; -lig- B1 B2 B3
[4] homuncionis A B3 ; homutionis B1 ; homuntionis B2
[5] apparatione A ; appa[ ]ne B1 (3 or 4 letters have been erased, and the reviser has noted *aricione* in the margin) ; -riti- B2 and contents-list of B2 ; -rici- B3 and contents-list of B3
[6] brendini A ; brendeni B1 B2 B3 and contents-list of B2 and of B3
[7] diormitium A B1 ?B2 (-mi't- B1) ; -micium B3
[8] praecipit A ; pre'cipit B1 ; precepit B3. Illegible in B2.

There was a certain religious brother named Genereus the Englishman, a baker, who while engaged upon the work of baking heard those words coming from the mouth of the saint. And after the end of a year, on the same day of the month, the saint said to the same Genereus the Englishman : ' I see a marvellous thing. Behold, the woman of whom I spoke in your presence a year ago is now meeting in the air the soul of her husband, a pious layman, and is fighting for it along with holy angels against the hostile powers. Through the help of the angels, aided by the righteousness of the mortal man himself, his soul, snatched from the battling of demons, has been brought to the place of eternal rest '.

[III 11] Concerning an apparition of holy angels whom Saint Columba saw at the passing of the blessed Brenden, coming to meet his soul. Brenden was the founder of the monastery that is called *Birra* in Irish

Again, when the venerable man lived in the island of Io, one day in the early morning he summoned his attendant Diormit (whom we have often mentioned), and gave him an order, saying : ' Let the sacred ministries of the Eucharist be quickly made ready. For today is the blessed Brenden's natal day '. ' Why ' said the attendant, ' do you order this solemn rite of the Mass to be prepared, for today ? No one has come to us from Ireland bringing news of the death of that

⁹ brendini A ; -deni B1 B2 B3
¹⁰ dies A ; dies est B1 B2 B3. Brenden's death was commemorated on 29 November (cf. Oengus 1905, p. 237). The year of his death is variously given ; see p. 80.

113a 'Vade tum' | ait sanctus, 'meae obsecundare jusioni debes. Hac enim nocte praeterita vidi subito apertum caelum, angelorumque choros [1] sancti Brendini [2] animae obvios discendere,[3] quorum luminosa et inconparabili [4] claritudine totus eadem hora inlustratus est mundi orbis'.

De angelorum visione [5] sanctorum qui sancti Columbani episcopi mocu-Loigse [6] animam ad caelum evexerant

QUADAM ITIDEM DIE, dum fratres sé calciantes mane [7] ad diversa monasterii opera ire praepararent, sanctus econtra ea die otiari [8] praecipit, sacraeque oblationis obsequia praeparari, et aliquam quasi in dominico prandioli adjectionem fieri. 'Meque' ait, 'hodie, quamlibet indignus sim, ob venerationem illius animae quae hac in nocte inter sanctos angelorum choros vecta 113b ultra siderea caelorum spatia ad paradisum as|cendit, sacra oportet eucharistiae celebrare misteria'.

Et hís dictís fratres obsequntur, et juxta sancti jusionem eadem otiantur die, praeparatísque sacrís ad eclesiam ministeriis quasi die sollempni albati [9] cum sancto pergunt. Sed forte, dum inter talia [10] cum

---

[1] choros A ; choros innumerorum B1 B3 ?B2
[2] brendini A ; -deni B1 B3. Missing in B2.
[3] discendere A ; desc- B1 B3. Missing in B2.
[4] inconparabili A, apparently altered from *incorporabili* by the text hand at the time of writing ; incomparabili B1 B3 ;]bili B2
[5] visione A B1 B2 and contents-list of B2 and of B3 ; visoine B3
[6] mocu loigse A ; moculoigse B1 B2 B3 and contents-list of B3 (-loi′g-B1) ; moculigse contents-list of B2. The family name mocu-Loigse indicates origin in the tribe that gave its name to county Leix, in Leinster. Cf. MacNéill 1911, p. 78.
[7] *mane*. Here, probably, the time meant is after Prime. It is not implied that Mass was to be celebrated at the next canonical hour ; perhaps Sext was the hour of celebration that Adomnan had in mind.
[8] *otiari*, and *otiantur* 113b, imply that by Columba's order the monks refrained from carrying out the heavy work of the day. Adomnan does

holy man '. ' Yet go ', said the saint ; ' you must obey my command. For in this past night I have seen the sky suddenly opened, and companies of angels coming down to meet the soul of Saint Brenden. Their shining and incomparable brightness in that hour lit up the whole circle of the world '.

[III 12] Concerning a vision of holy angels
who were carrying to heaven the soul of
the holy bishop Colman mocu-Loigse

Also on a certain day, when the brothers were putting on their shoes in the morning, preparing to go to the various labours of the monastery, Saint Columba on the contrary gave orders that they should not go to work on that day, and that the rites of the sacred obla-tion should be prepared, and that there should be the addition of a small meal, as on a Lord's-day. ' And I ', he said, ' although I be unworthy, must celebrate today the sacred mysteries of the Eucharist, in veneration of the soul that in this night has ascended to paradise beyond the starry spaces of the heavens, carried between holy companies of angels.'

After these words, the brothers obeyed, and accord-ing to the saint's command did not go to work on that day ; and when the sacred ministries had been prepared, they went with the saint to the church, clothed in white, as on a solemn feast-day. But when in the course of

---

not say that they were ordered to refrain from all work (*requiescere*). His words involve the assumption that on ' solemn days ' similar relaxation was customary.

⁹ albati A B1 B2 ; abbati B3
¹⁰ talia A B1 B2 ; alia B3

2K

modolatione [1] officia illa consueta decantaretur depre-
catio in qua sancti Martini [2] commemoratur [3] nomen,
subito sanctus ad cantatores [4] ejusdem onomatis ad
locum pervenientes : ' Hodie ' ait, ' " pro sancto Columbano episcopo " decantare debetis '. Tunc omnes qui
inerant fratres intellexere quod Columbanus episcopus
lagenensis carus Columbae amicus ad dominum emigra-
verit. Et post alicujus temporis intervallum aliqui de
lagenica [5] commeantes provincia ea nocte eundem obisse
114a   nuntiant episcopum | qua sancto ita revelatum est.

De angelorum apparatione [6] qui obviam
animabus sancti monacorum Comgelli [7]
discenderant [8]

ALIO IN TEMPORE vir venerandus cum in Iova conversaretur insula quadam subitatione incitatus signo
personante collectís fratribus : ' Nunc ' ait, ' oratione
monacís abbatis Comgilli [9] auxiliemur, hac in hora in
stagno dimersís vituli.[10] Ecce enim hoc momento in aere
contra adversarias belligerant potestates, animam alicujus hospitis simul cum eís dimersi eripere conantes '.

Tum post lacrimosam et intentam orationem cito
ante altarium surgens inter fratres pariter in oratione

---

[1] modolatione A ; -dul- B1 B2 B3
[2] *Martini.* Here, we think, Adomnan implies that in the Commemoration of the dead the name of Martin of Tours came first in the section of
bishops (as it does in the Stowe Missal) ; and that Columba interrupted
the Commemoration before the bishops' section began, and ordered that
Colman's name should be added at the end of that section. In the commemoration list of the Stowe Missal (II, p. 16), a Colman is mentioned,
after Findbarr, among the bishops.
[3] commemoratur A ; commemoraretur B1 B2 B3
[4] cantatores A ; the letters *ta* have later been deleted by over-pointing
(not by text hand). cantores B1 B2 B3   [5] lagenica A B2 B3 ; -ge'n- B1
[6] apparatione A ; -riti- B1 ; -rici- B3 and contents-list of B3. Illegible
in B2. This chapter-heading is omitted in the contents-list of B2.

this service that customary prayer was chanted, with melody, in which the name of Saint Martin is mentioned, suddenly Saint Columba said to the singers, when they came to the place of that name : ' Today you must sing, " For Saint Colman, the bishop ".'

Then all the brothers who were present understood that Columba's dear friend Colman, a bishop of the Lagin, had departed to the Lord. And after the lapse of some time, travellers from the province of the Lagin reported that the same bishop had died on the night on which it had so been revealed to the saint.

[III 13] Concerning an apparition of angels
who descended to meet the souls of monks
of Saint Comgell

At another time, while he lived in the island of Io, the venerable man suddenly sprang up, summoned the brothers with the sound of the bell, and said to them : ' Let us now aid with prayer abbot Comgell's monks, that have been drowned in the lake of the calf, in this hour. For see, at this moment they are fighting in the air against hostile powers that are trying to carry off the soul of a guest who has been drowned along with them '.

Then after tearful and earnest prayer he rose quickly, before the altar, among the brothers who were likewise prostrated in prayer, and said with joyful

---

[7] comgelli A B3 and contents-list of B3 ; congelli B1.   Illegible in B2.
[8] discenderant A ; des- B1 B3 and contents-list of B3.   Illegible in B2.
[9] comgilli A ; congelli B1 (with the *con* symbol) ; comgelli B3.   Missing in B2.
[10] *stagno vituli*.   This is a translation of Loch-láig, an Irish name of Belfast Lough.   Comgell's monastery, of Bennchor (Bangor), was on the south side of that loch.

prostratos, laetificato [1] vultu : ' Christo ' ait, ' grates
agite ; nunc enim sancti angeli sanctis obviantes animabus et ipsum hospitem ereptum a daemonum belli-
114b gera|tionibus quasi victoriales liberarunt belligeratores '.

De angelorum manifestatione alicujus
Emchathi [2] animae obviantium. .

ALIO IN TEMPORE vir sanctus ultra Brittanniae dorsum
iter agens secus Nisae [3] fluminis lacum subito inspiratus
spiritu sancto ad fratres pariter commeantes : ' Pro-
peremus ' ait, ' sanctis [4] obviam angelís qui, de summís
caeli regionibus ad praeferendam alicujus gentilici
animam emisi, nos illuc usque pervenientes exspectant,
ut ipsum naturale bonum per totam vitam usque ad
extremam senectutem [5] conservantem priusquam moriatur [6] oportune babtizemus '.

Et haec dicens sanctus senex [7] in quantum potuit
comites festinus praecedebat, donec in illum devenit
115a agrum qui Airchartdan [8] nuncupatur. | Ibidemque
quidam repertus senex Emchatus nomine audiens a
sancto verbum dei praedicatum et credens babtizatus
est ; et continuo laetus et securus cum angelís obvian-
tibus ei ad dominum commigravit. Sed et filius ejus
Virolecus [9] credens cum tota domu [10] est babtizatus. .

[1] laetificato A ; leti- B1 ; liti- B3. Illegible in B2.
[2] emchathi A B3 ; emchati B1 B2 and contents-list of B2 ; emdathi
contents-list of B3. See p. 160.
[3] nisae A ; nesse B1 : nese B2 B3. Cf. note under 81b.
[4] sanctis A B2 ; sanctus B1 B3
[5] senectutem A B1 B2 ; -tam B3
[6] moriatur A B1 B2 ; moreatur B3
[7] *senex*. According to Bede's reckoning, Columba came to Britain and
visited the Picts in 565, when he was about forty-five years old. He could
then have been called *senex* in comparison with his younger followers. But
Adomnan says that Columba came to Britain when he was in his forty-
second year, and implies here that when he visited the province of the

countenance : ' Give thanks to Christ ; for now holy angels, coming to meet the holy souls, have, like victorious warriors, rescued also that guest, snatched from the battling of demons '.

[III 14] Concerning a manifestation of angels coming to meet the soul of one Emchath

At one time, when the holy man was making a journey on the other side of the Spine of Britain, beside the lake of the river Nes [Ness], he was suddenly inspired by the Holy Spirit, and said to the brothers who travelled along with him : ' Let us hasten towards the holy angels that have been sent from the highest regions of heaven to conduct the soul of a pagan, and who await our coming thither so that we may give timely baptism, before he dies, to that man, who has preserved natural goodness through his whole life, into extreme old age '.

Saying this, the aged saint went as fast as he could, ahead of his companions, until he came to the farmland that is called Airchartdan [Urquhart]. And a certain old man whom he found there, Emchath by name, hearing and believing the word of God preached by the saint, was baptized ; and thereupon, gladly and confidently, with the angels that came to meet him he departed to the Lord. And his son Virolec also believed and was baptized, with his whole house.

Picts he was physically an old man. This seems to require that the visit was made several years after 563. See p. 78.

[8] air chart dan A (one word, slightly spread) ; aircardan B1 B2 B3 (-a'n B1). This appears to be an Irish form of a British name. See pp. 106, 157.

[9] virolecus A B3 ; viroletus B1. Illegible in B2. See p. 161.

[10] domu A ; domo B1 B3 ?B2

De angelo domini qui alicui fratri lapso de
monasterii culmine rotundi [1] in roboreti
campo oportune tam cito subvenerat. .

ALIO IN TEMPORE, vir sanctus dum in tegoriolo [2] suo
scribens sederet, subito ejus inmotata [3] facies, et hanc
puro de pectore promit vocem, dicens : ' Auxiliare,
auxiliare '.   Duo vero fratres ad januam stantes, videlicet Colgu [4] filius Cellachi et Lugneus [5] mocu-Blai,[6]
causam talis subitae interrogant vocis.   Quibus vir
115b venerabilis hoc dedit res|ponsum, inquiens :   ' Angelo
domini qui nunc inter vos stabat jusi ut alicui ex fratribus de summo culmine magnae domus laps[o] [7] tam cito
subveniret, quae hís in diebus in roboreti campo fabri-
catur '.   Hocque consequenter sanctus intulit famen,
inquiens :   ' Valde ammirabilis et pene indicibilis est
angelici volatus pernicitas, fulgoreae ut estimo caeleritati
parilis.   Nam ille caelicola qui hinc a nobís nunc illo viro
labi incipiente avolavit quasi in ictu oculi priusquam
terram tangeret subveniens eum [8] sublevavit ; nec ullam
fracturam aut lessuram ille qui cicidit [9] sentire potuit.
Quam stupenda inquam haec velocissima [10] et oportuna
subventio, quae dicto citius tantís maris et terrae inter-
jacentibus spatiis tam celerrime effici potuit '. . |

---

[1] *monasterii rotundi.* This building is called *magna domus* in 115b. It
appears to have been a communal house of the monastery. See 31a, and
p. 113.
    [2] tegoriolo A ; tuguriolo B1 B3 ?B2 (-i'olo B1)
    [3] inmotata A ; inmutatur B1 B2 B3
    [4] colgu A ; co'lgius B1 ; colgius B2 B3. Cf. 35b.
    [5] lugneus A B2 B3 ; lugne'us B1
    [6] mocublai A B1 B3 ; moccublai ?B2
    [7] lapsae A ; lapso B1 B2 B3
    [8] eum A B2 B3 ; illum B1
    [9] cicidit A ; ce'c- B1 ; cec- B2 B3
    [10] velocissima A B1 B2 ; vol- B3

[III 15] Concerning an angel of the Lord, who
came very quickly and opportunely to the
rescue of a brother as he fell from the top
of the round monastic house in the plain
of the oakwood [Durrow]

At one time, when the holy man sat writing in his
hut, suddenly his face changed, and he uttered from
his pure heart this cry : ' Help, help ! '

Two brothers, standing at the door, namely Colcu
son of Cellach, and Lugne mocu-Blai, asked the reason
of this sudden exclamation. The venerable man gave
them this answer, saying : ' One of the brothers was
falling from the highest point of the great house that is
at the present time being built in the plain of the oakwood, and I bade an angel of the Lord, that stood but
now between you, to go with all speed to his rescue '.
Then the saint added this utterance : ' Exceedingly
marvellous and almost beyond description is the swift-
ness of angels' flight, equal as I think to the speed of
lightning. For the heavenly one who flew away from
us just now, when that man was beginning to fall, came
to the rescue as though in the twinkling of an eye, and
held him up before he touched the ground ; and he
that fell was unable to feel any fracture or injury. How
amazing, I say, was this timely and most rapid rescue
which, more quickly than words, could be made so very
speedily, when so great spaces of sea and land lay
between ! '

116a ## De angelorum multitudine sanctorum visa
ad beati condictum viri de caelo
discendentium [1]

ALIO ITIDEM IN TEMPORE quadam die vir beatus in
Iova conversans insula fratribus congregatís cum ingenti
animadversione denuntiavit, ad eos dicens : ' Hodie in
occidentalem nostrae campulum insulae solus exire
cupio. Nemo itaque ex vobís me sequatur '. Quibus
obsecundantibus solus quidem ut voluit egreditur,[2] sed
frater quidam callidus explorator alia means via in
cujusdam monticelli cacumine, qui eidem supereminet
campulo, sé occulte conlocat, videlicet illius causam
solitariae beati egresionis viri explorare cupiens. Quem
cum idem explorator de monticelli vertice in quodam
116b illius campuli colliculo stantem et expan|sís ad caelum
manibus orantem, oculosque ad caelos elevantem, con-
spiceret, mirum dictu et ecce subito res miranda
apparuit ; quam idem supra memoratus homo, ut
estimo non sine permisu dei, de propioris monticelli
loco oculís etiam corporalibus aspexerat, ut nomen
sancti et ejus honorificantia [3] quamvis ipso nolente ob [4]
hanc manifestatam visionem postea magis in populís
devulgaretur.[5] Nam sancti angeli caelestis patriae cives
mira advolantes subitatione sanctum virum orantem
circumstare coeperunt albatís [6] induti vestibus. Et post
aliquam cum beato sermocinationem viro illa caelestis
caterva quasi sé exploratam sentiens ad summa citius
repedavit caelorum.[7]

[1] discendentium A ; desc- B1 B2 B3 and contents-list of B2 and of B3
[2] egReditur A (the R results from an alteration by the text hand,
perhaps from o) ; egre'd- B1 ; egred- B2 B3
[3] honorificantia A B1 ; -cancia B3 ; -centia B2
[4] ob A B2 B3 ; ad B1   [5] devulgaretur A ; div- B1 B2 B3
[6] albatís A ; albatis B1 B3 ?B2 (altered from *abbatis* in B3)

[III 16] Concerning a multitude of holy angels
seen when they descended from heaven to
a conference with the blessed man

At another time also, while the blessed man lived
in the island of Io, one day he admonished the assembled
brothers, with great severity, and said to them : ' Today
I wish to go out alone, to the western plain of our island.
Let none of you therefore follow me '. They obeyed,
and he did go alone as he desired ; but a certain
brother, a cunning spy, going by another way, took up
a position secretly on the top of a little hill that overlooks that plain, wishing to detect the cause of that
solitary expedition of the blessed man.

From the top of the little hill the spy saw him
standing on a certain knoll of that plain and praying,
with his hands outstretched to the sky, and his eyes
raised to heaven, and then, strange to tell, behold
suddenly a marvellous thing appeared, which the man
from his position on the nearby hill looked upon, even
with bodily eyes ; as I think, not without the permission
of God, in order that the name of the saint, and his
renown, should, although against his will, afterwards
be spread more widely among the peoples, because of
this vision made manifest. For holy angels, citizens of
the heavenly country, flew down with marvellous
suddenness, clothed in white raiment, and began to
stand about the holy man as he prayed. And after
some converse with the blessed man, that heavenly
throng, as though perceiving that they were watched,
quickly returned to the highest heaven.

---

⁷ *caelorum.* This chapter can hardly be dissociated from the belief
prevailing in the ancient Irish church that angels became visible to men in
the form of birds. Cf. Plummer 1910, I, p. cxlvii.

117a   Beatus | et ipse vir post angelicum condictum reversus
ad monasterium, iterum collectís fratribus cum quadam
non mediocri objurgatione inquirit quis de illís esset
transgressionis [1] obnoxius. Quibus consequenter se
nescisse protestantibus ille conscius sui inexcussabilis
transgressus ultra non [2] sustenens [3] delictum celare suum
flexís genibus in medio fratrum choro coram sancto
veniam supplex precatur. Quem sanctus seorsum
ducens, ingeniculanti [4] cum grandi commendat com-
minatione ut nulli hominum de illa angelica visione in
diebus ejusdem beati viri aliquid etiam parvum occultum
aperiret. Post egresum vero de corpore sancti viri illam
caelestis coetus apparationem [5] fratribus cum grandi
intimavit protestatione.[6] Unde hodieque et locus illius
117b   angelici con|dicti rem in eo gestam suo proprio protes-
tatur vocabulo, qui latine potest dici colliculus angelorum, scotice vero Cnoc-angel.[7]

Hinc itaque animadvertendum est, et non neglegenter [8] perscrutandum, quantae et quales ad beatum
virum himalibus [9] plerumque noctibus insomnem, et in
locís remotioribus aliis quiescentibus orantem, angelicae
fuerint et suaves [10] frequentationes quae nullo modo
venire in hominum notitiam potuere, quae procul dubio
valde numerosae fuerant : si etiam quaedam ex ipsís
quoquo modo ab hominibus vel in die vel noctu explorari
potuerint, quae absque dubitatione paucae admodum

---

[1] transgressionis A B1 B2 ; -onibus B3
[2] non A B1 B2. Omitted in B3.
[3] sustenens A ; -tin- B1 B2 B3
[4] ingeniculanti A B1 B2 ; -lati B3
[5] apparationem A ; -riti- B1 B2 ; -rici- B3
[6] *pro*|*testatione*. In A, the letter *p* was originally written, and was
altered by the text hand to the *pro* symbol, by adding a horizontal line
through the shaft.
[7] cnoc angel A, with two over-dashes above *cnoc* ; cnoc angel nuncupatur B1 ;]nuncupatur B2 ; cnocangel nuncupatur B3. A's reading,

The blessed man himself also, after his conference with the angels, returned to the monastery. The brothers were assembled again, and with severe reproof he asked which of them was guilty of a transgression. Thereupon they protested their ignorance ; but the one who was conscious of his inexcusable trespass was able to conceal his sin no longer, and with bended knees he prayed humbly for pardon, before the saint, in the midst of the company of the brothers. The saint led him aside, and charged him under severe penalties, as he knelt, to expose to no one, during the days of the blessed man, anything secret, however little, of this angelic vision. But he, after the holy man's departure from the body, revealed to the brothers, with strong affirmation, that apparition of a heavenly assembly. And hence even today the place also of that angelic conference bears witness to the event that occurred in it, in its proper name, which may be rendered in Latin ' knoll of the angels ', and in Irish *cnoc angel*.

From this it is to be noticed and earnestly considered, of what extent and nature were the pleasant visits of angels to the blessed man, often when he was awake on winter nights, and when he prayed in remote places, while others rested ; visits that could never come to the knowledge of men, but that without doubt were very numerous : even although certain of them were, by some means or other, in the day or in the night, discernible to men, which were without question very

---

taken too literally, would imply that the name rendered in Irish was not an Irish name.

[8] neglegenter A ; neglig- B1 ; neclig- B3. Illegible in B2.
[9] himalibus A ; hiem- B1 B2 B3
[10] suaves A B1 B2 ; suases B3

ad earum conparationem angelicarum frequentationum
quae videlicet a nemine sciri [1] poterant.

Hoc idem similiter et de quibusdam luminosís mani-
118a festationibus | annotandum,[2] quae a paucís exploratae
inferius craxabuntur. .

De columna luminosa sancti viri
de vertice ardere visa

ALIO IN TEMPORE iiii.[3] ad sanctum visitandum
Columbam monasteriorum sancti fundatores de Scotia
transmeantes in Hinba [4] eum invenerunt insula ;
quorum inlustrium vocabula Comgellus mocu-Aridi,[5]
Cainnechus [6] mocu-Dalon, Brendenus mocu-Alti,[7]
Cormac [8] nepos Leathain.[9] Hí uno eodemque con-
sensu elegerunt ut sanctus Colum [10] coram ipsís in
eclesia sacra eucharistiae consecraret misteria. Qui
eorum obsecundans jusioni simul cum eís die dominica ex more post evangelii lectionem eclesiam in-
greditur. Ibidemque dum misarum sollemnia cele-
brarentur sanctus Brendenus mocu-Alti, sicut post |
118b Comgello [11] et Cainnecho [12] intimavit, quendam crinio-
sum igneum globum et valde luminosum de vertice
sancti Columbae ante altare stantis et sacram oblati-
onem consecrantis tamdiu ardentem et [13] instar alicujus
columnae sursum ascendentem vidit donec eadem
perficerentur sacrosancta ministeria. .[14]

---

[1] sciri A Bı B2 ; scrire B3
[2] an notandum A (for one word) ; ad notandum Bı B3 ;]dum B2
[3] .iiii. A ; quatuor Bı B2 B3   [4] hinba A ; himba Bı B2 B3
[5] mocuaridi A B2 B3 ; mocua'rdi Bı. See 49b, 50a.
[6] cainnechus A B3 ; cainecus Bı ; caichechus B2. He was the founder
of Aghaboe. See 16a, 63a.
[7] brendenus mocualti A B2 B3 ; brende'nus mocualti' Bı. He founded
Cloin-fertae (Clonfert). His death is entered in A.U. under 576=577.
[8] cormac A ; cormaccus Bı B2 B3 (altered from -acus Bı). See 17a.

few in comparison with those angelic visitations that could be known to none.

This same thing is likewise to be noted also of certain manifestations of light, observed by a few, and to be written below.

[III 17] Concerning a column of light seen to glow from the head of the holy man

At another time, four holy founders of monasteries crossed over from Ireland, to visit Saint Columba, and found him in the island of Hinba. The names of these illustrious men were Comgell mocu-Aridi, Cainnech mocu-Dalon, Brenden mocu-Alti, Cormac grandson of Léthan. They chose, all with one accord, that Saint Columba should consecrate the sacred mysteries of the Eucharist in the church, in their presence. He obeyed their command, and on the Lord's Day according to custom he entered the church, along with them, after the reading of the Gospel. And there, when the rites of the Mass were being celebrated, Saint Brenden mocu-Alti saw (as he afterwards told Comgell and Cainnech) a kind of fiery ball, radiant and very bright, that continued to glow from the head of Saint Columba as he stood before the altar and consecrated the sacred oblation, and to rise upwards like a column, until those holiest ministries were completed.

---

[9] leathain A ; letha'ni B1 ; letani B2 ; lethani B3. This chapter seems to belong to the tradition of Columba's visit to king Brude, and suggests that Adomnan knew of the legend that other Irish abbots accompanied Columba on that journey. See p. 22.

[10] colum A, with an over-dash above ol ; columba B1 B2 B3

[11] comgello A B2 B3 ; congello B1

[12] cainnecho A B3 ; cainne'co B1 ; cainecho ?B2

[13] et A ; ad B1 B2 B3   [14] ministeria A ; misteria B1 B2 B3

De spiritus sancti discensione [1] sive visitatione
quae in eadem [2] insula tribus continuís
diebus et [3] noctibus super venerabilem [4]
mansit virum

ALIO IN TEMPORE cum sanctus vir in Hinba [5] commaneret insula gratia sancti spiraminis super eum
habunde [6] et inconparabiliter effussa per triduum mirabiliter mansit [7] ; ita ut per tris [8] dies totidemque noctes
intra [9] obserratam et repletam caelesti claritudine
119a domum manens nullum ad se acce|dere permitteret,
neque manducans neque bibens. De qua videlicet
domu [10] inmensae claritatis radii per rimulas valvarum
et clavium foramina erumpentes noctu visebantur.[11]
Carmina quoque quaedam spiritalia [12] et ante [13] inaudita
decantari ab eo audiebantur. Sed et multa quaedam, ut
ipse post coram paucís admodum professus est, occulta
ab exordio mundi arcana aperte manifestata [14] videbat.
Scripturarum quoque sacrarum obscura quaeque et
dificillima plana et luce clarius aperta mundissimi cordis
oculís patebant. Baitheneumque [15] alumnum [16] non
adesse querebatur, qui si [17] forte adesset illo [18] in triduo
vel de praeteritís vel de futurís deinceps seculís ab ore
viri beati quaedam plurima ab aliis ignorata hominibus

[1] discensione A ; des- B1 B3 and contents-lists of B2 B3. Missing in B2.
[2] eadem A B3 and contents-list of B2 ; ea'dem B1 ; eade contents-list
of B3. Missing in B2.
[3] et A ; totidemque B1 B3 and contents-lists of B2 B3. Missing in B2.
[4] venerabilem A B1 and contents-list of B3 ; -bile B3. Missing in B2 ;
illegible in contents-list of B2.
[5] hinba A ; himba B1 B3 ; im[B2   [6] habunde A B1 ; ab- B2 B3
[7] mirabiliter mansit A ; mansit mirabiliter B1 B3 (-bi'l- B1) ; man[B2
[8] tris A ; tres B1 B2 B3
[9] intra intra A ; intra B1 B3. Missing in B2. The second *intra* in A
has been crossed out with a horizontal line, not according to the text hand's
custom. The ink of the deleting line is indistinguishable in the facsimiles
from that of the text.   [10] domu A ; domo B1 B2 B3
[11] visebantur A B1 ; vide- B3. Missing in B2.

[III 18] Concerning a descent or visitation of the Holy Spirit remaining over the venerable man, in that same island, for three continuous days and nights

At another time when the holy man was living in the island of Hinba, the grace of the Holy Spirit was poured out upon him abundantly and in an incomparable manner, and continued marvellously for the space of three days, so that for three days and as many nights, remaining within a house barred, and filled with heavenly light, he allowed no one to go to him, and he neither ate nor drank. From that house beams of immeasurable brightness were visible in the night, escaping through chinks of the door-leaves, and through the key-holes. And spiritual songs, unheard before, were heard being sung by him. Moreover, as he afterwards admitted in the presence of a very few men, he saw, openly revealed, many of the secret things that have been hidden since the world began. Also everything that in the sacred scriptures is dark and most difficult became plain, and was shown more clearly than the day to the eyes of his purest heart. And he lamented that his foster-son Baithene was not there, who, if he had chanced to be present during those three days, would have written down from the mouth of the blessed man very many mysteries, both of past ages and of ages still to come, mysteries unknown to other men ;

---

¹² spiritalia A ; spiritualia B1 B3. Illegible in B2.
¹³ ante A B1 B2. Omitted in B3.
¹⁴ manifestata A B2 B3 ; manifesta B1
¹⁵ baitheneumque A B2 B3 ; baithe'neu'mque B1
¹⁶ *alumnum*, i.e. ' foster-son ' or ' pupil '. Cf. 11b.
¹⁷ si A B1 B2. Omitted in B3, and added somewhat later in very fine writing.   ¹⁸ illo A B2 B3 ; illi B1

119b misteria discriberet,[1] aliquantas | quoque sacrorum [2] explanationes [3] voluminum. Qui tamen Baitheneus,[4] in Egea [5] insula venti contrarietate detentus usque quo illi trinales illius inconparabilis et honorificae visitationis dies et totidem noctes terminarentur, adesse non potuit. .

> De angelicae lucis claritudine [6] quam Virgnous
> bonae indolis juvenis, qui postea [7] deo [8] auctore
> huic praefuit eclesiae, super sanctum Columbam
> in eclesia fratribus himali [9] nocte in cubiculís
> quiescentibus [10] discendere [11] viderat : cui [12]
> ego indignus licet deservio

QUADAM HIMALI [13] nocte supra memoratus Virgnous [14] in dei amore fervens eclesiam orationis studio aliis quiescentibus solus intrat, ibidemque in quadam exedra [15] quae oratorii adherebat parieti devotus orabat. Et post aliquantum quasi horae intervallum unius vir veneran-
120a dus [16] Columba eandem | sacram ingreditur domum, simulque cum eo aurea lux de summa caeli altitudine

---

[1] discriberet A ; des- B1 B2 B3

[2] sacrorum A B1 B2 ; sanctorum B3

[3] explanationes A B2 B3 (-aci- B3) ; -num B1, unaltered, although *es* has been written in the margin by the reviser.

[4] baitheneus A B2 B3 ; baithe'neus B1

[5] egea A B2 B3 ; ege'a B1. See p. 152. ⁚

[6] claritudine A B1 and contents-list of B2 and of B3 ; claritate B3. The whole chapter-heading is illegible in B2.

[7] postea A ; post B1 B3 and contents-list of B2 and of B3

[8] deo A B1 B3 and contents-list of B2 ; de contents-list of B3

[9] himali A.; hiemali B1 and contents-list of B3 ; hyemalis B3. Illegible in contents-list of B2.

[10] quiescentibus A B1 and contents-list of B3 ; quiestibus B3. Illegible in contents-list of B2.

[11] discendere A ; des- B1 B3 and contents-list of B3. Illegible in contents-list of B2.

[12] *cui.* In A, in the space between the columns, before *cui*, there is a dot that appears to have been made by the text hand, and serves as a placing-point ; the confused order of the sentence probably resulted from a marginal addition made by Adomnan in the manuscript from which

and also a number of interpretations of the sacred books. But Baithene was detained in the island of Ege [? Eigg] by contrary winds, and was unable to be present until those three days and nights of the incomparable and glorious visitation had come to an end.

[III 19] Concerning the brightness of angelic light that Virgno, a young man of good ability (who by God's guidance was afterwards the ruler of this church, which I, although unworthy, serve) saw descending upon Saint Columba in the church, on a winter night, while the brothers rested in their sleeping-chambers

One winter night, the above-named Virgno, fired with the love of God, entered the church alone for the sake of prayer, while others slept. There, in an exedra that adjoined the oratory wall, he prayed devoutly. After some space of time, as it were of one hour, the venerable man Columba entered the same sacred building ; and along with him there entered a golden light,

---

both A and the B texts are derived. Assuming that there was such an addition, the text of A should have read : *bonae indolis juvenis (qui postea deo auctore huic praefuit eclesiae, cui ego indignus licet deservio) super sanctum Columbam . . . discendere viderat.* This is the order followed by B1, ?B2, B3, and the contents-list of B2 and of B3. The parenthesis was needed to identify Virgno as the abbot of Iona (see p. 90).

[13] himali A ; hiemali B1 B3. Illegible in B2.

[14] virgnous A B3 ; virgno'us B1. Illegible in B2. *Virgno* was the British (or N.B.) form of a name that had become, in Irish speech, *Fergno* in Adomnan's time.

[15] *exedra.* See p.112 .

[16] venerandus A B2 B3 ; venerabilis B1

discendens [1] totum illud eclesiae spatium replens ; sed
et illius exedriolae separatum conclave,[2] ubi se Virgnous
in quantum potuit latitare conabatur, ejusdem caelestis
claritas luminis, per interiorem illius cubiculi januam
quae ex minore patebat parte erumpens, non sine aliquo
formidabili repleverat terrore. Et sicut [3] nullus aesteum [4]
et meridianum solem rectís et inreverberatís potest
intueri oculís, síc et illam caelestem claritudinem ille
Virgnous [5] qui viderat sustenere [6] nullo poterat modo,
quia valde oculorum reverberabat aciem illa luminosa et
inconparabilis effussio. Quo fulminali et formidabili
splendore viso in tantum idem supra memoratus frater
120b exterritus erat, ut nulla in | eo virtus remaneret.

Sanctus vero Columba post non prolixam orationem
egreditur eclesiam ; Virgnoumque valde timoratum ad
sé crastina advocat die, hisque brevibus conpellat consulatoriis [7] verbís : ' Bene O [8] filiole ' ingeminans, ' hac
praeterita nocte in conspectu dei placuisti, oculos ad
terram depremendo [9] claritatis timore perterritus ejus.[10]
Nam si non ita [11] fecisses, illa inestimabili obcaecarentur
tui luce visa oculi. Sed hoc non neglegenter [12] observare
debebis, ut talem hanc lucis manifestationem nemini
umquam in mea denudes vita '.

Haec itaque praedicabilis et ammirabilis res post [13]
beati viri transitum multís eodem Virgnovo narrante
innotuit. Cujus scilicet Virgnovi sororis filius Com-

---

[1] discendens A ; des- B1 B2 B3
[2] *conclave*. Here probably the meaning is figurative, but the normal
meaning is a compartment that can be locked.
[3] sicut A ; sicuti B1 B2 B3
[4] aesteum A ; estivum B1 B3 ?B2
[5] virgnous A B3 ; virgno'us B1. Illegible in B2.
[6] sustenere A ; -tin- B1 B2 B3
[7] consulatoriis A ; -sol- B1 B2 B3
[8] o A B3 ; ó B1. Omitted in B2.
[9] depremendo A ; -prim- B1 B2 B3

descending from highest heaven and wholly filling the inside of the church. Also the enclosed space of the exedra, in which Virgno tried to conceal himself as well as he could, was filled with the brightness of that heavenly light, which streamed through the partly-open inner door of that room, not without some effect of terror. And just as none can look with direct and undazzled eyes upon the summer midday sun, so also Virgno, who saw that heavenly brightness, could not at all endure it, because the brilliant and incomparable radiance greatly dazzled his sight. When he saw this flashing and terrifying effulgence, that brother was so greatly overcome by fear that no strength remained in him.

Saint Columba left the church after praying for a short time ; and on the following day he summoned to him the awe-stricken Virgno, and spoke to him in these few reassuring words : ' You have been well-pleasing, little son ; you have been well-pleasing ' he repeated, ' in the sight of God, this last night, in lowering your eyes to the ground, through dread of his brightness. For if you had not done so, your eyes would have been blinded by seeing that inestimable light. But you must diligently observe this, never in my life-time to disclose to any one this so great manifestation of light '.

So, through the narration of that Virgno after the passing of the blessed man, this memorable and wonderful thing became known to many people. His, that is Virgno's, sister's son, the honourable priest Comman,

---

[10] perterritus ejus A ; ejus perteritus B1 B2 B3 (-te'ri- B1 ; -terri- B2)
[11] non ita A ; ita non B1 B2 B3
[12] neglegenter A ; neglig- B1 B2 ; neclig- B3
[13] post A B3. Omitted in B1 ; illegible in B2.

manus, honorabilis prespiter, mihi Adomnano [1] de hac
121a supra visione craxata [2] aliquando sub testificatione |
enarraverat ; qui eam enarratam ab ore ipsius Virgnovi
abbatis et avunculi sui ab eo in quantum potuit visam
audierat. .

De alia prope simili celsae claritudinis visione [3]

ALIA ITIDEM nocte quidam de fratribus Colgius
nomine, filius Aido [4] Draigniche,[5] de nepotibus Fechreg,[6]
cujus in primo [7] fecimus mentionem, cassu ad januam
eclesiae aliis dormientibus devenit, ibidemque aliquandiu
stans orabat. Tum proinde subito totam videt eclesiam
caelesti luce repleri, quae scilicet fulgoralis lux dicto
citius ab ejus recessit oculís. Sanctum vero Columbam
hora eadem intra eclesiam orantem ignorabat. Postque
talem subitam luminis apparationem [8] valde per-
timescens domum revertitur.

Postera die sanctus illum advocans asperius objur-
121b gavit, inquiens : ' De caetero prae|cavere debes, filii,[9]
ne quasi explorator caeleste lumen quod tibi non est
donatum inspicere coneris, quia té effugiet ; et ne alicui
in meís diebus quod vidisti enarres '. .

[1] adomnano A (with space after *ad*) ; á domnano B1 ; a domnano
B2 B3
[2] craxata A ; caraxata B1 B2 B3
[3] visione A B1 ?B2, and contents-list of B2 and of B3 ; visioi˜e B3
[4] aido A B2 B3 ; ai′do B1
[5] draigniche A ; draignichae B1 B2 B3
[6] fechreg A ; fechrech B1 B3 ; fecreh B2. See 22b.
[7] primo A ; primo libro B1 B2 B3
[8] apparationem A ; -riti- B1 B2 ; -rici- B3
[9] filii A ; fili B1 B2 B3

once related to me, Adomnan, in testimony, the vision that I have above set down. He had heard it told by the lips of his uncle, the abbot Virgno himself, by whom it was seen, in so far as he was able to see it.

[III 20] Of another nearly-similar vision of light from above

On another night also, one of the brothers, Colcu by name, of whom we made mention at the beginning, son of Aid Draigniche, of the descendants of Féchre, chanced to come to the door of the church, while others slept, and standing there prayed for some time. And then he saw that the whole church was suddenly filled with heavenly light. Quicker than speech, this flash of light vanished from his eyes. He did not know that Saint Columba was at the same hour praying within the church, and after this sudden apparition of light he was much afraid, and returned to his dwelling.

On the following day the saint summoned him, and sharply reproved him, saying : ' Henceforth take great care, my son, not to attempt like a spy to observe heavenly light that has not been granted to you, for it will flee from you ; and not to relate to any one, in my time, what you have seen '.

De alia parili divinae lucis apparatione. .[1]

ALIO ITIDEM IN TEMPORE vir beatus cuidam suo sapientiam discenti alumno nomine Berchano,[2] cujus cognomentum [3] Mes-loen,[4] non mediocriter quadam denuntiavit die, inquiens : ' Caveto, filii,[5] ne [6] hac sequenti nocte juxta tuam semper consuetudinem ad [7] meum appropinques hospitiolum '. Qui hoc audiens contra interdictum ad domum beati viri in noctis silentio aliis quiescentibus accessit, callideque explorans oculos e regione ad clavium foramina possuit, estimans scilicet, ut res probavit, aliquam intus caelestem visionem sancto 122a manifestari. | Nam eadem hora beati viri illud hospitiolum caelestis [8] splendore claritudinis erat repletum, quam non sustenens [9] intueri transgressor juvenis ilico aufugit.

Quem die crastina sanctus seorsum dicens cum magna severitate objurgans haec ad eum profatur verba, dicens : ' Hac in nocte, filii,[10] coram deo peccasti ; nam tuae infitialis[11] explorationem calliditatis a spiritu sancto celari vel abscondi posse inaniter putasti. Nonne ad mei hostium hospitioli té illa in hora appropinquantem et inde redeuntem vidi ? Et nisi ego eodem momento pro té orarem, ibidem ante januam aut cadens morireris,[12] aut tui de suís foraminibus oculi eruerentur. Sed tibi [13] hac vice propter me dominus pepercit. Et hoc scito,

---

[1] apparatione A ; -riti- B1 B2 and contents-list of B2 ; -rici- B3 and contents-list of B3   [2] berchano A B2 B3 ; bercha'no B1
[3] cognomentum A B1 B2 ; -mento B3
[4] mesloen A B1 B2, with three over-dashes in A ; mosloen B3, with s altered from l.   [5] filii A ; fili B1 B2 B3
[6] ne A ; de B1 B2 B3   [7] ad A ; ne ad B1 B2 B3
[8] *caelestis.* After this word, in A, two letters, apparently *pa*, (perhaps a beginning of *patriae*) were written and erased by the text hand.

[III 21] Concerning another like apparition
of divine light

At another time also the blessed man one day gravely admonished a pupil of his, who was studying philosophy, called Berchan, surnamed Mes-loen, and said : ' Beware, my son, of coming near my lodging this night, as you are accustomed always to do '. But he, hearing this, came to the blessed man's house in violation of the interdict, in the silence of the night while others rested. And craftily spying he set his eyes opposite the holes for the keys, supposing that within the house some heavenly vision was being manifested to the saint, as the event showed to be true. For in that hour the blessed man's lodging was filled with the glory of heavenly brightness ; the youthful transgressor could not bear to look upon it, and immediately fled away.

On the following day, the saint took him aside, and reproving him very severely spoke to him these words : ' In this night, my son, you have sinned before God ; for you have vainly imagined that the crafty spying that you have denied could be concealed or hidden from the Holy Spirit. Did not I see you in that hour coming to the door of my lodging and going away from it ? And if I had not at that moment prayed for you, there before the door either you would have fallen and died, or your eyes would have been torn from their sockets. But this time the Lord has spared you for my sake. And

---

⁹ sustenens A ; -tin- B1 B3. Missing in B2.
¹⁰ filii A ; fili B1 B3. Missing in B2.
¹¹ *infitialis*. This word implies that Columba had charged Berchan with frequent spying, which Berchan had denied ; and suggests that Adomnan has omitted part of the story.
¹² morireris A ; morereris B1 B2 B3   ¹³ tibi A B2 ; tui B1 B3

quod in tua evernili [1] patria luxoriose [2] vivens exprobra-

122b tionem facies tua omnibus patietur diebus | vitae tuae.
Hoc tamen a domino orans inpetravi, ut quia noster sis
alumnus lacrimosam ante exitum agas penitudinem, et
a deo misericordiam consequaris '. Quae omnia secundum verbum beati viri ita ei postea contigerunt, sicuti de
eo profetata sunt. .

De alia angelorum sancto manifestata viro [3] apparatione,[4] quos sanctae ejus animae obviare incipientes quasi mox de corpore viderat migraturae

ALIO IN TEMPORE dum vir beatus in Iova commaneret
insula, quadam die sancta facies ejus subita mirifica et
laetifica hilaritate efloruit ; oculosque ad caelum elevans
inconparabili repletus gaudio valde laetificabatur. Tum
post modicum alicujus momentioli intervallum, illa
sapida et suavis laetificatio in mestam convertitur

123a tris|tificationem. Duo vero viri qui eadem hora ejus
tegorioli [5] ad januam stabant, quod in eminentiore loco
erat fabricatum, et ipsi cum eo valde tristificati, quorum
unus Lugneus [6] erat [7] mocu-Blai, alter vero Pilu [8] nun-
cupabatur Saxo, causam ipsius subitae laetationis [9] in-
quirunt et illius subsequentis [10] mestitiae. Ad quos
sanctus síc profatur : ' Ite in pace, nec illius laetaminis [11]
causam nec etiam tristificationis a me nunc inquiratis
manifestari '.

[1] evernili A ; hiberniali B1 (altered from probably *hibernili*, following
the reviser's marginal note, *ali*) ; hibernali B2 ; hibernili B3

[2] luxoriose A ; -xur- B1 B3. Missing in B2.

[2] viro A B2 B3 and contents-list of B2 and of B3   Omitted in B1.

[4] apparatione A ; -riti- B1 B2 and contents-list of B2 ; -rici- B3 and
contents-list of B3.

[5] tegorioli A ; tuguri'oli B1 ; tugurioli B2 ; tugurrioli B3. See p. 109.

[6] lugneus A B2 B3 ; lugne'us B1   [7] erat A. Omitted in B1 B2 B3

be sure of this, that while you live luxuriously in your home in Ireland, your face shall bear a mark of reproach, during all the days of your life. But this I have obtained from the Lord by prayer, that because you are our pupil you may do tearful penance before your death, and obtain from God mercy '.

All these things happened to him afterwards as they had been foretold of him, in accordance with the word of the blessed man.

[III 22] Concerning another apparition,
revealed to the holy man, of angels whom
he saw on their way to meet his holy soul,
as if it were about to depart from the body

At another time while the blessed man lived in the island of Io, one day his holy face lit up with sudden mirth, strange and joyous. Raising his eyes to heaven, he rejoiced greatly, being filled with incomparable gladness. Then, after the brief space of a moment, that sweet and pleasant joy was turned into dull sorrow.

Two men were at that time standing at the door of his hut that had been constructed on higher ground. One of them was Lugne mocu-Blai, and the other was called Pilu the Englishman. They too were made sorrowful by his sorrow ; and they asked the cause of his sudden joyfulness and of the sadness following it. And the saint addressed them thus : ' Go in peace. Do not ask me now to explain the cause, either of that gladness, or yet of the sorrow '.

---

8 pilu A B3 ; pilum B1. Illegible in B2.
9 laetationis A ; leticie B1 B2 B3
10 subsequentis A B1 ; -tes B3. Illegible in B2.
11 laetaminis A ; leticie B1 B3 ; leti[B2

Quo audito inlacrimati ingeniculantes prostratís in
terra [1] vultibus supliciter rogant, scire volentes aliquid
de illa re, quae hora eadem sancto erat revelata. Quos
valde tristificatos videns : ' Quia vos ' ait, ' amo, tristi-
ficare nolo. Promittere prius debetis ne ulli hominum
123b sacramentum quod inquiritis | in vita mea prodatis '.
Qui continuo secundum ejus commendationem prumte [2]
promiserunt ; et post talem promisionem vir venerandus
sic ad eos proloquitur : ' Usque in hunc ' inquiens,
' praesentem diem meae in Brittannia [3] perigrinationis [4]
terdeni conpleti sunt anni. Interea multís ante diebus a
domino meo devote postulavi, ut in fine tricensimi [5]
hujus praesentis anni [6] me de meo absolveret inculatu,[7]
et ad caelestem patriam ilico advocaret. Et haec fuit
mei [8] causa laetaminis,[9] de qua vos me mesti interrogatis.
Angelos enim sanctos de excelso vidi misos throno ad
meam de carne animam obvios educendam. Sed ecce
nunc subito retardati ultra nostrae fretum insulae stant [10]
in rupe, scilicet volentes ad me de corpore advocandum
124a appropiare, | sed propius accedere non permittuntur,
mox ad caelorum summa repedaturi. Quia dominus
quod mihi totís viribus roganti donavit,[11] ut hac in die
ad ipsum de mundo transirem, multarum magis eclesiarum pro me orationes exaudiens dicto citius inmotavit.[12]
Quibus scilicet eclesiis exorantibus sic a domino donatum
est ut, quamlibet contra meam voluntatem, quatuor ab

---

[1] terra A ; terram B1 B3. Missing in B2.
[2] prumte A ; prompta B1 B2 B3
[3] *brittannia.* In A, the final *a* has been altered from the *ae* symbol,
probably by the text hand.   [4] perigrinationis A ; -reg- B1 B2 B3
[5] tricensimi A ; -ces- B1 B3. Illegible in B2.
[6] *praesentis anni.* This means A.D. 593. See 124b.
[7] inculatu A ; -col- B1 B2 B3   [8] mei A ; mee B1 B3 ; mëe B2
[9] laetaminis A ; leti'cie B1 ; leticie B3 ; Jucentie B2, deleted by points
below.   [10] stant A ; stantes B1 B2 B3   [11] donavit A B1 B2 ; dan- B3
[12] inmotavit A ; immutavit B1 B3 ; intimavit B2

When they heard this, they knelt, weeping ; and with faces bowed to the ground they humbly implored that they might learn something of the matter that in this hour had been revealed to the saint. Seeing that they were very sorrowful, he said : ' Because I love you, I am unwilling to cause you sorrow. First you must promise not in my life-time to betray to any person the secret about which you ask '. Thereupon following his injunction they promised readily ; and after this promise the venerable man thus spoke to them, saying : ' Thirty years have been completed of my pilgrimage in Britain, down to this present day. Meanwhile, for many days past, I have earnestly requested of my Lord that in the end of this present thirtieth year he would release me from my residence, and at once call me to the heavenly country. And it was this that caused my gladness, about whose cause you sadly question me. For I saw holy angels sent from the high throne to meet and conduct my soul from the flesh. But see now, they have suddenly been held back, and are standing on a rock beyond the strait of our island ; they wish to approach, in order to summon me from the body, but they are not allowed to come nearer, and will presently return to the highest heavens. Because what the Lord granted me when I asked it with my whole strength, that I should pass to him from the world on this day, he has changed, more quickly than speech, answering in pre-ference the prayers of many churches for me. And it has so been granted by the Lord to the prayers of those churches that, although against my will, four more years

hac die mihi in carne manenti superaddantur anni. Haec
talis mihi [1] mesta retardatio hodiernae tristificationis
non inmerito causa fuit. Quibus videlicet [2] iiii.[3] futurís
deo propitio terminatís in hac vita annís subita emigra-
tione nulla praecedente corporis molestia cum sanctis
mihi obviaturís illo in tempore angelís ad dominum [4]
laetus emigrabo '. Secundum haec verba vir venerabilis,
124b quae non sine magno gemitu et merore ut | traditur
necnon et ingenti lacrimabilitate proloquutus est, quatuor postea annís in carne mansit. .[5]

De transitu ad dominum sancti
nostri patroni [6] Columbae

ANNORUM SUPRA iiii.[7] memoratorum [8] termino jam
appropinquante, post quorum conpletionem [9] finem
praesentis vitae veridicus praesagator sibi futurum fore
multo ante praesciebat tempore, quadam die mense
maio, sicut in priore secundo scripsimus libro,[10] ad
visitandos operarios fratres sanctus senex senio fessus
plaustro vectus [11] pergit. Ad quos in occidua insulae
Iovae laborantes parte síc ea die exorsus est loqui, dicens :
' In pascali sollemnitate nuper apreli [12] peracta mense
125a desiderio desideravi | ad Christum dominum, sicut et
mihi ab eo concessum erat si malluissem, emigrare. Sed

---

[1] talis mihi A ; mihi talis B1 B3. Illegible in B2.
[2] videlicet A B2 B3 ; scilicet B1
[3] .iiii. A ; quatuor B1 B2 B3
[4] dominum A B3 ?B2 ; deum B1
[5] mansit. Columba lived, according to Adomnan, until after a day in
May (124b), thirty-four years after the beginning of his pilgrimage (123b) ;
i.e. until May 597. See p. 89.
[6] nostri patroni A and contents-list of B2 and of B3 ; ac venerabilis deo
dilecti patroni nostri B1 B3 ?B2. The title in A is written in large letters,
comparable with those in 1a.
[7] .iiii. A ; quatuor B1 B2 B3
[8] memoratorum A B1 ?B2 ; meoratorum B3

from this day shall be added to my sojourn in the flesh. This delay, grievous to me, was justly the cause of my sorrow today. After the end of the four coming years in this life, by God's favour I shall, with a sudden departure and no preceding bodily distress, joyfully depart to the Lord, with the holy angels who will come to meet me at that time '.

In accordance with these words which the venerable man pronounced, as it is said, not without great lamentation and grief, and also with much weeping, he remained in the flesh for four years afterwards.

[III 23] Concerning the passing to the Lord of our holy patron Columba

When the end was drawing near of the four years above-mentioned, after the completion of which the foreteller of truth had long ago foreknown that his present life would come to a close, one day, in the month of May, as we have written in the preceding second book, the saint went, drawn in a wagon (being an old man, weary with age) to visit the labouring brothers, at work in the western part of the island of Io ; and on that day he began to speak to them in this manner, saying : ' At the Easter festival recently held, in the month of April, I desired with desire to depart to Christ the Lord, as had indeed been granted by him to me, if I had so chosen ; but I chose rather to put off a little

---

[9] conpletionem A ; complet- B2 B3 ; complect- B1

[10] *libro.* See 75b–76a.

[11] *plaustro vectus.* In A, these words have been written by the text hand in smaller letters (similar to those of 108a), probably over an erasure of which some trace is visible in the facsimiles in 123a.

[12] apreli A ; apri'li B1 ; aprili B2 B3. Cf. E.S., 1, p. 107.

né vobis laetitiae festivitas in tristitiam verteretur, diem
meae de mundo emigrationis paulo diutius protellari
mallui '.

Hís ab eo mestís monaci familiares auditís interim
dictís valde tristificati sunt ; quos in quantum poterat
verbís coepit consulatoriis [1] laetificare. Quibus finitís ut
erat in vechiculo [2] sedens ad orientem suam convertens
faciem insulam cum insulanís benedixit habitatoribus.
Ex qua die, ut in supra memorato craxatum [3] est libello,
viperarum venina [4] trisulcarum linguarum usque in
hodiernum diem nullo modo aut homini aut pecori
nocere potuere. Post ejusdem benedictionis verba
sanctus ad suum revehitur monasterium.

125b   Tum proinde paucís diebus transactís, | dum misarum
sollempnia ex more dominica celebrarentur die, subito [5]
susum [6] elevatís oculís facies venerabilis viri florido
respersa rubore videtur ; quia sicut scriptum est, ' Corde
letante vultus floret ' [7] ; eadem namque [8] hora angelum
domini supra volitantem [9] solus vidit intra ipsius oratorii
parietes ; et quia sanctorum angelorum amabilis et
tranquillus aspectus gaudium et exultationem electorum
pectoribus infundit,[10] haec [11] fuit illius subitae causa
laetitiae beato infusa[e] [12] viro.

De qua scilicet causa inspiratae laetationis [13] cum qui
inerant ibidem praesentes inquirerent, hoc eís sanctus
responsum sursum respiciens dedit : ' Mira et incon-

---

[1] consulatoriis A ; -sol- B1 B3. Missing in B2.
[2] vechiculo A ; vehiculo B1 B3 (-hi'c- B1). Missing in B2.
[3] craxatum A ; carax- B1 B2 B3   [4] venina A ; venena B1 B2 B3
[5] subito A B1 B2. Omittted in B3.   [6] susum A ; sursum B1 B2 B3
[7] *floret*. This quotation differs from the Vulgate text of Prov. xv. 13.
[8] namque A B1 B2 ; nanque B3
[9] volitantem A B1 B3 ; voluntatem B2
[10] *sanctorum* to *infundit*. This passage is a close quotation from the version
by Evagrius of the Life of Antony ; see Brüning 1917, p. 245.

longer the day of my departure from the world, so that the festival of joy should not be turned for you into sorrow '.

Meanwhile the monks of his congregation that heard him speak these sad things became very sorrowful ; and he began to cheer them, as well as he could, with comforting words. After which, still sitting in the wagon, he turned his face to the east, and blessed the island, with the islanders its inhabitants. And from then to the present day, as has been written in the above-mentioned book, the poison of three-forked tongues of vipers has not been able to do any injury to either man or beast. After the words of this blessing, the saint was carried back to his monastery.

Then after a few days had passed, while the rites of the Mass were being celebrated on a Lord's-day according to the custom, the venerable man lifted up his eyes, and suddenly his face was seen to flush with a ruddy glow ; for, as it is written, ' The countenance glows when the heart is glad ' ; and in fact at the same moment he alone saw an angel of the Lord hovering above, within the walls of the oratory itself ; and because the calm and lovely sight of holy angels fills the hearts of the elect with joy and exultation, this was the cause of the sudden gladness that filled the blessed man.

When those that were present there asked about this, the cause of the gladness inspired in him, the saint, gazing upward, gave them this reply : ' Wonderful and

---

[11] *Haec* in A has a large coloured initial letter ; B1 also begins a new sentence with *Hec*. B1 B2 B3 had begun a new sentence at *Et quia*.

[12] infusa A B1 B2 B3 ; but the context requires *infusae*.

[13] laetationis A ; leticie B1 B2 B3

parabilis angelicae subtilitas naturae.   Ecce enim angelus
domini, ad repetendum aliquod deo carum misus de-
possitum, nos desuper intra eclesiam aspiciens et bene-
126a dicens rursum | per parasticiam [1] eclesiae reversus nulla
talis vestigia exitus reliquit '.[2]

Haec sanctus, sed tamen de qualitate illius depositi ad
quod misus est angelus requirendum nemo de circumstantibus recognoscere potuit.   Noster vero patronus
sanctam propriam a deo sibi commendatam animam
depositum [3] nuncupavit ; quae sicuti inferius narrabitur
alia senís intervenientibus [4] continuís diebus dominica
nocte ad dominum emigravit. .

Vir itaque venerabilis in fine ejusdem ebdomadis, hoc
est die sabbati,[5] ipse et ejus pius minister Diormitius [6] ad
proximum pergunt benedicendum horreum.   Quod
intrans sanctus cum benedixisset, et duos in eo frugum
sequestratos [7] acervos, hoc intulit verbum cum gratiarum
actione, inquiens : ' Valde congratulor meís familiari-
bus monacís, quia hoc etiam anno, si quoquam a vobís |
126b emigrare me oportuerit, annuum sufficientem habebitis
[panem] '.[8]

Quo audito verbo Diormitius [9] minister tristificari
coepit et síc dicere : ' Hujus anni tempore, pater, sepius
nos contristas, quia de tuo transitu crebro commemoras '.
Cui sanctus dedit responsum : ' Aliquem arcanum
habeo [10] sermusculum, quem si mihi firmiter promiseris
nemini ante meum denudare obitum, de meo tibi egressu
aliquid manifestius intimare potero '.   Quam cum talem

---

[1] *parasticiam.*   See p. 112.
[2] reliquit A B1 B3 ; requirit B2
[3] *depositum.*   Cf. the Life of Antony, quoted in Brüning 1917, p. 246.
[4] intervenientibus A B1 B3 ; intuenientibus B2
[5] *sabbati :* i.e., the twenty-four hours from vespers on Friday to vespers
on Saturday.   See p. 120.
[6] diormitius A B2 B3 ; -mi'cius B1

incomparable is the fineness of angelic nature ! See, an angel of the Lord, sent to recover a deposit dear to God, looking down upon us within the church and blessing us, has returned through the roof-courses of the church, leaving no trace of that departure '.

This the saint said, but yet none of those standing by could know of what kind that deposit was, to recover which the angel had been sent. Our patron, however, described as a ' deposit ' his own holy soul, entrusted to him by God, which, as will be related below, departed to the Lord after an interval of six consecutive days, on the Lord's-night following.

In the end of the same week, that is, on the Sabbath day, the venerable man himself, and his devoted attendant Diormit, went to bless the nearest barn. After entering it, and blessing it and two heaps of grain that were there in store, the saint spoke thus, and rendering thanks said : ' I greatly congratulate my family of monks, because in this year also, if I have to depart from you to any place, you will have enough [bread] for the year '.

When the attendant Diormit heard this, he began to be sorrowful, and to speak in this manner : ' This year, father, you very often sadden us, because you frequently speak of your passing '. The saint gave him this answer : ' I have a few secret words concerning my departure that I shall be able to communicate somewhat more plainly to you, if you will faithfully promise me not to disclose them to any one before my death '. After the

---

7 *sequestratos.* This means either ' stored ', or ' held in reserve '.
8 panem B1 B2 B3. Omitted in A.
9 diormitius A B2 B3 ; -mi'cius B1
10 habeo A B2 B3. Omitted in B1.

2M

minister promisionem juxta voluntatem sancti flexís
genibus terminasset, vir venerandus consequenter síc
profatur : ' Haec in sacrís voluminibus dies sabbatum
nuncupatur, quod interpraetatur requies. Et vere mihi
est sabbatum haec hodierna, quia hujus praesentis
127a laboriosae vitae | mihi ultima est, in qua post meas
laborationum molestias sabatizo. Et hac sequenti media
venerabili dominica nocte, secundum eloquia scripturarum, patrum gradiar viam. Jam [1] enim dominus
meus Jesus Christus me invitare [2] dignatur ; ad quem
inquam hac mediante nocte ipso me invitante emigrabo.
Síc enim mihi ab ipso domino revelatum est '. Haec
mesta minister audiens verba coepit amare flere, quem
sanctus in quantum potuit consulari [3] conabatur.

Post haec sanctus horreum egreditur, et ad monasterium revertens media resedet [4] via. In quo loco
postea crux molari infixa lapidi [5] hodieque stans in
margine cernitur viae. Dumque ibidem sanctus, ut
praefatus sum, senio fesus paululum sedens requiesceret,
127b ecce albus [6] occurrit cavallus [7] | oboediens servitor, qui
scilicet lactaria bocetum inter et monasterium vascula
gestare consueverat. Hic ad sanctum accedens mirum
dictu caput in sinu ejus ponens, ut credo inspirante deo
cui omne animal rerum [8] sapit sensu quo juserit ipse
creator, dominum a sé suum mox emigraturum et ipsum
ultra non visurum sciens, coepit plangere ubertimque
quasi homo lacrimas in gremium sancti fundere, et valde

[1] Jam A ; Ita B1 B2 B3
[2] *secundum eloquia* to *invitare*. This passage follows closely the words of
the Life of Antony . See Brüning 1917, p. 246.
[3] consulari A ; -sol- B1 B2 B3   [4] resedet A ; -sid- B1 B2 B3
[5] *lapidi*. This was the stone of a hand-mill. See p. 115.
[6] *albus*. In A, the *l* has apparently been begun as a *b*, and altered by
erasure.   [7] cavallus A ; caballus B1 B2 B3
[8] rerum A. Omitted in B1 B2 B3. Reeves by mistake gave B3's
reading as *brutum*.

attendant had completed that promise on bended knees, according to the saint's desire, the venerable man made a statement to this effect : ' This day is called in the sacred books " Sabbath ", which is interpreted " rest ". And truly this day is for me a Sabbath, because it is my last day of this present laborious life. In it after my toilsome labours I keep Sabbath ; and at midnight of this following venerated Lord's-day, in the language of the Scriptures I shall go the way of the fathers. For now my Lord Jesus Christ deigns to invite me. To him I shall depart, I say, when he invites me, in the middle of this night. For so it has been revealed to me by the Lord himself '. The attendant hearing these sad words began to weep bitterly, and the saint tried to comfort him, as well as he could.

After this, the saint left the barn, and returning towards the monastery sat down midway. In that place a cross that was later fixed in a mill-stone is seen, standing by the roadside, even today. And while the saint sat there, resting for a little while, being (as I have said above) weary with age, behold, a white horse came to him, the obedient servant who was accustomed to carry the milk-vessels between the cow-pasture and the monastery. It went to the saint, and strange to tell put its head in his bosom, inspired, as I believe, by God, before whom every living creature has understanding, with such perception of things as the Creator himself has decreed ; and knowing that its master would presently depart from it, and that it should see him no more, it began to mourn, and like a human being to let

spumans flere. Quod videns minister coepit illum
flebilem repellere lamentatorem. Sed sanctus prohibuit
eum, dicens : ' Sine hunc, sine nostri amatorem, ut in
hunc meum sinum fletus effundat [1] amarissimi plangoris.
Ecce tu, homo cum sis et rationalem animam habeas,
nullo modo scire de meo exitu potuisti, nisi quod tibi ego
ipse nuper [2] manifestavi. Huic vero bruto et inrationali |
128a animanti, quoquo modo [3] ipse conditor voluit, egresurum
a se domnum [4] manifeste revelavit '. Et haec dicens
mestum a sé revertentem equm benedixit ministratorem.

Et inde egrediens, et monticellum [5] monasterio
supereminentem ascendens, in vertice ejus paululum
stetit ; et stans ambas elevans palmas suum benedixit
cenubium,[6] inquiens : ' Huic loco quamlibet angusto
et vili non tantum Scotorum reges cum populís, sed
etiam barbararum [7] et exterarum gentium regnatores
cum plebibus sibi subjectís, grandem et non mediocrem
conferent honorem. A sanctis quoque, etiam aliarum
eclesiarum, non mediocris veneratio conferetur '.

Post haec verba de illo discendens [8] monticellulo et
ad monasterium revertens sedebat in tegorio [9] psalterium
128b scribens. | Et ad illum xxx. tertii [10] psalmi versiculum
perveniens ubi scribitur, ' Inquirentes autem dominum
non deficient omni bono ' [11] : ' Híc ' ait, ' in fine cessan-
dum est paginae. Quae vero sequuntur Baitheneus [12]

---

[1] effundat A ; fundat B1 B2 B3   [2] nuper A B1 B3. Omitted in B2
[3] modo A ; modo ut B1 B2 B3   [4] domnum A ; dominum B1 B2 B3
[5] monticellum A B1 B2 ; -tec- B3. This hill was outside the boundary
of the monastery, therefore not the Cnoc nan Carnan, but more probably
Sgùrr an Fhithich, near the middle of the western rampart. See p. 112.
[6] cenubium A ; -no'b- B1 ; -nob- B3. Illegible in B2.
[7] barbararum A. Omitted in B1 B2 B3
[8] discendens A ; des- B1 B2 B3
[9] tegorio A ; tugurio B1 B2 B3 (-gu'r- B1). This hut, Columba's
writing-house, was within the rampart of the monastery, and near, if not
at, the south-western gate. See pp. 108ff.

tears fall freely on the lap of the saint, and foaming much, to weep aloud.

When he saw this, the attendant began to drive away the weeping mourner ; but the saint forbade him, saying : ' Let him, let him that loves us, pour out the tears of most bitter grief here in my bosom. See, man though you are, and having a rational soul, you could by no means know anything of my departure except what I myself have even now disclosed to you. But to this brute and unreasoning animal the Creator has, in what way he would, revealed clearly that its master is going to depart from it '. Thus speaking, he blessed his servant the horse, as it turned sadly away from him.

Going from there, he climbed a small hill overlooking the monastery, and stood on its summit for a little while. And as he stood he raised both hands, and blessed his monastery, saying : ' On this place, small and mean though it be, not only the kings of the Irish with their peoples, but also the rulers of barbarous and foreign nations, with their subjects, will bestow great and especial honour ; also especial reverence will be bestowed by saints even of other churches '.

After these words, he descended from that little hill, returned to the monastery, and sat in the hut, writing a psalter. And when he came to that verse of the thirty-third Psalm where it is written, ' But they that seek the Lord shall not want for anything that is good ', he said : ' Here, at the end of the page, I must stop. Let Baithene write what follows '.

---

[10] xxx tertii A ; tricesimi tercii B1 B2 B3 (-ii B1 B2)

[11] *dominum* to *bono*. In B1, *d' . n~ . d' . o . b .* ; the Vulgate (Ps. xxxiii. 11) reads *minuentur* instead of *deficient*.

[12] baitheneus A B2 B3 ; baithe'neus B1

scribat '. Sancto convenienter congruit decessori novis-
simus versiculus quem scripserat,[1] cui numquam bona
deficient aeterna. Successori vero sequens patri spiritalium [2] doctori [3] filiorum, ' Venite filii audite me ;
timorem domini docebo vos ', congruenter convenit, qui
sicut decessor commendavit non solum ei docendo sed
etiam scribendo successit.

Post talem superius memoratum terminatae versum
perscriptum [4] paginae, sanctus ad vespertinalem [5] do-
129a minicae noctis [6] misam [7] ingreditur eclesiam. | Qua [8]
continuo consummata [9] ad hospitiolum [10] revertens in
lectulo resedet[11] pernox ubi[12] pro stramine nudam habebat petram, et pro pulvillo lapidem [13] qui hodieque quasi
quidam juxta sepulchrum ejus titulus stat monumenti.[14]
Ibidem itaque resedens [15] ultima ad fratres mandata solo
audiente ministro commendat, inquiens : ' Haec vobís
ó filioli novissima commendo verba, ut inter vos motuam[16]
et non fictam habeatis [17] caritatem cum pace. Et si ita
juxta sanctorum exempla patrum observaveritis, deus
confortator bonorum vobís auxiliabitur, et ego cum ipso[18]
manens pro vobís interpellabo ; et non tantum praesentis vitae necessaria ab eo sufficienter amministra-
129b buntur, sed etiam | aeternalium bonorum proemia

---

[1] versiculus quem scripserat A ; quem scripserat versiculus B1 B2 B3
(scri′p- B1)
[2] spiritalium A ; spiritualium B1 B2 B3
[3] *doctori.* Transposition signs in A are intended to place this word
before *qui sicut* below. They are entered (shaped like a superscript *u*,
below *oc,* and before *qui*) by the text hand. In B1 B2 B3 the text is as in A,
but without any sign of transposition. The transposition was ignored in
the shortened version and in P.
[4] perscriptum A B2 B3 ; pres- B1
[5] vespertinalem A ; -ale B1 B2 B3
[6] *dominicae noctis.* ' Sunday night ' began at or after the vespers of
Saturday ; in this case, on Saturday, 8 June, A.D. 597. See p. 67.
[7] misam A ; officium B1 B2 B3. Cf. p. 122.
[8] qua A ; Quo B1 B2 B3

The last verse that he wrote aptly befits the holy predecessor, who will never lack eternal good things. And the verse that follows, ' Come, my sons, hear me ; I will teach you fear of the Lord ', is fittingly adapted to the successor, the father of spiritual sons, a teacher, who, as his predecessor enjoined, succeeded him not in teaching only, but in writing also.

After he had written the former verse, at the end of the page, the saint entered the church for the vesper office of the Lord's-night. As soon as that was finished, he returned to his lodging, and reclined on his sleeping-place, where during the night he used to have for bed, the bare rock ; and for pillow, a stone, which even today stands beside his grave as a kind of epitaph. So while reclining there, he gave his last commands to the brothers, in the hearing of his attendant alone, and said : ' I commend to you, my children, these latest words, that you shall have among yourselves mutual and un-feigned charity, with peace. If you follow this course after the example of the holy fathers, God, who gives strength to the good, will help you ; and I, abiding with him, shall intercede for you. And not only will the necessaries of this life be sufficiently provided by him, but also the rewards of eternal good things will be

---

[9] continuo consummata A ; -ato B2 B3 ; consumato continuo B1, with pen-marks, possibly indicating transposition, above and below the first *c*.

[10] hospitiolum A ; hospiciolum, B2 B3 ; hospicium B1.

[11] resedet A ; -sid- B1 B2 B3

[12] *pernox ubi*. This is to be interpreted as *ubi pernox* ; although as it stands *pernox* could be construed with *resedet*.

[13] *lapidem*. See p. 89.

[14] *titulus monumenti :* i.e. an ' epitaph ' that indicated the manner of Columba's life.

[15] resedens A ; -sid- B1 B2 B3

[16] motuam A ; mu'tuam B1 ; mutuam B2 B3

[17] habeatis A B1 ; habehatis B3. Illegible in B2.

[18] ipso A B1 B2 ; ipse B3

divinorum observatoribus [mandatorum] praeparata [1] tribuentur '.

Huc usque extrema venerabilis patroni verba quasi de hac tediali perigrinatione [2] ad caelestem patriam transmeantis brevi textu narrata deducta sunt. .

Post quae [3] felici appropinquante novissima paulisper hora sanctus conticuit. Tum proinde media nocte pulsata personante cloca festinus surgens ad eclesiam pergit, citiorque ceterís currens solus introgresus juxta altare flexís in oratione genibus recumbit. Diormitius [4] minister tardius prosequtus eodem momento eminus totam intrinsecus eclesiam angelica luce erga sanctum repleri videt. Quo ad januam appropinquante eadem lux visa ocius recessit ; quam etiam alii de fra|tribus pauci et ipsi eminus adstantes viderant.

Diormitius [5] ergo eclesiam ingrediens flebili ingeminat voce : ' Ubi es, pater ? ' Et necdum allatís fratrum lucernís per tenebras palpans sanctum ante altarium recubantem invenit, quem paululum eregens [6] et juxta sedens sanctum in suo gremio possuit caput. Et inter haec coetus monachorum cum luminaribus adcurrens patre viso moriente coepit plangere. Et ut ab aliquibus qui praesentes inerant didicimus, sanctus necdum egrediente anima apertís susum [7] oculís ad utrumque latus cum mira vultus hilaritate et laetitia circumspiciebat, sanctos scilicet obvios intuens angelos. Diormitius [8] tum sanctam sublevat ad benedicendum

130a (margin)

---

[1] prae|parata A ; mandatorum preparata B1 B2 B3. With the B reading, cf. the Vulgate, John xiii. 34, xiv. 21. It is clear that either *mandatorum* or *praeceptorum* (cf. John xv. 10, 12) must have been what Adomnan wrote, or meant to have written.

[2] perigrinatione A ; pereg- B1 B2 B3

[3] Post quae A ; Post que B1 ; Postque B2 B3

[4] Diormitius A B2 B3 ; Diormicius B1

[5] Diormitius A B2 B3 ; Diormicius B1

bestowed, that are prepared for those who follow the divine commandments '.

We have carried down to this point, briefly told, the last words of the venerable patron, when he was, as it were, crossing over to the heavenly country from this weary pilgrimage.

After them the saint was silent for a little, as the happy latest hour drew near. Then, when the beaten bell resounded at midnight, he rose in haste and went to the church and, running, entered in advance of the others, alone ; and bowing his knees in prayer he sank down beside the altar. In that moment Diormit, the attendant, following later, saw from a distance the whole church filled inside with angelic light about the saint. As Diormit approached the doorway, the light that he had seen quickly faded. A few more of the brothers also had seen it, when they too were a little way off.

So Diormit entering the church cried in a tearful voice : ' Where are you, where are you, father ? ' And groping in the darkness, since the lamps of the brothers had not yet been brought, he found the saint lying before the altar. Raising him a little, and sitting down beside him, he placed the holy head upon his lap. Meanwhile the company of monks ran up with lights ; and when they saw that their father was dying they began to lament. And as we have learned from some men who were present there, the saint, whose soul had not yet departed, opened his eyes, and looked around on either side, with wonderful joy and gladness of countenance ; for he was gazing upon the holy angels that had come to meet him. Then Diormit raised the holy right hand,

---

[6] eregens A ; -rig- B1 B2 B3   [7] susum A ; sursum B1 B2 B3
[8] Diormitius A B2 B3 ; Diormi'cius B1

sancti monachorum chorum [1] dexteram manum. Sed |
130b et ipse venerabilis pater in quantum poterat simul suam
movebat manum ; ut videlicet quod voce in egresu non
valebat animae etiam motu manus fratres videretur
benedicere. Et post sanctam benedictionem taliter
significatam continuo spiritum exalavit. .

Quo tabernaculum corporis egreso facies rubens et
mirum in modum angelica visione exhilarita [2] in tantum
remansit, ut non quasi mortui sed dormientis videretur
viventis. Tota interim personabat mestis plangoribus
eclesia. Sed non praetereundum videtur quod eadem
hora beatae transitus animae cuidam everniensi [3] sancto
revelatum est.

In illo namque monasterio quod scotica nominatur [4]
131a lingua Cloni-|finchoil [5] quidam homo erat [6] sanctus
senex, Christi miles, qui Lugudius [7] vocitabatur, filius
Tailchani,[8] justus et sapiens. Hic itaque primo mane
cuidam eque christiano militi, Fergnovo nomine, suam
enarravit visionem cum ingenti gemitu dicens : ' Hac
praeterita nocte media sanctus Columba multarum
columna eclesiarum [9] ad dominum transit.[10] Et in hora
beati exitus ejus [11] Iovam insulam, ad quam corpore
numquam perveni, totam angelorum claritudine in
spiritu vidi inradiatam, totaque spatia aeris, usque ad [12]

---

[1] chorum A B2 B3 ; cetum B1
[2] exhilarita A ; -rata B1 B2 B3
[3] everniensi A ; hiber- B1 B3 ; hyber- B2
[4] nominatur A ; nuncupatur B1 B2 B3 (numc- B1)
[5] cloni | finchoil A, with two over-dashes above *cloni* ; clonifincoil B1
B2 B3 (-coi'l B1). In Thesaurus 1903, p. 280, it is suggested that *Cloni*
should here be read *Clóin*, the nominative singular. But since the B texts
agree with A in reading *cloni*, i.e. the nominative plural, the presumption
is that that was what Adomnan wrote. In that case, the lenited *f* in A would
have to be emended to unlenited *f*. The lenited *f* would have been correct
only if the preceding word were *cloin*, and already locally used as a feminine
noun : in O.I., it was masculine (see Thurneysen 1946, p. 676, translators'
note 50).

to bless the saint's company of monks. And the venerable father himself at the same time moved his hand, as much as he was able, in order that he might be seen to bless the brothers even by the movement of his hand, a thing that in the departure of his soul he could not do by voice. And after the holy benediction thus expressed he presently breathed out his spirit.

When that had left the tabernacle of the body, his face continued to be ruddy, and in a wonderful degree gladdened by the vision of angels, so much that it seemed like the face not of a dead man, but of a living sleeper. Meanwhile the whole church resounded with sorrowful lamentations.

And it appears right that this should not be omitted that was revealed to a certain saint in Ireland, in the very hour of the passing of the blessed soul. For in the monastery that in the Irish tongue is called *Cloni-finchoil*, there was an aged holy man, a soldier of Christ, righteous and wise, who was called Luguid, son of Tailchan. In the early morning he related a vision that he had had, to a man who was likewise a Christian soldier, by name Virgno ; and said, with great lamentation : ' In the middle of this last night Saint Columba, the pillar of many churches, has passed to the Lord. And in the hour of his blessed departure I saw in the Spirit the whole island of Io (where I have never come in the body) lit up with the brightness of angels ; and all the spaces

---

[6] homo erat A ; erat homo B1 B2 B3
[7] lugudius A B2 B3 ; lugu'dius B1
[8] tailchani A ; talcani B1 B2 B3
[9] eclesiarum A ; eccles- B1 B2 ; ecclis- B3
[10] transit A ; -iit B1 ; -iit B3. Missing in B2.
[11] beati exitus ejus A ; exitus ejus beati B1 B2 B3
[12] ad A B1. Missing in B2 ; omitted in B3.

ethera caelorum, eorundem angelorum claritate inlus-
trata, qui ad sanctam ipsius animam praeferendam [1] de
caelís misi discenderant [2] innumeri. Altisona quoque
131b carminalia et valde | suavia audivi angelicorum coetuum
cantica, eodem momento egresionis inter angelicos
sanctae ipsius animae ascendentes [3] choros '.

Hanc angelicam manifestationem Virgnous,[4] ut prae-
dictum est, qui ab ore sancti illius senis cui revelata erat
indubitanter didicerat, hísdem diebus de Scotia remigans
Hinba in insula [5] reliquiis [6] diebus vitae suae permanens
sancti Columbae monacís sepius enarrabat. Qui videlicet Virgnous, post multos in subjectione inter fratres
inreprehensibiliter expletos annos, alios xii.[7] in loco
anchoritarum [8] in Muirbulc-mar [9] vitam ducens anchoriticam [10] Christi victor miles explevit.

Hanc praedictam visionem non solum paginís in-
132a scriptam repperimus, sed et [11] [ab] aliquibus | expertís
senioribus quibus ipse Virgnous retulerat sine ullo
didicimus cunctamine.

Eadem quoque hora aliam visionem aliter revelatam
unus ex eís qui viderant, Christi miles, valde senex, cujus
nomen [12] etiam potest dici ' ferreolus ', scotice vero

---

[1] praeferendam A ; perf- B1 B2 B3
[2] discenderant A ; des- B1 B3. Missing in B2.
[3] ascendentes A ; -entis B1 B2 B3
[4] *Virgnous.* So also below, and in 132a ; but above, in the dative,
Fergnovo ; cf. under 119b, and p. 139.
[5] hinba in insula A ; in insula himba B1 ; in ins[B2 ; insula himba B3
[6] reliquiis A ; -quis B1 B2 B3   [7] xii A ; duodecim B1 B2 B3
[8] anchoritarum A ; anachoret- B1 ; anachorit- B3. Illegible in B2.
[9] in muir|bulc mar A, with four over-dashes ; in mui′rbule mäar B1 ;
in muirbulc mäar B2 ; in muirbulc B3. The over-dash above *in*, in A,
shows that *in* was thought to be an Irish word (the preposition *i n-*), and
bulc, to be the O.I. dative of *bolc* : ' in the great sea-bay '. It is implied
that this place of anchorites was in the island of Hinba. See p. 154.
[10] anchoriticam A ; anachore′t- B1 ; anachorit- B2 ; anachoret- B3
[11] et A ; et ab B1 B3 ; ab B2
[12] nomen A ; nomen latine B1 B2 B3

533 LIFE OF COLUMBA

of the air, as far as the ethereal skies, illumined by the shining of those angels, who, sent from heaven, had come down without number, to bear aloft his holy soul. Also I heard, sounding on high, the songs, tuneful and very sweet, of the angelic hosts, at the very moment when his holy soul went forth among the ascending companies of angels '.

In those same days Virgno rowed over from Ireland, and he remained for the rest of his life in the island of Hinba ; and he very often described to the monks of Saint Columba this manifestation of angels of which, as has been said above, he had learned indubitably from the mouth of the holy old man to whom it had been revealed. After completing irreproachably many years in subjection among the brothers, this Virgno completed other twelve years as a victorious soldier of Christ, leading the life of an anchorite, in the place of the anchorites, in Muirbolc-már.

We have not only found the foregoing vision set down in writing, but we have learned it with no uncertainty [from] some elders who knew of it, since Virgno himself had told it to them.

Another vision, differently revealed at the same hour, was told with strong asseveration to me, Adomnan, then a young man, by one of those that had seen it, a

Ernene,[1] gente mocu Fir-roide,[2] qui inter aliorum sancti
Columbae monacorum reliquias, et ipse sanctus monacus,
in dorso Tómme [3] sepultus cum sanctis resurrectionem
exspectat, mihi Adomnano [4] illo juveni [5] in tempore cum
grandi retulerat testificatione, dicens : ' Illa in nocte qua
sanctus Columba de terrís ad caelos felici et beato fine
transiit, ego et alii mecum viri [6] laborantes in captura
piscium [7] in valle piscosi fluminis Fendæ [8] subito totum
132b aerei inlustratum caeli spatium videmus. . Cujus mi|ra-
culi subitatione permoti oculos ad orientem [9] elevatos
convertimus, et ecce quasi quaedam pergrandis ignea
apparuit columna, quae in illa nocte media susum [10]
ascendens ita nobis videbatur mundum inlustrare totum
sicuti aesteus [11] et meridianus sol. Et postquam illa
penetravit columna caelum, quasi post occassum solis
tenebrae succedunt. Hujus itaque claritudinem luminosae [12] et praedicabilis columnae non tantum nos qui
simul in eodem loco ineramus cum ingenti ammiratione
vidimus, sed et alii multi piscatores qui sparsim per
diversas fluminales piscinas ejusdem fluminis piscabantur,

[1] ernene A ; erne'ne B1 ; aernene B2 ; arrene B3. Adomnan's
translation *ferreolus* (grammatically a diminutive of *ferreus*) shows that he
thought that *Ernene* was derived from *iarn* ' iron ', representing a Goidelic
stem *isarno-*, with short *i*.

[2] mocu fir roide A, with five over-dashes ; mocufirroide B1 B2 (-ro'ide
B1) ; mocufirroive B3. The name means ' family of Fer-Roide ' ; and if
that is ' of the husband of Ród ', the stress-accent would be on the syllable
rōi, as in B1. After *mocu*, an initial consonant was (sometimes, at least)
lenited : A's dotted *f* may be correct. It was overlooked by Reeves, and
in Thesaurus 1903, p. 280.

[3] tómme A, with one over-dash above the second syllable ; thome B1 ;
come B2 ; tome B3. *Dorsum tómme* stood for O.I. *druimm-tómme*, later
-tuamma, with nasalized *t* ; it is now Drumhome, a parish in Donegal. See
p. 106. Cf. Reeves 1857, p. 238.

[4] adomnano A (with a slight space after *ad*) ; á domnano B1 B2 ; a
domnano B3

[5] juveni A B2 B3 ; inveni B1

[6] viri A B1 B2. Omitted in B3.

[7] *laborantes in captura piscium.* This was on ' the venerable Lord's-

very aged soldier of Christ, of the family mocu Fir-roide, whose name, in Irish *Ernene*, can also be rendered ' man of iron '. He (himself a holy monk) lies buried among the remains of other monks of Saint Columba, and awaits the resurrection with the saints, in the ridge of Tóimm. He said : ' In that night when Saint Columba passed, by a happy and blessed end, from earth to heaven, I and other men with me, at work on the catching of fish in the valley of the river Fendea, which abounds in fish, saw the whole space of airy heaven suddenly lit up. Startled by the suddenness of this miracle, we raised our eyes and turned them to the region of the rising sun ; and behold, there appeared what seemed like a very great pillar of fire which, rising upwards in that midnight, seemed to us to illumine the whole world like the summer sun at midday. And after that pillar pierced the sky, darkness followed, as after the setting of the sun. Not only was the brightness of this luminous and remarkable pillar seen, with great amazement, by us, who were together in the same place, but many other fishers also, who were fishing here and there among the various pools of the same river, were,

---

night ', 127a ; and evidently Adomnan expresses no disapproval of fishing on Sunday. See pp. 25ff.

⁸ fendæ A ; fendé B1 B2 ; fende B3. The meaning is ' white goddess ' ; see pp. 141-2. The river was apparently the Finn, in Donegal, a tributary of the Foyle. Reeves 1857, p. 239, suggested that the place was Gleann Finne, in the parish of Kilteevoge.

⁹ *orientem.* Iona was to the north-east of the Finn, the direction of sunrise in June.

¹⁰ susum A ; sursum B1 B2 B3

¹¹ aesteus A ; esti'vus B1 ; estivus B2 B3

¹² luminosae A ; -ose B2 B3 ; luminis B1

sicut nobis post retulerant, simili apparatione [1] visa

133a magno pavore sunt | perculsi '. .

Harum igitur trium [2] miracula visionum eadem transitus hora venerandi apparentium patroni aeternos ei a
deo conlatos protestantur honores.   Ad propossitum
revertamur.[3]

Interea post sanctae egresum animae ymnís matutinalibus [4] terminatís sacrum corpus de eclesia ad hospitium, unde paulo ante vivens venerat, cum canora
fratrum reportatur psalmodia.   Honestaeque ternís
diebus et totidem noctibus honorabiles rite explentur
exequiae ; quibus in dei sapidís [5] laudibus terminatís,
sancti et beati patroni venerabile corpus mundís in-
volutum sindonibus [6] et praeparata possitum in rata
busta [7] debeta [8] humatur cum veneratione, in luminosa

133b et aeternali resurrecturum | claritudine. .

De supra memoratís ergo tribus illís exsequiarum
diebus, more peractís eclesiastico, quod nobís ab expertís
traditum est hujus prope finem enarrabitur libri.

Quidam [9] namque aliquando unus de fratribus
coram venerabili viro sempliciter [10] loquens :   ' Ad
celebrandas ' ait ad sanctum, ' tuas post tuum obitum
exequias, ut putatur, totus harum provinciarum populus

[1] apparatione A ; -riti- B1 B2 ; -rici- B3
[2] *trium.*   The light in the church, 129b-130a, is included in the number.
[3] ad propossitum revertamur A ; -osi- B1 B2 B3.   This sentence is
written in coloured ink in B1 B3.
[4] *ymnís matutinalibus.*   This means the canonical hour next after the
midnight office.   See Gougaud 1932, p. 330.   At Bangor (in the seventh
century) and at Tallaght (in the ninth), there was an interval for sleep
between these offices.   We do not know whether an interval was normal
at Iona.   In the middle of summer there would hardly have been time
for it.
[5] sapidís A.   Omitted in B1 B2 B3.
[6] *sindonibus.*   This word was derived from the Vulgate Gospels' account
of the burial of Jesus.
[7] in ratabus|ta A ; in rata busta B1 B3 ;]ta busta B2.   The words, or
word, *rata busta* have not been satisfactorily explained.   *Busta* may be the

as they told us afterwards, struck with great terror, through seeing a similar apparition '.

These three miraculous visions, appearing in the very hour of the passing of the venerable patron, testify to the eternal honours conferred on him by God. Let us return to our theme.

In the meanwhile, after the departure of the holy soul, when the matin hymns were ended, the sacred body was carried back from the church, with the brothers' tuneful psalmody, to the lodging from which, alive, he had come a little while before. And for three days and three nights the funeral ceremonies were duly carried out in a worthy and honourable manner. When these had ended in the savoury praises of God, the venerable body of the holy and blessed patron was wrapped in clean fine cloths, and laid in the appointed burial-place that had been made ready, and was interred with fitting veneration, to rise again in bright and eternal light.

What has been handed down to us on good authority concerning those three days of funeral mentioned above, spent according to the custom of the church, shall be related here, almost at the end of this book.

A certain man, one of the brothers, on one occasion in the company of the venerable man spoke unthinkingly, and said to the saint : ' After your death, it is estimated that the entire population of these provinces will row over for the celebration of your funeral, and

---

accusative plural of *bustum* ' grave ' or ' tomb '. The jingle between *rata* and *praeparata* may have been intentional.

   [8] debeta A ; de'bita B1 ; debita B2 B3

   [9] Quidam A B2 B3 ; Cuidam B1 (a mistake of the decorator).

  [10] sempliciter A ; sim- B1 B2 B3

2N

hanc Iovam remigans replebit insulam '. Quod verbum audiens sanctus consequenter ait : ' Ó mí filiole,[1] non ut loqueris síc res probabit. Nam promiscuum populi vulgus nullo modo ad meas poterit exsequias venire. Mei soli familiares monaci mea sepulchralia conplebunt 134a et exsequialia honestabunt | officia '.

Quod verbum ejus [2] profeticum statim post transitum ipsius omnipotentia dei adimpleri fecit. Nam per tris [3] illas exsequiales dies et noctes grandis sine pluia [4] facta est ventosa tempestas ; qua fortiter prohibente nullus hinc et inde navicella [5] vectus transfretare poterat. Et post consummatam beati sepultionem viri continuo tempestate sedata et cessante vento totum tranquillatum est equor.

Perpendat itaque lector quanti et qualis apud deum praedicabilis patronus honoris habeatur, cui aliquando in carne mortali conversanti deo dignante oranti tempestates [6] sedatae sunt et maria tranquillata ; et rursus quando necesse habuit, supra memorata occassione, orta flamina ventorum et ventosa cum voluit concita [7] sunt | 134b equora ; quae subsequenter, ut superius dictum est, expletís ejus sepulturae ministeriis in magnam conversa sunt tranquillitatem.

Hic itaque nostro praedicabili patrono vitae terminus fuit ; ista meritorum exordia. Qui, secundum sententias [8] scripturarum, aeternís comes triumphís patribus additus,[9] apostolís et profetís consertus, numero aggregatus albatorum milium [10] agnino in sanguine suas

---

[1] filiole A B1 B2 ; filioli B3
[2] ejus A B1 B2. Omitted in B3 (as the result of erasure and rewriting).
[3] tris A ; tres B1 B2 B3
[4] pluia A ; pluvia B1 B2 B3
[5] navicella A B2 ; navice'lla B1 ; navi cella B3
[6] tempestates A B1 B2 ; tep- B3
[7] concita A ; concitata B1 B3. Missing in B2.

fill this island of Io '. Upon hearing this, the saint said : ' My child, the event will not prove to be as you say ; for a miscellaneous crowd of people will not be able to come to my funeral. Only my family of monks will fulfil the offices of my burial, and worthily perform my funeral rites '.

The omnipotence of God caused this prophetic saying of his to be fulfilled immediately after his death. For during those three days and nights of the funeral a great storm of wind blew without rain, and forbade any one in a small ship to cross the strait in either direction. And after the burial of the blessed man had been completed, straightway the storm was stilled, the wind ceased, and the whole sea was calmed.

Let the reader consider in how great and high honour with God the memorable patron is held, at whose prayer once while he lived in mortal flesh, God granting it, storms were stilled, and seas were calmed ; and again, when he had need, on the occasion mentioned above, at his wish blasts of wind sprang up, and stormy seas were raised ; which afterwards, as has been said above, when the services of his burial were complete, were changed into a great calm.

This was the end of our memorable patron's life ; these were the beginnings of his rewards. Being, in the language of the scriptures, added to the fathers as a sharer in eternal triumphs, united to apostles and prophets, and joined to the number of the thousands of

---

[8] sententias A B2 ; -enciam B1 ; -encias B3

[9] *Hic* to *additus*. This part of the paragraph is based upon passages from Evagrius's Life of Antony ; the part from *apostolis* to *labe*, (with its quotation from the Vulgate, Apocalypse vii. 14) upon a letter of Sulpicius Severus, concerning the death of Martin of Tours (in Halm's edition, p. 143). See Brüning 1917, pp. 246, 248.

[10] milium A B3 ; mi'lium B1 ; militum B2

sanctorum qui laverunt stolas, agnum ductorem comitatur ; virgo inmaculatus, ab omni intiger [1] labe, ipso domino nostro Jesu Christo dignante, cui est cum patre honor virtus laus gloria et imperium sempeternum,[2] in unitate spiritus sancti, per omnia saecula saeculorum. .[3] |

135a Post horum trinalium lectionem libellorum, quisque dilegens [4] annotet lector quanti et qualis meriti sanctus sepe supra memoratus praesul venerandus, quantae et qualis apud deum honorificantiae,[5] fuerit estimatus [6] ; quantae et quales angelicae ad ipsum et luminosae frequentationes fuerint ; quanta in eo profetalis gratia ; quanta dialium efficientia virtutum ; quanta et quam frequens eum divini luminis claritudo in carne mortali adhuc commorantem circumfulserit. Quae etiam post egresum animae de tabernaculo corporis almissimae,[7] sicuti quibusdam electís ostensum habetur conpertum, 135b locum in quo ipsius sancta pausant [8] ossa | usque hodie eadem caelestis claritas frequentare non cessat, et sanctorum frequens visitatio angelorum.

Et haec etiam eidem beatae memoriae viro a deo non mediocris est conlata gratia, qua nomen ejus non tantum per totam nostram Scotiam, et omnium totius orbis insularum maximam Brittanniam, clare devulgari [9] promeruit in hac parva et extrema ociani [10] brittannici commoratus insula, sed etiam ad trigonam usque

[1] intiger A ; -teg- B1 B2 B3
[2] sempeternum A ; sempit- B1 B2 B3
[3] saeculorum A ; seculorum amen B1 B2 B3
[4] dilegens A ; -lig- B1 B2 B3
[5] honorificantiae A ; -centie B1 B2
[6] *quantae* to *estimatus*. These words are omitted in B3.
[7] almissimae | A (-*mae* written later, with a different pen, by the text hand) ; sanctissime B1 B2 B3
[8] pausant A B1 B3 ; pausent B2   [9] devulgari A ; div- B1 B2 B3
[10] ociani A ; occe'ani B1 ; occeani B2 ; oceani B3

white-robed saints who have washed their robes in the blood of the Lamb, he attends the Lamb his leader ; a virgin unstained, free from every flaw, by the grace of our Lord Jesus Christ himself, who has, with the Father, honour, power, praise, glory, and everlasting dominion, in the unity of the Holy Spirit, through all the ages of the ages.

After the reading of these three books, let every attentive reader observe of how great and high merit, how greatly and highly deserving of honour, our venerable holy superior so often named above was esteemed in the sight of God ; how much and in what manner he was visited by shining angels ; how great in him was the grace of prophecy, how great the power of divine miracles ; how great and how frequent was the brightness of divine light that shone about him, while he still lived in mortal flesh. And even after the departure of his most gentle soul from the tabernacle of the body, this same heavenly brightness, as well as the frequent visits of holy angels, does not cease, down to the present day, to appear at the place in which his holy bones repose ; as is established through being revealed to certain elect persons.

And this great favour also was conferred by God on that man of blessed memory, that, although he lived in this small and remote island of the Britannic ocean, he merited that his name should not only be illustriously renowned throughout our Ireland, and throughout Britain, the greatest of all the islands of the whole world ; but that it should reach even as far as three-cornered

Hispaniam, et Gallias, et ultra Alpes [1] pininas [2] Italiam sitam pervenire, ipsam quoque romanam civitatem, quae caput [3] est omnium civitatum, tantus et talis honor noscibilis [4] eidem sancto inter cetera divinae donationis munera condonatus scitur a deo, qui sé diligentes amat, 136a et eos qui eum sapidís [5] magnificant | laudibus magis ac magis glorificans inmensís sublimat honoribus. Qui est benedictus in saecula. . Amen. .

[6] Obsecro eos quicumque voluerint hos discribere [7] libellos, immo potius adjuro per Christum judicem saeculorum, ut postquam deligenter [8] discripserint [9] conferant et emendent cum omni diligentia ad exemplar unde craxerunt,[10] et hanc quoque adjurationem hoc in loco subscribant. .[11]

Quicumque hós virtutum libellos Columbae legerit pro me Dorbbeneo deum deprecetur, ut vitam post mortem aeternam possedeam.[12]

---

[1] alpes A B1 B2 ; alpas B3
[2] pininas A ; penninas B1 B2 B3 (-ni'n- B1)
[3] *caput*. This passage is partly modelled upon words, used in a somewhat similar context, in Evagrius's Life of Antony : *ipsi quae urbium caput est Romae*. See Brüning 1917, p. 246.
[4] noscibilis A B1 (-ci'b- B1) ; vocibilis B2 B3
[5] sapidís A. Omitted in B1 B3 ?B2.
[6] Before *Obsecro*, a line is left blank in A. B2 had a title in colour, of which [*Adjura*]*tio sancti adamnani* is visible in our facsimile. Reeves (1857, p. 458) read in addition : *ad s*[*criptore*]*m*.
[7] discribere A ; des- B1 B2 B3
[8] deligenter A ; dil- B1 B2 B3
[9] discripserint A ; des- B1 B3. Missing in B2.
[10] craxerunt A ; caraxave'runt B1 ; caraxerunt B3. Missing in B2. This sentence must have been derived from Adomnan's own colophon, but we should suppose that he would have written *craxaverint*.
[11] *Obsecro* to *subscribant*. This subscription appears to be modelled upon words translated by Jerome (in his *De viris illustribus*) from the Greek of Irenaeus. See Brüning 1917, p. 253, and cf. Reeves 1857, p. 242. After *subscribant* in B1 B2 B3, lists of Columba's companions and relatives follow immediately. See the Appendix, below.

Spain, and Gaul, and Italy situated beyond the Pennine Alps ; also the Roman city itself, which is the chief of all cities. So great and high honour of fame is known to have been bestowed upon that saint, among the other gifts of divine granting, by God, who loves those that love him, and, more and more glorifying those that magnify him with savoury praises, elevates them with boundless honours. And He is blessed through the ages. Amen.

I beseech all those that may wish to copy these books, nay more I adjure them through Christ, the judge of the ages, that after carefully copying they compare them with the exemplar from which they have written, and emend them with the utmost care ; and also that they append this adjuration in this place.

Whoever may read these books of the miraculous powers of Columba, let him pray to God for me, Dorbbene, that I may possess after death eternal life.

---

[12] *Quicumque* to *possedeam*. This signature of Dorbbene is in A only. It is written in red ink, after a line left blank, and with a wider outer margin, probably at a somewhat later time, by the text hand. The red ink used was too thick for free writing ; for that or some other reason the parchment did not take the ink very well. The last four lines of 136a are blank, and there is no writing in the second column.

Page 137 is not divided into columns. It contains the Lord's Prayer in Greek, derived from a text similar to that of the Greek Testament, Matt. vi. 9-13. The writing is based upon Greek uncials of the seventh century.

The writer was probably the same who wrote the text of A. There is no indication that his Greek version was taken from a version written by Adomnan. But it has some value as evidence of the study of Greek in the Irish church of Adomnan's time.

In the lower part of the same page, a relatively modern hand has written about twelve lines, which were later erased.

A hand-copy of the Greek prayer was given in Reeves 1857, pp. xx–xxii, with a discussion.

APPENDIX

After the Life, the B texts give, from the same manuscript source, lists of Columba's monks and relatives. These lists were composed, or completed, more than two full generations after Columba's death. Irish names in these lists are spelt in a manner comparable with Adomnan's spellings, but the genitive of *mac* 'son' which is *maic* in all the manuscripts of the Life, appears as *meic* in the list of relatives. This somewhat later spelling suggests that the lists may not have been composed during Adomnan's life-time.

Our text of the lists is that of B1 (folio 143ab), except that we have supplied our own punctuation and capital letters. We note all variants of spelling in B2 (so far as the writing is visible) and in B3, including variations in the accents over proper names. In these lists, B2 has no other visible accents except, regularly, the double accent on *filii*, for diaeresis ; and B3 has no accent.

Hec [1] sunt xii.[2] virorum nomina, qui cum sancto
Columba de Scotia primo ejus transitu ad Britta'nniam [3]
transnavigaverunt. Duo filii Brendin: [4] Baithe'ne, [5] qui
et Conin, sancti successor Columbe ; et Cobthach frater
ejus. Ernam [6] sancti avunculus Columbe. Diormi'cius [7]
ejus ministrator. Rus, et Fechno',[8] duo filii Rodain.
Scandal filius Bresail, filii E'ndei,[9] filii Neil. Luguid,
mocu-Theimne.[10] Echoid. Thocamnu,[11] mocufi'r-
Cete'a.[12] Cairnaan [13] filius Bra'nduib,[14] filii Meilgi.
Grillaan [15]

Sancti Columbe parentes.[16] Fedilmith [17] pater ejus,
filius Fergu'so.[18] Eithne [19] mater ipsius, filia filii
navis.[20] Ioge'n [21] germanus frater Columbe ju'nior.
Item tres germane sorores ejus : [C]uimne,[22] mater
filiorum meic [23] Decui'l,[24] qui nominantur Mernoóc,[25]
et Caschene,[26] et Meldal, et Bran qui sepultus est in
Dairu[27]-Calchaich.

---

[1] *Hec*, with large initial letter, in B1 B2 B3.
[2] xii. B1 ; duodecim B2 B3
[3] britta'nniam B1 ; brittanniam B2 B3
[4] brendin B1 ; brenden B3. Illegible in B2.
[5] baithe'ne B1 ; baithene B3. Illegible in B2. See p. 90.
[6] ernam B1 ; ernäan B2 ; ernaan B3. See 46a.
[7] diormi'cius B1 ; diormitius B2 ; Diormitius B3. He survived
Columba by many years (77b).
[8] fechno' B1 ; the accent is smudged, perhaps for erasure. fechno
B2 B3
[9] e'ndei B1 ; endei B2 B3. Ende is thought to have been the eponym
of Tir-nEnda, in the district of Raphoe, in eastern Donegal. Columba was
a great-grandson of Ende's brother, Conall Gulban, the eponym of Tir-
Conaill.
[10] mocu theimne B1 ; mocutheimne B2 ; mocu themne B3
[11] thocamnu B1 ; thocannu B2 ; tochannu B3. The hypocoristic name
To-channu may date from the seventh century (cf. Thurneysen 1946,
p. 111). His family, mocu fir-Chetea, seems to imply that he was not
closely akin to Columba.
[12] mocufi'r cete'a B1 ; mocufir cetea B2 B3
[13] cairnaan B1 B3 ; cairnäan B2
[14] bra'nduib B1 ; branduib B2 B3
[15] grillaan B1 B3 ; grilläan B2

These are the names of the twelve men who sailed over with Saint Columba from Ireland in his first crossing to Britain. Two sons of Brenden : Baithene, also called Conin, Saint Columba's successor ; and Cobthach, Baithene's brother. Ernan, Saint Columba's uncle. Diormit, his attendant. Rus, and Féchno, two sons of Ródan. Scandal, son of Bressal, son of Ende, son of Néll. Luguid, mocu-Theimne. Echoid. Tochannu, mocu fir-Chetea. Cairnan, son of Brandub, son of Meilge. Grillan.

Saint Columba's parents. His father, Fedilmith, son of Fergus. His mother, Aethne, daughter of Mac-naue. Columba's younger brother, Iogen. Also his three sisters : Cuimne, mother of the sons of Mac-decuil, who are named Mernoc, and Cascene, and Meldal, and Bran who is buried in Daire-Calcig [Derry].

---

[16] *Sancti Columbe parentes.* These words are in coloured ink in B2, and perhaps in B1 and B3.

[17] Fedilmith B1 ; fe'dilmith B2 ; Fedelmith B3. The *F* is large in B1 B3, and decorated in B1. For Columba's parentage, see 4a.

[18] fergu'so B1 ; ferguso B2 B3

[19] eithne B1 B3 ; Aeithne B2

[20] navis B1 B3 ; navís B2

[21] ioge'n B1 ; iogen B2 B3. Cf. Reeves 1857, p. lxxi. For the element *Ivo->Io-, Eu-*, in personal names, cf. MacNeill 1909, p. 345.

[22] euimne B1 ; cuimne B2 B3

[23] meic B1 B3 ; meíc B2

[24] decui'l B1 ; decuil B2 B3

[25] mernoóc B1 ; mernöoc B2 ; mernooc B3. Doubled vowels stood for long single vowel-sounds, and were not understood by medieval scribes. Thus B2, and probably also B1, here mark double *o* for diaeresis.

[26] caschene B1 ; cascene B2 B3

[27] dairu B1 B3 ; dauru B2

Consobrini sancti Columbe.[1] Mincholeth [2] mater filiorum Ena'[in],[3] quorum unus Colmaan [4] dicebatur. Sinech [5] mater virorum mocu-Cein [6] Cu'ile [7] Aque, quorum nomina sunt Aidanus monachus qui sepultus est hi Cuil-uisci, et Chronïi [8] moccu-[C]ein [9] qui sepultus est in Daurmaig ;[10] a'via Tocummi mocu-Cein,[11] qui valde senio fessus presbiter sanctus in Iova [12] insula presentem finivit vitam.[13] Amen. Deo gratias.[14]

[1] *Consobrini sancti Columbe*. This rubric may originally have stood in a margin, and have been intended to apply to all Columba's sisters' sons. It is in coloured ink in B2, and perhaps in B1 and B3. The text hand of B2 wrote *sancte*, and afterwards corrected it to *sancti* in black ink. Reeves mistakenly made the words part of the preceding sentence ; he rendered as a comma after *calchaich* a punctuation sign that in B3 is used only as a major stop.

[2] *Mincholeth*. B1 and B3 have a large initial *M*. Probably this is a corruption of *Minchloth*.

[3] ena'~ B1 (presumably for *ena'm*, the *m* being an erroneous reading of *in*) ; enain B2 B3. The sons of Enan were thought to have given their name to the church of Cell mac-nEnain, now Kilmacrenan, in Donegal. Cf. Reeves 1857, p. 192.

[4] colmaan B1 ; colmäan B2 ; calmaan B3
[5] Sinech B1 B3 ; sineth B2
[6] mocu cein B1 ; mocuceiin B2 ; mocu ceiin B3, wrongly read by Reeves as *mocucei in*. The mocu-Céin have been equated with the Cianacht (cf. MacNeill 1911, p. 76).
[7] cu'ile B1 ; cuile B2 B3
[8] chronïi B1 ; conrïi B2 ; chonrii B3
[9] moccuoein B1 ; mocucein B2 ; moccucem B3
[10] daur maig B1 B2 B3
[11] mocu cein B1 ; mocu[B2 ; mocucem B3
[12] iova B1 ?B2 ; iona B3. See p. 1.
[13] Much later accounts say that another sister of Columba was the mother of Comgan, Diarmait's son, and of six other sons (Oengus 1905, pp. 78, 161, 168).
[14] amen. Deo gratias B1. Illegible in B2 ; omitted in B3.

Saint Columba's kindred. Mincholeth, mother of the sons of Enan, one of whom was called Colman. Sinech, mother of the men of the mocu-Céin of Cul-uisci, whose names are Aidan the monk who is buried in Cul-uisci, and Conrí mocu-Céin who is buried in Daurmag [Durrow] ; and grandmother of To-chumme mocu-Céin who ended the present life in the island of Io as a holy priest, worn out with age. Amen. Thanks be to God.

Indexes

General Index

The indexes were planned, and most of the slips were written, while my husband and I were working on the text and translation. The indexing of introduction and notes is mine, and I am responsible for any omissions or inconsistencies. The General Index includes all proper names and Irish words (including many elements of proper names) occurring in the Latin text, notes, and introduction. The translation has not been indexed, since names in it can be readily located from the text. For names or words that occur in the text, the references are, first to the text, by page and column of MS A (as printed in the outer margins) or Appendix (pp. 546-8), and then to introduction and footnotes by page number, references to notes being followed by *n*. Since the references to MS A always consist of a number and the letter *a* or *b*, it can be seen at a glance whether the name or word occurs in the text or not. Purely textual notes have not been indexed.

Irish names have been indexed under the vernacular nominative form, and the actual forms used in MS A are shown within brackets at the end of the item. When a regular latinized form is fully established by the text, it is given first within the brackets, in the nominative case and without particular references, followed by exceptional and vernacular forms, with references. The names of ancient authors and works have been sparingly included. Modern authors have been included only where the reference was to the author rather than to his published work.

M.O.A.

Abbor-doboir (Aberdour, Aberdeenshire), p. 158
ached, M. (' field '), 63a, p. 131
Ached-bou (Aghaboe, county Leix), monastery of, 63a, pp. 122, 150 ; founder of the, *see* Cainnech. (Irish nom. *Ached-bou* ; synonym, *campulus bovis*)
acht (' but '), p. 171
Actus Silvestri, pp. 23, 186*n*
adaig (' night '), p. 155
Adam, 84b, p. 92
Adamnan, pp. 92, 136 ; *see* Adomnan
Ad Candidam Casam (Whithorn), p. 77
Add, river, Argyllshire, p. 39
Adomnan, abbot of Iona, by name, 9a, 50a, 120b, 132a, pp. 8, 16, 27, 29, 51, 54, 60, 63, 73, 74, 76, 83, 104, 110, 202*n* ; speaking of himself personally, but not by name, 13b, 15b, 26ab, 98b-103b, 119b, 130a, 131b-132a, 133b. Aldfrith, king of Northumbria, his pupil and friend, 103b, pp. 54, 94. Birth, p. 92. Bishops, his attitude to, pp. 25, 102. Brude, son of Bile, brought to him for burial, pp. 96-7. Character, pp. 24, 97-8. Churches dedicated to him, pp. 94-5 ; *see* Forglen. Death, p. 96.

Easter and tonsure controversies, his attitude in, pp. 24, 26-7, 94, 96. Education, p. 93. Father, *see* Ronan, son of Tinne. Food, his attitude to, p. 29. Homeland, pp. 141, 312*n*. Iona, *see* under Io. Kindred, pp. 92, 136-7. King of Ireland his friend, p. 7. Law of, *see* Adomnan's Law. Life of (in Irish), pp. 29, 53, 56, 96-8. Mocu-Uais, his relations with, pp. 29, 98. Monastery founded by him, ? *see* Raphoe. Mother, *see* Ronnat. Name, pp. 92-3, 136, 164. Northumbria, his visits to, 103b, pp. 25, 27, 94, 96, 102, 461*n*. Relics, p. 99. Scholarship, pp. 96, 161. Spelling used by him, pp. 10-11, 64-5, 104-05, 124-61 passim, 545. Sunday, his attitude to, pp. 25-9. Synod in Ireland, his presence at, 101b, p. 457*n*. Works : *De Locis Sanctis*, pp. 92-4, 105, 111, 125, 216*n*, 337*n*, 390*n*, 456*n*. Life of Columba : composed in Iona, *see* under Io ; composition of, 3b, 10b, 104a, pp. 5-10, 14, 55, 57, 93, 96, 105, 121 ; sources of, 3a-4a, 9a-10a, 13b, 15b, 26ab, 45ab, 50a, 57a, 58a, 60ab, 84a, 120b-121a, 130a, 131b-132a, 133b, pp. 15-16, 19-23, 39, 68-9,

20   553

Index of Subjects

agriculture, 30a, 38a, 54b–55b, 98b–99b, 126a, pp. 114–15, 117, 119, 262n
anchorites, 50a, 131b, pp. 28, 90, 99
angels, 3b, 7b, 15b, 80ab, 104ab, 105b–117b, 122b, 123b–124a, 125b, 126a, 130ab, 131ab, 135ab, pp. 15–17, 497n
annals and annal-collections, pp. viii, ix, 37, 39, 41–2, 44, 53, 63, 66, 71, 76, 99–101
apples, 7a, 54a, 80b, pp. 89, 119
axe, 85b, p. 368
baker, 112a
baptism, 5b, 9a, 34b, 35a, 61a, 78a, 114b, 115a
battles mentioned by Adomnan, 4a, 8a–9a, 17b–19a, 50ab, 103b ; see also 108a
beggars, 83b–85b, p. 368
bell, cloca, 18a, 129b ; signum (perhaps the sound of the bell), 96b, 114a
bishops mentioned by Adomnan, 16b, 36b, 45b, 51a, 53ab, 106b ; cf. pp. 25, 101–2
boar, 74a, p. 7
boats, 5b, 35ab, 42a, 74b, 75b, 82a, 100a, 134a, pp. 116–17
books mentioned by Adomnan, 5b, 28a, 28b, 59a–60b, 76b, 99ab, 100a, 107a, 128ab
book-satchels, 59b–60a
bread, holy, 63a, p. 122 ; blessed as a charm, 56a, 58b
brochs (circular towers), pp. 31, 35, 83
bronze, 49b, 99a
brooch, p. 65
building work, 31ab, 54b, 75b, 100ab, 115ab
burial under a cairn, 35a ; burial of a hand, 37ab
butler, 23b
Byzantine musical notation, p. 173
cattle, 40b, 47a, 55b–57a, 65b, 66ab, 68a–69a, 76b, 84ab,
charms, stone, 7a, 79b, 80b, 81a ; bread, 56ab, 58b ; salt, 58b–59a ; water, 58b ; undefined, 57b
childbirth, 92b–93b
commemoration lists, 113b, pp. 25, 68–9, 134, 490n
cowl, 72a
crane, 48a–49a, pp. 24, 114

dead restored to life, 7a, 78a–79a, p. 7
death, avoidance of presence at, 108b, pp. 25, 476n
deer, 84ab
demons, 6ab, 7b, 36a, 41a, 61b–62a, 65ab, 66ab, 81b, 110a–111a, 112b, 114a, p. 16
deserts (remote places); 5b, 17a, 25b–26a, 95a
diminutives, Adomnan's use of, p. 368n
diseases and broken bones, 6ab, 7a, 37ab, 46a, 48a, 55b–58b, 61b–62a, 67a, 77ab, 79b, 81a, 92b, 102b–103b, 110b, 111a, p. 460n
dogs, 74a, 85a, pp. 7, 29
dove, 2ab
drought, 98b–99b, p. 8
druidism, p. 85
druids' fence, p. 84
Easter, 60a, 88ab, 124b, pp. 28–9, 45, 74, 96, 123 ; Easter controversy, 15b, pp. 24, 26, 60–1, 90–1, 94, 96, 98–9, 108, 123 ; see also tonsure
Easter tables, pp. viii, 46, 61, 101
elders, 3b, 11a, 14b, 38a, 39a, 57a, 99a, 106a, 111b, 132a. (majores, seniores ; = Irish sruthi)
Eucharist, 7a, 41b, 45b, 53a, 88b, 101b–102a, 112b, 113ab, 118ab, 125b, pp. 22, 25, 122–4, 353n, 467n, 476n, 488n; episcopal and presbyteral rites, 45b, p. 304n
fasts and fasting, 4b, 5b, 29b, 94a, 100a, 111a, p. 120, 122, 260n
fire, damage by, 35b, 59a
fire from heaven, 5b, 30ab
fishing, 67ab, 85b, 132ab, pp. 29, 70–1, 535n
food, 5b, 26b, 27b, 31b, 40b, 63a, 71ab, 84ab, 113a, 126b, pp. 29, 120, 122, 352n
fortresses mentioned by Adomnan, 40a, 49a–50b, 80a, 82b ; cf. p. 83
fosterage, 19a, 58b, 80ab, 105a
fragrance, miraculous, 38b
fratricide, 27b
funerals, 42b, 78b, 133a–134a
gardener, 23b
glass, 80a, 107ab
goat, 85a

581

Index of Latin Words

This is not intended as a glossary, the place of which, it is hoped, has been partly filled by the translation. The index is intended to draw attention to words or meanings which are rare, or which belong to medieval rather than classical Latin (Adomnan standing between the two), or which have been discussed in the foot-notes or need further comment. A few words have been included on account of their spellings. The forms are normally those of ms A. Words and meanings found in the Vulgate have not usually been given here ; most of them are contained in e.g. Lewis and Short's Latin Dictionary (1907). The references to the text may not be in all cases exhaustive, though it is hoped that they are nearly so.

2Q